Digital Course Materials

for

Living Sociologically
Concepts and Connections

RONALD N. JACOBS
ELEANOR TOWNSLEY

Carefully scratch off the silver coating (e.g., with a coin) to see your personal redemption code.

This code can be used only once and cannot be shared.

Once the code has been revealed, this access card cannot be returned to the publisher. Access can also be purchased online during the registration process.

The code on this card is valid for two years from the date of first purchase. Complete terms and conditions are available at **oup-arc.com**

Access Length: 6 months from redemption of the code.

Your OUP digital course materials can be delivered several different ways, depending on how your instructor has elected to incorporate them into his or her course.

BEFORE REGISTERING FOR ACCESS, be sure to check with your instructor to ensure that you register using the proper method.

VIA YOUR SCHOOL'S LEARNING MANAGEMENT SYSTEM

Use this method if your instructor has integrated these resources into your school's Learning Management System (LMS)—Blackboard, Canvas, Brightspace, Moodle, or other

- Log in to your instructor's course within your school's LMS.
- When you click a link to a resource that is access-protected, you will be prompted to register for access.
- Follow the on-screen instructions.
- Enter your personal redemption code (or purchase access) when prompted on the checkout screen.

VIA THE OUP SITE

Use this method if your instructor has NOT integrated these resources into your school's LMS, and you are using the resources for self-study only. **NOTE**: *Scores for any quizzes you take on the OUP site will not report to your instructor's gradebook.*

- Visit **oup.com/he/Jacobs-Townsley1e**
- Select the edition you are using, then select student resources for that edition.
- Click the link to upgrade your access to the student resources.
- Follow the on-screen instructions.
- Enter your personal redemption code (or purchase access) when prompted on the checkout screen.

VIA OUP DASHBOARD

Use this method only if your instructor has specifically instructed you to enroll in a Dashboard course. **NOTE**: *If your instructor is using these resources within your school's LMS, use the Learning Management System instructions.*

- Visit **register.dashboard.oup.com** and select your textbook.
- Follow the on-screen instructions to identify your specific course section.
- Enter your personal redemption code (or purchase access) when prompted on the checkout screen.
- Once you complete your registration, you are automatically enrolled in your Dashboard course.

*For assistance with code redemption, Dashboard registration, or if you redeemed your code using the wrong method for your course, please contact our customer support team at **dashboard.support@oup.com** or 855-281-8749.*

OXFORD
UNIVERSITY PRESS

Living Sociologically

Living Sociologically

CONCEPTS AND CONNECTIONS

Ronald N. Jacobs

Eleanor Townsley

New York   Oxford

OXFORD UNIVERSITY PRESS

Oxford University Press is a department of the University of Oxford.
It furthers the University's objective of excellence in research, scholarship,
and education by publishing worldwide. Oxford is a registered trade mark of
Oxford University Press in the UK and certain other countries.

Published in the United States of America by Oxford University Press
198 Madison Avenue, New York, NY 10016, United States of America.

© 2020 by Oxford University Press

Library of Congress Control Number: 2019950340

Printing number: 9 8 7 6 5 4 3 2 1
Printed in Mexico by Quad/Mexico

Brief Contents

Contents

CHAPTER 3 Doing Sociology: Research Methods and Critical Literacy 53

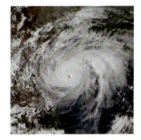

PART II: STRUCTURE AND CONTROL 81

CHAPTER 4 **Culture 83**

CHAPTER 5 **Socialization, Social Interaction, and Group Life 115**

CHAPTER 6   Deviance, Crime, and Punishment 147

PART III: DIFFERENCE AND INEQUALITY 177

PART IV: INSTITUTIONS AND ISSUES 277

CHAPTER 10   Marriage, Family, and the Law 279

CHAPTER 11 Science, Religion, and Knowing 309

CHAPTER 12 Health, Illness, and Medicine 343

PART V: CHANGE, ISSUES, AND THE FUTURE 435

Preface

Why Did We Write This Book?

Our students already live sociologically. They are drawn to topics of urgent sociological concern—race, class, gender, family, popular culture, health, and crime—by a need to understand the forces that shape their world, as well as a desire to change that world for the better. Yet they do not always find it easy to connect sociological concepts with real-world applications. Helping students make that connection is what we have sought to do with *Living Sociologically: Concepts and Connections*.

Students naturally want to know how the study of sociology can inform their career and professional choices. Throughout this textbook, we illustrate not only the ways in which sociologists live their profession, but also the rich and surprising ways in which sociological theories inform parenting and romantic relationships, political commitments, economic decisions, cultural expressions, and religious beliefs. Living sociologically is not only interesting— it's *useful*. Sociology provides not only big ideas to understand social life but also concrete tools for acting in the world with purpose and meaning. Sociology helps connect the individual level with the system level, revealing a layer of reality that is not always immediately obvious. We wrote *Living Sociologically* because we wanted a teaching resource that was grounded in the sociological tradition but also offered a more contemporary and practical approach to the discipline. By the end of the Introduction to Sociology course, our hope is that students will be critical rather than cynical, empirically committed rather than scientifically or politically dogmatic, and attuned to social relationships as well as individual stories.

Relational thinking

Living Sociologically offers a new formula to help students develop the relational thinking that is at the core of the sociological project. Five paired concepts structure the book and appear in every chapter, through extended case studies, compelling box features, and active learning exercises. The paired concepts aim to sensitize students to the idea that social things *always exist in relationship to other things*.

- *Inequality* does not exist without *privilege* that accrues to those who benefit from the disadvantage of other people. How particular relationships between inequality and privilege are organized through institutions, cultural norms, and patterns of behavior is a sociological question.

- *Structure* is inextricably linked to *contingency*. Critical sociological thinking means staying alert to unexpected contingencies that might disrupt the main social pattern.

- All *global* things occur in *local* contexts. Thinking across levels of scale is a fundamental sociological competence.
- There is no "us" without "them"; or, to put it sociologically, there is no *solidarity* that does not contain the possibility of *conflict* with those beyond the group boundary.
- Every act of *power* contains possibilities for *resistance* and social change when people say no and choose to follow another path of action.

We offer the paired concepts to help students get started with sociological thinking. But relational thinking does not stop there. Examples multiply quickly and students are good at identifying them. All categorical identities, for example, exist in relation to other identities. In fact, they presume them. The category "women" presumes "men," binary gender identities presume more fluid nonbinary gender identities, black presumes white, racial presumes multiracial, dominated presumes dominant, wealthy presumes poor. None of these categories is essential or necessary; rather, they are historically developed social institutions. *Living Sociologically* fosters a practical, comparative, critical awareness that social arrangements have a history, are made by people, and could be organized differently.

Intersectionality and Critical Social Literacies

Social relationships intersect in multiple and complex ways. More than ever before, students today recognize that they are positioned in overlapping relationships of privilege, solidarity, and power—relationships that are structured locally and globally. Thinking in relational terms helps students not only think intersectionally, but also link their individual experiences to the operation of multiple systems of oppression. *Living Sociologically* offers abundant opportunity for practice in thinking relationally and intersectionally.

While the paired concepts help students see the hidden aspects and complicated contexts of otherwise familiar social structures, scientific thinking and social research methods help them engage with these more complex realities. We want our students to become critical consumers and users of social information, and we want them to appreciate the power and potential of sociological research. The paired concepts work together with practical skills that use diverse data in different media to help students think critically. Throughout the book we provide active learning exercises connected to the paired concepts, affording students the opportunity to practice the habits of mind and concrete skills required to find good information. At the end of each chapter, we offer additional exercises for students to practice their data and media skills. In the ebook, we provide a set of Data+Media Literacy exercises where students further practice these skills and assess their own learning in a low-stakes environment. Instructors could also use these exercises as jumping-off points for class discussions or group activities.

Teaching with *Living Sociologically*

Living Sociologically combines what is useful from our experiences at a variety of institutions. We distill usable, high-quality, reliable teaching and learning resources for instructors and students alike. Our approach is designed for multiple settings: flexible enough that instructors facing different constraints will find it useful; rich enough that instructors with different interests can rely on it for detailed support when teaching the wider field; and inviting enough that students can follow exercises on their own if they desire.

Living Sociologically moves toward a new narrative for the Introduction to Sociology course that takes the best of new innovations in pedagogy and updates the standard formula. We include enough recognizable content to align with standard learning objectives, while offering new features that distinguish our book from other introductory sociology texts:

- a narrative that explains the changes that have taken place in sociological theory since the 1960s;
- an extended analysis of culture that considers new approaches in cultural sociology, including work on codes, narratives, mass media, social networks, and the public sphere;
- an extended focus on the range of research techniques contemporary sociologists use, including observation/ethnography, interpretive methods (textual analysis and cultural analysis), open-ended interviewing, survey research, historical-comparative methods, and experimental methods;
- a commitment to drawing connections between sociological subfields and anchoring them in particular real-world social processes; and
- an active learning approach that offers tools to students and instructors to succeed in their work.

A Contemporary, Applied, and Inclusive Introduction

The traditional model of three major theoretical perspectives followed by many introductory sociology textbooks relies very heavily on the Anglo-European history of sociology to describe the field. This is an important story, but we believe it needs to be placed in critical historical context. Today, most sociologists are also interested in "theories of the middle range" that are concerned with understanding concrete social practices, specific social contexts, and particular social outcomes.

Our aim is to present the foundational curriculum in sociology to all of the students in our increasingly diverse classrooms. We introduce the history and core ideas of the classical canon, we present extended criticisms of the canon, and we place these critiques in the context of broader currents in the academic field.

Last, as instructors who teach Introduction to Sociology every semester know, a unified social science does not exist. Moreover, there are important intersections between sociology, anthropology, economics, geography, psychology, history, literary studies, gender studies, and ethnic studies, and students are trying to figure them out. We believe the foundational curriculum in sociology should help students navigate these boundaries between fields, and to distinguish sociology from its closest colleagues and competitors. *Living Sociologically* contextualizes sociology within the story of the emergence of the social sciences and by identifying similarities and differences between social science disciplines. This interdisciplinary sensibility is woven through the text as we point to connections to other academic projects as well as applied settings for sociological research.

Chapter Structure

Every chapter of *Living Sociologically* has a specific focus and contains the following elements:

- An **opening vignette** that begins the chapter. In Chapter 1, "What Is Sociology?" we open with the decision by San Francisco 49ers quarterback Colin Kaepernick to sit during the national anthem and ask how a sociological perspective can help us understand it. This is used as a foundation to ask questions about sports, national pride, race, media, and celebrity. It also helps us introduce the five paired concepts. Similarly, in Chapter 13, "Politics, Media, and Social Movements," the vignette's examination of the role of the media in the extraordinarily charged US presidential election of 2016 foreshadows the even greater conflicts and confusions of the 2020 political season. This is used as a foundation to discuss other social movements and the institutional landscape of global and national power today. We explicitly link the case to the five paired concepts that organize the narrative of the textbook.

- Two or three **examples of contemporary research**, anchored in the discussion of a specific empirical focus. For example, in Chapter 1, "What Is Sociology?" we consider examples of the sociological imagination in published research and discuss classic works by Peter H. Rossi on homelessness and by William Julius Wilson on race and class in the inner city. In Chapter 8, "Race, Ethnicity, and Multiculturalism," we consider E. Digby Baltzell's *The Protestant Establishment* on the institutionalization of the WASP establishment, Noel Ignatiev's book *How the Irish Became White*, and Christina Mora's *Making Hispanics*.

- Box features that exemplify the five **paired concepts**. In Chapter 2, "American Sociology: Theories and Contexts," we discuss "Global and Local" by recovering the importance of immigrant sociologists to the development of the field in the United States. In Chapter 4, "Culture," we examine "Inequality and Privilege" through the lens of taxpayer support for cultural institutions. In Chapter 7, "Inequality, Mobility, and Social Change," we describe the development of Social Security to understand "Structure and Contingency." In Chapter 9, "Gender, Sexuality, and the Body," we discuss "Power and Resistance" in the context of the Stonewall Uprising and LGBTQ activism. And in Chapter 13, "Politics, Media, and Social Movements," the role of push polling in sowing division is highlighted as an example of "Solidarity and Conflict."

- **Career boxes** in each chapter encourage students to explore the relevance of sociological study to many different career fields.

- **Methods and Interpretation boxes** provide an opportunity to approach sociological questions with the critical thinking and research skill set and tools of a sociologist.

- **Case studies** at the end of each chapter apply the five paired concepts as analytical tools to understand a cultural, political, or social phenomenon relevant to the chapter's key themes. For example, in Chapter 4, "Culture," we analyze the social ritual of standing for the national anthem at sports events in the United States through all five of the paired concepts. In Chapter 12, "Health, Illness, and Medicine," we discuss the rise of commercial genetic testing as it influences understanding of health. In each case, the paired concepts encourage students to use their sociological imaginations to engage with complexity and contradiction.

- **Review sections** at the end of each chapter revisit the chapter's learning goals and provide lists of key terms, review questions, further readings, and suggestions for further exploration.

- **Practical Activities** at the end of chapters encourage students to use their sociological imagination, develop their media and data literacy, and discuss compelling questions and issues.

Teaching and Learning Support

Oxford University Press offers instructors and students a comprehensive teaching and learning package of support materials for adopters of *Living Sociologically: Concepts and Connections*.

Ancillary Resource Center

The Ancillary Resource Center (ARC) at www.oup.com/he/Jacobs-Townsley1e is a convenient destination for all teaching and learning resources that accompany this book. Accessed online through individual user accounts, the ARC provides instructors with up-to-date ancillaries while guaranteeing the security of grade-significant resources. In addition, it allows OUP to keep users informed when new content becomes available. The ARC for *Living Sociologically: Concepts and Connections* contains a variety of materials to aid in teaching:

- **Instructor's Manual**—A robust and innovative Instructor's Resource Manual that includes chapter summaries, chapter outlines, lecture suggestions, in-class activities and project assignments, discussion questions, and web resources, as well as tips for organizing and facilitating class discussions and cultivating engagement in the classroom

- **Test Bank**—Available in Word format and formats compatible with all major learning management systems, the test bank includes nearly 1,000 multiple-choice questions, as well as essay questions.

- **PowerPoint-Based Lecture Slides.**

- **Pop Culture Guide**—A valuable guide to media (movies, TV shows, podcasts) that can be used to demonstrate sociological ideas or concepts, organized by chapter. These come from multiple sources and include suggestions for clips as well as full-length features. Each suggested clip includes the concept being represented, the time stamp (if relevant), as well as the streaming service where the media can be accessed.

Digital Learning Tools

Living Sociologically: Concepts and Connections comes with exciting digital learning tools to ensure your students get the most out of your course:

- *In the News* is a resource for both instructors and students that provides current news articles on a weekly basis, along with low-stakes assessments that ensure student engagement and encourage students to connect the article to what they are learning in their course. These articles are selected specifically to relate to a particular sociological idea or concept, and are designed to demonstrate to students the sociological relevance of everyday events.

- *Media+Data Literacy Exercises*, developed by Ron Jacobs and Eleanor Townsley, are innovative, interactive exercises that help students build their data and media skills and assess their learning in a low-stakes environment. These exercises push students to critically analyze photos, charts, and graphs in an effort to highlight how easily information can be manipulated or misinterpreted. They can be assigned to students, or used as jumping-off points for class discussions or group activities.

Access to these tools is provided free to students with purchase of a new print or electronic textbook, through an access code or directly within the ebook. These and additional study tools are available at www.oup.com/he/Jacobs-Townsley1e, through links embedded directly in the enhanced ebook, via LMS integration, and in Dashboard. Additional tools are described below:

- **Enhanced ebook:** The enhanced ebook provides students with a versatile, accessible, online version of the textbook, with the *In the News* and *Media+Data Literacy Exercises* integrated on the appropriate pages though clickable icons that connect to each feature. Every new copy of the print text comes with an access code, which can be used to redeem Dashboard, premium ARC resources, or directly in your LMS, and the enhanced ebook will be available in all of these locations. (Please note: Students should check with their instructor before redeeming their code to determine if their instructor is using Dashboard or an LMS integration. If neither is being used, students can redeem directly on ARC.)

- **Online Study Tools:** Additional online tools are available at www.oup.com/he/Jacobs-Townsley1e for student use. For each chapter, these include interactive flashcards, a glossary, learning goals, and web links.

- **Digital Learning Tools: Delivery Options**
  - Learning Management System Integration: OUP offers the ability to integrate OUP content directly into currently supported versions of Canvas, D2L, or Blackboard. This integration brings all of the content listed here directly into your LMS, and quiz grades will report to your LMS's gradebook. Contact your local rep or visit oup-arc.com/integration for more information.
  - Dashboard delivers engaging learning tools within an easy-to-use cloud-based courseware platform. Prebuilt courses in Dashboard provide a learning experience that instructors can use off the shelf or customize to fit their course. A built-in gradebook allows instructors to quickly and easily monitor how the course as a whole and individual students are performing. Visit www.oup.com/dashboard or contact your Oxford University Press representative to learn more.

Format Choices

Oxford University Press offers cost-saving alternatives to meet the needs of all students. This text is offered in a loose-leaf format at a 30% discount off the list price of the text; and in an ebook format, through Redshelf, for a 50% discount. You can also customize our textbooks to create the course material you want for your class. For more information, please contact your Oxford University Press representative, call 800.280.0280, or visit us online at www.oup.com/he.

Acknowledgments

The authors would like to thank the many reviewers who provided substantive, helpful, and critical feedback throughout the development of this text:

Alabama
Matt Cousineau, Auburn University
Angela Ware, Auburn University

Arizona
Celeste Atkins, Cochise College

Arkansas
Rebecca Barrett-Fox, Arkansas State University
Linda Brady, Arkansas State University

California
Terri Anderson, University of California–Los Angeles
Jean Beaman, University of California–Santa Barbara
Shaneel Pratap, Evergreen Valley College

Connecticut
Erika Del Villar, University of Connecticut

District of Columbia
Sarah Stiles, Georgetown University

Florida
Stephen Lippmann, Miami University
Andrew Mannheimer, Florida State University
Richard Tardanico, Florida International University
Phillip Wiseley, Florida South Western State College

Indiana
Rachel Einwohner, Purdue University
Carmon Hicks, Ivy Tech Community College of Indiana
Stephanie Medley-Rath, Indiana University–Kokomo
Melinda Messineo, Ball State University
Carla Pfeffer, Purdue University North Central

Kentucky
Andrea Deal, Madisonville Community College

Massachusetts
Linda McCarthy, Greenfield Community College

Minnesota
Elizabeth Scheel-Keita, St. Cloud State University

Mississippi
Earnestine Lee, Alcorn State University

Missouri
George Carson, Ozarks Technical Community College
Joachim Kibirige, Missouri Western State University
Aurelian Mauxion, Columbia College

New Jersey
Patricia Stott, Kean University

New York
Marc (Jung-Whan) De Jong, Fashion Institute of Technology
Andrew Horvitz, SUNY New Paltz
Andrew Lindner, Skidmore College

North Carolina
Anne Hastings, University of North Carolina–Chapel Hill

Ohio
Amy Grau, Shawnee State University

Pennsylvania
Kaci Griffin, Temple University
Jess Klein, Robert Morris University
Teelyn Mauney, St. Francis University
Julie Raulli, Wilson College

South Dakota
Pamela Monaghan-Geernaert, Northern State University

Tennessee
Jessica Dalton-Carriger, Roane State Community College

Texas
Janet Armitage, St. Mary's University
Dawn Tawwater, Austin Community College
Dorothy Kalanzi, University of Texas at Arlington
Michael Ramirez, Texas A&M University–Corpus Christi

Virginia
Tom Linneman, College of William & Mary
Ashley Lumpkin, John Tyler Community College
Christa Moore, University of Virginia–Wise
Rachel Sparkman, Virginia Commonwealth University
Allison Wisecup, Radford University

Wisconsin
Sheena Finnegan, Wisconsin Lutheran College

9 anonymous reviewers

The authors and OUP are grateful to the Board of Advisors who provided valuable feedback on the manuscript, ancillary and digital program, and cover images:

Terri Anderson, University of California–Los Angeles

Rebecca Barrett-Fox, Arkansas State University

Jean Beaman, University of California, Santa Barbara

Linda Brady, Arkansas State University

Marc (Jung-Whan) De Jong, Fashion Institute of Technology

Andrea Deal, Madisonville Community College

Erika Del Villar, University of Connecticut

Rachel Einwohner, Purdue University

Sheena Finnegan, Wisconsin Lutheran College

Kaci Griffin, Temple University

Andrew Horvitz, SUNY New Paltz

Joachim Kibirige, Missouri Western State University

Jess Klein, Robert Morris University/University of Pittsburgh

Andrew Lindner, Skidmore College

Tom Linneman, College of William and Mary

Shaneel Pratap, Evergreen Valley College

Michael Ramirez, Texas A&M University–Corpus Christi

Rachel Sparkman, Virginia Commonwealth University

In addition, we thank those who attended our focus group at the American Sociological Association in August 2019 and provided substantive and useful feedback:

Debjani Chakravarty, Utah Valley University

Jeffrey Chin, Le Moyne College

Andrew Cognard-Black, St. Mary's College of Maryland

Andrew Horvitz, SUNY New Paltz

Aramide Kazeem, University of West Georgia

Lloyd Klein, Laguardia Community College

Monica Koziol, Harper College

John Musalia, Western Kentucky University

Timothy Radloff, East Stroudsburg University

Kevin Shafer, Brigham Young University

Jamie Washington, University of Maryland, Baltimore County

Jan Yager, John Jay College of Criminal Justice

Anne Eisenberg, SUNY–Geneseo

Albert Fu, Kutztown University

Hayley Pierce, Brigham Young University

Gwendolyn Purifoye, North Park University

Devparna Roy, Nazareth College

Judith Sedaitis, CUNY City Tech

The authors and OUP also sincerely thank the scholars and instructors who created the high-quality resources that accompany this text:

Rebecca Barrett-Fox, Arkansas State University (Test Bank; ebook assessments; Dashboard Quizzes)

Ian Callahan, SUNY Albany (In the News)

Andrew Horvitz, SUNY New Paltz (Instructor's Manual and PowerPoint lecture slides)

Nickie Michaud Wild, Upper Iowa University (Pop Culture Guide)

About the Authors

Ronald Jacobs (PhD, UCLA) is professor of sociology at the University at Albany, State University of New York. He is coeditor of the *Oxford Handbook of Cultural Sociology* (2012), coauthor of *Cultural Sociology* (Blackwell, 2012), coauthor (with Eleanor Townsley) of *The Space of Opinion: Media Intellectuals and the Public Sphere* (OUP, 2011), and author of *Race, Media, and the Crisis of Civil Society: From Watts to Rodney King* (Cambridge, 2000), as well as author of numerous journal articles and book chapters. He is cofounder and coeditor of the *American Journal of Cultural Sociology*, and he has served on the editorial boards for *Sociological Theory, International Journal of Sociology and Social Policy, Qualitative Sociology, Sociological Forum*, and *American Journal of Sociology*. In addition to teaching an introductory sociology course, he regularly teaches courses on sociological theory, mass media, and the sociology of culture.

Eleanor Townsley (PhD, UCLA) is the Andrew W. Mellon Professor of Sociology and the director of the curriculum to career program, Nexus, at Mount Holyoke College. She is coauthor (with Ron Jacobs) of *The Space of Opinion: Media Intellectuals and the Public Sphere* (OUP, 2011) and coauthor of *Making Capitalism without Capitalists: The New Ruling Elites in Eastern Europe* (Verso, 1998), as well as author of numerous journal articles, book chapters, and book reviews. She has served on the editorial boards for *Sociological Theory* and the *American Journal of Cultural Sociology*. Eleanor regularly teaches Introduction to Sociology as well as courses on media, organizations, inequality, the public sphere, and research methods. She is the recipient of two teaching awards and was named one of Princeton Review's "300 Best Professors" in 2012.

Both authors are dedicated teachers. With the exception of her time as a dean, Townsley has taught Introduction to Sociology every semester for the last 20 years, while Jacobs continues to offer Introduction to Sociology to classes with enrollments of over 400 students a semester. Both have taught at a variety of colleges and universities in different parts of the United States: Santa Monica Community College, UCLA, SUNY Albany, Rice University, the University of Pennsylvania, and Mount Holyoke College.

PART I THE BASICS

What Is Sociology?

Before kickoff against the Green Bay Packers on August 26, 2016, San Francisco 49ers quarterback Colin Kaepernick refused to stand during the national anthem. His silent but powerful gesture was meant to protest police violence against African Americans, as well as the larger history of oppression against racial minorities in the United States. At first, the protest went largely unnoticed; in fact, Kaepernick had remained seated during the playing of the national anthem at the previous two games. But Kaepernick's protest erupted into a national story after a fan tweeted a picture. Explaining his motivation, Kaepernick said, "I am not going to stand up to show pride in a flag for a country that oppresses black people and people of color. To me, this is bigger than football and it would be selfish on my part to look the other way."

In an attempt to defuse the controversy, the 49ers organization issued a statement saying that although the national anthem was a special opportunity to honor the country, they respected the rights of individuals to exercise their freedom of expression and choose whether or not to stand. But indignation exploded around Kaepernick and his stance. People who disagreed with his protest argued that Kaepernick was disrespecting the nation, its police officers, and members of the military. Angry fans burned jerseys with his number. Republican presidential candidate Donald Trump suggested that Kaepernick should be asked to leave the country for expressing "incorrect political views." Conservative political commentators suggested that Kaepernick was a spoiled rich athlete who had never experienced oppression. Others said that Kaepernick, who is biracial, was "not black enough" to complain about racial oppression. Iowa congressman Steve King even suggested that Kaepernick hated America and was sympathetic to Islamic terrorists.

Colin Kaepernick takes a knee
Between San Francisco 49ers Eli Harold and Eric Reid, Colin Kaepernick drops to a kneeling position at the beginning of the national anthem before an NFL game against the Seattle Seahawks, September 25, 2016.

Opportunities for Sociology Majors

Sociology is useful in many careers because it teaches critical thinking about social relationships and social systems. Sociology helps us see how individual and group behavior is influenced by the patterns of group life and also how individuals can shape wider social systems. Sociologists know how to use theoretical logic and data to analyze social problems and social puzzles. Sociological ideas and methods also help us imagine new ways to organize our social world.

There are countless examples of prominent and successful sociology majors, including former First Lady Michelle Obama, actors like Dan Aykroyd and Nina Dobrev, and writers, journalists, and poets, including Saul Bellow, Mitch Albom, Shelby Steele, and Linton Kwesi Johnson. Graduates of sociology programs include judges like Richard Barajas, retired chief justice of the Texas Supreme Court, as well as athletes and philanthropists like Alonzo Mourning of the Miami Heat. Business leaders who majored in sociology include Christopher Connor, executive chairman of Sherwin-Williams; Brad Anderson, former CEO and vice chairman of consumer electronics for Best Buy; and Alexis Herman, CEO of New Ventures and the former US secretary of labor.

ACTIVE LEARNING

Find out: Ask a parent, a teacher, or someone else who is in the workforce what kind of skills and abilities they think employers are looking for. Ask them what kinds of skills and abilities make people successful in their lives.

---

three sociologists, sociology was an intellectual perspective that promotes social understanding, human empowerment, and freedom.

If we put these claims together, we see that sociology is composed of three basic elements:

1. Sociology is interested in social facts, social actions, and social relationships. It looks at how individual actions are shaped by larger patterns that structure people's social lives.

2. Sociology is based on systematic research. Sociologists collect facts about the social world and are interested in explaining why things happen the way they do, and not otherwise.

3. Sociology hopes to provide people with a deeper understanding about the world around them, so they can empower themselves and try to make the world a better place.

The Sociological Imagination

The moral perspective shared by Mills, Bauman, Bourdieu, and others asserts that sociology should be a force for good. It holds that sociology should help us to recognize and challenge structures of domination and inequality; encourage greater understanding, tolerance, and empathy for different points of view; enable us to recognize that larger social forces shape our successes and failures; and prompt us to think critically about how the world around us came to be organized the way it is.

Sociological imagination The ability to see the connections between individual lives and wider social structures, and the way they affect each other.

For Mills, this kind of thinking defines the **sociological imagination**. "The sociological imagination," Mills (2000: 6) wrote, "enables us to grasp history and biography and the relation between the two in society." Mills wanted us to be able to connect our own private troubles to larger public issues. To do that, we need to understand not only how our society is organized, but also how it is different both from other societies in the past and other places in the present. Mills argued that we need to understand why certain types of people tend to be successful in our society, asking how successful people are selected and in what ways the characteristics of successful people change over time. Mills believed that sociologists were in the best position to provide good answers to these questions.

In his 1987 study, *The Truly Disadvantaged* (1987), William Julius Wilson offers a powerful example of the sociological imagination. Wilson's book explores the reasons for poverty in African American inner-city neighborhoods in the 1980s, despite the efforts of social welfare programs of the 1960s and 1970s to help people, and despite the victories of the 1960s Civil Rights Movement that helped to overturn racial discrimination in housing and other public policies. At the time when Wilson was doing the research for *The Truly Disadvantaged*, a number of influential social critics—among them journalists like Irving Kristol, politicians like Daniel Patrick Moynihan, and anthropologists like Oscar Lewis—argued that government welfare programs had created a "culture of poverty." These critics argued that this culture encouraged poor people to depend on welfare and discouraged them from working harder to improve their lives. By the late 1980s, politicians were using these arguments about the "culture of poverty" to propose policies dramatically reducing social welfare as a way to help people to "escape" what President Ronald Reagan called, in his 1986 State of the Union Address to Congress, "the spider's web of dependency" on government.

Wilson's book was an important intervention in the debate about race and welfare, because it used the sociological imagination to tell a more complicated story about what was happening in poor inner-city neighborhoods. Wilson's research showed that manufacturing and other low-skill jobs had left the cities, only to be replaced by service jobs that required more education. Women, who were entering the labor market in greater numbers, competed successfully with men for these service jobs. These factors made it much harder for the low-skilled and poorly educated men living in the inner city to find work. In addition, black middle-class families were taking advantage of anti-discrimination housing laws to move to better neighborhoods in the suburbs. As black middle-class families left the inner city, community institutions such as churches and schools were weakened. Young children living in the inner city had access to fewer positive role models, while teenagers were cut off from the kinds of informal social contacts that could help them get jobs. In other words, many of the problems that young African American men faced in the inner city were not of their own making. Rather, Wilson demonstrated, they were the result of deeper underlying structural changes in race, class, and gender relations.

Sociologists often use the idea of the sociological imagination to explain why what they do is important. Mills and the sociological imagination are featured in every sociological textbook written in the United States, and books like *The Truly Disadvantaged* are held up as examples of the kind of deep, systematic sociological research that needs to be part of the public conversation about important social issues.

The Discipline of Sociology

In the United States, sociology began to enter the university in the late nineteenth century. The first college course called "Sociology" was taught in 1875 at Yale University. The first sociology department was established at the University of Chicago in 1892. This history is similar to most of the social science disciplines. For example, economics, psychology, and political science departments were first created in American universities in the 1870s and 1880s. By the time the system of academic majors and distribution requirements had emerged (such a system was first established at Harvard University in 1910), there was broad agreement among educators that all college students should learn social science.

As one of the main social science disciplines in the university, sociology has always been committed to the idea that systematic and scientific research is the best way to understand the social world. Almost all of the early proponents of sociology were attracted to the prospect of developing a science of society. While most of the early sociologists were trained in other disciplines, such as philosophy, law, and theology, they embraced sociology because they believed that it offered a more scientific way of understanding the social world.

The goals of a scientific sociology are based on two related ideas: (1) if we want to understand a social issue, it is important to get the facts right; and (2) it is often quite difficult to get the facts right. What facts you collect depend on how you define the issue. For example, if we want to understand and respond effectively to the problem of homelessness, we need to define the problem. We need to know:

- how many homeless people there are,
- what kinds of people are more likely to become homeless,
- what homelessness is and how homelessness has changed over time, and
- how effective different social policies are at reducing homelessness.

This information can be difficult and time consuming to collect.

Social scientists do not have a definite answer to the question, "How many homeless people are there?" People move in and out of periods of homelessness, making it hard to count them as "homeless" or "not homeless." The most common strategy for counting the homeless population is to count the people who are either in the streets or in homeless shelters, even though most experts agree that this strategy results in undercounts (Shlay and Rossi 1992). It misses people who are living temporarily with friends and family but who are likely to be homeless soon. It misses people who managed to scrape up enough money to stay in a motel for a day or two. And it misses people sleeping in their cars, at temporary campsites, in abandoned buildings, and other places that researchers have a hard time locating.

Social scientists have used different strategies to try to overcome these measurement difficulties. Some have relied on local informants, asking them for their best estimate of the local homeless population. Others have tried to develop informed estimates of how many of an area's homeless population used shelters, and then produce an estimate for the total population based on a count of the shelter population. In a more sophisticated version of

Counting the Homeless in New York City
Workers from the Robin Hood Foundation, an organization that helps the poor, speak to a homeless person as they take part in a survey of homeless persons on the streets of New York. Hundreds of people fanned out across the city to conduct the survey just after midnight on February 9, 2016.

this approach, Rossi (1989a) combined a count of the shelter population with a systematic nighttime survey of the street population in Chicago. After interviewing both groups, Rossi used the results of the interviews to make a more informed estimate of the total homeless population in the city.

Knowing the exact number of homeless people helps to inform important questions, such as what causes homelessness or what the experience of homelessness is like. For example, Rossi (1989b) used the Current Population Survey (conducted by the United States Census Bureau on a monthly basis) to identify the number of extremely poor single people, arguing that this population was at the highest risk of becoming homeless. More recent research has tried to identify people who are poor and have precarious housing situations, arguing that this is a population at great risk of becoming homeless (Link et al. 1995). This focus on at-risk populations has produced a shift in the things being measured. For example, instead of trying to measure the precise number of homeless people, research now focuses on the factors that increase the risk of homelessness (Jencks 1995; Snow and Anderson 1993), the ways that an individual's life chances are impacted by periods of homelessness (Burt et al. 2001), and the coping strategies that homeless people use to get by and to maintain respect (Dordick 1997; Duneier 2000; Gowan 2010).

As we will discuss in Chapter 3, sociologists use many different strategies to collect accurate and useful information about the social world. They debate the strengths and weaknesses of different kinds of research strategies. They consider the problems that confront social researchers, and they propose different ways to deal with those problems. They actively seek out information that challenges what they expect to find in their research. This focus on **research methods** is one of the defining features of social science, and it is central to the practice of sociology.

Research methods Strategies to collect accurate and useful information about the world.

Sociology and Everyday Knowledge

Social-scientific knowledge is different than ordinary, everyday knowledge about the world. In most of social life, people tend to look for information that reinforces the beliefs they already have. For example, people who believe that the *New York Times* has a liberal bias will actively seek out and remember those stories that reinforce their belief, while ignoring those stories that are balanced. The same is true for people who believe that Fox News has a conservative bias. This tendency to look for information that reinforces personal beliefs is known as **confirmation bias**. Confirmation bias makes people overconfident in their judgments. It encourages people to believe that things are clearer and more certain than they really are, and it often leads to more polarized social attitudes. As an antidote to confirmation bias, sociology and the other social science disciplines are an important part of your college education.

Confirmation bias The tendency to look for information that reinforces prior beliefs.

While the discipline of sociology is part of the social sciences, it is also distinct from the other social science disciplines: psychology, economics, political science, and history. The main difference is that sociologists want to understand how different social things are related to one another, and (as we shall see in the next section) sociologists combine different levels of analysis to achieve that understanding. While psychologists focus primarily on individuals and small groups, sociologists want to see how larger social forces influence groups. While economists and political scientists focus on a single sphere of social life, like the economy or the political system, sociologists are interested in the relationships of different social institutions to one another.

While sharing the historian's interest in the past, sociologists are more interested in comparing different historical outcomes in order to develop general explanations about why things occurred the way they did. As we discuss in Chapter 2, sociology has always had grand ambitions. Rather than trying to understand a particular part of social life, sociology aims to develop a science of society itself.

Levels of Analysis

Level of analysis The size or scale of the objects sociologists study.

Sociologists think about social issues in terms of historical trends and structural patterns. Instead of relying on their own personal observations and opinions, they collect data systematically in order to identify patterns that were not obvious at the outset. They are also interested in combining different **levels of analysis** in their research. A level of analysis refers to the size or the scale of the research you are conducting. Sociologists study individuals, groups, neighborhoods, cities, nations, and global systems. They consider things that take place in a few seconds as well as larger processes that develop over many years. And they are often interested in the relationship between these different levels of analysis. For example, when sociologists study the actions of individuals, they want to know how those individual actions are connected to the wider organization of social life, and they want to know how the choices that are made today are connected to the choices that were made in the past.

Sociologists commonly define three levels of analysis. Microsociology is the level of individuals and small group interaction. Macrosociology is the level of large-scale structural patterns and historical trends, including the workings of the economic, political, and cultural systems. In between microsociology and macrosociology is the intermediate or **institutional level of analysis**. This is the level of analysis of specific institutions and social relationships.

Institutional level of analysis The intermediate level of analysis, between microsociology and macrosociology, of specific institutions and social relationships.

For example, when sociologists study divorce they are interested in the specific decisions that people make to stay married or get divorced, but they are also interested in how divorce rates are connected to larger social patterns, such as differences in education (Martin 2006). To use the language of the sociological imagination, while getting divorced is a "private trouble," the overall divorce *rate* is a "public issue."

The decision to file for divorce is shaped by the relationship between individuals who have strong feelings about each other—for better or worse. There are interactions between the two people in a marriage that are personal, and can be understood and analyzed at the microsociological level of analysis. But the challenge of marriage is often magnified by macrosociological factors, such as patterned differences in educational attainment. Other macrosociological factors will also add stress to a marriage. For example, there may be a lack of high-paying jobs in the city where the married couple lives, because of a shift in jobs to other parts of the country or the world. At the institutional level, an individual's choice to stay married or get divorced will be shaped by the general social belief that people should get married, as well as by government tax policies that encourage and reward marriage. Other patterns connected to gender, religion, health status, race, social class, and regional location can also influence an individual's decision to divorce. To study divorce and other social issues, sociologists will look for patterns and measure outcomes at every level of analysis and ask: How do causes at one level affect causes at another?

Microsociology

Microsociology examines the everyday interactions of individuals and small groups. It emphasizes all of the things that we have to do to coordinate our actions with the people around us to establish what sociologists call "a shared definition of the situation." In particular, microsociology focuses on the rules that we follow in social situations, as well as the strategies we use to bend those rules to our advantage.

For example, two drivers approach a four-way stop sign. Even though there is no way of knowing, each driver acts as if the other person knows the rules of the situation. The person who arrives first has the right of way. If both people arrive at the same time, the person on the right has the right of way. But there are other strategies that drivers use to navigate the interaction. Some drivers will "stop short," making it appear that they arrived at the intersection first even though they may not have done so. Other drivers will be excessively polite, always waving the other person through in any instance where there is a question about who arrived first. Many drivers will try to make predictions about the behavior of the other driver, based on the condition of the car that is approaching, the speed of the approach, or the age of the driver. They may give the right of way to poorly maintained cars, fast drivers, and young drivers, based on the assumption that their behavior will be less predictable. As we can see, even the ordinary activities of our lives are highly choreographed, requiring both social interpretation and cooperation from others around us.

The idea that social life is choreographed suggests that we are all actors on a stage, performing roles and responding to the performances of those around us. We have a clear sense of how we want to present ourselves, and we use a variety of "props" to signal that presentation to others. Are we wearing work clothes or casual clothes? Do we take charge, or do we blend into the background? We send out these signals with the hope that others will understand us, and will accept our self-presentation without challenging it. At the same time, we acknowledge other people's signals by adopting supporting roles that reinforce their self-presentations. If the performances are coordinated effectively and nobody's performance is challenged, then there is no problem and nobody is embarrassed. According to Erving Goffman (1922–1982), this kind of "impression management" is one of the most important features of social life.

Microsociology can help us see how individuals and groups collaborate with each other to create a "shared definition of the situation," as well as how everyday social interactions re-create patterns of inequality. One example is research showing that even though science teachers in middle schools are committed to treating all of their students equally, they actually spend significantly more time with the male students than the female students in their classrooms (Shumow and Schmidt 2013). To take another example, despite laws against racial discrimination in hiring for jobs, microsociological research shows that African American applicants receive a callback or a job offer about half as often as equally qualified white applicants; in fact, African American applicants with no criminal record receive a callback for a job about as often as a white applicant with a felony conviction (Pager 2007; Pager, Western, and Bonikowski 2009). All of these examples show how larger patterns of inequality are reproduced in the everyday interactions of individuals and small groups.

Microsociology can also help us ask better questions about the case we introduced at the beginning of the chapter. Football players wear a specific uniform and perform on a specific stage that is about athletic competition, rather than public

Microsociology The analysis of individuals and small group interaction.

Kaepernick, Reid, and Harold kneel during the National Anthem, October 6, 2016
San Francisco 49ers Eli Harold, Colin Kaepernick, and Eric Reid kneel during the national anthem before the team's game against the Arizona Cardinals in Santa Clara, California.

debate. When a player like Kaepernick veers off script, the unproblematic reproduction of a common sense of the situation is challenged. Different groups then respond to the challenge, taking their cues from each other about how to respond. Fans at the game are surrounded by tens of thousands of other fans. Fans watching at home usually watch together with other friends, and communicate with other fans on social media. Fans talk about the game and what happened the next day. In short, what fans focus on during the game, and the meanings they give to the game, are negotiated together with the other people with whom they are interacting. This is one reason that the protest of the anthem is a risky but effective strategy for challenging inequality.

Macrosociology

While microsociology examines the everyday activities of individuals and small groups, **macrosociology** explores how large-scale historical trends and structural patterns influence social life. We do not choose the society into which we are born. The opportunities we will have and the challenges we will face in our lives are not entirely of our own making. This is why the sociological imagination tells us to look at the relationship between biography and history. The choices we make in our lives matter, but they are structured by the society into which we are born as well as by our own position in that society.

Among the historical trends and patterns that macrosociologists examine, some of the most important are population patterns, differences in wealth and resources, and the organization of political and economic systems. Also important are power differences that are organized along the lines of race, gender, and class, legacies of military conquest, colonization and resistance, and religion and other cultural belief systems.

Macrosociological and microsociological perspectives complement each other, resulting in a more complete understanding of sociological life. If microsociological perspectives think about social life as if we are all actors on a stage, macrosociological perspectives show us how the stage we act upon was built in the first place. For example, if we return to the example of drivers at an intersection, macrosociologists would look at all the social structures that led people to arrive at the scene the way they did. The fact that they are driving is not an accident. It is based on political and economic factors that privileged the automobile industry over other systems of transportation. It is based on a specific history of cities and suburbs, where wealthier people left the cities to raise their families in "safer" and more economically and racially homogeneous neighborhoods. It is based on the global wealth and privilege of the Unites States, where car ownership and home ownership are reasonable goals for people to have. And it is based on general cultural beliefs about individuality and freedom, which in American popular culture have long been linked to cars.

Macrosociology The analysis of large-scale structural patterns and historical trends, including the workings of the economic, political, and cultural systems.

A macrosociological perspective can also help to explain why social protest by athletes attracts so much attention, particularly around matters of race. Professional sports are big business, and athletes are worshipped by their fans. In many countries, in fact, sports are treated as a national religion, so that when people cheer for their team they are actually cheering for their country and the values it represents (Dayan and Katz 1992). At the same time, sport and race have a complicated history in the United States. The racial integration of professional sports leagues was an important part of the historical fight for racial justice in America. African American athletes have been among the most famous celebrities in the country over the last 50 years, despite the fact that many of them grew up in impoverished, racially segregated communities. For many Americans, the success of these athletes is a "rags to riches" story that is part of the American Dream, and they get upset when successful athletes do not seem to be sufficiently appreciative of the good fortune they have had. However, the intersection of biography and history can make athletes (especially athletes of color) feel a responsibility to use their fame to speak against racial injustice. Using your sociological imagination can help you to better understand these competing expectations, and to ask good critical questions about public controversies when they develop.

Honoring a history of athletes' protest against racism
Tommie Smith, left, and John Carlos pose for a photo at San Jose State University campus on October 17, 2018. The statue honors their iconic, black-gloved protest celebrating the 50th anniversary of their medal ceremonies at the 1968 Olympic Games in Mexico City.

Institutional Perspectives

Social life is patterned and predictable because it is organized into institutions. An **institution** is an established system of rules and strategies that defines how people are related to each other and how they should act in a given social situation. Sociologists use the term in two ways; to refer to the coordinated activities of many different kinds of organizations in a particular domain (the overall social organization of religion, the family, or the economy), and to refer to specific organizations within a domain that follow and contribute to wider institutional logics.

Institution An established system of rules and strategies that defines how people are related to each other and how they should act in a given social situation.

How do institutions shape our lives? Schools, for example, define specific social roles (teacher, student, parent) and establish clear expectations about the behavior and responsibilities for each role. While people are free to act however they want, when they are in school they will be evaluated according to how well they meet the expectations of their role. In other words, everybody in the school has a clear understanding of how students, teachers, and parents are supposed to act.

Institutions often act as gatekeepers by controlling access to important social resources. Some institutions give out formal credentials, such as a school diploma, a driver's license, or a board certification to practice a profession. If you want one of these credentials, you have to take the right classes, learn the proper set of behaviors, and pass a test demonstrating that you know all the important rules that are associated with the credentialed role. In other cases, such as journalism, gatekeeping comes in the form of public access or public visibility. If you want media publicity, you need to know the rules and strategies that journalists use to define what counts as news, who counts as an authoritative source, and what makes a good news story (Gans 1979; Schudson 1981).

Classroom organization
Fourth-grade students in Seattle work on assignments as the teacher helps one child. The children know they are students who are expected to follow directions and sit and do their work when asked by the teacher. The classroom defines roles for both student and teacher behavior.

By defining different expectations for different types of people, institutional gatekeeping often reproduces social privileges and disadvantages. For example, because mothers have historically been expected to be the primary caregivers in the family, mothers (and women in general) have often been overlooked and devalued by gatekeepers in other institutions such as schools and the workplace (Epstein and Goode 1971). Institutional gatekeeping also helps wealthier and better-educated parents pass their advantages on to their children because institutional gatekeepers tend to recognize and reward privilege. Annette Lareau's study, *Unequal Childhoods* (2003), analyzes differences between middle-class and working-class parenting styles. She shows that, unlike working-class parents, middle-class parents encourage their children to communicate with adults, to ask questions, and to share their opinions. These children grow up expecting teachers, doctors, and other adults to take them seriously, and to treat them like present or future equals. More often than not, Lareau shows, these children are rewarded by these gatekeepers for the styles of interaction their parents taught them, because schools and workplaces tend to value this kind of assertiveness. In these examples, we can see microsociological, macrosociological, and institutional factors combining to produce specific social outcomes.

Thinking Relationally: The Paired Concepts

The social world is complicated. We are usually involved in multiple projects, and we are forced to respond simultaneously to many different demands. We cannot separate out each of these demands and projects, trying to think about them in isolation. Instead, the choices we make in one part of our lives have a cascading effect on the rest of our lives. This is why sociologists focus on the relationships between different social forces.

When we encourage you to think relationally, this means that we want you to try to avoid thinking about any *single* social force as if it exists in isolation. We don't live in a carefully controlled laboratory, where we can isolate a single factor to see how important it is. In real life, we have to respond to everything at once. Thinking relationally can help you to move through the world more effectively. To help you to begin thinking relationally, we offer you five sets of paired concepts. These paired concepts include many of the key terms that sociologists have developed for thinking about the social world.

We use the paired concepts throughout this book, to help you think like a sociologist. They will not only prepare you for more advanced undergraduate courses in sociology; they will also help you distinguish how a sociological approach is different from other approaches in the social sciences. Last, and most important, our belief is that the paired concepts will provide you with some useful tools for thinking about how to live in the modern world. The paired concepts are there to remind your that social forces do not exist in isolation, but instead exist in relationship to other social forces.

Solidarity and Conflict

Sociologists understand society as a kind of social fabric that connects us to each other. People want this fabric to be woven tightly enough that it comforts and supports them, but not so tight that it feels constricting. For example, if you stand too close to someone in an elevator, they will usually move away to increase social distance. We want to feel close to others, but there are rules about what counts as too close. As we move around in the social world, we identify with some groups but not with others. We are constantly making judgments about good and bad, appropriate and inappropriate, sacred and profane—and we know that others are making the same kinds of judgments.

When people make moral judgments between in-groups and out-groups, they create categories of "us" and "them." **Solidarity** is the sense of belonging and connection that we have to a particular group. It is the sense of "us" feeling connected together. Solidarity is one of the most powerful social forces, because the feelings of connection and community encourage us to cooperate with others and to act for the greater good. But solidarity also produces **conflict** because it always produces a "them." We can only feel connected to a group by drawing boundaries around it, and these boundaries only work by creating a division between inside and outside, by defining those outside the group who are both different from us and not connected to us.

The relationship between solidarity and conflict is easy to see in everyday life and can range from the mundane to the very serious. For example, as sports fans we not only root for "our" team, but we also root against the other teams, and particularly against our rival teams. It's fun. However, this kind of boundary-drawing can have considerably more serious consequences on a larger scale. For example, the concept of national identity can be used to encourage a people to think their own national group is superior to other national groups. Solidarity and conflict can also scale down. An example of this is the issues you might face when you try to integrate a new romantic partner into a long-standing friendship group. Old friends may not like your new partner, who may feel threatened by the solidarity between old friends. Boundary-drawing can create different levels of conflict, ranging from the vaguely awkward interactions between different groups of friends to the violent warfare that erupts between nations. The point is that solidarity and conflict are deeply interconnected, and the relationship between solidarity and conflict produces some of the most powerful social forces in our lives.

Power and Resistance

Sociologists understand **power** as a social relationship in which one individual or group is able to influence the conduct of other individuals or groups (Scott 2006: 127). In its most direct

Solidarity The sense of belonging and the connection that we have to a particular group.

Conflict Disagreement, opposition, and separation between individuals or groups.

Power A social relationship in which one individual or group is able to influence the conduct of other individuals or groups either directly through force or indirectly through authority, persuasion, or cultural expectation.

Greeting an acquaintance or introducing a friend
When a new person is introduced into an existing group of friends, solidarity is created. Greeting rituals like a handshake provide a patterned format for making the connection.

form, power operates by physical force or by the threat of force. Usually, though, power operates in other ways. You may follow an order because you believe that the person giving it is has a legitimate right to do so, like when a teacher asks you to complete a homework assignment or when you agree to pay your monthly phone bill. You may follow somebody's suggestion because they manage to convince you that they have a good solution to a common problem. You may act without much thought at all, either because it is something you have done many times before, or because everyone around you is doing the same thing. You may be powerfully attracted to a particular person, and willing to do virtually anything they ask you. Each of these relationships involves an exercise in power.

Resistance Opposition to the exercise of power.

Resistance is the other side of power. The exercise of power always produces resistance. People resent being forced to do things. They dislike feeling trapped. They do not like to feel powerless. They question whether the people ordering them to do something really have the right or the authority to do so. They argue about politics, and they get angry when they disagree with decisions made by elected politicians. Their leaders disappoint them, and they grow more cynical and distrustful of people in positions of power.

The relationship between power and resistance is a very complicated and open-ended relationship, which plays itself out in small-scale interactions, social institutions, and larger social structures. It is organized very much like a game, because each "move" by one player will influence the next move by the other. Making things more complicated is the fact that the different moves are not equally available to all players. For example, the use of force is mainly reserved for police, military forces, and other agents of government. Other people can use force, but this is usually met with considerable social criticism, and may even attract the attention of law enforcement. Many uses of power require both money and resources, which are distributed unequally throughout society. It is generally easier for privileged people to exercise power. At the same time, because the exercise of power produces its own resistance, these privileges are frequently challenged. For all these reasons, the relationship between power and resistance is a primary research interest of sociology as a discipline.

Inequality The uneven distribution of social resources.

Women marching in Los Angeles at the #MeToo women's march, November 12, 2017
The #MeToo march in November 2017 took aim at sexual abuse and misconduct charges within the entertainment industry and other workplaces. In 2017, an estimated half a million women marched in the United States and an estimated 7 million women marched in 60 countries around the world.

Inequality and Privilege

Inequality refers to the uneven distribution of social resources. Inequality exists in all societies, and for virtually every resource that people care about. Some of the key types of social inequality are organized around the distribution of income, wealth, education, food, health care, and access to power. Patterns of social inequality reflect key social divisions, including race, ethnicity, gender, age, social class, and geography. They also reflect past patterns of power and resistance, including colonization and decolonization and slavery and abolition.

Sociologists are interested in knowing how inequality is organized across time and place, since a key dimension of addressing inequality is to understand how it is created and sustained. Sociologists study inequality in single societies such as the United States; they compare how inequality is organized in different societies; they look at global inequality; and they track changes in inequality over time.

Inequality creates the social conditions for **privilege** because of the advantages that flow to people at the top of the hierarchy. People with privilege have more resources, and are able to segregate themselves from the less fortunate. In the United States and elsewhere, privileged people live in different neighborhoods, send their children to different schools, belong to different clubs, and work different jobs. Because they live almost completely different lives, surrounded by other people just like them, the well-off do not always see how inequality makes their privileges possible. Sociological research helps show how inequality and privilege are inextricably related to each other, locally, globally, and historically.

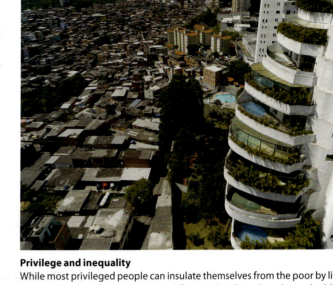

Privilege and inequality
While most privileged people can insulate themselves from the poor by living in different neighborhoods and attending different schools, in these luxury buildings in São Paulo, Brazil, residents can see the Paraisópolis favela from the swimming pools on their balconies.

Privilege The greater resources possessed by some individuals and groups compared to others.

Global and Local

Social life on our planet is increasingly interconnected. We buy things from all over the world, and we work for companies that have a global reach. Political conflicts thousands of miles away influence financial markets here at home. People everywhere watch the same movies and TV programs, play the same video games, and communicate with strangers over social media. The number of global migrants continues to increase, particularly to wealthier nations such as the United States, Canada, Australia, and Germany. Sociologists refer to this international integration of social life and increasing global interconnection as **globalization**.

Despite increased globalization, we still live much of our lives in specific **local** places. We spend months and years at a time without ever leaving the city in which we live. We spend most of our time with a small number of friends, family, and work colleagues. Although we might email and text friends from around the world, for most of us the majority of our communication is with people who live near us or work with us. Farmers' markets and farm-to-table restaurants are also increasing in popularity in the United States, particularly among the fashionable and the well-to-do. On internet travel forums, tourists offer suggestions about the best way to experience local cultures around the world. Despite the march of globalization, the lure of the local continues to present itself as a marker of authenticity.

Sociologists emphasize that the local and the global do not exist in isolation, but are related to each other. Global influences can be seen in almost every local setting, and they are themselves shaped by and adapted to local conditions. In Malaysia, for example, McDonald's sells a "Spicy Korean Burger." In the fashion industry, many of the global trends of the last 20 years first emerged in the styles created by

Globalization The interconnection of social life on the planet.

Local The specific particular settings of everyday life, including face-to-face relationships.

Global and local
McDonald's makes accommodations to local food cultures in different countries. It offers a McFalafel in Egypt, a McArabia in Morocco, a Wasabi Filet-o-Fish in Hong Kong, and a Nasi Lemak burger in Malaysia. This McDonald's Spicy Korean Burger, sold in Malaysia, is a burger with kimchi on charcoal buns in place of the classic sesame seed-sprinkled buns.

Social structures The seen and unseen regular, organized patterns of social life.

Contingency Openness in social life produced by human choices and actions.

teenage girls in the Harajuku neighborhood of Tokyo. In these examples and many others, local and global influences combine together into interesting new creations. People in today's world live globally and locally at the same time.

Structure and Contingency

While social life is patterned in many important ways, this does not mean that the patterns control us completely. As we move through the world, we are continuously reading and interpreting the social cues around us. We plan our actions, trying to predict their outcomes. We improvise, we try new things out, and we play with new identities. We may know the rules and the social conventions, but we do not always follow them. There is contingency, or openness, in action—outcomes are not completely determined by the regular patterns in social life that sociologists call **social structures.**

As we discussed earlier, some of the main patterns or structures that sociologists study are population patterns, political and economic structures, cultural belief systems, and power differences that are organized along the lines of race, gender, and class. These structures are created and re-created at all three levels of analysis—microsociologically, macrosociologically, and institutionally. People re-create social structures such as stereotypes when they cross the street to avoid people they perceive as threatening. They re-create structures such as employment and migration patterns when they move to a new city or a new country in search of work. They reproduce structures of status inequality when they treat doctors and judges with more respect than nurses and secretaries. They reproduce structures of gender inequality when they hand restaurant bills to men rather than women, and when they hold the door open for women but not for men. These structures are so deeply ingrained in our social environment that we hardly notice them.

However, because social structures have to be reproduced in our everyday actions, this means that they are connected to the openness of social life. **Contingency** refers to this openness and to the fact that a given outcome is never guaranteed, despite the likelihood that things will happen in a specific way. For example, while it is expected that someone will shake your hand if you extend it to them in greeting, there is never a guarantee that this will happen. While you are waiting patiently in line to buy a ticket, there is always the possibility that someone will cut in front of the line ahead of you. There is also contingency connected to institutional and macrosociological structures. A severe economic downturn or a catastrophic natural disaster can cause a massive increase in homelessness. International trade can be disrupted by bad weather and important news can be preempted by a celebrity event. This is why most organizations spend a lot of time developing contingency plans. No matter how much research and planning they do, it is impossible for them to predict perfectly what is going to happen.

When people act differently from expectations, they challenge social structures. One of the things that happens during times of great social change is that people are more likely to challenge existing structures and to create new ones (Swidler 1986). A goal for many sociologists is to make people more aware of social structures, so they can make a more conscious decision about which structures to reproduce and which ones to challenge. And sociologists also try to think about the role of contingency in their social research. No matter how much they know about social structures, they remain attentive to the ways that the contingent actions of individuals and groups can challenge and disrupt social structures and social outcomes.

These five paired concepts are connected to each other in important ways, and thinking about them together can help you understand the complex and dynamic nature of social life. For example, the relationship between "us" and "them" is connected to the exercise of power and resistance, and also to the organization of inequality and privi-

Structure and Contingency
Economic downturn, ill health, family dysfunction, and natural disaster are all events that can affect people's ability to find shelter. The lack of social resources and social care for people affected by such contingencies results in homelessness, with people sleeping on the sidewalk in very cold weather.

lege. The intermingling of the global and the local helps us to see social structures, to try out new things, to form different kinds of groups. When groups form into social movements that challenge the powerful, their actions highlight the contingency of social action and the possibility of challenging social structures.

Why Sociology?

Why sociology? There are many reasons to pursue a sociological life, but two literacy skills acquired by a study of sociology are especially important. First, sociology teaches a literacy of concepts. By developing a grasp of key sociological concepts and theories, you will be better able to identify how different social forces are connected in real life. Second, sociology teaches data and information literacy, by developing a range of research methods that help you think critically and creatively about how to get the facts right when asking social questions. Both of these are important skills valued by employers. They are also important for developing a deeper understanding about the world in which you live.

This is the larger promise of sociology: that it will inform the pursuit of human freedom and social justice. How? The goal is not to tell people what to think, but rather to help us all think more clearly and comprehensively about our shared social life. In the highly individualized societies that we live in today, this collective level of thinking is often missing or underdeveloped. By thinking about interactional norms, social scripts, organizational routines, and broader institutional principles, a sociological imagination can help us see the face of the "other" outside our own narrow circle, while illuminating our own complex positions in social relationships of solidarity, privilege, and power. Practically, sociologists do research on behalf of social movements, governments, nonprofit organizations, and businesses that help people make more informed decisions and think carefully about the social impact of their choices. Sociologists also create theories that help us think imaginatively about our shared social future. In short, sociology enables us to consider the human face of social action, and identify our own capacities to defend—or transform—social life.

LEARNING GOALS REVISITED

1.1 Define the sociological imagination.

- The sociological imagination is the ability to connect "biography with history"; that is, to connect our individual life story with the historical and cultural patterns of the society in which we live.

- The sociological imagination shows us how individual choices, like the decision to get divorced, might be affected by wider social forces such as economic change and the availability of jobs.

- The sociological imagination shows us that people's lives are sometimes shaped in surprising ways by social change; for example, William Julius Wilson's classic work showed the influence of structural change in race relations on inner-city poverty.

- The sociological imagination shows that people can resist larger social forces by acting in ways that change or challenge the social structure, or by forming social movements for social change.

1.2 Understand that there are different levels of social things; for example, individuals, relationships, and institutions.

- Early sociologists defined sociology as a new science of social facts, social action, and social relationships. They identified a special social domain that was different than the level of individuals alone.

- Sociologists identify different levels of analysis and different levels of scale in research. They define microsociological, macrosociological, and institutional levels of analysis.

- Sociologists are interested in how causes at one level affect causes and outcomes at other levels. For example, sociologists ask: How do small-scale interactions in classrooms or job interviews sustain or reinforce large-scale social structures? Or, how are local actions connected to global outcomes?

1.3 Understand that sociologists are committed to the norms of scientific and intellectual community and different methods for exploring the social world.

- Early sociologists like Émile Durkheim, Max Weber, and Albion Small were committed to the systematic and scientific study of social facts, social actions, and social patterns.

- Social-scientific knowledge is different than ordinary, everyday knowledge about the world because it self-consciously uses systematic strategies to collect accurate and useful information.

- Sociological research strategies are designed to eliminate or reduce bias, particularly confirmation bias, where people are more likely to think something is true because it confirms prior beliefs.

- A focus on research methods is one of the defining features of social science, including sociology.

- Sociology is distinct from the other social sciences that may focus on the political system or the economic system, because it is committed to multiple research methods to study the intersections between different dimensions of social life.

1.4 Understand that sociology is used in the worlds of work, politics, and other domains of social life.

- Sociologists are found in many different careers, including law, medicine, education, social work, the arts, public service, business, and more.

- Sociology teaches a literacy of concepts and a literacy of data and information. Both of these literacies involve concrete skills that are of interest to employers in many fields.

1.5 Understand that many sociologists pursue sociology as a way to secure human freedom and social justice.

- Sociology is a perspective on social life that promotes understanding, human empowerment, and freedom. This has been true from the early years of the discipline, and many sociologists pursue sociology as a way to pursue human freedom and social justice.

- Sociologists understand humans as individuals with free will who make judgments about good and bad, right and wrong. Sometimes people will choose to support the social structures and other times they will act to change them.

Key Terms

Confirmation bias 9
Conflict 15
Contingency 18
Globalization 17
Inequality 16
Institution 13
Institutional level of analysis 10
Level of analysis 10
Local 17
Macrosociology 12
Microsociology 11
Power 15
Privilege 17
Research methods 9
Resistance 16
Social structures 18
Sociological imagination 6
Solidarity 15

Review Questions

1. What is sociology? Describe the three basic elements of sociology.

2. What is the sociological imagination? Give an example of a research study that exemplifies the sociological imagination.

3. Why do sociologists believe that systematic and scientific research is the best way to understand the social world?

4. How is sociology different from other social sciences, such as psychology or economics?

5. What is microsociology? Give an example of a microsociological approach to understanding the world.

6. What is macrosociology? Give an example of a macrosociological approach to understanding the world.

7. What is an institution? How do institutions shape our lives? Give an example of an institutional understanding of the world.

8. Why do sociologists insist that we think about the social world relationally?

9. How are solidarity and conflict connected? Give an example of how solidarity produces conflict.

10. What is power? Why does the exercise of power always produce resistance? Give an example of resistance.

11. What is inequality? How does inequality help to produce privilege?

12. What is globalization? Give an example of how the global and the local are connected to each other.

13. Give an example of how people re-create social structures in their everyday lives.

14. What is contingency? How is contingency related to social structure? Give an example of contingency in action.

Explore

RECOMMENDED READINGS

Bauman, Zygmunt. 2008. *The Art of Life*. Malden, MA: Polity Press.

Bourdieu, Pierre. 2010. *Sociology Is a Martial Art: Political Writings by Pierre Bourdieu*. New York: New Press.

Goffman, Erving. 1959. *The Presentation of Self in Everyday Life*. New York: Anchor.

Mills, C. Wright. [1959] 2000. *Sociological Imagination*. New York: Oxford University Press.

Wilson, William Julius. 1987. *The Truly Disadvantaged*. Chicago: University of Chicago Press.

ACTIVITIES

- *Use your sociological imagination*: Are you a member of any kind of social group? Make a list of the ones you belong to. How many are there? Rank your list of groups in different ways, for example, by size or how strongly you feel connected to them. What are other groups that are different from but related to your group? Compare your findings with your classmates'.

- *Media+Data Literacies*: Are there any celebrities (politicians, actors, or musicians) that you think are persuasive? Explain why you find them persuasive. Where do you get information about celebrities? Using your sociological imagination, can you identify "gatekeepers" who might have shaped your opinions?

- *Discuss*: Why do you think you are in college right now when other people are not? Are there social reasons? What are they?

For additional resources, including Media+Data Literacy exercises, In the News exercises, and quizzes, please go to **oup.com/he/ Jacobs-Townsley1e**

2

American Sociology
Theories and Contexts

Are you already a sociologist? American sociologist Charles Lemert thinks you are, because you use ideas about the social world to navigate your life. This might be called common sense. For example, you might share the widely held view that college education is linked to increased income. But why? What is the source of your belief?

The difference between common sense and sociology is that sociologists use specific theories and methods to ask critical questions about social life (Lemert 2008). In this case, sociologists ask questions about how education works to produce differences in income. What is it about college education exactly that leads to higher average incomes among college graduates compared to nongraduates: is it the content of specific classes, the prestige of the particular institution, or the cultural knowledge learned at college that is important? Do the habits and mannerisms of educated people help college graduates navigate job interviews by signaling that they are the "right kind of people" for the job? Perhaps these are questions you will pursue in your own career as a teacher, a lawyer, a doctor, a politician, or . . . a sociologist?

Thinking Like a Sociologist

Sociological theories can refine our common-sense image of the world, by challenging us to think differently about things we believe we already know. For example, it is true that people with a college education usually do have higher incomes. But this is not only because people learn job-specific skills in college. College is also about status and credentials. For most of the 20th century, college attendance was a sign of privilege, and a way to access prestigious social networks. In the 1960s, US government programs were established to expand college enrollment in an effort to reduce social inequality.

Graduation
In today's global economy, a college degree is required for entry to most workplaces.

LEARNING GOALS

2.1   Understand that sociology developed as a way to explain social patterns and social change and is one of a family of social science disciplines located within the liberal arts.

2.2   Understand that knowledge is socially located and develops within particular intellectual and national traditions and different social networks and institutional settings.

2.3   Identify core theoretical concepts in the discipline.

2.4   Understand that the history of sociological theory is distinct from making theoretical arguments or applying theory to contemporary examples.

However, this was not a perfect solution for reducing inequality, because the people who are most likely to do well in school are those whose parents are well-educated, have good jobs, or both (Blau and Duncan 1967; Bourdieu and Passeron 1979, 1990; Lareau 2003). Sociological theories about inequality and privilege can help us better understand what might seem to be a common-sense relationship between college education and income. By asking critical questions, these theories encourage us to see the social world in new ways.

METHODS AND INTERPRETATION

Measuring the Effect of Education on Earnings

The US Census Bureau and the Department of Labor collect national data showing that education has an enormous impact on earnings for most of the US population. They report that "education levels had more effect on earnings over a 40-year span in the workforce than any other demographic factor, such as gender, race and Hispanic origin" (Julian and Kominski 2011). Figure 2.1 shows that in 2018, the median weekly earnings for workers with a Bachelor's degree ($1,198) were more than 60 percent higher than earnings for workers with only a high school diploma ($730) and more than twice the median weekly earnings of people with less than a high school diploma ($553).

There are exceptions to the general pattern of relationship between education and earnings. Some well-known people never attended college or dropped out, including Facebook founder Mark Zuckerberg, Microsoft founder Bill Gates, and Apple founder Steve Jobs. While these individuals are comparatively rare, they show how chance, contingency, and choice can play a role in individual life outcomes. In the language of sociology, these exceptions show that people's lives are not entirely shaped by social structures.

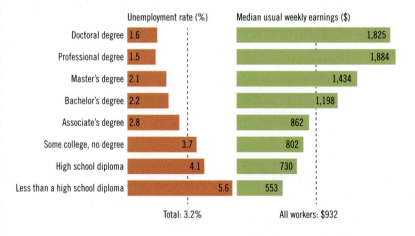

Figure 2.1   Unemployment rates and earnings by educational attainment, 2018.
Note: Data are for persons age 25 and over. Earnings are for full-time wage and salary workers.
Source: US Bureau of Labor Statistics, Current Population Survey.

ACTIVE LEARNING

Discuss: Ask your parents or another adult why they think college is important for career success. Be sure to ask what it is exactly about education that pays off for most people.

Critical Questions and the Sociological Imagination

A critical question relies on reason, theory, prior knowledge, and new evidence to reflect upon social actions. Critical questions allow for more than a yes/no answer. Sociologists who ask critical questions reject the idea that a given social outcome was inevitable. Instead, they seek to explain why something happened the way it did—and not otherwise. At their best, critical questions help us imagine new social possibilities.

Cultivating the ability to ask a critical question is fundamental to what C. Wright Mills (1916–1962) called the sociological imagination. As we discussed in Chapter 1, the sociological imagination is the ability to see the connections between individual lives and wider social structures.

C. Wright Mills

The sociological imagination implies that where you stand determines what you can see. Think about your position in a classroom. Perhaps you can see the front of the room, the instructor, or the students sitting in front of you? What you cannot see as clearly is yourself. To get a picture of where you are, you have to use your imagination to move outside your position and reflect on your surroundings. This imaginative ability to move outside of yourself, using your mind to view yourself as part of a wider social scene, is a mental capability called **reflexivity.**

The sociological imagination is based on reflexivity. It acknowledges that our perceptions are limited by our social positions. Our views are shaped by the time and place and bodies where we live. This is true for every person. We bring our experiences, knowledge, attitudes, and abilities into every social situation. And these experiences are shaped by the groups, families, and other institutions to which we belong. By asking critical questions about ourselves and our social world, sociology can help us extend our perceptions. The promise of the sociological imagination is that we will be able to see a much wider picture, tell much better stories, and take much more effective social action.

This chapter encourages you to apply the sociological imagination to sociology itself. In other words, we want you to think critically about sociology's history, so that you can see sociology from the viewpoint of sociologists themselves. To help you do this, we tell three stories about American sociology.

Reflexivity The imaginative ability to move outside of yourself in order to understand yourself as part of a wider social scene.

- The first story is about social theory, sociology, and the social sciences. From the beginning, sociology had big ambitions, trying to become the master discipline that would hold together all the social sciences. Because of these ambitions, theory has always been part of the work that sociologists produce.

- The second story is about the big ideas and important thinkers in the sociological tradition. Sociology originally developed in Europe and the United States during the late 19th and early 20th centuries, as an attempt to understand three key processes that were changing society: the Industrial Revolution, the spread of democracy, and the creation of nation-states. By the mid-1900s, particularly in the United States, there were three main perspectives in sociology: conflict theory, consensus theory, and symbolic interaction.

- The third story is about how sociology and sociological theory have changed over the last 50 years. During these decades, sociologists stopped organizing their work in terms of the "three-fold model" of conflict theory, consensus theory, and symbolic interactionism. As sociologists have become more concerned with culture, difference, and globalization, they have turned away from overarching theories that were supposed to apply to all societies. As a result, sociological theory now works to understand specific social problems rather than developing concepts that can be applied to any type of social analysis.

Social Theory, Sociology, and the Social Sciences

The French philosopher Auguste Comte (1798–1857) was one of the first sociologists. He was interested in how different types of scientific knowledge were connected to each other. Comte identified six "fundamental sciences": mathematics, astronomy, physics, chemistry, biology, and sociology. Of these six, Comte believed that sociology was destined to become the most important. Because social phenomena were the most complex, he argued, sociology needed to integrate all the other sciences into a single theory of social phenomena. If sociology could achieve this, Comte believed, then people would use its knowledge to create a new and better society.

Comte's ambitious agenda for sociological theory was influential for a long time. In fact, many sociologists in the 19th century believed that **social science** would eventually replace religion as the major intellectual force organizing in the world. They looked to sociology to develop a science of society itself, by establishing a master theory that could explain social phenomena.

Émile Durkheim (1858–1917), who is generally regarded as the "father of sociology" in France, believed strongly in this vision of sociology as the most important of the social sciences. At the Sorbonne in Paris, where Durkheim was a professor of education and sociology, his lectures on social science were required for all students (Jones 1986). As a key adviser for the French Ministry of Education, Durkheim helped spread sociology throughout the national curriculum.

At the center of Durkheim's vision was the idea that sociology was a distinct science, different from philosophy, psychology, or the natural sciences. Durkheim wanted sociologists to study **social facts,** which are the forces external to the individual that influence how people act, think, or feel (Durkheim [1895] 2014). Social facts are different from biological facts or psychological facts, because they exist outside of the individual's body or conscience. For example, in his study, *Suicide*, Durkheim (1997) showed that suicide rates were not simply the result of unpredictable, isolated, individual choices. Instead, they were related systematically to other social facts such as religion, nationality, gender, and marital status. We discuss Durkheim's theories in greater depth later in the chapter. For now, we want to emphasize two points. One, Durkheim insisted that social facts were the basic pieces of information that scientists needed to understand society. And two, Durkheim wanted to develop a single theory to understand and explain these social facts.

The same kind of grand vision motivated the work of Talcott Parsons (1902–1979), an American sociologist. Parsons, who led Harvard's Department of Social Relations (an influential collaboration of sociologists, anthropologists, and psychologists), worked to create a single theory for all the social sciences that could help support a democratic society.

Social sciences The disciplines that use systematic scientific and cultural methods to study the social world, as distinct from the natural and physical worlds.

Social facts Facts about the collective nature of social life that have their own patterns and dynamics beyond the individual level.

As we discuss later in the chapter, this pursuit of a single theory that could explain all social phenomena began to fall out of favor during the 1960s and 1970s. But it is an important part of the story of sociology. For most of its early history, sociologists were trying to accomplish two different things. They were trying to develop a general theory of society, and they were trying to explain the tremendous social changes that were taking place in the world.

Classical Sociology

Sociology emerged during a period of tremendous social change. The Industrial Revolution, the spread of democracy, and the creation of the modern nation-state were causing massive social upheaval in Western Europe, and their influence was spreading quickly throughout the world. Sociologists wanted to understand and explain these changes, which were making people interact in ways that had never happened before.

The Industrial Revolution

Most of the early sociologists lived in the immediate aftermath of the Industrial Revolution, which began in England around 1760. Before the Industrial Revolution, most goods were made by hand, by individuals or small groups of people, often working at home. After the Industrial Revolution, most goods were mass-produced in factories, with the use of machines to speed up and standardize the work process. The logic of marriage and families adapted to meet the needs of factory production. Scientific improvements in health and medicine extended life. Food became more plentiful. By 1850, the Industrial Revolution had spread throughout Europe and North America, reorganizing almost every part of social life. For this reason, some scholars have called the Industrial Revolution "the most important event in human history" (Hobsbawm 1996: 29).

Globalization A concept that refers to the growing social, economic, cultural, and political interdependence of the world's people.

The Industrial Revolution accelerated the process of **globalization**, which refers to the way that our actions and activities are linked across different regions and continents (Held 1999). Because factories were able to produce things faster and more inexpensively, factory owners searched constantly for new markets where they could sell their goods. Local markets grew into regional markets, and finally into global markets. All of this required increased coordination and administration across larger territories. As a result, social relationships became much more standardized across the world and between different groups of people. By standardizing time, currencies, weights, and other measures, an enormous expansion of global trade was made possible. New transportation technologies made it easier to move goods and people across great distances. New communication technologies made it easier to coordinate the activities taking place in these distant markets. All of this sped up and intensified the pace of global interconnection, blurring the boundaries between local and global events (Held 1999).

The new industrial landscape
This 19th-century engraving by Durand-Brager of Vivian's copper foundry in Swansea, Wales, depicts the pollution from open-pit mines and smoke from foundries that transformed the landscape.

Industrial division of labor
This 19th-century watercolor by I. F. Bonhomme shows women and children working in the coal-sifting room at the Blanzy mine, Saone-et-Loire, France. Women and children were among the first factory workers.

Machine technology
The industrial revolution witnessed rapid technological invention in new factories. This steam hammer was erected in James Nasmyth's foundry near Manchester in 1832. Today's factories can be cleaner but they are still based on industrial technology.

Urbanization A social process in which the population shifts from the country into cities, and where most people start to live in cities rather than rural areas.

The Industrial Revolution also encouraged greater **urbanization**, which refers to the growth of cities. For example, the population of London more than tripled between 1750 and 1850 from 700,000 people to more than 2.3 million. As more people moved into cities to work in factories, population density increased. New systems of public transportation made it easier for people to get to work, and allowed cities to spread across much larger territories. Cafés, coffeehouses, and pubs offered places where friends and strangers alike could meet, relax, and discuss the day's events. Crime increased, and professional police forces were created to control disorder and to act as a deterrent against theft and violence. Social inequality also increased. London was the wealthiest city in the world in the 19th century, but it was also a place of great poverty, where millions of people lived in overcrowded, unhealthy, and unpleasant slums. This was also true of American cities like New York and Chicago.

Taken together, industrialization, globalization, and urbanization changed the way that people interacted with each other. This new world was memorialized in the novels of Charles Dickens (*Oliver Twist*, *Hard Times*), Victor Hugo (*Les Misérables*), Upton Sinclair (*The Jungle*), and many others. Sociologists of the time also believed that they could help describe and explain these momentous social changes.

The Democratic Revolution

The second big change in the early days of sociology was the spread of democracy. Democracy refers to the rule of the people, and it has its origin in the city-states of ancient Greece. But democracy was not a very influential system of government before the 18th century. This began to change with the American Revolution (1776) and the French Revolution (1789), which replaced the rule of kings with the rule of the people.

The democratic revolutions that started in England, France, and the United States spread quickly. By 1850, movements for democracy could be found in most European societies. These movements challenged the rulers of those societies, who either had to forcefully maintain their control, or let the people have more say over political decisions.

Ideas about democracy combined with ideas about science began to change how people thought about modern society. Until the 17th century, Western societies had revolved around the institution of religion, and politics involved compromise between the king, landowners, and church leaders. But this arrangement was challenged throughout the 19th century, by intellectuals as well as revolutionary leaders of democratic movements. In fact, many intellectuals predicted that religion would eventually disappear completely in a new, secular society. Comte, Durkheim, and the other early sociologists believed that social science could help create a freer and more democratic society, one less reliant on religion and tradition. They hoped that sociology could help discover newer and better ways to create social order that more accurately reflected the wishes and desires of the people.

The Creation of Nation-States

The third great change during this era was the creation of nation-states. In a nation-state, a government has control over a defined territory; the people who live in that territory are citizens of the nation, united by a common identity, a common history, and a strong sense of social connection. Nation-states first emerged in Western Europe in the 16th and 17th centuries, and began to spread rapidly throughout the world in the 18th and 19th centuries (Mann 1993).

Nation-states were connected to industrialization and democracy in important ways. New communication and transportation technologies made it easier to govern across larger territories. Mass literacy and mass media meant that the people in these territories were reading the same things, learning new things and participating in a cultural world far greater than their local market. With the growth of citizen armies in newly democratic societies, governments were able to link the rights of citizenship with the duty of military service and sacrifice for the nation.

By the end of the 19th century, "the people" and "the nation" had become virtually interchangeable. With the growth of national education systems, national languages, literatures, holidays, and museums, national identity became one of the most powerful forms of common experience and belonging in modern social life (Anderson 2006; Weber 1946).

The growing power of nation-states was also associated with violence and domination. The most powerful industrialized nations used their superior military technologies to conquer new territories, leading to a vast system of colonialism that extended Western influence and control around much of the world. Believing that they were more advanced, these nations justified their conquests by claiming that they were bringing democracy and other modern benefits to "less civilized" parts of the world. Pseudoscientific arguments about the supposed superiority of the "European race" encouraged European nations to believe that other parts of the world were incapable of self-rule, and would be better off being controlled by the more advanced European nations (Smedley 1993). The European nation-states controlled almost the entire continent of Africa by the end of the 19th century, as well as India, much of Southeast Asia, and Australia. Racism, disrespect, poverty, and violence were regular features of life for indigenous people in these colonial territories.

The European Canon

Early sociological theorists struggled to describe and explain these vast, interlocking changes, among them Karl Marx (1818–1883) and Max Weber (1864–1920) in Germany, and Émile Durkheim in France. These three thinkers are

The patriotism of the colonies
Instead of resisting British colonial government, the colonized were asked to fight on behalf of the British Empire. In this 1917 postcard, a British and an Indian soldier pose next to the Red Ensign, an extension of British nationalism in a flag symbolizing Britain's overseas possessions.

Karl Marx

Canon The set of thinkers and ideas that serve as a standard point of reference for a scholarly or artistic tradition.

Capitalism An economic system based on the private ownership of property, including the means of material life such as food, clothing, and shelter, and in which the production of goods and services is controlled by private individuals and companies, and prices are set by markets.

Alienation A condition where humans have no meaningful connection to their work, or to each other.

especially important in sociology, and their combined work helped create the **canon** for sociological scholarship. This means they are a standard point of reference for many sociologists and their ideas continue to be used today.

KARL MARX. Karl Marx was one of the most influential intellectuals of the 19th century. His ideas about social and economic conflict changed the course of history. *The Communist Manifesto*, which he published in 1848 with Friedrich Engels, inspired dozens of socialist movements throughout the 19th and 20th centuries. Although he was trained as a philosopher, Marx is now viewed as one of the most important early sociologists.

Marx believed that society is shaped by the history of economic conflict. At any given time, Marx argued, there were two economic groups, or social classes. The dominant class, which controlled economic production, used that control in order to profit from the work of others. Everyone else lacked control over the conditions of their work. At the mercy of the dominant class, those who were dominated lacked true freedom. For Marx, the interests of the dominant class and the dominated class were fundamentally opposed. In order for the dominated class to become free, its members needed to overthrow the dominant class and set up a new system for organizing work. The problem was that the dominated class often failed to realize the true path to their freedom and happiness, a situation that Marx called "false consciousness."

Marx saw economic conflict as the central social fact determining every society, shaping social relationships between masters and slaves, landowners and peasants, factory owners and workers. In modern Western societies he described this fundamental economic conflict in terms of private property, or capital. **Capitalism** is a system that transforms the means of material life—food, clothing, shelter—into objects to be bought and sold on markets. A small class of capitalist owners control all the land, finance, factories, and machinery of production. Everyone else is destined to be a worker with no choice but to labor for capitalists for low wages under bad conditions. Instead of producing for their own purposes, Marx argues that capitalism strips workers of their humanity and creates **alienation**—a condition where humans have no meaningful connection to their work, or to each other. According to this view, all government, justice, cultural, and religious institutions are organized to support the rule of capitalists. For Marx, these are the defining features of the modern era: the domination of society by capitalists, the relentless expansion of production in pursuit of profit, and the exploitation of those at the bottom of the system. The key for overcoming this situation was the creation of a revolutionary class consciousness among the workers.

Marx's ideas remain influential today. The idea that economic inequality is a permanent feature of capitalist society, and in particular, that the economic interests of powerful corporations and a few extremely wealthy individuals shape the law and culture,

Mass worker action. The Manchester General Strike, 1926
The *Illustrated London News* captures the size and organization of the Manchester General Strike on May 15, 1926. Depicted here is the Great Procession of Corporation Tramwaymen starting from Albert Square and led by their band.

continue to resonate. While Marx's prediction in *The Communist Manifesto* that workers would inevitably rise up to overthrow capitalism and form a communist utopia seems unlikely in the early 21st century, there continue to be many movements for justice and economic equality that are inspired by Marx's writings.

Many sociologists have also been inspired by Marx's goal of using social science to improve the lives of the less fortunate. For example, the project of **public sociology** is a commitment to using sociological ideas in wider public conversations and struggles for social justice both in the United States and around the globe.

Public sociology A commitment to bringing sociological knowledge to a general public audience, and participating in wider public conversations and struggles for social justice.

MAX WEBER. Max Weber was also interested in understanding capitalism and modern society, but he took a different approach than Marx. While Marx wanted to produce scholarship that could help change the world, Weber believed that science needed to be separate from politics. While Marx's writings were deeply critical of capitalism, Weber argued that social science should limit itself to explaining, rather than evaluating, social outcomes. Finally, while Marx argued that material things like labor practices and economic

---

PAIRED CONCEPTS — Power and Resistance

Sociological Theorists in the Real World

Many sociological theorists have played important roles in politics and public life. For example, Émile Durkheim was an important advisor to the French Ministry of Education in the early 1900s, and Alexis de Tocqueville (1805–1859) served as minister of foreign affairs in France. Talcott Parsons was a frequent advisor to the US government during World War II. Robert Merton (1910–2003) conducted a number of studies for the US government about radio propaganda during the 1940s, and worked briefly as an adviser to the Pentagon (Simonson 2005: 11–12). More recently, the British sociological theorist Anthony Giddens was a consultant to governments around the world, and was one of the chief architects of the "New Labour" style of politics that led to the election of Tony Blair as British Prime Minister in 1997.

Other sociologists have entered political life not as government advisers, but rather as social critics trying to inspire acts of resistance to power. The most famous example is Karl Marx, whose writings against capitalism inspired labor movements and social revolutions around the world. In the United States, W. E. B. Du Bois (1868–1963) was a vocal critic of racial discrimination and police violence, a cofounder of the NAACP in 1909, and a leading voice trying to help organize African resistance against European colonial domination. C. Wright Mills was a well-known critic of the US government and its military throughout the 1940s and 1950s, and he was a major influence on the 1960s social movements that came to be known as "the New Left." More recently, the French sociologist Pierre Bourdieu (1930–2002) was one of the most influential critics of globalization and neoliberalism in Europe. His book *The Weight of the World* was a bestseller in France, and an inspiration to the waves of worker strikes and protest movements in France throughout the 1990s.

Anthony Giddens (left) and Tony Blair
British sociological theorist Anthony Giddens was a chief architect of the "New Labour" style of politics that led to the election of Tony Blair as Britain's prime minister in 1997. Giddens went on to serve as a consultant to governments around the world.

ACTIVE LEARNING

Think about it: Is there a time when a new idea or concept changed the way you thought about your life or about the world? How did it change your thinking?

Max Weber

Bureaucracy An organizational form with a clearly defined hierarchy where roles are based on rational, predictable, written rules and procedures to govern every aspect of the organization and produce standardized, systematic, and efficient outcomes.

Rationalization A major dynamic of modernity in which social relationships become more predictable, standardized, systematic, and efficient.

relationships were the most important issues, Weber argued that a good sociological explanation also needed to consider how ideas influence social actions.

Like Marx, Weber thought that capitalism was a central feature of modern society. What Weber added to the story, however, was a more nuanced sense of culture and organizations. For example, in *The Protestant Ethic and the Spirit of Capitalism* ([1905] 2011), Weber studied why capitalism developed first in specific Protestant communities in Europe and North America. He argued that religious ideas in those communities created the kinds of economic beliefs that were necessary for capitalism to flourish. Weber argued that many of the ways that people needed to act in a capitalist society were not "natural"—for example, the specialized division of labor, the investment of profit back into the business, and the desire to work longer than what is minimally necessary. When these principles became connected to religious beliefs and religious communities, they acquired a moral force that allowed them to spread quickly throughout society.

Weber was also interested in the organization of political authority, which had changed from traditional forms based on the divine right of kings to modern forms based on law and reason. Weber argued that one of the key developments in modern society was the creation of **bureaucracies.** In a bureaucracy, the organization is run according to formal rules and regulations rather than personal ties, traditions, or customs. Weber argued that all institutions in modern society—governments, militaries, corporations, and even cultural and religious organizations—were organized as bureaucracies.

Weber argued that the rise of bureaucracy was connected to the process of **rationalization**, in which all social relationships become more organized, standardized, and predictable. Rationalization made organizations much more effective in their operations, but it also led to a certain **disenchantment** in modern life, in which people blindly follow bureaucratic rules without any sense of passion or ultimate purpose.

Rationalization is still going on today. George Ritzer has written about the "McDonaldization of Society," in which more and more of our social life becomes predictable, standardized, systematic, and efficient—just like in a McDonald's restaurant (Ritzer 2013). But a rationalized world can be a tedious and dehumanizing place in which to live and work. This is obvious to anyone who has stood in line to renew their driver's license, or tried to get a question answered from a company's customer-service department.

ÉMILE DURKHEIM. The third key classical sociologist was Émile Durkheim. Like Marx and Weber, Durkheim was deeply interested in the way that economic change was shaping the

Waiting at the DMV
The tedium of waiting at the Department of Motor Vehicles is an iconic experience of bureaucracy in the United States. People sit in rows of chairs and wait their turn patiently before they proceed in an orderly manner to the counter where their applications can be processed.

division of labor and social life in industrial societies. Where Durkheim differed was in his focus on solidarity, which refers to the social ties that bind people together.

In *The Division of Labor in Society* (1893), Durkheim examined how solidarity was changing in industrializing, urbanizing nation-states such as France. In older societies, people were tied to each other through a strong sense of similarity, which Durkheim called **mechanical solidarity**. In these earlier societies people lived in the same place all their lives, and their social experiences were similar to those of the other people in their community. As a result, they tended to think the same way as everyone else, and they could assume that everyone in their society shared the same values and beliefs. This kind of social stability did not exist in modern industrialized societies.

Émile Durkheim

Durkheim believed that people still felt connected to one another in modern society, but it was based on something other than similarity. Instead, they were held together through a sense of social difference and interdependence. Because people work in increasingly specialized jobs, they know that they depend on other people's expertise, and this creates a kind of social connection. In other words, we feel connected to our doctor, our accountant, and the cashier at the local market, even if we do not know very much about them. Durkheim called this new form of social integration **organic solidarity.**

Durkheim believed that organic solidarity had certain advantages because it encouraged greater individuality and tolerance. But he also had concerns. Because modern societies were so large and changed so quickly, Durkheim worried that people would feel isolated and disconnected, a situation he referred to as **anomie**. Durkheim wanted sociologists to identify alternative sources of social connection that would promote solidarity. For example, Durkheim thought that national identity and national symbols could create a sort of common consciousness among the members of a nation-state, and as such the nation could be an important source of social solidarity that was similar to the mechanical solidarity of older societies (Durkheim [1893] 2014; Smith 2004). Durkheim believed that **collective representations**—the images we have of our own social groups like the nation, but also ethnicity, race, and religion—continue to produce social solidarity.

Durkheim's systematic approach to social analysis continues to be influential. Sociologists today study how people re-create a feeling of interdependence in our rapidly changing world, by examining the forms of social solidarity that exist at work, at play, in our close relationships, and in our worlds of social media. Sociologists are also studying the kinds of collective representations that bind people to society—not only during national holidays of commemoration like July 4 or Memorial Day but also during moments of national trauma like remembering September 11.

The Forgotten Canon?

In addition to Marx, Weber, and Durkheim, many other social analysts studied modern society. Among these are the "forgotten founders" who include lesser-known European theorists as well as prominent women and a range of theorists from non-European backgrounds (Lengermann and Niebrugge-Brantley 1998; Deegan 1990; 1991; 2002; 2014). This list includes thinkers like

Disenchantment The condition of rationalized bureaucratic societies characterized by the growing importance of skepticism and the decline of belief as a source of social action.

Division of labor A central principle for organizing the productive work in society that sorts different people into different work roles to ensure the production and reproduction of human life. This includes the separation of work and life into different, more specialized parts.

Mechanical solidarity A system of social ties that produces social cohesion on the basis of similar work and life in less complex divisions of labor.

Organic solidarity A system of social ties that produces social cohesion based on difference in complex division of labor.

Anomie The condition of feeling isolated and disconnected in the absence of rich social connection.

Collective representations Pictures, images, or narratives that describe the social group and are held in common.

Solidarity in Prayer, September 23, 2001
People pray holding American flags during a prayer service at Yankee Stadium for the victims of the World Trade Center terrorist attacks in New York in 2001.

Ibn Khaldûn (1332 CE/732 AH–March 19, 1406 CE/808 AH) in Northern Africa; Auguste Comte (1798–1857), Henri Saint-Simon (1760–1825), and Alexis de Tocqueville in France; Georg Simmel (1858–1918) and Karl Mannheim (1893–1947) in Germany; Harriet Martineau (1802–1876) and Herbert Spencer (1820–1903) in England; and Charlotte Perkins Gilman (1860–1935), Jane Addams (1860–1935), and W. E .B. Du Bois (1868–1963) in the United States. In this context, selecting Marx, Weber, and Durkheim as sociology's founders seems arbitrary and limited. Shouldn't we dismiss them as "dead white guys"? Perhaps.

PAIRED CONCEPTS

Inequality and Privilege

Forgotten Founders in Sociology

Ibn Khaldun is considered one of the premier philosophers of the Arab world. His scholarly output contains fundamental conceptual work in what we would recognize as the social sciences, specifically anthropology, economics, and sociology (Gates 1967; Haddad 1977; Dhaouadi 1990). Khaldun wrote prolifically on many topics, including six volumes of general sociology (Khaldûn 2004). Centuries before Émile Durkheim wrote about solidarity, Khaldun

Ibn Khaldun

invented the term 'asabiyyah to refer to the social cohesion among humans arising from group life.

There is evidence that 19th-century thinkers were aware of Khaldun's work but omitted reference to him and other non-European traditions in their theorizing. This is an example of how the classical sociological canon is Eurocentric in its exclusion of non-European voices and references.

Harriet Martineau was an English writer and early sociologist. She argued that the study of society must include key political and religious as well as social institutions. Martineau was popular and influential during her lifetime, and she wrote on a variety of topics, including political economy, taxation, the poor laws, travel, women's rights and education, and the abolition of slavery. In 1834 she traveled widely in America, observing its morals and manners. On her return to England she published *Society in America* (1837). For sociologists, Martineau's book about research methods, *How to Observe Morals and Manners* (1838), and her introduction and translation of sociological ideas in Auguste Comte's *Cours de Philosophie Positive* (1853), are particularly important.

Despite her influence, Martineau's ideas were not incorporated when sociology was institutionalized as an academic discipline in the late 19th century and into the 20th. Like other women authors and activists, Martineau

Harriet Martineau

the emancipation of slaves in the United States. Later in his career, he became a pan-Africanist and published many works on Africa, including *The World and Africa* (1947).

Although Du Bois's academic career almost precisely spans the formation and development of the discipline of sociology, his scholarly voice and output were disconnected from influential institutions in the discipline until recently. The context of this exclusion was the deep racial segregation of US society during his lifetime, and the way white privilege worked to preserve some voices in the new discipline of sociology rather than others. It is only in the last two decades that American textbooks have included him in the sociological canon.

W. E. B. Du Bois

was excluded. Historians like Michael Hill have argued that this reflects the pervasive gender inequality and masculine privilege of the early institutions of the discipline. Male founders excluded women's voices to make a scholarly case for their place in the university. Today, however, Martineau is considered to be one of the founders of the field of sociology (Giddens and Griffiths 2006; Hill 2002).

W. E. B. Du Bois was an American sociologist and civil rights activist. He was the first African American to earn a doctorate at Harvard, and he was a professor of history, sociology, and economics at Atlanta University. A prolific author and editor, Du Bois had a long and distinguished career, writing landmark studies on black culture, communities, and politics. These include *The Philadelphia Negro* ([1899] 1967), a landmark study on urban Philadelphia; *The Souls of Black Folk* ([1903] 1994); his influential chapter, "The Talented Tenth," in *The Negro Problem* (1903), which made a case for education and collective racial uplift; and *Black Reconstruction in America* (1935), which chronicled the continuing oppression and inequality that followed

ACTIVE LEARNING

Discuss: Do you think the ideas of people who are more powerful because of race, class, gender, or social position are more likely to be influential in society? Why or why not? Are there times when they may be less influential?

It is true that the classical sociological theories of Marx, Weber, and Durkheim are limited by a distinctly 19th-century European point of view. Marx did not comprehend the complexity of occupational and technical change. He also underestimated the power of nation-states, ethnicities, and religious identities to shape individual lives and world history. Weber underestimated the ability of religious traditions to adapt and thrive despite the onslaughts of secular life. Durkheim's references to "primitive" societies have been criticized for being Eurocentric and simplistic. Neither Marx, nor Weber, nor Durkheim really developed an adequate theory of race, gender, or colonialism.

While these men's theories have their limits, it is still the case that they operate as "classics" in sociology and enjoy a privileged status, in the sense that all sociologists are familiar with their main arguments (Alexander 1987: 11). By providing a common frame of reference, the classical theories make it easier for sociologists to communicate with each other. New theoretical movements in sociology often develop through arguments about the classical theorists, by reinterpreting what one or more of the classical theorists "really meant." This is just as true in the United States as it is in Europe, despite the fact that American sociology has its own distinctive history.

Sociology in America

Sociology existed in the United States in the late 1800s, but it was not as well organized as in Europe. William Graham Sumner was teaching sociology classes at Yale University as early as 1875. Frank Wilson Blackmar began teaching his "Elements of Sociology" class at the University of Kansas in 1890. Franklin Giddings began teaching courses in sociology at Columbia University in 1894, and he was the first person in the United States to be appointed a full professor of sociology. But American sociology really began to gain a distinct identity when the University of Chicago created a Department of Sociology—the first in the world—in 1892.

The Chicago School and American Sociology

Like the European founders, Chicago sociologists were interested in modern social life, especially immigration, urbanization, and crime. They used the

---

PAIRED CONCEPTS   **Global and Local**

The Importance of Immigration in American Sociology

Compared to their European counterparts, American sociologists in the early 20th century were much more interested in immigration. The cities in which American sociologists worked were major immigration destinations. As we discuss in Chapter 15, about 48 million people left Europe between 1864 and 1924, which was more than 10 percent of the population on the continent (Massey 1995). More than half of them came to the United States, and their arrival strongly affected cities throughout the Northeast and Midwest. In 1920, more than 40 percent of the population in New York City was foreign born. Boston (32%), Chicago (30%), Cleveland (30%), and Philadelphia (22%) had very large foreign-born populations. Sociologists living in those cities could not help but notice this massive influx of immigrants, and their research reflected this.

In fact, many early sociologists were themselves immigrants, and they had direct experience of the global population transfer from Europe to the United States. At the University of Chicago, Louis Wirth (from Germany) and Florian Znaniecki (from Poland) were both immigrants. Pitirim

Sorokin, who was a leading sociologist at Harvard University and the University of Minnesota, was a Russian immigrant. Mirra Komoravsky, a Barnard sociologist who was the second woman to serve as the president of the American Sociological Association, was also a Russian immigrant. Paul Lazarsfeld, the founder of Columbia University's Bureau of Applied Social Research, was an Austrian immigrant. Reinhard Bendix (University of California, Berkeley), Herbert Marcuse (Brandeis University), Max Horkheimer (Columbia University), and Erich Fromm (Columbia University, New School for Social Research) were German immigrants. Even today, sociology departments around the United States have significant numbers of faculty who emigrated from other countries, bringing a global perspective to their research and their teaching.

ACTIVE LEARNING

Find out: Are there any foreign-born sociologists studying at or teaching in your university? Try to visit their office hours, and find out how they think their experience as an immigrant has influenced their research and their teaching.

city of Chicago as a social laboratory to study social change in industrial society. Using a special kind of method—ethnography based on participant observation—Chicago sociologists painted a detailed portrait of early 20th-century American life (Deegan 2007).

The Chicago School of sociology is especially well known for developing a theory of the social self. Charles Horton Cooley (1864–1929) offered an early version of this theory, with his concept of the "looking glass self." Cooley ([1922] 2012:152) emphasized how society serves as a mirror people use to develop a self-concept as they reflect on how others see them. They react to their sense of others' social perceptions, often in ways that meet social expectations.

George Herbert Mead (1863–1931) developed a more complex theory of the social self, with his distinction between the "I" and the "me." For Mead, the "I" is the prior, pre-social part of the self. The "me" is a socialized version of the self (Mead 1967). So the statement, "I am hungry and Mommy feeds me" involves:

1. identifying the hunger;

2. identifying Mommy as a social object in the world who can feed me; and

3. recognizing that the "I" who is expressing hunger is also "me" for others— for Mommy.

This third step is a highly complex symbolic process. The child must place herself in the position of another—in this case, Mommy—to look back at herself. In that moment, the child uses her developing sociological imagination to see herself, her mother, and the relationship between them. She has stepped outside her self, using her capacity for reflexivity.

Influenced by these ideas about the social self, sociologists at the University of Chicago produced important empirical studies about life in the modern city. Key examples of this research include W. I. Thomas and Florian Znaniecki's *The Polish Peasant in Europe and America* (1918–20), a study of Polish immigrants and their families; Robert Park's (1922) study, *The Immigrant Press and Its Control* (1922), and St. Clair Drake and Horace R. Cayton Jr.'s 1945 study of race and urban life on the South Side of Chicago, *Black Metropolis* (Drake and Cayton 1993). By the middle of the 20th century, the Chicago School's focus on the social self came to be expressed as the theory of symbolic interactionism, which we describe later in the chapter. The method of urban ethnography is also widely used today in works such as *Slim's Table,* about working-class masculinity (Duneier 1992), and *The Stickup Kids,* about drug robberies in the South Bronx in the late 1980s (Contreras 2012).

Conflict, Consensus, and Symbolic Interaction

Following World War II (1939–1945), sociologists in the United States converged on three general models for thinking about society: consensus theory, conflict theory, and symbolic interactionism. **Consensus theory** was associated with the work of Talcott Parsons, who tried to develop a general theory of society that could be used by all the social sciences. Drawing on the European theories of Max Weber, Émile Durkheim, and Sigmund Freud, Parsons argued that modern American society was a *functional equilibrium*, a situation where things like money, political power, social influence, and cultural values tended to balance out, so that no single type of social resource could dominate society. Parsons also argued that all societies were converging toward a single modern form, in which each part of the social system became autonomous and self-organizing, designed to fulfill a specific function with maximum efficiency. Although he understood the social facts of inequality, Parsons's most important

Consensus theory Consensus theorists focus on social equilibrium, which is the way that different parts of society work together to produce social cohesion.

question (similar to Durkheim's) was: What factors contribute to stable social systems?

While Parsons was the dominant sociologist throughout the 1940s and 1950s, he was not without his critics. Many thought that his model of functional equilibrium was unable to explain social change. Others thought that his theory was insensitive to human domination, suffering, conflict, and inequality. In contrast to Parsons's argument that all societies were evolving naturally toward a single modern form, these critics insisted instead that the world's most powerful nations were imposing capitalism on the rest of the world.

By the end of the 1960s, these criticisms of Parsons had come together in the formation of a different model of society, based on **conflict theory**. Conflict theory, which was developed by sociologists including C. Wright Mills and Ralf Dahrendorf (1929–2009**)**, focused on power inequalities, domination, and the role of social conflict in social change. Conflict theorists argued that social structures emerged out of the conflicts between different groups. Instead of a functional equilibrium between different parts of society, conflict theorists emphasized that social structures were designed to reinforce the unequal distribution of power and resources. Ultimately, conflict theorists such as Mills wanted to understand how elites were able to maintain their control over society.

The tradition of **symbolic interactionism** cuts across both of these schools. Symbolic interactionism is interested in individuals, interactions, and interpretations. Herbert Blumer (1900–1987), a sociologist at the University of Chicago, synthesized earlier work by Mead and Cooley to define the three basic propositions that informed symbolic interactionism: (1) individuals act based on the meanings they have about the world; (2) those meanings develop through the social interactions they have with other people; (3) those meanings continue to develop and change, as the individual interprets the social interactions and experiences they have (Blumer 1968; Morrione 1988; Tamotsu 1988). While conflict and consensus theory emphasized the ways that structures shape actions, symbolic interactionism emphasized the ways that actions shape structures.

Erving Goffman (1922–1982) argued that people deliberately collaborate to maintain social order through interaction. His masterwork, *Presentation of Self in Everyday Life* (1956), uses a theatrical metaphor to explain how social encounters are scripted like plays. In this view, people are like actors who know how to perform in social life because social interactions are organized around scripts. We expect people to act according to those scripts—for teachers to behave differently than students, for prison guards to behave differently than prisoners, and for doctors to act differently than patients. In all these examples, Goffman's work has been used to explain how and why people follow social scripts and maintain social order. Importantly, however, the idea that social life is scripted has also been used as a critical tool for challenging social rules when they are found to be oppressive or constraining. This is what feminists do when they challenge scripts that say women do not have the same rights as men. It is what social activists do when they plan social protests. As these examples show, interactional theorists like Goffman provide tools for thinking about both conflict and consensus in social life.

By the middle of the 20th century, a standoff between the three perspectives came to dominate the story American sociology told about itself. The resulting three-fold model braided together the different strands of the broad sociological tradition from Europe and America by joining a focus on inequality and social values and connecting the analysis of large-scale social structures with smaller

---

Conflict theory Conflict theorists argue that social structures and social systems emerge out of the conflicts between different groups.

Symbolic interactionism A perspective associated with the Chicago School of sociology that argues that people develop a social self through interaction with others.

for Western nations to believe that they were civilizing non-Western societies, or bringing them into the modern world, instead of merely conquering and exploiting them.

Frantz Fanon

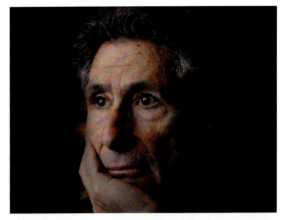

Edward Said

QUEER THEORY. Queer theory builds on feminism and other threads of critical social thought to challenge the supposedly stable identities of gender and sexuality. As developed by philosophers and gender theorists including Judith Butler, queer theory uncovers how deeply the logic of homophobia and heterosexism are embedded in social practice and social institutions, and how that logic helps maintain social order (Warner 1993; Turner 2000). At the same time, queer theory provides a broader critique of the social order. Similar to an intersectional perspective, a queer perspective points to the connections between different social categories and relationships and questions the limits of "the normal, the legitimate, the dominant" in every domain of human life (Halperin 1997: 62).

Judith Butler

Sociologists today are much more reflective about the exclusions and silences that are present in any given theory, and they are more likely to orient to a variety of different theories that can be used as tools to help them understand specific social questions. Students are also far more aware of silences and exclusions, and particularly of how expert social knowledge can work to exclude and marginalize people.

The Cultural Turn

Another development was the **cultural turn** in sociology, which began in the early 1970s but became a significant influence during the 1990s. In many respects, the cultural turn was a return to the **Thomas theorem**, one of the earliest theoretical statements of American sociology from the Chicago School. Formulated in 1928 by W. I. Thomas (1863–1947) at the Chicago School, the Thomas theorem argues that the way that people interpret a situation has real consequences for how they act. In other words, if we want to understand social life, we need to pay attention to the stories that people tell about themselves and the world around them. Today, there is a growing recognition that cultural issues are important for all sociological research (Hall, Grindstaff, and Lo 2010: 3).

While the cultural turn encouraged an attention to meaning and interpretation that had been emphasized earlier by symbolic interactionism, the cultural sociology that emerged in the 1990s was different in a number of ways. For symbolic interactionists, meanings are created by a social self, who is continually interpreting and reflecting upon her social interactions and social experiences. Cultural sociologists still study the meanings that people use to understand their lives. But they are also interested in the ways that meanings

Queer theory A critical perspective that identifies the logic of homophobia and heterosexism in social practice and social institutions, and how that logic works to maintain social order.

Cultural turn An interdisciplinary movement in sociology and other disciplines that emphasizes the collective cultural dimension of social life.

Thomas theorem The proposition that the way people interpret a situation has real consequences for how they act.

Cultural meanings
Andy Warhol disrupted artistic conventions in the 1960s with Pop Art renditions of ordinary objects like Campbell's Soup cans. In this 2012 image, an original Warhol painting is hung in the Campbell's Soup company corporate boardroom in Camden, New Jersey, framing specialty soup cans with art and sayings by Andy Warhol. What does Campbell's get from Warhol's art? What does the soup can symbolize?

circulate in collective memories, mass media, public rituals, and everyday objects. For example, brands like Disney, Nike, and Coca-Cola are known all over the world, as are icons such as the American flag, the Eiffel Tower, and the Olympic rings. There are clearly established ideas associated with most of these cultural objects, and there are frequent public conflicts over what they really mean. Are the Olympics about the spirit of competition, nationalism, or commercialism? Is the American flag a symbol of freedom or global power?

Increasingly, sociologists have come to recognize that these kinds of cultural conflicts are just as important as political or economic conflicts. Cultural classifications and conflicts are a central focus of Chapter 4, though they feature in many other chapters of this book as well.

Global Context

A key area of study for sociology today is globalization, which refers to the growing interdependence of the world's people. As we discuss in Chapter 4, globalization has economic, political, and cultural dimensions. The spread of global trade, and the enormous power of global finance and multinational corporations, are major forces in social life. The political dimensions of globalization are seen in the rise of international nongovernmental organizations such as Doctors Without Borders, the Red Cross, and Amnesty International, as well as regulatory bodies above the nation-state such as the United Nations and the International Criminal Court. Globalization can also be seen in migration patterns and patterns of global violence: both global migration and global terrorism have increased in recent years, as Figure 2.3 and Figure 2.4 illustrate.

To understand the global context of today's social world, sociologists should not assume that modern society is organized in terms of territorially distinct nation-states (Beck 2005, 2006). While nation-states continue to be important, they now act on a global stage alongside other important actors. For example, multinational corporations orient to a global market that is beyond the control of any single country. Global financial and environmental crises transcend national borders. New immigrant communities maintain a simultaneous involvement in their nation of origin as well as their nation of destination, creating transnational communities that challenge the boundaries between two or more nation-states (Faist 2000, 2004). Millions of stateless people and refugees fall between the boundaries of nation-states in the modern world system. Global civil-society organizations promote "universal human rights" by protesting against nation-states and corporations that violate those rights. Sociologists draw our attention to the "excluded others" of contemporary society, reminding us that the misfortunes and miseries of displaced, poor, and oppressed peoples are a side effect of the modern societies in which we live (Bauman 2004). While globalization is a central focus of Chapters 14 and 15, it is also a more general dimension of all social life that influences sociological research today.

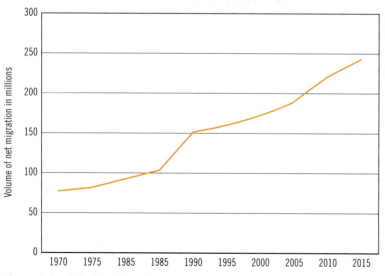

Figure 2.3 Global Net Migration, 1960–2015.
Source: World Bank Data.

Sociology Today

Contemporary sociologists engage creatively with the challenges of 21st-century social life. Some contemporary sociologists focus on producing empirically driven theories about particular institutions, historical events, and cultural structures. Some focus on race, gender, sexuality, and how these interact to produce different systems of hierarchy and social inequality. Other sociologists turn their attention to global power and post-colonial resistance. And many sociologists combine these different theoretical resources to analyze a particular problem or imagine a new kind of social relationship. All of them draw on the sociological tradition—the history of sociological thinking described in this chapter—to do their work.

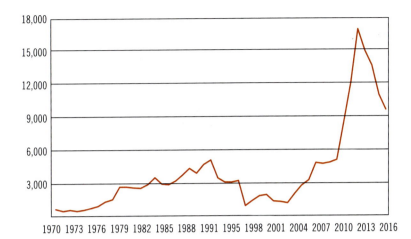

Figure 2.4   Incidents of Global Terrorism, 1970-2016.
Source: Global Terrorism Database.

Thinking Sociologically

The paired concepts we described in Chapter 1 are a useful way for understanding how sociologists think about contemporary society. They also provide a useful framework for organizing the history of sociological theory.

The paired concept of *solidarity* and *conflict*, for example, uses fundamental insights from the work of thinkers like Karl Marx, Émile Durkheim, and Talcott Parsons to analyze contemporary society. Thinkers like Jeffrey Alexander, Pierre Bourdieu, Michelle Lamont, and Michael Omi and Howard Winant focus on solidarity—what connects groups of people and what divides them. A major focus for these thinkers is the way categories and classifications divide "us" from "them," or "self" from "other." All these thinkers retain a hope for a more peaceful and equal human future in an increasingly violent and conflict-ridden world.

Contemporary sociologists who study *power* and *resistance* build on the sociological legacy of thinkers like Karl Marx, Max Weber, and C. Wright Mills. They do so by uncovering how contemporary power structures are organized in places such as the legal system, the criminal justice system, and the system of nation-states. We can also use the paired concepts of power and resistance to understand how feminist and intersectional theories think about institutions like marriage, the family, the education system, and corporate hierarchies. At the same time, sociologists who study collective behavior and social movements are interested in discovering how people mobilize and act to resist domination.

Inequality and *privilege* are also a major focus of contemporary sociology. Because resources are scarce and distributed unevenly, it is important to know who gets what and why. That is the central concern of the sociological subfield of **social stratification**. Stratificationists ask: Why are those with a college education more likely to earn high income than those without a college education? Why are poor people more likely to die in war than rich people? Why are men more likely to work in higher-paid occupations than women? How is the history of privilege and domination connected to the history of inequality and dispossession? These questions are being taken up by sociologists around the world, who are using theories about difference to think about patterns of inequality, exclusion, and marginalization.

Social stratification A central sociological idea that describes structured patterns of inequality between different groups of people.

The social changes of the modern period that gave rise to the discipline of sociology were also the beginning of the modern, global world system. Today, both *global* and *local* processes continue to shape contemporary social life. While the importance of global processes is increasingly apparent, sociologists also emphasize that individuals continue to live out their lives in particular locales. These include city neighborhoods and suburbs, workplaces and colleges, and also new settings like social networking sites, airports, and corporate boardrooms.

The last paired concept, *structure* and *contingency*, is at the heart of sociological theory. It refers to the idea that human life is both highly patterned and also historically open. We reproduce patterns in our everyday life: we follow scripts, we abide by institutional rules, and we support social order. But patterns can also be changed; they are shaped by our choices and actions. Karl Marx, for example, saw that capitalist society was turning many areas of life into objects to be bought and sold on markets. Yet he also believed the future could be changed, and he imagined a perfect society in which people came together to share resources equally and fulfilled every human being's potential. Émile Durkheim perceived that people understand themselves and society through inherited collective representations that symbolize who they are, but he also argued that these representations can be changed. And while Erving Goffman imagined social rules as a script that individuals used to maintain an orderly social life, his work has been fundamental in challenging those rules by helping people perceive the scripts so they can challenge them and write new ones.

Why Sociology?

Why choose sociology? In Chapter 1, we answered this question by focusing on individual skills and benefits that sociology offers. We pointed to the way that sociology can offer useful knowledge to help you understand your life and the world around you. We also emphasized the job skills that sociology can develop. In this chapter, we want to offer a more intellectual answer to the question of "Why sociology?"

The intellectual answer is that sociology offers useful concepts and theories for studying the rapidly changing and increasingly global social world in which we live. Sociology has developed valuable ways of thinking about social patterns and persistence and also social disruption, adaptation, and transformation. The concepts, exercises, and stories in this book are designed to aid in developing your sociological imagination. They are designed to provide the tools and the space to practice using them so that you will ask better questions and make better choices about your own future and the future of us all. In short, the sociological imagination helps us imagine a better future, and how to make our way in an increasingly uncertain world.

Sociology's focus on relationships also offers a counter-perspective to the highly individualistic emphasis of contemporary social life. In the United States, we are accustomed to thinking in terms of individuals and individual characteristics, experiences, and successes and failures. Sociology counterbalances this emphasis with resources for understanding social groups, organizations, institutions, and other social dimensions of human experience. These perspectives are important in a range of settings from public policy and management, to business, web design, and technical systems. A group perspective is also required in professional careers like teaching, social work, law, and medicine. In fact, sociologists can be found in all different kinds of careers and all over the world. They study everything, including education, immigration, politics, natural disasters, and the environment. They work in colleges and universities,

CAREERS

The Importance of Theory

Many career advisors today emphasize the importance of acquiring specific skills. According to common wisdom, people who get good jobs are the ones who know computer programming, website design, and other types of specific, technical knowledge. Fortunately, the study of sociology will teach you many of these technical skills.

Along with technical skills, today's workplace also requires people who have general theoretical skills. For example, a 2012 article in *Forbes* magazine wrote that the most important career skill is critical thinking, which as we have argued is a central aspect of sociological theory. Similarly, in his best-selling book *The World Is Flat*, Thomas Friedman argued that the "special sauce" that creates innovation in today's world is the ability to integrate technical skills with a broad-based liberal arts education in art, music, literature, and popular culture. A knowledge of theory is what helps people integrate these different kinds of knowledge and come up with innovative solutions to critical problems.

George Soros is one of the most well-known examples of a person who was able to use social theory to generate important new innovations in his career. Born in Hungary and educated in England, Soros moved to New York City in 1956 to work in the financial industry. As a graduate student at the London School of Economics, Soros had been deeply influenced by the theory of reflexivity, which was part of his philosophy training and which we wrote about earlier in the chapter in our discussion of the sociological imagination. Based on his understanding of reflexivity, Soros was convinced that most investors failed to understand how individual beliefs and biases changed the way that financial markets worked. Using a more sociological theory of markets, he founded Soros Fund Management in 1970. Today, Soros has a net worth estimated at $23 billion.

ACTIVE LEARNING

Find out: Describe an example where someone used critical thinking to change a situation. Make sure to define critical thinking in your answer.

government, prisons and social welfare agencies, hospitals, churches, and nonprofit organizations. They can be found throughout the business sector as well, working in marketing, communication, the creative industries, finance, and most other parts of the private sector. The central thread that connects all of their work is the application of the sociological imagination—the ability to ask good critical questions—about our shared social world.

CASE STUDY

W. E. B. Du Bois and the History of American Sociology

Sociologist Aldon Morris, in his book *The Scholar Denied: W. E. B. Du Bois and the Birth of Modern Sociology*, notes, "There is an intriguing, well-kept secret regarding the founding of scientific sociology in America. The first school of scientific sociology in the United States was founded by a black professor located in a historically black university in the South. This reality flatly contradicts the accepted wisdom" (Morris 2015: 1). Morris takes a critical look at the assumption made by most sociologists that the University of Chicago was the first important school of American sociology, as well as the

tendency of the history of American sociology to underplay Du Bois's significance.

Morris argues that the Du Bois–Atlanta School of Sociology deserves much more credit for creating scientific sociology in the United States, and that its contributions predate those of the Chicago sociology department by nearly two decades. Du Bois was the first African American to receive a PhD from Harvard University, where he studied with some of the leading philosophers and historians of his time. He spent two years studying at the University of Berlin, where he was one of the first

CASE STUDY CONTINUED

Americans to be exposed to the ideas of Max Weber, and where he received extensive training in statistics and quantitative social science methods (Morris 2015: 21). His 1899 book *The Philadelphia Negro* was the first empirical study of an urban black community in the United States, and was published well before any of the community studies for which the Chicago School became famous (Du Bois [1899] 1967). The research group he developed as an Atlanta University faculty member produced a significant number of empirical studies and important theoretical understandings about race and American life. The series of annual conferences he hosted tried to use social-scientific knowledge to develop practical proposals for addressing racial oppression. As Morris (2015: 89), argues, "these sustained scholarly activities signaled the presence of a groundbreaking sociology absent elsewhere in America."

Why were Du Bois's accomplishments overshadowed in favor of the Chicago School? A key factor had to do with *inequality* and *privilege*. Racial inequality in US universities meant that Du Bois, despite his many accomplishments, was never considered for a faculty position at elite universities such as Harvard University or the University of Chicago. Du Bois started his academic career at Wilberforce University, a small historically black college or university (HBCU) in Ohio, but he was frustrated by the fact that the school did not have a sociology department. He then spent about a year in an untenured position at the University of Pennsylvania, where he did the research that was ultimately published as *The Philadelphia Negro*. But this position offered no job security and actually prohibited him from teaching any students (Morris 2015: 56). Du Bois left to take up his position at Atlanta University, another important HBCU and the first university in the nation to place an emphasis on graduate education for African American students. But Atlanta University was a poor university, and it became progressively poorer as Georgia's state legislatures decided to withhold money from the university because of its refusal to racially segregate its students and faculty (Morris 2015: 57).

Du Bois's academic influence also suffered because of his *conflict* with Booker T. Washington, an influential African American of the time who had a different vision than Du Bois about how to improve race relations. (We discuss the differences between Du Bois and Washington in Chapter 8.) For now, we want to emphasize the harm of this conflict to Du Bois's influence in sociology. As it turns out, there were strong feelings of *solidarity* between Booker T. Washington and Robert Park.

Park had joined the University of Chicago sociology department in 1914; he was one of its most influential members for 20 years, and was one of the key people responsible for creating what became known as the Chicago School of sociology. Before he arrived at Chicago, however, Park had worked for nearly 10 years as Booker T. Washington's secretary, and he became the head of publicity for Washington's Tuskegee Institute. While Park was familiar with Du Bois's research and his intellectual status, he was also well aware of the conflict between Du Bois and Washington. Allied with Washington, Park systematically ignored Du Bois's scholarship, excluded him from his intellectual networks, and credited other scholars for ideas that Du Bois originally developed; most of Park's colleagues at the University of Chicago did the same (Morris 2015: 140–7).

More generally, the sociological studies of race being conducted at the University of Chicago benefited from *global* and *local* factors that were making the city of Chicago the most important social laboratory for studying race relations in the early decades of the 20th century. A primary factor was the Great Migration, in which millions of African Americans moved away from the South in order to settle into Midwestern cities like Chicago. Chicago sociologists studied the local conditions in their city, just like other sociologists in the United States studied the communities in which their universities were located. But Chicago came to be seen by the rest of the world as the most distinctively American city, and this helped reinforce the Chicago School of sociology's reputation as the most distinctively American version of sociological research.

While the *structure* of racism and inequality blocked Du Bois's path to a more elite academic position, there were other *contingent* factors related to the kinds of intellectual and political choices Du Bois made throughout his career. Put simply, Du Bois was never content to limit himself to academic scholarship. He was also a public intellectual, and he was deeply involved in politics. In 1905, Du Bois helped organize the Niagara Movement, which fought for full political and civil rights for African Americans. Du Bois was also a leader of the global Pan-African Movement, which sought to create a political organization that could unite all social movements fighting for racial equality, and which would serve as a global social movement advocating for political self-determination in Africa. Towards the end of his life, Du Bois moved to Ghana, where he received a state funeral upon his death in 1963.

CASE STUDY CONTINUED

There was also considerable *power* organized against Du Bois. He was opposed by Booker T. Washington, the most powerful African American leader of the time. He was opposed by Robert Park, the most powerful sociologist. He was opposed by the US government and the FBI, which targeted him as a communist and a subversive, and which took away his US passport in 1951. But Du Bois's *resistance* against those who opposed him was significant. He was an influential public figure and an effective political organizer, and he was an aggressive critic of those with whom he disagreed. And Du Bois had many allies, in intellectual as well as political life. There have always been sociologists who have aimed a critical eye at the history of the discipline and challenged the story that privileged the University of Chicago and marginalized Du Bois. Aldon Morris's book is a good example of this kind of intellectual resistance.

LEARNING GOALS REVISITED

2.1 Understand that sociology developed as a way to explain social patterns and social change and is one of a family of social science disciplines located within the liberal arts.

- Social thinkers like Marx, Weber, and Durkheim, as well as thinkers from the "forgotten canon" like W. E. B. Du Bois and Harriet Martineau, invented theories to explain social changes occurring in the modern era. This was the beginning of a sociological way of thinking that asserted that social life should be understood as a whole, complex, interacting system of political, economic, and cultural relationships.

- One of the most important insights of sociology is its insistence on the relational quality of social life. Sociology, for example, is related to disciplines like psychology, criminal justice, anthropology, history, and economics. Boundaries between these fields shift and change over time, and much good social analysis occurs at the rich disciplinary boundaries with other fields.

2.2 Understand that knowledge is socially located and develops within particular intellectual and national traditions and different social networks and institutional settings.

- Sociology developed as a discipline in response to the enormous social changes created by the industrial and democratic revolutions, colonial expansion, and the rise of the modern system of nation-states.

- The first department of sociology was founded at the University of Chicago in 1892 and was influenced by ideas from Europe, as were the departments at Harvard and Columbia. European thinkers and scholars also served on the faculty in Chicago.

- In the first half of the 20th century, the European legacy, along with the symbolic interactionist tradition developed at the University of Chicago, were synthesized into the threefold model of American sociology. This model began to unravel in the 1960s and 1970s with critics from within the discipline arguing for mid-range theory. Critics within and outside the discipline also pointed to the limitations of the white, male, European perspective of the field. With the cultural turn, and the rising need to address global concerns, a new global sociology was established.

- Many voices were excluded from early sociological institutions, particularly women's voices, but also scholars from non-European backgrounds. Today, some previously silenced voices have been recovered by historians, and new critical voices have entered the discipline, including feminists, critical race theorists, post-colonial theorists, queer theorists, and theorists of disability and intersectionality.

2.3 Identify core theoretical concepts in the discipline.

- Marx identified the economic system of capitalism as the most important feature of modern societies. Weber analyzed rationalization as the driving force of institutional and cultural change. Durkheim studied social facts and focused on the way group organization, such as the division of labor and collective representations, made social life possible. The Chicago School thinkers, who founded symbolic interactionism, identified the stable patterns of interactional settings in modern cities and institutions as a critical part of social life.

- Consensus theorists like Talcott Parsons emphasized the stability of systems and what held them together. Conflict theorists like C. Wright Mills analyzed the role of conflict in social change. Symbolic interactionists like Herbert Blumer analyzed how social meanings and social interaction play a part on both social equilibrium and social change.

- Contemporary critics of sociology, who also influence sociology, include feminists, critical race theorists, intersectional theorists, post-colonial theorists, and queer theorists.

2.4 Understand that the history of sociological theory is distinct from making theoretical arguments or applying theory to contemporary examples.

- Sociology is a way to think about social life. Using the sociological imagination, sociologists ask critical questions about social life, such as: Does more education guarantee a higher income? What is the connection between global processes and local communities?

- The tradition of social theory in sociology informs current sociology in deep ways. However, the history of sociological theory is not the same as doing sociology or inventing new social theory today. Contemporary sociologists use their sociological imaginations to apply theories to new global social realities or invent theories to explain them.

- Contemporary sociology has moved away from the grand idea that there can be one big master theory to explain the social world to developing "theories of the middle range." Contemporary social theory is more empirical and more cultural than earlier social theory.

Key Terms

Alienation 30
Anomie 33
Bureaucracy 32
Canon 30
Capitalism 30
Collective representations 33
Conflict theory 38
Consensus theory 37
Critical race theory 42
Cultural turn 43
Disenchantment 32
Division of labor 33
Feminism 41
Globalization 27
Intersectionality 42
Mechanical solidarity 33
Organic solidarity 33
Post-colonial theory 42
Public sociology 31
Queer theory 43
Racial formation theory 42
Rationalization 32
Reflexivity 25
Social facts 26
Social sciences 26
Social stratification 45
Symbolic interaction 38
Theories of the middle range 40
Thomas theorem 43
Urbanization 28

Review Questions

1. Define social theory. What is the difference between professional and amateur sociologists?

2. What is the sociological imagination and how is it connected to reflexivity?

3. What does it mean to say that sociology focuses on relationships?

4. What is the sociological canon? Who are the major figures in the canon? What is the forgotten canon and what does it tell us about inequality and privilege?

5. What conditions were the early sociological theorists trying to explain? How is that similar or different from today?

6. What is the three-fold model of sociology? How are conflict, consensus, and symbolic interactionist perspectives different?

7. Why did the three-fold model of sociology begin to unravel by the 1960s and 1970s? Identify three critiques of the three-fold model of sociology.

8. What is the cultural turn? Describe some ways that it shaped sociology.

9. What other disciplines are close to sociology in the modern academic field?

10. What do mid-range theorists do that is different from classical theorists?

11. What was the Chicago School of American sociology and why was it important?

12. What is the difference between the history of social theory and doing social theory?

Explore

RECOMMENDED READINGS

Abbott, Andrew. 2001. *Chaos of the Disciplines*. Chicago: University of Chicago Press.

Coser, Lewis A. 1977. *Masters of Sociological Thought*. New York: Harcourt Brace.

Deegan, Mary Jo. 2007. "The Chicago School of Ethnography." In *Handbook of Ethnography*, eds. Paul Atkinson, Amanda Coffey, Sarah Delmont, John Lofland, and Lyn Lofland (pp. 11–25). Newbury Park, CA: Sage.

Du Bois, W. E. B. [1903] 1994. *The Souls of Black Folk*. New York: Dover Publications.

Madoo Lengermann, Patricia, and Jill Niebrugge-Brantley. 1998. *The Women Founders: Sociology and Social Theory, 1830–1930, A Text with Readings*. New York: McGraw-Hill.

Mills, C. Wright. [1959] 2000. *Sociological Imagination*. New York: Oxford University Press.

Said, Edward W. 1994. *Culture and Imperialism*. New York, NY: Vintage Books.

Seidman, Steven. 2013. *Contested Knowledge. Social Theory Today*, 5th ed. New York: Wiley-Blackwell.

ACTIVITIES

- *Use your sociological imagination*: Sketch a diagram of what you can see in the room you are sitting in. Then sketch a diagram of the entire room as a map for someone else. Be sure to make a note of where you are on the map. How are the two sketches different? Why? What things did you have to think about to move from what you can see from where you sit to imagining the room as a map? Provide examples of those pictures.

- *Media+Data literacies*: Google the names of the major social theorists and forgotten theorists from this chapter. How many results are returned for each? Are there differences by gender or race?

- *Discuss*: Are the ideas of classical theorists relevant today? Why or why not?

For additional resources, including Media+Data Literacy exercises, In the News exercises, and quizzes, please go to **oup.com/he/Jacobs-Townsley1e**

3

Doing Sociology

Research Methods and Critical Literacy

On June 2, 2014, *USA Today* published a story with the headline "Lady-killers: Hurricanes with Female Names Deadlier." The story was about research from the University of Illinois published in the *Proceedings of the National Academy of Sciences,* that examined the number of people killed by the 94 hurricanes that hit the US coast between 1950 and 2012. Researchers found that hurricanes with women's names had killed nearly three times as many people as those with men's names. The explanation for this finding, according to the researchers, was that people did not feel as threatened by women, and so they tended to underprepare for hurricanes named after women.

While the original study was published in a respected scientific journal, not everyone was convinced that it was based on good research. Because hurricanes only began to get men's names after 1979, and because hurricanes had been getting less deadly over time, the supposed finding about men's and women's names was really a finding about better hurricane preparation by coastal cities since 1980. Eric Holthaus, a meteorologist for *Slate,* called the study a classic case of flawed research due to **confirmation bias**. Confirmation bias exists when researchers' methods produce findings that confirm the researcher's preexisting beliefs—in this case, about women being less threatening than men. And these were not even real women and men, but women's and men's *names*! Jeremy Freese, a sociologist at Stanford University, noted that the logic of the study's statistical model asked readers to believe that if Hurricane Andrew had simply been called Hurricane Diana, it would have caused 6,500 deaths instead of 60!

Hurricane Harvey
Hurricane Harvey was the second most costly hurricane recorded in the United States, causing about $125 billion worth of damage. But Hurricane Katrina was costlier—do you think it is because it had a woman's name?

LEARNING GOALS

3.1   Describe how sociology is a social science.

3.2   Define the major elements of the research process.

3.3   Describe a range of sociological research techniques.

3.4   Describe how social science, like sociology, is different from natural science.

3.5   Describe the difference between basic, applied, and public sociology.

Confirmation bias When research is biased to confirm the researcher's preexisting beliefs or hypotheses.

As sociologists and citizens, we need to ask two sets of questions about this case. The first set of questions is about the quality of the research itself. How can we evaluate the study? Did the researchers ask the right questions? Did they collect the right kind of data? Did they use the right methods to analyze the data they had? These questions are connected to a challenge we introduced in Chapter 1: when conducting social research, it can be difficult to get the facts right.

The second set of questions asks about the relationship between news media and social research. Why were newspapers so interested in reporting these results? How did they find out about the study? Why were the researchers interested in having their results published in the newspaper? In other words, how do people use social research in media, politics, and everyday life?

Social Research

Our society values a culture of evidence based on rules of logic and the scientific method. In the legal system, juries reach decisions based on eyewitness and expert testimony. Government agencies and corporations also base their decision-making on evidence, such as information about what a consumer will buy, what neighborhoods and communities need, or how a voter will choose candidates. Learning about the process of social research is important to developing the critical information and scientific skills we need as citizens, consumers, and workers.

Scientific statements are different from other kinds of statements. Unlike opinions or beliefs, scientific statements are based on research, which is systematic and empirical. Science is concerned with discovering how our world works *in fact*. Researchers think about the questions they are trying to answer, why those questions are important, and the best way to answer their questions. To do this, researchers proceed systematically. That is, researchers make every effort to locate the range of answers that other people have given for similar types of questions, and carefully evaluate what kind of new information they will need to collect to answer their questions. Researchers also consider the possibility that they will not be able to get all the information they would like, as well as the possibility that the information they do get will be imperfect. Finally, researchers search for different explanations for what caused the outcomes they observed. Researchers are also like detectives and philosophers in their use of the rules of **logic** to figure out if their

Logic Valid reasoning.

explanation is the best one. Some common logical arguments are that causes precede effects, 1 + 1 = 2, and that a person cannot be physically in two places at one time.

In addition to being systematic and logical, scientific researchers are especially interested in **empirical evidence**, or fact-based information, that might prove their explanation wrong. The idea that scientific statements can be proven to be true or false is fundamental to science (Popper 2005). This is why scientific statements are different from **beliefs** that may come through divine revelation or received tradition, or from **opinions** that may stem from common values or experience. While opinions and beliefs are a very important part of society, they are not subject to the same standard of **falsifiability** as scientific statements. Falsifiability requires scientists to conduct a systematic search for a falsifying logic or evidence that could prove that scientific statement is wrong. Scientific statements are also subject to verification using systematic scientific methods. The criticism made by the wider scientific community of the hurricane study reported in *USA Today* was based largely on the fact that the researchers relied on beliefs about women and men rather than scientific standards. Using logic, these researchers might have asked how a female-named hurricane could actually cause an increase in fatalities. This might have led researchers to consider alternative explanations for their findings. If they had pursued alternative explanations, they would have been likely to find a change in the pattern of naming hurricanes over time. Instead, the hurricane researchers considered neither evidence nor logical argument that could have challenged their sensational and newsworthy finding.

Researchers across disciplines and industries share a commitment to the scientific ideal, defined by falsifiability. The centralized research programs of the natural sciences are among the most developed versions of this idea of science based on falsifiability. So are government-sponsored rules about clinical testing for medical procedures or new drugs. While social science research is also committed to the ideals of the scientific community, social researchers face several challenges that other scientific researchers do not.

Social Research and Ethics

Sociology is a social science. This means that sociological knowledge should be based on good **social research**, defined as the systematic investigation of some aspect of the social world, which aims to contribute to our general understanding of society. Social research is conducted by social scientists, who work in universities, government agencies, and private companies.

In general, scientific studies are based on the model of the **controlled experiment**, in which a researcher controls the conditions of some outcome of interest and studies it systematically to isolate the causal logic that produces the observed effects. For example, if a botanist wants to know how light affects plant growth, she would divide a set of plants into groups, and control how much light each group receives. She can then compare the plants receiving different amounts of light. If the botanist wants to know how light and water interact to influence plant growth, then she would vary light and water both singly and in combination. Controlled experiments are not as common in social science as they are in natural science research, because there are widely shared legal and ethical rules about experimenting on people. Unlike the botanist, who can run the risk that a plant might die in an experiment, social scientists must be far more careful of the consequences of their research.

Empirical evidence Fact-based information about the social or natural world.

Beliefs Ideas about the world that come through divine revelation or received tradition.

Opinions Ideas about the world that stem from common values or experience.

Falsifiability The idea that scientific statements define what condition or evidence would prove them wrong.

Social research All the different strategies sociologists use to collect, measure, and analyze their data.

Controlled experiment Scientific method that systematically controls the factors that affect some outcome of interest and studies it systematically to isolate the causal logic that produces the observed effects.

PAIRED CONCEPTS Solidarity and Conflict

Race, Difference, and the Politics of Medical Research

For most of the 20th century, medical researchers did not account for differences in gender or race when recruiting research subjects; instead, most of their studies used white men. Doctors assumed that they could take the findings from that research and generalize it for the entire population. This began to change in the 1980s.

As Steven Epstein shows in *Inclusion: The Politics of Difference in Medical Research* (2007), health advocacy groups and civil rights leaders began complaining about the underrepresentation of women, racial minorities, and youth in clinical medical studies. After attracting public attention to this problem, these advocacy groups convinced health industry insiders and influential politicians to join their cause. The US Congress passed a law in 1993 mandating that clinical medical research must include underrepresented groups, and it must study medical differences based on gender, race, ethnicity, and age. Medical journal guidelines and medical school curricula also changed to reflect these social concerns.

The idea that social categories were relevant for medical research did not come from the medical community, but rather from the worlds of politics and social movements. Epstein shows how there was a gradual "categorical alignment" between social and medical research; medical researchers did not develop their own set of categories, but instead they used the categories of race, gender, and ethnicity that were being used in the US Census.

In demanding changes in the design of medical research, advocacy groups and politicians promoted greater equality and social justice in health outcomes. As Epstein demonstrates, however, these efforts had limits. By focusing on a small list of group identities that were politically deemed to be relevant, other factors were overlooked. The result is that medical research has not been very effective at identifying the full range of factors that lead to differences in health and health care. By focusing on racial, ethnic, and gender categories, it becomes harder to see how differences in wealth, power, and other social factors contribute to health disparities. There is also a danger of biological essentialism, in which people come to believe that differences in health are based on biological differences rather than social factors.

ACTIVE LEARNING

Find out: Use Google Scholar to search "gender bias in medical research" or "race bias in medical research." What do experts say today about the inclusion of race and gender in medical research? What other social factors do these experts say should be included in future medical studies?

studies that promoted national security or the economic interests of the United States (Rapaport 2013).

When social research involves "hot-button issues," such as drugs, health, crime, and sexuality (Kempner 2008; Kempner, Merz, and Bosk 2011), social researchers must be prepared to find themselves at the center of public attention, as politicians, journalists, and activists comment on their work. In these cases, researchers have to weigh questions about the effect of public attention on their research carefully, since they do not always control the way their research questions and findings are interpreted.

Science and Complex Societies

Despite the challenges and public controversies associated with social research, our world values scientific knowledge. Sociologists use many different types of data and evidence in their research, and all of them are collected with the goal of producing good scientific knowledge about social things.

Scientific knowledge is important because it is systematically reviewed, evaluated, and tested by a community of experts. Regardless of what kinds of research they are doing or what kinds of methods they are using, all scientists believe in the importance of **peer review**. Before they can publish their work or get funding for their research, scientific proposals and research findings are evaluated by experts in the field. This evaluation is usually anonymous; the reviewers' identities are kept private, and so are the identities of the people whose work they are evaluating. The goal of a good peer review process is to ensure the credibility and validity of scientific work. Peer reviewers consider five factors about the research:

March for Science
Citizens marched in Portland, Oregon, on April 14, 2018, to defend scientific standards for research. Does science need to be defended? Does this mean that scientific knowledge is no longer dominant and unquestioned?

1. Does the research ask important questions?

2. Does the research connect those questions to the appropriate research literatures?

3. Does the research collect the kind of data needed to answer the questions being posed?

4. Does the research use appropriate techniques to analyze the data?

5. Does the research generate appropriate logical inferences from the data being analyzed?

Peer review The process of review of proposed research or publication by the community of scientific experts in a profession or scientific field.

The hurricane study that we mentioned at the beginning of the chapter shows us how peer review in the scientific community works. A wide range of scientists identified problems with how the data were collected. They criticized the techniques that were used to analyze the data. They questioned whether the researchers' explanations had drawn on the correct theories. They identified alternative explanations for the findings, and they argued that these alternative explanations were much more plausible. This critical focus on the research process is typical of the way that the scientific community talks about research findings in the social sciences. The irony in this case is that the article had already been published in a credible scientific journal!

The Research Process

As scientists, sociologists aim to produce knowledge that is factually accurate, that is falsifiable, that contributes to our general understanding of social phenomena, and that can withstand the critical judgment of the scientific community. How do they go about doing this? What are the main steps in the research process for sociologists? What kinds of data do they use? What techniques do they use to analyze their data?

Most sociologists begin with a research question. Examples of research questions include: What causes some children to succeed in school while others fail? Why do some countries have higher homicide rates than others? How have beliefs about motherhood and childrearing changed in the last 50 years?

After identifying a research question, the next step in the research process is to find out what other researchers have written about the topic. The goal is to identify a useful contribution that your research can make to the scientific community. For some topics, there will be competing theories about a particular social phenomenon, and the new research can make a contribution by introducing new evidence that sheds light on which theory offers a better explanation. For example, when Douglas Massey and Nancy Denton published *American Apartheid* in 1993, there was a debate in the social science community about whether segregation in the United States was caused more by economic inequality or by racial discrimination. On the basis of their research, Massey and Denton argued persuasively that racial discrimination was the more important factor.

Another way to make a research contribution is to ask new or different types of questions about a particular social phenomenon. The paired concepts that appear throughout this book are useful for making this kind of research contribution. If most researchers are focused on inequality, for example, it might be helpful to study privilege. If most researchers studying a topic are focused on conflict, maybe you should try studying solidarity. If the dominant research focus is on structure, there are probably useful insights to be gained by paying more attention to contingency. This is the approach Robert Sampson and his colleagues took in his path-breaking research on the causes of delinquency. When virtually no researchers were asking about solidarity, Sampson showed that the level of violence in a community was connected to levels of trust and cooperative social action (Sampson, Raudenbusch, and Earls 1997). When most researchers were examining the structural factors that led children to become delinquents and adults to become criminals, Sampson asked whether there might be contingent turning points (such as getting married or joining the military) that could help set the juvenile delinquent on a different path (Sampson and Laub 1995).

Data and Measurement

One of the most important parts of the research process is identifying what kinds of evidence or data you will need to collect before you can answer your question. Sociologists use many different kinds of data. They talk to people, conduct surveys, observe people in their natural settings, look at mass media and social media, examine historical records, pore over government and other institutional records, and conduct experiments. For each type of data, there are established standards about the best way to collect, measure, and analyze evidence.

Sociological research methods are all the different strategies that sociologists use to collect, measure, and analyze data. Sociologists rely on an expansive set of research methods. One category of research methods is **quantitative,** where the goal is to collect numerical data that can be analyzed using statistical techniques. A survey of household income is one example of a quantitative study. When a researcher calls or texts you on your phone to ask what political candidate you favor, you are a participant in a poll, which is another kind of quantitative study. Quantitative methods offer powerful approaches to complex questions. And, in an era of big social data, when human populations and machines are generating an enormous amount of digital information, quantitative methods help us explore and map large social phenomena.

Statistical techniques also allow social researchers to mimic the logic of the controlled experiment. Using statistics, quantitative sociologists can hold some factors constant while examining how variation in other factors affects the outcome. Once they have identified important relationships between different social factors, they can also use statistical theory to determine how likely it is for those relationships to have occurred by chance. A statistical model can approximate a change in social condition to discover causal relationships. For

Sociological research methods All the different strategies sociologists use to collect, measure, and analyze data.

Quantitative methods Sociological research methods that collect numerical data that can be analyzed using statistical techniques.

example, we might ask if differences in earnings for the same work produce differences in happiness among employees. It would be unethical (and illegal) to manipulate social conditions and pay some employees less than others to discover the answer to this question. Another approach would be to survey people who do the same job about earnings and happiness, and compare reported happiness at different earnings levels.

Although not all information in the world can be meaningfully converted into numbers, the tools of quantitative methods can be applied to a wide range of situations. Sociologists use different kinds of measures for different things. The reason is that some social things are more numerical than others (Table 3.1).

How much money someone earns, for example, is a numerical question. Money can be counted. In the language of statistical measurement, money is a **linear** or **continuous** variable because it is numerical. By contrast, your sex is less inherently numerical. To be sure, sociological researchers assign numbers to sex categories in statistical models, traditionally coding men "1" and women "2" so groups can be compared. From a mathematical point of view, however, you cannot perform calculations on these numbers in the same way you can manipulate numbers representing money. For example, you cannot take a meaningful average of sex. Other researchers have raised questions about the social consequences of using only two categories for sex, when a substantial population does not identify with either category. Whatever the case, it remains true that unlike money, a numerical measure of sex in a statistical model is assigned simply so that statistical software can recognize the data. The numbers have no inherent numerical meaning. This is true for many social categories, including race and ethnicity, where there is no immediately obvious numerical meaning

Continuous or linear variable
A measure of inherently numerical phenomena that can be counted, divided, and multiplied, such as money or time.

Table 3.1 Levels of measurement

COMPLEXITY			
The interval between categories is known (interval) and zero is a true value (interval ratio).	You can perform higher mathematical operations on variables when the interval between categories is mathematically precise and where zero is a true value.	Continuous and interval ratio[1]	Income in dollars can run from $0 to $1,000,000 and more. Income can also be negative. Age begins at zero and increases in numerically precise units.
Categories are ranked higher or lower, but the distance between categories has no precise numerical value.	You can count occurrences in each category, and make comparative statements about higher and lower.	Ordinal (ranked)	Social class 1. Upper class 2. Middle class 3. Working class Opinion about desirability of a new tax 1. In favor 2. Neutral 3. Against
Categories are labels, not numerical values.	You can count occurrences in each category.	Nominal (categorical)	Mortality status 1. Alive 2. Dead Sex 1. Male 2. Female

Note: Levels of measurement determine what kind of statistical methods can be used to analyze data. Increasing numerical precision allows for more complex statistical analysis.

[1] The difference between interval variables and interval-ratio variables is rarely an issue in social science research. The difference rests on the idea that there is an "absolute value" denoted by numbers measured in increments from true zero. Interval-ratio variables include distance, age, time, and weight. With interval variables, there are equal intervals between numbers but there is no true zero. Variables include calendar years and IQ.

Representative sample A selection from a research population that contains all the features of the wider population from which it is drawn.

Snowball sample A selection from a research population taken by asking the first few research subjects to identify and recommend others for study.

Theoretical sample A selection from a research population that focuses a sample as research progresses and where the sampling strategy changes after the initial data have been collected, based on what is theoretically important.

Case study research Research that relies on a small number of cases that offer special insight into a particular social process and are studied in depth, typically using comparative methods.

Hypothesis A specific statement about the causal relationship between variables that is falsifiable, which means it is a statement that can be proved wrong on the basis of empirical evidence.

generator (a computer application that selects numbers randomly) to select the sample. In a random sample, every member of the research population has an equal chance of being selected. This means the sample is likely to be **representative** of the research population at large and mirror its central patterns and characteristics. This provides a strong basis for making a logical connection between what is discovered in the sample and what is really going on in the larger population. In other words, the random sample is a valid and reliable measure of what is occurring in the research population because it is less likely to be biased.

Although random samples provide a powerful basis for making population-level arguments, in many important cases it is not always possible to get a complete list of all the members in a research population. For example, you might be interested in studying people who are considering immigrating to a new country or thinking about changing their religion. You might be interested in the different strategies that people use to try to get on a reality television program. Or, you might be interested in the causes of genocide. In these examples, while the question is sociologically interesting and important, it is not possible to identify the entire research population, and you would need to use a different sampling strategy.

Sociologists use three types of nonrepresentative samples to collect data when it is not possible to identify the full population of interest to the research. In a **snowball sample**, the researcher begins with a few people who agree to participate in the research, and then asks those people to recommend other people they think would be willing to participate. Snowball sampling is effective when it is hard to get people to participate, which is a common issue when studying sensitive issues or vulnerable populations. A second strategy is a **theoretical sample**, where decisions about data collection change after the initial data have been collected, based on what is theoretically important (Glaser 1978). For example, when Sobieraj (2011) started interviewing social movement leaders and discovered that they were obsessed with attracting the attention of journalists, she changed her strategy to interview journalists as well, to see what they thought about social protesters. A third strategy is **case study research**, where a researcher selects a small number of cases that offer special insight into a particular social process. For example, when John Hall (Hall, Schuyler, and Trinh 2000) wanted to understand religious violence, he compared five famous cases from the Americas, Europe, and Japan in which members of religious movements turned to murder and suicide. In all five of his cases, the groups believed in apocalyptic narratives about the end of the world. But these beliefs did not cause violence all by themselves. The actions of murder and mass suicide were made more likely by escalating conflict with outsiders and authorities, and a public narrative about the danger of religious cults. Hall finds that a general paranoia about religious cults caused police to overreact to these religious groups, increasing the likelihood of violence.

WHAT IS THE HYPOTHESIZED CAUSAL RELATIONSHIP BETWEEN YOUR VARIABLES? A **hypothesis** is a specific statement about the causal relationship between variables. More than a hunch or a guess, a scientific hypothesis is a statement that is falsifiable, which means that your data can prove it wrong.

It is important to think critically about this issue of causality between variables, to make sure that your explanation seems realistic, and that it is supported by existing social theories. Sociologists criticized the hurricane study because it required assumptions that were not sociologically plausible. Even if it is true that people feel less threatened by women than they do by men, it does not make sense that they would prepare differently for a hurricane just because it had a woman's name. And it seems completely implausible that simply changing the name of a major hurricane from a man's to a woman's name could cost six thousand people their lives.

Just because two variables appear to be related (such as women's names and deaths during hurricanes), this does not mean that one factor is a **cause** of the other. This is a case of confusing **correlation**, which is when two variables share a pattern, for **causation**, which is when two variables share a pattern because one variable produces the pattern in the other. When an observed statistical relationship between two variables is mistaken for a causal relationship between them, it is called a spurious correlation. For example, there is a very strong statistical correlation between the consumption of margarine in the United States and the divorce rate in Maine (Figure 3.1). There is also a strong correlation between the number of honey-producing bee colonies in the United States and the marriage rate in Vermont (Figure 3.2). But it would be ridiculous to claim that these correlations are causal relationships, because there is no theoretical or logical basis for believing that one of the variables is actually producing a change in the other.

Another strategy sociologists use to explain the causal logic of their findings is **counterfactual reasoning**, where they try to imagine what factors might have led to a different social outcome. In everyday social life people use counterfactual reasoning all the time, particularly when they are thinking about important events in their lives (Kahneman, Slovic and Tersky1982). For example, military analysts use counterfactual reasoning ("What if Iran had nuclear weapons?" "What if China invaded Taiwan?") in order to develop a deeper understanding of the world, and to prepare more effectively for situations they might face in the future. When sociologists use counterfactual reasoning, they are also trying to develop a better understanding of the

Cause Something that produces an outcome. Technically, a cause is where a first event is understood to produce a material effect on a second event.

Correlation A correlation is an observed statistical dependence between two variables but it does not mean the variables are *causally* related.

Causation Causation occurs when two variables share a pattern because one variable produces the pattern in the other.

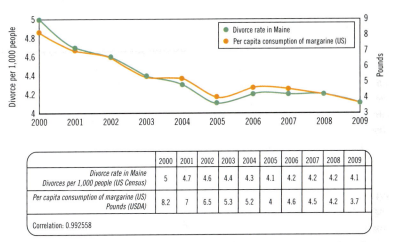

	2000	2001	2002	2003	2004	2005	2006	2007	2008	2009
Divorce rate in Maine Divorces per 1,000 people (US Census)	5	4.7	4.6	4.4	4.3	4.1	4.2	4.2	4.2	4.1
Per capita consumption of margarine (US) Pounds (USDA)	8.2	7	6.5	5.3	5.2	4	4.6	4.5	4.2	3.7

Correlation: 0.992558

Figure 3.1   Divorce Rate in Maine Correlates with Per Capita Consumption of Margarine (US).
Source: US Census; USDA.

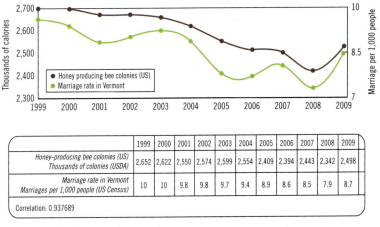

	1999	2000	2001	2002	2003	2004	2005	2006	2007	2008	2009
Honey-producing bee colonies (US) Thousands of colonies (USDA)	2,652	2,622	2,550	2,574	2,599	2,554	2,409	2,394	2,443	2,342	2,498
Marriage rate in Vermont Marriages per 1,000 people (US Census)	10	10	9.8	9.8	9.7	9.4	8.9	8.6	8.5	7.9	8.7

Correlation: 0.937689

Figure 3.2   Honey-Producing Bee Colonies (US) Correlate with Marriage Rate in Vermont.
Source: USDA, US Census.

What if?
The military practices counterfactual reasoning when it uses different scenarios for war-game simulations. Regular people also use counterfactual reasoning in everyday life when they ask "what if?"

Counterfactual reasoning
An analytical strategy for investigating the causal logic of research that asks what factors might have led to a different social outcome.

social world, particularly when they are studying important events in history. Max Weber insisted that counterfactual reasoning was one of the most important methodological tools for sociologists who were doing historical research.

ANALYZING YOUR DATA AND DRAWING CONCLUSIONS. Once data have been collected and analyzed, sociologists draw conclusions from their analysis. Most sociologists situate their findings in the context of previous research and specify what extra insight or factual understanding the new research adds. The contribution might be to change a theoretical idea, to discover a new social phenomenon, or to observe a change in a long-established trend. As we outline in the next section, there are many different strategies for collecting and analyzing social data and several different audiences for sociological research.

Three Common Strategies for Sociological Research

Most sociological research can be divided into three types of activities: talking to people, observing social settings, and examining publicly available data. For each of these activities, sociologists have developed quantitative and qualitative methods, different ways to collect data, and different approaches to explaining their findings. As you will see, there are trade-offs between different kinds of choices when designing research.

Talking to People: Survey Analysis, Interviews, and Focus Groups

If you want to know why people act the way they do, or what they think about a particular social issue, a good strategy is to ask them. Sociologists conduct **surveys**, where they ask defined questions to a large sample of the population. They do **in-depth interviews**, where they ask extended, probing, and open-ended questions to a smaller sample of people. And they conduct **focus groups**, where they

Focus groups
Researchers use focus groups when they want to see how people work together to make decisions and discuss issues.

METHODS AND INTERPRETATION

Major Surveys Conducted by Sociologists

Sociologists make extensive use of survey research conducted by the government, and have been active in the design of many government surveys. Some of the key government survey resources used by sociologists are the American Time Use Survey (2003–present), which measures the amount of time people spend doing various activities, such as work, sleep, leisure, and childcare; the Current Population Survey (1940–present), a monthly survey of households that provides data on the labor force; and the American National Election Study, a national survey of the American electorate that has been conducted every two years since 1948.

Sociologists have also conducted some of the largest and most important survey research projects in the country. The National Opinion Research Center (NORC) was created in 1941 at the University of Chicago, and focuses on large, national surveys. NORC created the General Social Survey (GSS) in 1974, which was conducted every year between 1972 and 1994, and has been conducted every other year since 1994. The GSS asks people their opinions on a wide range of social issues, and connects those responses with information about demographic characteristics such as age, race, gender, education, and socioeconomic background. The results from the GSS are available to the public, and they are used more often by sociologists than any other type of survey data. The NORC also conducts other important, ongoing surveys such as the National Longitudinal

Survey of Youth (1966–present), the Survey of Consumer Finances (1992–present), and the National Survey of Children's Health (2003–present)

The Detroit Area Survey was created in 1951 at the University of Michigan. Its purpose was to train social scientists in survey research and to collect reliable data on the Detroit community. Surveys were conducted nearly every year until 2004, when the research project ended. Each survey focused on specific social questions and issues connected to personal and public life, economic and political behavior, work, and family. Social scientists have published more than six hundred research articles using data from the Detroit area studies.

The Wisconsin Longitudinal Study was a long-term study of a random sample of 10,317 men and women who graduated from high school in Wisconsin in 1957. Survey data were collected during 13 different periods between 1957 and 2011, allowing researchers to study family dynamics, health and well-being, and other social aspects of people's lives over the life course.

ACTIVE LEARNING

Find out: Does your college, town, or state conduct regular surveys? Make a list of at least two sources and describe each briefly. Are the results of the survey publicly available? What questions do they ask? What questions do you think they should ask?

Discuss: Have you ever been asked to complete a survey? Do you typically respond to surveys? Why or why not?

gather groups of people together and facilitate a discussion about a particular social issue.

Survey research is a good research tool when you want to ask specific, defined questions of large numbers of people. If you want to know what kinds of people support the death penalty, what political candidate people prefer, or what kinds of rudeness people experience most often in their lives, you can find out by conducting a survey. Today, surveys are usually conducted over the phone or online.

A key advantage of survey research is that it allows sociologists to collect data from a large number of respondents. Surveys can rely on random sampling strategies to create representative samples. As a result, researchers can **generalize** their findings from the data analysis to the larger population in a way that is both valid and reliable. But survey researchers also face constraints. First, they have to decide in advance what questions they are going to ask, and they also have to decide what the possible answers will be. Survey researchers do not have a lot of flexibility to ask more probing questions, or to find out what

Surveys A sociological research method that asks a series of defined questions to collect data from a large sample of the research population.

In-depth interviews A sociological research method that uses extended, open-ended questions to collect data.

Focus groups A sociological research method that gathers groups of people together for discussion of a common question or a particular social issue to collect data.

Generalize To make the argument that the finding from a particular sample of people or a single research study applies to a wider research population.

the respondent really means by a response. It can be challenging to get people to answer sensitive questions, and survey researchers struggle with low response rates. In 2015, the average response rate for telephone surveys was below 10 percent, and the response rate for online surveys is even lower.

Researchers often use extended interviews when they want to ask more open-ended questions, or when they want to have the flexibility to follow the discussion wherever it may take them. Sociologists have used extended interviews to study how people think about the following issues: different parenting styles (Hays 1998; Lareau and Goyette 2014), racial identities (Lamont 2002; Young and Bhaba 2004), respect and stigma (Lamont et al. 2016), and poverty (Edin, Lein, and Jencks 1997). Extended interviews are particularly useful when researchers are talking with vulnerable populations such as the homeless, who may be more difficult to locate or less inclined to talk with a stranger on the phone. Extended interviews usually take more time and energy to complete than surveys, and they are more likely to use nonrandom samples. There is also a concern about **reactivity**, which is when the researcher has an effect on the behavior and the responses of the interview subject. The trade-off is that open-ended questions offer the possibility of gaining a more complete understanding of the people studied.

Reactivity When the researcher has an effect on the behavior and the responses of the interview subject.

A third way social scientists talk to people is by organizing focus groups. With a focus group, the researcher recruits people into the study, and then leads them in a group discussion about a particular social issue. While focus group research is commonly used by marketers to determine the effectiveness of an advertising campaign, it was actually invented by sociologists during the 1940s who were asked by the military to investigate how audiences viewed propaganda films. Focus groups allow the sociologist to see how people interact with each other, and how collective opinions develop within a natural setting.

Observation: Ethnography and Experiments

What individuals say can be very informative, but sometimes, what people tell us is not a very good measurement of how they will behave (Jerolmack and Khan 2014). For this reason, it is also important for sociologists to observe how people act in social life. The two most commonly used strategies for observing social action are ethnography and experiments.

Ethnography A sociological research method based on participant-observation in the field where researchers try to capture social life in all of its detail and complexity.

Participant-observation A research method of observing people in social settings by participating in those social settings with them.

Ethnography is a form of research that uses **participant-observation**, where researchers go into the field and participate in the everyday lives of the people they are studying. Rather than trying to isolate different variables, ethnographers try to capture social life in all of its detail and complexity. Ethnographers describe not only what people do, but also the full context in which they do it. This includes the mutual cooperation and coordination between different people, the subtle cues and gestures that people use, and the meanings that people attach to those cues and gestures. By immersing themselves in a social setting for a long period of time and providing a detailed description of how actions unfold in specific social contexts, ethnographers capture the interaction between structure and contingency much more fully than is possible with other methods. Ethnographies give us some of the most insightful accounts of social life we have, and they can be fascinating to read.

To understand what happens in ethnographic research, take the example of Loïc Wacquant's (2006) study of a boxing gym in inner-city Chicago. Wacquant, a French sociologist, wanted to study race and poverty in American cities. In order to get closer to the social world of the people he wanted to study, Wacquant joined a boxing gym and began training with other men from the neighborhood. While he had a much different social background than the other

Inequality and Privilege

Studying Doormen in New York

In New York City, there are more doormen than taxi drivers. Most doormen in the city are working-class immigrants who live in the outer boroughs. It is a good job, with an average salary of nearly $45,000. They are not easy jobs to get, because most doormen hold onto their jobs for decades, and it is not uncommon for veteran doormen to hold open positions for their friends and relatives. Doormen have an intimate relationship with the residents in their building, who generally speak of their doormen with great affection, lavishing them with gifts at the holidays. While the doormen have good jobs, they are surrounded by people who are much wealthier than they are. Sitting (literally) at the intersection of inequality and privilege, doormen witness, interact with, and support the lives of wealthy people in an intimate way while not enjoying the direct benefits of those privileges. Because of this, doormen make an excellent strategic research site for studying inequality. This is exactly what Peter Bearman did for his 2005 book, *Doormen*.

Bearman examines all aspects of the doorman's life, and the social setting in which he does his work. He looks at how doormen get their jobs, discovering how important referrals are, and how these social networks tend to exclude certain racial and ethnic groups. He examines why the doormen's union has been so successful. And he looks at the different challenges that doormen face in their work. How do they cope with long stretches of time with nothing to do? How do they deal with the rush of the holiday season? How do they deal with the particular preferences of specific tenants while still having all the tenants feel like they are being treated fairly? How do they make distinctions between "good tenants" and "bad tenants"? How do they deal with all the intimate knowledge they have about their tenants, while still maintaining an appropriate professional distance?

One interesting feature of Bearman's book is that it was based on a collective research project that he did with one of his undergraduate classes. In order to collect data for his research, Bearman and his students began by creating a representative sample of 287 buildings in New York City that had doormen. There were a total of 1,200 doormen working in those buildings, and Bearman recruited a sample of 212 to participate in his study. Each participant completed a questionnaire about their social background, their income, the duties of their job, and their income. Forty-three of the doormen participated in in-depth interviews that explored the job in greater detail. The in-depth interviews were supplemented by extensive participant-observation, interviews with tenants, and publicly available data about the doormen's union. By collecting multiple sources of data in this way, Bearman's study was able to identify patterns and similarities in how doormen interact with their tenants.

Doorman
A doorman opens a limousine door in Manhattan. Why do you think he wears a hat and a red jacket with golden braids and tassels? How does it separate him from other people on the street?

ACTIVE LEARNING
Find out: Can you think of a job that is similar to the doorman, in which people from much different social backgrounds interact regularly in a close and intimate setting? What would you need to do to collect the same kinds of data that Bearman did for his study of doormen?

boxers in the gym, Wacquant was eventually accepted as a regular member of the club. He became an "insider" who trained diligently, paid his dues in the ring, and represented the gym in boxing matches.

After several years as a participant-observer, Wacquant was able to discover that the inner-city boxing gym was a much more complicated and meaningful place than it appeared on the surface. The gym was much more than a place to train and develop skills as a boxer. It was also a "sanctuary," providing a buffer zone against the insecurity of the neighborhood and the general stress of every-day life (Wacquant 2006: 14). It was a place of discipline, pride, friendship, and social belonging, where people could reflect on the meaning of violence in their lives, while also standing apart from the criminal forms that violence usually took on the streets surrounding the gym.

Because ethnographers focus intensively on a single case, and because their goal is to uncover the many interconnected layers of the social environment, it is more difficult for them to isolate specific social processes or to generalize from their findings. In order to draw general arguments, they will either compare their findings with similar cases from other research, or they will consider how their findings either support or challenge other social theories. Michael Burawoy (1998) calls this the "extended case method," and he argues that this is the best way to connect ethnographic research to the larger body of social-scientific scholarship.

Experiments A sociological research method that controls the conditions of observation with the goal of isolating the effects of different factors on some outcome of interest.

Another way to observe social action is to conduct **experiments**. For example, a group of sociologists from Stanford University in the United States and from Hokkaido University in Japan conducted experiments about risk-taking and trust. (Cook et al. 2005). They found that Americans were far more likely to take risks than people from Japan, and that risk-taking was more important for building trust for the American participants. Other sociologists have used laboratory experiments to examine how people make moral judgments (Simpson, Harrell, and Willer 2013), and how they make status distinctions (Ridgeway et al. 2009).

Field experiments Research using experimental methods in natural settings outside of the laboratory.

Sociologists also conduct **field experiments**, which use experimental methods in natural settings outside of the laboratory. In one interesting field experiment, white, Latino, and African American job applicants were given equivalent résumés and sent out as job applicants in New York City (Pager, Western, and Bonikowski 2009). The results of this study revealed that African American applicants were about half as likely to receive a callback or a job offer as equally qualified white applicants, and that African American and Latino applicants with no criminal record fared about as well on the job market as white applicants who had just been released from prison.

Analysis of Publicly Available Data Sources: Media Reports, Government Documents, Official Statistics, and Big Data

Comparative-historical methods A set of research methods that uses comparison of events and processes in the past to understand the development and operation of social things.

In many types of sociological research, it is not possible to talk to people or to observe their behavior directly. This is the case for **comparative-historical** sociologists, who study events that took place in the past. For example, Richard Lachmann compared people living in different cities in England, France, Italy, Spain, and the Netherlands from the 12th through the 18th centuries in order to explain why capitalism developed in some parts of Europe but not in others (Lachmann 2000). Likewise, in his study of slavery, Orlando Patterson compared how slavery was organized in 66 different societies throughout the world over a period of nearly two thousand years (Patterson 1982).

To do comparative-historical research, sociologists rely on data from the past. They go into historical archives, which are typically housed in museums and libraries. They consult the work of other historians. They rely on official records, such as census data, bank transactions and other commercial records, newspaper reports, and legal documents. They read autobiographies, diaries, and letters written by the people they are studying.

Content analysis A sociological method to systematically evaluate and code text documents in which word frequencies or other textual features can be turned into quantitative variables.

Comparative-historical researchers are not the only sociologists who use publicly available data. Other researchers use **content analysis** to systematically evaluate and code text documents so that word frequencies or other textual features can be turned into quantitative variables. When there are official records of the outcomes we want to study, there is less of a need to talk to people or observe their behavior. If the answers we seek are quantitative—for example, which kinds of people are most likely to get arrested, get the highest test scores in school, or be unemployed—there are public data sources we can turn to for the answers.

One of the advantages of using publicly available data is that there is less concern with reactivity, where the researcher affects the social phenomenon she is studying. Because we are not interacting with the people we are studying when we use publicly available data, there is little chance that we will directly influence their responses or behavior. A possible drawback with publicly available data, however, is that we have to depend on what other people thought was important enough to collect, store, and share. This is a **selection effect**, which means that the way information is selected shapes what information we have. For example, in France, Italy, and the Netherlands, official census data do not collect information on race and ethnicity. It is important to think critically about these sources of bias and omission when we use data selected by other people.

With the rise of the internet and the rapid expansion of social media, sociologists are also beginning to analyze **big data**, which is data produced by our technological ability to capture the behavior of humans (and machines and others) over huge populations and time spans. Researchers interested in studying violence against women can now access geotagged reports of violence, which anyone with a GPS-enabled smartphone can upload to social media platforms such as Egypt's HarassMap (Belyea 2011). In addition to relying on opinion surveys, researchers now have access to more than 100 million daily social media posts (King 2011).

In fact, over the last 30 years, a great deal of cultural material has been produced and stored in digital formats. This shift has presented opportunities for sociologists, who are beginning to develop new techniques for collecting and measuring culture using big data and automated text analysis. Sociologists can now use automated text extraction programs and automated text-classification programs to assign values to variables, or code, their data (Bail 2014).

It is still important to think critically about the origins and limitations of the data. For example, there is ongoing debate about how representative social media data really are. Not everyone has access to computers and smartphones, and the people who post regularly on social media sites are not necessarily representative of the larger population (Hargittai and Walejko 2008). A lot of social media data are collected by private companies, who are not always willing to grant access to social scientists doing research. There are also enduring ethical concerns about protecting privacy and guaranteeing informed consent when analyzing any data.

Regardless of the type of research you are doing, you need to think about the limitations of your data and the possible sources of bias that might have influenced it. Sociological research is challenging to do well, both because there are so many different kinds of sociological questions and also because there are so many different ways to collect and analyze data. Recognize that no research is perfect or provides the final answer, and for this reason you need to try to be transparent about what you are doing so that future sociologists can build on and test your research findings. You need to think about the fact that the social world you are studying is changing as you are studying it, and that the people you are studying often change their behavior in response to social research.

Selection effect The bias produced in data by the way the data are chosen, or selected.

Big data Refers to the large amount of data produced by our technological ability to capture the behavior of humans (and machines and others) over huge populations and time spans.

Global and Local

Citizen Science: Using Local Data to Understand Global Patterns

Citizen science is scientific research conducted by amateur scientists or community members. Some associations that contribute to scientific observation include those that publish amateur astronomical observation, data collected by bird watchers and butterfly counters, and more recently citizen oceanographers who track marine debris and community conservationists who take photos of roadkill to assess the impact of traffic on wildlife (Vercayie and Herremans 2015).

In the age of the internet and smartphones, citizen observers can contribute a wide range of local data to build up a picture of global patterns. At the same time, crowdsourcing scientific data can also create new social challenges. For example, a British organization called Speedwatch relies on community volunteers to "monitor the speeds of vehicles using speed detection devices" and then report those observations to police (Speedwatch n.d.). In this case, citizens contribute to police surveillance of motorists.

Social researchers have also expressed concern about the rise of crowdsourced data collection online. Anonymous researchers who perform a small piece of an overall task for very little pay are neither acknowledged nor compensated for the results of their work (Brown 2015). Other critics raise the spectre of experimentation on online subjects without obtaining consent or thinking about protecting human subjects (Wood 2014; Goel 2014).

Citizen science
In an example of citizen science, volunteers in Costa Rica assist with a project that aims to protect sea turtles.

ACTIVE LEARNING

Discuss: Can you think about information that ordinary citizens could collect that would be hard for social researchers to access otherwise? Can you imagine a socially useful purpose for this information?

You need to recognize that the topic you are studying may be controversial and politically charged, and that other people outside of the world of sociology may have an interest (and not necessarily a benign interest) in your findings. In short, you need to pay attention to the social nature of sociological research.

The Social Nature of Social Research

As sociologists, we want to be aware of the ways that social relationships influence the practice of research. Scientists are organized into groups and networks. These groups can form among people who are asking the same kind of question, interested in a particular theory or developing a particular kind of research technique, or studied with the same teacher. Like all groups, scientific research teams have leaders and followers, and they are often influenced by rivalries with other groups.

The social organization of science organizes how people do their research. As people join specific research teams, they learn and adopt common assumptions about what counts as a good research question, what kinds of data are best for answering these questions, what are the preferred techniques for analyzing and interpreting these data, and what are the most important theories that can help explain the research findings (Kuhn 1979; Lakatos 1978). As we discussed in Chapter 2, scientists do not generally abandon a theory they support just because there are inconvenient facts that challenge their expectations. They will usually try to revise their theories in order to defend them against competing theories and competing research groups (Alexander 1990). This is particularly true for the social sciences, where there tends to be a large number of competing theories trying to explain the same phenomena (Gorski 2004; Reed 2011).

Scientific research is also social in the sense that particular types of people are more likely than others to become professional researchers. White people and wealthy people from privileged backgrounds have a greater chance of entering graduate school and completing a PhD. Group leadership and status differences are also important, with the top scientists receiving most of the awards, recognition, and resources (Merton 1968).

The Challenge of Studying People

Sociological research presents special challenges because we are studying people who are similar to us. Even when we are studying people who lived in the past or in other places, we can imagine what their lives are (or were) like. We have sympathy for the challenges they face, decisions they make, and their successes and disappointments. We need this sympathy in order to understand social life in its full complexity. The problem is that it is hard to understand the lives of the people we are studying without comparing them to our own lives. This creates a basic challenge of interpretation. Are we using our lives to understand their society, or are we using their lives to understand our own society? It is often difficult to disentangle these two goals.

A second challenge is that people often change their behavior in response to social research. We learn about social research from newspapers, blogs, magazines, books, friends, experts, and other people, in a broader process sociologists call **institutional reflexivity**. Institutional reflexivity makes it harder to replicate important research findings, precisely because of the way that people change their behavior after being exposed to those findings. For example, research in the sociology of education shows that teachers call on boys more often than girls, give them more feedback on their work, and generally pay more attention to them (Sadker and Sadker 1995).

Institutional reflexivity The phenomenon where people change their behavior in response to social research.

But this finding has been integrated into teacher training programs, and many teachers now consciously try to be more equitable in the way they treat boys and girls. To the extent that they succeed in their attempts, then future research on gender and education may not be able to find the same levels of difference in the attention boys and girls receive from their teachers. The earlier findings were not "wrong" just because they couldn't be replicated by newer research. Rather, the newer research reflected the fact that teachers had absorbed the lessons of the older research, and changed the way they taught.

The final challenge for sociological research is the special ethical responsibility we have when studying vulnerable

The effects of studying people
When education research revealed that teachers more often call on boys than girls in classrooms, many teachers self-consciously attempted to moderate their behavior and be aware of the gender dynamics of classroom discussions.

The Baby Einstein Phenomenon

Institutional reflexivity does not only happen when individuals are exposed to social research. Businesses can also get involved, trying to expose people to research findings and then selling a product that is connected to those findings.

The story of Baby Einstein begins with a 1993 study by a team of psychologists, which showed that listening to Mozart improved the spatial reasoning ability of college students, and which also showed that music training improved the nonverbal cognitive ability of three-year-old children (Rauscher, Shaw, and Ki 1993; Rauscher et al. 1994). Described as the "Mozart effect," the research was reported widely in the media and a series of popular books (Campbell 1997, 2000), which overstated the findings and claimed that the research demonstrated that listening to classical music makes your smarter.

Amid all this hype about the Mozart effect, a stay-at-home mother and former teacher created a video called *Baby Einstein* in 1997. Playing classical music in the background, the video showed children playing with educational toys, interspersed with images of numbers and words. The video was a huge commercial success, marketed around the world and generating millions of dollars of revenue. Other videos followed, and at its peak the Baby Einstein brand was worth nearly $400 million, with parents throughout the world trying to give their children the purported benefit of the Mozart effect.

At the same time, some researchers mounted a campaign against Baby Einstein. Arguing that the Mozart effect did not really exist, these researchers argued that parents were being misled by false advertising. They argued that the videos had no effect on children's intelligence. If anything, the extra time spent in front of the television was bad for child development. In 2007, public health researchers published a study showing that toddlers did not get any intellectual benefit from watching educational media, and that infants who watched these videos actually scored lower on language development tests (Zimmerman, Christakis, and Meltzoff 2007). The American Academy of Pediatrics reminded parents that infants and toddlers should be discouraged from watching television. Groups filed complaints with the Federal Trade Commission, and the Baby Einstein Company responded by removing many of the claims it had been making in its advertisements. Baby Einstein videos were no longer produced after 2009, and public belief and interest in the Mozart effect faded rapidly after that.

Intelligent babies?
The Baby Einstein phenomenon argued that scientific research proved that babies who listened to classical music would be more intelligent. Why do you think so many parents found this credible?

ACTIVE LEARNING

Find out: Did you watch educational videos as a child? Did they make research claims or cite any research studies? Do your parents or others remember those claims? Can you discover if those research studies actually say what the videos claim they say?

Discuss: Why do you think so many people bought into the Mozart effect? Do you think it's bad for children to watch television? Why or why not?

populations. Sociologists want their research to help the less fortunate in our society. When we study power, violence, inequality, crime and punishment, culture, health, or immigration, we are not only trying to get the facts right. We also hope that our research will help improve the world in which we live.

Basic, Applied, and Public Sociology

Most scientific disciplines distinguish between basic and applied research, and sociology is no exception. With **basic research**, the goal is to advance our knowledge and understanding about the world, by developing theories and testing them with empirical evidence. The primary audience for basic research consists of other scientists. Basic research is usually published in academic journals and books and funded by universities, government agencies, or by large science-focused nonprofits. Most of the work that sociologists do is best characterized as basic research.

The goal of **applied research** is to use empirical social science to solve practical problems in society. People who do applied sociology have advanced training and graduate degrees in sociology, but they are less likely to work in a university than sociologists who do basic research. Most applied sociologists work for private businesses, government agencies, or nonprofit organizations, or are self-employed as research consultants. The primary audience for applied research is the client who pays for their expertise, and the primary type of writing they do is the research report that they prepare for their client. There are many good jobs in applied research for people who have a graduate degree in sociology.

Basic research Research with the goal of advancing our fundamental knowledge and understanding of the world.

Applied research Research with the goal of solving practical problems in society.

CAREERS

Careers in Applied Sociology

There are many routes to a career in applied sociology. After receiving his PhD in sociology, Roy Feldman held academic positions at Harvard and MIT, where he served on the Institutional Review Board and specialized in program evaluation and organizational analysis. Feldman was hired as director of research for the American Institute for Research in the Behavioral Sciences, where he did research evaluating education, health, and human service programs. Feldman went on to create his own applied research company, Behavior Analysis, which does consulting work for foundations, community-based organizations, charities, schools, health service organizations, and private companies.

Marc Smith is an applied sociologist who does work with social media companies. After completing his PhD in sociology, Smith was hired to create and manage the Community Technologies Group for Microsoft's research division. Smith's research examines how groups operate in cyberspace, and he has helped develop important applications and data mining engines that other researchers use to study how people interact in online forums. Smith currently works as the chief social scientist for the consulting group, Connected Action, which helps clients collect and analyze social media and social network data.

Lindsay Hixon is an applied sociologist who works for the US Census Bureau in Washington, DC. After completing her PhD in sociology, Hixon worked as the assistant director for Capitalize on Community, a service-learning program at the State University of New York at Albany

focused on HIV prevention. She was hired by the Racial Statistics Branch of the US Census, where she analyzes population data on race and ethnicity.

The US Census
The US Census Bureau is a major employer of academic sociologists.

ACTIVE LEARNING

Find out: Contact the undergraduate advisor or the chair in your sociology department, and ask what kinds of applied sociology jobs are available in the area you live. See if you can find some job postings on LinkedIn or another employment site. What kinds of research skills do those jobs require? Think about the kind of classes that will help you develop those skills.

Pepper Schwartz
A well-known public sociologist, Pepper Schwartz studies gender and social relationships. She speaks widely in the media and serves as a consultant for Perfectmatch.com, a dating website.

Public sociology A commitment to bringing sociological knowledge to a general public audience, and participating in wider public conversations and struggles for social justice.

The goal of **public sociology** is to bring sociological knowledge to a general public audience and to participate in public debates about important social issues. With public sociology, the primary audience consists of the general public, as well as journalists and media organizations who set the agenda for public debate. Public sociology is published on the websites of major news organizations, in commercial (nonacademic) books, and on radio and television talk shows. The classroom is also an important place where public sociology happens, given the tens of thousands of undergraduate students who take sociology courses each year (Burawoy 2005).

There are many well-known examples of people doing important public sociology today. William Julius Wilson has written several best-selling books about race and poverty, and he writes regular opinion columns for leading news organizations. Pepper Schwartz has appeared on *The Today Show*, *The Oprah Winfrey Show*, and *Good Morning America*, and she is the relationship expert for Perfectmatch.com. Mitchell Duneier taught an online version of his introductory sociology course to more than forty thousand students in 2012, and then very publicly stopped teaching the course because of his concerns about state funding for public universities.

In reality, the boundaries between basic research, applied research, and public sociology shift over time. Many sociologists try to do more than one of these, and over the course of a career they may cycle between all three. The public sociologists who have the most impact are often people who have established their reputation doing basic research, and hold positions at prestigious universities. Basic research can have important policy implications, and academic sociologists are frequently hired as consultants by government agencies and businesses. People who are employed full-time as applied sociologists often maintain an academic affiliation with a sociology department, and many academic departments offer graduate degrees specializing in applied sociology. Like basic researchers, people who do applied sociology can also have an impact as public sociologists.

Regardless of what type of sociology you choose to do, there are questions about your research methods that you should always try to answer. Are you asking the right questions? Are you collecting the right data? Are you using the best research technique to examine the data you have collected? Are you being systematic in your approach? What are the potential limitations of your research and what can you do to avoid them? Have you considered logical alternative explanations for your findings? Have you taken the proper steps to protect the people you are studying and to ensure their informed consent? Have you thought about how your findings might be received by the general public, and whether you are interested in participating in public debates related to your research? Thinking about these questions will help you do more effective social research. It will help you evaluate other sociological research you confront, in your studies as well as in everyday life. And it will help you sharpen your data and information literacy skills.

CASE STUDY

Doing Sociology in Society (Including Society Online)

If research is a basic process of finding out new information, then we all do research all the time. We do research when we seek someone's address or telephone number. We do research when we are looking for a job or searching for a deal on a car. We do research when choosing what classes to take at college or what major to declare. This chapter encourages you to develop an awareness of formal sociological research methods. Sociological research methods help you analyze social institutions and social processes in a way that is systematic, logical, and empirically sensitive. Research methods are central to developing a critical sociological imagination.

Let's take a social media site as a case study to think about research methods. Do you have a Facebook account? If not, you are in a minority. In the first quarter of 2019, Facebook reported 2.38 billion active users. Facebook is the most popular website worldwide. As a major generator of social data, Facebook makes public reports on this information, and it also analyzes these data and applies them to real-world puzzles.

Seen through the lens of the five paired concepts in this book, we can say first that Facebook is both a *local* and a *global* institution that connects people from all over the world. On Facebook, people's everyday social networks include friends and classmates at the same school who share details about local social events, as well as far-flung family members. In this way, Facebook enables *solidarity* to grow. People can maintain intimate relationships in a new way by following the growth of one another's children, marking major social events such as births and deaths, and sharing intimate life details online. At the same time, Facebook has become important in organizing human *conflict*. People use Facebook to organize social protests and demonstrations. At the individual level they friend and unfriend each other online, spread nasty rumors about others, or upload unflattering photos of their enemies. In all these ways, Facebook provides a platform where people connect, and it also collects social data on those connections.

Owing to its size, Facebook has significant *power* that is difficult to *resist*. Facebook has the ability to leverage, or take advantage of, the social data people generate on its social media platform. Facebook uses this information to organize its own business practice and to sell information about its users to other organizations and corporations. Facebook also conducts independent experimental research on its users, and thus is subject to widespread concerns over research ethics. Facebook

Facebook
Facebook is well known as a social networking site, but it is also a major site of social research. Social data and social research are fundamental to Facebook's business and many other connected businesses.

generates profits by selling information to advertisers who can then very precisely target consumers by analyzing their social characteristics and individual behavior online, as well as the social characteristics and behaviors of their social networks. To be sure, targeted advertising is efficient for both businesses and consumers, but critics express concerns about privacy and data security on Facebook.

A further anxiety about the dominance of Facebook centers on *inequality* of access when Facebook shares information about social characteristics with other organizations. While it might be annoying that an advertisement for a pair of shoes you were browsing on another website keeps appearing when you are on Facebook, it is far more problematic if certain opportunities are never even made available to you because you do not match a specific profile. The question is: Do more *privileged* people get directed to some resources and opportunities while less privileged users do not? Given the size and dominance of Facebook online, it is reasonable to ask if the site is using the vast amounts of social data it generates to amplify relationships of privilege and inequality in society.

A related question is: If everyone you know uses Facebook to communicate, what are the costs of not

CASE STUDY CONTINUED

having a Facebook account? Can you imagine a situation where you cannot participate in social life if you do not have a Facebook account? Science fiction and social critics have raised the specter of this kind of society, one in which all information is known and all actions are scripted based on algorithms that define human life. In this scenario, scientific data are used to completely define humans, and there is no way to break out of preexisting social *structures*. In this nightmare of total constraint, there is no role for *contingency,* chance, or choice in shaping human lives. While we are a long way away from this bleak possibility, it does illuminate why so many critics are concerned about the commitment to human subject protections, research ethics, and overall

institutional power of a social media and research platform like Facebook.

Facebook is a fun social media platform that many of us use to keep up with family and friends, and it is also a complex organization with many social functions. One important function is that Facebook is a research organization that owns a platform that generates an enormous amount of social data. Social media platforms like Facebook also provide platforms for field experiments and pose questions about the importance of research ethics and data security. As Chapter 4 will show, Facebook is a key part of the global culture where people engage common cultural values and create cultural meanings.

LEARNING GOALS REVISITED

3.1 Describe how sociology is a social science.

- Sociology uses the research methods and scientific techniques of scientific research. Sociology is committed to logical, empirical research. Sociologists test empirical hypotheses using systematically collected data.

- Sociology shares the ethical commitments of scientific research that seek to prevent and avoid harm to human subjects.

- Sociologists submit their research to peer review by the wider scientific community.

3.2 Define the major elements of the research process.

- Define a research question and explore the history of research on the topic. Consider how the question fits into previous research and what kind of study is appropriate to answer the question. Will it be a quantitative or qualitative study?

- Define the variables.

- Operationalize variables by specifying valid, reliable measures. Think about what kind of evidence or data will best answer the research question.

- State a hypothesis about the expected causal relationship between variables.

- Collect the data. Will people be interviewed or observed in the field? Is an experimental design possible? Can different methods be combined?

- Analyze the data. What did you find?

- Was the hypothesis confirmed or falsified?

- What conclusions can you draw? What does this study add to the research literature and wider understanding of the topic of the research?

3.3 Describe a range of sociological research techniques.

- Sociologists use a range of research techniques to collect and analyze social data. These include asking people questions using surveys, in-depth interviews, and focus groups and also observing people using participant-observation methods like ethnography. Some sociologists use field experiments to observe social behavior. Comparative-historical methods and case studies are used to study different times and places.

- Many sociologists analyze publicly available data ranging from government documents to big data produced by computer programs and people using social media.

3.4 Describe how social science, like sociology, is different from natural science.

- Sociologists (like other social scientists, and some natural scientists like medical researchers) study living people, including vulnerable populations. This can constrain the research questions that can be pursued, the kind of data that can be collected, and the choice of methods that can be used.
- There is a very high standard for any kind of experimental design for studying living human subjects.

3.5 Describe the difference between basic, applied, and public sociology.

- Basic research in sociology advances knowledge and understanding about the world, by developing theories and testing them with empirical evidence. Its primary audience is other scientists, it is published in academic journals and books, and it is funded by universities or government agencies.
- Applied research in sociology is used to address practical questions and to solve practical problems in society. People who do applied sociology are more likely to work in private businesses, government agencies, or non-profit organizations, or to be self-employed as research consultants, than to work in a university setting. The primary audience for applied research is the client who pays for their expertise.
- The goal of public sociology is to bring sociological knowledge to a general public audience and to participate in public debates about important social issues. With public sociology, the primary audience consists of the general public, as well as journalists and media organizations who set the agenda for public debate. Public sociology is published in the mass media but also includes the sociology classroom.

- The boundaries between basic, applied and public sociology shift constantly.

Key Terms

Review Questions

1. What is scientific about sociology? How is social science different than natural science?

2. How is scientific research systematic, logical, and empirical?

3. How are scientific statements different from beliefs or opinions?

4. What is the difference between correlation and causation?

5. Are random samples better than other kinds of samples? Why?

6. What is the difference between a survey question and an open-ended question, and when would you use each?

Explore

RECOMMENDED READINGS

Luker, Kristin. 2008. *Salsa Dancing into the Social Sciences: Research in an Age of Info-Glut*. Cambridge, MA: Harvard University Press.

Spradley, James. 1979. *The Ethnographic Interview.* New York: Harcourt Brace Jovanovich.

Weber, Max. "Science as a Vocation." In *From Max Weber: Essays in Sociology*. New York: Oxford University Press.

ACTIVITIES

- *Use your sociological imagination*: If you were interested in the relationship between education and earnings and wanted to study it, in what different ways could you operationalize the variables "education" and "earnings"?

- *Media+Data literacies*: Go to the website for the United States Census. Using the Factfinder tool, describe the area where you live. What is a census tract?

- *Discuss*: Should there have been additional penalties for Facebook or OKCupid when it was found they manipulated their customers to research emotional behavior? Why or why not? What sort of sanction might be effective?

For additional resources, including Media+Data Literacy exercises, In the News exercises, and quizzes, please go to **oup.com/he/ Jacobs-Townsley1e**

PART II STRUCTURE AND CONTROL

Culture

It is not unusual for parents to dislike the cultural activity of teenagers. From the Sex Pistols in the 1970s, NWA in the 1980s, Marilyn Manson in the 1990s and early-2000s, down to the present day, teenagers have turned to music as a way of bonding with their friends and expressing their difference from their parents.

Music is not the only area where parents and their children disagree about hobbies or lifestyles. In the media, video games are frequently criticized as a dangerous waste of time, even though they generate more than $10 billion in revenue every year (McKernan 2013). Skateboarding is banned in public spaces throughout the country. This generational suspicion of teenage hobbies and lifestyles has long been a part of American life. For example, when comic books became popular among American youth in the 1950s, the United States government actually set up a special Senate subcommittee to study how dangerous they were (Lopes 2009).

The conflict over culture also works in the other direction. Teenagers and young adults do not want to share their lifestyles and hobbies with their parents. Consider Facebook, which was launched in 2004 as a social network for college students. Initially limited to Harvard undergraduates, Facebook quickly expanded and within two years had become absolutely central to the social life of high school and college students, and continued to grow from there. As of March 2019, Facebook reported 2.38 billion active users.

Yet many of the students who drove the early success of social media believe that their parents are ruining Facebook. A 2013 Pew Research Center study found that teenagers were tired of Facebook, and they were more interested in new social media sites that their parents had not yet discovered. As one college student commented, "Yeah, that's why we go on Twitter and Instagram [instead of Facebook]. My Mom doesn't have that" (Soper 2013; Madden et al. 2013).

Miley Cyrus

LEARNING GOALS

4.1   Define culture and identify the difference between material and ideal culture.

4.2   Understand that meanings are made in cultural context.

4.3   Describe how culture defines the moral quality of people, institutions, objects, and events.

4.4   Identify the connection between culture and power: identify ideologies, stereotypes, cultural hierarchies, and cultural resistance.

4.5   Distinguish different types of culture.

Why do adults care so much about their children's hobbies? Why do high school and college students cringe when their parents start listening to the same music or using the same social media that they do? Why do teenagers and their parents both try to cultivate a lifestyle that expresses their true identity? Last, what can these lifestyle choices and conflicts tell us about the society in which we live?

In this chapter we consider the important role that culture plays in social life. We begin by discussing how sociologists define culture and how they study it. We discuss how people use culture in everyday life, then consider the relationship between culture and power. Last, we consider the many different types of culture that circulate today.

How Do Sociologists Study Culture?

Most sociologists agree that culture is a basic dimension of social life, and important to include in their sociological research. But what is culture? Is it the beliefs and values inside our heads? Our everyday habits and customs? What we see in the museum? What we post on Instagram? Is there anything that is *not* culture? Raymond Williams (1921–1988) defined culture as "a whole way of life," meaning that the web of culture was so wide that it included virtually everything in society (Williams 1983). Because culture is everywhere, figuring out how to study it can be a real challenge.

What Is Culture?

Culture The entire set of beliefs, knowledge, practices, and material objects that are meaningful to a group of people and shared from generation to generation.

We can define **culture** as the entire set of beliefs, knowledge, practices, and material objects that are meaningful to a group of people and shared from generation to generation. While "culture" can refer to objects like a book, a house, or a work of music, it can also refer to cultural practices, such as reading, designing a house, or singing the national anthem at a football game. When we study culture, we are studying how people make their lives meaningful, how they share those meanings, and how they use those shared meanings to do things collectively with other people.

Culture is something we have to learn as members of society. While many scientists believe that we have an innate biological ability to learn language and culture (Chomsky 2006), we still have to learn the specific culture into which we are born. As we live our lives we gradually learn the shared meanings that connect us to our family, friends, and larger society. This ongoing process of learning the social meanings of our culture is known as **socialization** (Chapter 5).

Socialization The ongoing process of learning the social meanings of a culture.

The shared meanings of culture can change depending on which people are sharing them and how they are using them. Many students believed that Facebook was an indispensable part of their social lives, until their parents started using it. Music fans sometimes abandon bands if they become too popular, because they equate popularity with "selling out." Even the meanings of words and phrases can change, if groups start using them for different purposes.

HOW DOES CULTURE DEVELOP? Cultural meanings develop in relationships. Language provides the basic model for how this works, and it has provided the framework for how many sociologists think about culture. From linguistics, we know that words get their meaning through their relationship to other words (Saussure 1998). One of the most basic relationships is similarity and difference. We know the meaning of something because it is similar to or different from something else. Building on these basic relationships, the meaning of words can derive from the larger sequence of words and the social context in which they are used. If somebody tells you to "delete your cookies," for example, the sequence and the social context tell you that they are talking about your computer rather than your snack. The **symbolic meaning** of a word can be shaped by its relationship with other cultural images, emotions, meanings, and associations. For example, while the word "red" identifies a particular color worldwide, its symbolic meaning changes depending on the cultural context. In Japan, red symbolizes happiness, whereas in South Africa it is the color associated with mourning.

> **Symbolic meaning** The broader cultural content of a cultural object, idea or, event, which is based on the other images, emotions, meanings, and associations that come from the larger culture.

There are symbolic meanings for all types of culture, and not just for language. Sociological research on fashion has shown how everything we wear has additional layers of symbolic meaning (Aspers and Godart 2013). Silk and cashmere are associated with luxury, while polyester and boxy tailoring are associated with convenience, frugality, and lower quality. A Prada handbag conjures different meanings than a generic purse from Walmart, despite the fact that the two bags may look very similar. Like all culture, fashion develops in relationships of similarity and difference. To be fashionable one needs to wear clothes that are similar enough to other clothes recognized as stylish, but different enough to identify the wearer as a clever and original person (Aspers 2010).

PATTERN AND VARIATION. Over time, cultural patterns develop by placing beliefs, practices, and cultural objects into groups of similar things and groups of different things. These groupings develop into **classification systems**, which create increasingly complex identifications of similarity and difference. As people become more fully immersed in a given culture, they become more sophisticated in the kinds of classifications they can identify. Most of us can recognize the difference between basic kinds of music—classical versus pop, rock versus hip-hop, and so on. But for true experts, their "insider status" is based on their ability to identify and classify distinctions that other people cannot hear (Bennett 2009). The distinctions are already there, in the system of cultural classification, but only the true insiders can see them and make them visible for the rest of us.

> **Classification systems** Elaborate and nuanced identifications of similarity and difference based on cultural patterns that develop over time when people place beliefs, practices, and cultural objects into groups of similar things and groups of different things.

Priscilla Parkhurst Ferguson shows how cultural patterns of similarity and difference develop over time in her book *Word of Mouth: What We Talk about When We Talk about Food* (2014). She argues that how we talk about food is just as meaningful as what we choose to eat or how we choose to eat it. For example, in the 1960s, most middle- and upper-class Americans were taught that French cooking techniques and French ingredients provided the most authentic

Omakase sushi
Omakase sushi is an elaborate and expensive presentation of this Japanese delicacy. For most diners, the food they eat at a fancy restaurant has different meanings from the food they eat at home.

expressions of good food. Today, though, the reverence for classical French food has been replaced by a new language, which focuses on creativity, the blending of different food cultures, and the use of locally sourced ingredients. This new language about food, Ferguson argues, tells us a lot about who we are and how our cultural identities are changing. To be sure, there is still a value to eating traditionally American food on the Fourth of July or at Thanksgiving, but there are now also critical, global, and more environmentally and health-conscious standards of consumption.

Ideal Culture and Material Culture

While cultural patterns allow groups to share meanings and to do things with other people, they do not completely determine shared meanings. Culture itself is always changing, because individuals and groups are constantly trying to distinguish themselves by using culture in new ways. The ways that shared meanings change over time can provide important evidence about how people in a society understand themselves and the world around them.

One way to think about the many different types of culture is to distinguish between ideal culture and material culture. **Ideal culture** refers to all the social meanings that exist in nonmaterial form. This includes language, values, beliefs, and norms. **Material culture** refers to all the cultural objects that are produced by a social group or a society. Material culture includes objects that we find around us, such as furniture, clothes, toys, and cars. Most shared meanings include elements of both material and ideal culture.

Ideal culture All the social meanings that exist in non-material form, such as beliefs, values, expectations, and language.

Material culture All the cultural objects that are produced by a social group or a society.

IDEAL CULTURE: LANGUAGE, VALUES, BELIEFS, AND NORMS. Ideal culture is based on language, which is the way that people in a society communicate with one another. Linguistics, the study of language, documents how language is organized, the rules for its use, expectations about what words mean, and how different words are related to one another. In fact, linguists have argued that reality is literally unthinkable outside the categories and rules of language.

Language is one of the most powerful ways for a society to store culture and to transmit shared meanings from one generation to the next. Most societies take pride in their language or languages, and they take significant steps to preserve its heritage and purity. However, languages can be suppressed through colonization or other forms of ethnic violence. For example, most indigenous languages in North America are endangered or extinct (Gordon 2005). The point is that language is important for maintaining group identities.

Mandarin Chinese
Mandarin Chinese is spoken by more than one billion people around the world.

METHODS AND INTERPRETATION

Measuring Culture Using Big Data

Since the late 20th century, cultural material has been produced and stored in digital formats, resulting in a world shaped by big data. This big data environment presents opportunities for sociologists, who are developing techniques for collecting and measuring culture using automated text analysis.

One such technique for measuring culture is topic modeling. Topic models use mathematical algorithms to code a large number of texts into a group of categories or "topics." Topics are the underlying structural patterns that describe the data. Before topic modeling, most researchers who wanted to analyze a large body of texts would begin with a predefined set of variable values, and then they would have several researchers assign a value to every text they were studying. This method is common to most quantitative analysis, where researchers code the values of variables that describe the data. In addition to being time consuming and expensive, however, there are two additional problems with this approach when applied to large bodies of text data: it is very hard to decide in advance what the underlying values of the variables are; and it is very difficult to establish high levels of agreement between multiple coders. With topic modeling, however, the researcher begins by telling the computer how many topics to find. From there, the computer program identifies the specified number of topics, tells the researcher the probabilities of specific words being used for each topic, and alerts the researcher to how the different topics are distributed across the different texts in the sample (Mohr et al. 2013).

One useful feature of topic modeling is that the computer algorithm it is based on is one of the central principles about culture, which is that the meaning of a word depends on its relationship to other words. Simply put, the computer takes a very large population of texts, and looks for clusters of words that appear together. The idea of clustering relies on a basic idea about relationships of social distance. Using a mathematical algorithm to define the details, clustering asks: Do specific words appear close together or far apart? Are the words in relationships of similarity or relationships of difference?

In one study, researchers collected 8,000 newspaper articles about government funding for the arts in the United States, and used a computer algorithm to identify the 12 most prevalent topics and the 100 words most commonly associated with each topic (DiMaggio, Nag, and Blei 2013). They also compared how these topics were distributed in different newspapers, finding that conservative papers were more likely to use conflict-related topics. In a Dutch study of four million news articles published between 1950 and 2014 in *De Telegraaf*, waves of intense hype in the news were found to share a consistent pattern. They consisted of a "small lead, a sharp and narrow peak, and a slow decline." Waves of intense news hype became more political rather than less political over time, and news waves were found to be more prevalent in the 1950s, declining through the 1960s and 1970s, only to rise again in the decades that followed (Van Atteveldt et al. 2018). These kinds of studies demonstrate how topic modeling can illuminate very large data sets and is also faster and more efficient, cost effective, and objective than traditional techniques of content analysis (Jacobi, Atteveldt, and Welbers 2015). Other scholars are exploring how topic modeling and other forms of automated text analysis can be effectively combined with qualitative methods to more accurately trace how meanings change over time (Bail 2014).

ACTIVE LEARNING

Find out: List three kinds of businesses or other workplaces that rely on the automated analysis of massive amounts of social data to do their work. Identify a description for an entry-level position in each kind of institution.

Language shapes how we express ourselves, and how we make ourselves understood to others. When new words enter the language, they signal important social changes and important new meanings that bind people together. When the word "bureaucracy" (from the French word *bureau*, which means both "desk" and "office") first entered the English language in the late 18th century, its arrival reflected the growing importance to society of officials and administrators. Today, words such as "clickbait," "live-tweet," and "smartwatch" reflect the growing influence of social media in everyday life.

Some words in a language help define a society's **values**, which identify the basic standards that people use to define what is important, desirable, right,

Values General social ideas about what is right and wrong, good and bad, desirable and undesirable, important or unimportant.

and morally good. Values point to a society's ideals. They help us think about what it means to live a good life.

Sociologists have long compared the values of different countries. One of the earliest sociological studies, Alexis de Tocqueville's (1805–1859) *Democracy in America* ([1835, 1840] 2003), compared French and American values in the 19th century. Tocqueville found that the Americans he studied had a distinct set of values, which emphasized individualism, hard work, economic success, and religious and political freedom.

Since 1981, the World Values Survey Association, an international network of social science researchers, has surveyed values around the globe, examining the extent to which those values are changing. Using these survey data, social scientists have argued that there are two important dimensions that explain most of the value differences in the world: the difference between traditional and secular-rational values, and the difference between survival values and self-expression values (Inglehart and Welzel 2005). In the first dimension, **traditional values** emphasize religion, family, national pride, and obedience to authority, while **secular-rational values** place less importance on family and religion and more importance on individualism, science, and critique. In the second dimension, **survival values** emphasize economic and physical security, while **self-expression values** place more importance on tolerance, political participation, personal happiness, and environmental protection. The United States is characterized by self-expression values and traditional values, while European countries such as Denmark and Sweden combine self-expression values and secular-rational values. China combines secular-rational values and survival values, whereas Pakistan and Morocco combine traditional values and survival values.

Ideal culture also includes **beliefs**, which are all the things we think are true, even in the absence of evidence or proof. We cannot "prove" that God exists, or that we love our children, or that there is such a thing as a "just war," and yet people hold strong beliefs about these and other fundamental social issues. As Émile Durkheim pointed out, beliefs are primarily social, and come from the groups to which we belong.

Social differences between groups and societies are often expressed as differences in belief. Within societies, significant social conflicts often develop between groups that maintain different beliefs about important social issues. In recent years, major social conflicts have divided Americans based on their beliefs about abortion, gay marriage, sex education, globalization and immigration policy. Some sociologists have argued that there is a profound **culture war** in America, based on these fundamental differences in belief (e.g., Hunter 1991; Ellison and Musick 1993). Other sociologists have argued that a culture war requires significant conflicts over basic values. While there may be important differences in belief, they argue, survey research shows strong agreement among Americans about basic values such as individualism, equality, tolerance, and hard work (Hunter and Wolfe 2006; Demerath and Yang 1997).

Between societies, conflicts over beliefs can create deep divisions. While global conflicts are often influenced by differences in wealth and power, they are also based on basic differences in belief. In such conflicts, there is no evidence or data that can resolve the dispute. The shared beliefs unite each side together in solidarity, just as they heighten the conflict with those who have different beliefs.

Ideal culture is also expressed in **norms**, which are the common set of expectations about how people should behave in any specific situation. Norms,

---

Traditional values Widely held social beliefs that emphasize the importance of traditional religion, family, national pride, and obedience to authority.

Secular-rational values Widely held social beliefs that emphasize the importance of individualism, science, and critique.

Survival values Widely held social beliefs that emphasize the importance of economic and physical security.

Self-expression values Widely held social beliefs that emphasize the importance of tolerance, political participation, personal happiness, and environmental protection.

Beliefs All the things we think are true, even in the absence of evidence or proof.

Culture war A profound, society-threatening conflict over values.

Norms Shared expectations, specific to time and place, about how people should act in any particular situation.

which are necessary for people to coordinate their activities with one another, are learned through the process of socialization and enforced through social interaction. While norms point to overarching social values, they are not universal rules of behavior. Norms are particular to time and place, and connected to specific societies and specific cultures. What we consider to be polite, considerate, or "normal" behavior comes from wider cultural ideas as they are lived in particular settings.

Sociologists distinguish many different kinds of norms. There are social distance norms that specify how close or distant someone can be with another. These vary widely depending on the status and identity of the individuals involved. Other norms govern behaviors of people of different ages or different sexes. One important distinction is between folkways and mores. **Folkways** are common sense and fairly unserious expectations of behavior. Covering your mouth when you yawn, for example, might be considered a folkway. **Mores** are more serious expectations about behavior that reflect central values. For example, in US culture, while adultery is not against the law, it is considered a serious breach of social norms.

All norms are socially enforced through **sanctions**, which reward people when they act in the expected way, and punish them when they do not. Many of these punishments are formal sanctions, which are written down in specific rules about what the expected behavior is, as well as the consequences for violating the rules. But a lot of norms are enforced by informal sanctions, where other people give us feedback about our behavior. Most norms about politeness and rudeness are enforced by informal sanctions (Smith, Phillips, and King 2010). For example, if you cut in front of somebody in line, they may confront you or shake their head in disapproval. Over time, as people experience these formal and informal sanctions, they come to internalize our culture. We begin to police ourselves, and we feel guilty or wrong when we violate social norms.

MATERIAL CULTURE. Culture also shapes the meanings we attach to the objects we interact with in our social lives. Even ordinary objects that may not necessarily capture our interest contain social meaning. Consider the toaster. As Harvey Molotch (2005) shows in his book *Where Stuff Comes From*, the toaster is associated with breakfast, at least in the United States and other English-speaking countries. There are almost no toasters in Italy, for example, because breakfast there consists of other kinds of foods such as pastries or fruit. In the United States, the meaning of the toaster is connected to the ideas of progress and convenience, because toasters arrived in the early 20th century, just as the bread slicer was invented and home kitchens were wired for electricity.

It can be difficult to separate material culture from ideal culture, because cultural objects always have symbolic meanings. We have already discussed how this works for a variety of cultural objects, such as music, social media, clothes, kitchen appliances, and food. But it is also true for paintings, buildings, furniture, pictures, flags, religious objects, and every other object we confront in our lives. These objects help us understand ourselves and the world around us (Woodward 2012: 671).

As we discuss later in the chapter, the production, distribution, and consumption of cultural objects is one of the biggest parts of the global economy. Enormous industries are devoted to making objects that we want to buy, while others are devoted to advertising these objects to us and suggesting what they should mean in our lives.

Folkways Common sense and fairly unserious norms.

Mores Norms that define serious expectations about behavior that invoke central values.

Sanctions Actions that punish people when they do not act in a way that accords with norms.

The meanings associated with toasters
The toaster is one of the most common kitchen appliances found in the home. It is generally associated with breakfast.

Culture and Power

Because culture is such an important part of social life, it is connected to all of the paired concepts we introduced at the beginning of this book. Shared meanings are possible because they are organized into common patterns and relationships, but these meanings are always changing due to the different ways that people combine cultural objects and symbolic meanings. Cultural objects circulate globally, but their actual meanings often vary depending on the local context in which they are being used. Culture brings people together, but it is also a source of inequality as well as privilege. Shared values are a source of solidarity, but disagreement over values produces conflict. While we will explore each of these paired concepts later in the chapter, let's first examine the relationship between culture, power, and resistance.

Cultural Power

On May 25, 2017, a short video at a NATO Summit in Brussels showed President Trump apparently shoving the prime minister of Montenegro out of the way so he could get to the front and center of a group photograph. Like other major world leaders, Trump knew that the power of his position allowed him to choreograph the event. The *Washington Post* reported that Sean Spicer, then the White House press secretary, told reporters "that spots for the 'family photo' for which the leaders were preparing were predetermined, as is usually the case— implying that Trump was not trying to get a better position … but rather that he was heading for the position reserved for him." (Schmidt 2017). Spicer was correct that posed photos displaying hierarchies of power are standard, organized features of the exercise of legitimate authority. They mark the occasion, document who was there, and signal the status of each participant.

World leaders who can stage these kinds of public events and command media attention have a special kind of cultural power, because they control the means of symbolic production (Alexander 2006). Their access to resources (such as formal political and military power) means they can stage events for the sole purpose of getting media publicity. Importantly, they use these events to put forward interpretations of the world that they hope will become shared meanings in the larger society (Boorstin 1961; Dayan and Katz 1992). In this case, the event and the photo were intended to underline the dominance of the United States in NATO. In an increasingly sophisticated social media environment, however, there is no guarantee that people will accept the meanings that are intended.

Paralleling the official photograph and narrative of the NATO event was an alternative negative narrative of what happened. This began with critical Twitter commentary and was then picked up by journalists and other commentators on TV and radio (CNN 2017). While the prime minister of Montenegro, Dusko Markovic, stated, "This was an inoffensive situation, I do not see it in any other way,"

Cultural Power
Donald Trump shoving the prime minister of Montenegro out of the way during a group photograph, May 25, 2017.

the video of Trump "brushing by" or "shoving" Markovic went viral on Twitter with an interpretation that it was offensive (CNN 2017). The video was replayed endlessly and drew negative press around the world. Comedians in the United States and many other countries criticized Trump's actions and especially his rude manner, riffing on the "America First" message he delivered at NATO (Schmidt 2017). The point is that while it is true that privileged, powerful people have more resources to advance their agendas than others do, in a world of social media they are not always able to fully control the message.

IDEOLOGY. Ideology is any system of shared meaning that is used to justify existing relationships of power and privilege. In other words, ideology is culture in the service of power (Thompson 1991). The concept of ideology was first introduced in sociology by Karl Marx (Chapter 2), who argued that the dominant class used culture to get people to believe things about the world that were against their true interests. Marx argued that ideology distorted people's beliefs, and prevented them from recognizing what they needed to do to improve their lives. Sociologists influenced by Marx's theory of ideology were particularly critical of religious beliefs and ideas about national patriotism, because these ideas made it harder for people to see how they were being exploited in their everyday lives (Adorno et al. 1950).

> **Ideology** A system of shared meaning that is used to justify existing relationships of power and privilege.

Ideology operates in two different ways. First, it works through misdirection. By focusing attention on issues that will not have any impact on people's material well-being, ideology creates cultural conflicts between groups that have the same economic interests and who should be allies with one another. In the late 19th and early 20th centuries, for example, business owners used anti-immigrant and racial ideologies to encourage conflicts between white, immigrant, and African American workers, as a strategy for weakening labor unions (Lieberson 1981). In recent years, many social scientists have argued, political parties in the United States have used controversial issues such as abortion, illegal immigration, and gay marriage to distract voters' attention and to make it harder for them to form alliances based on shared economic interest (Gitlin 1995; Frank 2004). Analysts observing the 2016 US presidential election, for example, observed that many poor and working-class voters opted for Donald Trump (a wealthy, white New York businessman) because he represented an alternative to a cosmopolitan vision for a diverse, secular, more globally integrated American society, albeit promoted by a wealthy, white, female career politician (Hillary Clinton).

Sociologist Arlie Hochschild (2018) conducted ethnographic interviews with people who eventually voted for Donald Trump in 2016. Hochschild argues that these voters felt the loss of the American Dream. They wanted to return to an earlier version of America in which good jobs, home ownership, global power, Christian heterosexual marriage and family, and white dominance (or at least an end to what they saw was political correctness around race and gender) prevailed. This is why they chose a candidate who apparently empathized with their loss (Hochschild 2018).

The American Dream
Buying a home is associated with living the "American Dream." In recent years, severe economic downturns have challenged that idea.

This is the second way ideology works, by making certain beliefs seem like "common sense" so they cannot be challenged easily. For example, ideologies about sex and gender have encouraged people to believe that fathers are supposed to be the breadwinners in the family and mothers are supposed to take care of the children (Connell 1995). Other ideologies, drawn from religion, have encouraged people to assume that same-sex marriages are unnatural. Still other ideologies establish expectations about success and failure. The ideology of the American Dream, for example, encourages people to believe that their successes and failures are entirely of their own making, and to see social policies in terms of individual stories of fairness and luck. This makes it harder for people to perceive that their life chances are shaped by structural forces beyond their control, such as population movements due to war or climate change, or economic restructuring resulting from automation, international competition, or the behavior of financial markets (Messner and Rosenfeld 2007). If people accept these ideologies, it changes the way they think about themselves and can limit the decisions they make. In other words, ideologies make it harder for people to develop their sociological imagination.

STEREOTYPES. Stereotypes are a form of ideology that encourages people to believe in the natural superiority or inferiority of different groups of people. Throughout history, stereotypes have been used to reinforce and justify systems of inequality, particularly those that discriminate against women and minority groups. In the United States, for example, women were not allowed to vote until 1920, because of stereotypes claiming they were too delicate and emotional to participate in politics. The African slave trade was frequently justified by racial stereotypes suggesting that people of African descent were uncivilized and lacked the natural intelligence to take care of themselves. Many of these stereotypes persist today as informal systems of prejudice, long after the legal systems of discrimination have been eliminated. (We discuss racial and gender stereotypes in more detail in Chapters 8 and 9.)

As systems of cultural power, stereotypes get distributed by people who have an interest in using them to reinforce their own advantages over other groups in society. Those who successfully propagate stereotypes are able to do so because they have access to the **means of symbolic production**, the organized social resources for creating, producing, and distributing communications. These resources include education, literacy, museums, and libraries as well as the media. When stereotypes become instruments of cultural power, they result in formal laws and informal sanctions used to single out specific groups for unfair treatment. Criticizing stereotypes and challenging prejudiced beliefs is one way we can use culture creatively to resist cultural power when we think it is illegitimate or wrong.

CULTURAL POWER, KNOWLEDGE, AND SELF-CONTROL. While stereotypes are used to discriminate against specific groups, there is another kind of cultural power based on knowledge and self-discipline. This kind of cultural power was first analyzed by the French philosopher Michel Foucault (1926–1984), who produced pioneering historical research about madness, punishment, and sexuality. For Foucault, power operates by producing and organizing systems of knowledge about people's activities. These knowledge systems, or **discourses**, define what we count as normal, and what kinds of meanings we attach to people who are "not normal."

Stereotypes A form of ideology that encourages people to believe in the natural superiority or inferiority of different groups of people.

Means of symbolic production The organized social resources for creating, producing, and distributing communications.

Discourses Organized systems of knowledge and power that define what meanings we count as normal, and what kinds of meanings we attach to people who are "not normal."

Structure and Contingency

The Protocols of the Elders of Zion

The Protocols of the Elders of Zion is the most infamous example of anti-Semitism published during the 20th century. First circulated in Russia in the late 19th and early 20th centuries, the *Protocols* were a central part of a 1905 propaganda campaign in which more than 2,500 Russian Jews were targeted and killed. The *Protocols* later became an important part of Nazi propaganda in Germany, and were used as historical evidence to justify their persecution of the Jews. In the United States, the wealthy industrialist Henry Ford paid for the printing of 500,000 copies of the book in the 1920s.

While *The Protocols of the Elders of Zion* was treated as historical evidence and used to justify anti-Jewish stereotypes, it was actually a fabricated document, in which the writer claimed to have witnessed a secret meeting in which Jewish leaders made plans for world domination. Despite the fact that the meeting had never happened, the book drew on existing stereotypes about Jews and a supposed international Jewish plot to control the world.

The Protocols of the Elders of Zion was not only a hoax, it was also a forgery. Key parts of the *Protocols* plagiarized the work of the French writer Maurice Joly, who had written a fictional political satire in 1864, called "Dialogues in Hell between Machiavelli and Montesquieu." Joly's book was originally plagiarized by a German anti-Semitic writer named Herman Goedsche, who changed Joly's plot into a story about a mythical Jewish conspiracy. A single chapter from Goedsche's novel was rewritten as an eyewitness account of a supposedly real meeting that had taken place, renamed *The Protocols of the Elders of Zion*, and printed in Russia in 1897. The pamphlet was translated from French into Russian in 1903 and then circulated more widely in 1905, when Russian officials decided to release it as part of their anti-Jewish propaganda campaign. At this point, the pamphlet took on a new life, and it spread throughout the world.

The truth about the *Protocols* was first noticed by an Irish journalist named Philip Graves, who wrote a series of newspaper articles in 1921 documenting the plagiarism and the forgery. In the same year, the American journalist Herman Bernstein published a book documenting the hoax. Despite this, in Germany the *Protocols* continued to be taught in schools as a work of history well into the 1930s, and the pamphlet continues to fuel conspiracy theories about international Jewish conspiracies to this day. The Southern Poverty Law Center (2004) reports that the *Protocols* were available at Walmart as recently as 2004. In most of the world, however, the *Protocols* are now recognized for what they were: a work of anti-Semitic propaganda, which stole the structure of a fictional story and modified it for sinister purposes.

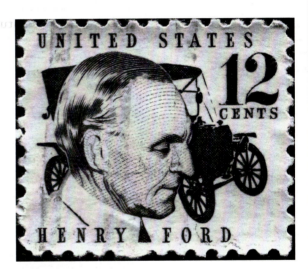

Henry Ford
American icon and car manufacturer Henry Ford helped to finance the distribution of anti-Semitic literature in the United States.

ACTIVE LEARNING

Discuss: How would you know if something that was presented to you as fact taught to you might be propaganda? What kinds of questions could you ask to discover if a historical or other factual claim is true or false?

Discourses produce cultural power by defining who needs to be watched, how they are to be watched, and how they are to be disciplined. Discourse also produces cultural power by encouraging us to watch over ourselves, to be always on the lookout for signs that there is something wrong with us, and to turn to specific sources of knowledge and guidance to cure ourselves of any problems or weaknesses we identify within ourselves.

Surveillance
Discourses of surveillance encourage people to watch over others, and to expect that they are being watched too.

Foucault argued that the discourses of surveillance and rehabilitation have made self-control more important than ever. In the prisons, schools, and mental hospitals that he studied, Foucault saw that surveillance was replacing violence as the main form of power. Because people knew that they were always being watched, they learned to control their own behaviors in order to stay out of trouble. Today, systems of surveillance have spread throughout society, and people have learned to accept them as a normal part of life. We know there are cameras watching us in stores and in public streets, and we know that everything we do on the internet can be traced and recorded (Ericson and Haggerty 2006). Public safety campaigns such as the "If You See Something, Say Something" anti-terrorism campaign spearheaded by the New York Metropolitan Transportation Authority and later adopted nationwide by the Department of Homeland Security, reminds us that the people around us are also watching (Doyle, Lippert, and Lyon 2012). We accept this as part of the cost of living in the modern world, and we learn to carefully monitor our own behavior so as not to arouse suspicion. In the process of accepting these shared meanings about the world, we exercise power over ourselves on behalf of these larger cultural systems.

The second cultural change Foucault identified was the discourse of rehabilitation, or the influence of therapy and self-help as forms of self-discipline. His research on madness shows how prisoners became objects of treatment: they were not just dangerous people who needed to be locked up, they were people with pathologies who could be treated and rehabilitated (Foucault 1988). Tracing the history by which madness was gradually redefined as a mental illness that could be treated by pharmaceuticals, psychology, and other therapies, Foucault shows how this language of rehabilitation and therapy gradually spread throughout society. Today, people read self-help books, use self-help apps, and see therapists to try to identify pathological and self-destructive tendencies that are holding them back and causing unhappiness in their lives (Giddens 1991). They search for drugs and other kinds of cures that can help treat these destructive tendencies (Conrad 2007). They make themselves into objects of study, and they turn themselves into projects of rehabilitation and redemption.

CULTURAL HIERARCHIES AND CULTURAL POWER. Cultural power is also exercised in **cultural hierarchies** that enforce particular ideas about what counts as "good" or worthwhile culture. The examples we introduced at the beginning of the chapter demonstrate the exercise of power in one kind of cultural hierarchy. When adults criticize popular music, video games, comic books, or skateboarding, they are making judgments about the kinds of interests and tastes that should be encouraged and rewarded. When they try to enforce cultural hierarchies, they are attempting to impose a set of shared meanings about how people should be spending their time and what their tastes should be. This includes cultural hierarchies that assert definitions of the right kind of clothes, language, food, religion, education, body type, car, phone, dance moves, movies, houses, families, leisure activities, and many more.

Cultural hierarchies Socially organized inequality based on ideas about what counts as "good" or worthwhile culture.

Sociological researchers examine how people use conflicts over culture to try to enforce their own cultural tastes and preferences on an entire society. Politicians frequently attack the arts and culture during elections, as a way of appealing to voters and mobilizing constituencies who might not otherwise vote for them (Kidd 2010). Conflicts over culture tend to increase when a large number of immigrants move into a community, threatening the lifestyle and tastes of the residents who already live there (Gusfield 1962; Tepper 2011). Wealthier and more privileged people regularly use their own tastes and cultural preferences as a way of excluding people with different social backgrounds, who are made to feel inferior because their cultural preferences get criticized for being tasteless and uncivilized (Bourdieu 1984). We explore this relationship between cultural preferences and social class in more detail in Chapter 7.

Resisting Cultural Power

As we have emphasized throughout this book, attempts to exercise power always meet resistance. Where cultural power is concerned, we need to recognize that people are never completely brainwashed by the shared meanings of culture. As the sociologist Harold Garfinkel (1967) pointed out, social actors are not "cultural dopes."

Cultural tastes
Our cultural tastes and preferences give signals about the kinds of people we think we are, and the types of culture we think are valuable.

They do not blindly follow rules, and they do not mindlessly accept the shared meanings of culture. People often recognize when cultural power is being used against them. They develop strategies for resisting that power, and they have the ability to take control of the cultural meanings they use in their social lives.

ACTIVE AUDIENCES. As we know from earlier discussions of structure and contingency, the fact that our social life is patterned and organized into structures does not mean that those structures completely control us. Culture may provide shared meanings that we use to interpret the world and to do things with other people, but this does not mean that we accept those shared meanings uncritically or without modification. People are active, skillful interpreters of the world. They have the ability to recognize and resist cultural power.

The British sociologist Stuart Hall (1932–2014) talked about cultural power and resistance in terms of two stages of meaning, which he referred to as encoding and decoding. During **encoding**, people with power try to create forms of material and ideal culture that encourage us to adopt specific shared meanings. In the example of the NATO summit photo shoot discussed earlier, President Trump sought to encode the dominant, central position of the United States and its president into the photo. But the success of these encoded meanings depends on the process of **decoding**, which refers to how the cultural messages are interpreted by specific people.

People do not always accept the encoded meaning of a cultural message. If they distrust or dislike the person delivering the message, they are more likely to reject the intended meaning. In this case, the NATO photo, which might have faded into obscurity in a short time, is now forever associated with the social criticism around Trump's actions at the photo shoot, and arguably Trump's behavior and manner in global political affairs more generally. This is a negative characterization of Donald Trump as an individual, and insofar as he is seen as the legitimate representative of the American people, it is a negative characterization of American culture as a whole. Ideologies are only successful when people decode the messages similar to the way they were encoded. In these kinds of situations, where people recognize and reject encoded meanings, it is harder to exercise cultural power.

Encoding The process through which people with power try to create forms of material and ideal culture that encourage cultural consumers to adopt specific shared meanings.

Decoding The process in which cultural messages are interpreted by specific people.

Culture Jamming
Culture jamming is a strategy of criticizing corporate advertising, to try to get people to think more critically about the cultural products that surround them. This antismoking ad campaign, sponsored by the California Department of Health Services, is an especially vivid example of culture jamming.

CULTURAL CRITICS. Cultural and institutional resources are available to help people challenge and resist cultural power. As we discuss in Chapter 13, social movements work to challenge and criticize official cultural messages, and suggest alternative ways to think about social issues. The sociological imagination can teach us to recognize unstated assumptions, to evaluate arguments based on logic and evidence, and to move through the world with both a healthy skepticism and a creative attitude about how things could be different from the way they are. Critical thinking about culture can also be part of the discussion in institutions like churches, social clubs, reading groups, and community organizations.

The idea of democracy is based on the idea of good critical argument, and expert cultural critics have become important figures in modern society (Alexander 2006). In music, art, architecture, fashion, politics, and every other type of culture, critical cultural experts help us evaluate cultural objects and cultural performances. They explain to the audience what the artist or the performer is trying to accomplish, and they explain the larger context we need to properly evaluate the object. They help us decode the intended meaning of the encoded message, and they show us the techniques or tricks that are used to try to get us to accept that encoded message.

Other critics, such as opinion columnists, call attention to the ways media shape the public conversation. Some media critics engage in culture jamming, where they deliberately invert or undermine the intended messages of mainstream media. All these critics help us develop our ability to decode the meanings of our culture. They encourage us to be skeptical of people who have cultural power, and they help us see how ideological messages get encoded with intended meanings. In doing so, they can help us resist cultural power.

MULTICULTURALISM AND THE CONTEMPORARY WORLD. Cultural power can be easier to exercise in societies where people have limited exposure to other cultures, and where they are intolerant of people who have different social and cultural backgrounds. Stereotypes are reinforced through **ethnocentrism**, which is when people assume that their society is superior to others and when they use their own cultural standards to judge outsiders. Ethnocentrism and stereotypes exist in all societies, and they are often challenged by critics and social movements. When ethnocentrism is not challenged, it can lead to **xenophobia**, which is the fear and hatred of strangers who have a different cultural background. History is full of tragic examples where cultural power was used to fuel ethnocentrism and xenophobia. Ethnocentrism and xenophobia encourage racism, violence, disrespect, and even genocide.

Social scientists recognize the dangers of ethnocentrism, and to counter those dangers many of them have argued in favor of cultural relativism and multiculturalism. **Cultural relativism** is the idea that we should not try to evaluate other cultures according to our own standards; instead, we should try to understand those other cultures and engage them on their own terms as we relate to them from a very particular position in our own culture. The

Ethnocentrism When people assume that their society is superior to others and when they use their own cultural standards to judge outsiders.

Xenophobia Fear and hatred of strangers who have a different cultural background.

Cultural relativism The idea that all meaning is relative to time and place.

principle of cultural relativism was developed by anthropologists in the early 20th century, and it has become a basic principle guiding research in the social sciences, including sociology.

Since the 1960s, many critics and social movements have used the principle of cultural relativism to argue in favor of social policies based on **multiculturalism**. A society committed to multiculturalism celebrates and protects all the different cultural practices and traditions of its people. Arguments about multiculturalism and cultural relativism have helped challenge stereotypes and overturn laws that singled out specific groups and treated them unfairly (Chapter 8). Arguments about multiculturalism have also helped change immigration laws in many countries (Chapter 15).

Multicultural worlds
The Dragon Boat Festival, a traditional Chinese occasion, is celebrated by many people in cities around the world. Here, dragon boat racers compete in New York City.

Multiculturalism A society's commitment to the celebration and the protection of all the different cultural practices and traditions of its people.

While multiculturalism promotes social tolerance and cultural relativism, it has not eliminated ethnocentrism or xenophobia. In fact, where multiculturalism has been successful, its advocates have encountered backlash and resistance. Using the language of a "culture war," these critics try to convince people that the fight against cultural relativism is a battle for the soul of their society. In France and Turkey, there have been fierce battles over the rights of Muslim women to wear headscarves, because of the belief that these cultural expressions threaten national culture (Korteweg and Yurdakul 2014). In the United States, there have been political fights about bilingual education policies, based on the argument that "real" Americans need to speak English (Valenzuela 1999). In Australia and Canada, critics have argued that multiculturalism threatens national identity and solidarity. Throughout Europe and North America, these criticisms have helped reduce public support for official multicultural policies (Joppke 2004). At the same time that opponents of multiculturalism worry about the negative effects that immigrants will have on the safety and prosperity of their societies, however, there are also large segments of the population that seek to welcome and support immigrants.

Types of Culture in Today's World

There are many different kinds of culture in the world today. Some people live lives very similar to the lives their parents and grandparents lived, while others embrace an emerging global culture and pursue novelty and constant change. There is also cultural traffic between groups that once had little contact, a process in which cultural elements are shared, adopted, critiqued, and transformed. Different types of culture are not necessarily mutually exclusive. Many people engage in traditional, modern, and global cultures as they live complex and rich cultural lives.

Global Culture

Globalization is the process of international integration in many domains affecting cultural, economic, and political relationships and made possible by changes in transportation, telecommunications, media, and information technology. **Global culture** is a product of globalization and refers to beliefs, knowledge, practices, and material objects that are shared all around the world. A good example of global culture is global material culture, where billions of people worldwide have access to the same fashion, cuisine, music, film, literature, television, and social media. These shared material objects along with the information and ideas that circulate globally create the possibility of shared meanings and relationships.

Some cultural objects began in small, local enterprises and have now become global brands. McDonald's was created in 1940 as a single restaurant in California, but today it is a global chain with more than 35,000 restaurants in 120 different countries. Coca-Cola began as a medicinal drink sold by an Atlanta pharmacist in 1886, but today it is the most recognizable drink in the world, available in every country except for Cuba and North Korea. Ugg boots, which is a fashionable global brand worth over $1 billion and worn all over the world, began as a cheap form of footwear in Australia and New Zealand. Nike started in Oregon in 1964 as a local distributor of Japanese running shoes, but today it is a global brand that sells more than $25 billion in sports apparel each year. For all of these companies, more than half of their revenue comes from outside of North America. These companies have global strategies for design, production, marketing, and distribution. They create and market their products to be consumed by the world.

Globalization The process of international integration in many domains affecting cultural, economic, and political relationships and made possible by changes in transportation, telecommunications, media, and information technology.

Global culture Beliefs, knowledge, practices, and material objects that are shared all around the world.

McDonald's is global
McDonald's is a global business with a global brand. In what ways does this McDonald's Restaurant in Bangkok, Thailand, look both similar to and different from McDonald's restaurants in the United States?

While companies like Coca-Cola and Nike can manufacture identical products that they distribute globally, the people who create global culture often adapt their product for specific local markets. McDonalds sells their French fries and Big Macs everywhere, but in India they also sell the McSpicy Paneer, a cheese-based burger that caters to the large vegetarian population. When Disney began building a new theme park in Shanghai in 2012, it created new cartoon characters and programs specifically geared for the Chinese market. The formula was the same, but it was modified to better meet the specific cultural tastes of the new market. In these instances, global culture is created through a combination of global and local influences.

A major concern about global culture is **cultural imperialism**, which happens when a small number of countries dominates the market for culture and destroys smaller local cultures. Historically, American companies have been the most successful at creating global culture, and the concern about cultural imperialism is often expressed as a concern about American cultural power. The media critic Herbert Schiller (1991: 34) once described American television as

Cultural imperialism When a small number of countries dominate the market for culture and destroy smaller, local cultures.

a "cultural bomb," eradicating local cultures and replacing them with American sitcoms and cartoons. Even when products are adapted to fit local cultural needs, like the case of the McSpicy Paneer, there is a concern that the American company is displacing the local tradition, especially when profits flow back to the corporate headquarters located in the United States.

While concerns about global culture are important, other research shows that there are limits to cultural imperialism. People around the world may recognize and desire the global brands, but they still have strong preferences for locally produced culture, especially when it comes to food and beverages (Nielsen 2016). Outside of the United States, audiences consume domestic, national media, and this is especially true in countries, like India, with long histories of domestic cultural production. In other words, while people recognize and have access to American media, they also consume and sometimes prefer culture that is produced in their own country (Bekhuis 2014; Tunstall 2007: 449). The same is true for food, music, literature, and other forms of material culture; while there are definitely global brands and people will choose them for price and quality, people show a long-standing preference for cultural products that are more closely connected to their local or national culture (Nielsen 2016; Corse 1997; James 1996).

Cultural imperialism is also limited by cultural policies that privilege local and national products. In France, current laws require that 40 percent of all television content be produced in France. Laws in Australia and Canada are similar, requiring that between 50 and 60 percent of media content must be produced domestically (Borkum 2016; Office of the United States Trade Representative 2017). In Sri Lanka, a tax is imposed on all imported film and television content. In Iran, many policy-makers want to create a "halal internet," which means an internet that adheres to Islamic law and so is free from the influence of Western and non-Islamic media (Carrington 2013). Iran's internet strategy is modeled after China's well-known "great firewall," where the Chinese government monitors all foreign internet material and blocks content that it does not want its citizens to be able to access (Yang 2011).

Globalization also influences nonmaterial culture because it has made it easier for languages, values, beliefs, and norms to circulate around the world. Research by the sociologist John Meyer has identified the existence of a **world society** that shares cultural norms about progress, science, democracy, human rights, environmental protection, and a host of other basic values (Meyer 2010). World society theorists argue that these basic values are recognized by governments around the world, and are reinforced by international bodies such as the United Nations. The values of world culture are also expressed in national constitutions, national parks services, national education and science policies, and national professional associations, which express the same basic principles in most places in the world (Benavot et al. 1991; Baker and Letendre 2005; Drori et al. 2003; Frank and Meyer 2007; Meyer et al. 1997; Meyer 2010).

Individuals, groups, and governments can criticize or reject the norms and values of world culture, but when they do this there is a good chance they will face formal or informal sanctions from the global community and resistance internally from citizens with access to world culture (Beck 2006). Powerful nongovernmental organizations such as Greenpeace, Oxfam, Doctors Without Borders, and the Red Cross and Red Crescent organizations publicize violations of world culture, and push for sanctions against offending groups and governments (Table 4.1).

World Society The view that there is a common global culture consisting of shared norms about progress, science, democracy, human rights, and environmental protection.

Table 4.1 International Nongovernmental Organizations

ORGANIZATION	VALUES	GOALS
Amnesty International	Human rights	Legal rights of imprisoned; ending abuse
Médecins Sans Frontières (Doctors Without Borders)	Medical	Medical assistance to zones of conflict, disasters, epidemics, etc.
Heifer International	Hunger	Provide livestock for breeding/food
TED	Academia	Access to knowledge across disciplines
Habitat for Humanity	Housing	Build and rehab homes for those in poverty
Oxfam	Poverty	Food security, natural disasters, sanitation
Wikimedia Foundation	Knowledge	International internet knowledge base
Free the Children	Child labor	End childhood exploitation/slavery
Anti-Slavery International	Slavery	End forced labor/marriage, human trafficking, etc.
CeaseFire	Violence	End cycle of urban gun deaths
Clinton Health Access Initiative	Medicine	Negotiate prices for HIV/AIDS and malaria drugs
PlanetRead	Literacy	Education and ending illiteracy in India
World Wide Fund for Nature	Conservation	Biodiversity protection/sustainable development
Root Capital	Microfinance	Small business loans to developing world
Injaz Al-Arab	Entrepreneurship	Mentor youth in Middle East/North Africa
Escuela Nueva	Education	Improve schools/outcomes in Latin America
Reporters Sans Frontières	Press freedom	End censorship/imprisonment of journalists
Transparency International	Corruption	Expose government corruption, bribery, etc.
Danish Refugee Council	Refugees	House refugees from conflict areas
Apopo	Landmines	Belgian organization that trains rats to detect landmines as well as disease

Source: http://theglobaljournal.net/2012/Top100NGOs/.

Although critics argue that the idea of world society is just another form of cultural imperialism, in which the values of the West are imposed on the rest of the world (Carney, Rappleye, and Silova, 2012), evidence suggests that the existence of a world society with shared cultural norms does not mean that all people share the same values or even that they follow all the same norms. Public opinion surveys show that there is uneven global support for the values of world culture (Welzel and Inglehart 2009). For example, while there is strong global support for the principle of democracy, support for women's rights and sexual freedom are weaker in many parts of the world. There is also a concern that the values of world society do not have much influence on how people behave. People can easily and cynically recite the values of human rights, democracy, and environmental protection even as they violate those principles in their everyday actions (Baiocchi 2012).

Despite anxieties about cultural imperialism and an emergent global culture, the forces of cultural diversity are very strong in world society. People resist global culture, they criticize it, and they create cultural policies designed to protect local culture. They change the meanings of global culture, by using it in unexpected ways and by combining it with their own local tastes and fashions. They maintain pride in their cultural heritage, and they celebrate the cultural traditions of others. As we discuss in the following sections, the creators

Global and Local

The History of Manga

Although Japanese comic art, or manga, predates the 20th century, its modern form came about as a result of Japan's defeat in World War II, when comic books were brought into the country by American soldiers. Younger Japanese citizens were influenced by the superhero themes and nationalistic viewpoints of the American comic books, and by the desire of Japanese artists and intellectuals to revive prewar cultural forms. These two influences melded and produced something entirely new.

The Atomic Age—the period following the detonation of the first nuclear bomb in 1945—itself was a significant influence on manga, specifically the work of Osamu Tezuka, known for his *Mighty Atom*. His work was based on Western cinematic approaches to character interaction. Manga has also been the inspiration for anime, which are animated cartoons based upon the manga drawing style. *Mighty Atom* was adapted for television under the title *Astro Boy* in Japan and there have been several English-language versions, feature films, video game adaptations, and re-releases of the manga in Japanese and English. Manga is a good example of cultural traffic because it originated in Japan, was influenced by contact with the United States and Europe, and then returned to these places through English and other language adaptations.

Manga stories aimed at boys (shōnen manga) tended to focus on stereotypical "boys'" interests, such as science fiction, action, sports, etc. (although, interestingly, the superhero genre did not dominate, as it did in American comics). Girls' stories were more domestic and humorous in nature (shōjo manga). Although mid-century manga artists tended to be men, by the 1960s, audience demand for manga grew and more women artists entered the genre.

Although the right-to-left reading style of the Japanese language has become a challenge for translations into languages that read left-to-right, this has not prevented manga from becoming popular in markets outside of Japan. In 2012, for example, Otaku news reported that annual manga sales in Japan were about $5 billion, the European and the Middle Eastern markets combined were about $250 million, and the American manga market was at $120 million. Artists outside of Asia have picked up the drawing style, and "Amerimanga" (original English-language work) has proliferated. Today, animation throughout the world shows clear traces of the manga influence.

Manga
A popular global cultural form, manga has origins in pre-20th-century Japanese culture.

ACTIVE LEARNING
Find out: Ask three of your friends what their favorite film, television show, or book is. How many are global? How many are local? How can you tell? Who produces and distributes the cultural object? Are they local or global organizations?

of material culture frequently draw on these sources of cultural diversity, in their attempts to create something new and different. Subculture, high culture, DIY (Do It Yourself) culture, and even popular culture are continuous sources of cultural change and innovation.

Dominant Cultures and Subcultures

For any given society, there is one common culture that everybody recognizes and shares. It is for this reason that we can talk about French culture, American culture, or even global culture. But within this shared culture, there are many smaller cultures that influence how we understand the world. We each belong to many different groups, and each of those groups is held together by its own culture. These groups are not all equal, though. Some groups are more organized and have more power, money, and influence than others. In the world of culture, these differences often show up as conflicts between dominant cultures and subcultures.

Dominant culture The ideas, values, beliefs, norms, and material culture of society's most powerful groups.

The **dominant culture** consists of the ideas, values, beliefs, norms, and material culture of society's most powerful groups. Because dominant groups control the means of symbolic production, they are able to make sure that their culture circulates prominently throughout the society. We learn about the dominant culture from schools, the media, museums, national monuments and national holidays, and our interactions with business and government.

The dominant culture is an ideology because it makes it appear that the culture of the dominant group is in fact identical to the culture of the entire society. Historically, in the United States, the dominant culture has been the culture of white, educated, wealthy, heterosexual men who are involved in business and professional life. The dominant culture does not eliminate other cultures, but it treats them as smaller, more distinctive, and only connected to specific groups within society. We learn about women's history, African American literature, and reggae music, but when we learn about these forms of cultural expression, they are identified with specific subgroups of society. By contrast, the cultural expressions of the dominant group do not get marked in a similar way. They are just "American culture."

Subcultures The ideas, values, beliefs, norms, and material culture of all the nondominant groups in the society.

Subcultures are the ideas, values, beliefs, norms, and material culture of all the nondominant groups in a society. A subculture's members set themselves apart as being somehow distinctive and different from the mainstream culture of the society, and attach considerable importance to their common identity as members of a distinctive group. Their shared culture allows them to easily identify other members of the group, through the use of their subcultural language, style, and set of norms.

Because subcultures emphasize their uniqueness and difference from the mainstream society, they are often marginalized by mainstream society. But subcultures can also become major influences on the larger culture, such as hip-hop and comics. In fact, as the sociologist Richard Hebdige has argued, there is a complicated relationship between youth subculture and popular culture (Hebdige 1979). In their clothing choices, musical preferences, and behavior, youth subcultures create forms of cultural expressions that often mock adult, mainstream society. In other words, subcultures are important sources of social criticism. Subcultural groups like skateboarders and graffiti artists ask important questions about

Skateboard
Beginning as a subculture, skateboarding has developed as an influential commercial culture, as seen in this image from the 2015 Van Doren Invitational skateboard competition sponsored by the popular shoe brand.

Solidarity and Conflict

Music and Social Protest

Music can be a powerful way to build solidarity, and virtually every country in the world has a national anthem that is played or sung at public events. But music can also provide a place for expressing social criticism, bringing together groups of people who participate in social movements and subcultures that are critical of the dominant culture.

The music of activism and social protest has a long history. In the United States, leaders of the abolitionist movement developed their own culture of protest music, which they used to popularize antislavery sentiment during the 1830s and 1840s. Singing was an important part of abolitionist meetings, and abolitionist songbooks allowed dispersed groups to sing the same songs. The Hutchinson Family Singers, a popular group of entertainers who performed throughout New England during the 1840s, helped popularize these songs and spread the abolitionist message throughout the region (Gac 2007).

As Eyerman and Jamison (1998) show in their book *Music and Social Movements,* music continued to be used as an expression of social protest throughout the 20th century. In the 1920s, the leaders of the American labor movement distributed songbooks for their members to use during meetings and demonstrations. In the 1950s and 1960s, the folk singer Pete Seeger's version of "We Shall Overcome" became the anthem of the Civil Rights Movement. The 1969 Woodstock Music Festival became one of the most famous events associated with the 1960s hippie subculture, and the musicians who performed there translated the movement's social criticisms into popular songs that united a generation of students who were trying to change the world. Reggae music was a powerful force responsible for the global spread of the Rastafarian movement, which criticized racism and Western colonialism while preaching the importance of pan-African unity (Murrell 1998).

More recently, hip-hop music has continued this focus on social criticism in music. The genre of "conscious rap"

first appeared in the early 1980s, with the release of Grandmaster Flash's "The Message," a social commentary on race and the challenges of contemporary urban life. By the late 1980s conscious rap had become an important critical voice in the African American community. Chuck D, the leader of the group Public Enemy, declared in 1989 that conscious rap had become the "Black CNN." Today, the tradition of social criticism continues in conscious rap, with artists such as Mos Def, Lupe Fiasco, and Talib Kweli. Like the folk music and reggae artists who preceded them, conscious rappers help spread the sociological imagination in the larger world of popular culture, by identifying social problems and giving a name to feelings of alienation and unhappiness (Eyerman and Jamison 1998: 138)

Talib Kweli
Talib Kweli is a social critic who works in the hip-hop genre. Conscious hip-hop identifies social problems and expresses cultural feelings of alienation while also creating shared identity and solidarity among listeners.

ACTIVE LEARNING

Reflect: What kind of music do you like? Why do you like it? In what way is it connected to your identity? How do you feel similar or different from others because of the music you listen to?

who controls public space (Beal 1995; Snyder 2009). The 1960s hippie subculture and the 1970s punk subculture strongly rejected the dominant values of the time, encouraging their members to reject materialism and to be deeply suspicious of governments and corporations (Brake 2013).

CASE STUDY CONTINUED

particular sports event and the solidarity it invokes are legitimate and important. Those who *resist* the ritual by failing to stand or challenging the sacred meaning of the song itself are sanctioned. When NFL player Colin Kaepernick knelt in public during the anthem in 2016 to protest police brutality, he was condemned by many in the media and and he and other players were derided by Donald Trump.

The joint singing of the song also highlights the *privilege* of American cultural power in a global world. The initial singing of the "Star-Spangled Banner" at that 1918 Red Sox game, for example, took place against a global backdrop of World War I and in a domestic context of massive industrial unrest, which included the bombing of the Chicago Federal Building initially blamed on the International Workers of the World, a radical labor organization that protested economic *inequality* in the United States and around the globe. The singing of the song, as well as the solidarity and power it generates, have both global and local dimensions. As a war song, the "Star-Spangled Banner" places the image of the embattled nation at the center of public sporting events on an almost daily basis. As *ESPN Magazine* wrote, "The anthem is a show, and a show of force. Every year, the Pentagon approves several hundred requests for military flyovers. … At lesser events, even at the high school level, a color guard is often on hand with the flag as the anthem is played. A game without the anthem is likely one that doesn't matter much" (September 11, 2011). Singing the anthem is a *local* expression of national solidarity that reminds participants of their belonging to a powerful military nation with *global* power. The flag itself references an international system of nations and flags. In fact, for other countries, national anthems are typically played only at international sporting events.

Finally, the ritual itself is also highly socially *structured* by norms as it invokes the central values of the American nation. People are asked to stand for the national anthem. Nearly everyone stands. People place hands on their hearts, turn to face the flag, and maintain a respectful expression on their face. Some audience members salute. As with any ritual, however, there is always a possibility of *contingency* and the possibility that the event will not unfold in the expected way. When people disrupt or resist a ritual, they can create a different social meaning, and a different social pattern. Colin Kaepernick did this when he knelt in protest—a form of protest that has been repeated at sporting events around the nation. In another example, Goshen College in Indiana made headlines in 2011 with its decision to sing "America the Beautiful" instead of the militaristic "Star-Spangled Banner" because it is a better fit with the college's pacifist Mennonite tradition.

Cultural moments like singing the anthem at sporting events are important moments in social life. They reveal much about how social interaction is structured and reveal fundamental dynamics of group life. As Chapter 5 will show, the five paired concepts offer a way to understand both the way culture works to shape individuals and also the operation of groups.

LEARNING GOALS REVISITED

4.1   Define culture and identify the difference between material and ideal culture.

- Culture is the entire set of beliefs, knowledge, practices, and material objects that are meaningful to a group of people and shared from generation to generation.
- Culture can refer both to material objects like a book, house, or work of music, and also to the actions and words of people doing things to share meaning by reading, designing a house, or singing the national anthem with others at a sporting event.

4.2   Understand that meanings are made in cultural context.

- Words, ideas, and cultural objects get their meaning through relationships to other words, ideas, and cultural objects.
- How similar or different a word, idea, or cultural object is to another is an important, fundamental way that social things get their meaning. This is elaborated in longer sequences of words and meanings.
- Symbolic meanings are shaped by the association of a word, idea, or cultural object with

other cultural images, emotions, meanings, and associations.

- There are symbolic meanings for all types of culture, and not just for language.
- Cultural relativism is the idea that cultural meanings are relative to time and place (i.e., context). Social scientists taking a position of cultural relativism assert that we should not try to evaluate other cultures according to our own standards. Instead, we should try to understand those other cultures and engage them on their own terms as we relate to them from a very particular position in our own culture.

4.3 Describe how culture defines the moral quality of people, institutions, objects, and events.

- Cultural hierarchies define some cultural objects, people, institutions, and meanings as good and others as bad or not good.
- Different people contend over the meanings of different cultural things, arguing about what is good or appropriate. For example, parents and children often disagree about the value of cultural things, from music to video games.

4.4 Identify the connection between culture and power: identify ideologies, stereotypes, cultural hierarchies, and cultural resistance.

- Ideology is a system of shared meaning that is used to justify existing relationships of power and privilege. Ideology is culture in the service of power.
- Ideology misdirects attention away from power and creates an idea that the way things are is common sense and therefore right.
- Stereotypes are a form of ideology that asserts the superior value of one group of people, institutions, or objects over others. They are linked to racism, ethnocentrism, and xenophobia. Stereotypes are often conveyed and reinforced through literature, films, and music.

- Cultural hierarchies are a form of organized cultural power in which some groups are able to define the dominant culture, which is often understood as common sense.
- In modern societies, one important form of cultural power is exercised through self-policing, and physical and psychological therapies where individuals evaluate and alter themselves to meet cultural norms.
- Cultural power is met in many cases by the cultural resistance of individuals, critics, and organized social movements. Existing cultural meanings are powerful but they can be and have been changed.

4.5 Distinguish different types of culture.

- Material culture refers to cultural objects.
- Ideal culture refers to ideas, actions, and meanings.
- Global culture is a product of globalization and refers to the shared beliefs, knowledge, practices, and material objects that are shared all around the world.
- Local culture intersects global culture to interpret and alter the meanings of words, ideas, and cultural objects. Global brands like McDonald's or Disney, for example, produce local versions of their successful formulas to cater to the local tastes of consumers.
- The dominant culture consists of the ideas, values, beliefs, norms, and material culture of society's most powerful groups.
- Subcultures are the ideas, values, beliefs, norms, and material culture of all the non-dominant groups in the society.
- Popular culture refers to objects of material culture industrially produced and distributed for the masses.
- Commercial culture refers to cultural commodities that exist to be bought and sold. These commodities are controlled by large and increasingly multinational corporations.
- High culture refers to all of the cultural products that are held in the highest esteem by a society's intellectuals and elites.

Key Terms

Review Questions

1. What is the difference between material and ideal culture?
2. List three different kinds of culture and provide an example of each.
3. How does dominant culture work as an ideology? Give an example.
4. How does a stereotype about a social group work as a moral standard? Give an example.
5. How is global culture different than local culture?
6. What is a discourse of power and how does it encourage our self control?

Explore

RECOMMENDED READINGS

Alexander, Jeffrey C. 2003. *The Meanings of Social Life: A Cultural Sociology*. New York: Oxford University Press.

Back, Les, Andy Bennett, Laura Desfor Edles, Margaret Gibson, Ron Jacobs, and Ian Woodward. 2012. *Cultural Sociology: An Introduction*. New York: Wiley-Blackwell.

Bourdieu, Pierre. 1984. *Distinction: A Social Critique of the Judgement of Taste*. Cambridge: Harvard University Press.

Hebdige, Dick. 1979. *Subculture: The Meaning of Style*. New York: Routledge.

Lopes, Paul. 2009. *Demanding Respect: The Evolution of the American Comic Book*. Philadelphia: Temple University Press.

Mukerji, Chandra, and Michael Schudson. 1991. *Rethinking Popular Culture: Contemporary Perspectives in Cultural Studies*. Los Angeles: University of California Press.

Smith, Philip, and Alexander Riley. 2008. *Cultural Theory: An Introduction*. 2nd ed. New York: Wiley-Blackwell.

ACTIVITIES

- *Use your sociological imagination*: Cultural capital is knowledge and consumption of socially valued things. Do you have cultural capital? What is it? Have you ever felt excluded by another person's cultural capital? How did that work?

- *Media+Data literacies*: Go to the reference section in your library and find a dictionary that gives historical information on words. Look up the words "culture" and "individual." How have they changed over time? Do you have any theories about why they changed?

- *Discuss*: McDonald's in Australia serves the Aussie Burger with an egg, bacon, and pickled beetroot on it. In India, McDonald's makes the vegetarian McSpicy Paneer. Do you think these are examples of cultural imperialism? Are they the same in both cases? Why or why not?

For additional resources, including Media+Data Literacy exercises, In the News exercises, and quizzes, please go to **oup.com/he/ Jacobs-Townsley1e**

"A MOVING 12 YEAR EPIC
THAT ISN'T QUITE LIKE ANYTHING ELSE IN THE HISTORY OF CINEMA"
-ANDREW O'HEHIR, SALON

PATRICIA
ARQUETTE

ELLAR
COLTRANE

LORELEI
LINKLATER

ETHAN
AND HAWKE

Boyhood

Written and Directed by
Richard Linklater

5

Socialization, Social Interaction, and Group Life

One of the most critically acclaimed films of 2014 was *Boyhood*. The film follows the coming-of-age of a boy named Mason, from the time he is six years old until he is 18. Mason goes to school, fights with his older sister, and looks on as his divorced parents form new relationships. As a teenager, Mason develops an interest in photography, experiments with drugs and alcohol, has his first serious relationship, graduates from high school, and begins college. Critics and audiences loved the film because it captured something both fundamental and universal about social life: the process of growing up.

In literature, the coming-of-age story has always been popular. Classics like *Jane Eyre*, *Great Expectations*, *The Adventures of Huckleberry Finn*, *The Catcher in the Rye*, and *To Kill a Mockingbird* are about young people learning how to live in society. Just like in *Boyhood*, the characters in these stories struggle to navigate different kinds of social groups, social settings, and social institutions. They face moral dilemmas, they make mistakes, and through these mistakes they become more mature.

In this chapter, we discuss how the social self develops, and we consider the different agents of socialization that help bring this about. We examine the relationship between socialization and social interaction, and we explore how the socialization process changes over the course of our lives. Finally, we look at the different ways that group dynamics influence social life, considering informal groups as well as large, formal organizations.

Boyhood, a modern coming-of-age story
Coming-of-age stories are important because they capture something universal and important about being human: growing up.

LEARNING GOALS

5.1   Define socialization and the process of normalization.

5.2   Identify the primary agents of socialization that operate over the life course.

5.3   Understand the difference between a status and a role and describe how interactional performances sustain the social self.

5.4   Define groups and distinguish different kinds of groups.

5.5   Distinguish networks from bureaucracies as distinct organizational forms of group life in modern societies.

Socialization and Selfhood

Socialization All of the different ways that we learn about our society's beliefs, values, and expected behaviors; the ongoing process of learning the social meanings of a culture.

In sociology, the process of growing up and learning how to live in society is called socialization. **Socialization** refers to all of the different ways that we learn about our society's culture: its beliefs, values, and expected behaviors. Socialization begins when we are infants, and it continues throughout our lives. Socialization happens when we are with our family and our friends, when we are watching television or using social media, and when we are at school or at work. It is an interactive process, because we are helping to socialize others at the same time that we are being socialized ourselves.

Nature and Nurture

When sociologists talk about socialization, they focus on the social environment. But they also recognize that biology plays an important role in who we become. Our genetic makeup influences our height, weight, health, response to stress, and other factors that impact our lives and our fate.

But biology is not destiny. What really matters is the *interaction* between our genes and our social environment. Take height, for example. While your height is influenced by your genetics, it also depends on the quality of your nutrition and health care (Grasgruber, Cacek, Kalina, and Sebera 2014). The consequences of being short or tall are related more to our social environment than our biology. In most contemporary societies, taller people are more likely to be seen as attractive, more likely to have positive interactions with other people, and more likely to have higher self-esteem (Freese 2008). These consequences are connected to the social meanings placed on height, rather than the biological nature of height itself.

Nature and nurture also interact when we respond to stressful events in our lives. Our genetic makeup influences whether we react to stress positively or negatively. Some people are naturally more resilient and resourceful in the way they deal with problems, while others have a tendency to become withdrawn or depressed (Ising and Holsboer 2006). But the frequency with which people experience stressful events is connected mainly to their social environment. People who live in poverty, for example, face extremely stressful events on a regular basis, testing their ability to respond to stress much more often than people who live with privilege.

Regardless of biological makeup, people who are socially isolated have a much more difficult time functioning effectively in society. Children who are too isolated have problems with short-term memory and language development, and are more likely to develop learning disorders, emotional problems, issues with aggression, and social withdrawal (Rubin and Ross 1982). Adults who are socially isolated have worse physical and mental health, and they tend to die younger than people who have stronger social attachments to family, friends, and community (Cornwell and Waite 2009). Genetics has some impact on how we respond to these situations of social isolation, but it is the experience of social isolation itself that is the most powerful factor that limits our ability to develop our social selves.

The Social Self

As social beings, we are not the only creatures who need to learn how to live in society. Even animals have learned how to live in society. People train their dogs to behave around other dogs and people. Even squirrels and pigeons have adapted to human society, congregating in open spaces where discarded food is plentiful and where pedestrians are more likely to feed them. In fact, squirrels were deliberately introduced into northeastern cities in the United States, beginning with Philadelphia in the 19th century, by social reformers who thought it was important for people to be exposed to nature (Benson 2013; Van Zuylen-Wood 2012).

While dogs, pigeons, and squirrels can learn to function effectively in human society, there are important ways in which our own socialization is quite different from theirs. While animals can change their behavior to adapt to the social world around them, they do not actually learn the values and the culture of our society. They do not try to imagine how others are feeling before they act; they do not spend a lot of time considering how others might respond to their actions; nor is there evidence that animals engage in processes of reflection and self-assessment. They don't feel guilt, shame, or pride. They don't try out different personalities, or pretend to be something they are not. They don't worry that they are wasting their lives or failing to fulfill their true potential. In short, animals do not have a **social self**.

Squirrels
Squirrels, a species that has adapted well to city life, seem to understand human behavior.

THE LOOKING-GLASS SELF. Charles Horton Cooley (1864–1929) developed one of the earliest theories of the social self, which he referred to as the **looking-glass self**. Cooley argued that the self is shaped by the social interactions we have, and the interpretations we make of those interactions. When we interact with other people, we imagine what they are thinking about us, and wonder if they are evaluating or judging us. On the basis of this imagined judgment, we have an emotional response. In this process, society serves as a mirror—a looking glass—we use to develop our sense of self throughout our lives.

Social self An individual's self-awareness and self-image as a product of social experience.

Looking-glass self A concept that describes how we develop a social self based on how we think other people perceive us.

Our looking-glass self develops gradually. Each interaction we have adds to our previous self-understandings. This is why early childhood socialization is so important. Early negative experiences teach us to look for clues that people don't like us, while positive experiences in early childhood give us confidence in future interactions. As our looking-glass self becomes more established, we start to look for evidence in future social interactions that confirms our sense of self.

MIND, SELF, AND SOCIETY. Our social self becomes more complicated as we grow older, and we begin to have internal conversations between self and other. George Herbert Mead (1863–1931) argued that children younger than three years old can only develop a very limited social self, because they lack the ability to step outside of themselves and think about the perspective of other people. They might be able to imitate the actions of the people around them, but they cannot really take on the role of the other. Once they enter the **play stage** of development, at around three years old, they begin to engage in role-playing games, pretending to be their parents or other significant people in their lives. This is an important step in the socialization process, because it is when children have to imagine themselves as other people.

By the time they are about seven years old, children begin to enter the **game stage** of development. For young children, learning how to play games is a crucial skill for making friends (Frankel 1996). Children learn how to choose games that other people want to play. They learn how to solve problems and respond to arguments that happen when the game is being played. They can only do this, Mead argued, if they can take the perspective of the **generalized other**, which means that they think about how they appear to "society in general." In other words, when children play games they are learning the expectations and standards of their social group, and they are learning to see themselves from the viewpoint of the typical child. They are beginning to reflect upon who they are in relationship to the world around them, and they can begin to make decisions about the kinds of people they want to become.

Play stage A stage of social development when children around three years old begin to engage in role-playing games.

Game stage A stage of social development when children are around seven years old and begin to make friends, learn to pick games that other people want to play, and learn how to avoid or to quickly resolve arguments that arise when a game is being played.

Generalized other The rules of society that the child internalizes through the process of socialization.

Id The unconscious part of the mind, which seeks immediate pleasure and gratification.

Superego The moral part of the mind, which acts as the conscience.

Sigmund Freud (1856–1939) also wrote about the internal dialogue between mind, self, and society. Freud's theory of the social self proposed that there were three interconnected parts of the mind: ego, superego, and id. The **id** is an unconscious part of the mind, which seeks immediate pleasure and gratification. The **superego**, by contrast, is the moral part of our mind, which acts as our conscience. Similar to the generalized other, the superego is our internalized image of society, with its rules for behavior. Within our mind, the superego acts to suppress any urges by the id that are considered wrong or socially unacceptable, by making us feel guilt. The superego is what tells you not to take candy from a baby, or to act violently against someone because they look at you the wrong way.

Early childhood
Playing games is an important part of early-childhood socialization.

In between the id and the superego, Freud argued, is the **ego**. The ego tries to strike a realistic balance between the instinctual urges of the id and the uncompromising morality of the superego, trying to determine the most practical course of action for a given situation. The ego allows us to delay gratification when that is in our long-term interests, and it provides us with important defense mechanisms that prevent the superego from allowing us to feel so much guilt that we endanger ourselves.

CULTURE, NORMALIZATION, AND THE SELF. Mead and Freud both viewed socialization as a force of social control. Our internalized image of society's rules and expectations encourages us to act in appropriate ways, and makes us feel guilty when we do not do so. The generalized other that we carry inside our head is there to remind us what behavior is expected of us. Our superego disciplines our instinctual urges and makes us want to be "normal" members of society.

As we discussed in Chapter 4, the social construction of normal and pathological behavior is a form of cultural power. We feel guilty when we act in ways that are considered not to be normal. We read self-help books and we seek out therapists to help us identify our pathological tendencies. We are encouraged to believe that these pathological tendencies are holding us back in our lives and causing us unhappiness. Michel Foucault described this as **normalization** ([1977] 1995), which refers to the way that discourses about the normal and the pathological identify the kinds of behaviors that will attract special attention, as well as the forms of rehabilitation that deal with people who are deemed to be "not normal."

In today's society, normalization is big business. As sociologist Eva Illouz shows in her book *Saving the Modern Soul* (2008), the language of therapy and self-help is deeply ingrained in our lives. Psychotherapy and mental health counseling is a global industry with annual revenues in excess of $15 billion. Everywhere we turn, there are experts and products available to help us work on our social self, improve our socialization, and cure any imbalances we (or they) may discover.

Agents of Socialization

Agents of socialization are the people, groups, and organizations that teach us about society's beliefs, values, and expected behaviors. Sociologists have identified five agents of socialization that are important for most people today: family, school, peer groups, media, and the workplace. These agents of socialization impact us in different ways as we grow up.

FAMILY. For most children, the family is the most important agent of socialization. The family is our first social group. It is where we establish our first social and emotional bonds. It is where we learn how to communicate and how

Ego The part of the mind that balances the demands of the id and the superego to determine the most practical course of action for an individual in any given situation.

Normalization The process through which social standards of normal behavior are used to judge people and to reform those who are determined not to be normal.

Agents of socialization The people, groups, and organizations that most powerfully affect human socialization. The five primary agents of socialization are family, school, peer groups, media, and the workplace.

Self-help books
Self-help books are a commercially successful part of a global therapeutic culture, as seen in this Malaysian bookstore. Such books enable people to match their behavior to defined social norms. They are part of a cultural process of normalization.

Families
Families are primary agents of socialization, in early childhood and throughout the life cycle.

to interact with other people. It is where we first learn about the rules of appropriate social behavior, and it is where we begin to learn the shared beliefs and values of our culture. The bonds we form with our parents and siblings are particularly strong, and they leave a deep imprint on our social self.

For the first five years of our lives, we spend most of our time with our family. As we discuss in Chapters 9 and 10, these early years provide important moments of gender socialization, when we learn about the different social expectations that exist for women and men. Young children observe which of their parents does the cooking, who does the cleaning, who takes out the trash, who leaves in the morning to go to work, and who stays home to take care of them. They notice the different kinds of clothes their parents wear, and the different kinds of relationships their parents have. Pretending to be "Mommy" or "Daddy" is a common activity during the play stage of development.

The family also begins to socialize children about the values and expectations of the larger society. Different parenting styles reflect cultural differences. In countries such as China and Japan, children are taught about the importance of obedience and cooperation, and parents tend to maintain stricter control over their children's behavior (Jordan and Graham 2015). By comparison, in countries such as the United States and Australia, children are taught more about the importance of individuality, personal happiness, and self-expression.

SCHOOL AND PEER GROUPS. Entering school is a major change for children, as they enter a new social environment. They quickly have to learn the rules, expectations, and culture of their school. All schools have a curriculum, which consists of subject areas and instructional goals. But there is also a **hidden curriculum**, which consists of the rules of behavior children need to learn to function effectively in the school and the larger society (Giroux and Purpel 1983). This hidden curriculum is really about socialization.

Hidden curriculum The rules of behavior students need to learn to function effectively in the school and the larger society.

What kind of socialization do children get at school? They learn how to be on time, how to listen to an authority figure, and how to ask questions without being disruptive. They learn how to work hard, when they are supposed to compete with their classmates, and when they are supposed to cooperate. They learn what kinds of behaviors are rewarded, and what kinds are punished. Schools are one of the most important institutions in our society, and we discuss them in more detail in Chapter 14.

Peer groups Groups of people of similar age who share the same kinds of interests.

School-age children also spend more time with **peer groups**, which consist of people of a similar age who share the same kinds of interests. Peer groups become an important agent of socialization throughout the school-age years. Many adolescents and teenagers spend more time with their peer groups than they do with their families (Larson and Richards 1991). Peer groups help us form a social self that is separate from our parents.

As we discussed in Chapter 4, peer group subcultures develop their own set of values and expected behaviors that can be completely separate from the world of adults, which can create conflicts between parents and their children. Many parents worry about **peer pressure,** which occurs when peer groups encourage adolescents and teens to engage in behaviors that they would not do if their parents were watching. Peer pressure has been linked to risky social behavior such as underage drinking, drug use, and shoplifting (Lewis and Lewis 1984). Peer pressure is also a big factor in early sexual activity, gossip, and bullying, which often cause great emotional distress, anxiety, and depression (Fried 1998).

Peer groups
Peer group interactions are an important part of the school experience. Did your peer group look like this stock image? How was it similar or different?

Peer pressure Peer groups encourage adolescents and teens to engage in behaviors that they would not perform if their parents were watching.

In adolescence, children begin to pay more attention to inequalities and social differences. Sociological research shows that the peer groups that form in school tend to be homogeneous, composed of individuals who are similar in race, gender, and social class (Shrum, Creek, and Hunter 1988). Because peer group identities form by drawing boundaries between different groups, the similarity within peer groups has the effect of intensifying social differences. In her book *"Why Are All the Black Kids Sitting Together in the Cafeteria?" and Other Conversations about Race* (1997), Beverly Tatum argues that these peer groups provide an important opportunity for students to establish and affirm their group identity. For minority students, peer groups allow them to secure a racial identity that is free of the negative racial stereotypes that circulate in media and the larger society. For more privileged students, the peer groups they form help them develop and learn subtle ways of signaling their privilege to others (Khan 2012). Regardless of the specific social background, membership in peer groups helps children define and understand their position in the larger society.

MEDIA. School-age children are voracious media consumers. According to research by Roberts and Foehr (2004), average media exposure increases rapidly in elementary school, from about four hours per day in second grade to about eight hours per day in fifth grade. These patterns hold constant through the teenage years. In fact, children "spend more time with media than any single activity other than sleeping" (Roberts and Foehr 2008: 11). More recent data from Common Sense Media show that children ages 8 to 18 spend nine hours a day in front of a screen, not including time for school or homework. This combines time spent watching traditional and time-shifted television as well as time on a game console, computer, or another multimedia device. Importantly, their parents also report spending 9 hours a day on screens (Common Sense Media 2016a, 2016b).

Digital natives
Very young children use media and media technologies with ease.

Like peer groups, media help us form a social self that is separate from our parents, and media can be a source of conflict between parents and children. Many parents and educators are concerned that media encourage children to embrace a more materialistic lifestyle focused on consumption (Schor 2004). Others are concerned that media expose children to inappropriate levels of sexual imagery, and promote sexist and degrading beliefs about women (Corsaro 2005: 276). There is also concern about media violence, and the possible effects that this exposure has on children's behavior (Anderson and Bushman 2018; Barker and Petley 2001).

Most sociological research shows that media exposure cannot completely change our values and behaviors, because media are only one agent of socialization among many. But media are always there. We talk with friends and family about the television shows we are watching . We show them YouTube videos and websites we have discovered. We check our smartphone every time a new notification appears. As Todd Gitlin argues in his book *Media, Unlimited*, we have come to expect that media images, sounds, and stories will be there for us on command. Living with the media, Gitlin (2001: 5) argues, is one of the main things that humans do.

Adult Socialization

Most people are deeply influenced by the big events in society that take place when they are adolescents. At a time when people are developing a distinctive social self that is separate from the family, these years have a significant impact on how we think about ourselves and our place in society. According to the sociologist Karl Mannheim (1893–1947), youth is a time when generations form. Mannheim (1952) defined a **generation** as a group of individuals who are a similar age, who get swept up by the same historical events that take place during their youth. Members of a generation do not all understand these events in the same way, but their own personal coming-of-age story will tend to focus on the same big events.

In the United States, for example, the "millennial" generation is composed of those Americans born between 1982 and 2004 (Strauss and Howe 2000). Millennials came of age during the September 11, 2001, attacks on the World Trade Center and the Pentagon, and they grew up in a climate of war. Those who entered the job market did so in a period of sharp economic decline; the job prospects for millennials were more uncertain than those of the preceding generation. Millennials are less trusting than older generations, less religious, more supportive of gay rights, and more supportive of legalizing marijuana (Pew Research Center 2014). Millennials are also the first generation to grow up with the internet and other forms of social media, and as a result they have been called the first group of "digital natives" (Pew Research Center 2014).

While generational identity is formed during our teenage years, the process of socialization continues to shape us throughout our adult lives. As we grow up, the agents of socialization act on us differently. Some adults live in **total institutions**, such as prisons, nursing homes, or the military, which control every aspect of their lives. For others, the workplace becomes a major agent of socialization. Family socialization changes, too, as people become parents and begin to raise children. Many adults experience significant disruption during their lives, particularly those who experience events such as unemployment and divorce. As people grow old and retire, they have to learn to adjust to a society that treats them differently than it did when they were young. As people adjust their lives in response to these new circumstances, they have to adjust their attitudes and behaviors accordingly, which is a transition that sociologists call **resocialization**.

Generation A group of individuals who are of a similar age and are marked by the same historical events that take place during their youth.

Total institutions Institutions like prisons, nursing homes, or the military that control every aspect of their members' lives.

Resocialization The process through which we adjust our lives, attitudes, and behaviors in response to new circumstances.

WORKPLACE. As we finish school and begin our careers, the workplace becomes an important agent of socialization. Every profession has informal rules and expected behaviors that can only be learned on the job. "Just doing a good job" is not enough for career success.

As people spend more time working in a particular profession or career, they begin to internalize the values of the workplace. Police officers who have been on the job for a long time become more distrustful of the public at large, and they tend to become secretive in their dealings with the larger society (Crank 2004). Investment bankers believe they are smarter and harder-working than everyone else, and they value short-term risk-taking and Ivy League degrees (Ho 2009). Doctors value expertise, and they believe that their specialized ability to diagnose and treat illness means that their medical judgment should not be questioned (Freidson [1970] 1988). These values are learned and reinforced on the job, as part of workplace socialization.

Work
For many adults, experiences in the workplace have a significant impact on the development of the social self.

Because social status is linked closely with occupational prestige, our experiences in the workplace have a significant impact on the development of our social self. People who are successful in their jobs tend to have more self-confidence. They also benefit from the material advantages of job success, which makes it easier for them to take care of their families, deal with medical issues, and plan for their retirement. On the other hand, people who experience unemployment face considerable stress and disruption in their lives, and they have to deal with the stigma that is associated with not working.

DIVORCE, UNEMPLOYMENT, AND DISRUPTION. Adult resocialization happens most intensely during significant disruptions. Two of the most serious causes of disruption are unemployment and divorce. When people lose their jobs, they may be forced to give up their home and move to a neighborhood with fewer advantages. They are more likely to lose contact with their friends and peer groups. They get sick more often, suffer more serious health issues, and often lose their health insurance just when they have the greatest need of it. Unemployment places great stress on families as well, and often leads to divorce.

Divorce also usually requires resocialization. While divorce creates emotional and social difficulties for children (Wallerstein 1991), it also creates challenges for members of the adult couple who are separating. When couples marry, they rearrange their entire social worlds, sharing the same family and friends, and they value their identity as a spouse (Vaughan 1990). When the marriage ends, individuals have to redefine all of those relationships, establish new social routines, and create a new identity as a single person. At least one of the partners will have to find a new place to live, and often both partners will do so. There are also economic consequences, as women who get divorced usually end up poorer than they would have been if the marriage had lasted (Peterson 1996). This is all a very painful and public process. Not only do friends, family, and peers know what is happening, but so does the phone company and the Internal Revenue Service.

In fact, any significant disruption during our adult years will be associated with resocialization. When you go to college you have to learn the new routines of the campus community, and when you get a job you have to learn different routines and different values. Parents reorganize their lives to take care of their children, and then reorganize it again when their children grow up and leave home. If you suffer a serious illness or injury, you may find that things you took for granted become difficult or even impossible. Resocialization is a common part of adult development.

RETIREMENT AND OLD AGE. For most people, the final period of resocialization comes with retirement and old age. This phase of life is much longer than it used to be, because people are living longer. In the United States today, the average age of retirement is 64 for men and 62 for women (Munnell 2015). On the other hand, for a person who is 65 years old in the United States today, the average life expectancy is 82 for men and 85 for women (Copeland 2014).

For most people, aging and retirement create challenges for the social self they developed over the previous decades. People who have spent more than half their lives working often get depressed if they cannot find a new identity away from work (Schlossberg 2009). Aging also poses a challenge for people whose sense of self is attached to their role as a parent. By the time most people reach retirement age, their children are grown, and they may have to readjust to the role of being a grandparent. Media are not much help either. Despite the fact that half of the viewers of television are at least 54 years old, most media celebrate youth and offer few positive images of older people.

Retirement also creates financial challenges that demand adjustments in our social routines. Many older workers are pushed out of their jobs earlier than they would like, due to pervasive age discrimination in the workplace (Roscigno, Mong, Byron, and Tester 2007). While the Social Security system was established in the 1930s to provide retirement benefits to older Americans, it does not provide enough income to allow many retirees to maintain their standard of living. The vast majority of Americans fail to save enough money during their working lives to maintain their standard of living after they retire (Ghilarducci 2008). In other words, most retirees need to learn to live with less. This often means selling their house and moving to a different community, changing their eating habits, traveling less, and reducing other types of consumption.

Aging brings other challenges as well. Chronic illness, weakness, and the loss of mobility make people less confident in public spaces, and they often respond by spending less time outside of the house. The death of friends means that the peer groups of older people often get smaller. With the death of a spouse, many people find themselves living alone for the first time in decades. As they near the end of their lives, many adults discover that they can no longer live independently, and they have to accept the fact that they need others to take care of them. Whereas the elderly once

Retirement
Retirement is a major source of resocialization for most adults.

Inequality and Privilege

Different Styles of Parenting

Family socialization varies depending on the social class background of the parents. In Chapter 1, we mentioned Annette Lareau's book *Unequal Childhoods* (2003). Lareau's research examines how working-class and professional parents socialize their children according to a different set of values and expectations. Working-class and poor parents emphasize the "natural growth" of their children. They are less involved with their children's activities; they are less likely to include their children in adult socializing; and they give their children a lot of unstructured free time to play. This choice is not entirely voluntary, as these parents often work long hours and do not have the money to pay for organized social activities.

Professional parents have a different parenting style. Instead of giving their children free time to discover their interests, these parents have a style that Lareau calls "concerted cultivation." They enroll their children in multiple organized activities, with the hope that their children will discover what they are good at. They invest considerable time and money to ensure that their children are exposed to organized sports, art, music, and a variety of educational enrichment activities. Last, they try to direct their children toward activities that will look good on a college application.

Lareau also found that professional parents communicate with their children in a different way than working-class parents. Using the style of concerted cultivation, professional parents encourage their children to communicate with adults, ask questions, and share their opinions. They socialize their children to be assertive, and to expect to be taken seriously in the adult world.

This socialization pays off later in life when children begin school, and also later when they enter the workplace.

Concerted cultivation

Concerted cultivation is a parenting style fostering middle-class culture. More-privileged parents pay for private music lessons and a range of athletic and academic experiences for their children in the hopes that it will pay off in their social development and success. Think about the extracurricular activities you had access to in high school. Why do you think schools and parents supported them?

ACTIVE LEARNING

Find out: Interview someone who is a parent and not in your sociology class. Ask them about their views on parenting. Do they think children should be in multiple extra activities outside of school? Ask the reason why. Applying Lareau's ideas of concerted cultivation and natural growth, what kind of parenting strategy would you say this person has?

moved in with relatives when they could no longer care for themselves, today they are more likely to move into retirement communities, assisted living facilities, and nursing homes. As they lose their independence, the elderly struggle to maintain the social interactions and the connections that had once helped nourish and reproduce their social selves.

Interaction and the Social Construction of Reality

We are socialized and create a social self through all the social interactions that occur over the course of our lives. Collectively, these social interactions create the social reality to which the social self belongs. There are common patterns

Life-Course Research on Socialization

The *Up* series, produced by ITV and the British Broadcasting Corporation (BBC), was one of the most famous television documentaries ever made. The first installment of the series, *Seven Up!*, was released in 1964. The director of the documentary followed the lives of 14 seven-year-old children, who were selected to represent a variety of social backgrounds in England. The goal of the series was to catch up with the children every seven years, and to see how their lives developed. Almost all of the children have agreed to continue participating in the project. The latest installment, *63 Up*, was released in 2019.

The *Up* series does a remarkable job of showing the power of socialization. Already at age seven, the children from wealthy families have plans to attend elite prep schools and universities. The children of privileged parents ended up living mostly privileged lives, while the children of working-class parents mostly ended up living working-class lives. The influences of religion, race, and gender socialization were already apparent in the seven-year-olds, and they continued to exert a powerful influence. But the disruptions that took place in their adult lives also had a significant impact on the development of their social selves. Divorce was a particularly powerful event in the lives of the adult characters, but the series also shows the influence of unemployment, homelessness, and illness. Influenced by the *Up* series, similar documentary projects have been undertaken in more than 10 different countries.

While the *Up* series is a powerful demonstration of socialization through the life course, sociologists have criticized certain features of the documentary series. As Mitchell Duneier has pointed out, the director asked leading questions to some of the subjects in the film, and he makes claims about their life-course trajectories that cannot be supported by the data (Duneier 2000). The director of the series has agreed with these criticisms, admitting that the assumptions he made about social background and life outcomes did not always turn out to be correct (Apted 2009).

Social scientists have also conducted research that examines socialization over the life course (Kuo et al. 2019; Vaillant 2012). Among sociologists, the most famous life-course study is probably Glen Elder's *Children of the Great Depression* (Elder 1998). In this study, Elder follows 167 people in Oakland, California, who were born in 1920–21, and then another group of children born in 1928–29. Beginning his research when they were in elementary school, Elder follows them through the 1960s, to see how the Great Depression of the 1930s influenced their lives. While the economic crisis was a major factor for all of his research subjects, Elder found that people were more resilient if they went to college, if they had a stable marriage, or if they entered the military.

ACTIVE LEARNING

Reflect: Are there events that define your own socialization? What are they? How do you think these events will matter in your life moving forward?

Discuss: Do you have a sense that your generation is a group? Do you feel you belong to it? In what contexts does that matter?

Status A specific social position that an individual occupies in the social structure.

Ascribed status A status assigned to people by society, which is not chosen and which cannot be changed easily.

Achieved status A status that can be earned through action.

to this process that help create shared beliefs and expectations. While these social patterns can be very stable, people also sometimes struggle over shared meanings with different beliefs about what is right and wrong, appropriate or inappropriate.

Status and Role

Interaction with other people provides us with important clues about our different statuses and roles. **Status** refers to a specific social position that an individual has relative to other people. Sociologists distinguish between **ascribed status** and **achieved status**. An ascribed status is something that is assigned to us by society, which we do not choose and which we often cannot change. Important examples of ascribed status include race, gender, family origin, and age.

Structure and Contingency

What Is the Meaning of Fair Play? The 2012 Olympic Badminton Controversy

During the 2012 London Olympics, a scandal erupted when four of the teams in the badminton competition appeared to deliberately lose their matches during early-round play. Like many Olympic sports, badminton uses a round-robin format in which the results from early matches are used to determine seeding for later matches. In principle, teams should want to win their matches, so they will have a higher seed and get to play weaker opponents during the "knockout" rounds that advance teams into the semifinals and the finals. But sometimes teams make different strategic decisions.

In the badminton matches that caused the scandal, the teams from China, South Korea, and Indonesia had already qualified for the knockout round, and decided that they would be in a better position if they lost their matches. The players were making errors on basic shots, and no rallies lasted more than four shots during one of the matches. There was an obvious lack of effort by the competitors. Fans booed during both matches, and the referees interrupted play several times to issue warnings to the competitors. A disciplinary committee disqualified the teams the next day, charging them with violating the spirit of fair play. British and American journalists praised the decision, arguing that fans had paid good money to watch the matches and the play of the competitors demeaned the sport as well as the Olympic spirit.

Not everyone accepted this social construction of reality. All four teams protested their disqualification. The Chinese players said they were just trying to preserve energy for the next round. The South Korean players said they were responding to China's actions, and trying to increase the odds of having two South Korean teams advance into the final match. The Indonesian players said they thought they would have a better chance of advancing to the final if they didn't have to play the Chinese team in the knockout round.

All of these players rejected the idea that they were violating the spirit of fair play. Their goal was to win the entire Olympic competition, and they had made a strategic decision that they thought would improve their chances. Sports experts noted that athletes often preserve their energy in the early rounds to make sure they are fully prepared for the later rounds, and they questioned whether the badminton matches in question were really any different. Furthermore, China and South Korea were trying to increase the chances of having an all-Chinese or an all-Korean final. Were their decisions based on bad sportsmanship or patriotism?

The 2012 Olympic Badminton Controversy
An official talks to women's-doubles pairs from South Korea and China after they allegedly made deliberate mistakes to lose the match in order to avoid meeting another team from their own country in the next round.

ACTIVE LEARNING

Discuss: Socialization is a part of the social construction of reality because it teaches us "what everybody knows" and provides a "cultural common sense." Whose common sense do you think should have prevailed in the Olympic badminton scandal of 2012? Why?

Achieved status is something that we earn through our own actions. Achieved statuses include things like our jobs and hobbies.

Our status often changes as we move through the life course, like when we transition from being a student to a teacher or from a child to a parent. Other statuses remain mostly the same, such as our race and our family of origin. At any given time we will have many different statuses. Some of them will be important all of the time, while others will only matter in specific situations.

Role conflict
Because people occupy multiple statuses, they often experience role conflict. A common conflict is between work and parenting roles.

Code-switching Adapting behavior to meet different role expectations across interactional contexts.

Role The set of expected behaviors associated with a particular status.

Role strain When the different expected behaviors associated with a status are in tension with one another, individuals experience strain trying to meet expectations.

Role conflict When there are competing expectations coming from different statuses and role expectations clash, individuals become conflicted.

Dramaturgical theory A theory of society developed by Erving Goffman that refers to social life as a series of theatrical performances.

Statuses can also change between interactional contexts. Elijah Anderson's classic study *The Code of the Street* (1999) documented how inner-city youth in Philadelphia switched between what they called "decent" and "street" behavior to adapt to different role expectations on the street, at home, and at school. Anderson called this behavior of adapting to different role expectations in different interactional contexts **code-switching**.

Roles refer to the expected behaviors that are associated with each status. Roles emerge in social interaction, as people decide which statuses are the most relevant for the situation. Sometimes roles are clearly defined. In the classroom, a teacher is expected to define the objectives of the lesson, to follow a syllabus, and to treat all students with equal respect. But role expectations are not always this straightforward. There can be **role strain**, which occurs when the different expected behaviors associated with a status are in tension with one another. Parents feel role strain frequently, as they balance the demands of offering love and support for their children with the need to establish clear rules their children need to follow and enforce discipline when those rules are broken. There can also be **role conflict**, which happens when there are competing expectations coming from different statuses. A working parent experiences role conflict when the expected behaviors associated with the workplace come into conflict with the expected behaviors of a parent.

Performance and the Social Self

As the sociologist Erving Goffman (1922–1982) observed, we are all actors on the stage of social life. Our statuses define specific roles for us to play in different situations, and we have to perform those roles in a way that is true to our social selves. At the same time, we are always giving other people clues about the roles they are supposed to be playing, and we provide them in-the-moment information about whether they are playing those roles effectively or not. Goffman's book *The Presentation of Self in Everyday Life* (1959) introduced the **dramaturgical theory** of society, which refers to social life as a series of theatrical performances.

Goffman argued that people want to convey a particular image of themselves in their interactions with others. To do this effectively, they prepare for their social interactions the same way an actor would prepare for a performance. They practice the role they expect to play. They select their costume carefully, so it will convey the right image. They pay careful attention to the cues they get from others, to see if their performance is succeeding. They improvise when their performance is not succeeding, or when it takes an unexpected turn.

Goffman made an important distinction between front-stage and backstage actions in the presentation of self. The front stage is where our social interactions take place. As actors in social life, we are always aware of the fact that we are being watched when we interact with others. We take notice of the setting where the interaction takes place, and we do everything we can to present ourselves in a particular way. But there is also action and preparation that takes place backstage, where we can step out of character and prepare for our front-stage performance without fear of ruining our presentation of self.

David Grazian captures the theatrical qualities of social life in his book *On the Make*, which is a study of nightlife in Philadelphia (Grazian 2008). As Grazian describes it,

> Table servers, bartenders, hostesses, cocktail waitresses, sommeliers, and exotic dancers draw on studiously rehearsed scripts when interacting with customers. Publicists fabricate anniversaries, celebrations, and other pseudo-events in order to artificially boost the exposure and popularity of otherwise fledgling restaurants and nightspots, while female "reality marketers" serve their clients by posing as ordinary patrons with the single-minded purpose of engineering an exciting atmosphere electrified by the staged allure of sexual abandon and nocturnal pleasure. (p. 227)

Nightlife
Urban nightlife is a complicated and theatrical social space, where people are actors as well as spectators.

The young people who attend these nightspots are just as careful in their backstage preparations (Grazian 2008: 95–133). Women wear revealing clothing, spend hours doing their hair and makeup, and try to present themselves with a "more sophisticated" look in order to gain admission into exclusive nightclubs. Men prepare just as carefully, donning expensive jeans and shoes that they only wear when they go to the clubs, and spending much more time than usual on their personal grooming. Men and women both prepare for their night out by getting together with their friends for "pregaming," which consists of drinking and devising strategies for increasing their odds of getting into the clubs. They may even create fake identities, with stories about one another that can be used when talking with strangers in the clubs.

As a theatrical performance, our presentation of self needs the cooperation of others to be successful. Most of the time, people go along with our presentation of self, because they don't want to embarrass us, or because they know that they also rely on others to go along with their own presentations of self. But there is no guarantee that our performances will succeed. People might misinterpret or deliberately reject our performances. When Grazian interviewed bouncers for his research, they thought that most college students were naïve kids who didn't deserve admission into the club. This made it difficult for those students to present themselves as sophisticated and trendy.

Social Interaction in a Digital Age

The amount of time people spend using media technologies to interact with each other has increased dramatically over the last 20 years. According to the Pew Research Center, 92 percent of teenagers go online daily, and 24 percent say that they are online "almost constantly" (Lenhart 2015). Social media networks have a major impact on socialization and group life.

Many of us have experienced the effects that digital media have on social interactions. As soon as class ends, most students (and teachers) immediately reach for their phones to check their email, text messages, and other social media. We increasingly turn to Facebook and Twitter to get our news. Internet forums allow us to interact with other people in complete anonymity, and also allow us to try on different personas and pretend we are anyone we want to be.

Power and Resistance

Challenging Gender Stereotypes with the SlutWalk Campaign

In an attempt to reduce sexual assaults, police have been known to warn women that wearing sexually provocative clothing may attract the wrong kind of attention. In a 2011 meeting with college students, for example, Toronto police officer Michael Sanguinetti said that women who wanted to prevent being raped should "avoid dressing like sluts." Sanguinetti later apologized for his statement and was disciplined by the Toronto Police Department, but his comments sparked a worldwide movement of "SlutWalks."

The women who organized the first SlutWalk in Toronto were fed up with the "blame the victim" mentality that surrounded sexual assault cases. They argued that women who were assaulted were victims, regardless of their self-presentation. "The idea that there is some aesthetic that attracts sexual assault or even keeps you safe from sexual assault is inaccurate, ineffective, and even dangerous," said Heather Jarvis, who was one of the co-organizers of the initial SlutWalk in Toronto (Stampler 2011).

The objective of the SlutWalk was to publicly challenge the idea that women who dressed a certain way were to blame if they were victims of sexual assault. Some women attended the protest wearing jeans and T-shirts, while others wore bikinis, fishnet stockings, stiletto heels, and other costumes. Participants gave speeches promoting women's empowerment and carried signs against victim blaming, and survivors shared their testimonies. There were nearly three thousand participants in the first Toronto SlutWalk, and the movement spread to cities throughout the world. Facebook groups have sprouted up in connection with the walks, with the goal of creating a global dialogue where women can feel comfortable discussing sexual assault without fear of blame.

SlutWalk
The SlutWalk protest challenges the cultural idea expressed by police officials and many others that women deserve to experience violence if they dress a certain way.

ACTIVE LEARNING

Discuss: Do you think the clothes we wear send social messages to others? In particular, do they send messages about gender to others? How do you think the women who organized the SlutWalk campaign wanted to challenge or disrupt those messages?

In her book *Life on the Screen: Identity in the Age of the Internet* (1996), the sociologist Sherry Turkle examined how computers and the internet were changing how people thought about themselves and their identities. She found that digital media allow us to communicate and form relationships with anyone in the world. The fictional characters we inhabit in virtual role-playing games are just as meaningful to us as the identities we inhabit and present in "real" social life. In fact, Turkle argues, these virtual identities can play an important therapeutic role, because they encourage us to see that we can be many different selves, and that none of those alternate selves is any more or less "real" than the others. This was the main point of Goffman's s dramaturgical theory: we are always playing a role in social interaction. We are always performing.

More recently, Turkle has expressed a concern that our interactions in the digital world might be damaging our ability to form meaningful social relationships. The reason is that virtual relationships are less demanding than real friendships. In her book *Alone Together: Why We Expect More from Technology and Less from Each Other* (2011), Turkle calls this the "Goldilocks effect" of social media. We want to have social relationships, but only on our terms.

Others are worried that social media encourage us to be less tolerant in our social interactions. We are all familiar with the internet troll, who posts deliberately inflammatory material with the sole purpose of upsetting people and turning every discussion into a flame war. In his book *Republic.com* (2001), Cass Sunstein argues that internet forums encourage social polarization, by allowing people to be exposed only to things that interest them and to people who agree with them. As these like-minded people interact, they encourage each other to develop more extreme versions of the positions they already hold. These developments threaten democracy, Sunstein argues, because they make it less likely that we will respect different beliefs or join groups where people hold views that are different from our own.

Together alone and online
Are digital interactions easier than face-to-face relationships?

Group Life

Most of our social interaction takes place in groups, and social learning occurs in groups. Some of these groups consist of people we know very well, while others consist of casual acquaintances and others are made up of people who have never met each other. Groups can be loosely organized and informally regulated, or they can be complex, formal organizations with official rules and procedures. Taken together, the groups we belong to affect who we become, and what opportunities we have in our lives.

Group Size

The number of people in a group has a major influence on the behavior of its members, independent of any other characteristics of the group. For instance, a **dyad** (a group of two people) is fundamentally different than any other kind of group. The sociologist Georg Simmel (1858–1918) argued that a dyad is the most unstable kind of group, because the withdrawal of even one person will destroy its existence. Dyads are intensely personal, because there is no way to shift responsibility or attention onto a third person. The romantic couple is the classic example of the dyad.

Dyad A group of two people with one relationship.

As soon as a group becomes a **triad**, consisting of three people, then group dynamics get a lot more complicated. Triads have more stability, because when two of its members have a conflict they can appeal to the third person to help resolve the situation. Triads also develop more complicated power dynamics than dyads. One of the members can deliberately create conflicts between the other two, or alliances can form, where two of the members agree to isolate the third. For children, an important part of their socialization involves learning how to navigate the power dynamics that exist in triads and larger groups.

Triad A group of three people with three relationships.

Solidarity and Conflict

The Stanford Prison Experiment

The Stanford Prison Experiment is one of the most famous social psychology experiments of the 20th century. The study was conducted in 1971 by Stanford psychology professor Philip Zimbardo. Funded by the US Office of Naval Research, the goal of the study was to learn about how conflicts develop between military guards and prisoners. Specifically, the researchers wanted to know whether abusive behavior was caused by the social setting of the prison or the inherent personality characteristics of the guards.

In the study, 24 male students were randomly assigned the role of prisoner or guard, and placed in a makeshift prison that had been created in the basement of the campus psychology building. The prison simulation was designed to last two weeks. Guards worked for eight-hour shifts, and were allowed to go home when they were not on duty. Prisoners had to remain in the prison during the entire period of the study. Prisoners were given identification numbers, and they were only allowed to refer to themselves or to other prisoners by using these numbers.

Trouble began on the second day of the experiment, when some of the prisoners began to taunt the guards, refusing to follow instructions or come out of their cells. In order to force compliance, guards attacked the prisoners with fire extinguishers. From this point forward, guards used physical and psychological harassment in order to maintain control. Prisoners were forced to do pushups for minor rules violations. Guards removed mattresses from some of the cells, forcing prisoners to sleep on the concrete. Other prisoners were denied access to bathroom facilities, and were limited to the use of a bucket placed next to their beds. Guards became increasingly sadistic, and prisoners exhibited signs of extreme stress. The experiment was ended after six days.

Today, the Stanford Prison Experiment is considered an ethically flawed study, because it neither adequately protected its research subjects, nor did enough to ensure informed consent. But the experiment showed clearly how social settings that create in-groups and out-groups also produce solidarity and conflict. The prisoners and the guards in the study internalized their roles, bonding with other members of their group and quickly growing to dislike the members of the other group. The research study also showed how in-group and out-group conflicts are shaped by differences in power. Having all the power in the situation, the guards were able to morally distance themselves from their actions by dehumanizing the prisoners.

While the Stanford Prison Experiment was an artificially created research study with serious design flaws (Blum 2018), similar dynamics have developed in real-world prison contexts. When Amnesty International publicized the physical and psychological abuse of war prisoners committed by US soldiers at the Abu Ghraib

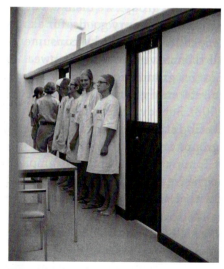

Prison Roles
Even though students knew the experiment was role-play, results suggested that even the experimental prison culture that was created altered people's behavior in negative ways.

Stanford Prison Experiment, 1971
The Stanford Prison Experiment divided students into guards and prisoners.

prison in Iraq in 2003, Zimbardo argued that the social factors that led his research subjects to act like sadistic prison guards were the same ones that led the military guards to act the way they did. Zimbardo appeared as an expert witness for one of the defendants in the Abu Ghraib trial, and he wrote about the similarities between Abu Ghraib and the Stanford Prison Experiment in his best-selling 2007 book, *The Lucifer Effect: Understanding How Good People Turn Evil.*

ACTIVE LEARNING

Think about it: Given findings from the Stanford Prison Experiment, what kind of training and support do you think prison guards need?

The relationship between in-groups and out-groups offers a powerful demonstration of the paired concept of solidarity and conflict. In order to feel pride in our in-group, we need an out-group to look down upon. In-group solidarity grows stronger by drawing clear boundaries that exclude members of out-groups. This boundary drawing and exclusion creates social tension between in-groups and out-groups, increasing the likelihood of conflict. This dynamic can be seen in relatively harmless contexts, such as rivalries between sports teams, as well as far deadlier conflicts stemming from ethnic and religious divisions.

Social inequality influences how in-groups and out-groups form. It is common for people to look at powerful and privileged groups as positive reference groups to be emulated, and to think about less privileged groups as negative reference groups that should be avoided. Dominant in-groups define what counts as normal and desirable in society, often by identifying specific out-groups as abnormal or undesirable. The members of those stigmatized out-groups get treated as less valuable, and are often subjected to humiliating social interactions that injure their self-respect (Margalit 1996). Historically, racial, ethnic, religious, and sexual minorities have been targeted as stigmatized out-groups. Other stigmatized out-groups who have suffered humiliation and exclusion include people with physical and mental disabilities (Goffman 1963), the homeless (Phelan et al. 1997), refugee groups (Bauman 2003), and people who are obese (Saguy 2014).

Bureaucracy in Group Life

Groups can be organized in different ways with different consequences for group life. A **bureaucracy** is an organized group with a clearly defined hierarchy, specific rules and procedures that govern every aspect of group life, and official documentation of everything considered important. Leadership in a bureaucracy follows a clear organizational structure and hierarchy of managers and workers. People know who they are reporting to, and what their specific responsibilities are. This is also true in military bureaucracies and in the civil service where there is a clear line of report or an explicit chain of command.

Bureaucracies have many advantages for group life. They define statuses and role expectations clearly, and by sorting jobs into departments based on specific tasks, workers are placed into groups of people who have similar knowledge, skills, and resources. This enables people to do their work within the

Bureaucracy An organized group with a clearly defined hierarchy that relies on specific written rules and procedures to govern every aspect of the organization.

Against bureaucratic cultures
In the tech industry, bureaucracy has come to be seen as the enemy of success and innovation. Many of today's tech companies try to design their offices in a way that they believe will encourage innovation and creativity.

Moral indifference When we distance ourselves from the consequences of our actions for others.

Social network A group organized through social ties between individuals that works through the connections that link individuals to one another.

consequences of their actions. This is a key feature of bureaucracy, which insists that decisions get made according to specific rules and "without regards to persons" (Weber 1958: 269). But the unintended consequence of this impersonal decision-making is that it encourages **moral indifference**, which happens when we distance ourselves from the consequences of our actions. In a bureaucracy, we treat people as categories and we treat every situation in terms of the appropriate rule that is supposed to apply. This is not a situation that encourages us to care about the well-being of others.

In his book *Modernity and the Holocaust* (1989), Zygmunt Bauman (1925–2017) reminds us that most of the perpetrators of the Holocaust during World War II were bureaucrats. The number of people who actually fired rifles at Jewish children and dropped poison into gas chambers was relatively small. The majority of people involved were sitting at their desks drawing up blueprints, composing memoranda, and talking on the telephone. They never had to see their victims, and they never considered whether the orders they were following were right or wrong. In fact, when the high-ranking Nazi leader Adolf Eichmann was brought to trial in 1961 for crimes against humanity, his defense was that he was "just following orders."

We experience the moral indifference of bureaucracy in our everyday lives. We are frustrated but not surprised when bureaucrats insist on strictly following the rules when they are dealing with us, and when they ignore any special circumstances that might get them to make an exception for us.

In Silicon Valley, the home of technology giants such as Apple and Google, bureaucracy has come to be seen as the enemy of success and innovation. In place of an older bureaucratic model, these companies are creating more decentralized networks, in order to encourage collaboration, allow people to try out new solutions to problems, and take greater responsibility for their actions.

Social Networks in Group Life

Networks are another form of organized group life. One familiar example of a network phenomenon is a social media post, or meme, that goes viral. The most popular memes get shared by hundreds of millions of people. This kind of sharing and connection happens through social networks.

A **social network** is a set of connections that link individuals to one another. Today, when we think of social networks we usually think of social media such as YouTube, Facebook, Twitter, or Instagram. But social networks existed long before the invention of the internet, and the study of social networks has always been an important part of sociology. In fact, Simmel's discussion of dyads and triads was arguably the first study of network structure and the social relationships they enable.

A network is held together by social ties between individuals. These ties can vary in intensity, from strong to weak. We have strong ties with our family and friends, and we generally have weaker ties with our neighbors, classmates, and coworkers. Each network will have its own structure, depending on how the different social ties are organized. Some individuals may occupy a position of **network centrality**, which means that they have direct ties with a lot of people in the network, while others may be only indirectly connected to a few people.

Networks influence all aspects of social life. In politics, people who have a position of network centrality are more easily able to influence the opinions of other people in the network (Katz and Lazarsfeld 1955; Rossi et al., 2016). In the business world, a new product or idea is more likely to be successful when there are early adopters who have high social status or high levels of education and positions of network centrality (Rogers 1962). People who want to be entrepreneurs are more likely to be successful if they can broker a connection between two different networks that do not share any ties (Burt 1995). Networks even influence our health and well-being (Clark, Algoe, and Green 2017). If your friend's friend's friend loses weight, you are likely to lose weight, too, even if you have never met them and they live hundreds of miles away from you (Christakis and Fowler 2009).

> **Network centrality** A network position with many individual direct ties with many people in the network, or someone who is highly influential in a network.

SOCIAL NETWORKS IN A DIGITAL AGE. The world of social media is a world of networks. How do these online social networks influence the rest of our social lives? Initially, there was a general concern that social media would isolate us from the "real world," allowing us to stay at home in our pajamas, abandoning our close friends in favor of virtual communities and online networks. But the picture that has emerged is more complicated. According to the Pew Research Center, people who use social networking sites have more close ties and are less likely to be socially isolated than the average American (Pew Research Center 2018). Facebook users are more politically engaged than the average American. Facebook also makes it possible for people to revive and maintain the distant, weak, and indirect ties that are so useful in the job market. Overall, the internet appears to help build **social capital**, which refers to the group ties and network attachments people have and the sense of trust and security that they get from their group memberships and network attachments.

> **Social capital** Group ties and network attachments people have and the sense of trust and security that they get from their group memberships and network attachments.

Social media
Facebook and other social media have become an important way of creating and maintaining our social networks. Are Facebook networks different than networks IRL (in real life)? How?

Getting a Job: The Strength of Weak Ties

If you are trying to get a job, it always helps to be related to the boss. This is an example of a strong network tie. But strong ties embedded within dense networks are not the only resources that are useful. In fact, in one of the most important sociological findings of the last 40 years, Mark Granovetter found that weak ties are particularly helpful in securing a job.

In his book *Getting a Job: A Study of Contacts and Careers* (1974), Granovetter studied 282 men in the United States, in order to discover how they got their jobs. He found that people relied mainly on their social contacts to get information about professional job opportunities, rather than using more formal resources such as job postings or employment agencies. Most social contacts came from family or work. Surprisingly, the social contacts that people saw the most frequently were not the ones who provided the most useful information. Rather, the most helpful contacts were the people they saw occasionally (more than once a year but less than twice a week). People they saw once a year or less were more useful social contacts than people they saw every week (Granovetter 1973: 1371).

How can these weak ties be so useful? The answer is that the weaker and more indirect ties in our network travel in different circles than we do. Because of this, they have access to information we do not have. By comparison, our close friends and relatives are much less likely to bring us new information. Not only do we see them all the time, but they also have strong direct ties with our other close friends and family members. In this kind of dense network, people tell the same stories, and the information they share is fully contained within the network. Strong ties can still be important career resources, but only by linking us with their friends, the friends of their friends, and so forth. In fact, Granovetter (1973: 1372) found that chance encounters with friends of friends often yielded surprising new information that people used to get a new job. Weak ties are an important source of useful new information, and they are what make social networks so powerful (Miller 2016; Grant 2014).

Networking
Our social networks are an important source of information about good jobs.

ACTIVE LEARNING

Find out: Who is central in your social network? How do you know? Can you tell by looking at your Facebook or LinkedIn account or your phone? Do you have a lot of weak ties? Do you maintain them? How?

The online media and digital technology that organize many of today's social networks are not equally available to everyone. The poorest people in our society are less likely to have internet access. Older populations are less likely to use Facebook or other social networking sites. As social networks increasingly use social media to communicate and maintain their social ties, these vulnerable populations become more socially isolated. Expensive data plans and high-speed internet connections that are required to use these newer media technologies create a serious risk that the media-augmented social networks will end up reproducing inequality and privilege.

Caitlyn Jenner and Gender Socialization

Media systems do not inevitably cause inequality, but they often shape and amplify existing inequalities. This is evident in the story of Caitlyn Jenner's 2015 transition from a man to a woman. Using the five paired concepts, we consider what Jenner's story tells us about socialization and group life.

By dubbing her the most famous transgender woman in the world, the cultural media response to Jenner's story of changing gender was generally positive. Jenner was congratulated and commended in popular magazines; on current affairs, news, and television talk shows; and on social media platforms. She was awarded the 2015 Arthur Ashe Courage Award at the ESPY (Excellence in Sports Performance Yearly) Awards sponsored by ESPN and ABC. In all these forums, Jenner made clear that she was a person with *power* who was using her relative privilege and position to *resist* traditional gender hierarchies to express *solidarity* with transgender people and other sexual minorities. Her expressed aim was to use her celebrity to resocialize broad publics around gender issues.

As many critics have pointed out, however, the sympathetic response to Jenner's story is inextricably bound up with her status as a wealthy, *privileged* celebrity. As a man, Bruce Jenner had won Olympic gold for America as a decathlete in the 1970s. As the father of six children, he later found fame as an author and media personality, most notoriously on the reality show *Keeping Up with the Kardashians*. Unlike other transgender people who might struggle with the financial cost of gender reassignment surgery and the cultural stigma of being a gender minority, Jenner had access not only to economic resources but also to the means of symbolic production. She exercised a great deal of control over how and where her story was told by carefully arranging positive publicity through sympathetic interviews and glamorous photo shoots. The *inequality* and subordination other transgender people routinely suffer were not as evident in Jenner's case. Moreover, as CNN reporter Emanuella Grinburg (2015) pointed out, Jenner's story and the visibility she brought to trans issues did not automatically make other trans people safer or more economically secure.

Jenner's resistance of gender scripts in group life, and her attempt to change the out-group status of trans people, also were not *globally* accepted. While Jenner was an Olympic champion and an influential, well-known American television personality in a global media landscape, her story remained culturally specific and *local*. Most sympathetic media coverage occurred in North America (and to some extent in Europe). Jenner's story had a much more limited appeal in other countries, with most international newspapers offering little coverage beyond a single story. Although the reality television show covering Jenner's transition, *I Am Cait* (2015–2016), was banned in Nigeria and later removed from the air across Africa (Morales 2016), international news coverage of these negative reactions remained muted. Within the United States, conservative politicians and commentators resisted the credibility and appropriateness of Jenner's narrative, rejecting the idea that gender scripts can be rewritten. As former heavyweight boxing champion Evander Holyfield said after Caitlyn Jenner received her ESPY award, "I just know that's Bruce Jenner, and I'll leave it at that" (ESPN 2015).

A different set of critics, including feminists, have also been cautious in parsing the impact of Jenner's story on the public conversation about women, inequality, and trans people. These critics observe that Jenner's performance of womanhood is extremely traditional and upholds an unattainable appearance-based standard for women. They emphasize that Jenner was born and socialized as a boy, enacted masculine gender scripts, and successfully lived and interacted as a man for most of her life. The implication is that her male socialization does not fully equip her to understand the lived consequences of being a woman. Still others have pointed out that Jenner enjoys wealth, power, and respect that other transgender people do not, and that she seems unaware of the issues of class, power, and sex discrimination that less privileged people confront in their everyday interactions. Other gender critics argue that the media focus on Jenner's story has institutionalized an overly narrow understanding of trans people that reduces all trans experience to the single issue of surgical transition from a male to a female body that fits into traditional gender categories. In all these ways, Jenner's story sheds light on underlying cultural *conflicts* about gender and gender socialization and their intersections with wealth, privilege, and celebrity in American society.

Last, Jenner's story raises enduring questions about the degree to which social *structures* constrain or enable us. Agents of socialization, including the family, school, peer groups, and the media, created expectations around sex and gender that Bruce Jenner followed successfully for much of his life. What Caitlyn Jenner's story shows clearly, however, is the flexibility of these structures. Despite a successful life as a man, Jenner was able to resist and eventually change the gender she was assigned at birth, a fact that testifies to the *contingency* of socialization. Jenner's argument that she is now who "she was truly meant to be" reverses a commonsense understanding of the relationship between structure

and contingency to assert that gender institutions, gendered scripts for interaction, and agents of socialization are themselves contingent.

These questions of how far structures constrain us, and how much our actions can change structures, is at the heart of the following discussions of social inequality organized around class, race, and gender, and the complex intersections among these dimensions of inequality.

LEARNING GOALS REVISITED

5.1 Define socialization and the process of normalization.

- The process of growing up and learning how to live in society is called socialization. Socialization refers to the ways that we learn about our society's beliefs, values, and expected behaviors. It begins when we are infants and continues throughout our lives. Socialization is an interactive process, where we are helping to socialize others at the same time that we are being socialized ourselves.

- The social environment and our biology interact to determine who we become as human beings.

- The looking-glass self refers to the way the social self is developed by using society as a mirror—a looking glass.

- Children progress through stages of development in which they learn to take on the roles of other people until they develop the generalized other, which is the internalized norms and expectations of society.

- Normalization is the way that social standards of normal behavior get used to judge people and to reform those who are determined not to be normal. Normalization can be something that happens to you, but it is also something you do to yourself.

5.2 Identify the primary agents of socialization that operate over the life course.

- There are five primary agents of socialization: family, school, peer groups, media, and the workplace. Each operates with varying degrees of influence over the life course.

- Socialization and social learning also occur over the life course as people refine their sense of self, learn new things, and undergo processes of resocialization.

- Total institutions (like prisons or the military) effectively resocialize their members into the norms and expectations of those institutions.

5.3 Understand the difference between a status and a role and describe how interactional performances sustain the social self.

- A status is a specific social position, and a role is a set of expected behaviors associated with that status. An individual *occupies* a status and *plays* a role.

- An ascribed status is something that is assigned to people by society, while an achieved status is something that can be earned.

- Role strain occurs when the different expected behaviors associated with a single status are in tension with one another. Role conflict happens when there are competing expectations coming from more than one status.

- People perform their social self in social interaction and construct social life in the same process. In interaction, individuals display their own statuses and cultural understandings; engage with the statuses and cultural understandings of others; and co-construct social meanings and social life.

- Group life cannot exist without social interaction and the accomplishment and performance of our social selves.

5.4   Define groups and distinguish different kinds of groups.

- Groups are collections of individuals and vary in size from very small two-person dyads to millions of people.

- As groups grow in size, the number of relationships they contain increases exponentially and becomes highly complex.

- Primary groups are small groups based on face-to-face interaction, while secondary groups are larger, more impersonal, and usually organized around a specific activity or interest.

- A reference group is any group that people use to help define how they fit in society by providing standards we can use to measure ourselves.

- An in-group is a reference group that a person is connected to in a positive way and feels bonded to, while an out-group is a reference group toward which a person has a negative connection.

5.5   Distinguish networks from bureaucracies as distinct organizational forms of group life in modern societies.

- A bureaucracy is an organized group with a clearly defined hierarchy that relies on specific written rules and procedures to govern every aspect of the organization.

- A social network is a group organized through social ties between individuals and works through the connections that link individuals to one another. Network ties can vary in intensity, from strong to weak. Networks are more decentralized than bureaucracies and tend to have flatter authority structures.

- Bureaucracies can foster moral indifference because they treat people as categories and understand every situation in terms of the appropriate rules that are supposed to apply.

- Influence in networks is defined through network centrality—a network position with many individual direct ties to many people in the network.

- Social capital refers to the group ties and network attachments people have and the sense of trust and security that they get from their group memberships and network attachments.

Key Terms

Achieved status 126
Agents of socialization 119
Ascribed status 126
Bureaucracy 135
Code-switching 128
Dramaturgical theory 128
Dyad 131
Ego 119
Game stage 118
Generalized other 118
Generation 122
Hidden curriculum 120
Id 118
In-group 133
Looking-glass self 117
Moral indifference 138
Network centrality 139
Normalization 119
Organizational culture 136

Review Questions

1. What is the difference between a role and a status?

2. Compare and contrast the difference between bureaucracy and a network as a form of group life.

3. In what ways can bureaucracies foster moral indifference?

4. Why did Simmel think dyads were less stable than triads?

5. How might parents suffer from role strain or role conflict?

6. When is an in-group a reference group?

7. Briefly describe Erving Goffman's dramaturgical theory of society.

8. What is the difference between an ascribed and an achieved status?

9. Does college have a hidden curriculum? What is it?

10. What is the generalized other and why is it important?

11. What is the relationship between the looking-glass self and the social self?

12. What is the superego and how is it related to the ego?

13. What is resocialization and when does it happen?

Explore

RECOMMENDED READINGS

Freud, Sigmund. [1930] 2010. *Civilization and Its Discontents.* New York: W. W. Norton.

Gitlin, Todd. [2002] 2007. *Media Unlimited: How the Torrent of Images and Sounds Overwhelms Our Lives (Revised Edition).* New York: Picador.

Grazian, David. 2008. *On the Make: The Hustle of Urban Nightlife.* Chicago: University of Chicago Press.

Herbert Mead, George. 1967. *Mind, Self and Society.* Chicago: University of Chicago Press.

Illouz, Eva. 2008. *Saving the Modern Soul: Therapy, Emotions and the Culture of Self-Help.* Berkeley: University of California Press.

Lareau, Annette. 2011. *Unequal Childhoods: Class, Race, and Family Life, 2nd Edition with an Update a Decade Later.* Berkeley: University of California Press.

Tatum, Beverly. 2003. *"Why Are All the Black Kids Sitting Together in the Cafeteria?" and Other Conversations about Race.* New York: Basic Books.

Turkle, Sherry. 1995. *Life on the Screen: Identity in the Age of the Internet.* New York: Simon & Schuster.

Turkle, Sherry. 2011. *Alone Together: Why We Expect More from Technology and Less from Each Other.* New York: Basic Books.

ACTIVITIES

- *Use your sociological imagination*: What do you think the similarities and differences are between the process in which you were socialized and those of people in your parents' generation?

- *Media+ Data literacies*: How do people who did not grow up with personal computers, the internet or smart phones learn how to use them?

- *Discuss*: In what ways can bureaucracies foster moral indifference? Do you think social networks also foster moral indifference? Why or why not?

For additional resources, including Media+Data Literacy exercises, In the News exercises, and quizzes, please go to **oup.com/he/ Jacobs-Townsley1e**

6

Deviance, Crime, and Punishment

In 2012, a woman in Beverly, Massachusetts, was sentenced to serve six months in prison for providing alcohol to teenagers during a party at her house. It was the first time in the state that somebody had received a jail sentence for violating the "social host law" in a case where a fatality was not involved. When the sentence was announced, the district attorney explained that the case "sends a clear message to adults who think they can control a gathering of underage drinkers or that by providing young people with a place to drink that they are keeping them safe" (Arsenault 2012).

The district attorney claimed that the laws regulating underage drinking were clear, and that they were necessary to protect children, but the truth is a little more complicated. Most states, including Massachusetts, allow parents to serve wine to their children during religious ceremonies. Other countries have much more relaxed laws about underage drinking. In England, children can begin drinking with their parents in restaurants once they turn 16. In France and Italy, there is no age restriction for children drinking with their parents. All three of these countries have less of a problem with adolescent binge drinking than the United States does. In fact, a 2004 study in the *Journal of Adolescent Health* found that children whose parents introduced drinking to them at home were significantly less likely to develop problems with binge drinking and alcoholism (Foley et al. 2004).

Why are Americans more worried than people in other parts of the world about underage drinking? Why is underage drinking viewed as a social problem, while adult drinking is viewed by many people as normal? How do people decide what counts as "normal drinking" and what counts as "problem drinking"? How do societies respond to drinking problems? Do they rely on criminal prosecution, education,

Scales of justice
A metaphor of balance and fairness, the scales of justice convey the application of law, regardless of privilege or favor. Do you think the scales are a fitting image to describe justice? Why or why not?

LEARNING GOALS

6.1   Define deviance and understand the social functions of deviance.

6.2   Distinguish between deviance, crime, and punishment.

6.3   Understand that deviance is socially constructed.

6.4   Distinguish different categories of crime and the challenges of measuring crime.

treatment, or social pressure? Are these social responses standardized, or do they vary depending on social factors such as race, class, age, and gender?

This chapter explores how some actions get defined as normal, while others are seen as dangerous. We begin with a discussion of **deviance**, which consists of any behavior that is outside social boundaries for what counts as normal and acceptable. We consider the social construction of deviance, what the existence of deviance does for society, and what the consequences are for people who get labeled as deviant. We then explore **crime**, which is deviant behavior that is defined and regulated by law. Here, we consider different types of crime as well as the different organizations that are responsible for enforcing the laws and prosecuting criminal offenders. Finally, we explore the different ways that crime is punished.

Deviance Any behavior that is outside social boundaries for what counts as normal and acceptable.

Crime Deviant behavior that is defined and regulated by law.

Deviance

The boundaries that distinguish normal behavior from deviant behavior are socially constructed. They are shaped by our culture, learned during our ongoing socialization, and reinforced in our everyday interactions. It is usually easy to tell when we do something that other people think is deviant. They may give us a stern look, stand back from us, or say something to us. If they think our deviance is serious enough, they may even call the police.

What counts as deviant behavior depends on the social context. Things that are considered deviant in some places or at some times are considered normal in others. Americans visiting China are often shocked at the driving behaviors they find, most of which would be considered highly deviant in the United States. Cutting people off, swerving into oncoming traffic, running red lights, driving on the sidewalk, and driving the wrong way down a divided highway are perfectly acceptable in China, as long as it keeps traffic moving. Visitors to Japan are often surprised to see people wearing

Deviance has a context
In Japan, it is considered impolite not to wear a mask in public if you are sick.

Structure and Contingency

Is Chewing Gum Deviant?

The context of chewing gum
Barack Obama chews nicotine gum as a way to control the urge to smoke. Do you think his gum chewing breaches social expectations? Is it an important breach?

The mass production of chewing gum began in the 1860s, when the former president of Mexico, Antonio López de Santa Anna, brought a substance called *chicle* with him on a trip to New York. Following a practice that had begun centuries earlier with the Mayans and the Aztecs, Santa Anna used the chicle, derived from the sap of a tree, as a chewing gum.

While many adults in Mexico chewed chicle just like Santa Anna, public gum chewing by adults had been viewed as a deviant act in 16th-century Aztec society where the practice originated. The Aztecs thought that men who chewed chicle in public were effeminate, and that the women who did this were sexually promiscuous (Matthews 2009). Most Aztec adults did chew chicle in private, but they avoided doing so publicly so they would not be labeled as deviants.

Thomas Adams, an American inventor who was working with Santa Anna, did not know about the history of chicle in Aztec society, nor did he know about the social meanings that Aztecs attached to public gum chewing. In fact, Adams did not even think about chicle as a source of chewing gum. Initially, he tried to transform chicle into a rubber substitute that could be used for tires. When this failed, he used it to create a chewing gum product. His Chiclets chewing gum proved to be very popular with American consumers. Adams soon partnered with William Wrigley, and helped create the Wrigley gum empire.

In the early years of the industry, Americans thought that chewing gum was a woman's activity, but Wrigley aggressively marketed his product to men. Wrigley organized the first-ever nationwide direct-marketing campaign in 1915, mailing sticks of gum to every address listed in the US phone book. By the 1920s, the average American was chewing more than a hundred pieces of gum per year. Wrigley also gave free gum to US soldiers during World War I, using this marketing strategy to associate his product with masculinity and patriotism. The "gum-chewing soldier" became a global ambassador for the product, and in much of Europe the practice of chewing gum came to be associated with American culture.

But gum chewing continued to be considered a deviant activity in certain places. In France, gum chewing has often been viewed alongside Hollywood films and comic books as an uncivilized feature of American culture that any self-respecting French citizen would want to avoid (Kuisel 1996). In Singapore, the government passed a law in 1992 that banned the use, distribution, and sale of chewing gum. People caught selling gum in Singapore face fines of up to $100,000, and prison sentences of up to two years. The law against gum is presented as evidence of Singapore's commitment to efficiency and cleanliness.

Sometimes, gum chewing is only seen as a deviant activity in specific contexts. In 2014, President Obama was criticized throughout China for chewing gum during the Asia Pacific Economic Cooperation Summit in Beijing. As a former cigarette smoker, Obama often chewed Nicorette gum as a way to control his smoking urges. But the Chinese press criticized Obama's behavior as disrespectful toward Chinese leaders and inappropriate for a formal political event. Obama was criticized for the same behavior during a 2014 visit to France and a 2015 visit to India.

ACTIVE LEARNING

Find out: Are there times and places that chewing gum is inappropriate? List two such times or places. Compare your list to your classmates'. Can you see any patterns?

surgical masks in public places; in fact, in Japan it is considered to be very inconsiderate not to wear a mask if you are sick. In Virginia, by comparison, it is illegal to wear a mask in public, and if you want to wear a surgical mask you have to carry a doctor's note that explains why it is necessary.

The boundary that distinguishes the normal from the deviant often changes over time. When Harvard University opened in 1636, breakfast consisted of bread and beer; today, this same breakfast would be a violation of the university's alcohol policy, and it would land you in the school's counseling center so someone could discuss your drinking problem with you. The behavior that used to be normal is now a deviant act that requires intervention. Things also change in the opposite direction, from deviant to normal. In the early 20th century, women who went to the beach in the United States were expected to wear long one-piece garments as well as stockings, and if they did not do so they ran the risk of being arrested. These laws and social norms no longer exist, and today women's swimwear is an $8 billion global industry.

Why Does Deviance Exist?

Deviance exists in every society, despite social efforts to combat and control deviance. Sociologists, however, argue that societies *need* deviance. The presence of deviance helps reinforce the boundaries between acceptable and unacceptable behavior, and in the process it sets the standard for what is normal. Deviance is an important part of our ongoing socialization, and an important source of social change. Many of the most innovative and revolutionary figures in history were considered to be highly deviant and even dangerous in their own times. Social change, after all, requires that people decide to do things that are not normal.

THE SOCIAL FUNCTIONS OF DEVIANCE. Émile Durkheim was the first sociologist to notice that deviance exists in all societies. As he argued in *The Rules of Sociological Method*, crime and deviance are basic features of a healthy society (Durkheim 1982: 98–103). Just like our bodies need pain and sickness to help establish boundaries of healthy and unhealthy behavior, Durkheim argued, societies need crime and deviance to establish social boundaries. If your knee starts hurting, this is a sign that maybe you need to exercise a little less. If people are glaring at you, it is a sign that you might need to control your behavior.

In our everyday socialization, deviance helps us draw boundaries. Parents, schools, peers, and media tell us what they expect of us, but they also highlight examples of behavior that is "over the line." The line is always moving, as social norms change and behaviors that used to be punished begin to pass unnoticed. There is no handbook for us to consult to see how these norms are changing. Deviance functions as a substitute for that handbook. This is why psychologists say it is normal for children to test the rules and boundaries that adults set for them. In their everyday interactions, kids see that the boundaries are often changing, and not always enforced consistently. There is a **zone of permitted variation** around the rules, and it is in this zone that much experimentation and change can occur.

While it is natural for us to test these boundaries in order for us to know the limits, we are still expected to develop enough self-control so that we will avoid getting into trouble. According to **social control theory**, people who have strong social bonds and attachments in their community are less likely

Zone of permitted variation
A social space around a boundary where rules can be contested.

Social control theory A theory that people who have strong social bonds and attachments in their community are less likely to engage in deviant behavior.

Moral panic When an event, situation, individual, or group comes to be defined as a threat to social values.

Solidarity and Conflict

The Moral Panic over School Bullying

Sociologist and criminologist Stanley Cohen defines a **moral panic** as a situation in which a "condition, episode, a person or group of persons emerges to become defined as a threat to societal values and interests" (Cohen 2002: 1). According to Cohen, moral panics have a number of common features, and they develop in a similar way. First, there is an event that captures public attention and gets defined as a serious threat to society. The sense of danger increases when "moral crusaders" enter the scene, and begin to demonize the offenders and stoke the sense of outrage. Moral crusaders are important because they manufacture a feeling of public danger that is out of proportion to the actual threat (Hall et al. 1978). This encourages media to sensationalize the story. Politicians and police further define the threat and suggest solutions. The public follows along closely, swept up in all the excitement and drama. Interest in the episode eventually subsides, but not before reinforcing specific cultural values and marking the limits of social tolerance.

School bullying provides a good example of a social problem that enters the public consciousness through moral panic. Bullying is a concern for many parents and educators, and it has been an issue of concern for almost as long as there have been schools. While school bullying has been a constant concern, however, public discussions about it usually erupt when there is a moral panic.

One such moral panic over school bullying was set in motion by the 2010 suicide of Phoebe Prince, a student at South Hadley High School in Massachusetts. A recent immigrant from Ireland, Prince was targeted by students shortly after her arrival in South Hadley. In addition to being bullied at school, she was also taunted on Facebook and other social media sites. Students, teachers, and administrators at the school were well aware of the bullying, and chose to do nothing. Prince killed herself on January 14, 2010, after a student followed her home from school, called her a "whore," and threw a can of soda at her from a moving car.

The day after Prince's suicide, students led a candlelight vigil for Prince. The local news covered the story, interviewing students and parents who emphasized that Prince had been bullied, and that bullying was a big problem at the school. The story gained national attention after the local district attorney filed felony charges against the six high school students who were most clearly involved in the bullying of Prince. National media converged on South Hadley, publishing articles with titles like "The Untouchable Mean Girls" and "Bullied to Death?" The story became global news. Four months later, the Massachusetts government passed an anti-bullying law. In August 2010, the US Department of Education hosted a Bullying Prevention Summit, which brought together politicians, policy-makers, and researchers to discuss possible solutions to the bullying crisis in American schools.

The moral panic over school bullying eventually subsided. Newspapers covered the criminal verdicts for the teenagers charged with Phoebe Prince's death, but the sentences of probation and community service did not attract much public attention. Nevertheless, the Phoebe Prince case had lasting effects in communities around the nation. Students, teachers, and parents united together against bullying, and school administrators developed clear anti-bullying policies.

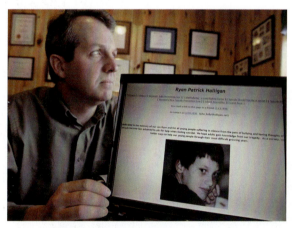

Cyber bullying
Cyber bullying is a major social issue, and a concern regularly brought to public attention by pediatricians and journalists. Here, John Halligan shows a web page devoted to his son, Ryan, who killed himself after enduring online bullying.

ACTIVE LEARNING

Discuss: Who benefits from the creation of a moral panic? In the school bullying example, who and what was the threat to the public? Who were the villains in the story? Who were the heroes?

to engage in deviant behavior. In his book *Causes of Delinquency*, Travis Hirschi argued that people who have strong bonds with their parents and schools were much more likely to follow the rules, because they would not want to jeopardize those relationships by engaging in deviant behavior (Hirschi 1969). In other words, Hirschi argued, it is not enough simply to know the rules. We also have to care about how breaking the rules will damage our relationships with other people. Too much deviant behavior can be an indicator that people do not have strong enough attachments to society.

Deviance can also serve to bring people together. As Durkheim argued, deviant acts arouse strong collective feelings among people who believe that important social norms are being violated. This shared collective indignation creates social solidarity (Durkheim [1893] 2014). When people hear news about identity theft, cyberbullying, or drug use, their concern is not only for themselves or their families. They worry about where their society is headed. They talk about the issue with friends, neighbors, and casual acquaintances. They may even attend a community meeting, or join a civic group to try to deal with the social threat. All of this serves to reinforce their bond with the larger society.

DEVIANCE AND SOCIAL CHANGE. Many of history's great innovators and revolutionaries were viewed as deviant people in their own societies. Socrates, one of the most important philosophers of ancient Greece, was arrested and eventually executed after being accused of corrupting the minds of Athenian youth. Galileo was arrested and convicted for heresy in Italy in 1633, for publishing his evidence that the Earth revolved around the Sun. The civil rights leader Martin Luther King Jr. was targeted for years by the Federal Bureau of Investigation (FBI), branded a communist by Southern politicians, and ultimately assassinated. Malala Yousafzai, an Afghan girl who broke the expectation that girls remain uneducated, was shot by the extreme organization called the Taliban for attending school. Malala went on to become a global symbol of hope for educating girls. The story of her life, *I am Malala* (2013), became a bestseller. She is currently attending Oxford University in England.

The link between deviance and innovation is not surprising. Innovation happens when people think differently and push boundaries. This does not mean that all deviance leads to constructive innovation. If somebody cuts in front of you in line, this does not make them a revolutionary; they may just be an inconsiderate jerk. But if everybody followed the rules, societies would never change. Some rule-breaking behavior ends up making society function more effectively.

To explain how deviance can lead to changes that improve society, Durkheim turned to the theory of evolution. Plants and animals are constantly mutating; over time the species adopts the changes that help them survive better. The same thing happens in society, where other individuals and groups adopt innovative deviance. The challenge is that we can usually only recognize innovative deviance after the fact. If society were able to eliminate all deviant behavior, it would not

Deviance and social change: the 1963 March on Washington
Law enforcement targeted Martin Luther King Jr. as a criminal, but his social protests are now understood to be positive acts of social change and social justice in the Civil Rights Movement. Here King marches with colleagues on August 28, 1963.

PAIRED CONCEPTS **Power and Resistance**

What's Wrong with Graffiti?

Graffiti refers to unauthorized writings or drawings that appear in public places. While archaeologists have found examples of graffiti in the ruins of ancient Greece, modern forms of graffiti really began to appear in the 1960s, as a form of illicit street art displayed in urban areas (Snyder 2009).

In New York, graffiti became part of a subcultural art scene. It developed into a form of cultural and political expression where outsider artists (i.e., people who were not recognized as artists by museums and galleries) could gain recognition. Modern graffiti took three main forms: tags, which are the artist's signature; throw-ups, which consist of two-color outlined text; and pieces, which are more ambitious multicolored murals. Graffiti artists competed with each other to place their work in the most visible places, such as subway cars, train tunnels, bridges, and freeway overpasses. Some of the most highly regarded graffiti artists became famous, and the subcultural movement spread to cities around the world.

But graffiti was considered vandalism by law enforcement authorities, who perceived that criminals were defacing property they did not own. By 1980, police departments around the country began to crack down on graffiti writers (Austin 2001). The mayor of New York City created an anti-graffiti task force in 1995, arguing that the presence of graffiti caused more crime. Since its creation, the Anti-Graffiti Task Force has made more than 2,800 arrests in New York City.

But the attempt to control and eliminate graffiti has met with resistance. Graffiti artists continue to do their work, despite arrests and despite repeated instances where the authorities paint over their work. The art community has also challenged the assertion that graffiti is equivalent to vandalism. Instead, they argue, graffiti is a legitimate form of artistic expression, worthy of being shown in museums and art galleries. Graffiti artists have benefited from this artistic credibility, and many of them have translated this credibility into successful careers as professional artists and designers. In some cities, the local government has even decided to encourage graffiti artists instead of prosecuting them. In Melbourne, Australia, for example, there are approved outdoor locations throughout the city where graffiti is both allowed and encouraged. Aiming to become the street art capital of the world, Melbourne sees graffiti as an important part of the tourist economy. These images of respectability challenge the earlier attempts to define graffiti as a deviant subculture and a problem to be eliminated.

Art or vandalism?
This wall mural in Flushing, New York, celebrating neighborhood diversity, is clearly a work of art. There are different interpretations of graffiti. Do you think all graffiti is art?

ACTIVE LEARNING

Think about it: Should art ever triumph over the private property rights of others? What about public property? Are there some places where graffiti is more wrong than in other places?

---

only be eliminating the inconsiderate behavior of unpleasant people. It would also be eliminating the future Galileos, Yousafzais and Kings.

DEVIANT SUBCULTURES. People who push boundaries and break rules may feel threatened by the negative attention they receive, but they can also receive social support and encouragement if they are part of a **deviant subculture**. As we discussed in Chapter 4, members of a subculture set themselves apart

Deviant subculture A group of people who set themselves apart as being different from the larger mainstream culture of the society.

Yakuza boss with his champion fighting dog
The yakuza is a Japanese crime syndicate whose subculture includes elaborate social rituals that define group life. This includes dog fighting, which has deep roots in yakuza culture.

as being different from the larger mainstream culture of the society. Because subcultures emphasize their differences from that society, it is not surprising that many of their behaviors get labeled as deviant. However, deviant subcultures can also be trendsetters and sources of social innovation.

According to sociologist Claude Fischer (1975), deviant subcultures spread with the growth of cities. Because cities have more diverse populations, with in-migration from many different communities and countries, people in large urban areas are more likely to find highly specialized, unconventional, and innovative subcultures than they would in smaller, more homogenous towns. These subcultures allow individuals to invest their energy and create community in a way that is self-consciously set apart from "normal" society. It is for this reason that artists, intellectuals, students, political dissidents, and other experimental communities have tended to congregate in cities. Deviant subcultures still feel social pressure to conform, but they have more social supports to resist these pressures.

Deviant subcultures embrace their difference from the larger society, and they help people resist the strong social pressures to conform. In some cases, as we saw with the example of graffiti, they actively challenge the idea that they are engaging in deviant behavior, by offering new interpretations about what they are doing (e.g., graffiti is not vandalism, but art). Today, social media makes it easier than ever to create and sustain deviant subcultures that challenge social conformity.

Not all deviant subcultures are committed to innovation, or to expanding the boundaries of what is considered "normal." The Italian Mafia, the Japanese yakuza, the Chinese triads, and other crime syndicates around the world have elaborate initiation ceremonies and strict codes of conduct that bond their members together and help them coordinate their activities. The same is true of hate groups such as the Ku Klux Klan or the Aryan Brotherhood. These groups are also deviant subcultures.

The Social Construction of Deviance

Normal and deviant behaviors are both socially constructed. There is quite a lot of cultural variation, and things that are considered deviant in some places are treated as normal in other places. Specific individuals and organizations have more power than others to label things as deviant. And different societies use different strategies to deal with deviance, such as punishment, banishment, education, treatment, and medical intervention.

DEVIANCE AND CULTURAL VARIATION. As we described earlier in the chapter, the identification of deviance depends on the social context. Even within the same society, the definition of the normal and the deviant is always changing. While the definition of deviance varies from one society to another, we can identify some general historical and cross-cultural patterns.

Most societies make distinctions between "everyday deviance" and more serious behaviors. Serious threats like violent crime spark the kind of collective indignation that produces moral panics. But the more typical encounter with deviance is more likely to make us annoyed than afraid (Smith, Philips, and

King 2010). Somebody bumps into us in the crowd, talks too loudly, uses inappropriate language, or cuts in front of us in line. We may shake our head or give them a disapproving stare, but we don't call the police or alert the media. We get annoyed about the social boundaries that are being violated, but we get over it.

While deviance exists in all societies, there are still differences in how much behavior a given society will define as deviant, as well as the amount of tolerance there will be for deviant behavior. In a study of 33 nations, Gelfand et al. (2011) found patterned differences between "tight" and "loose" societies. In tight societies, such as India, Malaysia, and Singapore, there are strong social norms and a low tolerance for deviant behavior. In contrast, loose societies such as Brazil, Israel, and the Netherlands have weak social norms and a high tolerance for deviant actions.

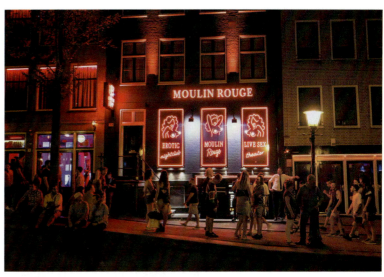

The Moulin Rouge Bar and Sex Shop, Amsterdam
Compared to most other countries, the Netherlands has a relatively high tolerance for deviance and has a well-developed and legal red-light district.

Large-scale historical changes also influence the social construction of deviance. For example, the rise of capitalism (Chapter 14) led to significant changes in the social construction of deviance, by encouraging people to think about profit-seeking behavior as desirable rather than immoral. The rise of democracy (Chapter 13) encouraged people to emphasize the importance of individual rights and freedoms, and to view actions that violated individual rights as deserving of criticism and punishment. The point is that what is considered deviant changes across time and place. This is an example of cultural relativism (Chapter 4).

THE POWER TO CALL THINGS DEVIANT. During our childhood and adolescent socialization, our families and schools have the power to define behavior as either normal or deviant. Our parents teach us the rules they expect us to follow, and that there are consequences for breaking those rules. Schools teach us specific subjects like English and math, but, they also teach a hidden curriculum that consists of all the different rules of behavior we need to learn to function effectively in the school and the larger society (Giroux and Purpel 1983). The hidden curriculum teaches us that there are consequences for being late, being disrespectful, and not doing work that is assigned to us (Chapter 5). These understandings of normal and deviant behavior are intended to help us become successful in our adult lives, and they are similar to the social expectations that we will find in the workplace.

Mass media and social media also have considerable power to label things as deviant. It often appears that the media are obsessed with crime, violence, and other forms of deviance. Nearly one-quarter of all local news stories are about crime and deviance (Graber 1980; Lotz 1991; see Heath and Gilbert 1996 for a review). Some of the most popular shows on television today focus on criminal investigators (*NCIS, Criminal Minds, Hawaii Five-O, The Mentalist*), police officers (*Blue Bloods*), and the FBI (*The Blacklist*). And books about high-profile crimes have been enormously popular since the early 20th century.

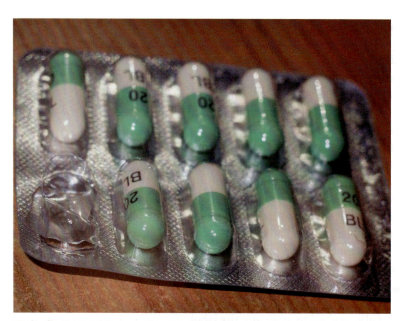

Medicalization and therapeutic cultures of deviance
Many people turn to doctors, therapists, and the pharmaceutical industry to help them deal with what they define as deviant behaviors.

of behavioral and drug therapies. People who are unhappy or depressed are diagnosed as having abnormally low levels of serotonin, and prescribed antidepressants. Increasingly, people turn to doctors, therapists, and the pharmaceutical industry to try to improve themselves, or at least to become more "normal."

In their book *Deviance and Medicalization*, Peter Conrad and Joseph Schneider show how the process of medicalization began as an attempt by the medical establishment to treat deviance and to rehabilitate deviant individuals (Conrad and Schneider 1992). Madness was redefined as mental illness in the early 19th century, and by 1900 psychiatry had developed as the science of mental disease. In the United States, the National Institute of Mental Health was established in 1949. Alcoholism began to be redefined as an illness in the 1940s, and opiate addiction in the 1960s. Child abuse was redefined as a mental disorder during the 1960s and 1970s. Eventually, crime itself came to be redefined as a mental disorder, and criminals found themselves subjected to a variety of behavioral modifications, drugs, and even surgical interventions designed to cure them of their illness (Conrad and Schneider 1992).

Because our beliefs about deviance are socially constructed and often change over time, the medicalization of deviance carries significant risks. When society becomes more tolerant of behaviors that were once considered deviant, the medical interventions that were originally intended to "cure" people are revealed as unnecessary and cruel actions that destroyed people's lives. In fact, as Conrad (2007) shows, this was the experience that gay men suffered for decades. Homosexuality was deeply stigmatized by psychiatrists in 1952, when it was listed as a sociopathic personality disturbance in the *Diagnostic and Statistical Manual of Mental Disorders* (*DSM*). Throughout the 1950s and 1960s, medical professionals used a variety of different behavioral therapies to try to "cure" gay men. In the 1970s, though, gay activists began to challenge psychiatrists about this diagnosis of homosexuality, and by 1987 the classification of homosexuality as a disorder was removed from the *DSM*. By this time, though, thousands of individuals had been subjected to dangerous and unnecessary medical interventions. Some men, such as the famous mathematician and computer scientist Alan Turing, had to endure chemical castration in the attempt to "cure" their homosexuality.

Laws Attempts by governments to establish formal systems of rules about how people are allowed to behave, as well as a system of punishments for when they break those rules.

Criminal justice system All the government agencies that are charged with finding and punishing people who break the law.

Crime

Crime is a special category of deviant behavior, which is defined, regulated and penalized by law. **Laws** are attempts by governments to establish a formal system of rules about how people are allowed to behave, as well as a system of punishments for when they break those rules. The **criminal justice system**

CAREERS

The Criminal Justice Field

Careers in the criminal justice field have always been one of the most popular destinations for undergraduates who major in sociology, and there is evidence that this interest is increasing (Senter et. al. 2014). One survey of sociology majors found that 7.7 percent of them planned to pursue careers in criminal justice after they graduated (American Sociological Association 2006: 27). An additional 11 percent plan to go to law school, where many of them will pursue careers as prosecuting attorneys and defense attorneys.

The job of police officer is one of the most common jobs in criminal justice. Key duties of police officers include patrolling, traffic control, assisting with fire and medical emergencies, investigating accidents and crime scenes, testifying in court hearings, and participating in public safety awareness campaigns. Jobs for police officers are relatively plentiful in communities nationwide.

Many sociology graduates who concentrate in criminal justice take jobs as probation officers, parole officers, and correctional treatment specialists. Correctional treatment specialists work with prisoners to develop rehabilitation and treatment plans. They develop educational and training plans to improve job skills, and they determine whether any mental health counseling or drug treatment is necessary. They make recommendations about release, and they develop rehabilitation and treatment plans that will continue after the prisoner is released. Parole officers work with prisoners after they have been released, to increase the likelihood that they will successfully return to society. They meet regularly with the ex-prisoners and their families, provide counseling, and ensure that the conditions of release are being followed. Probation officers also supervise people who have been placed on probation instead of being sent to prison. They meet regularly with the offenders, making sure that they are meeting the conditions of their probation, not a danger to their community, and progressing in their rehabilitation and treatment.

Sociology majors also pursue research-based careers in criminal justice. They work as crime analysts in local police departments, as social scientists in state departments of criminal justice services, and as research analysts in federal departments such as the FBI and the Department of Justice. These jobs require strong quantitative research skills, and typically require graduate-level training in sociology.

For sociology majors who go to law school, there are many opportunities to practice criminal law. Criminal defense attorneys represent their defendants in criminal courts at the federal, state, and local level. They can work for private law firms or they can work for the state, as public defenders. Prosecuting attorneys work for the government, trying to secure convictions against people charged with committing crimes. For both prosecuting and defense attorneys, their work involves collecting police reports, interviewing witnesses, examining the crime scene, looking for additional evidence, performing legal research, and preparing for court trials.

Last, there are roles in organizations advocating for prisoners and their families both within and outside the formal system of criminal justice. They include jobs as social workers, researchers, lawyers, and policy-makers. Organizations such as the Sentencing Project, the American Civil Liberties Union, the Equal Justice Initiative, and the Prison Activist Resource Center are all committed to providing legal and social resources for prisoners and their families. They also are involved in thinking about alternative models, such as restorative justice models, that avoid the negative consequences of the current system of incarceration.

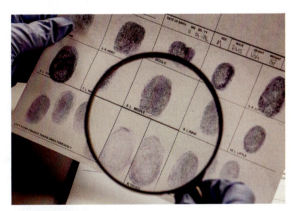

Criminal justice
Many students choose to double-major in criminal justice and sociology, eventually occupying positions as probation officers, parole officers, correctional treatment specialists, social workers, lawyers, policy-makers, researchers, and advocates for prison reform inside and outside the criminal justice system.

ACTIVE LEARNING

Find out: Go to the library or look online and find two entry-level job ads for a career in the criminal justice field. What are the duties and responsibilities needed for the jobs? What characteristics or qualities would recommend you as a good candidate for these jobs?

consists of all the government agencies that are charged with finding and punishing people who break the law. This includes the legislators who make the laws, the courts that determine if a person is guilty of committing a crime, and the correctional authorities that are responsible for punishing the guilty offenders.

Not all law-breaking behavior is defined as crime. The majority of legal cases are regulated by **civil law**, which is law that deals with disputes between individuals and organizations. Civil cases are filed by private parties rather than by the government. They still take place in the courts, but instead of focusing on punishing the wrongdoer, civil cases are concerned with restitution, which usually comes in the form of financial compensation paid to the aggrieved party. Examples of civil cases include things like property disputes, custody proceedings, and medical malpractice suits. As Émile Durkheim pointed out in *The Division of Labor in Society*, civil cases are much more common than criminal cases in modern society.

While civil cases are more common, it is the criminal cases that get the most public attention. The goal of a criminal case is to punish the offending person, to make a strong public display that will discourage others from engaging in the same kind of behavior, and to reassure the public that the most serious forms of deviance will not be tolerated. As we have seen, media coverage of criminal cases can produce the kind of public outrage and indignation that is often associated with moral panics.

Categories of Crime

In the Unites States, the FBI publishes crime statistics based on official data from the Uniform Crime Reporting (UCR) Program. UCR data comes from law enforcement agencies around the country, and is divided into Part I offenses and Part II offenses (Table 6.1).

Part I offenses are considered to be the most serious crimes that occur regularly, and that are most likely to be reported by the police. Homicide, aggravated assault, rape, and robbery (i.e., stealing something by using force or the threat of violence) are defined as **violent crime**. Burglary (entering a home or business to commit theft) motor vehicle theft, larceny (other forms of theft), and arson are defined as **property crime**.

Property crime is much more common than violent crime, as Table 6.1 shows. Historically, the property crime rate peaked in 1980, and has been declining consistently since 1991. The violent crime rate peaked in 1991, and has been steadily declining since then. According to Richard Rosenfeld, the declining crime rate was sudden, unexpected, and significant; by the year 2000, in fact, the homicide and burglary rates had fallen to lower levels than at any time since the 1960s (Rosenfeld 2002: 25).

Several factors explain why the crime rate has fallen over the last 30 years:

- The aging population meant that after 1980 there were fewer young people. This was an important factor because older people are less likely to commit serious crimes (Rosenfeld 2002: 27).

- Economic growth during the 1990s helped reduce unemployment and gave people better opportunities for finding legal work (Rosenfeld 2002: 30).

- The market for drugs began to shrink after 1990 (particularly the market for crack cocaine), which led to a reduction in firearm violence in the inner cities (Rosenfeld 2002: 28–29).

Civil law Law that deals with disputes between individuals and organizations. Most legal cases are civil cases.

Violent crime Defined by the Uniform Crime Reporting Program as homicide, aggravated assault, rape, and robbery.

Property crime Defined by the Uniform Crime Reporting Program as burglary (entering a home or business to commit theft) motor vehicle theft, larceny (other forms of theft), and arson.

Table 6.1 Crime rates, per 100,000 Inhabitants, 1998–2017

YEAR	VIOLENT CRIME RATE	PROPERTY CRIME RATE
1998	567.6	4,052.5
1999	523.0	3,743.6
2000	506.5	3,618.3
2001	504.5	3,658.1
2002	494.4	3,630.6
2003	475.8	3,591.2
2004	463.2	3,514.1
2005	469.0	3,431.5
2006	479.3	3,346.6
2007	471.8	3,276.4
2008	458.6	3,214.6
2009	431.9	3,041.3
2010	404.5	2,945.9
2011	387.1	2,905.4
2012	387.8	2,868.0
2013	369.1	2,733.6
2014	361.6	2,574.1
2015	373.7	2,500.5
2016	386.6	2,451.6
2017	382.9	2,362.2

Source: FBI: UCR 2017.

- Changes in police practices—such as targeted policing of high-crime areas and the use of DNA evidence—have led to more effective crime prevention (Telep and Weisburd 2012).
- A massive increase in the size of the prison population (Levitt 2004).

While most social science research and public attention focus on Part I offenses, the UCR also collects data for crimes that are considered to be less serious, and are defined as Part II offenses. Part II offenses include simple assault (i.e., where no weapon is used), forgery and counterfeiting, fraud, embezzlement, buying or receiving stolen property, vandalism, illegal possession of a weapon, prostitution, sex offenses, drug abuse violations, gambling, driving under the influence, violation of liquor laws, drunkenness, disorderly conduct, vagrancy, and loitering. Data for Part II offenses only includes those cases where arrests are actually made, which presents an inaccurate and distorted picture of how often those crimes are committed. In fact, social scientists have criticized all of the UCR data for presenting an inaccurate and distorted measure of the crime rate, because it only includes those criminal cases that the police know about and decide to investigate and therefore only captures a proportion of all crime (Anderson 2015: 23–25).

Another category of crime is **hate crime**, which refers to violence and intimidation against people because of their race, ethnicity, national origin, religion, gender identity, sexual orientation, gender, or disability. Attempts to

Hate crime Acts of violence and intimidation against people because of their race, ethnicity, national origin, religion, gender identity, sexual orientation, gender, or disability.

METHODS AND INTERPRETATION

Measuring the Crime Rate

The **crime rate** is defined as the number of criminal offenses that are committed per 100,000 people in the population. The violent crime rate and the property crime rate have both declined since the 1990s. In 2017, the violent crime rate was 382 offenses per 100,000 population, and the property crime rate was estimated at 2,362 offenses per 100,000 population. Crime rates are not uniform, and some places have higher crime rates than others. St. Louis, Missouri, had a violent crime rate of 2082 per 100,000 population in 2017 (the highest in the nation), but in Irvine, California, the violent crime rate was only 61 per 100,000 population (the nation's lowest).

The crime rate is not a perfect measurement, because it does not measure all the crimes that actually take place. Crimes like murder, aggravated assault, auto theft, and arson are more likely to be reported and investigated by the police, while crimes like buying stolen property, vandalism, and gambling are much less likely to be reported or investigated. International comparisons are nearly impossible to make, because the police in different countries have different levels of resources and community trust. In Mexico, for example, it is estimated that fewer than 25 percent of crimes are reported to the police (Edmonds-Poli and Shirk 2012). Even within the same country, the quality of the crime data that is collected may vary. Some cities do a better job of identifying crime than others, and some cities enjoy more trust among their citizens than others. These differences influence the quality of crime data. It is important to realize that all crime rates are estimates.

In the United States, the Department of Justice uses two strategies to estimate the crime rate. The first is the UCR Program. Data for the UCR comes from nearly eighteen thousand city, county, state, tribal, federal, and university law enforcement agencies, which voluntarily report data on crimes that are brought to their attention. The FBI examines the reports that come in, looking for large deviations that may indicate errors. Beginning in 1988, the UCR began converting to a National Incident-Based Reporting System (NIBRS), in an effort to standardize the data collection effort and to collect more information about each incident.

Recognizing that not all criminal offenses are reported or entered into the UCR, the Bureau of Justice Statistics began the National Criminal Victimization Survey (NCVS) in 1973. The survey is conducted twice yearly, using a nationally representative sample of forty-three thousand households. Households stay in the sample for three years. The survey collects data on all the crime that the household experienced, regardless of whether the incident was reported to the police. In addition to the information about the victims, the offenders, and the crimes that were committed, the survey also covers questions about the experience victims had with the criminal justice system, the self-protective measures that the household uses, and the reasons that victims give for reporting or not reporting a crime. This allows researchers to estimate the proportion of each crime type that is reported to the police. It also allows researchers to track changing public attitudes toward crime and the police.

ACTIVE LEARNING

Discuss: What do you think are the reasons why individuals may not want to report crime to the police?

Crime rate Calculated in the United States as the number of criminal offenses committed per 100,000 people in the population.

prevent and punish hate crimes began as early as 1871 in the United States, with the passage of the Ku Klux Klan Act that was designed to fight white supremacy organizations after the end of the American Civil War. The 1968 Civil Rights Act also contained provisions designed to prevent hate crimes, by making it illegal to hurt or intimidate someone on the basis of their race, religion, or national origin. Protections for sexual orientation and disability were added in the 1980s. The Hate Crimes Statistics Act was passed in 1989, which required the Department of Justice to collect and publish data on hate crimes. In 1994, two additional hate crime laws were passed: the Violence against Women Act, which authorized special police units and prosecutors focused on gender-related hate crimes; and the Hate Crimes Sentencing Enhancement Act, which authorized harsher sentences for hate crimes, as compared with other violent crimes (Grattet and Jenness 2001).

Table 6.2 Breakdown of 2017 Hate Crime Incidents, Victim Type by Bias Motivation

BIAS MOTIVATION	PERCENTAGE	FREQUENCY
Single-Bias Incidents		**7,106**
Race/Ethnicity/Ancestry	57.6%	4,131
Religion	21.8%	1,564
Sexual orientation	15.7%	1,130
Disability	1.6%	116
Gender	0.6%	46
Gender identity	1.7%	131
Multiple-Bias Incidents[1]	1.0%	69
Total	**100%**	**7,175**

[1] A *multiple-bias incident* is an incident in which one or more offense types are motivated by two or more biases.

Source: FBI: UCR 2017.

The most recent data show that there were 7,106 single-bias hate-crimes reported in 2017 (Table 6.2). The top three bias categories were race (57.6%), religion (21.8%) and sexual orientation (15.7%); 48.7 percent of the racially motivated hate crimes were directed against African Americans, and 60 percent of the religiously motivated hate crimes were against Jews. For the years in which the FBI has collected data, the number of hate-crime incidents peaked in 2001, with 9,730 incidents.

The final category of crime we will discuss here is **white-collar crime**, which refers to financially motivated nonviolent crime, usually committed by business professionals in the course of doing their jobs. Examples include accountants who embezzle money from their employer, financial advisors who steal the money of their clients, or government workers who accept bribes. The concept of white-collar crime was first introduced in 1939 by the sociologist Edwin Sutherland. Sutherland was concerned that the criminal justice system focused too much on street crime and other low-status offenders, and tended to ignore the offenses that were more likely to be committed by high-status individuals.

White-collar crime may be nonviolent, but it causes enormous damage. In the United States, estimates suggest that one in every four households has been victimized by white-collar crime, with annual costs of between $300 billion and $600 billion (Kane and Wall 2005). While the average loss in a case of street robbery is about $1,000, the average loss in a case of embezzlement is $1 million (Payne 2011: 48). Single cases of white-collar crime can have a national and even a global economic impact. In one of the most infamous recent cases, when Bernard Madoff's fraudulent investment firm collapsed in 2008, the financial damages he caused were estimated at between $10 billion and $20 billion. Madoff's victims included banks, hospitals, universities, charities and individuals around the world.

Today, new categories of white-collar crime are emerging, as an increasing proportion of economic transactions are coordinated through computer networks. **Cybercrime**, or crime conducted using computer networks, is today worth about $400 billion per year. "Phishing" attackers target more than one

White-collar crime Financially motivated nonviolent crime, usually committed by business professionals in the course of doing their jobs.

Cybercrime Crime conducted using computer networks.

The Global Drug Trade

While most police departments are organized at the local, state, or national level, crime does not always respect these boundaries. Bernard Madoff's investment fraud hurt people around the world, despite the fact that his company was located in the United States. Many sophisticated cybercrime organizations are located in Eastern Europe and former Soviet states (Broadhurst et al. 2014). In secure and encrypted internet forums, criminals worldwide buy and sell stolen identity documents and fake credit cards. It is difficult to police these kinds of organizations, because the victims are located far away from the offenders.

The illegal drug trade is another form of global crime, which has managed to grow and thrive despite the efforts of international police forces. Recent estimates suggest that the global drug trade is a $300 billion industry, with most of the revenue coming from the sale of cannabis, cocaine, and opiates (Chawla et al. 2005: 127). This is four times larger than the wine and beer industry, and it is more than 10 times larger than the coffee and tea industry. North America accounts for 44 percent of all drug sales, followed by Europe (33%) and Asia (11%). In North America, per capita expenditure on illegal drugs is more than $300 per year.

In a study of the heroin and cocaine trade, Peter Reuter found that there is a complicated global network linking production, distribution, and sales (Reuter 2009; see also Chawla et al. 2010). Most of the production takes place in poor countries. Myanmar and Afghanistan produce 80 percent of the world's supply of opium. Bolivia, Colombia, and Peru produce all of the cocaine, with Colombia responsible for nearly two-thirds.

In his research, Reuter found that the actual producers and refiners of the drugs receive 2 percent or less of the revenues. The majority of the earnings go to a very large number of low-level retailers selling the drugs in wealthy countries located in North America and Europe. The largest fortunes are made by a small number of global cartels, who control the distribution of the drugs and supply the retailers located in wealthy nations.

The global distribution networks have used a variety of different strategies to avoid the efforts taken by local and national authorities to stop the flow of drugs. Drug cartels have come to exploit transnational immigrant networks as a way to coordinate smuggling activities and avoid detection (Reuter 2009: 17). The ability to speak a non-native language makes it more difficult for local police to use wiretaps, and helps the smuggling networks escape notice. The use of family networks makes it easier to identify and trust new recruits; references from family members already in the organization are more trustworthy, and the cartel can easily identify family members in the sending country that they can hold hostage if the new recruit decides to steal their money or drugs. In other words, the global distribution network relies on the existence of local networks connecting sending and receiving countries.

Law enforcement officials showing the results of a drug bust Kamala Harris, center, here California's attorney general, announces the takedown of a California-based drug trafficking organization during a news conference in Fresno, April 14, 2014. On the table are bags of crystal methamphetamine that authorities say the organization smuggled in, along with cocaine, from Mexico.

ACTIVE LEARNING

Think about it: Are drug addicts deviant? Do you think drug addicts are criminals or sick? How are drug addicts treated by others in our society?

hundred thousand internet users every day, tricking people into giving away valuable personal information to criminals masquerading as friends, employers, government agencies, or other trustworthy groups. Another new type of computer fraud is ATM skimming, in which a small card-reading device is attached to an ATM machine in order to steal bank account information. These types of fraud often lead to **identity theft**, in which criminals use stolen personal and financial information to assume a person's identity in order to obtain credit and other financial advantages in that person's name. Over 17 million Americans were victims of identity theft in 2016, according to the Bureau of Justice Statistics (2019).

Policing Crime

In modern societies, the **police** enforce the law, prevent crime, pursue and bring to justice people who break the law, and maintain social order. As an agent of the state, the police are one of the only groups in society (along with the military) that is authorized to use physical force or violence to achieve its objectives (Terpstra 2011). This places considerable moral responsibility on police officers, who are licensed to use coercion against citizens and to intrude on the private lives of others (Waddington 2002).

For someone to be labeled a criminal, they first have to be pursued and apprehended by the police. Police are constantly making decisions about what crimes are worth pursuing, where crime is most likely to occur, when they should make an arrest, and when they should give a warning to people they find breaking the law (Rumbaut and Bittner 1979). Police also have to decide how they will divide their time among their various responsibilities (Wilson 1968). After all, police do more than pursue criminals. They help stranded motorists, direct traffic, give directions to people who are lost, try to settle domestic disputes, and provide many other services to the community in the course of their day.

Over the last 30 years, the way that police set their priorities has been shaped by the **broken windows theory** of deviance. First described in a popular 1982 article by George Kelling and James Q. Wilson, the broken windows theory argues that ignoring small crimes and minor violations creates a spiral of increasing deviance and more serious criminality. In other words, if people see broken windows and graffiti in their neighborhood, they will assume that nobody cares about the community, and that the neighborhood is unsafe. This becomes a self-fulfilling prophecy. If people stay off the streets, believing them to be unsafe, the streets will actually become more dangerous. The decreased levels of informal social control allow more serious crime to move into the neighborhood (Kelling and Wilson 1982).

Influenced by the broken windows theory, police began to focus on preventing less serious crime, as a way of creating a sense of social order and preventing more serious crime from developing. New York City adopted a "zero-tolerance" policy to policing in the 1990s, aggressively patrolling against graffiti, vandalism, begging, drunkenness, and disorderly behavior. Misdemeanor arrests increased by 70 percent, and more serious crime decreased. Police departments around

Identify theft When criminals use stolen personal and financial information to assume a person's identity in order to obtain credit and other financial advantages in that person's name.

Police A group of people authorized to enforce the law, prevent crime, pursue and bring to justice people who break the law, and maintain social order.

Broken windows theory A theory of policing stating that ignoring small crimes and minor violations creates a spiral of increasing deviance and more serious criminality.

Broken windows theory
The broken windows theory of policing assumes that smaller crimes like broken windows lead to more serious crime. This theory resulted in more intensive policing in poorer communities and communities of color.

the nation took notice, and shifted their policing practices to try to follow New York City's success. While social scientists dispute how much of the crime reduction could be attributed to the new police practices, the general consensus is that they had a statistically significant impact (Messner et al. 2007).

Because police have so much discretion in their work, the decisions they make about where to look for crime and when to make arrests are hugely consequential. Often, these decisions reinforce existing relationships of privilege and inequality. Of particular concern is **racial profiling**, which refers to the police practice of targeting an individual because of their race or ethnicity. Sociological research has shown that police are much more likely both to treat people as potential criminals when they are patrolling in poor and minority communities and to make arrests in those neighborhoods (Tomaskovic-Devey and Warren 2009). Police have long used race as an indicator of suspicion, targeting minorities for questioning and arrest (Kennedy 1997).

Racial profiling The police practice of targeting an individual because of their race or ethnicity.

African Americans are arrested more often than other Americans. There were 7,537,750 arrests reported by law enforcement in 2017, and while African Americans are 13 percent of the US population, they made up 27.2 percent of all arrests (Federal Bureau of Investigation 2017). African Americans were disproportionately arrested in every category. Particularly noteworthy is the disproportionate African American share of the arrests for drug violations (27.4%), disorderly conduct (29.5%), and vagrancy (27.3%). Such arrests suggest how the broken windows theory of deviance has led African American communities to be targeted.

Race influences police practices even more in routine traffic stops and encounters with pedestrians. A study of the New York Police department found that 85 percent of all New Yorkers who were stopped and frisked between 2005 and 2008 were African Americans (Center for Constitutional Rights 2009). In the nation as a whole, research shows that African American drivers are more than twice as likely as white drivers to be arrested during a traffic stop, and they are nearly three times as likely to be subjected to a police search during a traffic stop (Durose, Smith, and Langan. 2005). This phenomenon, which is sometimes referred to as "driving while black," leads to fear, anger, humiliation, and distrust of police by many in the African American community (Harris 1999).

In his book *Race, Crime, and the Law*, Randall Kennedy (1997) argues that racial targeting by the police ends up making African American communities more dangerous. The unwanted attention creates resentment and distrust among African Americans toward the police. As a result, African Americans are less likely to seek out the police when they need help, to cooperate with police investigations, and to venture out into communities where police will see them as "out of place." This leaves many African American communities more isolated, and more vulnerable to criminal victimization, with heightened rates of robbery and homicide.

Surveillance

Surveillance Monitoring other people's activities, often by using video cameras and other media technologies.

Surveillance is monitoring other people's activites, often by using video and other media technologies. Many of us are first exposed to the idea of surveillance in books, films, and television series such as *Black Mirror, 1984, V for Vendetta,* and *Minority Report*. Popular culture tends to represent surveillance as a threat to society, portraying it as part of a dystopian future world in which the government monitors every aspect of citizens' lives.

Table 6.3 Arrests by Race, 2017

OFFENSE CHARGED	WHITE	BLACK OR AFRICAN AMERICAN	AMERICAN INDIAN OR ALASKA NATIVE	ASIAN	NATIVE HAWAIIAN OR OTHER PACIFIC ISLANDER
Murder and nonnegligent manslaughter	44.8	52.5	1.2	1.4	0.2
Rape[1]	67.7	28.2	1.9	1.8	0.4
Robbery	46.6	51.1	1.0	0.9	0.4
Aggravated assault	62.7	32.8	2.5	1.7	0.3
Burglary	69.6	27.8	1.2	1.1	0.3
Larceny-theft	69.1	27.7	1.8	1.1	0.2
Motor vehicle theft	70.5	25.8	1.8	1.5	0.4
Arson	70.8	25.4	1.7	1.8	0.2
Violent crime[2]	59.9	36.0	2.2	1.5	0.3
Property crime[2]	69.3	27.6	1.7	1.2	0.2
Other assaults	65.9	30.4	2.1	1.3	0.3
Forgery and counterfeiting	65.3	32.2	0.9	1.4	0.2
Fraud	67.4	30.0	1.3	1.2	0.1
Embezzlement	60.0	37.5	0.8	1.5	0.2
Stolen property; buying, receiving, possessing	66.3	30.7	1.4	1.2	0.4
Vandalism	68.2	28.0	2.3	1.2	0.2
Weapons; carrying, possessing, etc.	53.8	43.9	1.1	1.1	0.3
Prostitution and commercialized vice	56.1	37.5	0.4	5.7	0.3
Sex offenses (except rape and prostitution)	70.8	24.8	2.0	2.1	0.3
Drug abuse violations	70.2	27.4	1.2	1.1	0.2
Gambling	39.9	49.7	0.7	7.9	1.8
Offenses against the family and children	65.8	28.1	5.3	0.8	*
Driving under the influence	81.7	14.0	2.1	1.9	0.3
Liquor laws	76.4	15.6	6.4	1.5	0.1
Drunkenness	73.9	14.3	10.6	1.0	0.2
Disorderly conduct	64.7	29.5	4.8	0.9	0.2
Vagrancy	68.8	27.3	2.6	1.1	0.1
All other offenses (except traffic)	69.0	27.5	2.3	0.9	0.3
Suspicion	38.0	20.1	39.8	1.2	1.0
Total proportion of arrests by race	**69.5**	**26.6**	**2.4**	**1.2**	**0.3**

[1] The rape figures in this table are an aggregate total of the data submitted using both the revised and legacy Uniform Crime Reporting definitions.

[2] Violent crimes are offenses of murder and nonnegligent manslaughter, rape, robbery, and aggravated assault. Property crimes are offenses of burglary, larceny-theft, motor vehicle theft, and arson.

Source: FBI: UCR "Arrests by Race and Ethnicity 2017."

Surveillance
Surveillance cameras in public spaces are a standard expectation of urban life. We know we are being watched, but we cannot always see the people who are watching us.

Ideas about surveillance also come from historical writings about crime and deviance. Writing about prison design in the 1700s, the philosopher Jeremy Bentham described a "Panopticon," in which a single guard positioned in a tower could view inside every jail cell and monitor the activities of all the prisoners at all times. Prisoners would not be able to see into the guard's tower, but they would be aware that at any given moment they might be being watched. Because they could never know whether they were being watched, they would have to act as if they were. As a result, Bentham argued, prisoners would end up policing themselves.

According to Michel Foucault, Bentham's ideas about the Panopticon created a new form of power in modern society, based on the principle of surveillance. We know that we are being watched, but we cannot see the people who are watching us, nor can we know when they are watching us. So we have to act at all times as if we are being watched. This makes the exercise of power both more economical and more intense. Not surprisingly, Foucault argued, the principle of the Panopticon has been extended from prison design to many other spheres of life, such as work and education. Eventually, with the use and spread of closed-circuit cameras, the surveillance model of the Panopticon extended into public spaces such as streets, airports, train stations, shopping malls, and the internet.

Research by sociologists and criminologists has found that the use of surveillance technologies is not a very good way to reduce crime. The place where video surveillance seems to be most effective is in parking lots, as a way of deterring vehicle theft (Welsh and Farrington 2009). Besides this specific use, though, studies in the United States and England have consistently found that the use of video surveillance does not have a statistically significant impact on crime (Welsh and Farrington 2009). A review of a US National Security Agency surveillance program concluded that it was not an essential tool for preventing terrorist attacks (Swire 2015).

Punishment

Punishment A social response to deviance that controls both deviant behavior and the offender, and that aims to protect the social group and its social standards.

Punishment is a social response to deviance that controls the deviant behavior and the offender, and protects the social group and its social standards. There is a social pressure to punish people who get labeled as deviant, and even stronger pressure to punish people who are accused of committing a crime. But there is a lot of variation in how people get punished, and what people think they are accomplishing when they punish deviants and criminal offenders.

Punishment as a Public Display of Morality

For much of history, punishment was both a violent and a public event. Public executions were common well into the 19th century, and they were popular events attended by entire families (Smith 2008: 37–38). The techniques of public punishment were often gruesome. During the 1300s in England, one technique of punishment involved attaching the convict to a piece of wood, dragging him to the place of execution, hanging him almost to the point of death, disemboweling him, beheading him, chopping his body into four pieces, and then displaying the body parts in public locations. Burning at the stake was a common practice until about 1800. In France, the last public execution by guillotine was 1939 (although the guillotine remained in use until 1977 and the death penalty was only abolished in 2007). Public executions by hanging also lasted until 1939 in the United States, and the death penalty continues to this day in many US states.

According to Émile Durkheim ([1893] 2014), violent and public forms of punishment are a way for a community to express its moral outrage toward acts that offend collective social values. By making the punishment public, the community was able to reinforce its moral beliefs in a way that also reaffirmed the social solidarity that held them together. Durkheim argued that this form of punishment would become less common in modern society, because the type of organic solidarity that held people together would be based more on trust and interdependence between individuals than on similarity of life and shared experience. In modern, diverse societies, people could no longer rely on their similarities or assume that they shared all beliefs and values. In this situation, Durkheim argued, maintaining trust and interdependence required a form of punishment that was more like conflict resolution, where the goal was restitution for the aggrieved party rather than public punishment of the offending party.

Public forms of punishment became less common throughout the 19th and 20th centuries. Many people found public executions to be cruel and uncivilized, and they campaigned for a system of punishment that granted more dignity and respect toward criminals (Spierenberg 1984). Fearful that the crowds that attended public executions were unpredictable and often violent, government authorities decided that it would be safer and more effective to punish prisoners in private (Foucault 1977).

Rehabilitation An approach to punishment that seeks to improve offenders and restore them to society.

Punishment and Treatment

Influenced by the medicalization of deviance, **rehabilitation** became an important part of punishment during the 20th century. Incarcerated people were encouraged to develop job skills, and to work with medical professionals to resolve any psychological issues that might prevent a successful reintegration into society. People who were convicted of crimes often received sentences that mandated treatment for things like substance abuse, personality disorders, and impulse-control problems. The goal was to help them

The public hanging of Rainey Bethea, August 14, 1936, in Owensboro, Kentucky
Punishment is a public display of morality. A huge crowd of over 15,000 people gathered to witness the public hanging of 26-year old Rainey Bethea, a black man found guilty of the rape and murder of a white woman, in 1936. Public outrage over the execution made Bethea's death the last public hanging by legal authorities in the United States.

Criminal recidivism The likelihood that a person will engage in future criminal behavior.

Parole A process through which prisoners who appear to have reformed themselves can earn an early release from their prison sentence.

Incarceration A form of punishment in which the offender is confined in prison.

successfully reenter society, and to reduce the likelihood that they would engage in future criminal behavior, or **criminal recidivism**.

The goal of rehabilitation led many criminal justice systems to develop alternative systems of punishment. In the United States, the National Probation Act of 1925 allowed courts to sentence criminal offenders to probation instead of sending them to prison. A person who is placed on probation agrees to be subject to supervision by a probation officer, and to follow the conditions of probation set by the court. Typical conditions include community service, regular meetings with the probation officer, periodic drug testing, avoiding certain people and places, and appearing in court during requested times. Violation of the conditions of probation can increase the probation time, incur fines, or in some cases result in probation being revoked and the person being sent to jail.

Parole is another form of punishment that was designed to encourage rehabilitation. With **parole**, prisoners who appear to have reformed themselves can earn an early release from their prison sentence. Prisoners who earn parole have a period of probation after they are released, where they have to meet regularly with a parole officer and demonstrate that they are fully rehabilitated. The system of parole was first created in Australia during the 1840s, and was adopted by criminal justice systems around the world during the 20th century.

Incarceration

Incarceration is a form of punishment in which the offender is confined in prison. Prisons have been used as a form of punishment since the time of ancient Rome. England built prisons in distant colonies in North America and Australia during the 17th and 18th centuries. Prison ships were also used during that time, as a way of confining criminals in a faraway place.

The modern prison developed during the 19th century, when public forms of punishment began to be viewed as cruel and uncivilized. Viewing existing prisons as disorganized and corrupt, an international prison reform movement proposed new standards in which prisoners would each be housed in a separate cell, receive healthy food and living conditions, and be watched over by professional guards (Smith 2008: 61–69). The prison reform movement was connected to the rehabilitation model, and focused on education, vocational training, and psychiatric treatment.

During the 1970s, the rehabilitation model of punishment was the subject of significant criticism by politicians as well as social scientists. Among the many criticisms were claims that rehabilitation does not reduce criminal recidivism, that it weakens the deterrent effect of punishment, and that it ignores the structural causes of crime such as poverty and inequality (Sundt 2002). Many criminal justice systems abandoned rehabilitation. The US Congress abolished federal parole in 1984, emphasizing instead longer and less flexible prison sentences (Clear 1994).

The emphasis on longer prison sentences has caused a significant increase in the US prison population. In 1978, there were 294,400 prisoners in federal and state prisons in the United States; by 2009, this number had increased by a factor of five to 1,555,600 (Carson and Golinelli 2013). Today, the US prison population is more than 2.2 million, which is the largest in the world. The United States has a prison population rate of 693 prisoners per 100,000 of national population (Table 6.4), which is more than seven times higher than countries in North America, Europe, and Asia.

Despite the fact that the violent crime rate has been decreasing since the 1990s, the incarceration rate has increased because of "tough on crime" policies

Inequality and Privilege

Punishment and Plea Bargaining

Fewer than 10 percent of all criminal cases go to trial. Instead, they get resolved through **plea bargaining**, in which the defendant pleads guilty to a lesser charge that has been negotiated by the prosecuting and defense attorneys (Devers 2011). In the United States, plea bargaining has been the dominant form of resolving criminal cases since the 19th century (Fisher 2003). Plea bargaining is an advantage for the criminal justice system because it reduces costs (Savitsky 2012). Plea bargaining also benefits the prosecuting and defense attorneys, because both parties to a plea bargain count the outcome as a victory (Alschuler 1968, 1975). Prosecutors record a conviction and defense attorneys can claim a lesser penalty than the defendant was charged with in the first place.

There are three kinds of criticisms that legal scholars and social scientists have made about plea bargains (Alkon 2014). First, the plea bargaining system is too coercive. Defendants are pressured to accept plea deals by police, prosecutors, and even their own attorneys, in a way that weakens their right to a fair trial. Second, plea bargains largely eliminate the moral component of crime and punishment. For the accused, the plea bargain becomes a cynical game about getting the best deal, rather than an opportunity to make a confession of guilt or to fight for justice. For victims, the plea bargain denies their opportunity to testify about how they were wronged, and it denies them the opportunity to witness the sentencing and punishment of the offender.

The third (and most common) criticism of plea bargaining is that it reinforces social inequality. The vast majority of poor defendants rely on court-appointed lawyers. These lawyers have huge caseloads, and usually do not have enough time to consult with their clients in a meaningful way or to develop a defense strategy. Instead, they take the first plea deal that is offered to them, which is usually a worse deal than plea offers that are made to wealthier clients who have higher-priced attorneys representing them (Alkon 2014).

There is also an important racial dimension to plea bargains. For example, in a study of misdemeanor marijuana arrests, researchers found that African American defendants were less likely to receive reduced-charge offers, and more likely to receive plea bargain offers that included jail time (Kutateladze et al. 2014). For defendants who had no prior record, African Americans and Latinos are less likely than white defendants to have felony charges against them dropped during the plea bargaining process (Schmitt 1991). These structural differences lead to the disproportionate and unequal incarceration of racial minorities, in a way that dramatically increases social inequality. This is especially concerning given the massive increase in plea bargaining over time and the fact that over 90 percent of criminal cases never go to trial (Clarke 2013).

ACTIVE LEARNING

Think about it: Do you think plea bargaining is fair? Why? What would you do if you were charged with a crime with a very long sentence and were offered a plea bargain that included a shorter amount of time in jail? How would you make the decision? Who would you talk to?

Table 6.4 Incarceration Rate per 100,000 National Population, Selected Countries, 2018

Australia	172
China	118
Canada	114
South Korea	109
France	100
Germany	75
Sweden	59
Japan	41
United States of America	655

Source: World Prison Brief. Institute for Criminal Policy Research.

Plea bargaining A process in which a defendant pleads guilty to a lesser charge that has been negotiated by the prosecuting and defense attorneys.

The United States has the largest prison population in the world
Nearly one-quarter of the world's prison population of about nine million is held in the United States, with approximately 700 of every 100,000 Americans in prison and jails. Russia and China are the other two countries with high prison populations, but their rates of incarceration are not as high as that of the United States.

that led to more prison sentences and longer prison sentences for nonviolent drug-related crimes (Tonry 1995). These policies had the biggest impact in poor, minority communities, where police were much more likely to make arrests for drug violations (Pager 2003). Police continue to arrest African Americans for drug violations at twice the rate of whites (Federal Bureau of Investigation 2017), despite the fact that the rate of drug use is the same for the two groups, and despite the fact that whites are actually more likely than African Americans to sell drugs (Rothwell 2014).

Most sociologists who have studied the growing prison rate agree that it has impacted African American men particularly hard (Pager 2003; Western 2006). Among African American men born since the late 1970s, nearly 25 percent had gone to prison by their mid-30s; among those who never completed high school, nearly 70 percent ended up in prison. This has had a devastating impact on African American urban communities. Prisons are usually located far away from urban African American neighborhoods, making it difficult for families to stay connected. There is also a significant financial strain, since more than half the fathers in prison had been the primary source of income in their households (Western and Petit 2005). As Bruce Western has shown, the growth of the prison population has been an important factor contributing to rising inequality between African Americans and whites in the United States (Western 2006).

The system of punishment and the rapid growth of the prison population is something that sets the Unites States apart from the rest of the world. The Unites States is the only Western country in the world that still uses capital punishment, or the death penalty (Garland 2008). The Unites States is much more likely to treat juvenile offenders as adults and to imprison them (Tonry 2007). Prison sentences are much longer in the Unites States than they are in Europe, resulting in an aging prison population. Unlike in Europe, prisoners in the Unites States are not allowed to vote while they are in prison (except for Vermont and Maine), and they are prohibited from certain types of jobs once they are released (Uggen, Manza, and Thompson 2006).

The US system of mass incarceration is also extremely expensive. Each new prison cell costs between $25,000 and $100,000 to build, depending on the inmate security level (Gottschalk 2007). Many experts and policy-makers question whether this is a good financial investment, and they fear that the cost of incarceration is taking money away from schools, hospitals, and other important social services (King and Mauer 2002). Pointing to countries like Germany and Finland, which have enacted policies to reduce their incarceration rates, a growing "decarceration" movement is campaigning for new criminal justice policies that reduce the number of prisoners in the United States (Tonry 2014).

Critics have described the US system of mass incarceration as the **prison-industrial complex**. Coined by the intellectual and activist Angela

Prison-industrial complex A profit-making system that uses prison labor and prisons to support a wide array of economic activities.

Why Are Crime Stories So Popular?

Crime and deviance—and the social control responses to them—define moral boundaries. To explore this idea, we conclude the chapter with a brief examination of a particular kind of crime story, the "police procedural." Originating in the 19th century, these gritty crime dramas developed alongside mystery and detective fiction genres. As their name suggests, procedurals focus on investigative police procedure. They typically highlight teamwork among investigators to solve a crime, usually a violent murder or rape, which is laid out for the audience in grisly, realistic detail (Hausladen 2000: 18).

Today, police procedurals make up a substantial slice of network television programming. Several well-known police procedurals are also *global* franchises. This means they adapt the basic format to different places around the world to connect to local audiences. *Law & Order,* for example, ran in the United States from 1990 to 2010. There were five American spinoffs: *Law & Order: Special Victims Unit* (1999–), *Law & Order: Criminal Intent* (2001–2011), *Law & Order: Trial by Jury* (2005–2006), *Conviction* (2006), and *Law & Order: LA* (2010–2011). Overseas, there were two *Law & Order* shows set in Moscow (adaptations of *Special Victims Unit* and *Criminal Intent*), and a version of *Criminal Intent* set in Paris called *Paris enquêtes criminelles.* Last, *Law & Order: UK* (2009–2014) offered a British take on *Law & Order* with more of a focus on forensics. Clearly, the contemporary police procedural holds very wide appeal.

Fascination with crime stories is not a new phenomenon. Historians emphasize that "stories of crime and punishment play a central role in the storytelling matrix of most cultures" (Turnbull 2014). Such stories are powerful because they distinguish right from wrong and separate the good guys from the bad guys. Police procedurals are like other crime stories because they invoke *solidarity* among those on the side of good—the police, responsible citizens, and innocent community members—in fundamental *conflict* with those who are evil, namely the criminals who hurt others and violate the community.

Viewers of police procedurals are invited to take the perspective of the police officer who brings criminals to justice. A unifying theme of these stories is that the law protects the social good regardless of social status. In some stories, the criminals are portrayed as poor, violent, and/or dangerous. There are often racial, ethnic and/or nationalist dynamics that reveal relationships of *inequality* in wider society. Urban gangs that are black or Latinx, for example, or crime families associated with Italian, Chinese, or Russian immigrants are staples of the genre. The role of the police in these stories is to justify, enforce, or overcome these racial-ethnic dynamics in the name of the social good. In other stories, where the criminal is *privileged* because they are wealthy, educated, powerful, or white, the narrative emphasizes that no one is beyond the law. Criminals who believe they are superior to the police or who think they are above the social rules of the community inevitably discover that they are no match for the relentless, systematic process of police investigation. In contrast to both kinds of criminals, the police protagonist in the story is invariably depicted as a citizen-hero doing good in a complex world. They are good guys who represent the best interests of society.

Importantly, police procedurals are also important stories about the legitimate exercise of lawful *power*. Criminals are bad because they transgress fundamental social boundaries—and the police procedural can be used to question or reflect on those boundaries. As it has developed historically, the police procedural has complicated questions of right and wrong. In episodes about corrupt police, for example, a more nuanced analysis is offered where *resisting* authority might be a legitimate course of action, as long as justice is done in the end (Riordan 2018). In the well-known storyline where some police officers (or lawyers or politicians) are identified as criminals, the story's conflict is resolved when they are brought to justice. As a recent review suggests, the "detectives at the heart of the best procedurals believe that they are the last best hope for justice in a compromised world" (Riordan 2018).

Police procedurals also rely on a narrative tension between *structure* and *contingency*, especially in their focus on investigating every detail of the crime. In police procedurals, even the most brilliant criminals cannot control every contingency. They are inevitably foiled by an unknown witness who sees them or by the DNA evidence that places them at the scene. They might be brought down by their own emotional weakness or by the brilliant police officer who makes connections between the details of multiple cases to identify the perpetrator. At the same time, police procedurals also rely on the idea of a structured, understandable world and the belief that the tenacious, detail-oriented police investigation will identify the criminal and solve the crime. This tension between structure and contingency is a central part of the appeal of criminal investigation.

CASE STUDY CONTINUED

The drama of crime
Law & Order had five American spin-offs as well as versions adapted around the world.

Importantly, police procedurals tell fictional stories. They close the moral breach created by terrible crime. In the real world, the story is very different. Not only are crimes underreported, but the majority of crimes that are reported to police are never solved. According to FBI data, in 2015 (the year for which data are most recently available) only about one-quarter of violent crimes are ever solved, and fewer than 10 percent of property crimes are solved (Gramlich 2017). Whatever the case, there is no doubt that the moral drama captured by the police procedural holds a wide social fascination because it defines the boundary of the deviant—separating right from wrong, good from bad, sacred from profane.

Davis in 1997 and subsequently elaborated by a range of prison reformers and social scientists, the prison-industrial complex is understood as a profit-making system that uses prison labor and prisons to support a wide array of economic activities from private prisons, to corporations that rely on prison labor, to construction companies that build new prisons, to the food service industry that feeds the enormous prison population (Harcourt 2012; Davis 2001). Theorists of the prison-industrial complex observe that the massively disproportionate incarceration of black men in the contemporary United States parallels its earlier slavery system (Pelaez 2008; Friedmann 2012; Childs 2015).

LEARNING GOALS REVISITED

6.1 Define deviance and understand the social functions of deviance.

- Deviance is any behavior that is outside social boundaries for what counts as normal and acceptable by a social group.

- Deviance helps social groups define and reinforce the boundaries of normal and acceptable behavior because it is the occasion when social standards are defined and articulated.

- Social control theory states that people who are strongly tied to their communities are less likely to engage in deviant behavior.

- Deviance is also one key to social change and social growth because it helps change social

standards by suggesting different or new possibilities.

- Deviance plays a role in socialization as children test the boundaries of what is acceptable behavior.

6.2 Distinguish between deviance, crime, and punishment.

- Crime is deviance that is defined and punishable by law.

- The criminal justice system consists of all the government agencies that are charged with finding and punishing people who break the law. This includes the legislators who make the laws, the courts that determine if a person is guilty of committing a crime, the correctional authorities that are responsible for punishing the guilty offenders, and the police who investigate crime and find lawbreakers.

- There are actions that are considered deviant because they transgress a boundary but they are not illegal. Other acts are illegal but are not heavily stigmatized.

6.3 Understand that deviance is socially constructed.

- What is considered normal behavior is socially constructed and varies across time and place. There are many examples demonstrating that what is considered deviant behavior, what is defined as a crime, and what is punished as a crime is both socially constructed and culturally relative to time and place.

- People who are defined as deviants are often stigmatized in a way that has consequences for their life outcomes. Once they are labeled as a deviant, this may influence them to engage in additional deviant behaviors or to join a deviant subculture.

- Some deviance is defined medically, and whether or not it is subject to criminal sanction is a matter of social context and social judgment. The social construction of drug use is a good example because in our society it can be defined as both medical and criminal, depending on the context.

- Over the last two hundred years, modern societies have shifted from public and sometimes gruesome punishment of criminal offenders to more private punishments and later a focus on rehabilitation of offenders in the hopes that they could reenter society and refrain from engaging in criminal behavior.

6.4 Distinguish different categories of crime and the challenges of measuring crime.

- There are different types of crimes. Violent crimes such as homicide, aggravated assault, rape, and robbery, and serious property crimes such as burglary, motor vehicle theft, larceny, and arson, are measured in the Uniform Crime Reports published by the FBI

and are considered to be the most serious offenses. Part II offenses are considered less serious and include simple assault (where no weapon is used), forgery and counterfeiting, fraud, embezzlement, buying or receiving stolen property, vandalism, illegal possession of a weapon, prostitution, sex offenses, drug abuse violations, gambling, driving under the influence, violation of liquor laws, drunkenness, disorderly conduct, vagrancy, and loitering.

- Other categories of crime include hate crimes such as gay-bashing, white-collar crimes like insurance fraud or embezzlement and cybercrimes such as identity theft.

- Civil law, which deals with disputes between individuals and organizations, is aimed at restitution of harm and as far as possible repairing a relationship or contract that has been broken. Criminal law is different because its focus is the punishment of the wrongdoer and the protection of the community and community values.

- Even the best crime data, such as that collected in the Uniform Crime Reporting Program, has serious drawbacks. One challenge is that a lot of crime is never identified or reported. A second problem is that the statistics are typically based on successful arrests and/or prosecutions, which means that those cases that do not result in arrest are not counted. A third concern is that some crimes like murder, aggravated assault, auto theft, and arson are more likely to be reported and investigated by the police than crimes like buying stolen property, vandalism, and gambling. Finally, international comparisons are nearly impossible to make, because the police in different countries have different levels of resources and community trust.

Key Terms

Broken windows theory 165
Civil law 160
Crime 148
Crime rate 162
Criminal justice system 158
Criminal recidivism 170

Review Questions

1. What is recidivism?

2. What is the difference between crime and deviance?

3. What is the prison-industrial complex?

4. Can cybercrime be white-collar crime? Can you think of an example?

5. What is the difference between primary and secondary deviance? Are they connected?

6. Explain how labeling theory works to define criminal behavior. Do you think labeling people has effects in other parts of life, too, like the family or classrooms?

7. How is crime related to social norms and values?

8. Why is it difficult to measure crime?

9. Does crime serve any social function?

10. Why do societies punish offenders? Does it work?

Explore

RECOMMENDED READINGS

Becker, Howard S. [1953] 2015. *Becoming a Marihuana User*. Chicago: University of Chicago Press.

Davis, Angela. 2001. *The Prison Industrial Complex* (audio CD). Chico, CA: AK Press.

Durkheim, Émile. [1893] 2014. *The Division of Labour in Society*. New York: Free Press.

Kennedy, Randall. 1997. *Race, Crime, and the Law*. New York: Random House.

Smith, Philip. 2008. *Punishment and Culture*. Chicago: University of Chicago Press.

ACTIVITIES

- *Use your sociological imagination*: Members of which groups are more likely to be arrested for illegal drug use in the United States? How can you find out?

- *Media+Data literacies*: Go online to discover the crime rate statistics for your county. Use search terms such as "Your county [your county name] crime rates." Are you surprised at the finding? Why or why not?

- *Discuss*: Minor acts of deviance are very common. Have you ever committed an act of deviance? Have you ever seen someone else commit an act of deviance? Was it punished?

For additional resources, including Media+Data Literacy exercises, In the News exercises, and quizzes, please go to **oup.com/he/ Jacobs-Townsley1e**

PART III DIFFERENCE AND INEQUALITY

A FUTURE TO BELIEVE IN

BERNIESANDERS.COM

7

Inequality, Mobility, and Social Change

In 2015, Vermont senator Bernie Sanders announced that he was running for the nomination of the Democratic Party to become President of the United States. While few experts believed that Sanders had a chance to win the nomination, he said that he was motivated to enter the race because of the "obscene level of wealth and income inequality" that he saw in the country. On his campaign website, Sanders (2016) argued that inequality in the United States had reached crisis proportions:

> The issue of wealth and income inequality is the great moral issue of our time, it is the great economic issue of our time, and it is the great political issue of our time. . . . This campaign is sending a message to the billionaire class: "you can't have it all." You can't get huge tax breaks while children in this country go hungry. You can't continue sending our jobs to China while millions are looking for work. You can't hide your profits in the Cayman Islands and other tax havens, while there are massive unmet needs on every corner of this nation. Your greed has got to end. You cannot take advantage of all the benefits of America, if you refuse to accept your responsibilities as Americans.

Sanders promised a significant increase in the minimum wage if he was elected president, and he proposed to make college tuition-free so that ordinary people could improve their lives. He promised to dramatically increase taxes on wealthy individuals and corporations. He proposed increases in parental leave, sick leave, and vacation time for workers. And he promised to increase government regulation of the finance sector, so that bankers would focus more on the public good instead of just making themselves rich.

Bernie Sanders, 2016 US Presidential Campaign
The choice of young Democratic voters in 2016, Bernie Sanders made the problem of inequality the centerpiece of his campaign.

LEARNING GOALS

7.1   Understand stratification as the way sociologists think about social inequality.

7.2   Distinguish types of stratification.

7.3   Develop an understanding of broad patterns of stratification in the United States and globally.

7.4   Comprehend the concept of mobility and distinguish different kinds of mobility, such as structural mobility and intergenerational mobility.

7.5   Consider factors that affect mobility and the stratification system, such as education, family background, and racial and gender differences, as well as social policy and social conflict.

Although Sanders began his campaign with almost no money and a huge deficit in public opinion polls, his message resonated with millions of Americans concerned about their economic prospects. Riding the wave of support from these voters, Sanders nearly won the nomination of the Democratic Party, and he made the topic of inequality critical to the 2016 US presidential election. Inequality continued to be a central issue in the contest for the 2020 Democratic nomination, and Sanders again announced his intent to campaign for the Democratic Party nomination.

Why does the topic of inequality provoke so much public interest and attention, especially in the current moment? How do ordinary people think about inequality? With whom do they compare themselves? What strategies do they use to try to improve their circumstances, and how confident are they in their ability to do so?

Inequality The unequal distribution of social goods such as money, power, and status.

This chapter explores social inequality and social mobility. **Inequality** refers to the unequal distribution of social goods such as money, power, and status. We begin by considering theories about inequality, and we discuss how patterns of inequality get organized into systems of stratification. We compare different stratification systems, and we describe how inequality is organized in today's world. Next, we turn to mobility, which refers to a change in a person's social status or a movement to a different place in the stratification system. We compare ways of thinking about mobility, and we discuss the social factors that contribute to increasing mobility. Finally, we consider how groups of people respond to inequality by creating movements for social change and demanding more effective social policies.

What Is Inequality?

By many measures, Singapore is the most expensive city in the world. A two-bedroom condominium in the city will cost more than $2 million. A gallon of milk is more than $10, and a gallon of gas is about $8. To live "comfortably" in Singapore, you will probably need an income of at least $200,000 per year. A person with an annual income of $60,000 in Singapore would feel very poor.

An interesting comparison to Singapore is Boise, Idaho, which is frequently described as one of the best and most affordable places to live in the United States. In Boise, a two-bedroom condominium averages about $170,000.

A gallon of milk is $2.50, and a gallon of gasoline costs about $2.40. You could live very comfortably in Boise with an income of $60,000 per year. A person making $200,000 per year would be near the top of the social hierarchy in Boise.

Boise, Idaho
Boise, Idaho, is often described as the best and one of the most affordable places to live in the United States.

Like most things in the social world, inequality is based on relationships and comparisons. It is not enough to know how much money you make, or what kind of house you live in, or how many televisions you own. We also have to know how you compare to the people around you. We need to know which people serve as your reference group and the criteria you are using to make your comparisons.

Is Inequality Natural or Social?

Philosophers and social theorists have long debated the causes of inequality. Some thinkers emphasize the natural differences in strength, intelligence, age, beauty, and technical skill that can lead to inequalities. The Greek philosopher Aristotle (384 BCE–322 BCE), for example, argued that good governments and good societies were those in which the naturally gifted were able to develop the virtue to lead their inferiors without exploiting them.

But most theories of inequality emphasize social causes. For the French philosopher Jean-Jacques Rousseau (1712–1778), the existence of social relationships leads to social comparisons, and ultimately to the desire for personal gain and advantages. We want to have higher status than other people, and we become jealous of those who have more prestige or wealth than we do. People may use their power and wealth to pursue their own private interests instead of the public good. These social causes of inequality, Rousseau argued, were more important than any natural differences in ability that may exist.

Karl Marx (1818–1883) also emphasized the social causes of inequality. As soon as people begin to cooperate and divide up necessary labor, he argued, inequality and exploitation will follow. The interests of those who control the work are in direct conflict with the interests of the workers under their control. As the dominant class, those who control the means of production organize society to their benefit. They invent ways to maximize their own profit and to exploit workers. For Marx, the history of society is the history of increasing inequality and exploitation.

Is Inequality Good or Bad?

Marx and Rousseau each held a negative view of inequality. They believed that equality created the conditions for human freedom, happiness, and self-fulfillment. Inequality, by contrast, was a source of slavery, misery, and wasted potential. They saw inequality as a social problem to be solved, either through better social policies, social movements to mobilize popular support for more social equality, or social conflicts.

There is abundant evidence for the negative effects of inequality. At the individual level, inequalities in income are associated with differences in health, educational attainment, and family stability (Neckerman and Torche 2007).

Inequality between groups is associated with an increase in political violence
Demonstrators in Paris, France, light a car on fire during a December 2018 protest of the Yellow Vests—a movement against the political elite protesting the rising cost of living in France as the prices of gas, housing, and other necessities continue to climb with no relief for working families.

Categorical inequality The inequality between social categories or social groups.

Relative deprivation A form of inequality between groups where people believe that they are being treated unequally in comparison to another group they view as similar to themselves.

Davis–Moore theory of inequality The theory that some level of inequality is necessary to motivate people to do the most difficult and important jobs in a society.

Marginal productivity theory The theory that inequality is a way of rewarding people who make a greater contribution to society, by encouraging them to work hard and use their talents.

Inequality also harms social development and the collective good. Inequality between groups, which Charles Tilly calls **categorical inequality**, is associated with an increase in political violence (Tilly 1999). **Relative deprivation** is another form of inequality between groups. It happens when people believe they are being treated unequally in comparison to another group they view as similar to themselves. Sociological research shows that increases in relative deprivation lead to higher levels of crime (Lea and Young 1984), and that for many people relative deprivation has a bigger impact on a person's quality of life than their objective circumstances (Firebaugh and Tach 2012). Cross-national research also suggests that high income inequality in a society is associated with negative health and wellness outcomes, such as higher rates of infant mortality, mental illness, drug use, and obesity. In other indicators, higher inequality is also associated with higher incarceration rates and homicide rates (Wilkinson and Pickett 2009).

But inequality is not always viewed as an evil that hurts society. While the Scottish philosopher Adam Smith (1723–1790) was concerned that extreme levels of inequality encouraged people to worship the rich and to scorn the poor, he thought that normal levels of inequality were unimportant as long as everyone in the society could satisfy their basic needs. Furthermore, Smith argued that normal levels of inequality encouraged people to work harder, leading to greater levels of innovation and economic productivity that benefit all. Many sociologists in the 1950s, like Kingsley Davis (1908–1997) and Wilbert E. Moore (1914–1987), held a similar view of inequality. The **Davis–Moore theory** argues that some level of inequality is necessary to motivate people to do the most difficult and important jobs in a society (Davis and Moore 1945). In economics, **marginal productivity theory** argues that inequality is a way of rewarding people who make a greater contribution to society, encouraging them to work hard and use their talents. According to these arguments, giving bigger rewards to the most productive and the most talented people benefits everyone.

Sociologists today are critical of the Davis–Moore and marginal productivity theories because these theories make unrealistic assumptions about the way the job market works. For example, people can only compete for vacant jobs, which means that there is a systematic bias in favor of people who discover such opportunities first—and this has nothing to do with who has the most talent (Sorensen and Kalleberg 1981). Other people are restricted in their job search by geographic ties to family or similar obligations that make a move difficult or impossible. In fact, most job markets are segmented, with a small number of prestigious, secure, and well-paid jobs and a larger number of less prestigious, insecure, and poorly paid jobs. Historically, minority groups have only been allowed to compete in the latter category, creating systematic biases in the job market (Kalleberg 2011). Even when a group is allowed to compete for vacant job openings in a part of the labor market where they were once excluded, they tend to receive less compensation for their talent and effort than other groups; this has clearly been the case for women and racial minorities (King 1992). These structured systems of inequality point to the need for a more sociological, multi-dimensional approach to the questions of talent, effort, and reward.

Inequality and Stratification

Stratification is a central sociological idea that describes structured patterns of inequality between different groups of people. It uses a metaphor from geology to describe how people are sorted into different social layers, or social strata, like the layers in a rock formation. Stratification touches virtually every social process and social institution. There are patterns of inequality in almost every area of social life—not only income, wealth, power, and prestige, but also employment, education, health, and participation in the arts. These patterns are shaped by family, gender, social class, race, ethnicity, sexuality, religion, nationality and ability. And the patterns of inequality are always changing, because societies are always changing.

Extreme stratification
The novel *Pride and Prejudice* described the stratification system in England in the late 1700s, where the extremely wealthy lived in castle-like manor houses.

Stratification A central sociological idea that describes structured patterns of inequality between different groups of people.

Types of Stratification

Stratification researchers examine the distribution of scarce but desirable resources, and how inequality emerges and is maintained. In most societies, inequality has multiple intersecting dimensions. For example, in societies where the first-born son inherits all the family wealth, inequality is based on a combination of age, gender, and inheritance. In societies where the most powerful people are members of a particular ethnic group, inequality is based on a combination of family and ethnic membership roles. By comparing the stratification systems of different societies, we can begin to identify which factors and combinations of factors are the most common, and how those have changed over time.

One comparative strategy is to define a small number of social classes that exist within the stratification system, and to compare the social characteristics and prospects for those social classes. Karl Marx and Ralf Dahrendorf argued that the most important features of inequality can be understood by distinguishing between two social classes: the dominant class, and the dominated class. Other sociologists have identified a larger number of social classes. In a recent study of the stratification system in contemporary England, British sociologists identified seven basic social classes (Savage 2015).

A different comparative strategy is to identify different ways of measuring inequality and stratification. Surveying the research literature in social stratification, David Grusky (Grusky 1994) identified four kinds of measurements common to sociological research:

Degree of inequality The level of concentration of a specific asset within the larger population.

Rigidity The degree to which movement is possible in a stratification system.

Ascriptiveness The degree to which characteristics at birth like race, gender, ethnicity, parents' background, or nationality determine life outcomes in a stratification system.

Crystallization The degree to which one dimension of inequality in a stratification system is connected to other dimensions of inequality.

Caste systems An extremely unequal stratification system in which people are born into a particular social group and have virtually no opportunity to change their social position.

1. **Degree of inequality** refers to the level of concentration of a specific asset within the larger population. For example, if we want to look at income stratification, we might want to know how much of the total income is controlled by the wealthiest 1 percent of the population.

2. **Rigidity** refers to how likely it is that people can move from one part of the stratification system to another. Rigidity measures whether people are likely to experience significant improvement (or decline) in their social situation over the course of their lives.

3. **Ascriptiveness** refers to the degree to which patterns of inequality are connected to traits that are present at birth, such as race, gender, ethnicity, parents' background, or nationality.

4. **Degree of crystallization** refers to how likely it is that somebody at the top (or bottom) of one inequality category will also appear at the top (or bottom) of other inequality categories. In other words, are the people with the most education also the ones with the highest levels of wealth, income, power, prestige, and health?

Caste Systems

The most extreme forms of stratification are found in classical **caste systems**, where people are born into a particular social group and have virtually no opportunity to change their social position. Caste systems are marked by high levels of inequality, rigidity, ascriptiveness, and crystallization. In a caste system, the group into which you are born completely defines your social standing, your life chances, and the kinds of people with whom you will be able to form relationships. One of the best-known caste systems is in India, but other historical examples include the American South during the period of slavery, the apartheid system in South Africa from 1948 to 1994, and China during the Yuan Dynasty (1271–1368).

In a caste system, there is a clearly defined hierarchy of social groups, or castes, which are defined by family background and measured in terms of racial or ethnic purity. Access to income, wealth, and other goods or services is completely determined by the caste into which a person is born. There are strict rules that forbid marriage to someone from a different caste. Friendships and even casual acquaintances are strongly discouraged and often forbidden for people who belong to different castes. The prohibitions against inter-caste contact are reinforced by extremely high levels of residential and occupational segregation, which means that your caste membership determines where you can live and what kind of job you can have. This also means that people from different castes rarely see each other in shared public spaces.

India's caste system has been the basis of Indian society for more than three thousand years. The Indian caste system was organized around a system of strict separation and social closure, in which people from different castes were assigned different and unequal positions in society. Marriages were traditionally arranged within castes by parents, and this ensured the reproduction of the caste system.

At the top were brahmins, who were mainly priests, scholars, and teachers, and at the bottom were shudras and the dalits. Shudras were limited to menial and undesirable jobs, and were forbidden to study sacred religious texts. Dalits, often described as "untouchables," were the only people in Indian society allowed to deal with the most ritually impure objects, such as waste and dead

Power and Resistance

Ending Apartheid in South Africa

Apartheid was a race-based caste system that existed in South Africa from 1948 until 1994. From the time that South Africa gained its independence from Great Britain in 1910, there had been racial segregation in housing and discrimination against black South Africans in the labor market. But racial inequality became much worse after 1948, when the Afrikaaner National Party won the national election. The National Party campaigned under the slogan "apartheid"; its goal was to separate society along racial lines, and to write laws that explicitly privileged the white minority.

Under the apartheid system, all South Africans were officially classified into one of four races: white, Bantu (black Africans), Colored (mixed race), and Asian (primarily Indian and Pakistani). The government passed laws that prohibited whites from marrying people from other racial groups. It set aside more than 80 percent of the land in South Africa for the white population, forcibly removing millions of non-whites from their homes and resettling them in impoverished minority-only spaces. There were separate public facilities for whites and non-whites, and non-whites were required to carry documents that showed that they were allowed to enter the white areas. Non-whites were prohibited from participating in national government. This discrimination produced extreme patterns of racial inequality. Average income for black South Africans was less than 10 percent of the average income for whites. On average, whites lived 20 years longer than blacks. Apartheid South Africa had the worst racial inequality in the world.

Black South Africans had long resisted and challenged racial discrimination in South Africa, and their resistance intensified under apartheid. In 1960, the South African police opened fire on a crowd of more than 5,000 black protesters in the town of Sharpeville, killing 69 people. The government banned the main black resistance movement, the African National Congress, jailing many of its leaders and forcing others to flee the country. Defenders of the apartheid regime tried to mobilize the international community in their favor, calling the African National Congress a terrorist and communist organization that was a threat to world order.

Despite the government's violence, protesters continued to challenge the apartheid system. Over time, they rallied world opinion against the apartheid system. South Africa was banned from the Olympics in 1964. The United Nations General Assembly denounced the apartheid system in 1973, and in 1976 the UN Security Council banned the sale of weapons to the South African government. Governments around the world imposed economic sanctions on South Africa, and a global divestment movement encouraged universities and other investors to pull their money out of companies that continued to do business in South Africa. Musicians and other performers stopped performing in South Africa, and many of them helped raise money for anti-apartheid groups.

By the end of the 1980s, the sustained pressure against the apartheid government led the Afrikaaner National Party to begin repealing many of the country's apartheid laws. The ban against the African National Congress was overturned. A new constitution gave all racial groups the right to vote, and formally ended the apartheid system. Nelson Mandela, who had been jailed for 27 years as the leader of the ANC, was elected president of South Africa in 1994. While South Africa still has some of the highest levels of economic inequality in the world today, and while racial inequality is still a significant problem, the country is no longer organized as a caste society.

Apartheid
Apartheid was a legally justified institution of racial segregation and subordination in South Africa that ran from 1948 to the early 1990s. The entrance to the Apartheid Museum, South Africa, shown here, evokes the memory of racism by re-creating the experience of separate entries for whites and non-whites to the museum.

ACTIVE LEARNING

Discuss: Are there laws in the United States that define race? What are they? What are their consequences?

animals. Within this hierarchy of castes developed a complex system of classification, with society separated into 3,000 distinct castes and 25,000 sub-castes, each defined by their occupation.

Stratification in today's India still retains strong influences from the caste system, but in other respects there have been important changes. The upper castes continue to dominate politics, education, and the economy. The lower castes continue to suffer from poor health, illiteracy, poverty, and social exclusion. But there are also changes. Caste-based discrimination was declared illegal by the Indian government in 1950. There is rising intermarriage between castes (Banerjee et al. 2013). The growth of non-Hindu groups in Indian society has further complicated the stratification system, while globalization and the growth of the industrial economy have introduced other forms of inequality, which are based more on class than caste.

Class Systems

In a class system of stratification, inequality is created primarily by differences in economic power. As Karl Marx observed of modern capitalism, at the top of the system are the people who own property and control economic production. Property owners create wealth for themselves by renting or developing their land, or by using proceeds from their land to invest in businesses. Business owners who control economic production also create wealth by keeping wages paid to their workers lower than the income they receive from their business ventures. According to Karl Marx, this is exploitation, since the value of the work performed by laborers that is not paid to the worker in wages is taken by the capitalist as profit. The lower the wages for workers, the higher the profits for the owners. Joining forces, property owners and business owners set the rules for the economy and enrich themselves. In a class system, the people with the most money have the most power, the most prestige, and the highest standard of living.

Compared with caste systems, class systems of inequality have less rigidity and less ascriptiveness. When class determines inequality, things like race, gender, ethnicity, or family background do not *directly* determine life chances; instead, what matters is access to material resources and control over economic production. These economic factors can reinforce older systems of inequality based on race, ethnicity, or gender. Family characteristics do not automatically create social privileges, as they do in a caste system. In a class system, the privileges one is born with have to be converted into economic resources and advantages.

Class systems of inequality have always been important, but in today's global economy the people who control economic production have more advantages than ever. They can search the world looking for the cheapest labor, which guarantees that their profits will be as high as possible. They can buy up property and other material resources

Class systems
In class systems, inequality is based on differences in economic power. This includes how much an individual owns and, importantly, how much power groups and institutions have to control what happens to them in the economy relative to other people.

all over the world, creating global businesses and global markets. Their wealth gives them global power and prestige, which means that virtually every society in the world has to deal with class-based inequality.

Status Systems

Class systems are not always stable on their own, because people do not always form alliances or join groups based solely on their economic interests. Max Weber argued that class systems function most effectively when they are organized around status groups. According to Weber, a **status group** is held together by a common lifestyle and shared characteristics of social honor. Like the in-groups we discussed in Chapter 5, people feel a bond of solidarity with other members of their status group, and they make social distinctions between their own status group and competing status groups.

In a status system, inequality is created when high-status groups join together to create a community of privilege and control. They belong to the same social clubs, live in the same neighborhoods, send their children to the same schools, and try to limit their friendships to people from the "right families" who have "good taste" and respectable jobs. As the political theorist Gaetano Mosca (1858–1941) wrote in *The Ruling Class* (1939), these high-status groups come to see themselves as being economically, intellectually, and morally superior. They believe they are the only ones who have the skills and character to control society. They aspire to create a society that is controlled by **elites.**

Status systems are similar to class systems in their levels of rigidity, but they have higher levels of ascriptiveness and much higher levels of crystallization of privilege across the entire spectrum of inequality categories. High-status groups live in a different world than everybody else, and even if outsiders do manage to gain access to that world, they are made to feel like they don't belong. (We discuss this in more detail later in the chapter, in our discussion of consumption and inequality.)

Because it is unusual for all high-status groups to be fully unified, status systems are also defined by elite conflict, in which high-status groups organize themselves into rival factions (Lachmann 2003). Sometimes competing elite factions are able to resolve their conflicts and consolidate their control. More frequently, however, they reach a stalemate, where the two factions are forced to share power despite the fact that they dislike and distrust one another.

Party Systems: Inequality through Meritocracy

In a **party system**, power and privilege come from the effective leadership of important organizations. The state socialist systems of the former communist countries of Eastern and Central Europe were organized as party systems. As we discussed in Chapter 5, organizational power increased with

Status group A group held together by a common lifestyle and shared characteristics of social honor.

Elites An elite is formed through high status behavior and the formation of institutions to create a community of privilege and control.

Party system A stratification system where power and privilege come from the effective leadership of important organizations.

Scroll and Key

The Scroll and Key Society is a secret society founded in 1842 at Yale University and is part of an elite status system. A privileged set of graduates from one of the most privileged universities in the world reproduces an even more elite community of privilege and honor in this secret society. Scroll and Key members include politicians, philanthropists, academics, and leaders in the arts and sciences.

the rise of bureaucracy. Bureaucracies allow people to complete their work more efficiently, develop greater expertise, and move more easily from one organization to another. Bureaucracy also forces people to follow the rules rather than exercise arbitrary power, in a way that can minimize conflicts and prevent the emergence of elite factions.

Party systems are less rigid and less ascriptive than other stratification systems. Hiring practices in a bureaucracy follow official rules, which reduces (but does not eliminate) the importance of "knowing the right people." Status and authority are based on party membership and also on possessing the technical expertise that is associated with the job, rather than the social characteristics and the family background of the person holding the job.

Party systems create inequality through **meritocracy**, which means that the people who control society are the ones who perform the best on examinations and other formal tests of ability. Despite the appeal of a society that rewards intelligence, skill, and effort rather than family background or family wealth, meritocracies are not perfect. When people get to the top of society by performing well on tests, they may believe that they are better than everyone else and that they deserve all the privileges they get. This can cause them to become unsympathetic toward people who are less successful. Meritocracy also pushes societies to subject children to testing in an effort to find and reward the "best and brightest."

A significant challenge of meritocracies is that they do not actually eliminate other sources of inequality, such as race, gender, or family background. Racism and sexism can work directly against merit. Families with more education and wealth also do particularly well in meritocracies, using their resources to make sure that their children do well on the high-stakes tests that are used to identify and reward talent. Some critics argue that meritocracy is no more than an ideology that justifies the wealth of the educated middle classes.

The Role of Consumption in Reproducing Inequality

As we discussed in Chapter 4, people with more education and wealth use their consumption to signal their privilege to others. First discussed by the social critic Thorstein Veblen (1857–1929) in his book *The Theory of the Leisure Class* (1899), **conspicuous consumption** happens when people buy things in order to display their wealth and social status. Today, conspicuous consumption might include buying an $8,000 Rolex watch, a $20,000 Hermès purse, or a $200,000 Bentley automobile. Nobody truly needs these things, but they are effective at signaling wealth and impressing other people.

Today, conspicuous consumption has led to an ideology of **consumerism** that encourages people to buy more than they need. In a consumerist society, people believe that buying things will make them happier. But problems arise when people cannot afford their consumption habits, and fall into debt.

Meritocracy Stratification systems where high position is held by those who perform the best on examinations and other formal tests of ability.

Conspicuous consumption A way to display privilege, wealth, and social status to others.

Consumerism A widespread ideology grounded in conspicuous consumption that encourages buying and consuming goods, including buying more than an individual needs.

Party systems create inequality through the ideology of meritocracy
The college entrance exam in China is the largest single high-stakes test in the world. In 2018, 975 million Chinese students registered for the exam.

PAIRED
CONCEPTS **Inequality and Privilege**

Marketing to the Super-Rich

For the wealthiest people in society, the experience of shopping is significantly different than it is for everyone else. Marketers of goods and services create specific campaigns for the super-rich that attempt to cater to their unique tastes and needs. We can see this distinction at work in the markets for travel and luxury goods.

For instance, most people make their travel decisions based on price. When searching for a plane ticket or a hotel room, they will usually buy the least expensive option that fits their itinerary. In these markets, the competition is fierce, and the profit margins are small. Companies need to sell large quantities of their product in order to make a profit.

But travel marketing is very different when it is targeted to the super-rich, for whom luxury and distinction are more important than price. Japan Airlines charges more than $20,000 for a first-class flight between Tokyo and London, which is nearly 20 times higher than the cost of a discounted economy fare. What does the rich traveler get for such an expensive ticket? Many airlines provide their first-class travelers a chauffeured car to the airport. Once at the airport, they get a special place to check in for their flight, and a separate and much shorter security line. They wait for their flight in a private lounge, with free food and drinks. They enter and exit the plane before everyone else, and their luggage comes off the plane first. While on the plane, they enjoy gourmet food and drinks and a private entertainment system from the comfort of an enclosed seat that converts into a bed. Some first-class cabins even have luxurious bathrooms that include a full shower. Because the profit margins are significantly higher for first-class seats than they are for economy seats, the airlines are happy to spend the money providing these extra amenities.

Some travel markets ignore the masses altogether and cater exclusively to the super-rich. The markets for luxury yachts and private aircraft only pay attention to people with a net worth—that is, wealth and income minus any debt owed—of $10 million or more. Despite the global downturn in the economy between 2008 and 2016, the market for yachts and private aircraft has remained strong, a testament to the growing inequality between the super-rich and everyone else.

Consumption as status markers
These luxury yachts docked in Italy are consumption markers for the super-rich. What consumption markers affect status in your world?

ACTIVE LEARNING

Find out: Consumption is also a social marker for those of us who are not super-rich. What does consumption look like at your school or in your workplace? Is there conspicuous consumption? Are there specific clothes, electronics, vacation destinations, or other consumption behaviors that define some groups? What does the marketing for these consumer goods look like? Pick one item and do some research to see if you can discover the relative size of the market for these items.

In her book *The Overspent American* (1997), sociologist Juliet Schor describes how consumerism increases inequality. In the past, people tried to "keep up with the Joneses," which meant that they were content if they had as much as their neighbors. Today, however, many take their cues from the lifestyles of wealthy and famous people they see in the media, despite the fact that those people have an income that is much higher than the average household. This creates a "culture of upscale spending," in which people set unrealistic consumption goals and obsess about the things they cannot afford.

As a result of this culture of upscale spending, most households have stopped saving money, and credit card debt has exploded. The typical American

lawyers, doctors, engineers, scientists, information technology officers, and others who typically have high-level educational credentials and professional expertise. This group enjoys financial stability, with good job security and salaries that often exceed $100,000 per year. They live in safe and comfortable neighborhoods, and they have high-quality employer-provided healthcare. They send their children to good schools, and they invest significant time and resources helping their children become successful.

Below the professional managers are members of the **middle class**, which is composed of people who have an annual income of between $60,000 and $90,000. Most people in the middle class have completed a college degree. They tend to come from one of the following three occupational groups:

1. Middle-level managers, such as branch managers, store managers, and human resource managers.

2. White-collar workers, who work in an office and perform specialized jobs for the organization. Examples of white-collar jobs include accountants, office managers and administrators, public relations specialists, and computer programmers.

3. Highly skilled blue collar workers, who do complicated and specialized physical jobs that are in high demand. Examples of these kinds of jobs include solar energy installers, elevator installers, oil drill operators, and commercial drivers.

As we discuss in Chapter 8, there are marked gender differences within these categories, with blue-collar workers being disproportionately male, white-collar workers in service positions disproportionately female (Groves 2011; Laughlin and Christnacht 2017), and women earning between 80 and 85 cents for every dollar men earn (Graf, Brown, and Patten 2019; Fontenot, Semega, and Kollar 2017).

Most middle-class workers have stable jobs and predicable salaries, which makes it easier for them to do the kind of planning that is necessary to achieve a middle-class lifestyle, such as saving for retirement. Their homes are smaller than those owned by people in the upper-middle class, their vacations are less fancy, they have significantly less investment income, and they are more likely to send their children to public schools.

The third group is the **lower-middle class**, which consists of families with a household income of between $15,000 and $60,000 per year. Among all the families with children in the United States, nearly one-third are in the lower-middle class (Kearney and Harris 2013). People in the lower-middle class have less job security, and they often perform fairly monotonous and unskilled work. Examples of lower-middle class jobs include cashiers, data entry positions, telemarketing and call center jobs, and fast food line cooks. These workers are often paid

Middle class A social class group below the upper-middle class composed of families with an annual income of between $60,000 and $90,000.

Lower-middle class A social class group below the middle class composed of families with a household income of between $15,000 and $60,000 per year.

Installing solar panels
Highly skilled blue collar workers, like this solar panel installation technician, are in very high demand and are typically members of the middle class.

hourly wages instead of a salary, which means that their income is less predictable because employers can cut back their hours. Many people in the lower-middle class work more than one job just to make ends meet. Their jobs are less likely to come with health benefits, retirement benefits, or opportunities for advancement, making it nearly impossible for them to plan for their future. For most workers in the lower-middle class, a single setback such as getting sick or needing a major car repair is enough to push them into poverty.

THE POOR. The US government establishes an official poverty threshold to measure who is living in poverty and who is eligible for government programs designed to help the poor. First developed in 1963, this measurement was set at three times the minimum amount of money it would cost to feed each member of a family, based on how much housing, health, and other essential services cost relative to food. Since that initial calculation, adjustments to the poverty threshold have been made by looking at changes in the prices paid for consumer goods and services. In 2017, the official poverty threshold for a family of four was $25,696, which some critics argue is too low (National Center for Children in Poverty 2019).

According to the US Census Bureau, in 2017 there were 39.7 million people living in poverty in the United States, which is equal to 12.3 percent of the total population (Fontenot, Semega, and Kollar 2018). Compared to the population at large, families living in poverty are more likely to be single-parent households, and they are more likely to be headed by women with young children. Women, children, and people with disabilities are overrepresented among the poor, and so are African Americans and Latinos. Nearly one-quarter of all families living in poverty are part of the **working poor**, which means that they are in poverty despite the fact that they include at least one person who worked for more than half of the year. Most of the working poor are employed in part-time jobs with low pay, no benefits, and no security, and often cycle between unemployment and part-time unemployment. About 30 percent of those in poverty did not work at least one week in 2017. The government defines long-term unemployment as being out of work for six months, and the Bureau of Labor Statistics reports that long-term unemployment remains stubbornly high since the 2008 recession, especially among African American men and Latinos. People who experience long-term unemployment in poor families find it extremely challenging to escape from poverty. In fact, once somebody has been out of work for a year, they only have a 10 percent chance of ever finding a job again. In his book *The Truly Disadvantaged* (1987), William Julius Wilson described this group as an **underclass**—a group of socially isolated people, usually living in impoverished urban neighborhoods, whose long-term unemployment forces them into welfare dependence, street crime, or the drug trade.

Working poor People and families in poverty despite having at least one person who works for a wage.

Underclass A social group described by William Julius Wilson that experiences long-term unemployment and social isolation, and often lives in impoverished urban neighborhoods.

Global Stratification

Global inequality is more extreme than the inequality that exists within nations (Milanovic 2010, 2016), and by many measures, global inequality is the worst it has been since the 19th century (Hickel 2016; Piketty 2014). Ten years after the global economic recession of 2008, 1 percent of the population owns 50.1 percent of all household wealth in the world. A recent Oxfam report documents that "61 people own the same as the bottom 50% of the world population" (Oxfam 2018; Credit Suisse 2017).

Global income inequality skews heavily in favor of countries in North America and Western Europe, particularly for people living in or near major

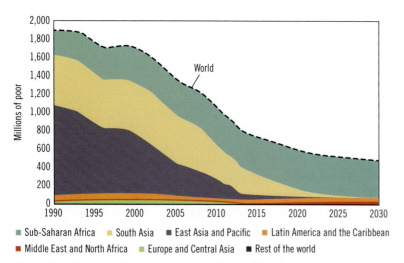

Figure 7.1   **Number of Extreme Poor by Region, 1990–2030.**
Source: PovcalNet (online analysis tool), http://iresearch.worldbank.org/PovcalNet/. World Bank, Washington, DC, World Development Indicators; World Economic Outlook; Global Economic Prospects; Economist Intelligence Unit.

cities. In fact, virtually everyone who can afford to buy a house or an apartment in a city like London, New York, Los Angeles, or Paris is a member of the global 1 percent. At the other extreme, global poverty skews heavily toward people living in poor nations in the Global South. The World Bank measures global poverty by looking at the proportion of the population living on less than $1.90 per day. As Figure 7.1 illustrates, the countries with the largest proportion of the population living below the global poverty threshold are mainly found in Africa, India, and parts of Southeast Asia. The global poverty population is disproportionately young, uneducated, and works in rural agriculture (World Bank 2018).

Colonialism   A global stratification system in which powerful nations used their military strength to take political control over other territories and exploit them economically.

Global patterns of inequality are connected to the history of **colonialism**, in which powerful nations used their military strength to take political control over other territories and exploit them economically. The major powers of Europe developed vast colonial empires that extended into North America, South America, India, Africa, and the Pacific. These began as early as the 1500s, and did not really end until the 20th century. The legacy of colonialism can be seen most dramatically in Africa, where Western European countries controlled most of the continent until after World War II, and where global poverty remains the most concentrated in the world even today.

Another way of thinking about global stratification is through the lens of **world systems theory**, which focuses on the different roles available to countries based on their level of economic power and development. First developed by the sociologist Immanuel Wallerstein, world systems theory argues that a country's position in the world economy determines the kinds of economic and social development strategies that are available to it. Advantages in the world system accrue over time, so nations that have been powerful in the past are likely to maintain their dominance. Wallerstein (2004) describes three positions in the world system: core nations, peripheral nations, and semi-peripheral nations.

World systems theory   A way to think about global stratification that emphasizes the relative positions of countries in the world economy as crucial determinants of inequality

At the top of the hierarchy are the core nations, which are the wealthiest and the most economically developed. The earliest to industrialize, these nations have the most diverse economies, and they are usually the first to develop new technologies. They were often colonial powers at an earlier time in history. Core nations compete with one another for global dominance, particularly in the areas of banking and trade. The core nations in the modern world system are the United States, Canada, Japan, China, Taiwan, Australia, New Zealand, and the nations of Western Europe (Chase-Dunn, Kawano and Brewer 2000).

At the bottom of the hierarchy are peripheral nations, which are the poorest and the least economically developed. These countries do not have diverse economies, and they usually make money by extracting raw materials and exporting them to the core nations. Peripheral nations have extremely high levels of inequality. While most of their population is poor and uneducated, a small group of elites own most of the land and are connected to multinational

Global and Local

Wealthy Chinese Students at Elite US Schools

In 2015, more than 300,000 students from China enrolled in US universities (Chen and Jordan 2016). These students came to the United States for many different reasons. Some found Chinese universities to be too rigid and uninspiring, and were excited by the American emphasis on creativity, originality, and entrepreneurship. Most believe that a degree from a US university will help them find better-paying jobs, either in the United States or in China. For the wealthiest Chinese students, however, going to an elite US university is viewed as their ticket to enter the global elite. The daughter of China's President Xi Jinping attended Harvard, which is the top choice among elite Chinese parents, followed closely by Yale, Stanford, Princeton, and MIT.

To improve their chances of getting their children into the most elite US universities, many wealthy Chinese parents have begun to send their children to US boarding schools. The Association of Boarding Schools now organizes events in Beijing and Shanghai, where wealthy Chinese parents can learn more about US prep schools (Gao 2012). By the time a wealthy Chinese student has completed prep school and college in the United States, their parents will have spent half a million dollars on their education.

There are significant economic motivations for American schools to accept large numbers of full-paying Chinese students. Because government funding for most state universities has decreased significantly, the influx of students paying out-of-state tuition is an important source of revenue. Prep schools and small private colleges need a certain number of full-paying students to remain financially viable, and they foster hopes that graduates from extremely wealthy families will eventually become generous donors. At the same time, these schools hope that the presence of foreign students will bring a more global perspective to their campus communities. By creating a cultural exchange between students from different countries, they hope to prepare all of their students more effectively for the diverse global economy.

The global market for college admissions
Elite private schools like Deerfield Academy in Massachusetts recruit students globally from among those who are willing and able to pay. Graduates of such "prep" schools are much more likely to gain entry to prestigious colleges and universities.

ACTIVE LEARNING

Find out: Does your school actively recruit international students? Research the reasons why they do so. You could begin your inquiry by consulting your school's admissions office or website.

corporations. Peripheral nations are usually dominated by core nations, whose multinational corporations exploit their cheap unskilled labor in order to produce products for export to the core nations. Peripheral nations are found primarily in Africa and parts of Asia and South America (Chase-Dunn, Kawano, and Brewer 2000).

Last, the middle position in the global system is occupied by semi-peripheral nations, which are positioned between the peripheral and the core nations. Semi-peripheral nations have diversified economies, but their industrial and technological development happened much later than that of the core nations. As a result, they usually remain dependent on the core nations for military protection, advanced scientific training, economic investment, and the regulation of global markets. Examples of semi-peripheral nations include Brazil, Mexico, Turkey, and India.

In today's global world, ambitious and talented students from peripheral and semi-peripheral nations often leave their countries to attend university and establish their careers in the core nations. In some instances, these students return home to help lead in the development of their countries. But many of them stay in the core nations, becoming a part of the global elite and leading to a brain drain that contributes to global stratification.

Social Mobility

The "rags-to-riches" story is a staple in Hollywood movies. *Joy* (2015) follows a single mother who invents a new kind of mop, becomes a celebrity on the Home Shopping Network, and ultimately becomes a business tycoon. *The Pursuit of Happyness* (2006) follows a salesman who, after a period of homelessness, manages to get an unpaid internship with a stock brokerage, and ultimately goes on to form his own multimillion-dollar financial firm.

Vertical social mobility Social mobility up or down in the socioeconomic stratification system.

Social mobility A change in a person's social status or a movement to a different place in the stratification system.

The rags-to-riches story describes a type of **vertical social mobility**, which happens when people change their position in the social stratification system. **Social mobility** that is vertical can include upward as well as downward mobility, but upward social mobility stories are much more common in popular culture. According to Lawrence Samuel (2012: 7), "upward mobility has served as the heart and soul of the American Dream . . . the prospect of 'betterment' and to 'improve one's lot' for oneself and one's children is much of what this country is all about."

In people's actual lives, upward mobility is much more gradual than the way it is presented in Hollywood movies. For people who have middle-class and upper-middle-class jobs, the most common experience of betterment is to move slightly upward within their social class position over the course of their lives. Although their salaries may gradually increase, their social class position remains the same. Significant vertical mobility is relatively uncommon.

Horizontal mobility Social movement in people's life that occurs without changing their overall position in the socioeconomic stratification system.

Intergenerational mobility The change in social status between different generations in the same family, or the change in the position of children relative to their parents.

However, many people do experience **horizontal mobility**, which happens when people experience change without altering their position in the socioeconomic stratification system. When people move to a new city to advance their careers, they have to meet new people, and they experience changes in their social standing and their social relationships. Another example of horizontal mobility is when a family moves to a new neighborhood in order to enroll their children in a better school district. Such parents are trying to create **intergenerational mobility**, which refers to changes in social status between different generations in the same family. In the next section of this chapter, we will discuss the social factors that are associated with successful intergenerational mobility.

Relative mobility The understanding of change in social position compared to other groups.

Absolute mobility Change in social position, regardless of what is happening with other people.

Most people care more about **relative mobility** than **absolute mobility**. Absolute mobility means that you have more things than you used to, but it does not take into account what is happening to other people. For example, most people in the United States today have better cars, computers, and televisions than their parents did. They live in bigger houses, travel more, and eat in restaurants more frequently. In absolute terms, people have more things than their parents once did.

Relative mobility is more sociologically meaningful, because it is based on your understanding of how well you are doing in comparison to other people. Upward relative mobility means that you are doing better than the people around you, or that you are doing better than you thought you were going to do.

If you live in a bigger house than the one you grew up in, but everyone you know has a bigger house than you do, you may not feel like you have experienced upward mobility. On the other hand, if you manage to find and purchase your dream house, then you will probably feel like you have experienced upward mobility.

Social Factors Associated with Mobility

Stratification researchers have identified three factors that are the most likely to increase social mobility: education, family background, and culture. These factors all interact with one another. In addition, social mobility is also higher in neighborhoods that have less residential segregation (Chetty

Social mobility
Mobility is about social distinctions. Most people care more about relative mobility than absolute mobility. They compare themselves to neighbors, friends, and family members rather than to some absolute standard.

et al. 2014). Social mobility is higher for people who do not experience major family disruptions, such as divorce or job loss (Conley 2005). Social mobility is also shaped by gender, race, ethnicity, sexuality, and other important social categories.

EDUCATION. Educational success is one of the strongest predictors of social mobility. In fact, sociological research for the last 50 years has shown that as much as half of all intergenerational mobility occurs through educational attainment (Blau and Duncan 1967; Black and Devereux 2011). Education is also associated with better outcomes in a range of domains, from the health of children and parents to the likelihood of criminal activity and voting (Lochner 2011). In short, if you want to improve your life and the lives of your children, the best strategy is to do well in school and make sure that your children also do well in school.

In today's society, getting a college degree is particularly important for mobility. Among adult children who have a college degree, nearly three-quarters have incomes greater than their parents'. For children born into low-income families, education is even more important. Among college-educated adults who were born poor, 96 percent end up earning more money than their parents (Haskins 2008).

It is also true that the relationship between education and mobility can reinforce inequality. Access to quality education is distributed unevenly, in a way that benefits the wealthy at the expense of the poor. Wealthy families are also better able to invest financial resources in their children's education. The result is that educational success is stratified by family income. Children from the wealthiest quintile (the top fifth of all families) are nearly five times as likely to complete a college degree as children from the poorest quintile (Haskins 2008). Among the top-ranked colleges and universities, nearly three-quarters of students come from families in the highest socioeconomic quartile (Haveman and Smeeding 2006). Students from poor and minority neighborhoods have fewer academic support resources in their high schools, tend to start their college search later than wealthier students, and are less aware of financial

Measuring Status Attainment and Social Mobility

The standard way to measure social mobility is to compare an adult person's position in the stratification system with that of their parents. But this strategy requires many additional choices: at what point in a person's life do we measure their social position? Do we compare their social position with both of their parents, or only one of them? And how exactly are we supposed to measure "social position"?

Among social scientists, there are two main strategies for studying social position. Economists focus primarily on income, assets, and other measures of financial wealth. Sociologists, on the other hand, prefer to focus on a person's occupation. A person's occupation, they argue, is a much better predictor of social position and a much better way of making comparisons with a person's parents. There are four compelling reasons for the effectiveness of this strategy. First, a person's occupation is highly correlated with their income as well as their level of educational achievement. Second, a person's occupation involves issues of identity, including judgments about the prestige of different kinds of work. Third, it is easier to collect reliable information about a person's occupation than it is to collect data about their income and financial resources. Finally, it is easier to collect the kind of historical data that is needed to compare adults with their parents. Most people know what their parents' occupations were, but they are unlikely to know much about their parents' income and finances.

In sociology, the most influential research strategy for measuring social mobility is the status attainment model created by Peter Blau and Otis Dudley Duncan (Blau and Duncan 1967). Blau and Duncan collected data on father's occupation, father's education, son's education, son's first job, and son's ultimate occupational status. They found that a father's occupation and education both have a direct and positive relationship on a son's education. But the effect of a father's status, while significant, was relatively small when compared with the effect that the son's actual educational achievements had on his first job and his ultimate occupational status. In other words, while a parent's background helps their child get to the starting line, the child has to finish the race on their own.

Because Blau and Duncan's original research is now more than 50 years old, sociologists have made important changes to their original model. For example, while the focus on fathers and sons may have made sense in the early 1960s, women and daughters are now routinely included in data collection and in theories about what causes social mobility (Goldthorpe and Payne 1986). Researchers now collect much more detailed educational and occupational histories (Blossfeld 1986), and they look more carefully at different outcomes between siblings within a family (Conley 2005). There is greater focus on the ways that consumption and other lifestyle factors influence stratification and mobility (Ganzeboom, Treiman, and Ultee 1991). And there is more comparative research, focusing in particular on the effects that different social policies can have on increasing social mobility (Neckerman and Torche 2007).

Occupational status
Compared to income or assets, occupation is usually a better predictor of social position and a better way of measuring intergenerational mobility than other factors.

ACTIVE LEARNING

Find out: One reason it can be hard to measure intergenerational income differences is that people are not always willing to talk about money—even in families. While parents talk to children about their children's economic situations, they are less likely to disclose their own financial situations to their children. Interview an older family member, or another adult from your parents' generation, and ask whether or not their parents talked to them about their own income and financial decisions. Then consider if you have had straightforward and detailed discussions with your parents about your parents' money and financial decisions, or if you have had (or will have) such conversations with your children. Do you think it would be a good idea to do so? Why or why not?

aid resources. These patterns do not completely determine life outcomes, since there is mobility in the system, but it is true that there are structures of inequality and opportunity that strongly shape life chances for different groups of people.

FAMILY BACKGROUND. Family background influences socialization, social opportunities, and social mobility. In virtually every country where there is data available, researchers have found that there is a significant relationship between parents' social and economic background and their children's educational and financial achievements (Bowles, Gintis, and Groves 2008).

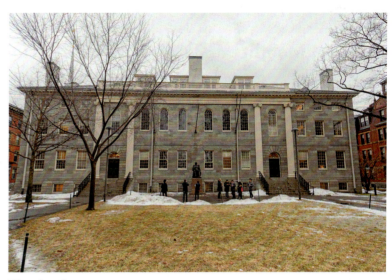

Elite education
Among the most prestigious colleges and universities, such as Harvard University, nearly three-quarters of the students come from the wealthiest quartile of families.

There are many reasons why family background shapes an individual's opportunities for social mobility. Wealthier parents can afford to send their children to better schools, and they can pay for tuition when their children go to college. Wealthy parents may even provide the down payment for purchasing an adult child's first home. All of this helps reduce the debt burden for children of privilege, saves them more money, and secures their futures more easily.

As we discussed in Chapter 5, parents with high levels of education have distinctive parenting styles. They teach their children to be assertive and to expect to be taken seriously in the adult world. This type of socialization starts paying off when children begin school, and continues to do so when they enter the workplace. More-privileged parents also teach their children to enjoy art, literature, and other forms of cultural capital that help them feel comfortable in the world of privilege.

CULTURE. Being comfortable with the cultural tastes and interests of the privileged is another way that people at the top of the stratification system reproduce their advantages. The sociologist Pierre Bourdieu (1986, 1998; Bourdieu and Passeron 1979, 1990) called this **cultural capital**. Usually, cultural capital reinforces social inequality. In certain circumstances, though, cultural capital can also be a source of social mobility. For ambitious children who come from low-income families, becoming familiar with art and classical music can contribute to upward social mobility (DiMaggio 1982). Children whose parents do a lot of reading in their spare time tend to experience higher levels of social mobility, when compared with children from a similar social background whose parents do not do as much reading (De Graaf, De Graaf, and Kraaykamp 2000).

In other circumstances, teachers and employers actively promote social mobility, by reinterpreting social disadvantages as advantages. While many employers prefer to hire people who share their background and interests, others believe that workers who come from disadvantaged backgrounds are more resilient, better able to handle setbacks, and more effective at operating with limited resources (Streib 2017). In jobs that require people to interact with a diverse

Cultural capital Education, cultural knowledge, and cultural consumption that signals privilege to others; the knowledge and consumption of culturally valued things.

CAREERS

Social Mobility and Career Planning

Effective career guidance is essential for helping people plan and make choices about their education, careers, and future lives. Guidance counselors are a critical resource for students to link the skills they are learning in school with career opportunities, especially those outside a student's own social networks. Social research suggests that students should start to think about careers as early as middle school, and should be in regular contact with professional guidance counselors through graduation (Curry, Belser, and Binns 2013). Effective career guidance is absolutely crucial for increasing social mobility, because poor and disadvantaged students are the least likely to have the social contacts and the cultural knowledge that will help them successfully navigate the complicated world of jobs and careers.

Guidance counselors are more effective when they take into account the patterns of social stratification and social opportunity. Most students look at prestige-based rankings when thinking about where to go to college, despite the fact that many of the most prestigious schools do a relatively poor job of admitting students from low-income families (Woodhouse 2015). In recent years CollegeNet has taken a different approach with its Social Mobility Index, which helps students identify the schools that most consistently graduate students from low-income backgrounds into promising careers.

Similarly, sociological research suggests that some high-paying jobs are better than others at hiring people from all levels of the stratification system. Many students want to work in top-tier investment banks, consulting firms, and law firms, because these jobs offer six-figure starting salaries. However, these employers aggressively target graduates from the most prestigious universities, ignoring the applications of students from other schools. In addition, even among the Ivy League graduates they interview, these firms tend to gravitate toward those students who combine good grades with the kinds of extracurricular activities and interests that signal a wealthy upbringing (Rivera 2015). These jobs may be glamorous and rewarding, but they are not always readily available to people who come from lower in the stratification system.

In contrast, huge investments are being made to increase the number of low-income and minority students entering careers in STEM (science, technology, engineering, and mathematics) fields. Jobs in these fields are forecast to expand rapidly over the next several decades, and on average they offer starting salaries that are 26 percent higher than those in non-STEM fields (Bidwell 2014). In some high-demand STEM fields, such as web development, computer user support, and environmental engineering, companies hire students as paid apprentices or interns while they are still in college and teach them the skills they will need to be successful in the industry (Harper and Lacey 2016). By comparison, for people who choose creative majors such as fashion, tourism studies, or communication, the people who get good jobs are more likely to be those who can afford to take unpaid internships in expensive cities, and who have social connections with industry insiders (Armstrong and Hamilton 2013).

Diversity in STEM careers
Huge investments are being made to increase the number of low-income and minority students entering careers in STEM. Why is it important to recruit diverse candidates into scientific careers?

ACTIVE LEARNING

Find out: The earlier you can connect with your school's career center, the more successful you will be in internship and job search. Career centers offer a range of programs and services, such as self-assessments, internship opportunities, and career information. Make an appointment at your campus career center to talk about your career goals with a counselor.

population, coming from a more disadvantaged background can be seen as an advantage. In these kinds of situations, people who come from lower positions in the stratification system can be successful, especially if they have done well in school and earned the credentials they need for the job.

Structural Mobility

Some high-paying jobs that are available today did not exist 10 years ago. **Structural mobility** happens when changes in society lead to larger changes in the stratification system. The US manufacturing sector has lost more than seven million jobs since 1979, taking away some of the best-paying and most secure jobs for men without a college degree. At the other end of the spectrum, between 1910 and 2000, jobs held by professionals, managers, salespeople, clerical workers, and service workers have increased from one-quarter to three-quarters of all US employment (Wyatt and Hecker 2006). These structural changes in the economy create both upward and downward mobility for entire classes of workers, creating significant opportunities for some and serious stress for others.

Periods of social crisis and rapid social change can also produce structural mobility. Major economic recessions cause widespread job losses, which can have lasting effects on entire generations of workers and their children. During the Great Recession of 2008 more than 8.7 million jobs were lost, with more than half of all adult workers in the United States experiencing unemployment, a cut in pay, a reduction in hours, or an involuntary period in a part-time job (Pew Research Center 2010a). In Japan, a 20-year economic decline that began in the early 1990s has created a "lost generation" doomed to career instability. For such workers, the bad luck of entering the workforce at the wrong time can have negative consequences that will last for their entire lives. Even after the economy begins to improve, they find themselves passed over in favor of new graduates and younger workers, who do not bear the stigma of long-term unemployment.

Structural Mobility
The 2008 economic recession led to widespread job losses and downward mobility. This was the result of the economic failure of institutions rather than individuals.

Structural mobility Changes in social position in the stratification system that occur because of structural changes in the economy and wider society.

Social Change and the Attempt to Create More Equality

The existence of inequality often creates resistance, conflict, and demands for social change. In his book *Weapons of the Weak*, James Scott shows how the disadvantaged use everyday forms of resistance to battle against inequality (Scott 1985). They drag their feet while they are at work, they engage in small acts of sabotage, and they gossip about the rich and powerful in their society. Constantly testing the authority of those who stand above them, they manage to create small spaces of freedom within the existing systems of inequality, in which they can maneuver and create advantages for themselves.

In fact, the experience of inequality is often connected to the hope of creating a more equal society. This is not true for all forms of inequality, to be sure. It is hard to get people to care about the inequalities that exist between the well-to-do and the rich (Frankfurt 1987). But many people do care about the poverty, violence, disrespect, and health disparities that fall disproportionately onto people at the bottom of the stratification system.

Social Policy

Governments have created social policies to address poverty, violence, and other undesirable consequences of social stratification. One of these social policies was the minimum wage law, which was first established in New Zealand in 1894, and then adopted by other countries around the world. Today, more than 90 percent of countries have established minimum wage laws. In 2019, Australia had the highest hourly minimum wage.

Another widely adopted social policy is the progressive income tax, in which poorer people pay a lower proportion of their income in tax, while wealthier people pay a higher proportion. The first progressive income tax was established in England in 1798. The United States established a progressive income tax in 1862; today, the US tax system has seven different income brackets, which begin at 10 percent and increase progressively up to a maximum of 37 percent of all income above $500,000 ($600,000 for married taxpayers filing jointly) (Table 7.1). Most countries in the world today have some version of a progressive income tax, as a way of trying to reduce inequality.

Other social policies are designed to redress historical inequalities based on race, gender, and ethnicity. Globally, women and racial minorities have been disproportionately harmed by poverty, violence, and discrimination, making these groups more vulnerable and limiting their opportunities for social mobility. The United States created a Civil Rights Division of the Department of Justice in 1957, in order to enforce laws prohibiting discrimination on the basis of race, color, sex, disability, religion, familial status, and national origin. At a global level, the United Nations, the US Department of State, and other national governments are engaged in diplomacy, foreign assistance programs, and partnerships with private organizations around the world to promote greater equality, by responding to historical structures of discrimination and inequality.

Social Conflict

Contentious politics The use of social conflict and other disruptive techniques to make a political point in an effort to change government policy.

Charles Tilly defines **contentious politics** as the use of social conflict and other disruptive techniques to make a political point and to change government policy. Contentious politics can be either nonviolent (demonstrations, protests, labor strikes, civil disobedience) or violent (destruction of property, rioting, civil wars, even terrorism). By disrupting ordinary events and focusing attention on specific issues, contentious politics force people in society to decide which side of the conflict they support, and pressure governments to respond.

Table 7.1 **US Tax Brackets and Rates, 2019**

RATE	FOR UNMARRIED INDIVIDUALS, TAXABLE INCOME OVER	FOR MARRIED INDIVIDUALS FILING JOINT RETURNS, TAXABLE INCOME OVER	FOR HEADS OF HOUSEHOLDS, TAXABLE INCOME OVER
10%	$0	$0	$0
12%	$9,700	$19,400	$13,850
22%	$39,475	$78,950	$52,850
24%	$84,200	$168,400	$84,200
32%	$160,725	$321,450	$160,700
35%	$204,100	$408,200	$204,100
37%	$510,300	$612,350	$510,300

Source: Internal Revenue Service. 2019.

Structure and Contingency

Creating Social Security

The question of economic security for large aging populations has been a perennial issue. Historically, the challenge of creating economic security was taken up by families, fraternal organizations, churches, trade unions, and charities. Eventually, governments created social policies to protect the economic security of their aged populations.

Government-created pension systems began to spread throughout Europe, Australia, and New Zealand between the 1880s and 1920s, through pension and social insurance programs established for workers and needy citizens. England, Sweden, and Denmark established "national minimums" in the 1930s, to support their citizens during old age, sickness, disability, and unemployment (Skocpol 1995: 313). The United States lagged behind these countries. It did not create any nationwide social insurance programs before 1935, and the programs it did create were less comprehensive.

In the United States, the attempt to create an old-age pension system goes back to the beginning of the nation. In 1795, Thomas Paine called for a system that taxed people who inherited property in order to pay an annual pension to every American aged 50 or older. In 1862, the Civil War pension plan was created to pay benefits to disabled soldiers as well as to widows and orphans of soldiers who had been killed or disabled during military service. This plan was extended in 1906, to cover all Civil War veterans who were aged 62 or older. But the Civil War pension program was relatively limited, including less than 1 percent of the total US population at the time.

While the United States could simply have copied European models of government-created pension systems, structural and contingent factors prevented this from happening. As Theda Skocpol has argued, the US government developed a much more decentralized policy than most European governments, with more bureaucratic decisions being made at the level of state and local governments. Most experts in the early 20th century doubted whether the federal government could manage a national pension system efficiently, and reformers worried that a large national government pension system would encourage political corruption (Skocpol 1995, 1996: 316).

The shock of the Great Depression in 1929 stimulated attempts to create a federal pension system in the United States. The Social Security Act of 1935 established a federal old-age insurance plan, established state-run unemployment insurance, and made money available for states to create assistance plans to help support poor mothers and their children. As these programs grew, federal government bureaucracies expanded and became more efficient.

Social Security became the largest and most successful of the social insurance programs established in the United States. Beginning as a federal program, Social Security was the only social insurance program that did not have to contend with powerful interests from state and local government. Supporters of Social Security used cultural strategies to convince the American public that it was a good system. Connecting it to a long tradition of dividing citizens into "worthy" and "unworthy" aid recipients, they described Social Security as a system that would reward retired workers after a long period of economic productivity (Skocpol 1996: 322). They also described it as a system in which workers would "earn" their pensions over the course of their working lives, glossing over the fact that current retirees' benefits are actually financed through current payroll taxes (Skocpol 1996: 323).

Social Security
Social Security is a strategy to guard against the contingencies of economic downturns for individuals, and especially to ensure that people will be supported in their old age.

ACTIVE LEARNING

Discuss: What social challenge do retirement schemes like Social Security solve? Have you started saving for your retirement? Why or why not? Does it make sense for everyone to start to save early for retirement?

PAIRED CONCEPTS   Solidarity and Conflict

A Short History of the Workers' Strike in the United States

When workers feel exploited, they can collectively refuse to work, which is known as a labor strike. But workers did not always have the legal right to engage in labor strikes. Strike efforts during the 18th and 19th centuries were often met with violence. England passed the Combinations of Workmen Act in 1825, which outlawed strikes and imposed criminal penalties for striking workers. British strikers who destroyed company property were often sentenced to death, and other strikers were exiled to penal colonies.

In the United States, strike activity increased dramatically during the 1870s, as did police violence against striking workers. The Great Railroad Strike of 1877 began in West Virginia, spread to five other states, and lasted 45 days before local, state, and federal troops forced the end of the strike, killing more than 100 people in the process. Private security forces shot and killed nine workers during an 1892 strike against the Carnegie Steel Company, and 8,000 Pennsylvania state militia were needed to end the rioting and the protests that ensued. A strike by railroad workers against the Pullman Company in 1894 was forcefully ended by 12,000 US Army troops, but not before it spread to include 250,000 workers across 27 states.

The violence directed at striking workers strengthened their solidarity and resolve, and convinced them of the need for a national labor movement. National strikes by rail, coal, and steel workers involved hundreds of thousands of workers. After decades of conflict, with government usually taking the side of business owners, the solidarity and sacrifices of workers finally began to pay off. The Wagner Act of 1935 guaranteed the basic rights of private-sector employees to organize into unions, to engage in collective bargaining in the attempt to improve working conditions, and to take collective actions (such as strikes).

Striking workers have continued to face challenges from employers as well as government. A 1947 law passed by the New York state legislature made it illegal for state employees to go on strike, and most states followed with similar laws. The Taft–Hartley Act of 1947 required workers to give 80 days' notice before going on strike, authorized the president to intervene in strikes that might lead to a national emergency, and prohibited federal employees from striking. A legal decision in 1989 ruled that employers were allowed to promise senior-level jobs to younger workers who were willing to break a strike. And companies have been allowed to respond to strike actions by using lockouts, where they tell their employees not to come to work until they are willing to accept management's contract offer. The larger unions have created strike funds that they use to pay their members during strike actions, but there is no question that successful strikes require high levels of solidarity among workers.

Workers strike in front of Verizon headquarters, New York City, 2016.
Do you think that workers are entitled to strike for better wages and conditions?

ACTIVE LEARNING

Discuss: Do you think direct action (like strikes and protests) is effective? Why do you think so? What are the alternative strategies to direct action? Are these available to everyone?

Social conflict over inequality also happens at a transnational level. While the Occupy Wall Street movement began in the United States in 2011 as a protest against economic inequality, the movement quickly spread, with a global "Day of Rage" in more than 80 countries. Antipoverty groups converge regularly on global finance meetings to denounce corporate greed and to press the world's wealthiest nations to make a real commitment to end global poverty. We discuss these kinds of social movements in greater detail in Chapter 13.

CASE STUDY

The Bachelor: Crystallizing Stratification on TV

Inequality is complex and contradictory. A person can be privileged in some ways but not in others. Dimensions of inequality intersect in different ways to affect individuals and groups. To end this chapter, we use the five paired concepts to explore inequality as it is represented on the hugely popular reality television show *The Bachelor*.

The Bachelor documents the search for a wife by an eligible bachelor. At the beginning of the season, he is presented with around 25 potential mates. The television audience watches and comments through a series of encounters as the female candidates are asked to leave or stay, usually with the presentation of red roses to successful candidates. The show has produced marriage proposals and marriages, and even a spinoff, *The Bachelorette*, where gender roles are reversed. *The Bachelor* also exemplifies the crystallization of several overlapping dimensions of stratification, and in particular, the way that different kinds of *inequality* reinforce each other.

The men selected to play the bachelor must be considered eligible. Thus the show illustrates both what is culturally valued as successful for men and what is considered desirable in the women who seek their favor. It is meaningful that all the individuals selected to play the bachelor are typically *privileged*, straight, wealthy, and (at the time of this writing) white. There are no male mates offered to the bachelor on *The Bachelor*. In fact, a major premise of the show is the inevitability of heterosexual marriage as an institution that secures the economic, social, and emotional future for both individuals. The show equates eligibility and desirability with heterosexuality, and it underlines the norm that heterosexuality and marriage are connected so that other alternatives seem unlikely or undesirable. Despite challenges and the promise to produce a gay "bachelor," the consensus remains that the "straights-seeking-love" formula works (D'Addario 2014).

The bachelors on *The Bachelor* are also considered eligible in economic terms. While they are not all rich, they have secure, typically well-paid professional jobs. Occupations range from banker and global financier to account executive and medical doctor. There have been a few athletes, an actor, and even a farmer, but the idea that wealth is important is emphasized in many ways. For example, the initial setting of the show is a lavish, 7,590-square-foot, six-bedroom, nine-bath mansion in California reputedly worth more than $8 million. As the show unfolds, dates and other social events occur in the mansion and other opulent surroundings around the world. The underlying message is that the eligible man is desirable because he is wealthy and privileged, and therefore it is reasonable that women will compete for his favor, even in a highly contrived media setting.

The competition between women, which is a major premise of the show, gives rise to rapidly shifting dynamics of *solidarity* throughout the season. The women make alliances of solidarity and then betray them to improve their own chances at winning a rose from the bachelor. The format of *The Bachelor* is designed to breed this kind of *conflict*, and it represents the way that setting up individuals to compete for scarce resources can create conflict, resentment, and even violent words and actions. Audience commentators are more than aware of this fact, posting their reactions to social media sites.

Despite the fact that audiences and cast members know the conflict between the women is manufactured, the competition for the bachelor and the conditions of this competition provide the drama that drives the show. The search for true love may not be the true goal of the show (gasp!), but there is certainly a lot at stake for contestants, including fame and lucrative careers.

Race and ethnicity are also important factors on the show. In recent years, the show has been widely criticized for a lack of diversity. As entertainment review *The Wrap* reported, "Though 2014 'Bachelor' Juan Pablo Galavis was Venezuelan-American, there still hasn't been an African American or Asian 'Bachelor' or

The Bachelor's rose presentation
Luxurious clothing and surroundings connect *The Bachelor's* narratives of heterosexual love and marriage to highly desirable markers of economic status and class reproduction.

CASE STUDY CONTINUED

'Bachelorette' in 32 seasons of the franchise. And even when non-white contestants are cast, they seldom go very far" (Verhoeven and Ali 2016).

This issue is exemplified in the case of Jubilee Sharpe, who dated bachelor Ben Higgins in the 20th season of the show in 2016. Jubilee's compelling biography reveals intersecting dimensions of inequality and privilege. *Reality TV World* reports that Jubilee "was active in the U.S. Army for 4.5 years . . . Jubilee prides herself on coming from a beautiful blended family. Born in Haiti, she was adopted at age 6 from an orphanage." It goes on to state, "She knows how to joke about *The Bachelor* franchise's diversity issue. After her elimination from the show, Jubilee posted on Twitter: 'The black girl on *The Bachelor*. Got no chance'" (Kwiatkowski 2016). Audience and industry reviews concurred that Jubilee's blackness was an issue on the show, and one of the reasons she did not get very far. As one audience member tweeted: "Am I the only one reading between the lines as to why these women don't 'see' Ben with someone like Jubilee?"

Social media commentary like this demonstrates *resistance* from fans and critics that pushes back against the *power* of the show's format to define what is normal or appropriate. It joins a range of other actions and protests about the whiteness of *The Bachelor*, including a class action lawsuit taken against the show in 2012 for lack of diversity. Jubilee joins critics in suggesting that the show is rigged and that her personal shortcomings don't explain why she left the show. At the same time, Jubilee's obvious audience appeal meant that she was also cast in *Bachelors in Paradise*, a spinoff of *The Bachelor*.

The Bachelor's representation of romance, sexuality, race, and marriage also has a *global* appeal. The format has been adapted in many other countries, with *local* versions airing over the last 14 years in Australia, Brazil, Canada, China, France, Finland, Germany, Israel, New Zealand, Norway, Poland, Romania, Russia, Switzerland, Slovenia, the United Kingdom, Thailand, Ukraine, and Vietnam.

Contingency is also an important part of the appeal of *The Bachelor*, since the show's action unfolds according to the bachelor's whims and desires. This is a central element in the dramatic tension of *The Bachelor*. Some commentators believe the show is fixed by its producers and directors, so the outcome is predetermined. Others think that the bachelor and the candidates for his hand overplay the drama of the show. Whatever the case, it remains the case that the *structures* that define the eligibility and desirability of the bachelor include heterosexual marriage, economic privilege, and whiteness.

LEARNING GOALS REVISITED

7.1 Understand stratification as the way sociologists think about social inequality.

- Stratification is the division of society into strata, or layers, of people with differential access to scarce but desirable things.

- Despite long-standing debates about the nature and ethics of inequality, there is considerable evidence for the negative effects of inequality on people in the lower categories of society.

7.2 Distinguish types of stratification.

- Different stratification systems organize inequality in a multitude of ways, with varying

consequences for different groups of people. There are several kinds of inequality, including economic, cultural, political, environmental, educational, racial, and gender inequality. All of these intersect in different areas of life. Stratification systems describe how these inequalities are organized.

- Stratification systems can be compared in terms of:

  a. the *degree of inequality*, or the degree to which scarce but desirable resources are concentrated in the hands of an elite group at the top of the system;

b. the *rigidity of inequality*, which refers to the degree to which it is easy or hard to move around in the system over a lifetime or between generations;

c. the degree of *ascriptiveness* in the system, which refers to the question of whether or not inherited statuses constrain movement in the stratification system over a lifetime or between generations; and

d. the *degree of crystallization*, referring to the degree to which inequality and privilege clump together across multiple domains.

- Traditionally, caste systems are highly crystallized, rigidly ascriptive stratification systems based on occupational assignment at birth. They display a high degree of inequality. Caste systems are becoming less rigid and unequal as a result of government policies and the operation of new economic forces in these systems.

- Class systems are based on inequality rooted in economic differences, in particular the ownership of property, control of legal institutions, and bureaucratic power. These can be compared with party systems, where institutional position is the primary determinant of social status in the stratification system; and status systems, where social groups are defined by lifestyle and consumption patterns.

7.3 Develop an understanding of broad patterns of stratification in the United States and globally.

- The distribution of wealth (including land, buildings, and intellectual property and earnings such as rents, salary, and other income) is highly unequal in the United States and around the world.

- The degree of inequality represented by the concentration of wealth in the hands of a tiny economic elite has become even more extreme over time.

- There is inequality between countries and also within countries.

- The United States is the wealthiest developed country in the world and also the country with the most extreme degree of internal economic inequality, understood as the distance between the poorest and richest.

- Economic inequality and class positions are measured in several different ways. For example, policy-makers and researchers might compare the top 1 percent as an economic elite with the bottom 50 percent of the population to describe economic inequality and the challenge of shared prosperity. Some sociologists might look at gender stratification by comparing the average earnings of women and men, while others might investigate differences in household income between class groups.

7.4 Comprehend the concept of mobility and distinguish different kinds of mobility, such as structural mobility and intergenerational mobility.

- Mobility is movement within a stratification system. Vertical mobility is movement up and down the hierarchy. In contrast, horizontal mobility describes lateral moves that do not affect overall socioeconomic location.

- Absolute mobility refers to the movement associated with the acquisition of things, while relative mobility describes movement compared to other salient groups.

- Intergenerational mobility compares social location relative to one's parents.

- Structural mobility is movement caused by some overall change in the stratification system, such as the shift from manufacturing to service occupations. Other sources of structural change that cause mobility in the system are economic depressions and recessions.

7.5 Consider factors that affect mobility and the stratification system, such as education, family background, and racial and gender differences, as well as social policy and social conflict.

- Social mobility is shaped by the nature of the stratification system, including how rigid and ascriptive inequality is, and how crystallized inequality is across the several dimensions of stratification (including education, political power, cultural influence, and economic wealth).

- Family background, education, and cultural capital all affect an individual's life chances in a stratification system.

- Gender and race organize stratification systems and shape the life chances of entire categories of people. Systems of gender and race inequality intersect with other kinds of stratification to shape individual life outcomes and group chances.

- Social policies such as old age pensions, unemployment insurance, progressive taxation, civil rights legislation, and universal public education are all societal efforts to shape the stratification system in more productive and more equal directions.

- Social conflict and direct action are ways that less powerful groups have asserted a need to change the stratification system or have resisted existing stratification systems. Such actions put pressure on government and other decision-makers to respond.

Key Terms

Absolute mobility 196
Ascriptiveness 184
Caste systems 184
Categorical inequality 182
Colonialism 194
Conspicuous consumption 188
Consumerism 188
Contentious politics 202
Cultural capital 199
Davis–Moore theory of inequality 182
Degree of Crystallization 184
Degree of inequality 184
Elites 187
Horizontal mobility 196
Income 190
Inequality 180
Intergenerational mobility 196
Lower-middle class 192
Marginal productivity theory 182
Meritocracy 188
Middle class 192
Net worth 190
Party system 187
Relative deprivation 182

Relative mobility 196
Rigidity 184
Social mobility 196
Socioeconomic status 190
Status group 187
Stratification 183
Structural mobility 201
Underclass 193
Upper-middle class 191
Vertical social mobility 196
Wealth 190
Working poor 193
World systems theory 194

Review Questions

1. What is the relationship between inequality and stratification?

2. What are the main ways to compare different stratification systems? Give examples of different systems.

3. Describe the broad patterns of stratification in the United States and around the world.

4. What is the difference between structural mobility and intergenerational mobility? Can intergenerational mobility be caused by structural mobility? How?

5. How does social policy affect stratification? Give an example.

6. If a country is rich, can it still have inequality? Explain.

7. How are gender and race stratification connected to class stratification?

8. Identify three differences between caste and class systems.

Explore

RECOMMENDED READINGS

Bourdieu, Pierre. 2000. *The Weight of the World. Social Suffering in Contemporary Society.* Stanford, California: Stanford University Press.

Domhoff, G. William. 2013. *Who Rules America? The Triumph of the Corporate Rich*, 7th ed. New York: McGraw-Hill.

Grusky, David, and Tamar Kricheli-Katz, eds. 2012. *The New Gilded Age.* Stanford, California: Stanford University Press.

Piketty, Thomas. 2014. *Capital in the Twenty-first Century*. New York: Belknap.

Sennet, Richard. 1972. *The Hidden Injuries of Class*. New York: Knopf.

Sennet, Richard. 2005. *The Culture of the New Capitalism*. New Haven, CT: Yale University Press.

World Bank. *2018. Piecing Together the Poverty Puzzle. Poverty and Shared Prosperity*. Washington, DC: The World Bank.

ACTIVITIES

- *Use your sociological imagination*: Can you identify any effects of structural changes on your own economic biography? What are they?

- *Media+Data Literacy:* Go to the library or go online and discover what the Gini coefficient is. Explain what the Gini coefficient summarizes. What is the Gini coefficient of the United States? Compare it with one other country.

- *Discuss*: In the five paired concepts, inequality is related to privilege. This means that where there inequality, there is always privilege. Most of us sit at the intersections of different kinds of privilege and inequality. Do you consider yourself privileged in any way in the stratification system? How?

For additional resources, including Media+Data Literacy exercises, In the News exercises, and quizzes, please go to **oup.com/he/ Jacobs-Townsley1e**

8

Race, Ethnicity, and Multiculturalism

On February 26, 2012, 28-year-old George Zimmerman shot and killed Trayvon Martin in a gated community in Sanford, Florida. Martin, a 17-year-old African American high school student, was in the community with his father to visit his father's fiancée. Zimmerman, an insurance fraud investigator who lived in the community, was a volunteer captain of the neighborhood watch. After calling the Sanford police department to report Martin as a "real suspicious guy," Zimmerman decided to follow Martin, despite the fact that the police dispatcher had asked him not to do so. After an altercation between the two, Zimmerman fatally shot Martin in the chest. Zimmerman claimed he was acting in self-defense. Martin was unarmed.

Trayvon Martin's family believed that their son had been racially targeted by Zimmerman, and they hired lawyers to pursue a wrongful death lawsuit. News of the case spread through the national media, and public protests against the killing took place across the country. More than two million people signed a petition calling for Zimmerman's arrest. Zimmerman was arrested and charged with murder, but a jury acquitted him of the charges.

In the six months between Trayvon Martin's death and George Zimmerman's acquittal, there was a national public discussion about **racial profiling**, which happens when police and private security target racial minorities for extra attention, based only on the perception that minorities are suspicious or dangerous. President Obama, noting that Trayvon Martin "could have been me 35 years ago," observed that the experience of racial profiling and race relations in the United States informs "how the African American community interprets what happened one night in Florida. And it's inescapable for people to bring those experiences to bear. The African American

Protest against the murder of Trayvon Martin, 2012
The murder of 17-year-old Trayvon Martin by George Zimmerman renewed the national outcry against racial profiling and the extreme violence directed at young black men in America.

LEARNING GOALS

8.1   Understand the way race is and has been socially constructed.

8.2   Understand the relationships and intersections among race and ethnic groups in the United States.

8.3   Perceive the relationship between racial privilege and racial inequality.

8.4   Understand current thinking about diversity and multiculturalism.

Race A system for classifying people into groups on the basis of shared physical traits, which people in society treat as socially important and understand to be biologically transmitted.

Ethnicity A system for classifying people into groups on the basis of shared cultural heritage and a common identity.

community is also knowledgeable that there is a history of racial disparities in the application of our criminal laws—everything from the death penalty to enforcement of our drug laws. And that ends up having an impact in terms of how people interpret the case."

Why did the Trayvon Martin case cause so much concern and public discussion? How were these discussions influenced by the history of racial and ethnic relations in the United States? How have attitudes about race and ethnicity changed over time?

This chapter explores the different ways that race and ethnicity shape our social lives. **Race** refers to a category of people who share specific physical traits, which people in society treat as socially important and understand to be biologically transmitted. We begin by discussing the different ways that race has been socially constructed, and the way it continues to be socially constructed despite the fact that there is no biological foundation for racial categories. We also distinguish between race and **ethnicity**, which refers to a group of people who have a shared cultural heritage and a common identity. After describing the main racial and ethnic groups in the United States, we then discuss how racism and racial discrimination have been used to reinforce inequality and privilege. Finally, we examine how multiculturalism and multiracial identities have begun to change social policies and attitudes about race.

The Social Construction of Race

When sociologists emphasize that race is a social construction, they are making two related points. First, race is not a biological category. As we will discuss, most scientists today agree that race is not a useful way to think about human genetic diversity. The second point is that race, despite not being a biological category, is still an important sociological concept. Race is a social construction that is a powerful force in social life. When W. E. B. Du Bois wrote in 1903 that "the problem of the Twentieth Century is the problem of the color line," he was making a prediction about how hard it was going to be to overcome racial thinking and racist actions. In most respects, his prediction has proven accurate.

Race and Biology

Beginning in the 1930s, a growing number of biologists and social scientists began arguing that race was not a useful concept for thinking about human genetic diversity. For any given set of racial classifications, they realized, there was more genetic variation within groups than between groups. There is also a tremendous amount of genetic overlap between different racial groups. The genetic differences between groups is not nearly as fixed as the idea of race suggests. The United Nations Educational, Scientific, and Cultural Organization (UNESCO) recognized this growing scientific consensus when it wrote in 1951 that "for all practical social purposes 'race' is not so much a biological phenomenon as a social myth."

By the 1970s, advances in genetics had revealed even more clearly the scientific problems that were associated with the race concept. A 1972 study by the geneticist Richard Lewontin found that racial categories had virtually no genetic significance, with more than 85 percent of human genetic variation present within any of the so-called racial groups. Later research discovered that all humans have genome sequences that are 99.9 percent identical. Standing on the White House lawn in 2000, the geneticist Craig Venter declared that "the concept of race has no genetic or scientific basis" (Weiss and Gillis 2000).

If the concept of race has been so completely discredited by biologists and geneticists, why do sociologists continue to study it? The answer to this question is connected to the Thomas theorem (Chapter 2), which holds that if people define a situation as real then it will be real in its consequences. In other words, race continues to play a powerful role in social life because individuals and groups continue to define race as a real thing. Race is embedded in social institutions, reproduced in social interactions, and embedded in language and culture. Governments throughout the world still collect data on the racial composition of their population. Individuals, groups, and communities continue to understand their identities in racial terms. And centuries of racial discrimination continue to shape the life chances and the opportunities that are afforded to different social groups.

In Chapter 2, we discussed racial formation theory, which analyzes modern Western society and particularly US society as structured by a historically developed "racial common sense." Racial stereotypes and institutionalized patterns of inequality are embedded in the fundamental fabric of modern social life at both the individual and the institutional level. These have been developed over the course of particular histories of power and conflict that connect ideas of race, immigration, language, and culture.

The Changing Understanding of Race over Time

Biologists and geneticists may have stopped using the concept of race, but they have not offered an alternative way to think about human variation. In everyday life, most people continue to use race as a way to think about the world, as they have for hundreds of years.

RACE BEFORE SCIENCE. Before the 17th century, farmers were the people most likely to talk about race, and they used the concept as a way of talking about different animal breeding lines (Smedley 1993: 39). But this began to change when European explorers began to have more frequent contact with foreign populations.

Initially, explorers viewed native peoples as "savages," because the indigenous people they met did not share the same religion or morality as the conquering explorers. The explorers began to view themselves as different from and superior to the populations they were meeting. But this feeling of superiority was based on religion and culture, rather than biology.

Racial thinking grew in the British colonies of North America, and it intensified with the growth of the African slave trade. By 1700 Britain had become the world's largest slave trader, with the majority of their slaves going to North America. The North American colonies quickly established a system of

Slavery
The buying and selling of Africans in a system of permanent slavery, as depicted in this 1824 image of a slave auction in the West Indies, defines the history of race in the United States and worldwide.

permanent slavery for those of African descent. Africans lost the right to testify in court, hold property, gather together in public places, travel without permission, get married, or receive an education (Nash 2014). Treated as property, these slaves produced the tobacco, sugar, and cotton that helped England become the world's greatest economic power.

Initially the North American colonists viewed the African slaves as irreligious and immoral savages, similar to the way they viewed the native populations; over time, though, they came to focus on physical differences. Associating dark skin with slave status, they came to see both free and enslaved African Americans as separate and permanently inferior. Over time, they developed a subtle ranking of inferiority among the different groups of "savages" (Smedley 1993: 106–10) and created a pseudoscience of racial classification.

THE ATTEMPT TO CREATE A SCIENCE OF RACIAL CLASSIFICATION. The earliest attempts to create a scientific classification of human diversity began in the 1730s and 1740s, as part of a larger attempt by early modern scientists to classify all living things. Humans were placed at the top of the hierarchy, just above apes. As the classifications continued to develop, people developed a ranking of different human groups, trying to identify which groups were the most advanced and which were the closest to the apes. Most of the early classifications focused on physical features, character traits, and geography. Johann Blumenbach, a German doctor and one of the most important of the early racial classifiers, proposed a system that divided humans into five groups associated with the major regions of the world. Blumenbach believed that the combination of climate, nutrition, and living habits caused the differences between these groups, and that over time these differences became part of the character of the different races. All of the people who created these early classifications were Europeans, and all of them placed the groups of European descent at the top of their hierarchies.

Racial determinism A dominant social theory in the 19th century that argued that the world was divided into biologically distinct races, and that there were fundamental differences in ability between the different racial groups.

By the middle of the 19th century, **racial determinism** had become the dominant theory explaining the achievements and failures of different human groups. Racial determinism was the idea that the world was divided into biologically distinct races, and that there were fundamental differences in ability between the different racial groups. Proponents of the pseudoscience of racial classification used a variety of strategies to try to demonstrate these supposedly innate biological differences. They measured skull size and shape, they looked for anatomical differences, they did psychological tests, and they measured things like physical strength, vision, and pulmonary capacity (Smedley 1993: 255–71). They developed elaborate techniques for measuring skin color, and they used new quantitative techniques to develop statistical portraits of different racial groups. When IQ tests were developed in the early 20th century, racial determinists used them to try to prove that there were inherent racial differences in intelligence.

THE CONCEPT OF RACE TODAY. Beliefs about race began to change during the 20th century, because of changes in science as well as in societies themselves. After a large influx of immigrants between 1890 and 1910, many Americans began to celebrate their nation as a "melting pot." At the same time, millions of African Americans began to move from the rural South to the industrializing North to seek better jobs and education, a movement known as the "Great Migration." Most important, perhaps, was the experience of World War II, in which people around the world were shocked by the atrocities that the Nazis committed in the name of racial purity and racial determinism (Smedley 1993: 273). With the US government publicly criticizing the racism of the Nazis, arguments about racial inferiority and racial determinism became less acceptable in public debates within the United States as well (Alexander 2006).

In the fields of science, even before biologists and geneticists began to question the scientific status of the race concept, anthropologists and sociologists had already begun to question the assumptions of racial determinism. Anthropologists such as Franz Boas (1858–1942) argued that race did not have anything to do with language, culture, or behavior, as these were all things that were learned and not inherited (Smedley 1993: 276–82). Boas insisted that any group superiority or inferiority was caused by differences in social environment and not by heredity. The sociologist W. E. B. Du Bois argued that the disadvantages suffered by African Americans were not caused by heredity, but rather by the consequences of two centuries of slavery (Morris 2015: 38). Writing in 1920, Du Bois argued that "there are no races, in the sense of great, separate, pure breeds of men, differing in attainment, development, and capacity" (Morris 2015: 45).

While many people in everyday life continued to believe in racial determinism, the work of social scientists such as Du Bois and Boas helped create a more sociological way to think about race. Rather than thinking about group differences in terms of heredity, the sociological approach tries to identify the social and historical factors that have caused these differences to exist. Linking these social factors to inequality and privilege, they try to identify the consequences of being a member of a minority group. They study how racial privilege gets institutionalized, in both formal and informal ways. They study how racial minorities resist power and prejudice, and they try to identify which social factors help this resistance succeed. They explore how racial group dynamics are influenced by local and global processes. In other words, while they reject biological theories of racial determinism, sociologists today still treat race as a real thing; from a sociological perspective, race is a category of group membership, which produces solidarity as well as conflict.

Race and Ethnicity

Ethnicity, another important category of group membership, is based on a shared cultural heritage and a common identity. Ethnic groups are held together by shared language, traditions, rituals, and behaviors. They can often identify a shared ancestry and a common history, and they have certain types of food, dress, and music that they associate with their shared ethnic identity. Membership in an ethnic group is usually recognized by group members themselves as well as by outsiders.

Symbolic ethnicity
Irish Americans celebrate their ethnicity by participating in St. Patrick's Day parades in cities like New York and Boston. For most people, though, Irish ethnicity does not involve any other form of affiliation.

Symbolic ethnicity The way dominant groups feel an attachment to specific ethnic traditions without being active members of the ethnic group.

The distinction between racial and ethnic groups is not always clear. Most racial groups have ethnic similarities based in shared cultural experience. African Americans, for example, have distinctive religious, musical, and artistic traditions that can be traced to their common ancestry and their shared struggle against oppression (Baker 1987). Many groups that are today considered to be ethnic groups, such as people of Jewish or Irish ancestry, were once thought of as racial groups. Because the boundaries between race and ethnicity are often so blurred, particularly for minority groups, scholars today often write about "racial and ethnic groups" as if they are a single category.

In most societies, majority groups tend to emphasize their ethnic identities and to ignore their racial identities or their racial privileges. The sociologist Herbert Gans referred to this as **symbolic ethnicity**, which refers to the way dominant groups feel an attachment to specific ethnic traditions without really being active members of the ethnic group (Gans 1979). Irish Americans express their Irishness by participating in St. Patrick's Day celebrations, but they do not actually need to belong to any Irish groups. Jewish Americans express their Jewish identity by celebrating Hanukkah, but they do not have to go to synagogue or join any Jewish organizations. According to Gans, symbolic ethnicity turns ethnicity into a kind of leisure activity. For these groups, their racial and ethnic identity is voluntary, rather than being ascribed by other people. This is a privilege of being in the majority group, as we discuss later in the chapter.

Racial and Ethnic Groups in the United States

The United States is a very diverse nation. A recent report by the US Census Bureau projected that the United States would become a "majority-minority" country by 2043, which means that the country's largest ethnic group (non-Hispanic whites) will make up less than 50 percent of the US population. There are other societies that are more racially and ethnically diverse than the United States, particularly those in sub-Saharan Africa. But the United States is much more racially and ethnically diverse than other wealthy countries in Europe and Asia.

Table 8.1 shows the current racial and ethnic composition of the United States, according to the Census Bureau. Non-Hispanic whites are the largest racial group, making up 60.4 percent of the population, African Americans are the next largest group at 13.4 percent, followed by Asian Americans at 5.9 percent, Native Americans at 1.3 percent, and Native Hawaiian and Other Pacific Islanders at 0.2 percent. In addition, the Census asks an ethnicity question to identify Hispanic and Latino American as an ethnicity. Latinos, who can be of

Defining and Measuring Race in Official Government Data

Since the first official census in 1790, the US government has collected data on the racial and ethnic characteristics of its population. But the categories it uses have changed in important ways over the last 225 years, and so have the strategies used to collect these data. Additionally, the US Census Bureau uses different data collection strategies than those used in other countries. A close look at the development of these different measurement strategies can help us understand how race is, and has been, socially constructed.

Until 1960, decisions about race were made by official census workers, based on their perceptions about the physical characteristics of the individual. At first, the Census had only three categories: "free white," "slaves," and "all other free persons." The 1820 Census created a new category for "free colored person," reflecting the growth of the non-slave African American population, as well as the fact that free African Americans had fewer rights than free whites. The 1850 Census eliminated the "slave" category, replacing it with the categories of "Black" and "Mulatto." The 1870 Census added the category of "Indian" to refer to Native Americans, and also began adding categories for Asian immigrants, who were identified by their nation of origin. The 1930 Census eliminated the category of "Mulatto." The 1970 Census provided for White, Black and Oriental, which narrowed the categories considerably. The attempt to count Latinos began in 1930 with the creation of the "Mexican" category, but this was eliminated in the 1940 Census after protests by the Mexican government. The 1970 Census added a Hispanic self-identification question, called the ethnicity question. This was a nonexclusive category, so that a person who self-identified as Hispanic by ethnicity was also counted as a member of one of the other racial groups.

Beginning with the 2000 census, all US citizens were allowed to report more than one race. US Census officials are even considering eliminating the word "race" from the 2020 Census, instead asking people to select all the "categories" that describe them (Cohn 2015). Other governments have made different choices about how to collect data about race and ethnicity. The Brazilian Census uses skin color (white, brown, and black) rather than race, reflecting the belief that race is a US concept that does not apply to Brazilian society (Telles 2002). France does not collect any census data on race, and French law prohibits the collection of official government data on racial characteristics.

→ **NOTE: Please answer BOTH Question 8 about Hispanic origin and Question 9 about race. For this census, Hispanic origins are not races.**

8. Is Person 1 of Hispanic, Latino, or Spanish origin?
☐ No, not of Hispanic, Latino, or Spanish origin
☐ Yes, Mexican, Mexican Am., Chicano
☐ Yes, Puerto Rican
☐ Yes, Cuban
☐ Yes, another Hispanic, Latino, or Spanish origin — *Print origin, for example, Argentinean, Colombian, Dominican, Nicaraguan, Salvadoran, Spaniard, and so on.* ↗

9. What is Person 1's race? *Mark ☒ one or more boxes.*
☐ White
☐ Black, African Am., or Negro
☐ American Indian or Alaska Native — *Print name of enrolled or principal tribe.* ↗

☐ Asian Indian   ☐ Japanese   ☐ Native Hawaiian
☐ Chinese   ☐ Korean   ☐ Guamanian or Chamorro
☐ Filipino   ☐ Vietnamese   ☐ Samoan
☐ Other Asian — *Print race, for example, Hmong, Laotian, Thai, Pakistani, Cambodian, and so on.* ↗   ☐ Other Pacific Islander — *Print race, for example, Fijian, Tongan, and so on.* ↗

☐ Some other race — *Print race.* ↗

US Census form
The decennial US Census collects data on a wide range of topics, including race, ethnicity, ancestry, nativity, and language. The Census is an important social institution that defines racial and ethnic categories.

ACTIVE LEARNING

Discuss: Do you think the US government should collect racial and ethnic data? Are there consequences of collecting the data? What are they?

any race, are 18.3 percent of the population and are the largest single minority group in the United States. Importantly, the Supreme Court has said that race is not limited to what the Census defines but also can extend to all other ethnicities, including Jewish, Arab, or Italian groups. Generally though, sociologists follow the Census categories to talk about race.

Table 8.1 Population of the United States by Race and Ethnicity, 2018

RACE	
White alone	76.5%
Black or African American	13.4%
American Indian and Alaska Native	1.3%
Asian	5.9%
Native Hawaiian and Other Pacific Islander	0.2%
Two or More Races	2.7%
Total population	100%
ETHNICITY	
Hispanic or Latino	18.3%
Non-Hispanic or Latino	81.7%
Non-Hispanic Whites	*60.4%*

Source: US Census Bureau: National Population Estimates; QuickFacts.

Native Americans

Although scientists continue to make new discoveries about the peopling of North America, there is general agreement that the first humans began arriving from Asia about fifteen thousand years ago. This migration was made possible by a drop in sea level that created a land bridge between Siberia and Alaska. While it is impossible to know the exact size of the Native American population before the 15th century, archaeologists estimate that it was somewhere between 10 million and 100 million people.

Theft of Indian land
The US government took land from indigenous peoples through violence and forced resettlement. This poster is a stark illustration of power relations on Western lands in North America from colonial times through the 20th century.

The arrival of European colonizers devastated the Native American population. Native Americans had no immunity to European diseases, and many of them died from smallpox, influenza, tuberculosis, and other infectious diseases carried across the ocean from Europe. While disease was the largest cause of death for Native Americans, many others died in wars with the European settlers. The forced removal from ancestral homes and resettlement of Native Americans onto "Indian reservations" far away from the population centers of the white colonial settlers further decimated the population. According to the 1900 Census, the Native American population in the United States was only 237,196.

The US government created the Bureau of Indian Affairs in 1824, with the goal of assimilating Native

Americans into mainstream American society and culture. Native American children were sent to boarding schools where they were taught English and punished for speaking their own languages, given new "white" names, forced to wear Western clothes, and received religious training in Christianity. Educators hoped that their students would not return to the reservations, even during their summer holidays, but would prefer instead to become part of the white community. Politicians predicted that the "American Indians" were a dying race that would soon disappear from existence (Champagne 2008: 1679).

Those Native Americans who stayed on the reservation lands suffered from poverty, health problems, substandard housing and transportation infrastructure, and high crime rates. These disparities continue today. More than one-quarter of the Native American population currently lives in poverty, and Native Americans have levels of education and labor force participation significantly lower than the US averages. They have the highest per-capita rate of violent victimization, the highest levels of alcohol and drug use, and the highest age-adjusted death rates of any racial or ethnic group in the nation (Sarche and Spicer 2008).

Since the 1970s, Native American communities have organized to make demands for stronger self-government, more cultural autonomy, and better economic self-sufficiency (Champagne 2008: 1681). Native Americans have been successful in the energy industry as well as the gaming and entertainment industry, bringing significant wealth to some communities. The Red Power Movement organized protests against the illegal takeover of Native American lands, and a number of tribes that had been terminated by the US government successfully campaigned to reclaim land and federal recognition (Champagne 2008: 1685–86). Efforts to preserve and reclaim Native American language and culture have led to a stronger assertion of Native American identity. Native Americans are also involved in social movements and join with other groups to preserve tribal lands, including the famous protest against the Dakota Pipeline at Standing Rock beginning in 2016. Over five million (5.2 million) people self-identified as Native Americans in the 2010 census.

White Ethnic Groups

The North American colonies were established by white settlers from England, who believed that white Europeans were at the top of the racial hierarchy. When the United States established its first citizenship law in 1790, it specified that only "free white persons" could apply for citizenship. Until 1965, immigration laws established clear quotas that were designed to ensure that the United States would remain a nation dominated by white Europeans.

As the sociologist E. Digby Baltzell (1915–1996) explained in *The Protestant Establishment*, the early history of the United States was dominated by a group of White Anglo-Saxon Protestants, or "WASPs," who were primarily of English, Scottish, and Welsh ancestry (Baltzell 1958). WASPs controlled the worlds of politics, business, and education. They lived in the same neighborhoods, had their own social clubs, and tended to marry among each other. They sent their children to elite boarding schools in the New England countryside, and then to elite universities such as Harvard, Princeton, and Yale.

Beginning in the late-1800s, large numbers of white European immigrants began arriving from Southern and Eastern Europe. Many of these immigrants were Catholic and Jewish, and most of them did not speak English. When they arrived, they were encouraged to learn English and to assimilate into American society. For the most part, these new white ethnic groups were blocked

Structure and Contingency

The Growth and Success of Native American Casinos

The US Constitution defines Native American tribes as separate and independent from the federal government and the states. While the Native American tribes have clearly suffered from colonization, forced migration, and appropriation of ancestral lands, their legal independence from federal and state governments has offered certain limited opportunities. The courts have consistently found that Native American tribes have the right to govern themselves. They have also prevented the states from taxing Native Americans living on reservation lands. By the 1980s, many Native American tribes began to develop strategies for economic growth that were made possible by their formal independence. One of the most significant and successful of their strategies has been the creation of a multibillion-dollar gaming industry.

Native American gaming operations began in the 1970s and 1980s, when several tribes in Florida and California began to open bingo parlors and poker halls. State police quickly moved in to close down these operations, which they claimed had larger prizes and longer hours of operations than state laws allowed. The Native American tribes filed lawsuits in federal court, claiming that states did not have any jurisdiction over economic enterprises taking place on tribal lands. The tribes won their lawsuits, setting the stage for expanded gaming operations.

Native American tribes continued to open bingo parlors, poker halls, and casinos throughout the 1980s, with significant establishments developing in California, Florida, Maine, Connecticut, and Michigan. State politicians and casinos in New Jersey and Nevada began to lobby Congress to try to limit the growth of Native American casinos. The federal government responded by passing the Indian Gaming Regulatory Act (IGRA) in 1988. This law stated that tribes could run small-scale gambling operations without any interference, but they could only operate full-blown casinos in states that already allowed those types of operations.

While the casino lobby believed that the IGRA protected their interests, Native American tribes argued aggressively and creatively for the right to establish casino operations in states other than Nevada and New Jersey. For example, the Mashantucket Pequot tribe in Connecticut won a lawsuit that allowed them to open casinos, based on the fact that the state allowed charities to run "casino nights" as a form of fundraising. The Pequots used this victory to transform their bingo hall into the Foxwoods casino, which today has annual revenues of nearly $10 billion. Other major casinos followed, built on Native American lands in Michigan, California, New Mexico, Arizona, Minnesota, and Oklahoma. By 2000, there were more than 200 casinos on Native American lands. Today, there are nearly 500 Native American casinos, which together account for more than 40 percent of all casino gaming revenue in the United States.

Foxwoods Casino, Mashantucket Pequot tribe, Connecticut
Many years after Native Americans were forced to resettle on reservations, the Supreme Court held that those reservations were not bound by regulations on gambling that held in other parts of the country. Indian casinos boomed since they faced little competition from legal gambling elsewhere. This was a contingent outcome of the way the legal arrangements for reservations were organized.

ACTIVE LEARNING

Find out: Are there Native American casinos in your state? If so, when were they established?

Discuss: Do you think the establishment of casinos means that Native American tribes that own casinos have assimilated to American culture?

from entering the WASP establishment. They were largely excluded from WASP neighborhoods, living instead in crowded urban areas. They were forced to take low-paying jobs, and they endured discrimination in the workplace that limited their career advancement. Harvard, Yale, and Princeton introduced subjective admissions criteria focusing on "character" as a way to privilege students who came from WASP families and to discriminate against the new white ethnic groups; in fact, all three universities established quotas limiting the number of Jewish students they would admit (Karabel 2005).

Over time, and particularly since the 1960s, the social forces that had maintained such strong divisions between different white ethnic groups began to loosen. Today, the children and grandchildren of white European immigrants speak English as their preferred language, and their experiences in college and the labor market are similar to those of children from WASP backgrounds (Alba 1990). Intermarriage rates between white Catholics, Protestants, and Jews have increased dramatically, to the point where the majority of US-born non-Hispanic whites now have an ethnically mixed ancestry (Alba 1990: 15).

New York City's Little Italy neighborhood, circa 1900
Little Italy, which is still a distinct neighborhood in New York, began as an ethnic enclave for Italian immigrants.

African Americans

The Atlantic slave trade brought more than one million black slaves into North America between 1720 and 1807. The system of slavery was responsible for much of the wealth created in the new nation during its first century. By 1830, slave-produced cotton was responsible for more than half the value of all exports from the United States (North 1961). By 1860, at the dawn of the Civil War, there were four million slaves; in the 11 Confederate states of the South, slaves were 38 percent of the population.

The system of slavery was extremely brutal and had profound consequences for African Americans. The legal system did not recognize slave marriages and family life, and slave owners routinely split up families. More than one-third of all slave children grew up in households where one or both parents were absent. Nearly half of all infants born in slavery died during their first year of life, and the average life expectancy of a slave at birth was only about 21 years. A typical workday for slaves was more than 10 hours long, and could be as long as 15 or 16 hours. Any perceived disobedience was punished with whipping, branding, and other forms of violence. Slave women were frequently raped and sexually abused. Runaway slaves could be killed without penalty. Slaves received no education, and it was illegal to teach them to read or write.

Even after the Thirteenth Amendment to the US Constitution outlawed slavery in 1865, the legacy of slavery continued to exert itself in the lives of African Americans. Southern states created a system of "Jim Crow" laws that enforced racial segregation in schools, public transportation, restrooms, drinking fountains, and all other public facilities. Violence and intimidation were a regular feature of life for African Americans in the South. Between 1882 and 1968 there were more than 4,000 lynchings (murders carried out by a mob) of African American individuals, usually by hanging, without any legal prosecution of the murderers.

Ethnic conflict
African American neighborhoods were destroyed by fires set by white rioters during the 1919 Chicago race riot. The five days of violence began with the murder of a black swimmer by a white man at a segregated beach on July 27, 1919.

During the Great Migration (1880–1960), millions of African Americans migrated from the rural South to the cities of the Northeast, Midwest, and West, only to be greeted by suspicion, hostility, and violence (Tolnay 2003). They found themselves limited to low-status and low-paying jobs, and they were forced to live in poor and racially segregated neighborhoods (Lieberson 1980). Deadly race riots took place in cities such as St. Louis (1917), Chicago (1919), and Tulsa (1921), with white mobs beating and killing African Americans and setting fire to their neighborhoods.

Throughout US history, African Americans have organized to resist racial violence, segregation, and injustice. Former slaves such as Frederick Douglass and Sojourner Truth were important leaders of the abolitionist movement. W. E. B. Du Bois helped create the Niagara Movement in 1905 and the National Association for the Advancement of Colored People (NAACP) in 1909, groups that fought against racial hatred and racial discrimination. Martin Luther King Jr., Ralph Abernathy, Rosa Parks, and other leaders of the Civil Rights Movement organized mass protests, boycotts, and marches throughout the 1950s and 1960s, to highlight racial injustice and discrimination, and to try to get the federal government to protect African American civil rights We discuss these resistance and protest movements in more detail later in the chapter.

Since the 1980s, the size of the black immigrant population in the United States has quadrupled, with the largest numbers coming from Jamaica, Haiti, and Nigeria (Anderson 2015). These immigrants are different in many respects from domestic-born African Americans. Their connection to a transnational Caribbean or African community has helped them adapt successfully to life in the United States, despite the fact that they have had to face racial discrimination based in the legacy of American slavery. In fact, black immigrants are employed at a higher rate than the overall native-born population (Thomas 2012). Black immigrants, and particularly African immigrants, are among the most highly educated immigrants. Despite this, they confront a racial wealth gap in the United States that results in a median household income far lower than would be expected on the basis of educational credentials (Asante-Muhammad and Gerber 2018). In this context, many immigrants consciously hold onto their cultural heritage and they encourage their children to do the same thing, as a way of distinguishing themselves from the larger African American population and as a strategy for shielding themselves from the worst forms of racial discrimination (Waters 1990). By holding onto their identities and maintaining their cultural autonomy, these groups contribute to the growing trend of multiculturalism, which we discuss later in the chapter.

Latinas and Latinos

As the United States expanded westward during the 19th century, it settled and conquered lands that had previously been controlled by Mexico. The end of the Mexican-American War in 1848 gave the US ownership of California, as well

Solidarity and Conflict

W. E. B. Du Bois, Booker T. Washington, and the Struggle to Define African American Politics

Since the end of the Civil War, African American leaders have argued about what the best political strategy is for fighting against racial discrimination and achieving full equality in US society. Was it better to demand an immediate end to all forms of discrimination, or to focus on specific improvements even if that meant that other versions of inequality would continue? Would it be more effective to make strategic alliances with white leaders and supporters, or to create a movement for empowerment that was led exclusively by African Americans? Was nonviolence always the best political strategy for expressing protest?

Many of these strategic choices can be traced back to the conflict between Booker T. Washington (1856–1915) and W. E. B. Du Bois, two of the most important African American leaders of the early 20th century. Washington was born in Virginia in 1856, and along with his mother was emancipated at the end of the Civil War. After teaching himself to read and eventually earning a college degree from the Hampton Institute, in 1881 he established the school that would become Tuskegee University.

In an 1895 speech, Washington described his political strategy for African American improvement, counseling patience in order to avoid a backlash by angry whites. In the short term, Washington argued, the best strategy for African Americans was to focus on education, job skills, and economic self-improvement. He argued that African Americans should delay their demands for full political equality; once they showed themselves to be responsible and reliable American citizens, he thought, they would be able to overcome white prejudice and be fully accepted into all parts of American society. Washington's approach received strong support from white politicians, business leaders, and philanthropists from the Northeast United States, whom he raised millions of dollars to support his project.

Washington's approach was strongly opposed by W. E. B. Du Bois. Born in 1868, Du Bois grew up in western Massachusetts, where his parents were part of a small community of free blacks living in the town of Great Barrington. He earned bachelor's degrees at Fisk and Harvard universities, and studied economics, political science, and social policy at the University of Berlin. Returning to the United States in 1894, Du Bois became the first African American to earn a PhD at Harvard. As a professor at Atlanta University, he created the first scientific school of sociology in the United States (Morris 2015). He was also one of the founders of the NAACP, and an influential journalist and public intellectual.

Du Bois argued that it was a mistake for African Americans to delay their demands for political equality, arguing that without voting rights and full social equality they would continue to be oppressed. He rejected the idea that African Americans should ignore the liberal arts and focus exclusively on practical job-related education. Du Bois argued that the most talented African Americans needed a classical education in order to reach their full potential and to become effective leaders and spokespersons. He also rejected the arguments of many white scholars, who claimed that Africans and African Americans had an inferior and pathological culture, and that they would be better off if they assimilated into the dominant white American culture (Morris 2015: 177). As editor of *The Crisis*, the official publication of the NAACP, Du Bois actively promoted the achievements of African American artists, musicians, and writers.

Booker T. Washington

ACTIVE LEARNING

Discuss: One element in Du Bois's argument with Washington rested in his belief that a free black people needed a liberal arts education that included history, philosophy, and the arts, and not only narrow vocational training for a job. This debate continues today. Do you think less advantaged and oppressed people should learn philosophy and history, or is it more important to get skills training for jobs? What are the pros and cons of each argument?

Immigration and work
Latino/a farm workers have been an important part of California's agricultural economy since the early 20th century.

as much of the land that would become New Mexico, Nevada, Utah, Wyoming, and Colorado. Mexicans living on those lands had the option to become US citizens, and most of them did so.

Mexican Americans living in the West and Southwest experienced prejudice and discrimination, and most white ethnic groups treated Mexican Americans as a racial minority group. Racially restrictive housing covenants barred Mexican Americans (as well as African Americans) from buying houses in "white" neighborhoods. Many school districts segregated Mexican American children from white children.

Despite these obstacles, Mexicans immigrated to the United States in large numbers, particularly after 1910. Mexican labor was crucial for the development of the agricultural economy in California, and also for the development of the railroad and the mining industry in the Southwest. When World War II caused labor shortages during the 1940s, the United States established the Bracero program to bring in Mexican contract workers. This pattern continues today, with more than 35 percent of the Latino population being foreign born.

Most sociologists refer to Latinos as an ethnic group, and they emphasize that Latinos can be of any race (Alba and Nee 2003). Complicating matters further, Latinos are more likely than any group to mark their race as "other" on the US Census (Bonilla-Silva [2003] 2018). But race is still a powerful influence on their lives. While many Latino immigrants did not experience race-based discrimination back in their countries of origin, once they arrived in the United States they found themselves grouped together with African Americans, treated as racial minorities, and segregated into minority communities (Portes 1995). This has had a negative impact on the educational resources available for their children, the kinds of jobs that are available to them, and the ability to improve their socioeconomic circumstances (Zhou 1997).

People of Mexican descent account for 64 percent of the Latino population in the United States, followed by Puerto Ricans (9.6 percent). But the Latino population in the United States has become more diverse since the 1980s, with large numbers of immigrants coming from Cuba, El Salvador, the Dominican Republic, and other countries in Central and South America (Stepler and Brown 2016).

In her book *Making Hispanics,* Christina Mora describes how an alliance formed during the 1970s to promote a pan-ethnic identity of "Hispanic" as a way to unite this diverse population (Mora 2015). Before that time, most Latino groups identified with their place of origin, with the dominant identities being Mexican American, Puerto Rican, and Cuban American. These groups were concentrated in different regions of the United States, and they had different political goals from one another. Gradually, an alliance formed between federal officials, grassroots activists, and Spanish-language broadcasters. These three groups worked together to promote the category of "Hispanic" as a common identity that could unite the diverse population of Latinos into a single ethnic group. Over time, Hispanic ethnic identity came to be adopted by Latinos

PAIRED CONCEPTS
Global and Local

Latino Computer Engineers from Colombia and Puerto Rico

The growth in the information technologies and telecommunications fields during the 1990s created a demand for specialized computer and software programmers, which could not be met by professionals already living and working in the United States. As a result, the US government increased the work visa quotas for foreign-born professionals. This policy, combined with greater enforcement of antidiscrimination laws, encouraged employers to actively recruit foreign-born minorities into professional positions in the computer engineering field (Alarcón 1999). Large numbers of foreigners were recruited into the software engineering field from China, India, and Latin America.

Among the Latin American computer engineers, the majority came from Puerto Rico and Colombia. Each group was motivated by a combination of global and local factors. Puerto Ricans are legal citizens, which allows them to travel freely between the island and the mainland to work legally in the United States. Many high-tech companies had opened offices in Puerto Rico during the 1970s, taking advantage of laws that exempted them from taxes when they relocated to the island. Puerto Rican universities invested heavily in science and engineering to meet this demand. But when these tax exemptions ended in the mid-1980s, most of these companies closed their Puerto Rican offices. As a result, large numbers of Puerto Rican computer engineers moved to the mainland United States to pursue professional career opportunities.

Colombian computer engineers were also concerned about the ability to find work in their professional fields, because of the deteriorating economic conditions in their country. Many of them were also worried about the growth of drug cartels and drug-related violence in Colombia. Fearing for their safety and that of their families, and feeling that they had very limited opportunities to find rewarding professional jobs in their home country, Colombian computer engineers emigrated to the United States to work in the information technologies industry (Rincon 2015).

In Colombia as well as Puerto Rico, transnational recruitment networks made it easier for technology companies and computer engineers to find each other (Rincon 2015). The global nature of engineering meant that university curricula had been standardized to meet the needs of transnational engineering companies. Many of the engineering professors in Puerto Rico and Colombia had trained in the United States, and they could use the networks they had developed there to help their students make professional contacts. Likewise, many of these students took advantage of internships and study-abroad programs to spend time in the United States.

Despite their high levels of education and their professional degrees, however, Colombian and Puerto Rican computer engineers often experienced racial discrimination once they arrived on the mainland United States to begin their jobs. Many of their coworkers treated them as less qualified and less intelligent because of their accents. They were subjected to racial and ethnic slurs, as well as police harassment, because of their skin color or accent. Despite the fact that many of these computer engineers viewed themselves as sophisticated and cosmopolitan, people in their local communities did not always see them this way (Rincon 2015).

ACTIVE LEARNING

Reflect: Using terms from Chapter 5, we can say that the Colombian and Puerto Rican engineers occupied an ascribed status of ethnicity that interacted with their achieved status of education in a complicated way. Can you list your own ascribed and achieved statuses? Do your statuses tend to work together, or do you sometimes find them in conflict with each other like the immigrant engineers in this example?

---

throughout North America, South America, and Central America, as television stations such as Univision transformed themselves from regional Mexican broadcasters to become a global Hispanic media empire. This is an excellent example of the self-conscious and intentional construction of an ethnic category.

Asian Americans

Asian Americans, including people from Hawaii and other Pacific Islands, are a diverse ethnic group with a long history of immigration to the United States. Chinese immigrants began arriving in large numbers during the California

Gold Rush in the 1840s and 1850s. Many of these immigrants later found jobs in the railroad industry in the 1860s, and Chinese workers played a large role in the construction of the transcontinental railroad. Japanese agricultural workers began arriving in the United States in the 1880s. Koreans and Filipinos began arriving in US states and territories in the early 1900s, where they worked on the sugar plantations in Hawaii.

Native Hawaiian and Pacific Islanders also have a long history in the United States, although it was not until 2000 that the category "Native Hawaiian and Other Pacific Islander" was added to the Asian race question in the US Census (Pew Research Center 2015a). A part of the legacy of US imperialism in the Pacific Ocean during the 19th and 20th centuries (Camacho 2016), American Samoa became a US naval station in 1878, and then an unincorporated territory in 1899 as part of an agreement between colonial powers in the Pacific. Guam and the Philippines were annexed in 1898 after the Spanish-American war; the Philippines went on to fight a war against US occupying forces from 1899–1902. Hawaii was a kingdom until the late 19th century, briefly a Republic, and then ceded itself to the militarily dominant United States in 1898.

Early Asian Americans faced significant hostility, prejudice, and violence in the United States, and they were denied protections that were available to US citizens. Chinese and Japanese immigrants were not allowed to own land in many parts of the country, and they were forced to live in crowded urban areas outside of white communities. The Chinese Exclusion Act of 1882 made Chinese immigration to the United States illegal, and denied citizenship to those already in the country. New immigration laws passed in 1917 and 1924 extended these exclusions to other Asian groups, and these laws remained in effect until the 1940s.

After the 1965 Immigration Act ended the system of racial, ethnic, and national quotas, the Asian American population increased, from 491,000 in 1960 to more than 11 million in 2010, as Vietnamese, Laotian, and Cambodian refugees joined the migrant stream in the 1970s. By the early 1980s, Asian Americans comprised more than half of all immigrants (*Historical Abstract of the United States* 2006: Table Ad98-105). Nearly half of all Asian immigrants have settled in three states (California, New York, and Texas), though large Asian American communities can be found in cities throughout the country.

Asian Americans have been a remarkably successful ethnic group. Compared to the US population as a whole, they have higher average incomes and higher levels of educational attainment. Nearly half of all Asian Americans have a college degree, as compared to only 28 percent of the US population. The median household income for Asian Americans was $81,331 in 2017, as compared to $61,372 for the US population (Fontenot, Semega, and Kollar 2018). Many Asian immigrants, especially those from India, are employed in high-skilled jobs and enter the United States on temporary H-1B visas for specialty occupation workers. Households headed by Indian immigrants had a median income of $100,000 in 2015 (Pew Research Center 2017).

Despite this success, Asian Americans still deal with prejudice and stereotypes. A recent study by the US Department of Housing and Urban Development found that one in five Asian Americans experience discrimination when trying to buy or rent a home. Asian American groups have filed lawsuits against Harvard and other elite universities in recent years, alleging that these schools have racial quotas limiting the number of Asian American students. Stereotypes about overly demanding Asian American parents circulate widely. Despite all their educational success, Asian Americans continue to be underrepresented as corporate executives, law firm partners, and in other top management positions (Zweigenhaft and Domhoff 2006).

Popular beliefs about Asian Americans as a successful "model minority" also hide the fact that there is still a good deal of poverty in many Asian American communities (Chou and Feagin 2008). One in eight Asian Americans live below the poverty level, which is about the same as the average for the total US society. Poverty rates are particularly high among Asian Americans from Cambodia (29.3 percent) and those of Hmong descent (37.8 percent).

Race and ethnicity in university admissions
Harvard University has faced protests and lawsuits charging discrimination against Asians and Asian Americans in the admissions process.

Race, Privilege, and Inequality

Inequality and privilege shape how people experience race and ethnicity. Minority groups experience **discrimination**, where they are treated in a negative and unequal way based on their race or ethnicity. Their choice of where to live is influenced by **segregation**, a social practice in which neighborhoods, schools, and other social organizations are separated by race and ethnicity. Discrimination and segregation reinforce social inequality by limiting the resources that are available to minority groups as well as the opportunities that are extended to them. Social conflicts erupt between minority groups trying to reduce or eliminate race-based inequality, and majority groups that have an interest in maintaining their privileges.

Discrimination Negative and unequal treatment directed at a particular group.

Segregation A social practice in which neighborhoods, schools, and other social organizations are separated by race and ethnicity.

The Privileges of Being in the Majority Group

Whites are the largest racial group in the United States, accounting for 60.4 percent of the population. They are also the most privileged racial group. Compared with people from other racial groups who have similar social characteristics (education, occupation, etc.), whites have higher incomes, live in safer neighborhoods, and have access to better schools (Shapiro 2005). They get lower interest rates on loans to buy houses and cars, and accumulate more wealth over their lifetimes (Oliver and Shapiro 2006). Whites are less likely to be pulled over by police or be treated with suspicion as potential criminals. In other words, there are a host of material and psychological benefits that come with white privilege. One of the most important of these benefits is simply not having to constantly think about race or be aware of racial privilege.

Social science research has measured the material aspects of white privilege. The median white household had more than $111,000 in wealth in 2011, as compared to $7,113 for the median black household and $8,348 for the median Latino household (Sullivan et al. 2015). In 2018, the real median household income of non-Hispanic whites in the previous year was $68,145 compared to a median household income of $50, 486 for Latinos and $40,258 for African

PAIRED CONCEPTS   **Inequality and Privilege**

How Irish Americans Became White

The Irish Catholics who began arriving in the United States in the 1800s were leaving a society in which they suffered significant religious and racial discrimination. In Ireland, they were not allowed to vote or attend university, banned from many occupations, and forced to live outside of the city limits in many towns. This racial discrimination, combined with a famine that swept through Ireland, encouraged nearly two million Irish Catholics to emigrate to the United States between 1800 and 1860.

Arriving in the United States, the majority of these Irish immigrants continued to face racial discrimination and stereotyping. Depicted in the press as ape-like barbarians prone to drunkenness, crime, and stupidity, they were forced to live in the poorest neighborhoods and limited to the lowest-wage and lowest-skilled jobs. Anti-Irish violence was common. Many Americans referred to Irish Catholics as "white Negroes," and believed that they were racially inferior.

But Irish Catholics managed to convince Americans that they were white. According to the historian Noel Ignatiev (2008), they did this by cooperating with other whites to suppress and exclude African American workers. Irish Americans took the lead in attacking African Americans and driving them out of neighborhoods in cities throughout the Northeast and Midwest, most notably during the New York City Draft Riots of 1863 and the Chicago race riot of 1919. By taking the lead in these acts of racial violence, Irish Americans were able to distance themselves from the African American population. In this way, as Ignatiev describes, they "earned" their white identities.

By the early 20th century, Irish Americans had gained political power in many cities. Al Smith was elected Governor of New York four times, and ran for President in 1928 as the nominee of the Democratic Party. Irish Americans were welcomed into white neighborhoods, and they frequently married people from other white ethnic groups. In fact, intermarriage rates were nearly 80 percent for third-generation Irish immigrants (Alba 1976). Today, the history of discrimination against Irish immigrants has been virtually forgotten (Waters 1990).

Alfred Smith, the first Irish American governor of New York

ACTIVE LEARNING

Discuss: For most of the last two centuries, the Irish were considered a race and African Americans were considered a race. Did race mean the same thing at the time? How can you tell? How did the Irish resist their racial classification? To what extent do you think Irish assimilation into American culture was based on defining themselves as not Black?

Americans (US Census 2018). The return on investment for completing a college degree is more than ten times higher for whites than it is for African Americans or Latinos (Shin 2015). Even poor whites benefit; a study by the Brookings Institution found that white children born into poor families have a much better chance of becoming wealthy by the time they are 40 years old than poor African American children do (Short 2014).

There are also nonmaterial benefits associated with white privilege. Whites are far less likely than racial minorities to think about structural obstacles that influence their lives, and far more likely to believe that they will be successful as long as they work hard (Kluegel 1990). They are much more likely to believe that schools, courts, the workplace, and other social institutions are fair (Patten 2013). They are more likely to receive small favors, like getting a free ride on the bus or getting a warning instead of a citation when they are pulled over by the police (Pinsker 2015). All of these small favors allow white people to move through the world without thinking about racial discrimination, assuming instead that most people are fair and good natured.

Racial Discrimination and Segregation

Racial discrimination and segregation are a central part of US history. As we discussed earlier in the chapter, discrimination was built into the laws and the official policies of the US government for nearly two hundred years. Immigration policies set quotas on minorities, barred Asian Americans from citizenship, and gave preferences to white ethnic groups. State and local governments enforced racial segregation in schools and neighborhoods, investing much more money in white areas of the city than minority areas. Interracial marriage was illegal in many states throughout the South and West. These laws and policies remained in place until the 1950s and 1960s, when a series of Supreme Court rulings declared that policies based on racial discrimination were unconstitutional.

Even though explicit policies of racial discrimination have been declared unconstitutional, informal policies of segregation continue to shape the life chances of racial minorities. One of the most important ways this happens is through residential segregation. Despite the fact that the 1968 Fair Housing Act made it illegal to use race as a criterion for making decisions about real estate rentals and purchases, **residential segregation** remains very high in the United States (Frey 2018; Massey and Denton 1993). Not all cities are the same, of course, and not all racial groups are affected equally by racial segregation. Frey's (2018) recent analysis of census data shows, for example, that despite small declines in residential segregation since 2000, very high levels of segregation persist in many cities, including Milwaukee, New York, and Chicago, and African Americans experience more extreme forms of residential segregation than other racial groups (Massey and Denton 1993; Frey 2018).

A variety of different strategies have been used to create and reproduce the system of residential segregation. **Redlining** was a practice where banks would not give mortgages to people who lived in minority-dominated neighborhoods (Jackson 1985). **Racial steering** was a practice in which realtors would encourage people to look for homes in specific neighborhoods depending on their race, as a way to ensure that the "desirable" neighborhoods were reserved for whites (Cashin 2005).

Residential segregation
A social practice in which neighborhoods are separated on the basis of group differences.

Redlining A practice where banks would not give mortgages to people who lived in minority-dominated neighborhoods.

Racial steering A practice in which realtors would encourage people to look for homes in specific neighborhoods depending on their race, as a way to ensure that the "desirable" neighborhoods were reserved for whites.

Residential segregation
Most cities and suburbs in the United States still have very high levels of residential segregation, so that most of the people that you see in your neighborhood look like you. Residential segregation is also connected to segregation in schools, churches, and other important social institutions.

Blockbusting A practice where real estate agents would go to a neighborhood where racial minorities were beginning to move in, convince white residents that their property values were going to decrease, and encourage them to sell their houses below market value. Realtors then sold those homes to minority buyers at inflated prices.

Blockbusting was a practice in which real estate agents would go to a neighborhood where racial minorities were beginning to move in, convince white residents that their property values were going to decrease, and encourage them to sell their houses (below market value) "before it was too late" (Hirsch 1983). The realtors would then turn around and sell those homes to minority buyers at inflated prices, because those prospective buyers had fewer options about where they were permitted to live.

Racial discrimination also continues in the workplace. African Americans are more likely to be unemployed than other racial groups, while average wages for African Americans and Latinos continue to be lower than those of whites (Pager and Shepherd 2008; Fontenot, Semega, and Kollar 2018). Experimental studies examining hiring decisions find a consistent preference for white job applicants when employers are presented with people who have similar qualifications (Pager 2007a, 2007b). Black men seem to have a particularly difficult time on the job market, having to spend more time looking for jobs and having a less stable employment history than white workers with similar qualifications (Tomaskovic-Devey, Thomas, and Johnson 2005).

There is also the everyday racial discrimination that racial and ethnic minorities experience in their interactions with store owners, police, and people in the street. As we discussed at the beginning of the chapter, President Obama commented on this everyday discrimination when discussing the murder of Trayvon Martin in 2012. Most African American men have had the experience of being followed by store owners and store security, and they have witnessed the nervous looks of white people when they enter an elevator or pass somebody in the street (Feagin and Sikes 1994). African Americans and Latinos who apply for a mortgage are 82 percent more likely to be rejected than whites who have a similar financial profile, and those who do get mortgages generally have to pay higher interest rates and additional fees (Pager and Shepherd 2008). On other major purchases, such as buying a car, research shows that salespeople are less flexible in their negotiations with racial minorities (Ayres and Siegelman 1995). These experiences of discrimination lead to material disadvantages for racial minorities, as well as a host of psychological and emotional consequences.

Consequences of Discrimination

Discrimination means that racial minorities get a lower rate of return for many of their efforts to improve their lives. Discrimination in housing means that racial minorities settle in less desirable neighborhoods, where their houses will be less profitable investments than similar homes purchased in "white" neighborhoods. Discrimination in credit means that they have to pay higher interest rates for bank loans, while discrimination in consumer markets means that they have to pay a higher price in stores. Employment discrimination means that they have a harder time finding work, are more likely to lose their jobs, and are more likely to receive lower wages than white workers. These patterns of discrimination are measurably worse for African Americans and Latinos than they are for other racial groups.

Racial discrimination forces people into poorer, more dangerous, and more poorly resourced neighborhoods, where they are more likely to be victims of violent crime. People who live in minority neighborhoods also have to deal with more aggressive police practices (Chapter 6). These include frequent interrogations of drivers and pedestrians, the frequent use of random sobriety checkpoints, and the tendency to make arrests instead of giving warnings for minor violations of the law (Tomaskovic-Devey and Warren 2009). Minority neighborhoods have fewer banks, fewer medical resources, and less access to healthy foods (Moore and Diez-Roux 2006).

Racial discrimination also creates long-term emotional and psychological consequences for the people who experience it. For example, the stress created by racial discrimination leads to physical and mental health problems that proliferate throughout their lives and across generations (Thoits 2010). Racial discrimination also makes people more distrustful of police, health care providers, and other mainstream social institutions. This makes their communities much more vulnerable during times of emergency and crisis.

Consequences of discrimination
Minority neighborhoods have fewer banks and medical resources, and less access to fresh food.

Colorblind Racism

The mechanisms that reproduce racial discrimination are less obvious today than they used to be. Expressions of overt racism are less common, and government policies of explicit racial discrimination have been declared unconstitutional. Many people today reject racism, and say that they treat everyone the same. As the comedian Stephen Colbert quipped, "I don't even see race, not even my own. People tell me I'm white, and I believe them, because I just spent the last six minutes explaining how I'm not a racist. And that is about the whitest thing you can do."

Colbert's joke refers to a phenomenon that sociologists refer to as **colorblind racism**. This is a situation where the refusal to discuss or notice race allows people to ignore the history, consequences, and continued existence of racial discrimination. In his book *Racism without Racists: Color-Blind Racism and the Persistence of Racial Inequality in America* ([2003] 2018), Eduardo Bonilla-Silva identified several common ways that colorblind ideologies allow whites to deny racial discrimination and inequality while ignoring their own substantial privilege. Through a framework of *abstract liberalism,* they think about all people as abstract individuals who have an equal opportunity to work hard and to be successful in their lives. Through *naturalization,* they explain away things like racial segregation, by claiming that different groups have a natural desire to live in homogeneous communities. Through *cultural racism*, they argue that poverty persists in minority communities because the people in those communities are lazy and have the wrong values. Through *minimization*, they argue that racism and discrimination are problems from the past that no longer exist. These explanations allow people to ignore the historical accumulation of race-based advantages and disadvantages. In short, Bonilla-Silva argues, colorblind racism allows people to "blame the victim" in a way that frees them from responsibility for past historical injustices and continued racial inequalities.

Colorblind racism A form of racism based on the refusal to discuss or notice race.

Racial Conflict

Violence and conflict have also been used to reinforce racial privileges and inequalities. In its most extreme form, racial conflict takes the form of **genocide**, which is the systematic killing of people on the basis of their race, ethnicity,

Genocide The systematic killing of people on the basis of their race, ethnicity, or religion.

National memorial to victims of genocide, Rwanda
The systematic killing of people on the basis of their race, ethnicity, or religion is called genocide, and it was shockingly frequent in the 20th century. In the Rwandan genocide of 1994 an estimated one million people were killed, including 70% of the ethnic Tutsi population.

Ethnic cleansing The forcible removal of an entire group of people from a society because of their race, ethnicity, or religion.

or religion. Colonial expansion from Europe in Africa, Asia, Australia, and North America had genocidal aspects. There have also been repeated genocides around the world in the 20th century. In 1915, the government of the Ottoman Empire (in what is today called Turkey) began systematically killing and deporting its Armenian population. Russia under Stalin systematically killed millions of Cossacks, Muslim peoples (including Chechens, Ingush, Crimean Tatars, Tajiks, Bashkirs, and Kazakhs), Jews, and Ukrainians. In the most infamous genocide of the 20th century, Germany systematically killed six million Jews. More recently, racial conflict in Rwanda led members of the Hutu ethnic majority to kill nearly 800,000 of the Tutsi ethnic minority in 1994. The United Nations has identified eighteen major acts of genocide perpetrated during the 20th century, resulting in total deaths estimated to be between 13 million and 35 million people.

A type of racial conflict that is closely related to genocide is **ethnic cleansing**, which happens when an entire group of people is forcibly removed from a society because of their race, ethnicity, or religion. Ethnic cleansing happens when the dominant group decides that it wants to create an ethnically homogeneous society. This happened in the 1990s during the war in Bosnia-Hercegovina. Before the war, Bosnia had been a multiethnic society consisting primarily of Serbs, Croats, and Bosnian Muslims. While there were occasional ethnic tensions between these groups, they had lived together peacefully for decades. This began to change after 1989, when Slobodan Milosevic came to power campaigning on a platform that favored a "Greater Serbia" and an ethnically pure Serbian nation. The campaign for ethnic cleansing began with violence, rape, and murder directed against the ethnic minorities residing in the territory. It continued with the forceful expulsion of the remaining minorities, and the murder of those who refused to leave. More than three million people were displaced, and an additional hundred thousand were killed. The United Nations considers both ethnic cleansing and genocide to be war crimes.

The competition for jobs and other material resources can also cause racial conflict. Sociological research has shown that racial violence between low-skilled workers tends to increase when the economy gets worse, or when there is an increase in the number of low-wage workers competing for the same jobs (Olzak 1994). This was clearly the case during the "Red Summer" of 1919, when white mobs in more than three dozen cities (mostly in the North and the Midwest) violently attacked African Americans. These outbursts of violence followed several years of building racial tensions, in which African American migrants from the South and soldiers returning from World War I found themselves competing with white ethnic groups for blue-collar manufacturing jobs. Hundreds of African Americans were killed in these race riots. In some cities,

Power and Resistance

Black Lives Matter

After George Zimmerman was acquitted in the 2012 shooting death of Trayvon Martin, anger about the verdict spread throughout the nation. People took to the streets and went on social media to express their anger and disappointment. Alicia Garza, an activist and writer living in Oakland, expressed her feelings in a post on her Facebook page, writing, "Black people. I love you. I love us. Our lives matter, Black Lives Matter." A friend of hers, Patrisse Cullors, reposted it with the hashtag #BlackLivesMatter. A third friend, Opal Tometi, also reposted it. The three women, who were all community organizers and political activists, talked about forming a social movement called Black Lives Matter. Using social media, they hoped the #BlackLivesMatter hashtag would bring people together who wanted to fight against racism in their communities.

The protest movement developed slowly, but it exploded in August 2014, when a police officer shot and killed Michael Brown, an unarmed African American teenager, in Ferguson, Missouri. In the following month, the hashtag #BlackLivesMatter was used more than 52,000 times; after the November 2014 decision not to indict the officer involved in the shooting, the hashtag was used more than 92,000 times in four hours (Demby 2016). There were more than two hundred demonstrations nationwide protesting the police shooting in Ferguson, with most of them being organized with the help of the Black Lives Matter Movement.

Since 2014, Black Lives Matter has become one of the most important protest movements fighting against racism and police violence. The hashtag has been used to express anger, organize protests, and bring visibility to additional cases in which African Americans died during interactions with police, such as the cases of Tamir Rice (2014), Eric Garner (2014), Freddie Gray (2015), and Sandra Bland (2015). It was also used to organize protests in 2015 after nine African Americans were murdered while attending church in Charleston, South Carolina. Yet disproportionate killings of black people by police have continued in the years since and show little sign of abating.

Today, Black Lives Matter is an established national movement committed to fighting violence against African Americans. It continues to be an important presence in social media, with more than 100,000 followers on Twitter and more than 100,000 page views on Facebook every month. The movement has local chapters in 28 different cities, as well as in Canada and the United Kingdom.

#BlackLivesMatter
The Black Lives Matter Movement is one of the most important movements fighting racism today. It emerged following the acquittal of George Zimmerman in the Trayvon Martin case, and gained momentum after the 2014 police shooting of Michael Brown in Ferguson, Missouri. The hashtag helps to organize protests and brings visibility to other cases where African Americans have died in encounters with the police.

ACTIVE LEARNING

Discuss: What do you think of the Black Lives Matter movement? Are you more aware of the extrajudicial killings of Black citizens in recent years? Do you think there are more killings or more media attention to these killings?

African Americans responded by creating armed resistance movements to ensure that similar violence would not happen in the future.

Another cause of racial conflict is racial profiling, in which police and civilians target minority populations and treat them more harshly than the majority group. In the US South during the era of Jim Crow, an African American was killed in public every four days, often for things as trivial as making boastful remarks or trying to vote. Minor offenses quickly escalated to public lynchings by a white mob, often with the support and cooperation of police officers and government officials. The goal was to terrify the African American population, scaring them into accepting the system of racial discrimination.

Today, racial profiling continues to be a problem, particularly for African American men. Police are much more likely to treat people as potential criminals when they are patrolling in minority communities, and they are much more likely to make arrests in those neighborhoods (Tomaskovic-Devey and Warren 2009). African American drivers are more than twice as likely as white drivers to be arrested during a traffic stop, and they are nearly three times as likely to be subjected to a police search during a traffic stop. Their interactions with police are also more dangerous: African American men are more than three times as likely to be killed during such encounters as white men (Sikora and Mulvihill 2002).

Multiculturalism and Diversity

Racial minorities do not passively accept the violence directed at them. Protest movements publicize practices of racial discrimination and violence, calling on governments to create more equitable policies and citizens to be more tolerant of diversity. Over time, these movements have successfully challenged official policies that reinforce racial privilege, and they have changed public opinion enough so that overt expressions of racism are less common or acceptable than they once were. Many societies now support policies of multiculturalism, which support and encourage the distinctive identities of the different cultural groups that exist in society. Multicultural policies explicitly reject the idea that some cultural groups are more valuable than others.

Assimilation and Racial Privilege

Assimilation When minority groups fully embrace the culture of the dominant group and lose their distinctive racial and/or ethnic characteristics.

Many societies expect racial and ethnic minorities to **assimilate** over time, which means that minority groups are expected to fully embrace the culture of the dominant group. In France, assimilation is required for immigrants who want to become citizens. This means that potential new citizens must display a strong knowledge of French language and culture, and their behavior must show that they favor the French identity over any racial, ethnic, or religious identity. There is no official recognition of minorities in France, to the point that the French government does not even collect data on the racial and ethnic characteristics of its population.

France is not alone; the goal of assimilation is built into the citizenship policies of many countries around the world. In the United States, immigrants who want to become citizens have to demonstrate that they can speak, read, and write English, and they have to pass a civics test about US history and its form of government. Similar citizenship tests are required in most nations in Western Europe, as well as Australia (Etzioni 2007). All of these tests and requirements are based on the belief that people who take the time to learn the history and culture of their society will be more likely to assimilate.

While early sociologists thought that assimilation was inevitable, most social science research today finds that assimilation has been limited and uneven. In the United States, white ethnic groups have assimilated more easily than non-white groups (Massey 1995). Residential segregation persists. There are **ethnic enclaves** throughout the country—geographical areas defined by high levels of ethnic concentration and cultural activities and ethnically

Ethnic enclaves Geographical areas defined by high levels of ethnic concentration and cultural activities and ethnically identified economic activities.

identified economic activities. Examples of ethnic enclaves are Chinatown in San Francisco, Koreatown in Los Angeles, Little Havana in Miami, and Spanish Harlem in New York City. These enclaves encourage the reproduction of ethnic identities rather than a process of assimilation.

There is considerable debate about how much assimilation is taking place, and whether assimilation is a desirable outcome for societies. According to Richard Alba and Victor Nee, new immigrant groups to the United States continue to learn English, settle in the suburbs, intermarry, and experience economic and educational success at rates that are similar to those achieved by white European immigrants of the early 20th century (Alba and Nee 2003). At the same time, though, Alba and Nee also note that children of Afro-Caribbean and darker-skinned Latino immigrants are not assimilating at the same rates into mainstream society; many of them, in fact, are assimilating into "oppositional cultures" that are alienated and segregated from mainstream society. In other words, the assimilation of new immigrant groups is being shaped unevenly by the racial distinctions and inequalities that already exist. This is a form of intersectionality (Chapter 2), where immigrant, ethnic, and racial status are interacting to shape outcomes differently for different groups of people.

Challenging Assimilation

The ideal of assimilation has always had its critics. The philosopher Horace Kallen (1882–1974) presented an alternative vision in 1915, which he called **cultural pluralism**. In an article titled "Democracy versus the Melting Pot," Kallen argued that society would be stronger if people had pride in their cultural heritage, and that they could maintain their unique cultural identities while still accepting the core values of the larger society in which they lived (Rose 1993). Similar debates about assimilation were taking place within the African American community. To put it simply, not everyone agreed that full assimilation was a desirable outcome (Jacobs 2000: 38-46).

By the mid-1960s, many racial minority groups had begun to challenge the ideals of assimilation much more forcefully. The Black Power Movement argued that specifically African American political and cultural institutions were needed to combat the racism of mainstream society. They argued that a movement devoted to Black Pride was needed to counteract centuries of history and culture that celebrated the achievements of Europeans and ignored the achievements of other groups. The Black Arts Movement and the academic field of African American studies sought to increase awareness of and pride in African American achievements.

Similar developments occurred among other racial and ethnic groups. The Chicano Movement of the 1960s continued the push for civil and political rights, but it also worked to increase awareness and pride in Latino achievements. This included a growing Chicano

Cultural pluralism An alternative to the idea of assimilation that imagines a society where people maintain their unique cultural identities while also accepting the core values of the larger society.

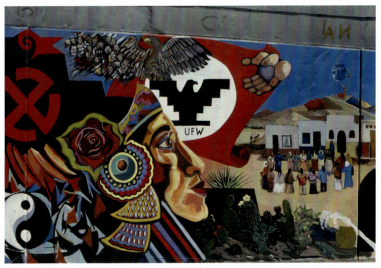

Chicano Mural Art
The Chicano Art Movement expresses pride in the Mexican American cultural experience and resists assimilation and loss of meaning. It is part of the ethnic studies movement that seeks to tell the history of racial and ethnic minorities in their own terms.

Art Movement, and the creation of an academic field of Chicano Studies that developed an explicitly Mexican American perspective on culture, literature, and history. Movements in Asian American Studies and Native American Studies developed in the late 1960s, with a similar goal of developing an ethnic perspective on culture and history. The National Association for Ethnic Studies was created in 1972, with the goal of telling the history of racial and ethnic minorities on their own terms. By the 1990s, the push for cultural pluralism was strong enough that the sociologist Nathan Glazer wrote an article with the title "Is Assimilation Dead?" (Glazer 1993). For many, multiculturalism was the new reality and the new ideal.

Multiculturalism (Movement and Policy)

Multiculturalism A culturally pluralist society that officially recognizes the existence of different cultural groups and identities, and that develops policies promoting cultural diversity.

Multiculturalism refers to a type of society that officially recognizes the existence of different cultural groups and identities, and that develops policies promoting cultural diversity. People who adopt a multicultural perspective argue that cultural pluralism is a far more common outcome than assimilation in today's society. Critics such as Charles Taylor are concerned that assimilationist policies threaten the dignity of minority groups, by asking them to reject their history and their cultural heritage (Taylor 1994). Instead of assimilation, multicultural policies explicitly acknowledge the distinctive identities of racial and ethnic minorities, and they invest resources to help disadvantaged groups preserve their culture.

Canada was the first country to adopt official policies of multiculturalism. The 1971 Multiculturalism Policy of Canada explicitly affirmed the value and the dignity of all Canadian citizens, regardless of their racial or ethnic origins, their language, or their religious affiliation. It affirmed the rights of all indigenous peoples, and it established two official languages, French and English. The goal of the new policy was to allow all citizens to have pride in their cultural heritage, to keep their identities, and to create better racial and ethnic harmony in a society that celebrates tolerance and mutual respect.

While other countries have adopted similar policies, multiculturalism has not been without critics. Critics fear that multiculturalism promotes cultural relativism, making it difficult to criticize behaviors that go against the grain of the national culture. The Netherlands adopted official national policies of multiculturalism during the 1980s, but after several high-profile incidents of violence, it now identifies itself as a society that is tolerant but not multicultural. The UK had a similar experience, with its prime minister, David Cameron, declaring in a 2011 speech that "state multiculturalism has failed." In the United States, there are no official policies of multiculturalism. There have been many US initiatives to promote cultural pluralism in education, culture, and the arts, but these efforts have also faced criticism and resistance.

Multiracial and Multiethnic Identities

The growing awareness of cultural pluralism and the influences of multiculturalism have encouraged many people to celebrate and take pride in the diverse cultural heritage that shapes their family history. Many people no longer feel the need to select only one racial or ethnic identity. Today, there are more high-profile multiracial and multiethnic celebrities than ever before—athletes like Tiger Woods and Derek Jeter, singers like Alicia Keys and Bruno Mars, actors like Keanu Reeves and Halle Barry, and politicians like Barack Obama.

Multiculturalism in the Workplace

The growing recognition and support for multicultural policies is creating change and opportunity in the workplace. Cultural awareness has become an important business tool, and many employers now recognize that they can enhance productivity and workplace unity if they can develop better cross-cultural awareness and respect.

Multiculturalism offers a number of clear business advantages. Instead of discriminating against specific groups because of racial or ethnic stereotypes, multicultural awareness allows employers to identify a larger pool of talented workers. Multicultural workforces encourage innovation, by exposing employees to different perspectives and experiences. They allow a business to identify a new market niche that it might have ignored, and to create a more successful advertising strategy focused on that niche. In addition, research shows that multicultural workplaces encourage higher levels of tolerance, which has a general social benefit (Gudykunst 2004).

Multiculturalism has also created new kinds of jobs. For example, the advertising industry has created new jobs in "multicultural marketing," which develop new advertising strategies focused on Asian American, African American, and Latino consumers. Most colleges and universities now have an office of multicultural affairs and multicultural services, and they hire social scientists to help advance diversity and promote multicultural awareness on campus. Many schools, police departments, hospitals, government service agencies, and nonprofit organizations now employ multicultural liaison officers, whose job is to communicate more effectively and respectfully with the diverse communities they serve. Many large corporations employ diversity officers, who are responsible for attracting, developing, and retaining a diverse talent pool of workers. Diversity officers often work with the multicultural marketing department, to make sure that there is a good strategy for communicating the company's brand in a way that addresses the needs of a diverse base of clients and consumers.

In addition to having good skills in research and communication, people who work in these jobs need specific skills that allow them to satisfy the multicultural mission of their positions. First, they need to have good foreign language skills. In the United States, fluency in Spanish is the most helpful, but with the growth of the Asian American population a knowledge of Chinese, Japanese, Korean, or Vietnamese is also valuable. In addition, they need to have a strong sociological understanding of the communities and their cultures. This sociological and cultural sensitivity will help them know when and how to change a marketing campaign so as not to accidentally offend people. For example, multicultural marketers encouraged Buick to rename one of its automobile models when it was released in Canada; recognizing that "Lacrosse" is a slang term for masturbation in Quebec, they changed that car model to the "Allure" (Associated Press 2003). Multicultural marketers also use a sociological perspective to understand different age cohorts within an immigrant or minority community, recognizing that there are likely to be different levels of generational acculturation.

Jobs that specialize in the multicultural workforce offer strong growth and good salaries. Multicultural marketers and liaison officers generally make between $40,000 and $70,000 per year, depending on their experience and the size of the organization where they are employed. Chief diversity officers are executive-level positions in most organizations, with annual salaries often in excess of $100,000.

Mucho Más Que Autos
Multicultural marketing is one of the fastest-growing segments in the advertising industry.

ACTIVE LEARNING

Find out: Search online using the term "diversity and inclusion jobs." What are the qualifications for the job? Do you think having a developed sociological imagination would be useful in this work? Why?

Alicia Keys in concert, 2017

Because of the growing visibility and influence of multiracial and multiethnic identities, the US Census Bureau decided in 2000 that it would allow people to select more than one racial category on their official census forms. Nine million people chose more than one race in the 2010 Census, a 32 percent increase since 2000. These trends are likely to continue, because nearly half of all multiracial Americans are younger than 18 (Pew Research Center 2015b). In fact, more than 10 percent of children born in the United States today have parents who come from different racial groups.

Not everyone who has mixed-race parents identifies as multiracial. At present, fewer than half of US adults who have a mixed-race background consider themselves to be multiracial. Many people of mixed-race heritage report that they still feel social pressure to identify with a single race (Pew Research Center 2015b). Others make a political choice to identify with a single identity. Recognizing the deep imprint that racism and racial thinking have had on society, they make a deliberate choice to adopt the stigmatized identity and help build a proud and powerful cultural identity around it (Appiah and Gutmann 1998). In his 2007 memoir *Dreams from my Father: A Story of Race and Inheritance*, Barack Obama describes how he came to see himself as an African American man with mixed-race heritage. On his own census form, in 2010, Obama selected only one race for himself and his family.

Civil rights leaders have expressed some reservations about the multiracial classifications that are now available on the Census. They are concerned that it will become harder to identify and enforce civil rights violations if people are allowed to indicate that they belong to more than one racial group (Perlmann and Waters 2002: 13). They are concerned that the rise of multiracial identities will weaken the strength of African American advocacy groups (Alex-Assensoh and Hanks 2000). Some scholars have suggested that using data based on subjectively defined categories will make the entire system of racial and ethnic data vulnerable to legal challenge (Harrison 2002).

Despite these reservations, however, most experts predict that the multiracial population will increase. Government agencies are now collecting data in a way that includes categories for multiracial identities; schools, businesses, and even public opinion pollsters are beginning to do the same thing (Hochschild and Weaver 2010). As multiracialism becomes a more visible and influential presence, it will have profound effects on politics and social life. For some, multiracialism will fundamentally challenge the basic premises of racial thinking, causing them to forcefully confront all forms of racial intolerance and discrimination. For others, who are defenders of assimilation or racial privilege, multiracialism will lead to a growing backlash against multiculturalism and cultural pluralism. And for yet others, embracing a multiracial identity will mean that racial and ethnic differences will become less significant in their lives. Understanding all of these effects, and how they are connected to one another, will require us to cultivate our sociological imaginations.

Intersecting Identities

As this chapter has shown, the classifications that describe racial and ethnic identities are complex and have changed over time. Pseudoscientific arguments about race continue to circulate, but there is no evidence that biological differences determine racial or ethnic identity. It is clear, though, that racial and ethnic identities have real social consequences in the world. People's actions make race and ethnicity real. Larger institutional systems that reproduce the racial and ethnic system, like the US Census, shift official categories to reflect a rapidly changing social reality, and individuals navigate this changing landscape as they form and re-form their identities.

To apply the five key concepts to think about the racial and ethnic system in the United States, we end this chapter with the case of Sofía Vergara. Vergara is best known for her role as Gloria Pritchett on the television show *Modern Family* for which she has won multiple Emmys and Golden Globe Awards. Vergara was already well known to Spanish-speaking audiences for her work on Spanish-language television during the 1990s. According to *Forbes Magazine*, Vergara was the highest-paid female television actor in the United States

Sofía Vergara

from 2012 to 2018, an accomplishment that rests as much on her many product endorsements and licensing agreements as on direct compensation for her TV roles .

When Vergara talks about her life, she includes accounts of the racial and ethnic system of the United States that has shaped her career. For example, in many interviews, she repeats the point that she is a "natural blonde":

> "I'm a natural blonde, but when I started acting, I would go to auditions, and they didn't know where to put me because I was voluptuous and had the accent—but I had blonde hair," she explained in a 2010 interview with *Self* magazine. "The moment I dyed my hair dark, it was, "Oh, she's the hot Latin girl.'"

This is a complicated story about the *structure* of the racial and ethnic hierarchy in the US entertainment business. According to Vergara, the casting agents had a stereotype of "the hot Latin girl" that they wanted the actress to fulfill, and her hair color was wrong since the stereotype assumes all Latinas are brunette. As an award-winning and critically acclaimed television actress and an influential voice in media discussions, Vergara uses her *power* in this story to introduce *contingency* into the category of Latina in the entertainment business. The story that she is a "natural blonde" was covered very widely in the entertainment media over several years and might be interpreted as a moment of *resistance* against the stereotypes that are used to typecast Latina actors and characters. Vergara joins a long line of prior critics who recall that Latina actresses have both been made to appear darker to exemplify a Latina stereotype, and in other cases "whitened" through hair bleaching and removal to avoid the stereotype (Molina-Guzmán 2010; Valdivia 2010; Rodriguez 2004). In all cases, the actions and decisions of gatekeepers in the entertainment industry have served to uphold the cultural perceptions of Latinas at any given time.

That said, Vergara is not above playing with stereotypes, and she has drawn wide criticism for doing so. For example, in 2012 the *Huffington Post* asks of Vergara's role in *Modern Family*, "As alluring as she is, has the Colombian actress taken the Latina stereotype too far?" They go on to suggest that Vergara is not only playing a comedic version of the stereotype but that she is reinforcing the stereotype because her performance supports very traditional understandings of gender and class *inequality*. For example, the authors quote a

CASE STUDY CONTINUED

Daily Beast interview where Vergara defends the Latina stereotype:

> I don't see anything bad about being stereotyped as a Latin woman . . . We are yellers, we're pretty, we're sexy, and we're scandalous. I am not scared of the stereotypes.

In another interview with *Esquire* magazine Vergara is quoted:

> Listen, I didn't know how to make coffee when I came to the United States. Because in Colombia the maids do it. . . . It's so different over there. You have the maid that cooks. The maid that irons the clothes. It's a hard adjustment. When I came to the United States and started working, my priority was not to buy a handbag but to spend my money on the maid and a nanny. Always. I always tell my guy friends who are complaining that their Latina girlfriends want a maid: "Listen, this is for your own good. You don't want a woman who is tired all day long, taking care of the kids, cooking, doing everything. She'll never be any fun. She'll never want to go out with you because she'll be exhausted. She'll never want to sleep with you. So this is an investment you're making for your love life. Think of it that way."

Striking a different note, *The Latin Times* cites critics who question Vergara's Latina accent, arguing that she exaggerates her accent to profit from the Latina stereotype she performs. This is a challenge of *solidarity* that suggests that Vergara does not do enough to counteract stereotypes of Latinas and instead profits by reinforcing them. In counterpoint to this criticism, Vergara and her son Manolo posted a satirical "behind the scenes" YouTube clip that purported to capture Vergara with a fake British accent when she was not on camera. All of these examples indicate *conflict* over the markers of Latina status in the US ethnic and racial system, and they are evidence that the media and other gatekeepers closely police ethnic and racial categories.

To be sure, the critical attention Vergara receives reflects her relative *privilege,* which stems from her enormous accomplishments and celebrity. It is also linked to a social context in which there is a rapidly growing Hispanic population in the United States and an organized and growing presence of Latino/as in Hollywood. This makes questions about Latina/o identity particularly salient.

Last, Vergara's biography is illustrative, not only in the way it illuminates intersections of language, accent, gender, and class with ethnicity, but also because it points to the way the racial and ethnic system in the United States is formed through the intersecting *local* and *global* histories that describe the immigrant experience in the United States. Vergara was born in Colombia, worked in the United States for most of her career, and became a naturalized US citizen in 2014. Vergara describes herself as Latina, which refers to people with origins in and connections with Latin America. This is sometimes distinguished from the term "Hispanic," which is defined as "people of Spanish-speaking origins," which would presumably also include Vergara, a native Spanish speaker. More recently, the newer popular category "Latinx," has come into use as a way to explicitly include a spectrum of gender identities and resist the gendered forms of the nouns "Latino" or "Latina" that come from Spanish, adding another layer of complexity to the system of racial and ethnic categories.

The Latina category is especially complex, and there is a vibrant public discussion about its boundaries and content. Vergara's biography illuminates the shifting boundaries of this category and the way it intersects with other systems for classifying people such as class, race, gender, and immigration status. This is true even as she plays with all these stereotypes in her comedic performances.

LEARNING GOALS REVISITED

8.1 Understand the way race is and has been socially constructed.

- The modern racial and ethnic system has been constructed through violent conquest, genocide, slavery, and lynching. Laws and other government policies and also scientific ideas and cultural beliefs all contribute to the reproduction of the racial and ethnic system in place.

- Restrictive laws that controlled immigration, marriage, education, housing, jobs, and voting together have defined the racial and ethnic hierarchy. Law enforcement through policing has also helped reproduce the racial system.

- Government policies of assimilation have helped destroy indigenous languages and cultural traditions among Native Americans, Chicanos, and African slaves as well as immigrant groups. These policies also deprioritize economic development and infrastructure on native lands and in racially segregated and economically depressed neighborhoods.

- Scientists, including social scientists, have contributed to the social construction of racial classifications. One example is the pseudoscientific classifications of racial determinists starting in the 1700s. Another contemporary example is the system of classifications in the US Census.

- The system of racial and ethnic categories has given rise to racial and ethnic identities forged in a context of shared experiences.

- Historically developed, systematic, institutional and individual racism results in fear, anxiety, intimidation, and backlash that consistently shape individual life chances in American society based on the assignment of racial status.

8.2 Understand the relationships and intersections among race and ethnic groups in the United States.

- Race and ethnicity are overlapping concepts. Race is a set of categories based on perceived biological differences, whereas ethnicity is a set of categories based on shared cultural heritage and common identities. Racial and ethnic categories intersect, and many people have intersectional identities. For example there are Latinos that identify as black and those who identify as white, and also those who identify differently depending on which country they are in. Ethnicity also intersects racial categories, with African, Latin American, Caribbean, and American people all identifying as black or African American.

- The US racial and ethnic system is measured officially by the US Census in an attempt to capture the nation's changing population characteristics and the changing understanding of those differences. Historically the census taker decided someone's racial status. Now individuals self-identify in a racial category or as "more than one race." Importantly, some groups of people "become white" over time, like the Irish, although this seems connected to the continuing existence of a non-white reference group, like African Americans.

8.3 Perceive the relationship between racial privilege and racial inequality.

- The racial system in the United States privileges white people at the expense of non-white people. This privilege is so pervasive and unremarked upon that most white people are unable to perceive it. White experience is one of not attracting negative attention because of one's race. Not being required to pay attention to race status is one of the privileges of being a member of a dominant white group.

- Symbolic ethnicity refers to the way dominant groups consume ethnic identity as a leisure activity since it has little concrete impact on their lives.

- Economic and political privileges accrue from inheriting white privilege. For example, most people in the United States occupy land that was originally taken from Native Americans who were decimated by the diseases of invading Europeans. War and forced resettlement onto reservations also resulted in the removal of Native Americans from ancestral lands.

- Racial privilege continues to be secured through organized restrictions on access to institutions like segregated and elite schools, fraternal and social clubs, and neighborhoods. Residential segregation and ethnic enclaves tend to reinforce racial boundaries.

- White privilege also operates in the labor market to protect jobs, especially good jobs, for members of the dominant racial group.

8.4 Understand current thinking about diversity and multiculturalism.

- Multicultural societies reject the idea that some cultural groups are more valuable than others and have explicitly adopted policies to officially recognize the existence of different cultural groups and identities. Multicultural societies develop policies promoting cultural diversity.

- The idea of cultural pluralism is an earlier version of multiculturalism that opposed earlier policies of assimilation and argued that people should take pride in their different cultural traditions while still accepting the core values of the larger society.

- Many social institutions in the contemporary United States such as schools, hospitals, government agencies, and nonprofit organizations have multicultural policies and employ professionals to promote diversity and inclusion.

Key Terms

Assimilation 234
Blockbusting 230
Colorblind racism 231
Cultural pluralism 235
Discrimination 227
Ethnic cleansing 232
Ethnic enclaves 234
Ethnicity 212
Genocide 231
Multiculturalism 236
Race 212
Racial determinism 214
Racial steering 229
Redlining 229
Residential segregation 229
Segregation 227
Symbolic ethnicity 216

Review Questions

1. What are racial determinists and why are their classification systems considered to be pseudoscientific?

2. Define residential segregation and name some of the practices that produce it.

3. What is the difference between race and ethnicity?

4. What is color-blind racism and how does it work to reproduce racial inequality?

5. Define racial privilege. How does it work?

6. What are the main ways that the US racial and ethnic system was created and maintained? Is it still being maintained today? How?

7. What is multiculturalism and how is it different than assimilation policies?

8. What are the major racial and ethnic groups defined and measured by the US Census Bureau?

9. How are immigrants similar to and different than African Americans and Native Americans?

Explore

RECOMMENDED READINGS

Alba, Richard, and Victor Nee. 2003. *Remaking the American Mainstream: Assimilation and Contemporary Immigration*. Cambridge, MA: Harvard University Press.

Bonilla-Silva, Eduardo. [2003] 2018. *Racism without Racists: Color-Blind Racism and the Persistence of Inequality in America*. Lanham, MD: Rowman and Littlefield.

Du Bois, W. E. B. 1994. *The Souls of Black Folk*. New York: Dover Publications.

Champagne, Duane. 2008. "From First Nations to Self-Government: A Political Legacy of Indigenous Nations in the United States." Special Issue on Indigenous Peoples: Struggles against Globalization and Domination, eds. James V. Fenelon and Salvador J. Murguia. *American Behavioral Scientist* 51(13): 1672–93.

Chou, Rosalind S., and Joe R. Feagin. 2008. *Myth of the Model Minority: Asian Americans Facing Racism*, 2nd ed. Paradigm Publishers.

Ignatiev, Noel. 2008. *How the Irish Became White*. New York: Routledge.

Mora, G. Christina. 2015. *Making Hispanics: How Activists, Bureaucrats, and Media Constructed a New American*. Chicago: University of Chicago Press.

Shapiro, Thomas. 2005. *The Hidden Costs of Being African-American: How Wealth Perpetuates Inequality*. New York: Oxford University Press.

ACTIVITIES

- *Use your sociological imagination*: The scale of genocide is difficult to grasp and the numbers can sometimes lead to moral indifference. One way to think about this is to try to translate the numbers into a context that is meaningful to you. So, for example, if the Nazis killed six million Jews, what proportion of the population of your state would that be? If you live in Massachusetts, where the population is 6.7 million, that means six in every 7 people would be murdered. It is a sobering exercise but an important way to think about the enormity of horror that people create.

- *Media+Data Literacies*: Look at the census categories in the Methods and Interpretation box. Do you fit easily into existing census categories? Why or why not? What might the consequences be of feeling like you don't fit? Do the race categories used by the census help socially construct race?

- *Discuss*: Do you think the United States is a multicultural or an assimilationist society? Why or why not?

For additional resources, including Media+Data Literacy exercises, In the News exercises, and quizzes, please go to **oup.com/he/ Jacobs-Townsley1e**

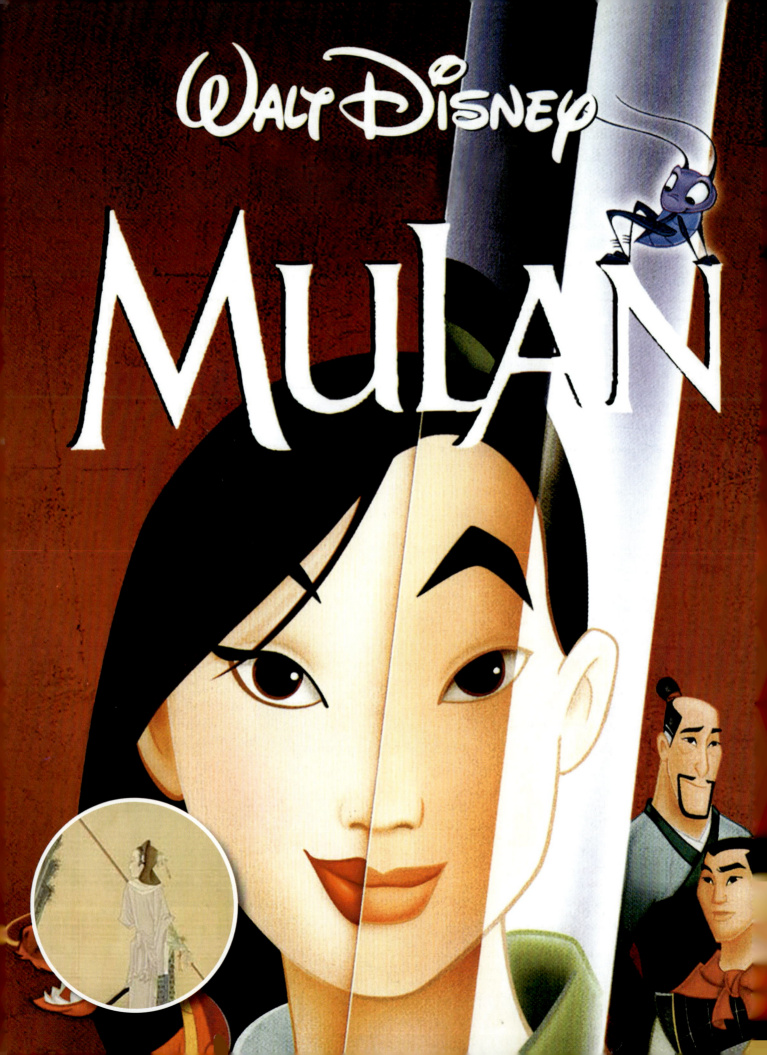

9

Gender, Sexuality, and the Body

In the 1998 Disney movie *Mulan*, based on a traditional Chinese ballad, the young Chinese girl Hua Mulan takes her father's place when the emperor sends out a call for soldiers to fight in a war. When her parents discover Mulan has gone to be a soldier, her mother asks Mulan's father to go after her because "she will be killed." Mulan's father replies, "If I reveal her, she will be." Mulan risks her life when she decides to make a gender switch and impersonate a soldier.

Mulan survives the war and returns to her family to take up her old life. Every version of the story says that Mulan sheds her soldier's armor to return to the role of daughter. Although she performed heroically in a man's role, and was believed to be a man by the soldiers who served with her, it is important to the story that Mulan really is, in the end, a woman. The story emphasizes that she was not ever really a man and reassures the viewer that she does not occupy the male role permanently.

The Disney version of the story also ends with a romance, as Mulan enters a relationship with a male soldier. Importantly, this romance connects Mulan's female body to her female role of daughter as well as her heterosexuality. In this way, the movie resolves the dramatic tension arising from the question of what will happen when it is discovered that Mulan has switched gender roles and fooled everyone into thinking she is a man. By returning to the traditional gender roles of daughter and heterosexual woman, the film's conclusion reinforces the stability of traditional gender structure, which links family roles with work roles and sexual roles.

Disney's Mulan and Hua Mulan
Disney's depiction of the mythical female Chinese warrior Mulan is depicted with both male and female characteristics, divided by a sword. Compare the Disney depiction with the traditional Chinese depiction (inset) from the 18th-century album of paintings *Gathering Gems of Beauty* (畫麗珠萃秀). Which facial features and elements of clothing were emphasized to define masculine and feminine gender?

LEARNING GOALS

9.1   Define the difference between sex and gender.

9.2   Describe the dimensions of gender inequality

9.3   Analyze how gender is socially constructed as a social and moral order.

9.4   Understand how sexuality and bodies are socially constructed through gender.

9.5   Consider how gender intersects with other dimensions of the stratification system like race and class.

In this chapter, we explore how institutions of sex and gender shape individual experiences and social life. We begin with a discussion of how sex, gender, and bodies are socially constructed. Focusing on gender scripts that define what is expected of women and men, we emphasize that sex and gender are broad institutional principles. We then explore gender and power, including divisions of labor and gender violence. We describe how sex and gender organize other social relationships and help reproduce racial and class-based systems of power. Last, we offer a brief history of the social organization of sexual desire and examine how recent social movements have introduced more fluid understandings of gender, sexuality, and bodies in the United States.

Sex, Gender, and the Body

Sex The status of male or female, which is assigned at birth and is associated with physical attributes such as chromosomes and anatomical differences.

Primary sexual characteristics The organs required for physical reproduction.

Secondary sex characteristics Physical features that emerge at puberty like body hair and breasts.

Gender The socially constructed roles for women and men that define expected behaviors for individuals of each sex.

Gender script A set of social norms that direct people to act in accordance with widely understood gender expectations.

Sex is the status of male or female, which is assigned at birth and is associated with physical attributes such as chromosomes and anatomical differences. **Primary sexual characteristics** are the organs required for physical reproduction, while **secondary sex characteristics** are features that emerge at puberty (such as body hair and breasts). In contrast to sex, **gender** refers to socially constructed roles for women and men that define expected behaviors for individuals of each sex. Gender difference extends beyond bodily difference to configure the social world. This results in widely understood differences between women and men in personal styles, emotional qualities, and intellectual and physical abilities. In short, the social institution of gender works to define women and men as different *because* they possess different sex characteristics.

While differences between people of different sex categories are well documented, many scholars and activists have argued that social practices tend to overemphasize differences between girls and boys. Scholars whose work is informed by feminism observe that people tend to emphasize and exaggerate sex differences among their children. For example, there is little reason to dress baby girls in pink and baby boys in blue, since sex status is not important to babies. Rather, dressing babies in gender-specific colored clothes is a social behavior performed by adults that underscores the classification of the baby as either male or female.

This behavior follows a **gender script** that directs parents to display the sex status of their baby. This is important because many social roles flow from the classification of a child as male or female, including family roles of sons and daughters. Parents and others might wonder if a son or daughter will join the family business, share a hobby with a parent, or follow their father into the military. A sociological perspective emphasizes that it is not the body of

Color-coded babies
Pink for girls and blue for boys.

Gender socialization
Family roles are powerful. There are alternatives to gender stereotypes, but women continue to be associated with unpaid housework in the family household.

the baby that is producing the gender effect. Rather, it is the social act of classifying the infant's body into a sex status as either male or female that shapes gender behaviors and related gender expectations. The color of a baby's clothes is a **gender cue** that tells other people what gendered behavior to expect in the future and how to orient their own behavior in the present.

Gender and Performance

In our society, people generally do not display their primary sex characteristics when in public. Instead, when we interact with others, we rely on gender cues (such as dress, speech, and manner) to indicate our sex status and its associated gender roles (Goffman 1959). This is a key insight of sociological theories of **gender performance**, which emphasize that performing social roles reproduces not only the gender roles themselves but also the widespread "common sense" that the current institutional arrangement of gender is natural, inevitable, and therefore morally justified (Garfinkel 1967).

In Chapter 2, we discussed the sociological tradition of symbolic interactionism that documents how meanings about the social world develop in the interactions people have with one another. As we saw in Chapter 5, social interaction is key to wider processes of socialization where people learn how to act in society. In **gender socialization**, individuals learn how to occupy the gender roles considered appropriate to their sex status.

Erving Goffman's work has been particularly influential in this tradition. Goffman emphasizes how social encounters are scripted like plays, and people are like actors who perform the well-understood scripts of social life. Scripts about sex and gender affect a wide variety of other social roles. There are specific social expectations organized around gender in family roles such as husbands, wives, mothers, fathers, daughters, sons, brothers, and sisters. Consider what gender expectations are connected to work roles such as manager, waitress, policeman, doctor, nurse, professor, or rock star. The gender expectations connected with these social roles are reproduced by all the agents of socialization: family, schools, peer groups, and especially mass media.

Mass media are very powerful in communicating gender scripts and role expectations. As we saw in Chapter 4, individuals in our society spend an enormous amount of time online, watching television, consuming a wide array of other

Gender cue Part of a social script that tells other people what gendered behavior to expect in the future and how to orient their own behavior in the present.

Gender performance Actions and behaviors that conform to widespread gendered understandings of social roles and social identities.

Gender socialization The social interactions and experiences through which individuals learn how to occupy the gender roles considered appropriate to their sex status.

Classifying Intersex Babies

Legal gender
Gender is produced and reproduced in official documents. Birth certificates, driver's licenses, passports, and many other official documents produced by governments, hospitals, workplaces, and educational institutions define both an individual's gender and the overall system of gender categories.

Estimates of children born with "atypical sex characteristics" (involving "abnormalities of the external genitals, internal reproductive organs, sex chromosomes or sex-related hormones") are about 1 in 1,500 (American Psychological Association [APA] 2017a). Such infants are understood to be **intersex,** or as having "disorders of sex development" (DSD). This biological fact raises the possibility that sex status is more socially contingent than is widely believed.

Importantly, however, our society does not recognize a naturally occurring third category. Rather, medical personnel and parents typically move to sort children born with atypical sex characteristics into one of the two traditional sex categories. By the end of the 20th century, criticism of unnecessary surgery performed on babies with disordered sex development had led to a move away from the idea that all sex nonconformity is a bad thing that needs to be corrected (American Psychological Association 2017a). Nonetheless, most babies with disorders of sex development are quickly treated to align with standard sex categories. One reason is that some intersex conditions are life threatening or have consequences for the fertility of the individual. In these cases, parents and doctors seek to quickly resolve the sex status of a child. In other cases, the reason for the intervention is less clearly a medical decision.

From a sociological point of view, thinking about how babies are assigned to a sex status at birth sheds light on the institutional reproduction of the binary system of sex and gender. Scientific and medical institutions are particularly important in this social process of sex classification, since they record sex for medical records and on the legal document of the birth certificate. Government agencies also reinforce and uphold the sex and gender system that divides humans into male and female. A child's sex status is registered on a birth certificate, which is proof of citizenship and other legal rights.

Historically, the government has used sex status to define who can marry whom, who can vote, who can own property, and who can serve in the armed forces. Other institutional gatekeepers have used sex status to decide who can be educated or perform particular jobs. While these regulations have changed over time—for example, women can now vote, go to college, and serve in the armed forces—it remains the case that the assignment of sex status at birth is highly consequential for an individual, since it also assigns them to a myriad of associated gender roles. And while it is increasingly possible for individuals to change the legal sex status on their birth certificates, it is not an easy, inexpensive, or straightforward process.

ACTIVE LEARNING

Think about it: Can you think of an example when sex status or a gender role is exaggerated? What do you think the reason is for the exaggeration? Are there social consequences of the exaggeration?

Intersex   The medical term for people born with primary sex characteristics that are not easily classified into the dichotomous male/female categories. More recently the term "disorders of sex development" (DSD) has been recommended by persons with intersex conditions.

media, and gender representations in mass media promote traditional gender stereotypes. A 2015 study from the Center for the Study of Women in Television and Film analyzed 2,300 characters in the top 100 grossing domestic films of 2014. Researchers found that only 12 percent of protagonists in domestic US films were female, and fewer than a third of all major characters were female (29%) or were speaking characters (30%) (Figure 9.1). Female characters were far more likely to be younger than male characters, and were far less likely to be defined by a work role, to be portrayed in a formal leadership position, or to play a character with goal-oriented behavior (Lauzen 2015). The report argues that on-screen differences are related to behind-the-scenes differences in who directs and writes films, since films with at least one woman writer or director have more female protagonists and more female speaking characters than films with all-male directing and writing rosters. Other research shows that films with independent female characters tend to have smaller budgets and have a correspondingly lower box office return (Lindner, Lindquist, and Arnold 2015).

As performed in both the media and everyday life, sex and gender are important for shaping social expectations and individual behavior. Knowing someone's gender is a cue for other people's social behavior. Additional social cues include class, race, age, and occupational status. These intersect with sex and gender to define how people understand themselves and act in everyday life.

Gender Stereotypes

The social psychologist Sandara Bem invented the Bem Sex Role Inventory (BSRI) in the 1970s by asking a sample of Stanford undergraduates what they saw as the characteristics of women and men (Bem 1974). From this research, Bem identified lists of masculine, feminine, and gender-neutral psychological traits. These are listed in Table 9.1.

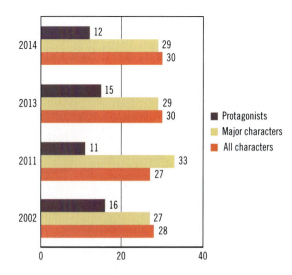

Figure 9.1   Historical comparison of percentages of female characters as protagonists, major characters, and all speaking characters.
Source: Martha M. Lauzen, "It's a Man's (Celluloid) World: On-Screen Representations of Female Characters in the Top 100 Films of 2014." Center for the Study of Women in Television and Film, 2015.

Table 9.1   Characteristics on the Bem Sex Role Inventory

FEMALE	MALE	NEUTRAL
Yielding	Self-reliant	Helpful
Cheerful	Defends own beliefs	Moody
Shy	Independent	Conscientious
Affectionate	Athletic	Theatrical
Flatterable	Assertive	Happy
Loyal	Strong personality	Unpredictable
Feminine	Forceful	Reliable
Sympathetic	Analytical	Jealous
Sensitive to other's needs	Leadership ability	Truthful
Understanding	Willing to take risks	Secretive
Compassionate	Makes decisions easily	Sincere
Eager to soothe hurt feelings	Self-sufficient	Conceited
Soft spoken	Dominant	Likable
Warm	Masculine	Solemn
Tender	Willing to take a stand	Friendly
Gullible	Aggressive	Inefficient
Childlike	Acts as a leader	Adaptable
Does not use harsh language	Individualistic	Unsystematic
Loves children	Competitive	Tactful
Gentle	Ambitious	Conventional

Source: PsyToolkit http://www.psytoolkit.org/survey-library/sex-role-bem.html#refs

CAREERS

Women, Men, and Social Networks

Women and men at work

Women and men at work are often employed in different roles. Even when they are employed in similar roles, the organizational culture and local gender norms can affect work experiences, including salaries, career development, promotion, work satisfaction, and networking styles.

Research on leadership, networking and careers provides evidence that women and men have different kinds of social networks, different approaches to social networking in the workplace, and different career outcomes as a result (Kanter 1977; Eagly and Johnson 1990; Ibarra 1993; Forret and Dougherty 2004; de la Rey 2005; van Emmerik et al. 2006; Misner, Walker and DeRaffele 2012). It might be tempting to explain these differences as the product of inherent differences in sex and gender. Men are characterized as direct, instrumental, and transactional in their networking styles, while women are characterized as indirect, expressive, and relational. The idea that women seek to build relationships while men seek to get down to business quickly aligns with the general gender stereotypes identified by the BSRI. It also points to the enduring influence of sex and gender—and beliefs about sex and gender—in shaping social action.

Sociological research on gender and networking explores the extent to which the specific organizational context shapes differences between women and men (Kanter 1977). Factors that affect gender difference include different opportunities for women and men in the organization, different network resources, and gender role socialization that results in different responses to similar behavior by men and women (Ibarra 1993). Workplace behavior for women is shaped by the number of women in the corporation, the availability of mentors and internal career paths, the functional roles women play in the organization, the effect of non-work roles on women (especially family roles), and the work culture of the organization. All these shape the network strategies of women and men.

ACTIVE LEARNING

Find out. Write down a list of the student and community organizations or clubs where you are a member. What is the gender composition of the organizations? Who leads? Do the women and men in the organization have different roles? Do they have different relational styles? Does the same behavior work for women as for men leaders?

Gender stereotypes

Widespread cultural understandings about the different and contrasting qualities associated with women and men.

Similar lists of masculine and feminine characteristics have been developed over time and are widely available online. Despite criticisms of the BSRI (Colley et al. 2009), the inventory has been used by a wide range of researchers to analyze how women and men conform to traditional **gender stereotypes** (Carver et al. 2013). The BSRI has also provided a baseline to consider how gender roles have changed over time (Twenge 1997).

The pervasiveness of gender as a social principle can also be seen in the widespread use of gender in social descriptions of objects well beyond the human body. For example, cars and ships are widely considered to be female and are referred to with the pronouns "her" and "she." As we saw in chapter 3, between 1953 and 1978, the US National Oceanic and Atmospheric Administration characterized hurricanes as female and gave them female names. Cats are typically characterized as female while dogs are often characterized as male. The planet Venus and the Moon are characterized as female while the Sun and the planet Mars are characterized as male. Some foods are considered

Which chair is feminine? Which chair is masculine?

more masculine than others. Some fabrics, furniture, and houses are considered more **masculine** or more **feminine,** depending on the degree to which they track supposedly male or female characteristics. Consider the differences between what Google search returns as images for male and female chairs or cars. Sociologists study how the cultural effect of these distinctions supports or challenges the intricate, detailed, and powerful system of gender that permeates every social institution.

Gender and Power

Bem (1993) and others have observed that stereotypes of men and women are not equal. Rather they are rooted in a context of male power, or **patriarchy,** where men and qualities associated with men are considered to be superior to women and to qualities associated with women. Patriarchy describes a society where men hold the powerful positions in political, economic, and cultural institutions. Despite gains in gender representation across major social institutions in the last 50 years and the extension of civil rights to sexual minorities in the United States, American society remains a patriarchy. Men dominate both houses of Congress, there has never been a female president, and very few women have been appointed to the Supreme Court. Men comprise the vast majority of the CEOs of major corporations, and men also control the means of symbolic production in the mass media as owners, producers, directors, and writers.

These patterns are evident worldwide, with some variation across countries. A small number of countries have gender quotas, including Rwanda, Andorra, and Cuba, where about half of all political representatives are women. In Sweden, where there is no gender quota, 44 percent of representatives are women. In the United States, by contrast, while women formally have equal political rights and also vote in elections in substantially higher numbers than men, only about one-quarter of congressional representatives are women. Despite this underrepresentation, this is nonetheless an historic high following the 2018 midterm elections. Looking at economic indicators tells a similar story. US census data show that despite the fact that American women have begun to outpace men in formal educational achievement, women still do different work than men (Beckhusen and Cooper 2018) and earn between 80 and 85 cents for every dollar men earn (Graf, Brown, and Patten 2019; Fontenot, Semega, and Kollar 2017). Female-headed households have lower earnings than

Masculine The set of personal, social, and cultural qualities associated with males and men.

Feminine The set of personal, social, and cultural qualities associated with females and women.

Patriarchy A social system rooted in male power, where men and qualities associated with men are considered to be superior to women and to qualities associated with women.

male-headed households, and women are still far more likely to live in poverty than men (Fontenot, Semega, and Kollar 2017). These statistics underline continuing gender inequality in social resources and institutional power in the United States.

Masculinity and Femininity

Gender theorist R. W. Connell argues that these patterns reveal a patriarchy that operates through **hegemony**, or the strategies that dominant groups use to maintain their power while making their views seem like "common sense" to the rest of the population. Masculine gender hegemony, what Connell refers to as **hegemonic masculinity**, refers to an ideal standard of masculinity that is used to justify all the ways our society is organized to reinforce the leading role of men. Hegemonic masculinity institutionalizes the common sense idea that women and men are different and unequal (Connell 1987; 1995). The idea of hegemonic masculinity has been very widely employed by gender researchers as a way to account for culturally pervasive patterns of gender inequality that emerge, even when women and men are formally equal before the law.

Gender theorists argue that hegemonic masculinity is the dominant form of masculinity in any given society and can vary across time and place (Connell 1995; Donaldson 1993). In some societies, for example, the dominant form of masculinity might emphasize military prowess, while in others it might be associated with wealth. Some societies expect men to show affection to each other through hugging and kissing, while in other societies this behavior is seen as less than masculine or deviant. In short, masculinity is culturally relative.

Connell (1995) further argues that there is a **hierarchy of masculinities** where some masculinities are seen as superior to others. Hegemonic masculinity is defined in relation to *marginal masculinities*, which are forms of masculinity where an individual cannot meet the hegemonic ideal of masculinity and are seen as somehow nonmasculine or feminine. In this perspective, gay men, transgender people, some non-white men, disabled men, and unemployed men may occupy a position of marginal masculinity compared to able-bodied, employed, straight white men. **Complicit masculinity** refers to a form of masculinity where an individual may not meet all the requirements of hegemonic masculinity but still benefits from the gender order in which they are viewed as masculine. The effect of complicit masculinity is to prevent challenges to the existing system.

A counterpart to the idea of hegemonic masculinity is the idea of **emphasized femininity**, where women perform in stereotypically feminine ways that conform to a patriarchal gender order. Other forms of femininity are defined by the extent to which they resist hegemonic masculinity. In every case, expectations around hegemonic masculinity and emphasized femininity are reproduced through gender performances in everyday social interactions, through explicitly defined gender roles, and in all social institutions.

The Gender Order

Together, hegemonic masculinity and emphasized femininity describe the cultural dynamics of the **gender order**, which refers to the way gender organizes, or orders, all of social life. The gender order is also a **moral order** because it defines what is right and wrong for women and men.

To be clear, the sociological insight about the moral force of social expectations does not imply that sociologists support any particular gender order—although it is true that most sociologists are aware of gender diversity and support gender

Hegemony. A form of power where dominant groups are able to make their worldview seem like "common sense" to the rest of the population.

Hegemonic masculinity A form of power that enshrines an ideal standard of masculinity and justifies all the ways our society is organized to reinforce the leading role of men.

Hierarchy of masculinities A social order where some masculinities are seen as superior to others, and all are superior to femininity.

Complicit masculinity A form of masculinity where an individual may not meet all the requirements of hegemonic masculinity but still benefits from the gender order in which they are viewed as masculine.

Emphasized femininity A counterpart to the idea of hegemonic masculinity, where women perform in stereotypically feminine ways that conform to a patriarchal gender order.

Gender order A characterization of society as fully organized by gender.

Moral order A social arrangement that is organized around widely understood and institutionally enforced ideas of right and wrong; the gender order is a moral order since it defines what is right and wrong for women and men.

equality. Rather, the sociological insight about the moral force of social expectations helps explain *why* people follow social scripts to maintain gender order. Most people follow the traditional script because it seems like "common sense" to do so. This is how hegemony works.

For example, for those people who understand themselves to fit easily into the patriarchal gender order, following the signs that designate male and female bathrooms seems natural and is not a burden. This is illustrated in a much-repeated field experiment from social psychology, where researchers place printed male and female bathroom signs on the glass doors of a building and observed as women and men self-sorted to use the door that matches their gender. Versions of this experiment have been used on elevators, trash cans, and other public accommodations, and they all show that gender conformity is a major way that the gendered social order is produced in everyday social interaction.

The workings of the gender order can also be seen in the social reaction

Bathroom politics
This all-gender restroom sign disrupts the moral order of binary gender. It combines features of "male" and "female" in the third figure, and connects all gender designations to disability via the fourth figure in a wheelchair.

that occurs when a person's behavior does not conform to gender expectations. When someone disrupts a gender script, others can find it threatening to their understanding of moral order. In some cases, tragically, the perceived threat is met with severe social censorship in the form of criminalization, medicalization, and violence. In the late 19th and early 20th centuries, for example, when women threatened male social power through campaigns for the right to vote, many suffragist leaders were imprisoned and brutalized. Rape and public sexual harassment aimed at women and some men are also forms of social control in the gender order. Gay, lesbian, bisexual, queer, and transgender people have historically been defined as deviant, sick, or illegal, suffering such consequences as harassment, physical violence, attempted resocialization, and incarceration in prisons and mental institutions. Importantly, these repressive social responses include state-sanctioned violence as well as informal violence and intimidation. They testify to the enduring relevance of the gender order in organizing many areas of social life.

Members of gender and sexual minorities argue that bodily difference, sex status, gender roles, and sexuality do not always align neatly. This insight challenges hegemonic masculinity and the traditional gender order because it questions the common-sense understanding of gender arrangements. This, in turn, creates a risk of social censorship (including violence) for members of gender and sexual minorities. This frightening prospect testifies to the *moral* nature of gender order.

On the other hand, the idea that gender is socially scripted is also a powerful critical tool for challenging the established gender order. Feminists do this by challenging gender scripts for women and men in the workplace, by

The battle for marriage
Marriage is a contentious issue. Successful social movements for same-sex marriage have been met with fierce resistance against non-heterosexual and non-heteronormative marriages. This remains the case despite the legal recognition of same-sex marriage by the Supreme Court in 2015.

Same-sex marriage
A crowd stands outside the Supreme Court waiting for the decision on the legalization of same-sex marriage in 2015.

arguing that women can do the same work as men and be paid the same wages. Gay men and lesbians challenge the idea that heterosexuality is the only appropriate form of sexual desire and the only basis for marriage and family formation. In the United States, there have been multiple social movements to extend civil rights to women, gay people, and transgender people and to change widespread public understandings of gender itself. Women won the right to vote only one hundred years ago. Same-sex marriage was recognized for the first time in Vermont in 2003 and was upheld at the federal level in 2012, when the Supreme Court struck down the Defense of Marriage Act (DOMA) that attempted to narrow the definition of marriage as a union between a man and a woman. Debate over same-sex marriage continues at the state level, despite widespread public support and hundreds of thousands of same-sex marriages (Pew Research Center 2012a; Schwarz 2015). Current conflicts over bathroom use illuminate issues around the status and rights of transgender people.

The use of public bathrooms by transgender people is contentious, with multiple US states proposing laws in recent years that regulate their access. One such bill in North Carolina, the Public Facilities Privacy & Security Act, was passed in March 2016. Among other clauses, it stated that individuals could only use restrooms that corresponded to the sex on their legal birth certificate. Supporters of the bill referred to it as "common sense" legislation while opponents described it as discriminatory. On March 30, 2017, the bill was repealed as a result of massive public protests and business boycotts of North Carolina. Whatever your position on these proposed laws, so-called bathroom bills illustrate the moral nature of gender, since they underline the fact that the gender order is about the moral meaning of bodily difference. Appeals to traditional gender arguments about bodies, sex status, and social roles are an attempt to regulate bodily practices in public restrooms. These conflicts also show that the gender order of society is subject to protest and change. In fact, extending rights for members of sexual minorities (like transgender people) are rarely institutionalized without struggle and resistance.

Divisions of Labor

We have seen that the gender order defines bodily differences and associated gender roles. Gender is also a central organizing principle of the **division of labor** in society, since it describes institutions of work and defines who does

Division of labor A central principle for organizing the productive work in society that sorts different people into different work roles to ensure the production and reproduction of human life.

what work. Where an individual lives and works is directly linked to economic outcomes, which means that the division of labor is an important key to understanding structures of stratification and inequality.

SEPARATE SPHERES. The idea of **separate spheres** can be traced back to the ancient Greek philosopher Plato. He distinguished the public sphere of the (male) citizen, called the *polis*, from the private sphere of family reproduction and economic production, called the *oikos*. The more modern idea that men and women occupy separate spheres dates to the early industrial era in Western Europe and North America, as economic production began to move outside the family household. Over time the theory of separate spheres stated that it was natural for men to occupy the public sphere of politics, economics, and law, while women were better suited for life in the domestic sphere of childrearing, family life, and housework.

The doctrine of separate spheres never fully described the historical experience of real women and men. Women from different class, race, and ethnic backgrounds always worked for wages in greater numbers than white women, and at the other end of society, upper-class women participated in public life and politics through elite cultural institutions. Nonetheless, the powerful idea that there is a natural separation between the public world of men's roles and the private worlds of women remains with us to this day.

One legacy of the idea of separate spheres is that women are naturally better equipped to care for children. This belief has had many social consequences. A major reason that publicly accessible, affordable, collective childcare was never institutionalized in the United States was because it was presumed that mothers and other adult women would care for children at home in the private household. Related to this was the idea of the **male breadwinner**, a social expectation that men should earn enough in wages to support a wife and family. This idea still resonates today, despite the fact that most families rely on two incomes and most adult women engage in paid labor. For much of the 20th century, the ideal family household consisted of a single male breadwinner who supported a nonworking wife and children. Classic television shows like *I Love Lucy* and *Leave It to Beaver* illustrated this family ideal.

The economic dependence of women on husbands or other male relatives was reinforced in many ways. Since married women were understood to have husbands who supported them, there were few careers open to them, even if they were qualified. In many businesses and in government jobs, it was official policy that women were dismissed or resigned when they married or became pregnant. The choice was between work *or* family, and most women chose family. This created an expectation that women were unreliable workers because of their family commitments.

This system also created a strong incentive for women to get married and stay married, even if there were serious problems with those marriages. It was the main way women secured their own economic status and the security and welfare of their children. Sociologists in the mid-1900s analyzed these arrangements in terms of functional role difference that suggested women and men were sorted and socialized into roles that suited them and supported the overall system. This echoed the separate spheres idea.

Of course, many families never fit this ideal model of the nuclear family, including single people, gay couples, and single-parent families (e.g., widows and widowers, unwed mothers). In addition, single women, unmarried mothers, working-class women, and many women of color had no choice but to work

Separate spheres The idea that there are and should be separate social domains for women and men.

Male breadwinner A social role for adult men based on the expectation that men should earn enough in wages to support a dependent wife and family.

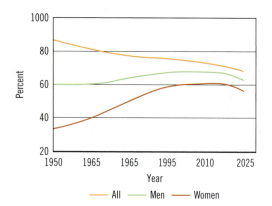

Figure 9.2 **US labor force participation, workers 16 years and over, actual and projected, 1950-2025.** Source: Based on data from Howard N. Fullerton Jr. 1999, "Labor force participation: 75 years of change, 1950–98 and 1998–2025," Monthly Labor Review, December 1999, 3–12.

Pink-collar jobs A term coined to describe the kinds of jobs done by women entering the labor force in the 1970s and 1980s.

Horizontal occupational segregation A pervasive pattern of gender segregation where women are concentrated into female-typed, lower-earning jobs.

to support themselves and their families. The consequences of the gendered division of labor between public and domestic spheres for these women were fewer economic opportunities, lower social status, and much lower wages than men.

The gendered division of labor based on the ideology of separate spheres changed dramatically as women began to enter the US labor force in larger numbers beginning in the 1970s. Labor force participation among US women age 16 and over in 1950 was 33.9 percent. This almost doubled to 59.8 percent by 1998 (Bureau of Labor Statistics 2017), as women's and men's labor force participation rates became much more similar (Figure 9.2). This change in the gendered division of labor also occurred in other wealthy industrial countries over the same period (International Labour Organization 2017).

Despite gains in economic independence for many women, however, gender continues to structure the division of labor in US society. Many of the jobs women entered in the 1970s were called **pink-collar jobs**. Pink-collar jobs typically had a very short internal career path, or offered no chance to be promoted into higher positions. They were support roles and clerical jobs dominated by women that required less experience and were therefore paid less than either white-collar work or well-unionized blue-collar jobs in manufacturing and the trades. As women began to enter professional and white-collar jobs in the 1980s and 1990s, there was a widespread expectation that the income gap between women and men would finally narrow. This did not occur. To this day, women in the United States earn around 80 cents for every dollar men earn (American Association of University Women 2016).

OCCUPATIONAL SEGREGATION. What accounts for the persistent gap in earnings between women and men in the last 50 years? About half the earnings gender gap is produced by **horizontal occupational segregation**. This is a pervasive pattern of gender segregation where women are concentrated into female-typed, lower-earning jobs (Blau and Kahn 2017). The evidence suggests that these jobs are lower paid *because* they are female typed. Women's jobs are more likely to be lower paid, even when they are nominally similar to men's jobs, requiring similar skills, education, and responsibility. "The median earnings of information technology managers (mostly men) are 27 percent higher than human resources managers (mostly women), according to Bureau of Labor Statistics data. At the other end of the wage spectrum, janitors (usually men) earn 22 percent more than maids and housecleaners (usually women)" (Miller 2016).

Historical analysis shows that the gender composition of an occupation is associated with pay differences

Occupational segregation
Women and men do different work. Although men were actually among the first typists, it was women who worked in the typing pools of post–World War II America.

(Levanon, England, and Allison 2009). Between 1950 and 2000, Miller (2016) reports, recreational jobs such as working in parks or leading camps transitioned from being primarily done by men to being primarily done by women, and wages declined 57 percent. Similar declines in wages happened "when women in large numbers became designers (wages fell 34 percentage points), housekeepers (wages fell 21 percentage points) and biologists (wages fell 18 percentage points)." However, traditionally female occupations that over time attracted more men saw wages *increase*. Miller goes on to note, "Computer programming, for instance, used to be a relatively menial role done by women. But when male programmers began to outnumber female ones, the job began paying more and gained prestige." As sociologist and expert on occupational segregation Paula England asserts, "Once women start doing a job, it just doesn't look like it's as important to the bottom line or requires as much skill. Gender bias sneaks into those decisions" (Miller 2016).

Other mechanisms that account for occupational gender segregation are differences in seniority and job search strategies, work preferences, and the self-selection of women into jobs that pay less but may provide more flexibility for family care and housework. These differences also account for some part of the gender gap in earnings. But even when they are doing the same job and performing identical work, women earn less than men, and this is true whether or not these are female- or male-dominated occupations (Hegewisch and DuMonthier 2015). This is also connected to patterns of **vertical occupational segregation** where men also tend to hold higher, better-paid positions within the same occupation as women. The most powerful and best-paid doctor in the hospital, the primary partner in the law firm, or the CEO of the company are all likely to be men.

Vertical occupational segregation A pattern in occupations where men tend to hold higher, better-paid positions within the same occupation as women.

To be clear, gender segregation in occupations does not produce a pattern where all individual women earn less than all individual men. Rather, it means that gender organizes the division of labor at several different levels, within and between occupations and over time. The point is that gender defines women's work as less valuable—at least in financial terms—*because* women do it.

THE SECOND SHIFT. Enduring beliefs about women's roles in the family and the workforce also translate into an unequal division of work at home for many women, who not only work for a wage but are also expected to fulfill traditional gender roles in cooking and housekeeping. As a recent article in the *American Sociological Review* states, "In recent decades, women have entered the labor force en masse, yet this trend has not been matched with a corresponding increase in men's share of unpaid household work, men's entry into traditionally female-dominated occupations, or substantial reforms to government and workplace policies" (Pedulla and Thébaud 2015; England 2010).

Pedulla and Thébaud's research shows that the institutional policies of employers have a powerful effect on gender roles in housework and childcare. When employers provide flexibility and family-friendly policies, women and men of all education and class levels report a preference for egalitarian work roles in the family household. When such policies are not in place, they disproportionately affect women's labor force participation and unpaid housework. In this situation, given uneven gender expectations about housework and childcare, many women self-sort into flexible, more family-friendly jobs that may be less well paid.

In her book *The Unfinished Revolution: Coming of Age in a New Era of Gender, Work and Family* (2011), Kathleen Gerson explores how young women and young men make choices when their egalitarian gender aspirations are difficult

Inequality and Privilege

Men in Pink-Collar Work

Nursing
Although nursing was long stereotyped as a female occupation, many men work as nurses, caring for patients in hospitals and other medical settings.

Historical analyses of gender shifts in the US labor force indicate that gender intersects with race, language, and immigrant status to shape occupational demographics. While white college-educated women appear to be the main beneficiaries of occupational feminization, men without the privileges of whiteness and citizenship are entering traditionally female occupations such as nursing and therapy.

When Mary L. Gatta and Patricia A. Roos compared occupations in the United States from the 1970s to the 1990s, they identified occupations where the gender composition remained *stable*, occupations that were *feminizing* because an increasing number of women were entering them, and occupations that were *masculinizing*

because an increasing number of men were entering them. They showed that in occupations that were feminizing, workers tended to be white, college-educated US citizens. Workers in feminizing occupations also tended to be workers in intact husband/wife families, and they tended to work in core industries. By contrast, those in masculinizing occupations showed higher percentages of workers below the poverty level, who were foreign born, Hispanic, and did not speak English well. Gatta and Roos concluded, "These data suggest that integration is occurring for very different reasons at different levels of the occupational hierarchy; while occupational feminization is providing primarily college-educated White women with the opportunity to move into traditionally high-paying, prestigious, male occupations, masculinization is occurring mainly for foreign-born, noncitizen, and Hispanic men" (2005: 387).

More recently, men of all ages and races have begun to enter traditionally female occupations, as have more college-educated men. Revisiting Gatta and Roos's earlier research, the *New York Times* reported "that from 2000 to 2010, occupations that are more than 70 percent female accounted for almost a third of all job growth for men, double the share of the previous decade" (Dewan and Gebeloff 2012). It is not that men were displacing women but that the overall size of these job categories continues to grow. Men in these jobs reported higher job satisfaction and a sense that these jobs are more recession proof than others. Previous research also suggests that such men might expect to benefit from a "glass escalator" where they are more likely to rise faster to better-paid and more powerful positions than women entering male-dominated occupations (Williams 1992), although this "escalator" seems to work better for white men than men of color (Wingfield 2009; Williams 2013).

ACTIVE LEARNING

Find out: Make a list of occupations where you would like to work. What are the occupational characteristics that appeal to you? Explore occupations at data.census.gov at the US Census website, and find out the gender composition of each occupation.

The second shift
Women often do housework while juggling other responsibilities.

to meet. The individuals she studied grew up in a context where women faced conflict between work and family roles, families were economically challenged by the declining availability of well-paid blue-collar jobs, and deep recessions resulted in the layoffs of many white-collar workers. Her research shows that men and women of this generation tend to avoid marriage and rely on their own efforts to build a career outside traditional workplaces. They may also fall back on traditional, unequal gender roles at home. Gerson concludes that the way gender works in the wider institutional environment significantly determines how individuals respond. For the most part, current employer policies constrain the aspirations of young women and young men to live more gender equal lives. The result is that many women continue to be responsible for what Arlie Hochschild and Anne Machung ([1989] 2003) called the **second shift** of unpaid housework and child care after returning home from their paid job.

Second shift The unpaid housework and child care women perform after returning home from their paid job.

Workplace Harassment and Sexual Exclusions in Work and Public Spaces

Gender discrimination in the workplace is illegal in the United States. Yet despite the Equal Pay Act of 1963, which held that there will be no pay discrimination on the basis of sex, women still earn less on average than men. Similarly, the Civil Rights Act of 1964 makes it unlawful to discriminate against any individual "with respect to his compensation, terms, conditions, or privileges of employment, because of such individual's race, color, religion, sex, or national origin." This set of laws also prohibits discrimination on the basis of pregnancy or for taking family and medical leave. **Workplace sexual harassment** is defined as unwelcome and offensive conduct based on gender that has become a condition of employment, or conduct that creates an intimidating, hostile, or abusive work environment. The US Equal Employment Opportunity Commission defines workplace harassment as illegal for a range of protected categories, including "race, color, religion, sex (including pregnancy), national origin, age (40 or older), disability or genetic information" (Equal Employment Opportunity Commission 2017).

Workplace sexual harassment Unwelcome and offensive conduct that is based on gender that has become a condition of employment, or conduct that creates an intimidating, hostile, or abusive work environment.

Despite the existence of legal protections, there is evidence that sexual harassment and gender discrimination in the workplace continue to be a challenge

METHODS AND INTERPRETATION

Gender Bias in Social Research

Joan Acker's classic article "Women and Social Stratification: A Case of Intellectual Sexism" appeared in the *American Journal of Sociology* in 1973. The article began with a list of sexist assumptions that guided social research on social inequality during the 20th century:

1. The family is the unit in the stratification system.
2. The social position of the family is determined by the status of the male head of the household.
3. Females live in families; therefore, their status is determined by that of the males to whom they are attached.
4. The female's status is equal to that of her man, at least in terms of her position in the class structure, because the family is a unit of equivalent evaluation . . .
5. Women determine their own social status only when they are not attached to a man.
6. Women are unequal to men in many ways, are differentially evaluated on the basis of sex, but this is irrelevant to the structure of stratification systems. (Acker 1973: 937).

Acker showed that these assumptions underpinned many major data collection efforts by research institutes, universities, and the US government. This was true despite the fact that according to the 1970 US Census, 11 percent of people in the United States did not live in families, and two-thirds of all households were either female headed or had no male breadwinner. Acker's analysis was important because it used the tools of logic and empirical evidence to document that very large social phenomena were simply not being seen, measured, or analyzed. Women were being rendered invisible by the practices of supposedly scientific social research.

Sociologists were not the only critics identifying systematic gender bias in research. Around the same time that Acker published her article, feminist historian Margot Conk (1978, 1989) documented that census takers in the early 20th century United States routinely "corrected" women's reported occupation if they were found to be in male-typed occupations like machinist or tailor. These systematic practices of gendered "correction" biased the data we have about the gender composition of historical occupations. In a slightly different

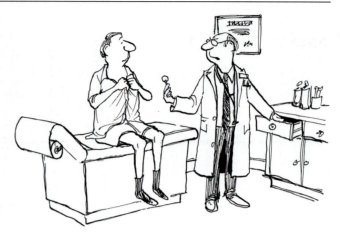

This drug has proven effective in testing of 500 women with your condition.

Gender bias in scientific research
Gender bias is a problem in scientific research because results that are true for men may not be true for women.

vein, feminist anthropologist Emily Martin (1990) documented the gendered language biologists use to describe human reproduction. She analyzed multiple scientific and medical texts to show that women's eggs were invariably described as passive and waiting to be fertilized while male sperm were described as active and engaged, and she described the consequences of this medical language on the ways in which medical practitioners and their female patients communicated about the reproductive process.

In each of these cases, feminist scholars pointed to pervasive gender assumptions that shaped how we understand fundamental human processes. Gendered biases in the Census shape the way we tell historical stories as well as the historical record we have to inform those stories. The gendered language of biological and medical science influences how we think about male and female roles in human reproduction. And, until quite late in the 20th century, problematic assumptions of sociological researchers effectively resulted in the exclusion of large parts of women's economic activity—and therefore all economic activity—from the analysis of inequality.

ACTIVE LEARNING

Discuss: Do you think the language of science can ever be completely neutral? Can you think of any practices that could help reduce cultural assumptions about gender that might bias scientific research?

Solidarity and Conflict

Feminist Politics

Intersectional solidarity?
Solidarity among different groups of women is crosscut by competing identities and affiliations. When activist Rachel Cargle (right) posted this image on her social media accounts advocating against patriarchy on behalf of all women in white spaces, she received considerable support. She reports that support was mixed in black social media spaces, where questions about racial solidarity were raised in counterpoint.

Feminist critiques have transformed politics around the world and positioned feminists in solidarity as well as conflict with others pursuing movements for group rights. Feminists participating in the student movement and the anti–Vietnam War movements, for example, argued that male activists excluded women in political activism. Feminists insisted that they needed their own organizations that developed a distinctively female and feminist social analysis. The second wave of the women's movement was a wide range of many organizations that reflected a broad range of cultural changes and social conflicts, including important internal criticisms of feminism itself.

These criticisms were connected to important social movements that developed in the last quarter of the 20th century. For example, black women and other women of color critiqued white women's organizations as insufficiently attentive to racial privilege (hooks 2000). Women from former colonies and developing countries identified the ways that women in the developed world benefited from colonial exploitation (Mohanty 1984). Working-class women criticized the upper-middle-class origins and assumptions of many feminist concerns, especially as college-educated women entered more lucrative careers in the 1970s and 1980s. Gay, bisexual and lesbian women argued that middle class white feminism was often heteronormative—assuming that **heterosexuality**, defined as sexual desire between males and females, as the only normal form of sexuality. Trans women have been criticized and excluded by some feminists who don't accept them as "real women." Disability activists have critiqued the assumption of the able-bodied inside activist organizations and social movements. As a result, feminism today concerns itself not only with women's roles, gender, and a critique of patriarchy, but also with the intersectional analysis of social inequality.

Intersectional analysis seeks to comprehend how different dimensions of inequality intersect for individuals and groups. An intersectional perspective emphasizes that individuals cannot be reduced to only one identity. Privilege and inequality are not simply additive, with a plus or minus sign appended to individuals depending on what race, class, or gender labels are assigned to them by social scientists. Different statuses, roles, and histories shape individual and group experiences by offering resources for social action as well as constraints upon it. In short, people's identities are more fluid than social science categories measure. An intersectional perspective works to understand all the complex, historical, and codeterming ways that principles of difference and power such as gender, race, and class shape the entire social system (Choo and Ferree 2010).

ACTIVE LEARNING

Think about it: Consider your own identity in intersectional perspective by making a list of the identities that describe you and/or inform your actions. Are there any privileged identities? Are there any less-privileged identities? Do you use different aspects of your identity at different times?

Heterosexuality Sexual desire and sexual relations between males and females.

following the intellectual and social advances earlier in the century. These years saw a reflourishing of feminist activism around issues of reproductive rights, work, family, and equal pay. In this period, access to education and other social institutions was more widely opened to women. Feminist scholars and scientists pointed out that patriarchal bias was embedded in supposedly neutral and scientific categories and supposedly universal historical, legal, and art traditions. Contraception, especially the birth-control pill, became widely available. Access to safe, legal abortion was affirmed by the Supreme Court in 1973 when they held that the constitutional right to privacy included the right of pregnant women to decide to have an abortion. Together with reforms in divorce and marriage law, these changes opened women's choices in education, work, and lifestyle. As a result, women began to enter paid work in larger numbers.

Arguing that women's roles are not reducible to the female body and traditional roles in social reproduction, the women's movement became a model for other social movements. The gay rights movement, for example, argued for civil liberties for gay men and lesbians on the basis that sexuality was not reducible to bodies and the gender roles they presumed. Gay liberation movements pushed this further to argue that sex and gender were more fluid than simple male/female, heterosexual/homosexual dichotomies would indicate. And later movements for trans liberation built on insights from queer theory and disability studies to challenge the basic idea that bodies are essential and unchanging.

Sexuality and the Body

Sexuality is based in sexual biology, and also includes social psychological elements such as attraction, emotion, and beliefs, patterns of sexual behavior, and cultural conditions, such as taboos and laws around sexual behavior. In short, sexuality is a socially constructed phenomenon that is not fully explained by socially defined gender roles or biologically defined bodies. However, all known human cultures set moral expectations around sexuality that define what is considered appropriate and inappropriate for that specific culture (Mead 1928). One example of this cultural specificity is the culture around romantic love, sex, and marriage in modern US society.

Romance

The idea that sexual relationships should be based on emotional intimacy and romantic love is a comparatively recent historical development. In many other historical periods and cultural contexts, sexual ties were organized through arranged marriages to ensure family succession, secure economic security, or make a profit. Sexuality and sexual relationships also have long been disconnected from marriage in the form of prostitution or sex for hire. The current American understanding of romantic love is highly culturally specific.

Although there is some debate about the emergence of romantic love in different cultures (Grunebaum 2007),

Romance

English artist Edmund Leighton's 1900 painting *God Speed* depicts the tradition of chivalry developed in medieval Europe. In these earliest forms, romantic love was connected with artistic and aesthetic expressions of respect and loyalty rather than sexual intimacy.

historical accounts identify its origins in medieval court culture and the traditions of chivalry developed in Europe from about the 12th century onward. In these earliest forms, romantic love was connected with artistic and aesthetic expressions of respect and loyalty rather than sexual intimacy.

It was in the period of modern capitalist development in the 18th and 19th centuries that romantic love and erotic love came to be linked with heterosexual marriage and reproduction. For example, Jane Austen's novels, such as *Pride and Prejudice* (1813) and *Sense and Sensibility* (1811), tell stories of romance triumphing over oppressive, old-fashioned social rules about marriage. Over the course of the 20th century, the idea that an individual could find self-realization in a romantic partnership became dominant in many Western cultures, including in the United States (Giddens 1992). Greater economic and cultural opportunities for women during this era allowed them to make choices outside of marriage and seek sex and intimacy without economic dependence on men (Shumway 2003). This development further emphasized the importance of romance and intimacy for sex and marriage, since men and women now had the choice of changing partners or not partnering at all.

Anthony Giddens argues that the rise of the modern idea of romantic love was also connected to literacy and media, especially novels (1992). These stories encouraged people to imagine themselves as individuals with emotions who could make lives of meaning. Romantic love became connected with ideas of happiness for the individual rather than family obligation, and was increasingly tied to the idea of self-realization. Many of these ideas about romance continue to be represented in popular stories on television and in films. The Disney version of the story of Hua Mulan, which began this chapter, is a good example of a modern romantic narrative that combines Mulan's desire for self-realization with family honor, romantic love, and traditional gender roles. Indeed, common-sense cultural understandings of sex, gender, and sexuality are deeply interwoven throughout global media culture and provide scripts for gender roles as well as cultural resources for thinking about sexuality and bodies.

Marketing Desire

Sex sells. Sexual imagery and narratives are a dominant feature of global media. Such imagery is especially important to advertising, and everything from washing machines to cosmetics to food items is linked to achieving happiness through a connection with sexual desire. Motorcycles and cars at auto shows have long been framed by scantily clad, young, typically white women, in an attempt to link sexual desire with the excitement of car ownership.

Although advertising and other media texts sometimes play with ideas about gender and push boundaries, the use of sexual imagery in advertising and other media texts more typically reflects hegemonic masculinity and emphasized femininity. In the workplace, men are typically represented in positions of power with women in subordinate roles. Families are represented as traditional nuclear families with male

Marketing desire
The #MeToo barcode hashtag makes the argument that women are products that are bought and sold on markets like any other.

Global and Local

Sex Work

Rights for sex workers
Protesters fight for rights for sex workers in London, April 7, 2018.

Protest against child trafficking in New Delhi, India, April 2009
Aimed at sitting members of Parliament during national elections, hundreds of parents and family members of missing children demanded that elected officials help trace missing children, whom they allege traffickers are selling into commercial sex work and hard labor.

The global prostitution industry is estimated to be worth $186 billion (Havocscope 2015). Local, regional, and global markets for sex have been linked to worldwide patterns of human trafficking for sexual exploitation. Equality Now (2017) estimates that approximately 20 million adults and children are bought and sold worldwide, with the overwhelming majority of these people being women and children who face lives of extreme degradation, brutality, and violence.

Mail-order brides
Colin Mingo and his wife, Lourdes, run a Find A Bride Agency. Here they pose in 1997 for the *Daily Mail* with their catalogs of Filipino women who hope to find a husband.

However, some women participate in sex work willingly. Kimberly Chin describes how the sex workers she studies migrate from one global city to another to perform paid sexual labor (Chin 2013). In other countries like Germany and the Netherlands, prostitution is legal. Both of these European countries are sex tourism destinations, where sex workers are registered and provided care by the national health systems. In sex tourism, vacationers—typically men—travel to visit other cities or countries with more permissive laws regarding prostitution than their place of residence (Hoang 2015). Sex tourism is a major part of the global sex industry.

A different organization of sex for material benefits are arranged marriages, sometimes referred to as the mail-order bride industry. Mail-order brides have a long history in affluent countries. During the 19th century in the United

States, women from the Eastern Seaboard contracted to marry single men on the Western frontier (Enss 2005). Today, men in affluent countries agree to marry women seeking to emigrate from countries in Asia and the former Soviet Bloc of Russia and Eastern Europe.

ACTIVE LEARNING

Discuss: What is the difference between mail-order brides and legal prostitution? Do you think mail-order contracts that exchange marriage for citizenship should be illegal? What about legal prostitution? Why or why not?

breadwinners and female homemakers still the norm. In advertising with more explicit sexual context, women are typically young, white, beautiful, and posed in ways that suggest they are sexually available.

There is also often a racial intersection, where white models are preferred to promote all products, including beauty and skin care products. This is a global phenomenon, with skin-lightening creams sold to whiten complexions (Elliot 2014). In fact, dieting, weight loss, and hair coloring and depilation products are promoted so women can achieve a youthful, whiter appearance. While these trends are subject to resistance and social critique, the skin-whitening industry alone is forecast to be worth $23 billion by 2020, with the Asia-Pacific region being the largest and fastest growing market (Global Industry Analysts, Inc. 2015).

Historians of advertising also observe that not only have white, middle-class images been the default in advertising for most of the 19th and 20th centuries, but so have heteronormative assumptions about sexuality and family (O'Barr 2012). Not until the late 1970s were gay characters represented in advertising. It was not until much later that multiethnic non-white people were represented. The attempt by advertisers and other creators of media texts to target specific demographics such as gay people, African Americans, and Latino/as is referred to as **multicultural marketing**. Such marketing campaigns target groups understood to be different from the majority group, appealing to them through specific messages tailored to their specific experiences. This development has produced greater variation in the media messages about sexuality and gender, but they are still limited by mainstream understandings (O'Barr 2012). Critics have also observed that the target-advertising model misses the variation within groups. For example, when characters coded as gay do appear in advertising they tend to be white, educated, attractive, and nonthreatening to the gender order in any other way (O'Barr 2012).

Heteronormativity

The traditional gender order is **heteronormative**, since it both assumes and enforces **compulsory heterosexuality**, or sexual desire between males and females. Heteronormativity explicitly links binary sex categories to gender roles at work, in the family, and in the nation, and also to heterosexual sex roles. Widespread cultural norms and social scripts for women and men are heteronormative, and as with other parts of the gender order, heteronormativity has been enforced historically through criminal and medical sanctions for individuals who stray too far from expectations.

Multicultural marketing Advertising that tailors specific messages to target minority groups.

Heteronormative A social order that assumes compulsory heterosexuality and links binary sex categories, to gender roles at work, in the family, and in the nation, and also to heterosexual sex roles.

Compulsory heterosexuality A social order in which sexual desire between males and females is understood to be the only normal form of sexuality, and is enforced through medical, legal, religious, and other social institutions.

The traditional wedding
The traditional wedding between a man and woman reinforces norms of heterosexuality and the wider binary gender order. Women and men dress in gender-stereotypical clothing, and the bride is often given away by her father to her husband. Can you think of any other heteronormative features of traditional weddings?

Many institutional and cultural mechanisms support heteronormativity. For example, until very recently in the United States, laws defined marriage as a union of a heterosexual man and heterosexual woman, and all adult women and men were expected and assumed to be married. Heteronormativity has also been institutionalized in the medical and legal systems through the recognition of two mutually exclusive sex categories and the related assumption that sexual relations between a biological man and a biological woman is the only normal kind of sexuality. Homosexuality was criminalized in many countries, and in the United States was widely viewed as a pathological condition, requiring policing, incarceration, or medication (Drescher 2015). It was not until 1973 in the United States that homosexuality was removed from the American Psychiatric Association's *Diagnostic and Statistical Manual of Mental Disorders* (*DSM*).

Social norms and laws have changed as well. Sodomy laws have been repealed in many countries, and there are efforts to expunge the criminal records of those who were imprisoned under these laws in the past (Medhora 2015). In addition, laws have been passed to protect the human rights of gay, lesbian, bisexual, and transgender people, to enable marriage, adoption, and inheritance, and to open roles in the workplace. Non–gender-conforming people also have expanded opportunities to serve as clergy and in the military (Drescher 2015), although new 2019 rules prohibiting trans people from joining and serving in US armed forces indicate how fragile some of these gains are. That said, it remains true that homosexuality is more widely accepted in the United States now than it once was (NORC 2011), and to some extent, so are other non-normative expressions of sex, gender and sexuality—especially among younger cohorts of Americans (Parker, Graf, and Igielnik 2019).

Gender dysphoria A diagnosis in the fifth edition of the *Diagnostic and Statistical Manual of Mental Disorders* to describe when people experience "intense, persistent gender incongruence."

Importantly, however, there are still medical and social definitions of gender and sexuality. According to the fifth-edition *DSM*, **gender dysphoria** is when people experience "intense, persistent gender incongruence." Opinion about its inclusion as a disorder is split within the psychological and psychiatric communities. Some practitioners think that "the diagnosis pathologizes gender noncongruence and should be eliminated. Others argue that it is essential to retain the diagnosis to ensure access to care" (American Psychological Association 2017b).

There is also criticism and resistance to the widespread liberalization of social norms around sexuality and gender-nonconforming behavior. For example, there is clear bias against lesbian and gay people. A report of global attitudes by the Pew Foundation also found that views on homosexuality were one of the most divisive issues worldwide and were heavily linked to religiosity (Pew Research Center 2007). It notes widespread tolerance toward homosexuality in Western Europe and much of the Americas, and less tolerance in Africa, Asia, and the Middle East.

Queer Identities beyond the Closet

Before the late 1960s and early 1970s, the social stigma associated with being gay led many gay men, lesbians, and other sexual minorities to lead hidden lives. Living "in the closet" was a metaphor for gay life for much of the 20th century. Sociologists who analyze changes in public perceptions and institutional responses to homosexuality refer to the period since the late 1960s as the "post-closeted" world (Seidman 2002). In the post-closeted world, variation and criticism within the gay community has entered into the wider public conversation. Important political differences among gay people and gender-nonconforming people have become part of a larger cultural conversation as well.

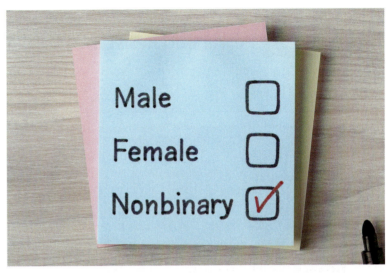

Sex, gender, and beyond
"Male" and "female" formally designate sex status, and can refer to bodies, behaviors, and a wide range of social objects. "Nonbinary" disrupts the dualistic assumptions these categories create about the world.

Steven Seidman's book *Beyond the Closet* (2002) compares what he calls the "gay rights" and "gay liberation" dimensions of political activism. Gay-rights activists seek to extend the civil rights afforded to every citizen to gay citizens. These include the right to marry, inherit, adopt, and serve in the armed forces. A result of this activity, according to Seidman, is the social construction of "the normal gay," who is much easier for wider society to assimilate than more challenging gender nonconformity of those who either choose not to adhere to the gender order, or who, for whatever reason, are unable to do so.

Queer theorists of nonbinary and genderqueer identities suggest that human experience is not actually fundamentally dichotomous; rather, gender identities and sexuality are far more fluid. They further note that binary thinking is an important way that the gender order is organized, with each binary category reinforcing the others. Theorists like Judith Butler, David Halperin, and Eve Sedgewick contend that to actively "**queer**" or "trouble" the binaries that traditionally describe sex, gender, and desire is a form of resisting the constraints of the traditional gender order (Butler 2006; Sedgewick [1990] 2008). In this view, the struggle is not about winning cultural acceptance, safety, and civil rights, as important as these are for many people. Rather, it is about challenging the binary organization of the entire gender order and the power relations and violence that underpin it.

Transgender activists also challenge binary categories. **Transgender people** are those whose gender identity does not correlate with the sex status they were assigned at birth. More broadly, the idea of gender fluidity and/or genderqueer identities suggests that identities and practices range over a spectrum from male to female, or even a matrix that defines gender and sexuality beyond that single linear dimension. This is important because gender identities also intersect with racial identities, economic status, nationality, language, and disability. Importantly, the expression of a gender

Queer Any idea or practice that actively disturbs the binaries describing a neat concurrence of sex, gender, and desire in society.

Transgender people People whose gender identity does not correlate with the sex status they were assigned at birth.

Power and Resistance

Stonewall

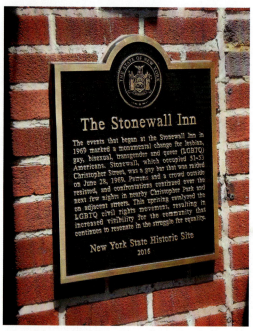

The Stonewall Uprising
This plaque on the Stonewall Inn in Greenwich Village, New York, commemorates the 1969 Stonewall Uprising against police harassment and abuse against the gay community.

Today, gay pride parades are held annually in communities all over the world. Some of these parades recall earlier traditions such as Mardi Gras or religious festivals. For the most part, however, they commemorate the 1969 Stonewall Uprising against police in New York City.

For most of the 20th century, the US legal system marginalized and criminalized gays, lesbians, and other sexual minorities. In 1969, patrons of the Stonewall Inn in Greenwich Village fought back against a police raid. In the days and weeks that followed, the gay community established newspapers, created safe spaces for the open expression of gay identities, and laid an important foundation for the movement for gay and lesbian pride. By directly resisting the exercise of police power and asserting a social identity that was positive and powerful, the Stonewall protests became the symbol for a much wider social movement for gay rights.

In the 1970s and 1980s, gay and lesbian activists continued to fight for positive representation and social rights. By the mid-1980s, tragically, a central focus of these actions was to raise awareness of the AIDS health crisis, amid a lack of action from the federal government. These actions resulted in a wider cultural recognition for the gay community and support for gay claims for civil rights. One concrete result of this was National Coming Out Day, October 11, which is a day of national awareness and support for a safe society for gay and lesbian people. National Coming Out Day now includes a range of fluid gender identities, genderqueer people, and transgender people.

ACTIVE LEARNING

Discuss: Do you think gay rights are related to women's rights? Why or why not?

identity does not necessarily imply a specific sexuality or bodily sex status. In the more open culture that defines the post-closeted world, a very wide range of social possibilities around sex, gender, and sexual identities have become possible.

Language and labels have also shifted quickly to capture cultural exploration around issues of sex and gender, and they are still in motion. Theorists of gender fluidity suggest that gender identity should be about an authentic sense of one's own experience and not be constrained by traditional gender social scripts. This means that while gender expressions are somewhat durable, the expression of gender identity may shift over the life course, over different social situations, or even over the course of a single day.

Gender Intersections at Mcdonald's

Happy Meal toys for boys and girls
Can you tell which Happy Meal toys were intended for boys, and which for girls? What gender stereotypes do these toys reflect and reinforce?

As a social principle, gender orders society by linking bodies to social and sexual roles. Above all, gender is a moral order that defines what is right and wrong and good and bad for women and men. Understanding the gender roles that shape our culture and our lives provides a lens through which to examine even seemingly trivial things. To conclude this chapter, we use the five paired concepts to analyze the case of how gender is constructed around toys included in the popular McDonald's Happy Meals.

McDonald's introduced the Happy Meal in 1979, and it was an instant success. Happy Meals became associated with family values. The meals included chicken nuggets or a hamburger, fries, a fountain drink and, importantly, a toy. By 2016, nearly 1.2 billion Happy Meals were sold in the United States each year.

The first toys included with Happy Meals were a "Mc-Doodler" stencil, a "McWrist" wallet, an ID bracelet, a puzzle lock, a spinning top, or a McDonaldland-character eraser. None of these toys were explicitly gender typed.

In 1987, McDonald's partnered with Disney to include Disney-themed toys, especially princess toys. These proved enormously popular and McDonald's has since partnered with brands including My Little Pony, LEGO, Teletubbies, Ty Beanie Babies, Hello Kitty, G.I. Joe, and more (Webley 2010). Many of these toys have been explicitly gendered with the idea that there are "girls' toys" and "boys' toys."

In 2014, a Connecticut 11-year-old named Antonia Ayres-Brown objected to the fact that McDonald's employees asked her and her brother if they wanted a "girl" or "boy" toy with their Happy Meals. Ayres-Brown wrote to the CEO of McDonald's to ask if he thought it was appropriate for "employees to ask customers if they want the 'girl toy' or the 'boy toy,'" pointing out that you wouldn't ask a job applicant if he or she wanted "a man's job or a woman's job" (Morran 2014). The response was that it was not McDonald's policy to ask that question. Ayres-Brown's father was a professor at Yale University, and with his help she conducted a study on how often McDonald's employees asked the girl toy or boy toy question. She found that they did so 79 percent of the time.

Ayres-Brown drew on different parts of her identities to shape her *resistance* to the gendering of Happy Meals toys. She used her relative *power* as a *privileged* middle-class daughter of a supportive, well-educated parent to resist what she saw as gender *inequality* produced by gender discrimination by McDonald's employees. Was the gender stereotyping that Ayres-Brown noticed in the awarding of Happy Meals toys a human rights violation? Ayres-Brown and her father suspected it might be and presented their findings to the Connecticut Commission on Human Rights and Opportunities in the hopes that the Commission would join the *conflict* and use their legal and cultural resources to help her case. The Commission declined to join Ayres-Brown's protest. In an article that she went on to write for Slate magazine in 2014, Ayres-Brown reported that "the commission dismissed our allegations as 'absurd' . . . All in all, this was a pretty humiliating defeat." Ayres-Brown had been looking for *solidarity* and allies, and she had been refused.

Nonetheless, Ayres-Brown continued to pursue the issue. She undertook a larger study in 2013, finding "that 92.9 percent of the time, the store, *without asking*, simply gave each child the toy that McDonald's had designated for that child's gender—a Justice fashion toy for girls and a Power Rangers toy for boys. What's worse was the trouble the children encountered when they immediately returned to the counter and asked to exchange their unopened toy: 42.8 percent of stores refused to exchange for an opposite-sex toy." Ayres-Brown reported her findings to McDonald's corporate headquarters again. This time, she received a letter from the company's chief diversity officer, Patricia Harris, saying, "It is McDonald's intention and goal that each customer who desires a Happy Meal toy be provided the toy of his or her choice, without any classification of the toy as a 'boy' or 'girl' toy and without any reference to the customer's gender. We have recently reexamined our internal guidelines, communications and practices and are making improvements to better ensure that our toys are distributed consistent with our policy" (Ayres-Brown 2014). Ayres-Brown counted this as a success and found clear evidence that McDonald's employer training addressed the issue.

From a sociological perspective, Ayres-Brown's argument raises complicated issues. Although the gender stereotyping of Happy Meals toys does not constitute a violation of human rights, as the Connecticut Commission on Human Rights determined, her argument rests on the fact that in the billions of interactions that occur at the point of check-out for Happy Meals at McDonald's restaurants every year, traditional gender stereotypes are enacted. This is likely to have a social impact, locally and globally. Gender socialization works at a *local* level in every interaction in which children learn about gender or are themselves treated as gendered individuals. These kinds of interactions are the fundamental materials of social life because they reinforce common-sense understandings about what toys boys and girls want, and teach children what gender roles are appropriate. As we have discussed in this chapter, the feeling of a cultural common sense is a powerful way that hegemony works in everyday life. People ask, "What's the big deal?"

Ayres-Brown's discovery that children requesting different toys were refused the toy of their choice suggests another way the gender order is institutionalized, namely through the efficient operation of fast food service. If toys are prepackaged as girl toys or boy toys, then it may be simply more convenient in the rapid-fire, stressful culture of fast food service to give only one toy and to make a quick guess about which one to give the child standing in front of you. In short, the gender effect can be produced through institutional processes without any negative or sexist intention on servers' part. This logic suggests that the answer to changing this situation is to introduce new employee-training guidelines and/or new routines for offering toys with the Happy Meal so kids can make a choice. This is what the McDonald's corporate office did.

Some might dismiss Ayres-Brown as an entitled student who focused on a trivial, unimportant issue and received media attention based on her relative social privilege (e.g., Otto 2014). However, women's issues are often dismissed as "trivial." A political focus on such smaller details is a way to engage the cultural power of gender. Not only is McDonald's a *global* corporation, but the choice of McDonald's to offer boy toys and girl toys reveals McDonald's as a participant in every local instance of a much larger global order of gender difference.

Finally, Ayres-Brown's critique demonstrates that every social interaction is *contingent*. Every transaction for a Happy Meal contains several possibilities around gender expression, stereotyping, and impact. Ayres-Brown's investigation confirms the findings of sociological research about gender in interaction, which holds that people act in gender-conforming ways and that our institutional routines and actions directly correspond to existing traditional *structures* of gender.

LEARNING GOALS REVISITED

9.1 Define the difference between sex and gender.

- Sex is the status of male or female, which is assigned at birth and is associated with physical attributes such as chromosomes and anatomical differences.

- In contrast to sex, gender refers to socially constructed roles for women and men that define expected behaviors for individuals of each sex.

- Primary sexual characteristics are the organs required for physical reproduction, while secondary sex characteristics are features that emerge at puberty like body hair and breasts. There is a lot of natural human variation in secondary sex characteristics.

9.2 Describe the dimensions of gender inequality.

- The understanding that women are different and lesser than men is enshrined in gender stereotypes that define what is male and what is female, with female roles and qualities being seen as less valuable than male roles and qualities.

- The gender division of labor mandates that women and men do different work in the family and the wider society. Women earn less money than men at every level of the occupational hierarchy and they also earn less when they do the same work. Women are also disproportionately responsible for housework and childcare, even if they also participate in paid labor. Historically this has provided an incentive for the economic dependence of women on men, typically in the institution of marriage.

- The patriarchal organization of social life can be seen in the predominance of men in formal positions of power in political, economic, and many cultural institutions.

- Male power and gender inequality operate through hegemony, a system where men dominate women by making male power and superiority appear as cultural common sense. Hegemonic masculinity relies on the distinctiveness of differences between men and women to secure male power. Hegemonic masculinity excludes and marginalizes other forms of masculinity and emphasizes femininity that complements the idea of male privilege and superiority.

9.3 Analyze how gender is socially constructed as a social and moral order.

- The gender order is based on the understanding that human bodies fall into a dichotomy of male and female sex status, defined at birth and continuing over the life course. Because it is understood to be a natural dichotomy, sex and gender are understood to be inevitable and therefore morally right.

- Sex status is used to define gender difference beyond bodily difference to configure every role and relationship in the social world. This results in widely understood differences between women and men in personal styles, emotional qualities, and intellectual and physical abilities. In short, the social institution of gender works to define women and men as different *because* they possess different sex characteristics. Gender differences therefore operate as moral differences because they define what is good and bad or appropriate or inappropriate behaviors for women and men.

- Sexuality is constructed through sexual biology, social psychological elements such as attraction and emotion, and cultural conditions like taboos and laws around sexual behavior.

- Widely shared gender scripts that are conveyed through socializing agencies such as the family, school, science, medicine, and media cue people to act in accordance with masculine and feminine social expectations.

- Those who fail to conform to gender scripts about sex status, sexual desire, and gender roles are punished. Punishment can take place informally through social sanctions (such as social exclusion, shunning, and bullying), and can include harassment and violence. Social punishment can occur formally in medical pathologization, institutionalization, and unwanted treatment and therapy. Criminalization includes sodomy laws or laws of civil exclusion that prohibit LGBTQ people from marrying, forming families, adopting, serving in military or clerical roles, or using a gender-appropriate bathroom.

- Social movements to expand civil rights and social recognition to gender minorities include the movement for women's suffrage, equal pay, reproductive choice, decriminalization and de-pathologization, gay marriage and family laws, and all policies that would ensure a safe and supportive social environment.

9.4 Understand how sexuality and bodies are socially constructed through gender.

- The gender order helps reproduce other orders of social difference such as the difference between heterosexuality and homosexuality by mapping the binary of sex status onto a new binary about sexual desire and family reproduction. The binary principle of the traditional gender order is an important way that sex, gender, and bodies are aligned.

- Genderqueer bodily practices and transgender people disrupt the moral force of the idea that bodily sex status, gender, and sexuality are linked in an essential set of binaries. They testify to fluidity in the sex and gender system and the multiple ways in which bodies and sexuality are socially constructed.

- The global prostitution industry is worth about $186 billion annually, and women and children are the primary people exploited through legal and illegal pornography and prostitution and in sex tourism worldwide.

- Marriage is another institution through which sexuality and bodies are organized. Marriage is a central institution in social reproduction, and plays a key role in the reproduction of many different kinds of social difference.

- Social struggles for and against gay marriage and bathroom access for transgender and genderqueer people are evidence of the way people have shaped and defined bodies in the modern gender order.

9.5 Consider how gender intersects with other dimensions of the stratification system like race and class.

- The control of sexuality and human reproduction through compulsory heterosexuality also underpins the reproduction of other communities. Controlling heterosexual sex through marriage where only individuals of the same race, nationality, language, or religion can marry ensures group identity through maintaining group boundaries. In short, control of reproduction through compulsory heterosexuality intersects the reproduction of other social orders of difference.

- Critics have drawn attention to the faulty assumption that all women inherently share the same interests. Gay and genderqueer activists criticized second-wave feminist organizations for being heteronormative. Other critics have pointed to the privileged, white, middle-class focus of much of the second-wave women's movement and the fact that white women have benefitted while their non-white sisters have been left behind. There has been a call for a more intersectional perspective on identity and political issues.

- Gender hegemony intersects the racial and national system in global advertising that upholds a white, Western ideal image of women. The enormous size of the global marketing for skin-whitening products is one example of the intersection of race and gender.

Key Terms

Complicit masculinity 252
Compulsory heterosexuality 267
Division of labor 254
Emphasized femininity 252
Feminine 251
Gender 246
Gender cue 247
Gender dysphoria 268
Gender order 252
Gender performance 247
Gender script 240
Gender socialization 247
Gender stereotypes 250
Hegemonic masculinity 252

Review Questions

1. How are sex and gender related to biological sex differences?

2. How are occupations segregated by gender?

3. What is the difference between horizontal and vertical segregation?

4. What is gender fluidity? How is it affecting laws about sex and gender in the United States?

5. What is the relationship between hegemonic masculinity, complicit masculinity, and emphasized femininity?

6. What is the "second shift"? Do employer workplace policies affect young people's strategies around housework? How?

7. What are the reasons that babies who are born intersex are corrected into one of two sex categories?

8. How has the movement for transgender rights affected the binary order of gender in the United States? Give an example.

9. What does it mean to say that the gender order is a moral order?

Explore

RECOMMENDED READINGS

Butler, Judith. 2006. *Gender Trouble: Feminism and the Subversion of Identity*. New York: Routledge.

Connell, R. W. 1987. *Gender and Power: Society, the Person and Sexual Politics*. Stanford, CA: Stanford University Press.

Connell, R. W. [1995] 2005. *Masculinities*, 2nd ed. Berkeley: University of California Press.

Giddens, Anthony. 1992. *The Transformation of Intimacy: Sexuality, Love and Eroticism in Modern Society*. Cambridge, MA: Polity

hooks, bell. 2000. *Feminist Theory: From Margin to Center*. Boston: South End Press.

Kanter, R. M. 1977. *Men and Women of the Corporation*. New York: Basic Books.

Sedgewick, Eve Kosofsky. [1990] 2008. *Epistemology of the Closet* (updated with a new preface). Los Angeles: University of California Press.

Seidman, Steven. 2002. *Beyond the Closet: The Transformation of Gay and Lesbian Life*. New York: Routledge.

ACTIVITIES

- *Use your sociological imagination*: Drawing on the Bem Sex role inventory and the pictures of chairs in the Gender Stereotypes section, explain why some chairs are seen as feminine and some are seen as masculine. How do you know? Ask others to describe the difference. Do they use a similar logic? What can you conclude about gender on this basis?

- *Media+Data Literacy*: Choose a simple media text, for example, a scene from the movie *Mulan* or another Disney movie or television show. What are the gender expectations of the women and men in the scene?

- *Discuss*: Do you think it will matter if the United States elects a female president? Why or why not?

For additional resources, including Media+Data Literacy exercises, In the News exercises, and quizzes, please go to **oup.com/he/ Jacobs-Townsley1e**

PART IV INSTITUTIONS AND ISSUES

10

Marriage, Family, and the Law

The greeting card industry is hugely profitable, with annual sales of about $8 billion in the United States alone. And as families have changed, so have the types of greeting cards that are available to purchase. There are now greeting cards designed specifically for divorced families, same-sex families, interracial families, single-parent families, families where the children are being raised by a grandparent, adoptive families, and families with transgender children or parents. While these new greeting cards reflect the profound changes that are taking place in the family today, they also illustrate the universal desire to reinforce the family bond and celebrate family members' milestones and achievements.

One such example of the movement to diversify greeting cards is "Mamas Day," which was started in 2011 by the collaborative nonprofit organization Strong Families Network. Each year, the group commissions black artists to create original art for greeting cards that honor the ways "Black mamas move heaven and earth to hold together their families and communities." Traditional greeting card companies have followed suit. Hallmark has expanded its range of LGBT-themed cards, and in 2015 they created a Mother's Day video featuring a family with a transgender son.

Despite the availability of online greeting card vendors, traditional paper greeting cards have a surprisingly enduring appeal. In fact, millennials now buy more greeting cards than people from their parents' generation did. Concerned that it is too impersonal to simply send a "Happy Birthday" post on Facebook, young people are turning to paper greeting cards to celebrate the milestones and the achievements of their friends and family (Nanos 2016). They may not be buying the same Hallmark cards as their parents—in fact, many of them are making their own cards, or turning to niche brands—but they continue to send out paper cards, particularly during important family events and holidays (Romalino 2014).

Mother's Day cards
Mother's Day cards have been transformed in recent years to reflect the experiences of diverse families and mothering.

LEARNING GOALS

10.1   Define family and kinship, and describe how kinship systems have changed over time.

10.2   Understand how the family is connected to systems of inequality, such as race, class, and gender inequality.

10.3   Define the nuclear family, and describe how divorce, single-parent families, and the delay in marriage have led to changes in the traditional nuclear family.

10.4   Comprehend the main feminist critiques of the family, and show how women's movements for greater equality have led to changes in family dynamics.

10.5   Describe the changes in attitudes and laws that have become more accepting of multiracial families as well as lesbian and gay families.

This chapter examines issues related to marriage and the family. We begin by considering the central role that family and kinship systems play in society. We discuss how marriage and family operate as social institutions, helping define gender roles and contributing to the reproduction of stratification systems. Next, we discuss how marriage and family have changed over time. We discuss how traditional families have largely been replaced by the nuclear family, and we discuss important trends in marriage, such as the rise of divorce, the decision by many to delay marriage, and the growth of transnational families. Throughout the chapter, we look at the different social and legal challenges that have tried to expand how people think about families and family life.

Family and Society

As societies change, our understandings about what counts as a family will also change. When Talcott Parsons wrote about the family in 1943, he distinguished between family of origin (the family into which you are born), the family of orientation (where you are raised), and the family of procreation (after you get married and have children). Today, these distinctions seem too old-fashioned to many people, because they assume that all families are mainly about having and raising children.

The US Census Bureau defines the family as "a householder and one or more other people living in the same household who are related to the householder by birth, marriage or adoption." This definition prioritizes a shared residence and a relationship that is either biological or legal in nature. Until recently, hospitals used a

Different kinds of families
A woman holds a sign representing different kind of families during a march to protest the World Congress of Families, in Verona, Italy. This US-based coalition defines family as strictly centering around a mother and father.

similar definition for their visitation policies, but many have since created more flexible visitation policies that are sensitive to the diversity of contemporary family forms.

A more recent and flexible definition is offered by the sociologist Philip Cohen, who defines **family** as "groups of related people, bound by connections that are biological, legal, or emotional" (Cohen 2014: 4). Although many families today are still connected through biological relationships, just as Parsons described and the Census Bureau defines, one of the most important aspects of "family" is the emotional bond that it promises. Most people hope that their family will provide them with social support, emotional intimacy and connection, and the reassurance that they are committed to one another. In a world that is always changing, the security of knowing that you belong to this kind of family is a huge blessing and a crucial resource.

Family A group of related people, who are connected together by biological, emotional, or legal bonds.

Family, Kinship, and Society

In 1996, Ancestry Publishing launched Ancestry.com, the first company to use the internet to help people trace their family history. By 2001 it had more than one billion records in its online databases, which subscribers could use to research and create their family tree. The company now has more than two million subscribers, most of whom pay between $200 and $400 per year.

The success of Ancestry.com points to the popularity of **genealogy**, which is the study of family history in order to document how family members are related to each other. As humans, we have always been fascinated by genealogy. The Bible is full of genealogical accounts, and there is evidence for the practice of genealogy in ancient Rome, India, Africa, and China. In fact, some anthropologists have argued that the practice of genealogy is universal to all known societies (Goodenough 1970). The family is always changing, but the desire to document a person's family tree is a near-constant.

Genealogy The study of family history in order to document how family members are related to each other.

Societies have different rules for who counts as a member of the family and the expected relationships between family members. These socially conditioned rules for thinking about family relationships are referred to as **kinship systems**. The words used to describe relatives, the rules about marriage, the attitudes about different kinds of relatives, and other kinship rules are among the most important elements of a society's culture.

Kinship system The set of rules that define who counts as a member of the family, the names that are given to different types of family members, and the expectations about how different family members will relate to one another.

We can learn a lot about a society by studying its kinship system. For example, what do we call a mother's brother's son? What are the roles he is expected to take in the family? In the United States today, we call this person a "cousin." Most people in the United States do not live in the same households as their cousins, and in fact they may only see their cousins a few times a year—at family events such as weddings or funerals, or at major holidays. We do not generally distinguish between our male and female cousins, though other family relationships

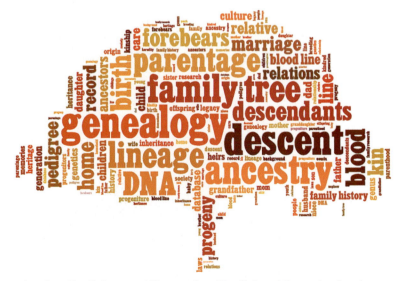

What does "family" suggest? The meaning of family is multilayered and evokes many social relationships and identities.

continue to have gender-specific designations (aunts vs. uncles, nephews vs. nieces, etc.). But there is nothing "natural" about the terms that are used to describe relatives, nor is there anything natural about the rights and responsibilities that are associated with different types of relatives.

Changes in kinship systems provide good evidence about changing power relationships in society. Before the 20th century, most European societies were **patrilineal**, which meant that they privileged the male line of descent. Names, titles, property rights, and family inheritance were traced only through the men in the family. Women took the name of their husbands when they were married. In matters of family inheritance, older daughters were passed over in favor of younger sons. Both men and women were expected to use marriage as a way of building wealth and resources for their families.

Today, many of these social rules and expectations have changed. Many societies have adopted **multilineal** systems, which trace both the maternal and the paternal lines of descent, giving equal significance to each. Family inheritance includes sons and daughters equally. Men and women are free to marry whoever they like, and they are expected to marry for love rather than for building strategic family alliances. We discuss these changes in greater detail later in the chapter.

Patrilineal A kinship system that privileges the male line of descent.

Multilineal A kinship system that traces both the maternal and the paternal lines of descent, giving equal significance to each.

The social benefits of family. Families provide intimacy and social support.

A sandwich generation
In multigenerational families, grandparents can support their grown children, but it can be hard for the middle generation to support their children and their parents at the same time.

INTIMACY AND SOCIAL SUPPORT. Regardless of how they are organized, all families are supposed to provide their members with social support. Evidence suggests that people who enjoy close relationships live longer and healthier lives. As we discussed in Chapter 5, people who are socially isolated and who lack adequate social supports are particularly vulnerable to the effects of stress. While family is not the only way to provide support and reduce isolation, it has historically been one of the most effective ways.

What kind of social support do families provide? Members of a family can share the daily tasks that are necessary for survival, such as getting food, cooking, cleaning, and caring for people when they are sick. These tasks are not shared equally, as we will discover later in the chapter, but there is usually at least some degree of cooperation involved. Families provide other material resources as well. In most societies, the care of infants, children, and the elderly is performed by various family members. When they can afford to do so, family members can provide financial assistance to other relatives. In fact, according to the National

CAREERS

Marriage and Family Therapists

There are many professions designed to support families with the pressures of family life. As these pressures increase, jobs in marriage and family therapy are in high demand. According to the Bureau of Labor Statistics, the number of jobs in marriage and family therapy is expected to grow more than 19 percent between 2014 and 2024. Today, there are more than 100 accredited programs in marriage and family therapy in the United States.

A person who wants to work as a licensed marriage and family therapist will need to complete graduate studies in marriage and family systems, mental and behavioral disorders, therapy techniques, and professional ethics. Most graduate programs have active internship programs where students gain real-world experience providing therapy to families. After completing the degree, passing a state licensing exam, and spending at least two years working under the supervision of a licensed therapist, new therapists will receive their professional license. In 2018, the median salary for a licensed marriage and family therapist was $50,090. (For more information, visit the website of the American Association of Marriage and Family Therapy at http://www.aamft.org/iMIS15/AAMFT/.)

Marriage and family therapists work in social service agencies, hospitals, outpatient mental health facilities, schools, and private practices. Clients typically see these therapists for an average of 12 sessions, fewer than most other types of therapy. About half of the sessions will be one-on-one, with the remainder being group sessions with the couple or the family. Because of the shorter number of sessions required and the high levels of success, more insurance companies are referring clients to marriage and family therapists instead of psychiatrists or psychologists.

Sociology provides a particularly good background for people who wish to pursue a career in marriage and family therapy, because of the emphasis on social relationships and social institutions. Graduate programs in marriage and family therapy encourage sociology majors and other undergraduate students who wish to enter the field to take courses in sociology of the family and gender, crime and deviance, domestic violence, culture and consumption, and research methods.

Marriage and family therapy
Marriage and family therapists work in social service agencies, hospitals, outpatient mental health facilities, schools, and private practices.

ACTIVE LEARNING

Find out: Go to the Bureau of Labor Statistics website for the Occupational Outlook Handbook (https://www.bls.gov/ooh/), and locate "marriage and family therapists," then click the search result for that profession. On the Marriage and Family Therapists page, click the Similar Occupations tab, then choose three other occupations. Compare them with marriage and family therapy in terms of job duties, education required to enter the profession, expected pay, and the ways that training in sociology would help you perform the job more effectively.

Association of Realtors, more than a quarter of first-time home buyers borrow money from family or friends to help with the down payment (Chen 2011).

Even more importantly, perhaps, families are a key source of identity and belonging. As we discussed in Chapter 5, the family is the most important agent of socialization for most people during the early years of their lives. The family is our first social group, where we learn the rules of appropriate social behavior and begin to learn the shared beliefs and values of our culture. The bonds we form with our parents and siblings are deep and impactful. Family is an important source of intimacy, a place where people expect to feel unconditional acceptance and emotional connections. We expect our family members to be on our side, and to love us unconditionally. When this expectation is not met, the result is often a sense of disappointment and betrayal.

FAMILY AND INEQUALITY. While families can be an important source of social support, they also reinforce social inequality. As we discussed in Chapter 7, parents shape the opportunities available to their children and the kinds of lives those children will have as adults. Wealthy parents invest in their children's futures, leaving those children with more opportunities and fewer debts as they begin their adult lives. Highly educated and successful parents socialize their children to be assertive, in a manner that increases their likelihood of success in school and in the workplace. More privileged parents expose their children to art, literature, opera, and other forms of high culture, which makes them more comfortable in the world of privilege and more likely to marry other people who come from a privileged social background. These dynamics of privilege and inequality link families to all the systems of stratification that operate in a society, at local, regional, national, and global levels. If anything, the role that family plays in social stratification is increasing, because highly educated, professionally successful, and high-earning people are more likely than ever to marry one another (Greenwood et. al. 2014).

There are also things that happen within families that create inequality. Historically, family dynamics have been a major source of gender inequality. In most societies, the work that adult men do has been rewarded with higher status and more money. While adult women were expected to do most of the cooking, cleaning, and care work in the home, they have had to do this without compensation or social recognition. Until very recently, family law in the United States granted husbands the right to exercise their authority over their wives and children in a manner that was free from government interference, except in cases of child endangerment. Sons have often received preferential treatment over daughters in educational opportunities, career expectations, inheritance rights, and the general distribution of power and status in the family (Blumberg 1991). Birth order has also been a source of family inequality, with many societies organized through a system of **primogeniture**, in which the first-born child (or, more commonly, the first-born son) inherits the entire family estate. Many social scientists believe that birth order continues to create inequality in modern society. Common stereotypes distinguish between the high-achieving first-born child, the rebellious or delinquent youngest child, and the overlooked or neglected middle child.

Last, as we will discuss later in the chapter, laws about who is allowed to get married grant special privileges to certain types of couples that are not available to others. For most of US history, family law only permitted legally identified males and females to marry, and also prohibited interracial marriages. These laws have changed, but only after significant conflict and resistance, and only after decades of economic and social disadvantages to those who did not fit the categories.

Primogeniture A system in which the first-born child (or, more commonly, the first-born son) inherits the entire family estate.

Housework inequality
Many women feel more responsible than others for housecleaning and childcare. Even women with full-time jobs often find themselves beginning a "second shift" of housework once they get home.

METHODS AND INTERPRETATION

The Debate about Birth Order Effects

Psychologists have long debated the effects of birth order on personality. The media tell us that first-born children are reliable, hard-working, and achievement oriented; middle children are more loyal and willing to compromise; and the youngest children are the most creative, rebellious, and attention-seeking (Gregoire 2015). Popular psychology abounds with parenting tips about how to treat each of these children, and with relationship tips about what is likely to happen to couples composed of different birth order combinations.

Despite the popular beliefs about birth order effects, however, the actual research remains inconclusive. Examining the available research on the effects of birth order on personality, Damian and Roberts (2015) found wildly inconsistent conclusions. A key problem is the range of differences in the ways researchers collect their data. Many studies fail to use representative samples, while many others rely on samples that are too small. Some studies control for the size of the family, while others do not. Some studies focus on the differences within families, while others study a cross-section of people from different families. Most studies do not account for the fact that first-born children are older, and that older children are going to act differently from younger children regardless of personality differences. Virtually none of the studies attempt to measure how stereotypes about birth order can influence behavior in a manner that is not connected to personality.

Ideally, research on birth order effects would use large, representative samples; combine between-family and within-family studies; try to control for family size, age of the different siblings, and other confounding factors; and try to figure out how stereotypes about birth order influence behavior. But these studies would be extremely expensive and complicated. Examining the studies that come closest to this ideal research design, Damian and Roberts conclude that there is little or no relationship between birth order and personality, and only a very small relationship between birth order and intelligence. This argument corresponds with other social science research, which finds a weak relationship between personality traits and social outcomes (Conley 2005).

However, when researchers shift their focus away from personality traits and toward social outcomes, they do find that there is a modest relationship with birth order. Research on educational attainment shows that there is a tendency for each subsequent sibling in the family to perform slightly worse in school (Black, Devereux and Salvanes 2005). Some research shows a relationship between birth order and adult financial success, but this relationship is stronger for men than it is for women (Black, Devereux, and Salvanes 2005). Sociologists caution, however, that we should not think about these effects in isolation from other events that take place within the life of a family (Conley 2005). The spacing between births matters, and so does the gender composition of siblings (Buckles and Munnich 2012). Big events like divorce, job loss, or the death of a parent can have massive effects on siblings, which are much larger than any isolated birth order effect. Birth order is not destiny. Its importance depends on how it is connected to the other events in our lives.

Birth order
The arrival of a new baby affects their older siblings. Research is inconclusive about the impact of birth order on personal development. Do you think your own birth order shaped your development? How?

ACTIVE LEARNING

Find out: Do a search for books and magazine articles about birth order effects. How many are you able to find? Now, do a similar search for books and magazine articles about the effects of divorce on children, and the effects of parent job loss on children. Compare the types of questions they ask, and the types of data they use to answer their questions. How are they similar, and how are they different? What do you think explains the differences?

Legal Biases in Favor of Marriage

A society's laws reveal how it thinks about different groups, how it plans to organize them, and what strategies it uses to hold them together (Unger 1976: 47). Where the family is concerned, the law shows consistent preferences that favor married couples over other kinds of social groups.

Married couples are afforded key rights that are not available to other couples. For example, a married couple is granted a special right of confidentiality, which prevents a person from being forced to testify in court against their spouse (Hamilton 2006). Married couples are granted special rights over their children that are not automatically extended to other people who have children. Any child born to a married woman is automatically treated as a legal child of both members of the married couple. For an unmarried couple, by contrast, the biological father does not have any automatic rights to the child. To have any custodial rights, he will have to prove he is the biological father, and complete a legal document acknowledging his paternity. Even after he does this, he will often have fewer custodial rights than the married partner of the biological mother; in cases where there is conflict, the courts overwhelmingly rule in favor of the legally married couple (Hamilton 2006: 39). In cases of adoption, there is a preference favoring legally married couples, and many states in the United States actually prohibit unmarried couples from adopting a child together.

Preferences that favor legally married couples have been built into laws that regulate employment, insurance, taxation, inheritance, and immigration. For immigration laws in the United States, a legally married spouse can apply for a visa immediately, and can come to live with their partner while their visa application is pending. For inheritance laws, a person will receive Social Security benefits upon the death of their legally married partner. A legally married couple can leave unlimited amounts of money to their spouse upon their death, without having to pay any estate taxes. Insurance laws require health insurance companies to provide family coverage to legally married couples, but there are no laws requiring them to provide family coverage to unmarried partners, even if they are living together. All of these laws create a situation in which there are clear social and financial benefits associated with marriage.

ACTIVE LEARNING

Find out: Visit the website of the US Census Bureau, and find the median household income for married couples with children under 18. Now see if you can find the median household income for unmarried couples with children under 18. Which figure is easier to locate? Which group has the higher median income?

Marriage and Family as Social Institutions

In 2008, hip-hop singer and producer Usher released "Prayer for You," a song inspired by his regrets that he had not slowed down from work to spend more time with his dying father, and by his father's final words, asking for his son's forgiveness that he had not been at home more when Usher was a child. Usher's song, a promise to be there every day for his son, is a message that resonates with many fathers. In the best-selling book *The Top Five Regrets of the Dying*, written by a palliative-care nurse, one of the most consistent themes among elderly men was the wish that they had spent less time at work and more time with their families (Ware 2011). For so many people, family is the thing that has the most meaning in their lives. There are strong social and legal supports in place that privilege marriages and families, and that reinforce their roles as some of the most powerful institutions in our society.

PUBLIC AND PRIVATE. As we discussed in Chapter 1, institutions provide us with a set of rules that help us think about how we are related to each other and how we should act in a given social situation. Families do this by encouraging us to distinguish between our private family life and the public world that exists outside of our homes. It is common for people to think about their family as a refuge from the larger public world. It is a place where they come home at the end of the day, and where they get intimacy from other family members who support them without reservations. The American poet Maya Angelou described this sense of family when she wrote that "I sustain myself with the love of family."

The family has also traditionally prepared people to become effective members of society. As the Chinese philosopher Confucius wrote more than twenty-five hundred years ago, "To put the nation in order, we must first put the family in order." He meant that strong societies depend upon strong families. There is widespread belief that people are much more likely to grow up to become good citizens and productive members of society if, when they are children, they are raised in supportive, stable, and healthy families.

The family is also used as a metaphor for describing public leaders, with the leaders becoming the "parents" of the society. Confucius wrote that the leader of government should be regarded as the father of the nation. Similarly, the ancient Greek philosopher Aristotle argued that a society's government was a natural extension of the family; if the family formed the root of human relationships, the society was the flower. In nations as diverse as China, the United States, and Ghana, schools teach students about the "founding fathers" of the nation.

GENDER ROLES AND FAMILY ROLES. One of the most powerful ways that families shape our lives is by defining and modeling gender roles. Young children learn about gender by watching their parents. They notice the different kinds of clothes their parents wear, and they pay attention to the way that parental roles are divided up: who does the cooking, who does the cleaning, who leaves in the morning to go to work, and who takes care of them during the day. If they have siblings, they pay careful attention to the different ways they are treated, particularly if there are different expectations for sons and daughters.

The choices that parents make about family roles are often shaped by existing systems of inequality. Gender inequality in the workplace will often encourage married couples to privilege the husband's career and to have the wife stay home to take care of the children (Budig and England 2001). As we discussed in Chapter 9, gendered expectations make women feel more responsible for housecleaning and childcare; even when they have full-time jobs, women often find themselves beginning a "second shift" of housework once they get home

Gender roles as family roles
A mother watches her daughter prepare food as she holds her baby (left), while a father repairs a toy truck with his son (right).

(Hochschild 2012). These gendered expectations are reinforced by media. Children are able to compare their own families with the kinds of families they see on television. Based on this comparison, they get clues about what a "typical" family looks like and whether their family is "normal."

How do media portray families? For the first 50 years of commercial television, most media families were similar to the family in *The Adventures of Ozzie and Harriet*, a comedy program that aired between 1952 and 1966. Set in Los Angeles, that show featured a white, heterosexual couple with two sons. The wife in the show did not engage in paid work, and spent most of her time in the kitchen. The husband had a job, and when he was at home he spent most of his time in the family room or in the yard of their middle-class suburban home. Both of the sons went to college, and both became lawyers. There were no financial struggles depicted on the show, nor was there any real conflict between the family members.

As we discussed in Chapter 4, there is still a strong tendency for media to underemphasize the diversity of family types, and to privilege traditional family roles. When compared to families in the real world, fictional media families are less likely to be racial minorities or interracial, less likely to have same-sex couples, and less likely to have single parents. They are also less likely to be poor, unemployed, chronically ill, overweight, or depressed.

Changes in Marriage and Family

As we pointed out at the beginning of the chapter, families are always changing. The nuclear family is still the most common type, but there is much more diversity in families than there used to be. Divorce has become relatively common since the 1960s, which has led to many changes in family life. People have started marrying later, and an increasing number of them are deciding not to get married at all. Because of globalization, there are more transnational families.

Traditional Families and Nuclear Families

Nuclear family. A traditional image of the family, which consists of a heterosexual couple living together with their children.

Today, when people think about the "traditional family," they tend to think about a **nuclear family**, which consists of a heterosexual couple living together with their children. This is the image of the family that we can find in television shows such as *The Adventures of Ozzie and Harriet*, *Modern Family*, and *The Simpsons*.

Social scientists used to believe that the traditional nuclear family was a universal feature of social life. In 1949, the Yale anthropologist George Murdock wrote that the nuclear family was the most natural way to care for infants and raise young children, and he argued that the nuclear family could be found in all societies (Murdock 1949). But cross-cultural research has challenged this belief. Anthropologists and historians have pointed out that the nuclear family was more common in Western societies than it was elsewhere. The Zincantecos of Southern Mexico did not have a term for family; for them, the basic social unit was the *house*, which contained as few as one or as many as 20 people, who were not necessarily related biologically (Vogt 1969). In other societies the most common form was the **extended family**, in which the household went beyond the nuclear family to include grandparents, aunts, uncles, and other relatives. In traditional China, to take one example, the social ideal was the four-generational joint family, which included all the sons and all their descendants living under

Extended family. A type of family in which the household includes parents, children, grandparents, aunts, uncles, and other relatives.

(a)

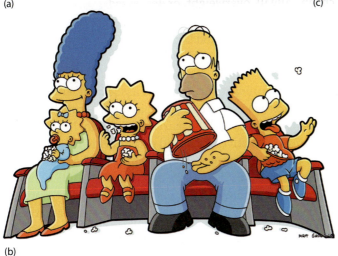

(b)

(c)

Media depictions of the family
Modern Family (a) presents a more contemporary family picture than previous TV shows because it includes cousins, same-sex spouses, divorce, and blended families. *The Simpsons* (b), which first aired in 1989, represents the heteronormative, intact, working-class nuclear family still prevalent at that time. The 1950s show *Ozzie and Harriet* (c) was an iconic representation of a heteronormative, intact, middle-class nuclear family that ran on network television from 1952 to 1966. We learn about families from families on TV that both reflect and provide a comparison for real life. Children learn cues about families from media representations, which are largely images of heteronormative nuclear families.

the same roof with their parents (Chen 2009). In many respects, then, the nuclear family as we know it today was an invention of modern Western society.

The nuclear family may not be universal, but the nature of modern society has made it much more common, even in places where the extended family was once the ideal. As more people moved to cities, where population densities are much higher, they settled in smaller houses and apartments, which made it more difficult to maintain the extended family. Industrialization also placed pressure on the extended family, by weakening the household economy, increasing residential mobility, and forcing people to move in search of better work (Parsons and Bales 1955). The movement toward universal education meant that children were spending more time in school and less time at home, reducing the need for the kind of extended childcare arrangements that took place in extended families. Rising standards of living also placed pressure on the extended family, because young couples were more easily able to move out of their parents' homes and find a place of their own. The existence of extended families declined rapidly in North America and Western Europe throughout

Multigenerational family dinner
The generational nature of family life is organized differently in different countries. In some countries families live with three and four generations. The norm in the United States, however, is one-generation households.

the 20th century; in Eastern Europe, Southern Europe, and East Asia, rapid economic growth since the 1970s has also been associated with the decline of the extended family (Ruggles 2012).

Culturally, the concept of the nuclear family did not enter the public consciousness until the 20th century. It first appeared in the *Oxford English Dictionary in* 1925, and in the *Merriam-Webster Dictionary* in 1947. By the 1950s, however, the idyllic image of the suburban nuclear family was being broadcast around the world, courtesy of American television. In fact, the 1950s were probably the high-water mark for the nuclear family, at least in North America and Western Europe. The median age of marriage for women in the United States was 20.3 in 1950 and 1960, the lowest in the nation's history; nearly 45 percent of all US households in 1960 consisted of married couples with children (Jacobsen, Mather, and Depuis 2012).

Divorce

Before the 1960s, there was significant social stigma associated with divorce. A couple who wanted a divorce would have to prove in divorce court that one party's faults were sufficient reason to end the marriage. Proving the fault often required one partner to hire a detective who could gather evidence and testify about the bad actions of the other partner, which meant that divorce was not really an option for poor people. The kinds of behaviors that could result in divorce included adultery, violence, abuse, mental illness, criminal conviction, alcoholism, and substance abuse. This fault-based divorce was the standard approach in virtually every country in the world. The exception was the Soviet Union, which established no-fault divorce in 1918.

Things began to change in the 1960s, as feminist researchers began to show how the social organization of the family was reinforcing male power. Where marriage was concerned, they pointed out, women who stayed home to raise children lacked the financial resources to hire private detectives, and so they had no way to get out of a bad or an abusive marriage if the courts required them to prove fault by their spouses.

In 1966 Herma Hill Kay, a member of the California Governor's Commission on the Family, proposed that California should adopt a system of no-fault divorce. No-fault divorce became California law in 1970, and by 1983, every state in the United States (except for South Dakota and New York) had adopted new laws that created some form of no-fault divorce. Today, most countries have laws that permit divorce by mutual consent, though many still require a period of legal separation before the divorce is legally granted.

As Figure 10.1 shows, the divorce rate in the United States increased dramatically between 1960 and 1980, reaching a peak of 22.6 divorces per 1,000 married couples in 1980. Since 1980 the divorce rate has gradually declined, but it is still significantly higher than it was in 1960. Today, approximately 2

Solidarity and Conflict

Disagreements over Parenting Styles

The nuclear family places more pressure on parents, because there are only two adults in the household who are available to take responsibility for household chores and supervising children. When both parents have jobs and there are no relatives nearby, parents often find themselves having to pay somebody to help them with childcare. And yet, as we discussed in Chapter 5, the ethic of intensive parenting in many families means that parents are more involved than ever in the day-to-day lives of their children. The stress that results can lead to disagreements about the best way to raise children.

Disagreements about parenting can emerge as soon as a child is born and continue until the child becomes an adult. Do you maintain a strict sleep schedule for your infant, or do you pick them up and comfort them when they begin crying? Do you set hard boundaries about behavior and enforce those boundaries regardless of the consequences, or do you try to negotiate with your children to convince them to behave the right way? What are your attitudes about your child's media use, or their study habits? Do you intervene when they are having social conflicts with peers, or do you let them work things out for themselves? Most couples have not discussed these questions with each other until they have actually become parents. And they are often surprised to find that they have different views on these issues than their partner.

Conflicts over parenting have a negative impact on all members of the family, and social research shows that they are associated with a higher probability of marital dissolution (Helland et al. 2014). Disagreement can escalate into conflict when one partner feels like they are not getting enough help from the other, or when there are major disagreements over parenting styles. Even in cases where the marriage does not end in divorce, there is clear evidence that parental conflict is associated with poorer academic achievement and increased likelihood of substance abuse for children (Musick and Meier 2010). In fact, some research suggests that for children whose parents fight a lot, it is better if the parents divorce than if they stay together (Amato, Spencer, and Booth 1995).

Conflicts over parenting styles also have an effect on friendships and other social relationships. Decisions about whether to breastfeed, whether to use cloth or paper diapers, when and how to enforce bedtime, or how permissive to be about media use can explode into friendship-ending fights. These conflicts place even more stress on the family. Parents need authentic and supportive relationships to help them deal with the everyday stresses of raising children (Luthar and Cicciolla 2015). When morally charged disputes about parenting styles destroy friendships, the nuclear family becomes more isolated than ever.

Parenting
When parents disagree about parenting, conflict can be introduced into the marriage that is difficult for children to navigate.

ACTIVE LEARNING

Find out: Ask your parents (or other parents you know) if they ever had disagreements over parenting styles, either with their partner, with friends, or with acquaintances. What was the nature of the disagreement? How was it resolved?

---

percent of married couples get divorced each year, and about 10 percent of the adult population is divorced at any given time (Stevenson and Wolfers 2007).

Divorce is not distributed randomly across the population, and it tends to reinforce existing systems of inequality. Most of the decline in the divorce rate has taken place among couples with more education (Amato 2010) (see Figure 10.2). Among heterosexual married couples who get divorced, wives tend to experience significantly larger declines in economic well-being than

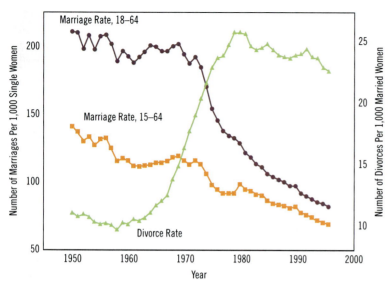

Figure 10.1 **Rates of Marriage and Divorce, 1950–2000.**
Source: National Bureau of Economic Research, 2009.

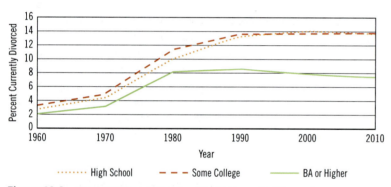

Figure 10.2 **Percent of Population Age 30–44 Currently Divorced.**
Source: Lundberg, Shelly, Robert A. Pollak, and Jenna Stearns, 2016. "Family Inequality: Diverging Patterns in Marriage, Cohabitation, and Childbearing," *Journal of Economic Perspectives* 30(2): 79–102.

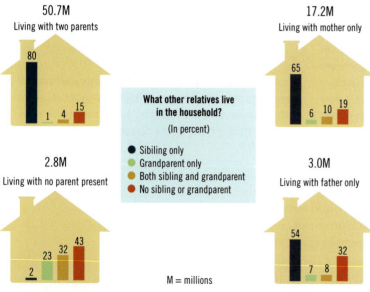

Figure 10.3 **Living Arrangements of Children under Age 18.**
Source: 2016 Current Population Survey Annual Social and Economic Supplement www.census.gove/hhes/families

their husbands, which means that divorce reinforces gender inequality (Bianchi, Subaiya, and Kahn 1999). And the negative consequences of divorce are often multigenerational. Children of divorced parents tend to have lower levels of educational success, lower levels of psychological well-being, and a higher likelihood of having their own marriages end in divorce (Amato 2010).

Single-Parent Families

Another recent change in American society is the increase in single-parent families. Around one-third (32 percent) of all children in the United States live in a single-parent household, as compared to only 13 percent of children in 1968 (Livingston 2018) (see Figure 10.3). Single-parent families are overwhelmingly headed by women, and they are strongly associated with childhood poverty. As a result, these families often live in poor, high-crime neighborhoods, with inferior schools and very few opportunities. In 2017, the Current Population Survey recorded that 30 percent of children living with single mothers are poor, compared to 17 percent of families living with solo fathers, while only 8 percent of children living in married-couple families live below the poverty line. There are significant racial differences as well: approximately 13 percent of white children live in single-mother families, as compared to 23 percent of Hispanic children and 47 percent of African American children (Livingston 2018).

Research by Edin and Kefalas (2005) shows how race, gender, and class intersect in the lives and choices made by many single mothers. Women living in poor neighborhoods often want to get married, but think they should not do so until they have financial stability. Unlike professional women, they do not struggle with decisions about whether to prioritize career or family, because they are often stuck in unsatisfying jobs with very

Structure and Contingency

"Bird-Nesting" as a Co-Parenting Strategy after Divorce

Since the 1980s, there has been a trend in favor of joint custody for divorcing parents with children. The most common arrangement is joint legal custody, in which one parent gets physical custody of the children but the other parent has legal visitation rights, and legal rights to participate in decisions about their children. In joint legal custody, the noncustodial parents usually have a financial responsibility to help pay for the costs of raising their children. In these types of arrangements, it is overwhelmingly the case that the mother will be the person who has physical custody, while the other partner will have joint legal custody.

A second type of arrangement is joint physical custody, in which both parents agree to a schedule where the children have regular opportunities to live with each parent. The parenting schedule might have the children living one week with one of the parents, and then moving the following week to live with the other parent. Another common arrangement is to spend weekdays with one parent and weekends with the other. Children might alternate weekends, and also have specific days each week where they live with each parent. The important principle is that they are spending enough time with each parent so that they can maintain close bonds with both of them.

While joint physical custody makes it easier for children to maintain a strong relationship with both of their parents after a divorce, it presents a number of challenges. The biggest problems emerge when the divorced parents do not get along, because each time children are handed off, there is a chance for an emotional argument to happen. This places a lot of psychological stress on children. Even when there are not conflicts between the parents, joint physical custody forces the children to be moving households continuously. Joint physical custody is also associated with lower child support payments, which means that sometimes the parent pushing for joint physical custody is more interested in reducing payments than in maintaining a close relationship with their children (Emery 2009).

One increasingly popular strategy is "bird's-nest" custody. In this arrangement, the children stay in the same household, and it is the parents who move in and out depending on whose turn it is to have custody of the children. The obvious benefit of this strategy is the stability it gives the children. They get to maintain close relationships with both parents, but they do not have to deal with the stress and disruption of constantly moving houses. This makes it much easier for them to maintain their friendships, and they don't have to worry about leaving their shoes or their homework at the wrong house. But bird's-nest custody has its own distinctive limitations. Most family therapists suggest that it is only a viable strategy for couples in an uncontested divorce, where there is minimal animosity between parents, and where both parents agree to live close to the children. Bird's-nest custody is usually more expensive, because it requires that there be three residences instead of two. Even in the best of circumstances, bird's-nest strategies can become awkward if one of the divorced parents enters a serious relationship. For all of these reasons, most of the social science research shows that bird's-nest custody is most effective as a temporary or a short-term solution (Silverman and Higgens 2003).

ACTIVE LEARNING

Find out: Not all families are the same, and the effectiveness of different custody arrangements will vary depending on the type of family that is experiencing a divorce. Choose two or three sources of social difference that you read about in previous chapters (e.g., race, class, gender, family background, education, etc.), and create a table comparing the advantages and disadvantages of each type of co-parenting strategy described here.

---

few opportunities for advancement. In fact, they view having children as the most meaningful thing they can do, and the most important source of identity in their lives. Edin and Kefalas find that disadvantaged women place more value on having children than do middle-class women. Confident in their ability to be effective and loving mothers, they are not interested in waiting until they find suitable partners to marry.

Delay and Decline of Marriage

Only 48.6 percent of all US adults were married in 2015, which was down from 72 percent in 1960 (Cohn et al. 2011) (see Figure 10.4). There is a fairly large

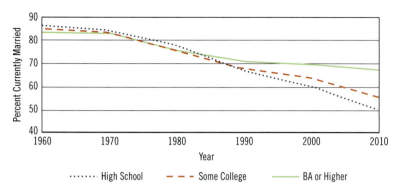

Figure 10.4   Percent of Population Age 30–44 Currently Married.
Source: Lundberg, Shelly, Robert A. Pollak, and Jenna Stearns, 2016. "Family Inequality:
Diverging Patterns in Marriage, Cohabitation, and Childbearing," *Journal of Economic
Perspectives* 30(2): 79–102.

Cohabitation. An arrangement in which romantic couples
choose to live together instead
of getting married.

racial disparity, with African Americans significantly less likely to marry
than other racial groups in the United
States (Raley, Seeney, and Wondra
2015). Looking from a global perspective, the decline in marriage is a widespread phenomenon among wealthy
countries throughout the world (Organization for Economic Cooperation and
Development 2018).

Divorce and single parenting have
contributed to the decline in marriage,
but so has the increasing popularity of
cohabitation, when romantic couples
choose to live together either before or instead of marriage. Nearly two-thirds
all marriages today were preceded by a period of cohabitation, "up from one-
third of marriages in the late 1970s" (Sutherland 2014) and only 20 percent of
marriages in the 1960s (Smock 2000: 3). Importantly, cohabitation is less likely
to end in marriage now than in the past (Sutherland 2014). Cohabitation is
slightly more common among people who have less income and less education;
it is also more common among people who are less religious, and who have more
egalitarian beliefs about gender roles (Smock 2000: 4; Ishizuka 2018). But it
is a fairly common practice among all social groups, with the exception of the
extremely religious.

There are many factors contributing to the rise in cohabitation. Changing
attitudes about sexuality (Chapter 9) mean that romantic couples can cohabit
without the disapproval of their parents and peers. Women who are working
are less likely to view marriage as an economic strategy, and women who reject
traditional attitudes about gender roles are less likely to view marriage as being
central to their identities (Cherlin and Furstenberg 1988). Children of divorced
parents tend to be more cautious about marriage, and they look at cohabitation
as a good way of hedging their bets (Thornton 1991). The same thing is true for
adults who have already been divorced themselves. And many couples who cohabit believe that they should wait to get married until they can afford to have
a "real" wedding, buy a house, and achieve financial stability (Gibson-Davis,
Edin, and McLanahan 2005).

While there are many good reasons for couples to choose cohabitation, sociological research shows that it is associated with an increase in family instability (Ishizuku 2018). The average duration of first cohabitation is two years,
with 40 percent ending in marriage and 27 percent ending in dissolution within
three years (Copen et al. 2013). Cohabitation also lacks the legal support and
protections that are associated with marriage, which means that partners
have fewer options if the relationship goes bad (Nock 1995). When cohabiting
couples dissolve their unions, there is strong evidence of negative economic
and psychological outcomes for both adults and children (Lee and McLanahan
2015; McLanahan, Tach, and Schneider 2013; Tach and Eads 2015).

One of the clearest consequences of cohabitation is that the people who do
end up getting married do so at a later age than previously. In the United States,
the median age at first marriage is now 27.8 for women and 29.8 for men, which
is an increase of nearly seven years since 1960 (US Census 2018). The age of first
marriage is even higher in Canada, Australia, Israel, Japan, South Korea, and
all of Western Europe (World Atlas 2019).

Boomerang Kids and Sandwich Parents

The delay in marriage means that more people are having children at an older age than they once did. There has been a significant increase in out-of-wedlock births in the last 40 years, but more than 60 percent of all births in the United States are still to married couples (Smock and Greenland 2010: 577). As a result, women's average age at first birth has increased significantly, from 21.4 in 1970 to 26.3 in 2014. The birth rate has increased the fastest among women aged 35 and older.

The wealthiest and most highly educated third of the population is the most likely to delay marriage and parenthood (Sassler and Cunningham 2008). By waiting until they are established in their careers before they have children, college-educated couples have more financial security and less stress in their lives during the period when they are raising their children. They are in a good position to invest time and money in their child's future, in a way that effectively transmits their privilege to the next generation. For these reasons, the delay in parenthood reinforces existing systems of inequality.

While the delay in marriage and parenting has definite advantages, it also comes with specific costs and risks. One of the biggest challenges for older parents is that they often become **sandwich parents**, which means that they are still raising their children at a time when their own parents are becoming elderly and need care. It can be very challenging to help two generations of family members simultaneously. Right at the time they are helping their children choose a college, they find themselves having to move their parents into an assisted-living facility—and trying to figure out how to pay for both. Excitement about the marriage of their own children can be tempered by concern over how their elderly and frail parents will be able to attend the celebration. Sandwich parents often feel a deep sense of guilt—stretched by the needs of their parents and children, they feel like they are failing everyone.

Since the 1980s, parents have also found themselves dealing with **boomerang kids**, which are young adults who move back home to live with their parents after a period of independence. Today, nearly one-quarter of young adults in their 20s and early 30s are living with their parents, and more than half are receiving some form of financial assistance from their parents (Parker 2012). There are many reasons for the increasing rate of boomerang kids. Young adults today have more student loan debt and marry later than previous generations. Since the global financial crisis of 2008, they are more likely to be unemployed or underemployed. As moving back home becomes less a sign of failure among their peers, some boomerang kids perceive the decision as a smart financial strategy that will set them up better for their future lives (Davidson 2014). For parents, though, the presence of boomerang kids threatens their ability to save effectively for their own retirements (Anderson 2015).

Sandwich parents The generational position where people are raising their children at the same time as their own parents are becoming elderly and need care.

Boomerang kids Young adults who move back home to live with their parents after a period of independence.

Boomerang kids
"Boomerang kids" are adult children who return to the parental household after a period of independence. In the United States, nearly one-quarter of young adults in their 20s and 30s live with their parents, and about half receive some financial assistance from their parents.

Transnational Families

International migration has increased significantly since the 1980s, with an

Transnational family. A household that is maintaining strong family bonds and simultaneous connections to multiple countries.

Remittances The money a migrant sends back from their new country to family members in their country of origin.

impact on families around the world. In the United States, nearly one-quarter of all the children under the age of 18 now live in immigrant families (Foner and Dreby 2011: 546). Many families that migrate are doing so in search of better work and opportunities for their children, and they often lack the economic resources to maintain connections with extended family (Espiritu 2003). Although new media technologies make it easy for people to communicate, distance still affects the number and intensity of interactions that people have with each other (Mok, Wellman, and Carrasco 2010).

Despite these challenges and difficulties, many migrants are creating **transnational families** who are maintaining strong family bonds and simultaneous connections to multiple countries. One of the ways they do this is through **remittances**, where the person who has emigrated regularly sends money back to family members in the country they left (Levitt 2001). We discuss remittances further in Chapter 15. In fact, many migrants plan to return to their countries of origin after their working careers are finished, which gives them extra motivation to maintain transnational ties.

The ability to maintain connections as a transnational family depends on who does the migrating, and whether the entire nuclear family emigrates. But each arrangement creates social pressures. When the entire nuclear family emigrates to another country, parents often worry that their children will reject their cultural heritage and become corrupted by the new society (Zhou and Bankston 1998). Children feel the pressure of the sacrifices their parents are making for them, and they can come to resent the expectation that they will help their parents translate documents, fill out forms, and help them conduct their everyday affairs (Menjivar 2000).

It is not always possible for families to emigrate together, which creates other kinds of challenges. Parents often leave their children behind, letting the children be raised by grandparents while the parents move elsewhere in search of better work (Foner and Dreby 2011: 551). In other instances, children are the ones who leave their parents behind. There is a long history of Central American youth coming to the United States to do agricultural work and sending remittances back home, and hoping that in the future either they can move back to Central America or their parents can move to the United States (Suarez-Orozco and Suarez-Orozco 2001). There is also a history of Asian children coming to the United States to attend school, with the hope that once their careers are established their parents can come and join them (Zhou 1998). These kinds of arrangements can create stress for the parent-child relationship, with parents struggling to maintain control over children (Glick 2010). On the other hand, family members who stay behind are often highly motivated to emigrate themselves. These desires reinforce the value of the family, and make family members more driven to do the things that are necessary to maintain family bonds.

Challenging Family Forms

In the United States, more than half of all adults are single and about 15 percent of them are living alone. The United States is not exceptional; in Europe, living alone is even more common. Some of this is due to structural changes in society. People are waiting longer to get married, and those who have good jobs can afford to live by themselves rather than getting a roommate or living with their parents. But a lot of it reflects a shift in preferences.

Global and Local

Korean "Wild Geese" Families

A distinctive form of the transnational family has emerged in Korea, where the mother takes the children to a foreign country for school while the father stays behind to work and support the family. This type of split-household transnational family started to become popular among wealthy Korean families in the mid-1990s, and the trend accelerated rapidly during the first decade of the 21st century. By 2007, there were more than 27,000 Korean students enrolled in foreign schools, with nearly half of them enrolled in elementary school. The United States is the most popular destination, followed by China, Canada, Australia, and New Zealand (Kim 2009: 170). In Korea, these families are called "kirogi," or wild geese families.

There are local and global forces driving the rise of wild geese families. Korea has an unusually intense school culture. Students begin attending after-school "cram schools" as early as elementary school, and by high school it is common for students to be in school or studying for 15 hours per day. South Korea's college-entrance exam, which is eight hours long, is one of the most difficult and stressful in the world. South Korea is consistently at the top of global education rankings, but this success comes with a cost. Recent research has found that South Korean children are among the least happy among all wealthy countries, with academic stress being the most significant contributing factor (Diamond 2016). Given this context, it is not so surprising that families wish to take their children to a different country for school, where they can be happier and more well-rounded as students.

For many South Korean wild geese families, the primary goal is to improve their children's English skills so they will be able to compete more successfully in a global world. In South Korea, studying English in a foreign country is a sign of social prestige and a marker of global citizenship. Memoirs written by wild geese children who attended elite US prep schools and Ivy League universities have been best-sellers in South Korea, offering up a blueprint for ambitious families wishing to join the global elite (Abelman and Kang 2014: 2). Many wild geese children have returned triumphantly to South Korea to become successful business leaders and politicians. Others have stayed in the United States, enjoying successful careers in elite law firms and global corporations.

At the same time, wild geese families face a number of significant challenges. The fathers who stay behind suffer from loneliness and depression, and the mothers often have a hard time settling in to the new country where their children are going to school (Reed 2015). Wild geese mothers and children have come under significant criticism in South Korea, where they are faulted for being too focused on material success, not concerned enough about the needs of the father, too selfishly focused on their own families, and not patriotic enough (Abelman and Kang 2014). This can make it harder for wild geese families to return to South Korea, placing additional stress on the family. And the situation is even worse for less-wealthy families who try the split-household transnational strategy. In these families, the father is often called a "penguin Dad" because he cannot fly and may go years at a time without seeing his wife or children.

Wild geese families
A young girl says goodbye to her father as she leaves with her mother and brother to pursue her education outside Korea.

ACTIVE LEARNING

Find out: Think about and list the different structural and cultural factors that help explain why "wild geese families" would be successful in American schools. Are these factors distinctive to wild geese families, or are there other immigrant groups that also display these kinds of structural and cultural advantages?

Living alone
Living alone is considered by some people to be an accomplishment and represents adult success.

In his book *Going Solo*, sociologist Eric Klinenberg shows some of the ways that the preference for living alone challenges traditional family forms (Klinenberg 2012). For many people today, the ability to live by themselves is a measure of becoming a successful adult—even a better measure, in fact, than getting married. Living alone gives people the freedom to do whatever they want, experimenting with different hobbies and lifestyle choices. For some people, the attraction of living alone is that it gives them complete sexual freedom. For others, it is the ability to focus on their careers and find their "true selves." Many young adults view living alone as a temporary phase, but they believe they are better off on their own than they would be if they settled for the wrong person by marrying too soon.

Living alone is not the only challenge to traditional ideas about family and social life. Feminist ideas have had a major influence too, encouraging people to think more carefully about the power, violence, and inequality that exists within marriages. Divorce and remarriage has led to an increase in blended families, in a way that challenges many traditional beliefs about the nuclear family. Social movements have successfully fought for greater acceptance of multiracial, gay, and lesbian families. Many of these challenges have resulted in overturning laws designed to give preferences to certain types of families over others.

Feminist Challenges to the Family

In her book *The Feminine Mystique*, Betty Friedan described the family as a prison that blocked women from their full development:

> Each suburban wife struggles with it alone. As she made the beds, shopped for groceries, matched slipcover material, ate peanut butter sandwiches with her children, chauffeured Cub Scouts and Brownies, lay beside her husband at night—she was afraid to ask even of herself the silent question—"Is this all?" (Friedan [1963] 2001)

Friedan argued that the equation of motherhood and femininity kept women from realizing their full potential, at the same time as it relieved men from the responsibility of doing any housework. Seeing the division of household labor through the lens of gender inequality, Friedan argued that women had the right to expect their husbands to do their fair share of the housework and to share the responsibility for childcare. Friedan's criticisms have been backed up by sociological research. Wives do most of the housework in the family, even when they are employed (Berk 1985; Bianchi et al. 2012). Wives who earn more money than their husbands compensate by doing extra housework, so their husbands will still feel like "real men" (Bittman et al. 2003). When husbands do contribute to housework, they do not feel accountable or responsible for how well they do it, leaving their wives to supervise the work and redo it when necessary

(Lyonette and Crompton 2015). The division of household labor becomes even more unequal when there are children in the family, which helps explain why motherhood reduces the wages of employed women (Budig and England 2001).

Inspired by the writings of Betty Friedan and other feminists in the 1960s and 1970s, women around the country began to join consciousness-raising groups to talk about the inequality, oppression, and unhappiness they were experiencing in their family lives. The National Organization for Women was founded in 1966, with Betty Friedan as its first president. The organization's founding statement included a demand for fundamental changes in gender relations within the family:

> It is no longer either necessary or possible for women to devote the greater part of their lives to child-rearing; yet childbearing and rearing, which continues to be a most important part of most women's lives—still is used to justify barring women from equal professional and economic participation and advance . . . we believe that a true partnership between the sexes demands a different concept of marriage, an equitable sharing of the responsibilities of home and children, and of the economic burdens of their support. (Freeman 1974)

Actively recruiting women to its cause, the National Organization for Women built a powerful political coalition to challenge gender inequality in the family. Rallying around the slogan that "the personal is political," they argued that the challenges women faced within their families were social issues that required organized resistance and fundamental social change.

Movements to create greater gender equality have led to real changes for many families. Changes in the law now require companies to grant maternity leave, making it easier for mothers to reenter the workforce after giving birth. Company policies that also extend parental leave to new fathers have allowed and encouraged men to become more involved in parenting. Many men have embraced the goal of creating more gender equality in the family, believing that this would be good for men as well as women; others have resisted the demands for greater gender equality, arguing that a woman's natural place is in the home, and that women's desires to have careers and participate in public life threaten their role as mothers and caregivers (Kimmel 2010). Regardless of their opinions about gender, work, and family, though, most people today are accepting of a variety of ways to organize housework and other family matters.

Blended Families

The prevalence of divorce and remarriage has also challenged the traditional nuclear family and led to new family forms. In the United States today, more than two-thirds of women and more than three-quarters of men remarry after divorce (Sweeney 2010: 668). As a result, 16 percent of all

The National Organization for Women
Founded in 1966, the National Organization for Women built a powerful political coalition to challenge gender inequality in the family and to rally support against gender stereotypes. This image from 2015 shows NOW supporters at a ticker-tape parade held for the champion US women's soccer team in New York City.

PAIRED CONCEPTS — Power and Resistance

Loving v. Virginia

The legal case that overturned laws against interracial marriage in the United States was filed in 1964 by the American Civil Liberties Union (ACLU) in Virginia on behalf of Mildred and Richard Loving. The couple had been married in 1958 in Washington, DC, in order to avoid Virginia's Racial Integrity Act, which made it a crime for whites and non-whites to get married. Returning to their home in Virginia, the couple was arrested and sentenced to a year in jail. The judge offered to suspend the sentence, if the Loving family agreed to leave Virginia and not return to the state together for 25 years. Leaving the house that they had built themselves, and separated from all of their friends and family in Virginia, they moved to Washington, DC.

After five unhappy years in Washington, DC, Mildred Loving wrote a letter complaining about her situation to the US attorney general, Robert F. Kennedy. Kennedy referred her to the ACLU, whose lawyers filed a motion to overturn the Virginia court decision, on the grounds that laws against interracial marriage violated the Equal Protection Clause of the 14th Amendment. The decision was upheld several times in Virginia, and lawyers appealed the decision until it came before the US Supreme Court.

In a unanimous decision in September 1967, the Supreme Court overturned the decision against the Lovings, and declared that laws against interracial marriage (which still existed in 16 states) were unconstitutional and unenforceable. Chief Justice Earl Warren wrote that "the freedom to marry, or not marry, a person of another race resides with the individual, and cannot be infringed by the State."

Today, *Loving v. Virginia* is viewed as a historic milestone that advanced civil rights. Three movies have been made about the case, and June 12 (the date of the Supreme Court decision) is celebrated around the country as "Loving Day." For their own part, Mildred and Richard Loving were not active participants in the Civil Rights Movement, and they were not particularly political in their everyday lives. As their attorney Bernard Cohen has described them, "They were very simple people, who were not interested in winning any civil rights principle. They just were in love with one another and wanted the right to live together as husband and wife in Virginia, without any interference from officialdom" (Siegel and Norris 2007).

Mildred and Richard Loving

ACTIVE LEARNING

Find out: While *Loving v. Virginia* declared that laws against interracial marriage were unconstitutional in 1967, the state of Alabama continued to enforce its ban until 1970, and did not remove anti-miscegenation language from its state constitution until 2000. Find out and describe the events that led Alabama to change its laws and its legal practices regarding interracial marriage between 1967 and 2000.

In many respects, then, society and law still continue to privilege monoracial families (Onwuachi-Willig and Willig-Onwuachi 2009).

Lesbian and Gay Families

One of the most significant challenges to the traditional image of the family has come from lesbian and gay families. Before the 21st century, marriages between same-sex partners were not legally recognized anywhere in the world (Biblarz and Savci 2010: 480). The Netherlands was the first country to legalize gay marriage, in 2000, and that was followed by similar rulings in Belgium, Canada, Norway, Sweden, Spain, and South Africa. In the United States, same-sex marriage was legally recognized for the first time in 2004, in Massachusetts. This was followed by Connecticut (2008), Vermont (2009), New Hampshire (2010), and New York (2011). After several years of legal disputes over whether states were required to recognize the validity of same-sex marriage licenses that had been granted in other states, the US Supreme Court ruled in 2015 that same-sex couples had the constitutional right to marry and to have their marriages legally recognized.

Along with the legal changes, the public acceptance of gay and lesbian families has increased significantly. In 2003, 58 percent of Americans were opposed to same-sex marriage; by 2015, at the time of the Supreme Court decision, fewer than 40 percent opposed it (Fingerhut 2016). Today, more than two-thirds of people in the United States believe that same-sex couples should have the same legal rights as heterosexual couples (Pew Research Center 2013). Similar to attitudes about multiracial families, support is strongest among those who are younger than 30 years old, which suggests that gay marriage may become less controversial in the future.

It took both solidarity and conflict for supporters of gay marriage to change public opinion and to get legal rulings in their favor. Some advocates argued that same-sex marriage was a basic civil right, which people were entitled to under the Equal Protection Clause of the US Constitution (Wolfson 2004). Others pointed out that marriage was an important source of family stability, which would encourage greater social cohesion, emotional support, and economic security if it was extended to same-sex couples (Sullivan 2004). Arguments like these were made in the mainstream media as well as in dozens of legal briefs that were filed with the courts.

As lesbian and gay families have become more visible, social scientists have examined how they are different from other types of families. Gay and lesbian parents have a more egalitarian attitude toward housework and parenting than traditional heterosexual parents (Fulcher, Sutfin, and Patterson 2008; Johnson and O'Connor 2002). The children of gay and lesbian parents hold more egalitarian and less stereotypical attitudes about gender and behavior (Biblarz and Savci 2010: 485). Overall, though, children raised by gay and lesbian parents have similar outcomes to children of heterosexual married parents, in terms of psychological well-being, friendships, and educational success (Biblarz and Savci 2010: 484; Cheng and Powell 2015).

Expectant parents
Two women hold a picture of an ultrasound celebrating the expectation of a new baby. Social acceptance of same-sex relationships, along with advances in reproductive technology, have allowed for the formation of nontraditional families.

CASE STUDY

Family Names

As families continue to change, and as people criticize and challenge different aspects of family life in society, things that were once taken for granted become more uncertain and more a matter of conscious choice. This is clear in the case of naming practices, and specifically with respect to the question of whether or not women will keep their own last names when they get married. Using the five paired concepts, we consider how naming practices can shed light on the relationship between family and society.

It was not long ago that a woman was unable to keep her unmarried name after getting married. This expression of men's *power* over women was built into the law. Before the 1970s, many states required a married woman to use her husband's last name in order to vote, get a passport, or have a bank account. In this context, the insistence on keeping one's unmarried name was an act of *resistance*. In fact, it was an important strategic action throughout the 1970s, encouraged by the women's movement as an act against patriarchal power within the family.

In the 1970s, a woman who decided to keep her name after marriage knew that it was a deeply political and controversial action, but she did it because she felt a strong sense of *solidarity* with others in the women's movement. At the same time, women knew that their decision was also likely to create *conflict*. There was often conflict with their husbands, whose friends disapproved of his choice and criticized him for not taking control of the family. There was also conflict with women who chose not to keep their name after marriage, who felt that people in the women's movement were criticizing them for not being more loyal to the movement. Over time, a backlash against the feminist movement grew in strength. Swept up in this conservative backlash, fewer married women during the 1980s made the choice to keep their unmarried names (Goldin and Shim 2004).

Today, a married woman's decision to keep her name has less to do with solidarity, and more to do with social dynamics related to *privilege* and *inequality*. Women are more likely to keep their names if they have a higher income, an advanced degree, or an established career, or if they live in a city (Kopelman et al. 2009). For these successful urban women, the choice to keep their name, just like the choice to marry, is a choice that cannot be separated from the fact that they have already made a name for themselves as successful individuals (Goldin and Shim 2004). The choice can still be a difficult one, and it can still involve awkward conversations with their partner, family, and friends. But their privilege means that they are not likely to feel pressured into making the decision. Women who marry less educated and less wealthy men, however, are more likely to be criticized and punished for their desire to keep their unmarried name (Shafer 2006).

The women's movement has had a *global* impact on how people around the world talk about gender and family. But the decision about whether or not a married woman should keep her name is also shaped by more *local* factors. In Japan, the law requires that a married couple should share their last name; the law does not specify which last name they should share, but an overwhelming majority choose to share the husband's name. In Quebec, Greece, France, Belgium, and the Netherlands, the law requires married women to keep their unmarried names (Koffler 2015). In Korea, Spain, and Chile, it is much more common for married women to keep their unmarried name than it is for them to adopt their husband's name.

While the decision about whether married women should keep their name is shaped by the history of the women's movement and the *structure* of gender inequality in the family, there have been many recent attempts to develop creative new solutions to the problem of family names. Some men, fully embracing the feminist critique of gender inequality in the family, are taking their wives' last names. Others are creating a hyphenated last name that combines both last names—Shawn and Beyoncé Knowles-Carter are probably the most well-known example of this choice. Others are creating entirely new last names, which combine different parts of the last names of the two partners. New strategies such as these represent the *contingency* that is present in all social situations and social choices.

LEARNING GOALS REVISITED

10.1 Define family and kinship, and describe how kinship systems have changed over time.

- A family is a group of related people connected by biological, emotional, or legal bonds. For many government statistics, such as the US Census Bureau, there is also an emphasis placed on living in the same household.

- A kinship system consists of the rules that define who counts as a member of the family, the names that are given to different types of family members, and the expectations about how different family will relate to one another. Rules about kinship provide some of the most important elements of a society's culture.

- Before the 20th century, most European societies were patrilineal and privileged the male line of descent. Names, titles, property rights, and family inheritance were traced only through the men in the family. Women took the name of their husbands when they were married. Both men and women were expected to use marriage as a way of building wealth and resources for their families.

- Today, many societies have adopted multilineal systems that give equal significance to both maternal and paternal lines of descent. Family inheritance includes sons and daughters equally. Men and women are free to marry whomever they like, and they are expected to marry for love rather than for building strategic family alliances.

10.2 Understand how the family is connected to systems of inequality, such as race, class, and gender inequality.

- Highly educated, professionally successful, and high-earning people tend to marry and form families with one another, in a way that reinforces social inequality. Wealthy parents use their money to invest in their children's futures, leaving them with more opportunities and fewer debts as they begin their adult lives. Highly educated and successful parents socialize their children to be assertive in a manner that increases their likelihood of success in school and in the workplace. They also teach their children about high culture, which makes them more comfortable in the world of privilege and more likely to marry other people who come from a privileged social background.

- For most of US history, family law only permitted opposite-sex couples to marry and prohibited interracial marriages. This prevented same-sex couples and multiracial families from enjoying the social and economic benefits of legal marriage. Legally married couples have privacy rights that are not available to other couples. They also get special benefits in matters of employment, insurance, taxation, inheritance, and immigration.

- The family unit can reinforce gender inequality. In most societies, the work that adult men do has been rewarded with higher status and more money. While adult women were expected to do most of the cooking, cleaning, and care work, they have had to do this without compensation or social recognition. Sons have often received preferential treatment over daughters in educational opportunities, career expectations, inheritance rights, and the general distribution of power and status in the family.

10.3 Define the nuclear family, and describe how divorce, single-parent families, and the delay in marriage have led to changes in the traditional nuclear family.

- Historically, the traditional image of the nuclear family has consisted of a heterosexual couple living together with their children. The nuclear family became more and more common in modern society, as people moved to cities, their children spent more time in school, and a rising standard of living allowed young couples to afford a home of their own.

- Changes in the law during the 1960s made it easier for couples to get divorced, and this led to a large increase in the divorce rate. Today, about 10 percent of the adult population is divorced at any given time. Among heterosexual couples, divorce tends to have a larger negative effect on the economic well-being of women. Children of divorced parents tend to have lower levels of educational success and psychological well-being, and a higher likelihood of having their own marriages end in divorce.

- More than one-quarter of all children in the United States today live in a single-parent household. Single-parent families are overwhelmingly headed by women, and they are strongly associated with childhood poverty.

- Only about half of all adults in the United States today are married, and the decline in marriage is a widespread phenomenon that is occurring in wealthy countries throughout the world. Divorce and single parenting have contributed to the decline in marriage, but so has the increasing popularity of cohabitation. Cohabitation presents both advantages and disadvantages for couples, but one of its consequences is that the people who end up getting married do so at a later age than they used to.

10.4 Comprehend the main feminist critiques of the family, and show how women's movements for greater equality have led to changes in family dynamics.

- During the 1960s and 1970s, many women began to join consciousness-raising groups to talk about the inequality, oppression, and unhappiness they were experiencing in their family lives. Describing the family as a prison that blocked women from their full development, they argued for a different understanding of marriage, which emphasized sharing the responsibilities of home and children, and committing to the equal support of both partners' career aspirations.

- Demands for gender equality have led to real changes for many families. The law now requires companies to grant maternity leave, making it easier for mothers to reenter the workplace. Company policies that extend parental leave to new fathers have allowed and encouraged men to become more involved in parenting. Many men have embraced the goal of creating more gender equality in the family, believing that this would be good for men as well as women. But there has also been a backlash, with some men arguing that a woman's natural place is in the home, and that women's desires to have careers and participate in public life threaten their role as mothers and caregivers.

10.5 Describe the changes in attitudes and laws that have become more accepting of multiracial families as well as lesbian and gay families.

- Interracial marriage was not fully legal in the United States until 1967, and it remained extremely uncommon before the 1980s. But attitudes have changed rapidly, and nearly 90 percent of Americans now support interracial marriage. Today, more than 10 percent of all children born in the United States have parents who identify with different racial groups, and more than one-third of the population has a close relative who is part of a multiracial family.

- Marriage between gay and lesbian couples was not legal anywhere in the world before the 21st century. The Netherlands was the first country to legalize gay marriage, in 2000, followed by similar rulings in Belgium, Canada, Norway, Sweden, Spain, and South Africa. In the United States, same-sex marriage was legally recognized for the first time in 2004, in Massachusetts, and was extended to the entire country after a 2015 Supreme Court ruling. Today, there is broad-based public support for gay marriage, with support being strongest among those younger than 30 years old.

Key Terms

Blended family 300
Boomerang kids 295
Cohabitation 294
Extended family 288
Family 281
Genealogy 281
Kinship system 281
Multilineal 282
Nuclear family 288
Patrilineal 282
Primogeniture 284
Remittances 296
Sandwich parents 295
Transnational family 296

Review Questions

1. What kinds of social support do families provide?

2. What kinds of social and legal privileges do married couples receive that are not available to unmarried couples?

3. How do families influence gender roles? Do family gender roles reinforce inequality? To what extent have family gender roles changed over time?

4. What social forces helped make the traditional nuclear family the most common type of family form in modern society? When was the high-water mark for the traditional nuclear family? What has happened to the nuclear family since that time?

5. What were the main factors that caused the divorce rate to increase between the 1960s and the 1980s? How does divorce tend to reinforce existing systems of inequality?

6. How do race, gender, and class intersect in the lives and choices made by many single mothers?

7. What are the main reasons for why cohabitation has been increasing among couples? What are the advantages and disadvantages of cohabitation, as compared to marriage?

8. What are the biggest challenges couples face when they delay the decision to get married?

9. Describe some of the different strategies that transnational families use to stay connected.

10. What were the main criticisms that women's groups made against the family during the 1960s and 1970s?

11. What are the main challenges that face blended families?

12. Describe how attitudes and laws about marriage have changed to become more accepting of multiracial families as well as lesbian and gay families. What were the main factors that led to these changes?

Explore

RECOMMENDED READINGS

Cohen, Philip N. 2014. *The Family: Diversity, Inequality, and Social Change*. New York: W. W. Norton.

Conley, Dalton. 2005. *The Pecking Order: A Bold New Look at How Family and Society Determine Who We Become*. New York: Vintage.

Edin, Kathryn, and Maria Kefalas. 2005. *Promises I Can Keep: Why Poor Women Put Motherhood before Marriage*. Berkeley: University of California Press.

Foner, Nancy, and Joanna Dreby. 2011. "Relations between the Generations in Immigrant Families," *Annual Review of Sociology* 37: 546–64.

Friedan, Betty. [1963] 2001. *The Feminine Mystique*. New York: W. W. Norton.

Klinenberg, Eric. 2012. *Going Solo: The Extraordinary Rise and Surprising Appeal of Living Alone*. New York: Penguin Books.

Smock, Pamela. 2000. "Cohabitation in the United States: An Appraisal of Research Themes, Findings, and Implications," *Annual Review of Sociology* 26: 1–20.

Wolfson, Evan. 2004. *Why Marriage Matters: America, Equality, and Gay People's Right to Marry*. New York: Simon & Schuster.

ACTIVITIES

- *Use your sociological imagination*: Go to a restaurant or coffee shop with one or two of your friends. Choose between 15 and 20 people who are seated together, and mark down whether or not you think they are a married couple. Are your guesses the same? What clues did you use to guide you in your choices?

- *Media+Data Literacy*: Choose three popular films or television shows where there is a married or an unmarried couple. How is the housework divided up in the household?

- *Discuss*: Do you think it is ever too late to get married? Is there an age beyond which people should not get divorced? Why or why not?

For additional resources, including Media+Data Literacy exercises, In the News exercises, and quizzes, please go to **oup.com/he/ jacobs-Townsley1e**

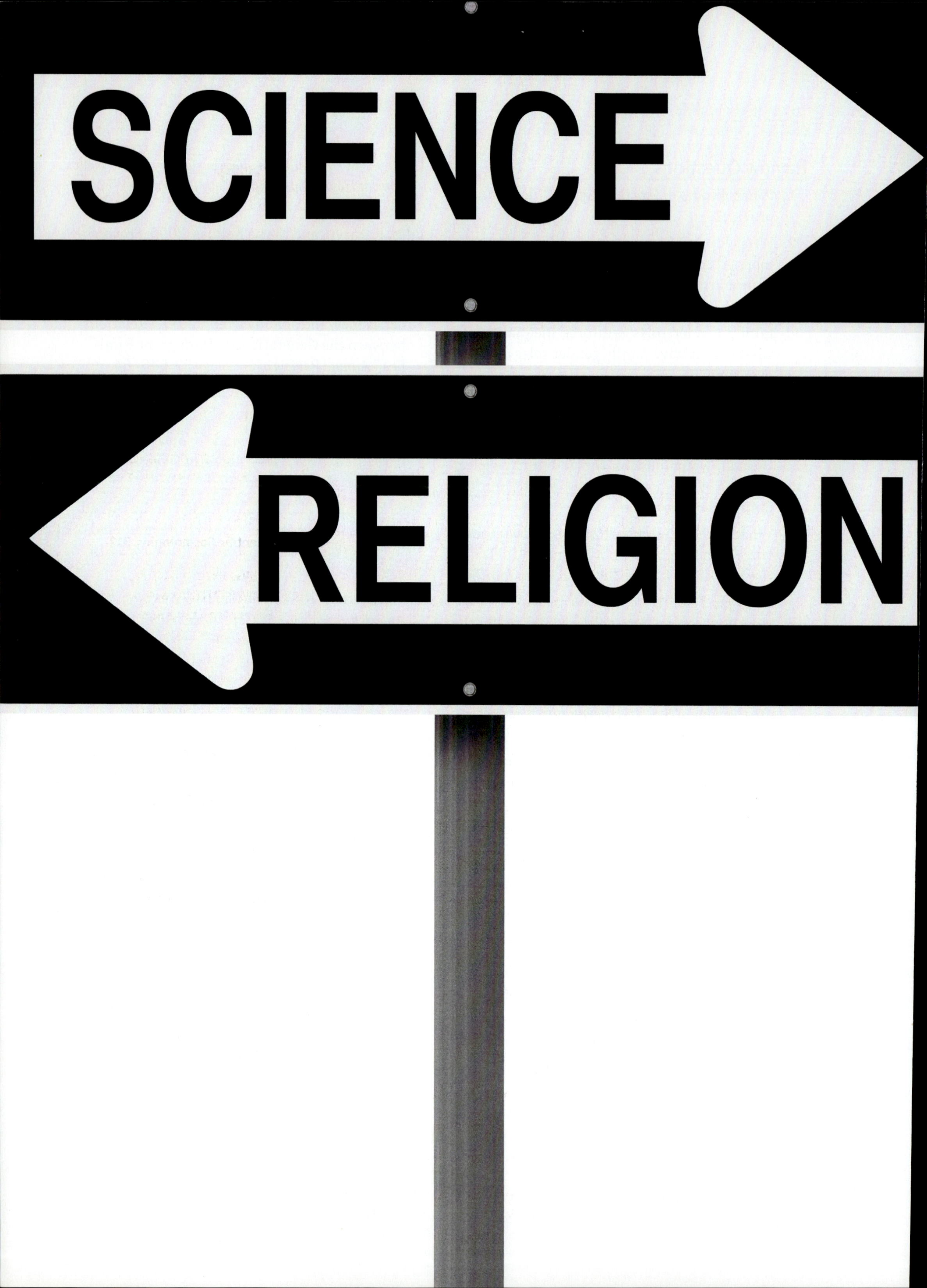
SCIENCE
RELIGION

11

Science, Religion, and Knowing

In November 2007, John Coleman drew national attention when he wrote a blog post calling global warming the "greatest scam in history." As a cofounder of The Weather Channel and one of the first national television weathermen in the country, Coleman was one of the nation's most well-known meteorologists. Coleman soon became a regular guest on conservative radio and television talk shows, where he argued that climate scientists had a political agenda, that they had manipulated data, and that the scientific consensus about global warming was closer to religious belief than to valid scientific knowledge (Homans 2010). Coleman emphasized his scientific expertise as a meteorologist, and he argued that "we scientists . . . have truth on our side" (Yale Climate Connections 2010).

Climate scientists fought back strenuously against Coleman's charges. They pointed out that Coleman's academic credentials were in journalism, not science. They further observed that research about global warming came from the scientific field of climatology, and not from meteorology, and that within the field of climatology the consensus about climate change was based on "solid settled science." The CEO of The Weather Channel released a press statement distancing itself from Coleman, noting that Coleman had no affiliation with their organization and reaffirming that their meteorologists supported the scientific consensus about climate change (Ariens 2014).

Scientists are deeply worried that people continue to doubt claims about global warming. Among scientists, there is very little disagreement about the facts of the matter. In fact, 97 percent of all actively publishing climate scientists agree both that climate change is occurring, and that human activities are the primary cause (Cook et al. 2016).

Science and Religion
Sociologists emphasize that although people sometimes think science and religion are very different, they have striking similarities. They are both ways of knowing the social world, provide comfort in times of stress, and offer practical ways to manage social life.

LEARNING GOALS

11.1   Describe the main differences between religious and scientific cosmologies.

11.2   Describe how religion and science are organized as social institutions.

11.3   Learn the history and the global impact of the five major world religions.

11.4   Define secularization, and discuss the main points of evidence for and against the secularization thesis.

11.5   Think about some of the ways that religion and science can coexist in contemporary society.

In 2005, the Yale School of Forestry and Environmental Studies organized a major conference to explore why scientific knowledge about climate change was not shared more widely among everyday citizens, policy-makers, and business leaders. An outcome of the conference was the creation of the Yale Program on Climate Change Communication. Its mission is to develop a comprehensive public education campaign about climate change and its implications. Its research associates conduct regular opinion polls focusing on public attitudes and beliefs about the environment. They have developed relationships and alliances with leaders from business, politics, religion, and journalism. And they have undertaken a grassroots education effort to try to connect with local communities and schools.

Program leaders quickly recognized that they needed to try harder to overcome the divide between religion and science. Noting that "scientists are not always seen as credible messengers by religious groups," they have come to terms with the fact that emphasizing science might not be the best way to change the minds of people who are suspicious about environmentalism (Abbasi 2006: 40). The partnerships they created with religious leaders have helped them craft a message about the ethical and religious obligation that people have to protect the environment.

This chapter examines religion and science as two important systems of knowledge that people have used to understand the world. We begin by introducing the concept of **cosmology**, which refers to the system of knowledge and beliefs that a society uses to understand how the world works and how it is organized. After comparing the main differences between religious and scientific cosmologies, we then focus more closely on how religion is organized as a social institution. We examine how the major religions have shaped the world, and we consider how religion has changed in society today. We also examine how science is organized as a social institution. We review the sociological research in this area, which has studied the values and beliefs of scientists, the social organization of scientific reward systems, the ways scientific labs are organized, and how scientific knowledge is produced. We finish by exploring how science and religion can coexist in the contemporary world.

Cosmology The system of knowledge and beliefs that a society uses to understand how the world works and how it is organized.

Religion and Science as Ways of Knowing the World

Humans have tried to understand the world around them for as long as they have had language, and they have developed theories about how the world was created. Archaeologists have discovered carvings and other physical objects

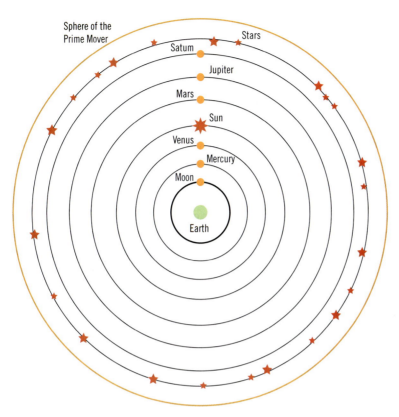

Figure 11.1   **Aristotle's Geocentric Universe, c. 350 BCE.**

that are more than twenty thousand years old that attempt to describe how the universe is organized. A Babylonian clay tablet from the sixth century BCE (currently displayed at the British Museum) depicts the world as a disc surrounded by a ring of water. In the fourth century BCE, the Greek philosopher Aristotle described a world in which Earth remained stationary in the center, while planets and stars circled it (Figure 11.1). Most of these theories were concerned with astronomy, trying to understand how the Earth is related to the rest of the universe. But there are also social cosmologies, which are theories about how societies were created, how they work, and how they are connected to the larger world.

Among the early sociologists, Émile Durkheim and Max Weber both wrote about social cosmology. In his book *The Elementary Forms of the Religious Life* (1912), Durkheim argued that there was a natural human proclivity to classify and categorize things, as a way of understanding our relationship to our society and to the larger world. Durkheim argued that the classifying impulse is shared by the earliest religious ideas as well as the most advanced scientific systems. Weber studied how religious cosmologies shaped social and economic life, through historical studies of Protestantism, Judaism, Confucianism, and Hinduism.

Religious Cosmologies

According to Weber, the main difference between religion and science is that religious cosmologies describe the world by making reference to mysterious, magical, and incalculable forces (Weber 1946: 139). **Polytheism** is a religious cosmology in which the world was created by a group of deities, who are responsible for many of the forces of nature and who often intervene in human lives. Ancient religions tended to be polytheistic. **Monotheism**, by contrast, is

Polytheism A religious cosmology in which there is a group of deities.

Monotheism A religious cosmology in which there is only one deity.

conflict, hunger, or unhappiness. Before science, most forms of utopian thinking described a period in the distant past, when people lived simply and primitively, but were happy and content. In contrast, scientific utopias describe an advanced world (usually in the future) in which people have conquered nature and managed to create a perfectly organized society. Francis Bacon, who was one of the first people to describe the scientific method, described such a utopia in his fictional work *New Atlantis*. Published in 1627, *New Atlantis* describes a mythical island where the most important social institution is a scientific college, called Salomon's House, where scientific experiments are undertaken in order to master nature and create a better social existence for the island's inhabitants. Psychologist B. F. Skinner imagined a similar kind of utopia in his 1948 novel, *Walden Two*, which describes a society organized around experimental science, in which new strategies for organizing the community are continually being tested. Skinner's view of the perfect society was one in which the scientific method came to organize all aspects of social life, replacing traditional forms of knowledge. *Walden Two* inspired a number of real-life utopian communities throughout the 1960s and 1970s. But utopian hopes for science are not as strongly held as they used to be, for reasons we discuss later in the chapter.

Today, science is a major industry, supported by governments and corporations around the world. Globally, more than $1.918 trillion was spent on basic scientific research in 2018, with the largest expenditures taking place in the United States, China, and Japan (NSF 2018). Organizations such as the Coalition for Evidence-Based Policy lobby politicians to increase government effectiveness by relying on scientific methods and rigorously collected evidence. In all levels of education, the highest priority is given to training in science, technology, engineering, and math. Scientists may try to create partnerships with religious leaders, as we discussed at the beginning of the chapter, but they do so with the belief and the confidence that scientific ways of knowing are the best way to produce reliable knowledge about the world and create social progress.

Provo Utah Temple
Religion is a social institution that provides a framework for social life. In Provo, Utah, 77 percent of people describe themselves as extremely religious, and 90 percent are associated with the Church of Jesus Christ of Latter-day Saints.

Religion as a Social Institution

Provo, Utah, is the most religious city in the United States, with 77 percent of the city's residents describing themselves as "extremely religious" (Newport 2013). More than 90 percent of the city's residents are affiliated with the Mormon Church. The city is home to Brigham Young University, the largest religious university in the United States, which is owned and operated by the Mormon Church. Social life at BYU is organized around religion, with more than 100 church organizations, known as "wards," organizing the majority of the social events. There is a

Measuring Religious Commitment

Social scientists who study religion need a way to measure how religious people are. But there are many different ways to measure religiosity. Should you measure how frequently people attend religious services, pray, or read religious texts? Should you measure how much time or money a person donates to their church? Should you measure how important religion is to a person, compared to other parts of their life? Does it matter if they treat their sacred religious texts as completely true and accurate? If more than one of these measures help define religiosity, what is the relative importance of each?

The most straightforward way to measure religiosity is to examine the frequency of prayer or attendance at religious services. One key source of information, the Baylor Religion Survey, asks people how often they attend religious services. They also ask people how often they pray alone outside of religious services. And they ask people how often they read sacred religious texts. All of these measures rely on self-reports, which creates problems for social scientists because there is a tendency for people to exaggerate how frequently they participate in religious activities (Hout and Greeley 1998).

Another strategy is to measure the amount of time or money a person donates to their church. The most typical question is based on a simple binary measure, such as the one that the Survey of Chicago Catholics asks: "Did you contribute money to your parish last year?" Some surveys ask people whether they tithe (i.e., give a fixed percentage of their income to their church), but these also tend to be measured in a binary yes/no fashion.

Other measures of religiosity focus on people's religious beliefs. The General Social Survey asks people whether they believe that the Bible is the actual word of God and whether it is to be taken literally. A global survey on religiosity asks a similar question, but tailors it to be specific to the religious beliefs and sacred texts of the people they are asking. The American National Election Studies ask people whether they consider religion to be an important part of their lives. The Baylor Religion Survey asks people how religious they consider themselves, ranging from "not religious at all" to "very religious." The Measuring Morality Study asks people how strongly they look to their religious faith for meaning and purpose in their lives.

Even after decisions have been made about which measures of religiosity to collect, there is still work to be done. How can the different measures be combined into a single scale of religiosity, when they are all measuring different things? Do the different measures all get weighted equally in the scale, or should different weights be applied depending on a theory about how important a given measure is for overall religiosity? These are complicated questions, which social scientists studying religion have been debating for more than 50 years.

ACTIVE LEARNING

Explore: The Association of Religious Data Archives is located at Pennsylvania State University. Its goal is to provide a central location for storing social science data on religion. Spend some time exploring their website, and particularly their section on religiosity (http://wiki.thearda.com/tcm/concepts/religiosity/). What do you think are the most important measures that should be included in research about religiosity?

major emphasis at the school on marriage, and more than half of all undergraduate students get married by the time they graduate. The school sees itself as a world ambassador for the Mormon Church, and it works hard to instill Mormon values among its students.

While most cities and universities are much less religious than Provo and Brigham Young University, religion continues to have a social presence in many places in the world. As a social institution, religion offers people a set of rules and strategies for how they should relate to each other and how they should act. Religion also provides people with organizations—churches, synagogues, mosques, and so forth—where they can spend time and interact with other people. Religions give their members a common identity, and a place where they can feel connected. And religious organizations frequently provide important social resources, such as education, counseling, spiritual guidance, and charity.

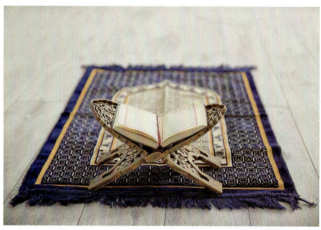

The elements of religion
Religious elements include ritual objects that are considered sacred, such as these objects used during the Catholic Liturgy, a chalice, wine and water cruets, and a bell (a). Prayer is a common religious practice. In Islam, practicing Muslims set the rhythm of the day by kneeling and praying five times a day. The prayer mat and Quran (b) are objects used for prayer. (c) Religious holidays bind people to religious communities and identities through ritual celebration. Simchat Torah is a Jewish holiday that marks the completion of the annual Torah reading cycle. Here, a man carries the Jewish Holy text, the Torah, as other members of the religious community celebrate.

Elements of Religious Institutions

In *The Elementary Forms of the Religious Life*, Émile Durkheim defined a **religion** as a unified system of beliefs and practices related to sacred things, which unite all of its adherents into a single moral community (Durkheim 2008). Looking at the elements of this definition, it is easy to see why religion has been such a powerful social force. As a system of beliefs and practices, religion is a source of culture and meaning. As a type of culture that is focused on sacred things, religion gives people a connection to a world bigger than themselves, as well as a sense of larger purpose. As a moral community, religion is an important source of social solidarity, social connection, and social comfort. Religion also provides a way for people to think about the presence of injustice and suffering in the world.

THE SACRED AND THE PROFANE. As a type of culture, religions divide the world into a group of sacred things and a group of profane things. Sacred things are set apart from the ordinary.

All religions have a set of sacred objects that serve as a point of focus for their adherents. In Judaism, this includes the Star of David, the Torah, and the tallit (prayer shawl). In Christianity, it includes the cross, holy water, and the Bible. In Islam, it includes the mosque, the crescent and star, and the Quran. These sacred objects are invested with significance, and they are not to come into contact with the ordinary, profane world. In Judaism, the Torah is never supposed to touch the ground, and a person who drops it is required to fast for 40 days. When Muslims enter the mosque for daily prayers, they are expected to remove their shoes so that dirt from the outside does not enter the sacred space.

According to the sociologist Peter Berger (1929–2017), religion establishes a sacred world that gives its members a sense of meaning, order, and protection against the fear of chaos. As he wrote in *The Sacred Canopy*, "Religion is the audacious attempt to conceive of the entire universe as being humanly significant" (Berger 1967: 28). In other words, by giving us access to a world of sacred things, religion gives us comfort in the belief that our ordinary, everyday lives are not meaningless.

RITUAL. For a religious institution, a **ritual** is an event where people come together to reaffirm the meaning of the sacred, to acknowledge its special qualities and its separateness from ordinary (profane) life. Ritual is the social part of religious belief, allowing people to gather and reaffirm their common beliefs and to share a powerful experience together.

In fact, Durkheim argued that ritual was so fundamental that it was an essential feature of all societies. Regardless of how religious a society might be, it still needed periodic rituals in which its members gathered together to reaffirm their shared beliefs, their sacred objects, and their most cherished values. In this sense, Durkheim argued, all societies need some form of religious practice.

RESPONSE TO SUFFERING AND INJUSTICE. If society is to exist as a moral community, we need an explanation for why the world is so imperfect, and for why good people suffer while evil people prosper. In his historical sociology of religion, Max Weber described this as the problem of **theodicy**, which is the attempt to explain why suffering and injustice exist in the world. Weber documented how ancient religions offered powerful explanations for suffering and injustice. Many of the earliest religions described a universe that was controlled by two competing forces of good and evil. Hindu religions explained the problem of theodicy in terms of karma, in which good actions would be rewarded and evil actions punished in later incarnations of the soul. Other religions have emphasized the distinction between life and afterlife, with good people being rewarded in the afterlife and bad people being punished.

Religious institutions have also responded to the problem of suffering in concrete ways, by creating organizations that take responsibility for doing care work. Charity is a major emphasis of most religious organizations, and adherents are often encouraged (and sometimes required) to give money in order to help the weak, the sick, and the defenseless. Many observant Jews today donate 10 percent of their income to charity, following the tradition from ancient biblical law. Observant Muslims follow the practice of *zakat*, in which they donate a percentage of their income to be redistributed to poor Muslims and to Islamic clergy. For Christians, the New Testament describes charity as the foundation of all Christian virtues. Charitable giving surges during major religious holidays. Research has consistently shown that religious people donate more time and money to charity than people who do not have a religious affiliation (Brooks 2003).

Because of their strong emphasis on charity, religious organizations have been and continue to be some of the largest and most significant providers of charitable social services. According to research by the sociologist Mark Chaves, more than 80 percent of all religious congregations in the United States are involved in some kind of social service provision, such as soup kitchens, homeless shelters, and food delivery to the elderly (Chaves and Eagles 2016). Many of the largest and most important charitable organizations in the world were started as

Religion A unified system of beliefs and practices related to sacred things, which unite all of its adherents into a single moral community.

Ritual An event where people come together to reaffirm the meaning of the sacred, to acknowledge its special qualities and its separateness from ordinary (profane) life.

Theodicy The attempt to explain why suffering and injustice exist in the world.

Religious responses to pain and suffering
Most religions emphasize charity, and religious organizations are some of the most significant providers of charitable social services. Many of the largest and most important charitable organizations in the world, such as the Salvation Army, United Way, and Caritas International, were started as religious charities. The Salvation Army is famous for their Christmas fundraising drives.

religious charities, with some of the better-known examples including United Way, Salvation Army, and Caritas International.

The Major Religions and Their Global Impact

As Figure 11.2 shows, nearly 70 percent of the people in the world are affiliated with Christianity, Islam, or Hinduism. For Christians, Muslims, and Hindus, there is a strong tendency to live in a place where they are in the majority; for other groups, there is a stronger likelihood that they will live in places where they are religious minorities (see Figure 11.2).

While the number of adherents is an important measurement, other studies of comparative religion focus on the global and historical impact of different religions. Using this metric, most religious scholars identify five major world religions: Judaism, Christianity, Islam, Hinduism, and Buddhism (Esposito, Fasching, and Lewis 2014).

JUDAISM. Although Judaism has fewer than 15 million adherents worldwide, it is still considered one of the major religions because of its historical influence.

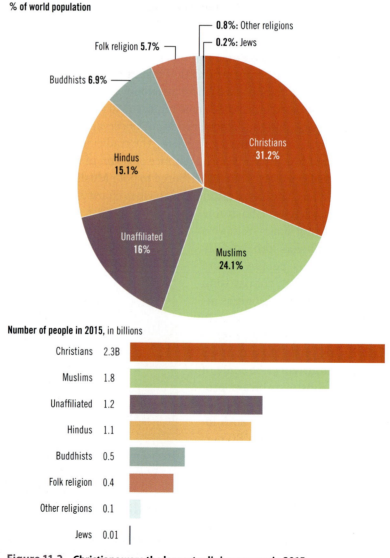

Figure 11.2   Christians were the largest religious group in 2015.
Source: Pew Research Center demographic projections.

Originating in the Middle East more than 3,500 years ago, Judaism is one of the oldest monotheistic religions, based on the belief that there is one all-powerful god who created the world. Judaism was a major influence on Christianity and Islam; in fact, all three are considered to be Abrahamic religions, in the sense that they all trace themselves to Abraham, and they all believe that God revealed himself to Abraham.

The sacred text in Judaism is the Torah, which consists of the first five books of the Hebrew Bible, which Christians call the Old Testament and Muslims call the Tawrat. The Torah tells the story of Abraham, his descendants, and the covenant between God and the Jewish people. The most important part of the religious ritual in Judaism involves the reading of the Torah, which is read in its entirety over the course of the year. The Torah includes some of the most famous stories in Western culture, including the story of Adam and Eve, Noah's ark, Moses and the exodus from Egypt, and the Ten Commandments.

As a religious group, the Jewish people have experienced a long history of persecution. As a community, their history has been one of repeated diaspora, in which they have been driven out of their ancestral homeland and forced to live in other places in the world. The Jews were forced to leave their homeland after the Assyrian destruction of Israel (722 BCE), the Babylonian destruction of Judah (597 BCE), and the Roman destruction of Jerusalem (70 CE). The Romans brought large numbers of Jews back to Rome as slaves, where they gradually dispersed throughout Europe within the lands of the Roman Empire.

From as early as the 12th century, Jewish communities in Europe and Russia were forced to live in segregated, poor, and extremely crowded communities (known as ghettos), where their movements were strictly regulated and their opportunities were limited to marginal occupations. Anti-Semitism was a common feature of European social life, with Jews suffering harassment, expulsion from communities, and even massacre. By the 19th century, however, conditions had improved for many Jews; they were granted civil rights in many countries, and they made tremendous contributions and achievements in the arts, the sciences, and the business world. But anti-Semitism continued in many parts of the world. Adolf Hitler came to power in Germany in 1933 on an anti-Semitic pledge to drive the Jews out of Germany and Europe. Hitler's Nazi government killed more than six million Jews between 1942 and 1945, a mass genocide that came to be known as the Holocaust, and which led to the creation of the first international trial for crimes against humanity.

The long history of diaspora and persecution led to an international movement of Zionism, which sought the establishment of a Jewish homeland in Israel, where Jews could live as a majority group instead of continuing to exist as a religious minority. Israel was established as a Jewish state in 1948, though it has faced challenges and conflicts from neighboring Arab countries since its creation. Today, more than six million Jews live in

Jewish neighborhood in Brooklyn, New York
Most American Jews are assimilated and live within the larger American population. In some American communities, however, Jews remain a distinct minority with a strong Jewish identity.

Israel, making it the largest Jewish population center in the world, and by far the most concentrated. The second-largest Jewish population (at 5.4 million) is found in the United States. While Israeli Jews are a majority group (at 75% of the national population), American Jews are a distinct religious minority (at less than 3% of the national population). As the sociologist Charles Liebman argued, American Jews face a continual tension between their commitment to assimilating into American society and their commitment to maintaining a strong Jewish identity (Liebman 1973).

CHRISTIANITY. With 2.3 billion adherents, Christianity is the largest religion in the world. There are significant numbers of Christians on every continent. In fact, more than one hundred countries are majority Christian, with most of them located in Europe, Latin America, sub-Saharan Africa, and North America (Pew Research Center 2017).

While there is a lot of diversity among Christians, they are held together by a common belief in monotheism, as well as a corresponding belief that Jesus was the Son of God who was sent to save humanity from sin. The sacred texts in Christianity include the Hebrew Bible (referred to as the Old Testament) as well as the New Testament, which records the life and teachings of Jesus and his early followers. Key rituals in Christianity include baptism, which is a ritual of moral purification and initiation; and the Eucharist or Holy Communion, which is a symbolic remembrance of the last meal Jesus had with his followers.

Christianity gained influence and spread rapidly after it became the official religion of the Roman Empire in 380 CE. In 1054, the religion was formally split into the Eastern Orthodox Church (based in Constantinople) and the Roman Catholic Church (based in Rome). A second major division occurred in the 16th century during the Protestant Reformation, which challenged the authority of the Roman Catholic Church by arguing that the religious faith of the individual was more important than church hierarchy and church traditions.

The Protestant Reformation produced a lot of innovation and diversity within the Christian church. Protestants created many new **sects**, which were smaller and more loosely organized groups of believers who disagreed with the established church and tried to create their own authentic expression of religious faith. Over time, several of these sects became more established **denominations**, which means that their sect began to develop a more established bureaucracy and a common set of ritual practices. By the beginning of the 20th century there were a number of clearly established "mainline" Protestant denominations, including the Baptist, Methodist, Lutheran, Presbyterian, and Episcopal churches. But the spirit of protest and innovation continues within Protestantism, with new sects and denominations forming all the time.

Christianity continued to spread throughout the world because of the colonization of Africa, South America, and Asia by the powerful nations of Europe and North America. All of these powerful nations were majority Christian, and they believed that their religious faith was one of the things that made them superior to other societies. It was common practice to send Christian missionaries to the newly conquered territories, in order to introduce Christianity to the native

Sects A smaller and more loosely organized group of religious believers who disagree with the established church and try to create their own authentic expression of religious faith.

Denomination A religious sect that has begun to develop a more established bureaucracy and a common set of ritual practices.

Martin Luther

PAIRED CONCEPTS   Global and Local

Catholicism in Africa

Historically, the Catholic Church has been centered in Europe. More than half of all Catholic parishes and more than 40 percent of all Catholic priests are located in Europe (Pattison 2015). Today, however, the majority of Catholics live outside of Europe, and the fastest-growing Catholic population is in Africa. In fact, while the global Catholic population is growing at less than 1 percent per year, the Catholic population in Africa is increasing at a rate of nearly 20 percent annually. Social scientists project that by 2050 there will be nearly 90 million more Catholics in Africa than there will be in Europe (Saenz 2005).

Demography is a large factor behind the growth of Catholicism in Africa (where birth rates are higher), but there are also other important social forces at work. Levels of religiosity are very high in Africa, and missionaries see the large populations of Africans involved with traditional religions as good candidates for conversion. Changes within the Roman Catholic Church since the 1960s encouraged greater tolerance and understanding of other religious beliefs, and there has been a more conscious attempt to blend African symbols and culture into the practice of African Catholicism. Since the election of Pope Francis in 2013, there has been a conscious attempt in the Vatican to increase the number of African priests who have important leadership positions in the Catholic Church.

Catholicism in Africa has certain distinctive elements that are connected to the local culture. In 1965, Cardinal Paul Zoungrana (from Burkina Faso) wrote that the mission of African Catholicism was "to bring the faithful to meet Christ according to their African soul" (Ilo 2017: 58). Instead of forcing converts to adopt the same style of worship practiced in Europe, African priests have tried to create new styles that are connected to local cultures and traditions. In sub-Saharan Africa, it is common for African priests and bishops to be formally established as tribal elders and leaders of the community (Nyenyeme 2017: 81). In Zimbabwe, African drumming has become a part of the Catholic Church service (Pasura 2016). In Congo, the Catholic mass includes an invocation of ancestors, which draws on elements from traditional African theology.

As African Catholicism has grown, it has had an important influence on the larger global culture of the Catholic Church. For a long time these influences were resisted by Vatican leaders, but in 2013 many experts predicted that an African priest would be elected pope. The 2013 election was ultimately won by an Argentinian-born priest, Pope Francis, who was the first non-European pope in twelve hundred years. Pope Francis has worked hard to increase the visibility and influence of African priests, and he has led a change in emphasis for the Vatican that is more closely aligned with the interests of the African church. This includes more emphasis on the issue of global poverty, a greater willingness to criticize global capitalism, and a more assertive stance about the need to address climate change.

ACTIVE LEARNING

Find out: See if you can find the latest bulletin from the Catholic church of your local parish (many of them are available online). What evidence do you see about attempts by the local church to deal with, incorporate, and/or discuss global changes taking place within the Catholic Church? Are similar kinds of discussion taking place in other local religious communities where you live?

---

populations. Today, Australia and New Zealand are both majority Christian, and so are the nations located in sub-Saharan Africa, South America, Central America, and the Caribbean. In fact, more than half of the world's Christians live in countries that were once conquered and colonized by European nations.

ISLAM. With 1.6 billion adherents, Islam is the world's second-largest religion. There are currently 49 countries that are majority Muslim, located primarily in Africa, the Middle East, and parts of Central Asia. Islam is also the fastest-growing religion in the world, and recent research suggests that Islam will become the world's largest religion at some point during the second half of this century (Lipka and Hackett 2017). There are two main denominations of Islam. Sunnis are the largest group, accounting for between 87 and 90 percent of the total; the remaining Muslims are Shia (Pew Research Center 2012b).

Great Mosque of Mecca
Mecca is considered the holiest of cities in Islam. Devout Muslims hope to perform the pilgrimage called the *hajj,* where they visit Mecca to pray and renew their sense of purpose in the world.

Islam is a monotheistic religion, based on a belief in Allah and organized around the teachings of the prophet Muhammad. Muslims believe that Allah sent a number of prophets to teach people how to live properly. They believe that the final prophet was Muhammad, who was born in Mecca (in present-day Saudi Arabia) in 570. They believe that Muhammad received revelations from Allah throughout his life, which he recorded in the Quran, the sacred text of the Islamic religion. The key rituals are organized around the Five Pillars of Islam, which include a declaration of faith (*shahadah*), praying five times daily (*salat*), giving money to help the poor (*zakat*), fasting during the month of Ramadan (*sawm*), and making a pilgrimage to Mecca (*hajj*).

Proselytizing The attempt by an individual or an organization to convert other people to their own religious beliefs.

Islam spread rapidly throughout North Africa and into the Iberian peninsula of present-day Spain, through a combination of military conquest and religious **proselytizing**. It continued to expand as the official religion of the Ottoman Empire, which was centered in what is modern-day Turkey and controlled large parts of the Middle East, North Africa, and southwest Europe for nearly six hundred years, beginning in the 13th century.

The Ottoman Empire ended after defeat in World War I, in a way that had profound social and political consequences for the Islamic world (Fawaz 2014). Millions of Ottoman soldiers and citizens were killed during the war, and railroads and cities throughout the region were destroyed, leading to economic collapse and widespread famine. Politically, the Islamic caliphate was dissolved, and England and France controlled the redrawing of national borders in the Islamic world. The British took control of Egypt, Iraq, and Palestine, while the French took control of Lebanon and Syria. But these new boundaries were shaped mainly by the political and economic interests of the victorious powers, without consideration for the social and cultural history of the regions being divided. The Balfour Declaration of 1917 promised to create a national home for the Jewish people in Palestine, which led eventually to the creation of the nation of Israel in 1948. The dream of a renewed Islamic caliphate has been a major source of Arab nationalism and religious conflict ever since the end of World War I. We examine these events in further detail later in the chapter, when we discuss religious conflict.

HINDUISM. There are slightly more than one billion Hindus in the world today, located primarily in South Asia. Hindus are a religious majority in India, Nepal, and Mauritius, which together account for 97 percent of all Hindus in the world. The four main denominations of Hinduism are Vaishnavism, Shaivism, Shaktism, and Smartism.

Hinduism is the oldest religion in the world, with archaeological evidence showing that it has been practiced for more than four thousand years. The most sacred texts are the Vedas, which were written by Hindu scholars between 1200 and 200 BCE. Hindus believe in a cycle of birth, death, and rebirth, governed by a principle of karma in which the consequences of our actions will eventually be rewarded or punished, either in this life or in a subsequent lifetime. Hindus also believe in the importance of meditation, in which we withdraw our mind and senses from the distractions of the world in order to achieve a transcendental state of consciousness that is better able to appreciate the ineffable nature of human existence.

Compared to the other world religions, Hinduism blurs the distinction between monotheism and polytheism (Doniger 2013). Hindu texts describe many different deities, and it is common for religious adherents to pray to different gods depending on the situation. But there are other texts that describe a single Supreme Being, Brahman, which lacks any determinable characteristics; while Brahman is beyond comprehension in its original essence, it takes on a variety of different forms so that humans will be able to relate to it.

Statues of Hindu deities in Kapaleeshwarar Temple, Chennai, Tamil Nadu, India
Hinduism is the oldest religion in the world and blurs the distinction between monotheism and polytheism. There are diasporic Hindu communities around the world.

Today, while most Hindus continue to live in India, there are large diaspora populations in cities throughout the world. Transcendental meditation, yoga, and other Hindu meditation practices have also become popular worldwide.

BUDDHISM. There are about 500 million Buddhists in the world, with more than 95 percent of them living in the Asia-Pacific region. Buddhists are a religious majority in Cambodia, Thailand, Burma (Myanmar), Bhutan, Sri Lanka, Laos, and Mongolia. Nearly half of the world's Buddhists live in China, where they make up nearly 20 percent of the population.

Compared to the other world religions, Buddhism is much more focused on personal spiritual development. Like Hindus, Buddhists believe in reincarnation and the principle of karma. Buddhism does not emphasize the relationship between humanity and god, but instead stresses the development of morality and wisdom through the practices of meditation and reflection. The main sacred texts are the Sutras, which contain the words and teachings of the Buddha, Siddhartha Gautama, and his quest for enlightenment during the sixth century BCE.

As Buddhism spread throughout Asia from the sixth century onward, its teachers interacted with local cultures, and distinct traditions of Buddhism developed in Korea, Japan,

The Tian Tan Big Buddha and Po Lin Monastery
Buddhism is focused on personal spiritual development. It is mainly found in Asia but has spread around the world. Here tourists visit the Tian Tan Big Buddha at the Po Lin monastery in Hong Kong to pray and to be blessed with good fortune.

China, Myanmar, and Tibet. Although Buddhism was virtually unknown in the West before the 18th century, globalization brought greater awareness of Buddhist beliefs and practices. Today, Buddhist centers can be found in cities throughout the world. Buddhist practices such as Zen meditation are extremely popular in the West, resonating with the New Age spirituality that we discuss later in the chapter. Buddhism was particularly popular within the hippie culture of the 1960s, and it continues to be popular among celebrities in the West, with well-known converts such as Keanu Reeves, Richard Gere, Steve Jobs, and Kate Hudson.

Modern Society and Secularism

Most of the social scientists and philosophers who lived during the 18th and 19th centuries would be shocked to learn that religion still exists today. Arguing that religion was based on ignorance and superstition, they were convinced that it would disappear in a modern world committed to science and reason. Voltaire, the French philosopher, once wrote, "Nothing can be more contrary to religion and the clergy than reason and common sense." Karl Marx viewed religion as a form of ideology, and wrote that "the first requisite for the happiness of the people is the abolition of religion." Sigmund Freud described God as an illusion, which had once been useful as a way to restrain the violent impulses of society, but which would no longer be needed in an age of science. All of these thinkers shared the view that religion was an outmoded form of fictitious knowledge, which would naturally disappear and be replaced by science.

The Secularization Thesis

Secularization thesis The argument that religion will become less important in modern society.

In sociology, the argument that religion would become less important in modern society is known as the **secularization thesis**. Secularization does not mean that religion will disappear completely or lose all of its legitimacy, but rather that it will become less influential.

There are two ways to think about secularization. At the level of the individual, secularization means that religious faith is declining, that people are less likely to attend church, or both (Finke and Stark 1998). In this sense religion will continue to exist in a secularized society, but there will be fewer believers and fewer people attending church services. At a more public or macro level, secularization means that religious leaders and religious organizations have less influence and less authority in public debates about social issues (Chaves 1994). In this version of secularization, we can expect to see less religious language in our schools, fewer religious references made by our political leaders, and fewer religious leaders quoted in our newspapers.

Evidence for secularization is strongest in Western Europe, at least for Christian churches, where levels of religious belief and attendance are much lower than they used to be (Gorski and Altinordu 2008: 62). Nearly three-quarters of Northern Europeans do not even attend church once per month, and the rates of attendance are declining throughout Western Europe (Brenner 2016). Most European nations have a separation of church and state, in the sense that governments are religiously neutral and there is legal protection for people to believe (or not believe) what they want. The highest authority in public policy debates is given to scientists and doctors. Religious content is not prominent in popular culture (Figure 11.3).

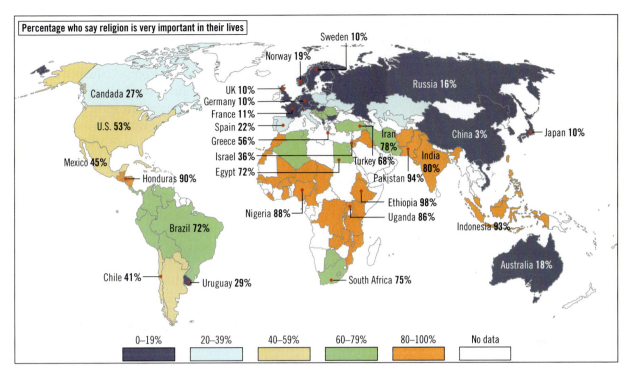

Figure 11.3   People in Europe and East Asia say religion is not very important to them.
Source: Pew Research Center surveys, 2008–2017. "The Age Gap in Religion Around the World."

In the United States, mainline Protestant churches have been losing members as well as political influence since the 1960s. Between 1965 and 1990, the Presbyterian Church lost about one-third of its members, the Episcopal Church lost about one-quarter, and the Methodist Church lost about 20 percent of its members. Churches throughout the country face financial crisis, with declining levels of donations and persistent staff shortages (Wuthnow 1997). The number of Americans who express no religious preference doubled during the 1990s, and continues to rise today (Hout and Fischer 2002).

While the mainline Protestant churches have experienced decline, the United States continues to be much more religious than most of Europe, and most sociologists argue that its history does not provide strong evidence for secularization. Survey research shows that while religiosity is slowly declining in the United States (Chaves 2017), more than 90 percent of Americans believe in God (Fahmy 2018), and around 35 percent continue to attend church weekly (Chaves 2017). Membership in evangelical churches has been on the rise since the 1960s, and conservative evangelical Christians have been a significant political force since the 1980s (Wuthnow 1989). Even among those Americans who express no religious preference, the vast majority maintain strong religious beliefs and consider themselves to be spiritual people (Hout and Fischer 2002; Fahmy 2018).

The Persistence of Religion

In fact, the evidence for the continuing importance of religion is very strong. Nearly 85 percent of the world's population maintains a religious affiliation, and 73 percent of the world's population lives in a country where people from their religion are a majority of the population (Pew Research Center 2012). Forty percent of all countries still had an official state religion in 2000, and

Pentecostal worship at the Brownsville Assembly, Pensacola, Florida, 2012
Pentecostalism is a renewal of and innovation in Christianity that emerged in 1910 in Los Angeles. Pentecostalism emphasizes a direct personal experience with the Holy Spirit, which is revealed in gifts of the spirit such as faith healing, prophecy, and speaking in tongues.

the available evidence indicates that this trend has been stable since 1970 (Barro and McCleary 2004). The sociologist Peter Berger, who helped develop the secularization thesis during the 1970s, admitted in 1999 that "the assumption that we live in a secularized world is false" (Berger 1999: 2).

NEW RELIGIOUS FORMS. One reason that religion continues to be important in society is because of the creation of new kinds of religious groups. Innovation and change have always been a part of the religious landscape, and such innovation has kept religion an important and relevant social force. In the Catholic Church, a new form of liberation theology developed during the 1950s (particularly in Latin America), with an emphasis on human rights and a criticism of global capitalism's indifference to the poor (Casanova 1994). Within Judaism, the World Union of Progressive Judaism (known in the United States as Reform Judaism) grew rapidly in popularity throughout the 20th century, with an emphasis on inclusiveness and progressive values (Kaplan 2003).

Religious change has also come from new forms of religion, which have developed as a response to modern society and as an attempt to understand it. One of the biggest of these new religious forms is Pentecostalism. First emerging in 1910 in Los Angeles, Pentecostalism emphasizes a direct personal experience with the divine, which is revealed in gifts of the spirit such as faith healing, prophecy, and speaking in tongues. The focus on personal transformation makes Pentecostalism extremely flexible and adaptable to local cultures (Thompson 2012). Today, there are more than 100 million Pentecostals in the world, and there is a large Pentecostal presence throughout South America, Africa, and Asia.

Another new religion is the Baha'i faith, which was established in Iran in 1863. An explicitly tolerant and pluralist faith, Baha'is believe that there is a truth and a validity in all religious faiths. Baha'is believe that all religions are trying to describe the same reality, but are limited by the culture and the experiences of their time. They believe that there is no conflict between science and religion, because both are trying to improve the human condition and shed light on the nature of human conduct. Baha'is strive for the abolition of all forms of prejudice, the end of

Yoido Full Gospel Church, South Korea
This congregation has more than 800,000 members.

global poverty and inequality, equality between men and women, and a world bound by the principle of justice. These messages have been enthusiastically embraced, and today the Baha'i faith is the second-fastest-growing religion in the world.

The focus on personal experience, pluralism, and tolerance is also shared by New Age spirituality, a type of informal religious practice that has become increasingly common in Western societies. New Age movements became popular during the 1970s, as a generation of people who had grown up during the 1960s sought a form of spirituality that was not connected to established churches (Roof 1993). These spiritual seekers were open to a wide variety of practices, combining the teachings from Hinduism, Buddhism, Jewish mysticism, neo-paganism, meditation, yoga, and other forms of spiritual practice. Instead of joining an established church, their goal was to find personal fulfillment, an inclusive and welcoming community, and a diverse variety of spiritual practices.

This kind of "quest culture" has influenced religious practices throughout the United States, with a growing emphasis on spiritual exploration and a culture of choice (Roof 1999). We can see this with the large numbers of people who describe themselves as "spiritual but not religious," the incorporation of yoga and meditation in established churches and synagogues, and even in the creation of lifestyle organizations such as Catholic Surfing Ministries, which organizes "sacramental surfing retreats" at beaches all along the East Coast of the United States.

Religion and Politics

Religion has always been connected to issues of power, conflict, and politics. The worldwide spread of Christianity was closely connected to the political power of the Roman Empire, and the spread of Islam was linked to the political history of the Ottoman Empire.

As secular governments work to establish a formal separation of church and state, they have sometimes found themselves in open political conflict with religious organizations. The Soviet Union had an official doctrine of state atheism, and had policies in place to control, repress, and ultimately eliminate religion. In China, from 1966 to 1976, government leaders seized the assets of churches, denounced religion as a worthless superstition, and declared that the open practice of religion was illegal. In France, for about five years after the 1789 Revolution, the new government passed anti-church laws, exiled and imprisoned thousands of priests, banned religious holidays, and converted churches to "temples of reason." Even today, the French policy of *laïcité* (secularism) bans the public display of religious symbols.

Religious organizations and adherents have resisted the attempts by secular governments to reduce the power and the visibility of religion. In China as well as the Soviet Union,

Religion and Politics
The French policy of *laïcité* is the core constitutional principle of French democracy, which states that France is a secular republic. France has banned the public display of religious symbols, and politics over wearing a headscarf or burkini (a burka designed as modest swimwear) continue to be contentious.

PAIRED CONCEPTS   Solidarity and Conflict

Religious Proselytizing

A central mission of many religious groups is proselytizing, which refers to the attempt by an individual or organization to convert other people to their own religious beliefs. Proselytizing is a significant source of solidarity for religious believers who practice it. Most proselytizing takes place in groups, where religious adherents reaffirm their common identity and their common bond through the collective practice of talking to others and trying to convert them.

Proselytizing has a complicated and ambiguous legal status. On the one hand, laws that protect the freedom of expression would seem to protect proselytizing, since it is a form of speech. Proselytizing is also a central component of many religions, so banning it would seem to violate the 1948 United Nations Declaration of Human Rights, which states that believers must be allowed to publicly manifest their religious beliefs (Danchin 2008).

On the other hand, proselytizing can often seem coercive, threatening, and intrusive to the people being proselytized. When government-supported missionary groups travel abroad, the aid they provide to the poor is often linked to the practice of proselytizing, in a way that can make it seem like material help is connected to religious conversion (Bandarage 2015). In countries where conversion from the official religion is illegal, proselytizers

actually put their targets at significant legal and physical risk. In the workplace, proselytizing has led to lawsuits, with courts having to decide whether the religious proselytizing is creating a hostile workplace that should be stopped, or an annoyance that will have to be tolerated (Wolf, Friedman, and Sutherland 1998).

Most laws protecting religious freedom recognize that proselytizing is a sensitive issue, and they have tended to avoid mentioning it explicitly as a protected practice (Danchin 2008: 259). Some courts have tried to distinguish between "proper" and "improper" proselytizing, suggesting that only proper proselytizing needed to be protected; but these courts have not been very clear about how to draw such a distinction (Danchin 2008: 273). There is also a concern about the history and the context in which proselytizing has taken place, particularly in places such as Africa, where proselytizing missionaries were part of the system of colonization by Western powers.

ACTIVE LEARNING

Find out: Search the internet for a lawsuit in your state about proselytizing (for example, you might search "Massachusetts lawsuit about proselytizing"). Describe the case. What were the main issues? What was the resolution of the case?

---

religious practice continued in secret during the period when repression was strongest, enabling a religious revival to occur as soon as the government became more tolerant. In France, there was widespread resistance to the attempts at de-Christianization during the 1970s (Anderson 2007). Today, the French policy of *laïcité* is very controversial, with many French citizens protesting that the policy is disrespectful to people who have deeply held religious convictions.

PUBLIC RELIGION. As the previous discussion makes clear, religion continues to be an important presence in society. While most democratic countries maintain a formal separation between government and religion, religion continues to be a meaningful part of people's lives, and it continues to be a source of influence in political life.

In his book *Public Religion in the Modern World*, sociologist Jose Casanova argues that most churches are unwilling to limit themselves to the spiritual issues that concern their adherents (Casanova 1994). Instead, they aggressively participate in social and political debates about public issues, affairs, and policies. Casanova refers to this as **public religion**, which happens when

Public religion A situation in which individuals and organizations make faith-based moral arguments about the public good.

individuals and organizations make faith-based moral arguments about the public good.

We can see examples of public religion all over the world. Religious groups have been a major force driving nationalist movements in places as diverse as India, Sri Lanka, Iran, Algeria, Egypt, and Israel (Friedland 2001). In the United States, Christian evangelicals have been an increasingly vocal part of the political scene, with a strong focus on issues surrounding reproduction, sexuality, and the public display of religious symbols (Lienesch 1993). Throughout Europe and North America, religious groups have challenged the "wall of separation" between church and state, arguing that religious perspectives have just as much right to participate in public discussions as scientific or legal ones (Joppke 2015).

RELIGIOUS FUNDAMENTALISM. One response to modern society has been the rise of religious fundamentalism, in which religious militants and "true believers" try to create an alternative to secular institutions and behaviors (Almond, Appleby, and Sivan 2003: 17). According to sociologists Michael Emerson and David Hartman, the term "fundamentalism" was first used to describe a form of conservative Protestantism that developed in the United States between 1870 and 1925, as part of a conflict with other Protestants who wanted to make the religion more relevant for a modern and progressive society (Emerson and Hartman 2006: 132–33). Today, however, religious fundamentalists are more likely to see themselves in direct conflict with the values and the political institutions of modern, secular society.

Contemporary versions of religious fundamentalism began to emerge during the 1970s, and today there are versions of religious fundamentalism among all of the major world religions (Emerson and Hartman 2006: 128). In the United States, Christian fundamentalists became a powerful political influence during the 1980s, fighting against abortion, homosexuality, and the spread of secular values in popular culture. In India, Hindu fundamentalists have used mob violence and intimidation to attack religious minorities in an effort to create a "pure" Hindu nation. In Iran, Islamic fundamentalists overthrew the secular monarchy in 1979, replacing it with an Islamic Republic in which Islamic laws are strictly enforced. Fundamentalist groups continue to be a significant presence in countries throughout the world. Jewish fundamentalist groups factor strongly in Israel, and Buddhist fundamentalist groups have been a part of religious conflicts in Thailand, Sri Lanka, and Myanmar.

Religious fundamentalist movements share a number of common features (Almond, Sivan, and Appleby 2003). They believe that their religion is under attack by modern society, and they identify selective features of modern society that they find particularly evil. They emphasize the truth

Conflict with secular society
Pro-life groups protest the US Department of Health and Human Services mandate of 2012 that requires all employers to provide free contraceptives, sterilization, and abortion-inducing drugs through their health plans. Many religious groups argued the mandate was an attack on freedom of conscience and religious liberty.

and accuracy of their sacred text, and they insist that the laws of this text have more authority than other national or international laws. They draw sharp boundaries between believers and nonbelievers, and they have strict requirements about how believers should behave. They have strongly conservative views about gender and family, believing that men and women have separate roles to play in society. They are intolerant of dissenting beliefs, and their goal is to have their own religious beliefs placed at the center of public life.

Some fundamentalist groups use violence to dramatize their cause, to announce their presence, and to strike at the symbols of the societies they are trying to overcome. However, the relationship between fundamentalism and violence is complex. While the frequency of religious violence has been increasing, the majority of fundamentalist groups do not use violence (Juergensmeyer 2003). Those that do use violence are more likely to appear in countries that restrict religious freedoms or favor one religion over the others (Iannaccone 1997). They are also more likely to appear in communities that have a lot of poverty, and in countries that fail to provide basic social services (Berman 2009).

Science as a Social Institution

In 2010, Lawrence Krauss, a physicist from Arizona State University published an article in *Scientific American*, titled "Faith and Foolishness: When Religious Beliefs Become Dangerous" (Krauss 2010). In the article, Krauss complained about the lack of scientific literacy in the United States, observing that the people who are the least willing to accept scientific reality are the same ones who are the most religious. Arguing that "religious leaders should be held accountable when their irrational ideas turn harmful," he warned that an unwillingness to publicly criticize religion will lead to bad public policies and the promotion of ignorance.

Why did Krauss care about the scientific literacy of ordinary people, and why did he think that publicly denouncing religion would lead to better public policies? As we discussed in Chapter 3, the goal of science is to produce knowledge that is factually accurate, falsifiable, and can withstand the critical judgment of the scientific community. The cornerstone of science is the principle of peer review, which means that scientific research needs to be evaluated anonymously by other scientific experts. Scientific advances do not require scientific literacy by the general population, and they definitely do not require the public criticism of religion.

Scientists care about public policy because they are members of society, and they believe that their society will be a better place if policy-makers listen to them. Many scientists realize that religion is an alternative way of knowing the world, and they know that religion has historically provided

March for Science
Thousands of protesters marched in 2017 to protest US federal budget cuts that threaten scientific research.

CAREERS

Women's Careers in STEM

Careers in science, technology, engineering, and mathematics (STEM) offer some of the best-paid jobs in today's economy. According to a recent survey, the average advertised salary for entry-level jobs in a STEM field was more than 25 percent higher than an entry-level job in a non-STEM field. Students who get degrees in a STEM field have a major advantage in the job market too; while nearly half of all entry-level jobs requiring a college degree are in STEM fields, fewer than 30 percent of all college graduates earn a college degree in a STEM field (Burning Glass 2014). Many politicians and experts argue that STEM education is the key to the future of the economy, and hundreds of millions of dollars are being invested in this effort.

Gender inequality continues to be a significant challenge in STEM fields. Women are 48 percent of the total workforce in the United States, but they are only 24 percent of the employees in STEM fields. Among those people who have a college degree in science or engineering, men are employed in STEM fields at twice the rate of women (Landivar 2013). And the disparities are even worse in fields related to engineering and computer science, which are the largest and fastest-growing parts of the STEM sector.

A 2010 research report by the American Association of University Women identified several key factors that are reducing participation by women in STEM fields (Hill, Corbett, and Rose 2010):

- There are still powerful stereotypes suggesting that women are not as good as men at math and science, which leads to an implicit bias against women pursuing these fields. For boys and girls who have the same abilities in math, the boys will consistently rate their own abilities higher than the girls will rate theirs. This has consequences for the courses they choose to take, as well as their behavior and self-confidence in science classes. It also influences the likelihood that they will express an interest in pursuing a STEM career.
- When faced with the stereotype that women are not as good at math, many talented girls respond by reducing their interest in STEM careers. In other words, if girls do not believe that they have the ability to do science or engineering, they will choose a different career, even when all evidence suggests that they have plenty of scientific aptitude.
- The culture of STEM departments in colleges and universities too often privileges men in the recruitment of students, the kind of informal socializing that takes place, and the opportunities for research collaborations with faculty. Women students and faculty often feel excluded in these environments, making it more difficult for them to receive effective mentoring or to succeed.
- The organization of family responsibilities falls more heavily on women, even when they are in STEM careers. This makes many tech companies less likely to recruit women, due to the assumption that they will be less productive workers when they have children.
- There is still rampant sexism in many tech companies. Successful women in the tech sector are perceived as more unlikeable than successful men, and if they try to be more likeable, they often find themselves dealing with unwanted sexual advances (Mundy 2017). They find themselves being dismissed and interrupted constantly, even by male workers who are much lower in the corporate bureaucracy.

To respond effectively to these challenges, social scientists suggest that teachers need to work harder to recognize and counteract stereotypes about gender and math. Schools need to develop aggressive outreach efforts to encourage girls to take STEM courses. Colleges, universities, and tech companies need to adjust their cultures in a way that makes them more welcoming to women. They need to address issues related to work-life balance, so they do not penalize women unfairly. Workers, social movements, and journalists need to publicize instances of sexism in the tech workforce, and they need

Women in STEM
Women are 48 percent of the total workforce in the United States, but they are only 24 percent of the employees in STEM fields. Evidence suggests that gender stereotypes and discrimination account for this pattern. In recent years, significant efforts have been made to recruit women into STEM fields.

to highlight the work of organizations offering better models for promoting gender equity in STEM.

ACTIVE LEARNING

Explore: Project Include is an initiative that was started by women CEOs in the tech sector. It is an advocacy group whose goal is to get more companies to implement gender diversity solutions based on inclusion, accountability, and comprehensiveness. Visit their website (projectinclude. org) and explore some of their activities, recommendations, and company case studies.

a type of authority that has often been in conflict with science. These are not their only motivations, of course. But it is important to study the social dimensions of science if we want to understand why scientists act the way they do.

The Sociology of Science

Research in the sociology of science examines how scientists do their work and how science is socially organized. One of the most important scholars in the sociology of science was Robert Merton (1910–2003). Merton was interested in the "extra-scientific elements" that influenced scientific interests, practices, and reward systems (Merton [1942] 1973). To study this, he collected data from the biographies and journals of scientists. He examined publication rates, inventions, the number of scientists in a given field, and the status markers associated with different scientists and scientific organizations. He looked at scientific publications, and tracked how different research problems changed over time.

Scientists work hard to convince the larger public about the virtues of science, and they do this by emphasizing a set of values and expectations about scientific practice. In his famous essay on the normative structure of science, Merton ([1942] 1973) identified four basic values in science. First, scientists are committed to the principle of universalism, which means that scientific findings are evaluated according to their objective truth rather than the personal qualities of a particular scientist. It also means that scientists are committed first and foremost to the advancement of science, which they hold to be more important than all other loyalties, including national identity. Second, they believe in the communal character of science, which means that they believe in full and open communication of scientific findings. Related to this, scientists are committed to the principle of disinterestedness, in the sense that they are supposed to be committed to the pursuit of scientific knowledge itself rather than the pursuit of personal success. Last, scientists are committed to the principle of organized skepticism, which means that they are supposed to demand proof of any claim that is made and to test competing explanations, rather than simply believing that one explanation is correct.

Matthew effect A tendency in science in which the most eminent scientists get most of the recognition and rewards for scientific research.

The normative structure of science frequently places scientists in conflict with nonscientists (Gieryn 1999). Scientists are suspicious of people in business who try to make money from new scientific technologies, particularly when those businesses make claims about their products that are misleading or not

Inequality and Privilege

Science and the Matthew Effect

In the world of scientific research, there is a tendency to reward those scientists who are already powerful and successful. Robert Merton (1968) called this the **Matthew effect,** relying primarily on research by sociologist Harriet Zuckerman (1937–). Merton named his theory after a passage in the Christian Bible from the Gospel of Matthew, which reads, "For whoever has will be given more, and they will have an abundance. Whoever does not have, even what they have will be taken from them." In other words, the rich get richer, and the poor get poorer. Merton argued that this was true in science, just as it was true in other parts of social life.

The Matthew effect in science works in several different ways. Examining the careers of scientists, Zuckerman (1977) found that those scientists who receive early recognition tend to be more productive throughout their careers than those who do not receive early recognition. Scientists who publish a prominent article early in their careers get a better first job, with better resources for them to set up their own research labs. Because they are located at more prestigious universities, they also develop more valuable social networks. They can collaborate with eminent senior colleagues, and they have the assistance of many postdoctoral and graduate student researchers to help them develop and conduct their research (Ebadi and Schiffauerova 2015). Because they are at more prestigious universities and better-resourced labs, they are more likely to get research grants.

The Matthew effect also influences collaborative research. In collaborative research and co-authored publications, the most eminent scientist in the group will get the most credit for the work (Perc 2014). Credit comes in a number of different forms. The big scientific prizes (such as the Nobel Prize) almost always go to the most eminent scientist in a research team (Zuckerman 1977). This scientist will get the most media coverage, and the most speaking invitations. Other scientists will associate the major findings of the research team disproportionately with the eminent scientist, so that over time the other members of the research team are virtually forgotten.

Historically, the Matthew effect has profoundly suppressed the careers of women scientists. Their contributions have consistently been ignored and denied credit, often disappearing altogether from the history of science (Rossiter 1993). Rossiter calls this the "Matthew Matilda" effect. For example, the biophysicist Rosalind Franklin was consistently denied recognition for her role in discovering the genetic structure of DNA, while her male colleagues James Watson and Francis Crick received all the recognition. Jocelyn Bell discovered pulsars as a graduate student in 1967, but the Nobel Prize for the discovery was awarded to her male supervisor, Anthony Hewish. Even Merton's theory of the Matthew effect was influenced by the Matthew Matilda effect. Despite the fact that Merton consistently credited the key research findings to Harriet Zuckerman, who was a Columbia University sociology professor as well as Merton's wife, the overwhelming credit for the theory of the Matthew effect in science has gone to Robert Merton (Merton 1988).

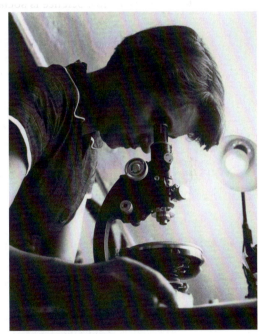

Scientific Recognition
The biophysicist Rosalind Franklin was consistently denied recognition for her role in discovering the genetic structure of DNA, while her male colleagues James Watson and Francis Crick received all the recognition. This is a common pattern in the history of science.

ACTIVE LEARNING

Find out: Talk to one of your professors, and ask them if they have had any direct experience with the Matthew effect in their own careers. Do they think the situation is getting better? What do they think could be done to reduce the influence of the Matthew effect in their field?

scientifically supported. They criticize people who politicize science, and they criticize politicians who make policy decisions that are not based on scientific principles. Last, scientists are critical of those who believe that religious knowledge is as valuable as science.

Many social factors shape the practice of science and the organization of scientists. There is an established hierarchy of scientific disciplines, which has been in place for nearly two hundred years. The physical sciences are at the top, the social sciences are at the bottom, and the biological sciences are in the middle (Smith et al. 2000). Scientists in high-status disciplines have more resources at their disposal, including higher salaries, better laboratory spaces, more research grant money and autonomy, and higher levels of authority. This leads to inequalities in the world of science. Like in other areas of social life, scientists who have more resources tend to act in ways that preserve their privileges.

Science and Technology Studies

The scholarly field of science and technology studies uses the tools of sociological research to ask questions about the production of scientific knowledge. How do scientists come to recognize something as a fact? What styles of writing do they use in their publications? How do they learn to use lab equipment? How do they learn to "clean" their data, eliminating pieces of information that are caused by human or machine error? When they confront data that challenge their hypotheses, how do they learn what is the most effective response? These kinds of questions focus attention on the ways that scientific knowledge is a social accomplishment.

From a sociological point of view, the production of scientific knowledge is shaped in significant ways by the dynamics of solidarity and conflict. The solidarity of scientists is reaffirmed in their choice of specialty topic, their use of specialized jargon, their membership in specific research networks and laboratories, and their choice to publish in specific scientific journals (Shapin 1995: 300–3). Their solidarity is also reaffirmed in their competition with rival research teams, scientific disciplines, and other producers of knowledge whose work they dismiss as "pseudoscience" (Panofsky 2014).

In their book *Laboratory Life: The Construction of Scientific Facts* (1979), sociologists Bruno Latour and Steve Woolgar visited a research laboratory in order to observe how scientific knowledge actually gets created. The scientists they studied wrote about their research in a way that emphasized a surprising moment of discovery, rather than focusing on the research procedures that were a key part of their work. They evaluated other people's research mainly in terms of the "reliability" of the researcher, which they measured by looking more closely at the record of grants and publications than at the research design of their studies. These scientists described their choice of topics in terms of what was likely to be trendy in the near future. They argued that the only way to properly study the substance they were investigating was to use expensive equipment that was available to a very small number of scientific labs. They produced a lot of very significant scientific findings, to be sure. But every part of their work was shaped by social dynamics. The focus on the social dimensions of scientific practice reminds us that scientists are real people, and that "doing science" is a craft that requires both skill and handiwork.

Structure and Contingency

The Invention of Velcro

Scientists and engineers do not spend their entire lives in the lab doing research or testing new products. They live in the world, and in their ordinary lives they sometimes stumble onto solutions to problems they had been trying to solve for a long time. Probably the most famous example of this is the discovery of penicillin in 1928, by the Scottish biologist Alexander Fleming. Fleming was experimenting with different treatments for the flu, when he left for a summer vacation with his family. When he returned to his lab after the vacation—having not cleaned it properly—he noticed a fungus surrounding one of the cultures he had left in a petri dish. Upon further analysis of the fungus, he discovered that it killed many different disease-causing bacteria. Fleming was awarded the Nobel Prize in Medicine for his accidental discovery of penicillin.

Sometimes scientists and engineers stumble across discoveries they didn't even know they were looking for. In 1941, an electrical engineer named George de Mestral was taking his dog for a walk on a mountain trail in Switzerland. When he returned home he noticed that his pants and his dog's fur were covered with cockle-burs. Curious about how the burs managed to attach themselves, he put them under a microscope to look more closely. Discovering that the hooks on the burs were attaching themselves to the loops in the fabric of his pants, he realized that there might be practical uses for such a fastening system. Mestral created a synthetic equivalent of the hook-and-loop system, which he patented in 1955 and trademarked with the name Velcro. Initial sales were slow, but they picked up in the 1960s after NASA began using Velcro in the manufacture of its space suits. Sports apparel manufacturers followed, and Velcro soon found its way into dozens of different products, ranging from clothes to automobile parts to medical devices. Today, more than 2.5 million miles of Velcro tape are produced and sold each year.

"Accidental" discoveries like these are not complete accidents, of course. In the case of penicillin, Alexander Fleming was actively trying to develop medicines to treat disease. Even though the fungus developed because Fleming didn't clean his lab properly, it was only because he was trained as a biologist that he was able to recognize what the mold was doing to the bacteria around it. As for Mestral, his training as an engineer meant that he was always on the lookout for solutions to potential problems, and he had the technical skill to turn his curiosity into real products. In both cases, the accidental discovery was structured by the socialization that comes with being a scientist.

Accidental discoveries
Velcro was invented in the 1940s by scientist George de Mestral. The idea came when he noticed how burrs attached to his dog. The ability to recognize the possibilities and create Velcro came from his training as a scientist and engineer.

ACTIVE LEARNING

Find out: Can you identify other important accidental discoveries? How did they get discovered? What social conditions made it more likely that the person who made the discovery would have realized what they had stumbled into?

The Crisis of Knowing, and the Importance of Belief

Because skepticism is central to the scientific worldview, it was probably inevitable that the rise of science would lead to a loss of certainty about how the world works. Science was able to launch a powerful attack on religion, tradition, and other forms of nonscientific knowledge, but those other forms of

Knowledge and belief
The skeptical attitude of science can undermine certainty about what we know. For knowledge to exist, however, belief is an important element. Scientists believe in scientific methods for reaching truth. All ways of knowing, including scientific ones, contain elements of belief.

Epistemology A branch of philosophy that explores how we know whether a statement or a fact is actually true.

Relativism The idea that truth depends on the group, the community, the society, and the culture to which a person belongs.

knowledge still influence people throughout the world. Religious organizations have pushed back against secularization, challenging the idea that scientific knowledge is the only thing that should be respected in public debates about social issues. The sociology of science has shown that scientists work in a realm of power and inequality, in which minority groups and new entrants struggle to gain recognition for their work. The utopian hopes for science have mostly disappeared, as societies continue to find themselves beset with hunger, poverty, injustice, inequality, pollution, natural disasters, and the effects of modern warfare.

Epistemological Doubts

Epistemology is a branch of philosophy that asks, "How do we know whether a statement or a fact is actually true?" For a scientific epistemology, we know that knowledge about the world is true when it offers a good description, explanation, and prediction of natural reality. Scientists recognize that the knowledge they produce is subject to revision. New facts emerge, new technologies allow us to see things we could not see before, and new experiments help us test competing explanations to see which one is actually correct. The scientist approaches each new piece of evidence with skepticism. But she also believes that, over time, science will yield progressively better knowledge about the world.

Not everyone believes in the superiority of scientific knowledge. Politicians, policy-makers, and businesspeople often criticize scientists for spending too much time in the lab and not enough time in the "real world." The result, they argue, is that science is not able to offer practical solutions for the problems people face. Religious conservatives argue that scientists do not respect people of faith. Using social media to publicize cases where scientists falsify data and act inappropriately, some people try to discredit the credibility of the scientific enterprise. Many scientists feel themselves to be under attack.

As scientific knowledge continues to be challenged by other forms of expertise, it becomes more difficult to be certain about what we believe to be true. People are more aware than ever that not everyone shares their epistemology, and this is true whether they believe in science, religion, common sense, or some other form of knowledge. Philosophers and other intellectuals argue that relativism is one of the biggest challenges facing the modern world. **Relativism** means that truth depends on the group, the community, the society, and the culture to which a person belongs. Ideas about universal truths that are the same everywhere and for everyone are less persuasive than they used to be (Stenmark 2015). But people are often unsatisfied with an epistemology of relativism, because relativism makes it extremely difficult to distinguish between good and bad.

Can Science and Religion Coexist?

As we saw at the beginning of this chapter, with the discussion of the Yale Program on Climate Change Communication, scientists and religious leaders are beginning to think about how they can coexist and cooperate to try to solve important social problems.

In recent years, some of the world's leading philosophers have begun to develop a theory of a **post-secular society**, in which religious ideas and scientific ideas need to learn from each other (Habermas 2008; Taylor 2007). They argue that the continued existence of religion does not have to be a threat to a secularizing society, and that the two can coexist more harmoniously if scientists stop attacking religious epistemologies. They argue that a modern society based on tolerance has to be more tolerant of religion. In fact, despite the presence of some scientists who continue to publicly criticize religion, sociological research shows that the majority of scientists believe that science and religion operate in separate spheres, and are not in conflict with each other (Ecklund et al. 2016).

The coexistence of science and religion
In post-secular society, theorists argue that science and religion should try to learn from each other. Science must be more tolerant of religious belief, which offers resources for moral learning and moral decision-making. Religion must embrace an attitude of tolerance toward science and scientific change and also accept the validity of law.

Theories of post-secularism argue that secular belief systems and scientific epistemologies have a lot to learn from religion. Religious writings have long focused on moral questions about how to live a good life or how to be a good person (Habermas 2008). Religion provides a "sense of fullness" and a commitment to a higher purpose that can motivate people to contribute to the common good, and this remains true in today's secular and scientific age (Taylor 2007). For many people, a belief in a higher power reduces anxiety and improves psychological well-being. Belief encourages people to act less selfishly toward others, and to remain engaged in the world. Many of the most important social movement leaders of the 20th century were religious, and there is good evidence that this continues to be the case today (Smith 1996).

At the same time, theories of post-secularism point out that a peaceful coexistence between science and religion requires that religious people also make accommodations. First, they need to embrace an attitude of tolerance toward religious and scientific ideas that are different from their own religious beliefs. Second, they need to accept the authority of their society's laws, even when those laws are different from tenets of their religious faith. Finally, they need to accept the reality that scientific knowledge has tremendous authority in modern society, and that scientists will play a crucial role in designing public policies. In fact, sociological research shows that religious people are just as likely as nonreligious people to seek out scientific knowledge and to accept its legitimacy, unless religion and science are making directly contradictory claims, or they are suspicious of scientists' moral agenda about a particular issue (Evans 2011).

Post-secular society A society in which religion and science coexist harmoniously, and where there is an attempt to create mutual learning and respect between religious ideas and scientific ideas.

CASE STUDY

Debating Evolution in Public Schools

One of the most famous trials in American history was a 1925 case, *The State of Tennessee v. John Thomas Scopes.* Commonly referred to as the "Scopes Monkey Trial," the case involved a high school teacher who had violated the Butler Law, which made it illegal to teach evolution in a public school. The trial received national publicity, both because the two sides were represented by high-profile attorneys and because it involved a highly charged conflict between science and religion. It was also the first US trial to be broadcast live over the radio.

One of the most unusual parts of the trial happened when the defense attorney (Clarence Darrow) called the prosecuting attorney (William Jennings Bryan) to the stand, in order to question him about whether the Bible should be interpreted literally, and whether it was reasonable to use the Bible to teach science. Bryan complained that the questions were intended "to cast ridicule on everybody who believes in the Bible"; Darrow responded that his purpose was "preventing bigots and ignoramuses from controlling the education of the United States." After two hours of this, the judge in the trial declared that the entire cross-examination was irrelevant to the case and should be removed from the official trial record. Scopes was found guilty, and the ruling was reaffirmed when it was appealed to the Tennessee Supreme Court.

Political, cultural, and legal opinions became much more supportive of teaching evolution during the 1960s. Congress passed the National Defense Education Act in 1958, which increased funding for science education and led to the creation of new textbooks

that included evolution. Tennessee repealed the Butler Law in 1967. In 1968, the US Supreme Court ruled that bans against teaching evolution were unconstitutional, because they violated the Establishment Clause of the First Amendment.

The origin of the Scopes Monkey Trial can be traced to the *power* of the church in Tennessee. The law against teaching evolution was sponsored by John Butler, who was a farmer, an elected politician, and the head of an influential religious organization called the World Christian Fundamentals Association. This law met immediate *resistance* from the American Civil Liberties Union (ACLU), which offered to defend any teacher in Tennessee who was willing to defy the Butler Act. This resistance was ineffective in the short term, as Scopes lost his legal case. But it proved to be effective in the long term,

The *conflict* between creationists and evolutionists created strong feelings of *solidarity* on both sides of the dispute. Five years after the Scopes trial, Christian organizations founded William Jennings Bryan University (known today as Bryan College) in Dayton, Tennessee, the town where the trial had taken place. The stated purpose of the college was to create a community of Christian learning, which provided "for the higher education of men and women under auspices distinctly Christian and spiritual." Secular and scientific groups also used the trial to create solidarity. The ACLU used the case to encourage more people to join their organization. The scientific community recognized the conflict as an opportunity to make millions of Americans aware of the scientific worldview. Even today, when the legal questions would seem to have been settled, the conflict over teaching evolution is a rallying call and a major source of fundraising. Religious groups continue to organize against teaching evolution, developing new legal challenges that will allow other theories to be taught alongside it.

The Scopes Monkey Trial was also shaped by the social organization of *inequality* and *privilege.* Dayton, Tennessee, was a small town of fewer than two thousand people in the 1920s. While the town had once had a relatively successful mining operation, by the 1920s its economy was in decline due to mining accidents and declining market prices for iron ore. In fact, the trial was in many ways a publicity stunt. Scopes was actually recruited by a group of local businessmen, who were convinced that the trial would bring tourism revenue into the town. Even today, the Scopes Trial Museum is the most popular attraction in Dayton, and the Scopes

The Scopes Trial of 1925
William Jennings Bryan interrogated by Clarence Darrow (standing right). Proceedings of the Scopes Monkey Trial were held outside due to the extreme heat of July 20, 1925. Photo by Watson Davis.

CASE STUDY CONTINUED

Trial Festival is the biggest tourism weekend of the year. As a small and poor town, though, Dayton could not control what people from more privileged backgrounds thought of them. When the famous Baltimore journalist H. L. Mencken wrote about the trial, he called the city of Dayton "Monkeytown." Describing the townsfolk as morons, hillbillies, and ignoramuses, Mencken criticized the trial as "a universal joke." The 1960 movie of the trial, *Inherit the Wind*, portrayed the people of Dayton as dangerous religious fanatics.

While the trial was intended to challenge a *local* law and to boost the local economy, it became a *global* media event. More than 150 journalists came to Dayton to cover the trial, traveling from places as far away as Hong Kong and London. Mencken's coverage of the trial was published in newspapers around the country, and the Chicago radio station WGN broadcast the trial live. More than 150,000 words were sent out about the trial every day via telegraph to journalists and writers around the world.

The different people who cooperated to bring about the Scopes trial were correct that the *structure* of the event would bring a lot of publicity. The attorneys were well-known celebrities who attracted a lot of media attention, and the ACLU was very skilled at creating the kind of publicity that would attract the attention of journalists around the world. But they could not contain the event. As people descended upon Dayton to participate in the media spectacle, the *contingency* of the event turned it into a carnival. A circus owner brought his trained monkey to the trial every day. Dressed in a suit and top hat, the monkey played a miniature piano outside the courthouse and posed for photographs with tourists. Bible salesmen roamed the streets, as did vendors selling stuffed monkeys, street performers, and ministers preaching against the evil of ice cream and coffee. *Time* magazine described the scene as a "fantastic cross between a circus and a holy war" (Moore and McComas 2016: 63).

LEARNING GOALS REVISITED

11.1 Describe the main differences between religious and scientific cosmologies.

- Religious cosmologies describe the world by making reference to mysterious, magical, and incalculable forces.

- Religious cosmologies include a moral component, in which they provide a framework to help people distinguish between right and wrong.

- Religious cosmologies provide their adherents with a theory about the meaning of human life that is grounded in belief, faith, and sacrifice.

- Scientific cosmologies are based on evidence, where the goal is to produce reliable knowledge about the world.

- Scientific cosmologies are based on the belief that people can create a better society if they cast aside older forms of knowledge and replace them with science.

11.2 Describe how religion and science are organized as social institutions.

- Religion is a unified system of beliefs and practices related to sacred things, which unites all of its adherents into a single moral community.

- As a social institution, religion has three elements: (1) the division of the world into groups of sacred and profane things; (2) a set of rituals, where people come together to reaffirm the meaning of the sacred; and (3) an explanation and a response to the existence of suffering in the world.

- As a social institution, science is committed to a set of values and expectations about good scientific practice. These values include universalism, the communal character of science, disinterestedness, and organized skepticism. Scientists are often critical of people in society who do not follow these values.

- Science is organized in a hierarchical way. Some scientific fields have higher status than others. Eminent scientists get most of the rewards and recognition. This creates a system of inequality and privilege within the world of science.

11.3   Learn the history and the global impact of the five major world religions.

- The five major world religions are Judaism, Christianity, Islam, Hinduism, and Buddhism

- Seventy percent of people in the world are affiliated with Christianity, Islam, or Hinduism. For Christians, Muslims, and Hindus, there is a strong tendency to live in a place where they are in the majority; for other groups, there is a stronger likelihood that they will live in places where they are religious minorities.

- Religion has always been connected to issues of power, conflict, and politics. The worldwide spread of Christianity was closely connected to the political power of the Roman Empire, and the spread of Islam was linked to the political history of the Ottoman Empire.

11.4   Define secularization, and discuss the main points of evidence for and against the secularization thesis.

- Secularization refers to the idea that religion will become less important in modern society.

- Evidence for secularization is strongest in Western Europe, where levels of religious belief and church attendance are much lower than they used to be and are still declining. The vast majority of European students attend secular schools, and most European nations have legal protection for people to believe (or not believe) what they want.

- The evidence for the continuing importance of religion is very strong in most of the world. Nearly 85 percent of the world's population maintains a religious affiliation, and 40 percent of the countries of the world still had an official state religion in 2000. Individuals and religious groups continue to make faith-based moral arguments about the public good.

Religious fundamentalism continues to be a significant social force.

11.5   Think about some of the ways that religion and science can coexist in contemporary society.

- Theories of post-secularism argue that the continued existence of religion does not have to be a threat to a secularizing society, and that the two can coexist more harmoniously if scientists stop attacking religious epistemologies.

- Theories of post-secularism also point to changes that religious groups and organizations have to make. They argue that religious people need to be tolerant toward religious ideas and scientific ideas that are different from their own religious beliefs. They need to accept the reality that scientific knowledge has tremendous authority in modern society, and that scientists will play a crucial role in designing public policies. And they need to accept the authority of their society's laws, even when those laws are different from tenets of their religious faith.

Key Terms

Cosmology 310
Denomination 320
Epistemology 336
Matthew effect 332
Monotheism 311
Polytheism 311
Post-secular society 337
Proselytizing 322
Public religion 328
Relativism 336
Religion 316
Ritual 316
Sects 320
Secularization thesis 324
Theodicy 317
Utopia 313

Review Questions

1. What are the main differences between religious and scientific cosmologies?

2. Describe the main features of religious institutions.

3. Why is Judaism considered to be one of the world's major religions?

4. What was the Protestant Reformation, and how did it influence the history of Christianity?

5. What are the main beliefs and rituals of Islam? How did the Ottoman Empire shape the history of Islam?

6. In what ways are Hinduism and Buddhism each different from the other world religions, in terms of their beliefs, rituals, geography, and history?

7. What is the secularization thesis? Describe the evidence for and against the secularization thesis.

8. What are some of the ways that religious groups have come into conflict with modern, secular governments?

9. What is religious fundamentalism, and why has it spread since the 1970s?

10. What are the four basic values and ideals of science? How does the normative structure of science put scientists into conflict with other groups in society?

11. How is the production of scientific knowledge shaped by the dynamics of solidarity and conflict?

12. How did the rise of a scientific worldview help create greater epistemological doubt?

13. What kinds of changes would scientific and religious organizations need to make if they wanted to create a post-secular society?

Explore

RECOMMENDED READINGS

Berger, Peter. 1967. *The Sacred Canopy: Elements of a Sociological Theory of Religion*. New York: Penguin.

Calhoun, Craig, ed. 2011. *Robert K. Merton: Sociology of Science and Sociology as Science. New York: Columbia University Press*.

Casanova, Jose. 1994. Public Religions in the Modern World. Chicago: University *of Chicago Press*.

*Khosrokhavar, Farhad. 2008. In*side Jihadism. New York: Routledge.

Latour, Bruno, and Steve Woolgar. 1986. *Laboratory Life: The Construction of Scientific Fact. Princeton, NJ: Princeton University Press*.

Smith, James. 2014. *How (Not) to Be Secular: Reading Charles Taylor.* Grand Rapids, MI: Eerdmans.

ACTIVITIES

- *Use your sociological imagination*: In her book *The Politics of Consolation*, sociologist Christina Simko argues that one of the key roles of American political leaders is to provide consolation after major national tragedies (Simko 2011). Look at the statements of political leaders after a recent national tragedy. Are their statements religious in nature, or are they based on a nonreligious type of theodicy?

- *Media+Data literacy*: Choose three television shows that have characters who are scientists or church leaders and compare how they are represented.

- *Discuss*: Do you think science and religion are becoming more or less accepting of each other? What is the evidence for your position?

For additional resources, including Media+Data Literacy exercises, In the News exercises, and quizzes, please go to **oup.com/he/ Jacobs-Townsley1e**

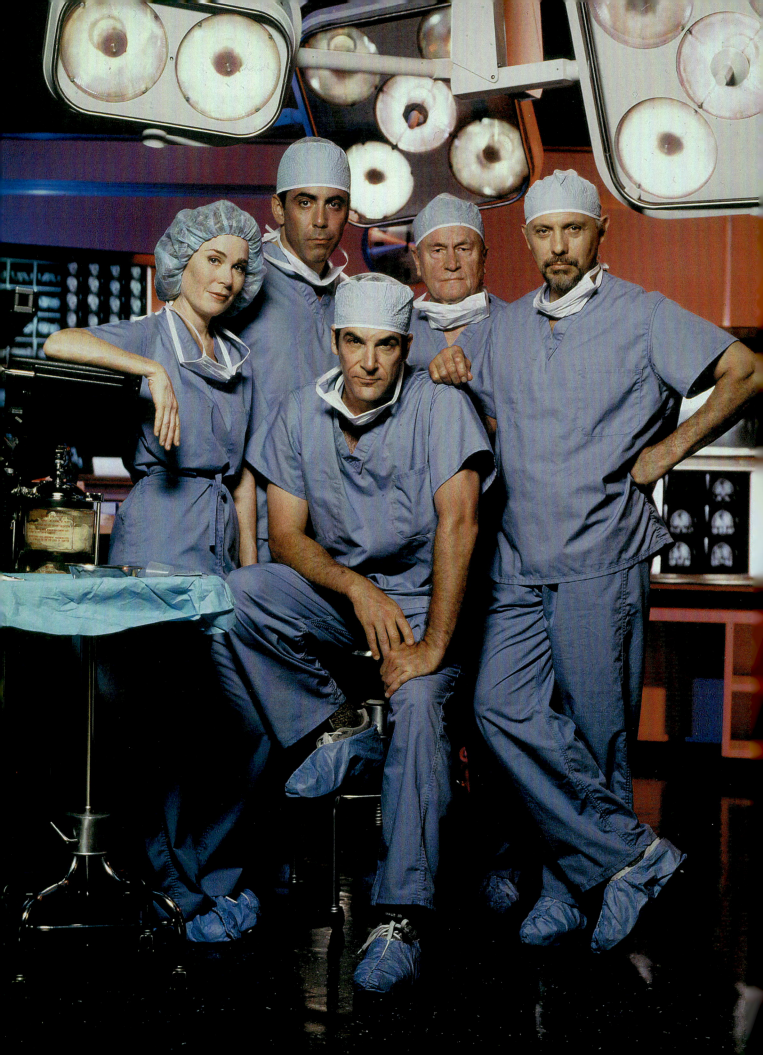

12

Health, Illness, and Medicine

Medical dramas like *Grey's Anatomy* and *Chicago Hope* are staples of network television in the United States. Stories revolve around doctors in white lab coats or blue surgical scrubs. They use surgery and drugs to respond to emergencies, heal mystery illnesses, and solve medical puzzles. Doctors and nurses might bring their skills to poor communities to help those with limited access to the medical system. In all these stories, the dominance of medical science, based in biological approaches to the body, remains unquestioned. When alternative medical practices are mentioned, they are usually regarded as problematic, or their benefits are explained using the language of medical science. Rarely are medical practices like hypnosis or spiritual healing shown in a positive light. Nor is the institutional organization of medicine and health care fundamentally questioned.

Unlike in the television shows, in wider society people pursue a broad range of medical practices. They try new exercise programs to improve their health and live longer. They change their diets, meditate, and use apps on their smartphones to remind them to count their steps or drink more water. Some people learn about self-care practices from family traditions, or are persuaded by friends that certain foods or supplements can make a dramatic difference in their lives. From the perspective of conventional biomedical institutions, these other health behaviors are defined as "complementary and alternative" medicine, and they include practices as varied as acupuncture, biofeedback, yoga, and traditional healers (Nahin, Barnes, and Stussman 2016). Between 1990 and 2002, the National Center for Health Statistics reported that the number of people who used complementary and alternative medical therapies in the United States "nearly doubled" (Su and Li 2011);

Doctors on TV
There is rarely any mention of complementary or alternative medical practices in media representations of medicine and health. Most doctors on TV programs such as *Chicago Hope* (1994–2000) are traditional medical practitioners grounded in surgery and biological science.

LEARNING GOALS

12.1   Know that health outcomes are stratified by race, class, gender, citizenship, education, geographical location, and income as well as the interaction between these factors for any given individual.

12.2   Identify how health and illness are shaped by social factors such as cultural beliefs, historical experiences, social institutions, and the physical and social environment.

12.3   Understand the way stigma, labeling, and medicalization affect the definition and experience of health.

12.4   Understand that the social responses to health, illness, and disability vary across time and place. There are different organizational and economic arrangements for health care, and these also change over time.

today, about one-third of the US population reports using alternative medical approaches to support their health (Clarke et al. 2015).

Complementary and alternative medical approaches are also a substantial part of the healthcare economy, accounting for "1.1% of total health care expenditures in the United States ($2.82 trillion) and . . . 9.2% of out-of-pocket health care expenditures ($328.8 billion)" (Nahin, Barnes, and Stussman 2016). Some people report using alternative medical approaches because conventional health care is too expensive (McMillen 2011). In other cases, conventionally educated doctors include alternative therapies alongside more traditional treatments. Some health plans now cover practices like massage and yoga, although other practices remain outside the umbrella of mainstream health care institutions. Clearly, approaches to health care and medicine are more varied than the picture of the doctor in the white lab coat that we see on TV.

In this chapter, we examine variation in health, illness, and medicine. We begin with a discussion of who gets sick. Genetics and environment are major determinants of health, but access to resources and cultural beliefs shape health and sickness too. Next, we consider the lived experience of being sick in groups and communities. We explore the various social responses to ill health, disease, and disability, and we ask how we decide who is healthy or not healthy. Focusing on the idea of social stigma, which was developed in Chapter 6, on crime and deviance, we discuss how some conditions are labeled as sick or pathological while others are regarded as normal. Last, we describe the social organization of medicine, hospitals, and other care facilities in the United States today. This includes a discussion of medical authority, medical and health education,

Yoga
The practice of yoga is associated with lowering stress, improving flexibility, and other health benefits.

health policy, and health insurance, all of which operate in the context of a global crisis of care. A diverse array of social institutions interlock to deliver a social response to health and illness in large, complex, modern societies.

Health

The **sociology of health and illness** examines the relationship between health and society, with a central focus on **health demography** which is the study of the distribution of disease and illness in a population. Sociological approaches emphasize that the social status of individuals, and cultural beliefs about illness and medicine, are important external factors that affect health. For example, it is a widely held cultural belief in many modern societies that ill health is the product of biological or natural conditions. This is in contrast to other people who might emphasize magical or religious causes. As scientifically committed researchers, sociologists agree that there are biological causes of disease, but they also show how social conditions like access to health care, environmental conditions such as pollution, and cultural beliefs about medicine also shape health outcomes.

Sociology of health and illness A field of sociology that studies the relationship between health and society.

Health demography The study of the prevalence, or the distribution, of disease and illness in a population.

Geography, Class, Race, Gender, Age, and Other Differences

One way to consider the demography of health is to compare groups by geographical differences or other social indicators such as class, race, gender, and age. For example, the World Health Organization (WHO), a division of the United Nations that oversees global health, reports that in 2017 there was more than a 30-year gap in average **life expectancy** between rich countries like Japan (82.7 years) and Switzerland (83.4 years) and poorer countries like Sierra Leone (50.1 years) and Angola (52.4 years) (World Health Organization 2016). Explanations of these differences center on complex interlocking social conditions and environmental factors, such as risk of famine and violent conflict, and differences in nutrition, education, health care, and disease prevalence. Compared to the African countries, Japan and Sweden are rich, privileged societies where most people enjoy plentiful food, safe social environments, high levels of education, affordable high-quality health care, and comparatively lower rates of disease. These shocking social facts about life expectancy are an important marker of the depth of global inequality.

Life expectancy The amount of time an individual can expect to live.

There are gender differences in health status and life expectancy that intersect with other social conditions to shape individual outcomes. For example, while women everywhere live longer than men on average, it remains difficult to disentangle the exact role of biological and social factors (Baierl 2004; Assari 2017; Zarulli et al. 2018). Important social factors include a higher rate of unhealthy behaviors like smoking and drinking among men, and higher likelihoods of accidental or violent death. For women, lower life-expectancy rates are associated with these behaviors as well as pregnancy and childbirth. In places where women become mothers at ages younger than 15 and can expect numerous pregnancies in their lifetime, the risk of death associated with pregnancy and childbirth makes it less likely that women will live longer than men on average.

There is substantial inequality within countries too, including rich countries like the United States (Milanovic 2016). Some of the most striking differences are connected to race and class, and they cut across gender and geography. For instance, WHO has reported that ". . . in the United States, infants born to African-American women are 1.5 to 3 times more likely to die than infants born

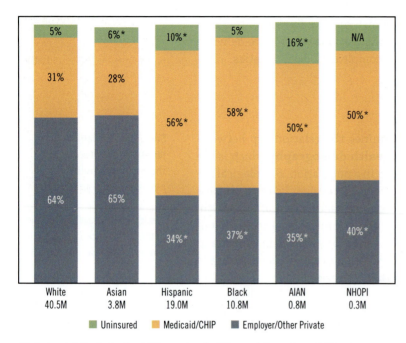

Figure 12.1 **Health Insurance Coverage of Children by Race/Ethnicity, 2014.**
Source: Kaiser Family Foundation analysis of March 2015 Current Population Survey, Annual Social and Economic Supplement.

to women of other races/ethnicities. American men of all ages and race/ ethnicities are approximately four times more likely to die by suicide than females. African-American men in the United States are the most likely, among all ethnic groups in the United States, to develop cancer—a rate of 499.8 per 100,000" (United States Centers for Disease Control and Prevention and National Cancer Institute 2019).

One major cause of differences between social groups is access to health care. A great deal of the observed variation in access and use of health care is related to people's varying economic resources (Pollack et al. 2013; Adler and Rehkopf 2008; Crimmins, Hayward, and Seeman 2004). In the United States, the impact of social class and geographical location are deeply entwined with race, and persistent inequalities between racial and ethnic groups remain a focus of public policy (Figure 12.1).

Genetics

Some individuals and groups are more prone to disease than others. Medical researchers have identified specific genes that shape individual chances of disease, including cancer. That said, genetics are not destiny.

For example, you can be born to short parents and be much taller than they are. That is an outcome produced by random variation in human reproduction. The role of individual social development is also important. If someone born to tall parents is deprived of nourishment and exercise as a child, they may never grow as tall as they might have otherwise. Indeed, as the comparison of average life expectancy between countries illustrates, access to nutritious food, safe environments, and physical activity can affect health outcomes. An individual may be genetically predisposed to live a long life, only to have it cut short by violence, preventable disease, accident, or starvation. While there is no question that genetic inheritance shapes the demography of health, it is also true that *social context always matters*. Medical researchers make this point by separating the study of **genetics**—the study of how genes function in the biological system—from the study of **epigenetics**—the study of how genes interact with wider natural and social environments. This is why doctors and nurses ask questions about family history during medical examinations. Family histories capture the interaction between the genetic and epigenetic—the biological inheritance and environment of social development of an individual.

The general idea that there is a connection between shared genetic heritage and social environments is widely accepted. Applying this idea to medical policy, however, has highlighted the fundamental complexity of racial and ethnic systems, differences in power, resources, and historical experience (Yancy 2007). On one hand, membership in a particular racial or ethnic

Genetics The study of how genes function in the biological system.

Epigenetics The study of how genes interact with wider natural and social environments.

category *may* reference a history of common experiences. It *might* capture shared social and natural conditions that shape health status epigenetically in the interaction of biological and environmental conditions. Because of the long and terrible relationship between scientific medical research, social policy, and institutional racism, scientific arguments about the biological basis of race should always earn critical sociological scrutiny.

Environment

Environmental impacts on health include both natural and social factors. For example, elevated levels of lead in a city's water supply, carcinogens released from industrial processes,

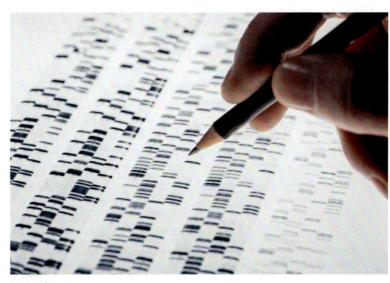

DNA gel
Scientists use gel electrophoresis as a technique to identify DNA fragments and study them at the molecular level. The technique has wide application in genetics and forensics.

and chemicals used in food production can all damage health. According to the National Institute of Environmental Health Sciences (NIEHS), the list of environmental factors that cause ill health includes pesticides, pollen, lead, mercury, and mold, as well as extreme weather, climate change, and cell phones. Climate change researchers, for their part, also show that some of the most lethal diseases affecting the world's population have been shaped by the migration of animal populations that carry and spread pathogens—germs or other infectious agents—among humans (Wu et al. 2016). Climate change has affected the availability of fresh water and farming land, which also has consequences for health and hygiene.

In addition, environmental health research focuses on health risks associated with occupational sites where there are chemicals, heavy metals, loud noises, or dangerous machinery or electronics. They support research on nontoxic, environmentally friendly design of workplaces and work processes, and they advocate for reducing chemicals and other pollutants in the natural environment. The NIEHS also studies environmental factors that may affect some populations more than others. For example, special attention is paid to environmental factors affecting pregnant women and the development of babies and young children, who are particularly vulnerable to chemicals and other toxins in their physical development (National Institute of Environmental Health Sciences 2019).

Environmental health
Health is a social fact. Humans create pollution that affects our health, although not everyone experiences the same level of environmental health risk. Those who are more privileged live healthier lives on average and can also choose to live in relatively cleaner environments. Do you think privileged people should be concerned about environmental health risks for people with less privilege? Why?

Race-Based Medicine

One of the most complex discussions about racial categories, genetics, and health occurred in the process of developing the heart disease drug BiDil in the early 2000s. The drug sparked controversy in the United States because it was tested on racially segmented populations, in this case African Americans. In previous scientific trials before BiDil, new drugs were tested on random samples of the US population that were racially heterogeneous.

In the conflict over BiDil, the point that race is not a biological category was made repeatedly by every stakeholder to the dispute. Doctors, pharmaceutical companies, and government officials all acknowledged that race is a historically evolved system of classifications, identity categories, and power relations. All parties pointed to the social inequalities in health care as the central causal factor producing racial disparities. All parties agreed with the argument that racial categories were not physiological categories and therefore should not be treated as physiological categories for the purposes of health research. Even NitroMed, the drug's producer, admitted that "race is an uncomfortable proxy for medical treatment." Despite all these statements, they used race as a proxy for physical differences anyway.

The authority to move to race-based drug testing was underpinned by a 2005 guideline published by the federal Food and Drug Administration. This guideline states in part that "differences in response to medical products have already been observed in racially and ethnically distinct subgroups of the U.S. population. These differences may be attributable to intrinsic factors (e.g., genetics, metabolism, elimination), extrinsic factors (e.g., diet, environmental exposure, socio-cultural issues), or interactions between these factors" (FDA 2016: 7). The idea that it was acceptable to racially segment populations for drug trials was also supported in a complex statement by the Association of Black Cardiologists, which argued that heart disease presents differently in the African American population than in others (Yancy 2007). As *Scientific American* (2007) summarized, "Absent better criteria, which may emerge from the work of genomics researchers . . . race may provide a valid measure of how a drug works in a segment of the population that is underserved by the healthcare system."

On the other side of the debate about race-based medicine, critics argued that the use of racial categories in biomedical research is problematic and polarizing (Roberts 2012; Kahn 2007, 2013; Bibbins-Domingo

and Fernandez 2007). For example, researchers and doctors at San Francisco General Hospital, Bibbins-Domingo and Alicia Fernandez (2007), argued that the decision to allow race-based drug trials was based on "flawed scientific interpretations" of the data. They said it represented a "setback in the scientific and policy discourse on medical therapeutics and race" and that it "hinder[ed] the efforts aimed at eliminating health and health care disparities." Johnny Williams's book *Decoding Racial Ideology in Genomics* (2016) suggests further that using race as a biological proxy in health research is continuous with a long history of genomic research, which is profoundly rooted in common-sense understandings of race.

A similar point is made by lawyer, sociologist, and civil rights activist Dorothy Roberts in her book *Fatal Invention: How Science, Politics, and Big Business Re-create Race in the Twenty-first Century* (2012). Roberts details how the biological myth of race has been resurrected to support supposedly cutting-edge research in genetics, and that the search for racial difference at the molecular level is part of a long history of scientific racism in the United States. Ethicist, historian, and legal scholar Johnathan Kahn makes a similar argument in his book *Race in a Bottle: The Story of BiDil and Racialized Medicine in a Post-genomic Age* (2013). His detailed history of racial categories in biomedical research identifies legal and commercial forces that work to unduly exaggerate racial differences and describe them as genetic differences. Kahn argues that this emphasis on genetics shifts the focus away from differences in social power and resources that create racial subordination, including

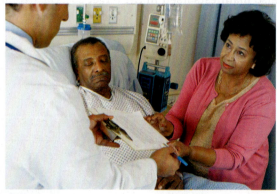

Race and Medicine
There are extremely large health disparities between black and white patients in the United States, especially in rates of cardiac disease. This was a major reason cited by the Association of Black Cardiologists in their statement supporting the testing of the heart disease drug BiDil.

METHODS AND INTERPRETATION CONTINUED

health disparities. Along with Roberts, Kahn fears the social consequences of redefining race as a set of biological categories.

Clearly, the questions of racial difference and genetics raised in the BiDil controversy are complicated. In the United States, they exposed deep divisions in scientific, medical, and legal opinion. Civil rights activists and ethicists challenged the use of racial categories in biomedical research, and remain wary of how these categories are used in scientific research protocols and federal drug policy. In contrast, supporters advocate the use of race categories as a crucial element in addressing racial disparities in health in the United States.

ACTIVE LEARNING

Reflect: How do you make a decision when scientific authority is split? Name three strategies you would use. Share with a partner in class.

A second dimension of environmental health are social factors, which some researchers measure using the idea of **allostatic load**, or the wear and tear on the body due to stress. A high allostatic load describes a state where the normal adaptive processes of a person's body "wear out or fail to disengage or shut off" (Seeman et al., 2004). People who suffer chronic stress have a higher allostatic load than others and are at increased risk for illness, such as heart disease (Logan and Barksdale 2008), and lower life expectancy (Duru et al. 2012; Geronimus et al., 2006). Researchers have begun to explore the idea that exposure to racism and/or economic inequality over the life-course increases the allostatic load of members in affected groups and harms long-term health outcomes (e.g., Upchurch, Rainisch, and Chyu 2015; Parente, Hale, and Palermo 2013; Juster, McEwen, and Lupien 2010). Such disadvantage is cumulative over the life-course and helps explain the deep disparities we observe between groups in the United States, especially racial groups (Shuey and Willson 2008). New work also documents the impact of particular historical experiences and economic events, such as experiencing the Great Depression, in increasing allostatic load with substantial impacts on cognitive function in old age (Hale 2017; see also Juster, McEwen, and Lupien 2010). Along with a focus on differences in economic resources and access to health care, the concept of allostatic load is a useful way to think about how the social environment, such as the extent of racism or poverty in a society, not only affects individuals directly but also manifests itself in the larger social patterns observed by sociologists of health and illness.

Allostatic load The wear and tear on the body due to stress.

An Intersectional Understanding of Health Disparities

An **intersectional health perspective** describes multiple systems of oppression that shape health outcomes (Mullings and Schulz 2006). The intersectional perspective was developed to account for the unique experiences of black women. Critical race theorists argued that when judges used perspectives that focused either on black people or on female people as separate categories, the experiences of people in intersecting categories like black women became invisible (Crenshaw 2016). This fundamental idea has since been extended to other intersections and social identities, including inequalities associated with age, language group, citizenship, and ability.

Health researchers influenced by an intersectional perspective are critical of standard medical models, which disconnect intersecting identities and treat them as abstract categories. As an alternative to mainstream biomedical approaches, intersectional researchers recommend attention to concrete, historical contexts and actual lived experience of particular people in all their

Intersectional health perspective A multilevel approach to health care and medicine that emphasizes the multiple systems of oppression that shape health outcomes and how they interact.

Inequality and Privilege

How Inequality Shapes Our Final Years

Not everyone makes it to old age. In his award-winning ethnography, *The End Game: How Inequality Shapes Our Final Years* (2017), Corey Abramson emphasizes that people who are poorer and socially disadvantaged are less likely to become old because they have "greater psychosocial stress loads, higher levels of violence, unequal treatment by medical institutions, and often the need to live or work in toxic environments" (135). If they survive to old age, Abramson observes, those who have had harder lives "are more beaten-up and worn down" when facing the physical challenges of aging.

For those who do make it to old age, challenges include decreasing energy and mobility, changing bodily appearance, and expanding health issues, and also the death of friends and family members. Abramson argues that being an "old person" is a social status that shapes many aspects of life. For example, the importance of a functioning body was emphasized by many of the elderly because it defined dependence and independence and therefore the opportunities available to them. As one man in a nursing facility said, "I just sit around all week dying, and watching others waiting to die" (137).

Abramson also emphasizes that aging is socially stratified, despite some commonalities. People with more privilege enjoy greater autonomy in their decisions about how to age. Abramson found that neighborhood resources such as education, social networks, and neighborhood services were more robust in affluent middle-class suburbs and much rarer in poor communities. Cultural differences also played a part in how seniors approached the challenges of aging. Important cultural resources like "language skills, knowledge of institutions, and general styles of interacting with authority figures," Abramson argues, "ultimately play a substantial role in mediating outcomes" (141). If people had previous negative experiences with local social workers or clinics, they were less likely to seek help when they needed it.

Abramson's research is important because it documents the subtle ways that pervasive inequalities in resources, social networks, and cultural experiences work over time to shape the experience of aging. As the US population continues to age, this is an increasingly urgent social justice issue.

The elderly homeless
Homelessness is a challenge at any age, but the elderly homeless are extremely vulnerable and experience reduced life expectancy.

ACTIVE LEARNING

Reflect: How do you understand the "categorical status" of old age? What are the social characteristics of the elderly and what role do they play? Are you making any plans to support yourself and your health in old age? Have you talked to your own family members about plans for aging?

Epistemic privilege The privilege that attaches to the knowledge of powerful people.

Multilevel approach to health and illness A part of an intersectional health perspective that emphasizes the systemic sources of health and illness as well as individual characteristics.

identities. An intersectional perspective also emphasizes the knowledge possessed by people in subordinate positions of power to describe and address their own health experiences. Many patients occupy different social positions than doctors. In the case of health disparities, intersectionality requires medical practitioners, researchers, and policy-makers to recognize their **epistemic privilege** as rooted in their own powerful positions. This privilege elevates the medical understandings and expertise that health practitioners bring to patient care rather than the knowledge the patient might bring to their own situation.

Last, the intersectional perspective is also different from a mainstream biomedical perspective in its emphasis on a **multilevel approach to health and illness**. This assumes that categories like race, class, gender, disability, and citizenship are not merely individual characteristics. Rather, they reflect social histories rooted in colonialism, slavery, segregation, and capitalist exploitation. These histories, which have determined the current distribution of material resources, are an important part of understanding health differences, making diagnoses, and supporting patients. In summary, intersectionality illuminates the need for policy and medical interventions that address interlocking systems of power at the structural and cultural levels as well as the level of the individual patient (Caiola, Docherty, Relf, and Barroso 2014).

Illness

There is no universal agreement about what it means to be "healthy" or "sick." Different people can interpret the same situation in different ways. WHO defines health as "a state of complete physical, mental and social well-being and not merely the absence of disease or infirmity" (World Health Organization 1946). This broad definition sets a high standard for human flourishing but does not help define health, disease, or disability for specific purposes.

To complicate matters, what counts as health, disease, or pathology varies over time. For example, osteoporosis is a disease where people lose bone density as they age. Osteoporosis was officially recognized as a disease by the WHO in 1994, when it "switched from being an unavoidable part of normal ageing to a pathology" (Scully 2004). On the other hand, some conditions are redefined as healthy rather than pathological. As we described in Chapter 9, the medical understanding of homosexuality changed over the course of the 20th century from being considered a biologically based endocrine disorder, to a mental disease, to eventually being de-pathologized in 1973. Although stigma and discrimination against gay people continue, being gay in the United States today is much more widely accepted than ever (Schneider 2015).

A second issue is that medical science is increasingly able to detect new diseases. This is a social benefit in some ways since medical conditions cannot be treated until they are identified. However, our expanded ability to identify new medical conditions raises social expectations about good health, and also highlights the role of commercial interests in pursuing new diagnoses for the purpose of pursuing profitable new drug therapies (Rose 2007a; Schneider 2015). One example is the success of Viagra for erectile dysfunction in men, and the search for "an equivalent market (that is, condition) in women" (Scully 2004; Moynihan 2003).

Ethical questions also arise around diagnoses of **medical risk**, or the predisposition to a disease. Insurance companies may register someone as having a genetic predisposition to a disease, even though they have no symptoms. Such a diagnosis can change someone's life even though they do not feel ill and are exactly the same person they were before the condition was diagnosed.

Medical risk Any condition or factor that increases the likelihood of disease or injury.

Defining health, disease, and illness is far from straightforward. What counts as a disease affects the technological and social resources dedicated to fighting disease and the social status of people afflicted. Ethical questions arise because modern medicine has powerful tools to intervene in people's lives. For example, should medical treatment or new health regimes be imposed on people who do not want them? And who defines what is normal and what is pathological?

Experiencing Illness Differently

Anne Fadiman's 1997 ethnography, *The Spirit Catches You and You Fall Down*, captures a disastrous clash of understandings around health, disease, and well-being. It tells the story of Lia Lee, the daughter of Hmong immigrants in

Disease A disorder in the structure or function of the human organism.

Illness experience The way in which illness is understood and managed by patients and their carers.

Cultural competence The ability to perceive and engage other cultural ideas. In medical settings cultural competence means the ability to meet the cultural, social, and linguistic needs of patients.

Cultural humility An approach to health care where medical professionals develop a stance that is open to the patient and that seeks to learn from them how they perceive the situation on an ongoing basis.

Acute disease A single or repeated episode of relatively rapid onset and short duration from which the patient usually returns to his/her normal or previous state or level of activity.

California. Lia developed an epileptic condition as a baby. Her parents understood her condition as one where her spirit left her body to engage with other spirits. In their view, Lia was an "anointed one" whose condition was as much a spiritual as a medical condition. In contrast, the American doctors at the hospital in California where Lia was treated defined epilepsy as a medical condition.

The doctors initially did not understand and could not reconcile themselves with the Lees' disregard for Western medicine, including the drugs that were prescribed for her condition. Lia's parents spoke little English and miscommunications deepened over time. At one point the doctors removed Lia from her parents and placed her in foster care. On the other side, Lia's parents had good reasons rooted in their own experiences to distrust Americans and Western medicine. As time went on, they came to distrust the hospital and the doctors, who they blamed for failing to understand Lia's condition. Caught in the middle, Lia's epileptic seizures got worse until she was left with severe and permanent brain damage. Doctors believed she would die within weeks. Her parents took her home to care for her, and Lia survived for decades.

Lia's tragic, traumatic story highlights the difference between what sociologists identify as the disease and the illness experience. **Disease** is a disorder in the structure or function of the human organism, in this case Lia's epilepsy. The **illness experience** is the way in which the illness is understood and managed by Lia, her family, and their community (Strauss and Glaser 1975; Pierret 2003).

Lia's story also sheds light on serious problems of cultural miscommunication and insensitivity in health care. Fadiman's book was read widely, and Lia's story became central to the movement to develop **cultural competence** in medical education. Health care providers are increasingly taught to engage the cultural knowledge of their patients and to critically examine their own beliefs and biases. The idea of **cultural humility** builds further on the cultural competence model. It recognizes that rather than becoming cultural experts in someone else's culture, health care professionals should develop a stance that is open to the patient and that seeks to learn from them how they perceive the situation on an ongoing basis (Tervalon and Murray-Garcia 1998; Prasad et al. 2016).

The sick role
How do we know this man is sick? Do you play the sick role when you are sick? Why or why not?

Being a Patient

Being a sick person changes your social status. If you have an emergency appendectomy or catch the flu, you might be relieved of work or family responsibilities. Appendicitis and flu are both **acute diseases,** which WHO characterizes as "a single or repeated episode of relatively rapid onset and short duration from which the patient usually returns to his/her normal or previous state or level of activity" (World Health Organization 2004). In these kinds of cases, it is understood that being sick is not your fault. You are expected to make an effort to get well and to seek competent technical help. Sociologist Talcott Parsons (1902–1979) identified this as occupying the **sick role**.

The sick role is a departure from normal role expectations. When you are sick, you seek health care. At that point, you become a patient. As a patient you are asked to submit to the care of others, giving up some of your privacy and autonomy as a result. You may be institutionalized in a hospital, and your meals, exercise, or drug therapy may be supervised. In the sick role, you are expected to surrender decision-making to others, and to depend on doctors and other health carers to cure the medical condition. When you recover, you return to your normal role.

The sick role does have serious limitations. One issue is that it characterizes acute illness better than chronic or long-term medical conditions. **Chronic disease** is defined as a permanent, nonreversible condition that might leave residual disability, and that may require long-term treatment and care (World Health Organization 2004). Rather than curing the disease, in this situation the goal is to manage the disease and maintain quality of life.

Many patients reject the sick role and the model of medicine and health care it presumes. Some people work with home remedies and lay people to address their sickness. Others are suspicious of mainstream medical expertise, medical authority, and the health care system more generally. They challenge the idea that patients should be passive in the sick role and instead become advocates and experts on their own conditions. Sociologists have documented that treatment of patients in the medical system is highly dependent on race, class, and gender, so becoming an expert in and advocate for one's own health can seem like good sense.

LABELING AND STIGMA. Being labeled as a sick person can carry social **stigma**—a form of dishonor, discredit, or shame associated with illness (Goffman 1963). A mild form of medical stigma may result in someone declining to shake your hand because they do not want to catch your cold. A more serious form can accompany extreme physical or mental illness where a person's social behavior is understood to be unpredictable or dangerous. This kind of stigma can result in the social avoidance of the sick person. A third form of stigma blames the individual for their illness. In addition to social rejection, people who are suffering can be given social messages that they are responsible for their own illness, such as alcoholism, obesity, heart disease, or sexually transmitted infection. There is strong evidence that when people internalize the negative social message that they are responsible for their own suffering, it can affect their social identity and social behavior, resulting in a worsening of the medical condition.

A particularly harsh example of this was the fear and widespread social rejection of gay men in the 1980s when the HIV epidemic was emerging (AVERT 2018). Stereotyped as a gay disease, HIV-AIDS was so stigmatized that patients were seen as unworthy of compassionate care or national concern (Figure 12.2). In fact, in the face of a burgeoning global AIDS crisis, then–US president Ronald Reagan barely discussed the disease publicly in eight years, and prevented his surgeon general, C. Everett Koop, from doing likewise; this silence allowed AIDS stigma and stereotypes to grow.

Stigma continues to be a causal factor in the lethality of AIDS. When people are stigmatized, they are socially marginalized, and they may fail to seek treatment or education (Sidibé 2012; UNAIDS 2017). Combating the negative effects of the stigma associated with different health conditions is a question of social justice, and an important part of any solution to public health challenges like AIDS.

Sick role An idea developed by Talcott Parsons to describe social expectations for the behavior of sick people.

Chronic disease A permanent, nonreversible condition that might leave residual disability, and that may require long-term treatment and care.

Stigma A form of dishonor, discredit, or shame associated with illness.

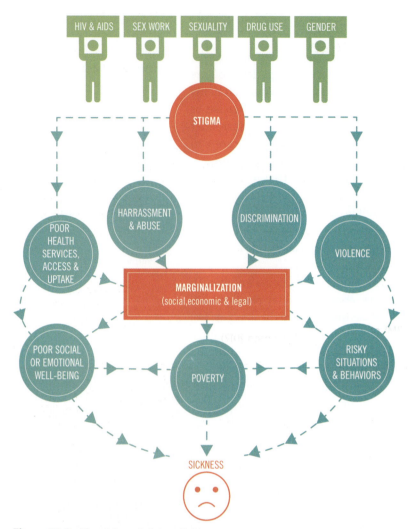

Figure 12.2 How Stigma Leads to Sickness.
Many of the people most vulnerable to HIV face stigma, prejudice, and discrimination in their daily lives. This pushes them to the margins of society, where poverty and fear make accessing health care and HIV services difficult.
Source: avert.org. Adapted from United Nations Development Programme stigma-sickness slope.

The stigma associated with illness sheds light on the way illness and deviance are connected. Like other forms of deviance, illness is a departure from social norms, and health is associated with social definitions of what is normal or socially standard. When people resist the stigmatizing power of negative labels, they question what is normal and can challenge public understandings of badness, wrongness, or pathology.

ABILITY AND DISABILITY. Definitions of "normal" and "pathological" defined in the context of disease also reflect social understandings of ability and disability. In the medical model, disability is defined as a physical or mental defect located in the individual. Disability scholars challenge this assumption. They argue that the medical model makes moral judgments about the value and quality of different ways of being human. This imposes normalized standards that can have perilous consequences for people labeled as disabled—from unnecessary surgery and medication to social exclusion and marginalization. This is a serious concern in a context of selective fertility and genetic testing for disability, because it raises questions about what kind of human beings have the right to be born (Scully 2004).

A medical perspective also makes it hard to see the ways that disability is distinct from illness or disease. Rather than progressing like an acute sickness, for example, a disability can be very stable—more an existential condition of human life than a medical condition. In this case, the goal is to live life rather than become a permanent patient occupying the sick role.

Strict boundaries between what is considered normal, abnormal, or disabled are also not self-evident. Who should define the difference between normal human physical variation and disability? "No-one's body works, perfectly, or consistently, or eternally" (Shakespeare and Watson 2001, p. 26), and some populations widely perceived as disabled do not consider themselves disabled at all. Deafness is one such example. Many in the deaf community consider themselves a linguistic and cultural minority rather than disabled, arguing that "deafness is not a pathology and therefore does not need to be 'fixed'" (Jones 2002). In this case, it is the medical model—which assumes a disability needs to be fixed—that causes suffering rather than the supposed disability itself.

Power and Resistance

Stigma and Size

In her 2013 book *What's Wrong with Fat?*, Abigail C. Saguy analyzes the public health crisis of obesity in the United States. She argues that fat is framed in a way that pathologizes the fat body. This creates social stigma that has negative social consequences for individuals deemed overweight. Saguy traces changing medical attitudes to evaluating fat in the United States to show how medical institutions use the power of measurement to define broad social understandings of what is normal.

For example, Saguy reveals how the Body Mass Index (BMI) has been used by public health authorities in arbitrary ways. While in 1985 the "National Center for Health Statistics defined overweight as having a BMI of 27.8 or more for men and 27.3 or more for women . . . the National Institutes of Health (NIH) lowered the cutoff to a BMI of 25 in both men and women in 1998 . . . causing 29 million Americans to become overweight overnight" (2013: 8). What began as a screening tool for health professionals to be used in conjunction with other medical tests to evaluate health was transformed over time to diagnose otherwise healthy individuals as unhealthy. This is true in both medical and popular uses of BMI. Saguy reports, "Based on BMI, actors George Clooney, Brad Pitt, and Matt Damon are all overweight, while Arnold Schwarzenegger is obese. Oprah Winfrey is technically 'obese' at her typical weight and was still technically 'overweight' at her lowest weight of 160 pounds at 5'7"" (2013: 8–9). In this context, Saguy asks if it is possible to arrive at a neutral understanding of a heavier body.

The fat acceptance movement has been vocally critical of unreasonable social expectations about weight. Founded in 1969 as a civil rights organization, the National Association to Advance Fat Acceptance asserts its vision as "a society in which people of every size are accepted with dignity and equality in all aspects of life." Activists

challenge the idea that losing weight is a moral obligation. They are also very critical of corporate attempts by brands like Dove, Aerie, or ModCloth to replace extremely thin models with heavier alternatives, which they see as a marketing ploy, pointing out that replacement models are still well within social norms of standard weight and beauty, "size 12s and typically white." As one body positive activist argues:

> Our bodies aren't something to be fixed. It's our culture that is in desperate need of repair. We deserve respect and access and representation right now. Those aren't things to be gained only if we change our bodies. (Thompson 2017)

Oprah at a 2018 Weight Watchers event in California.

ACTIVE LEARNING
Find out: Call a health insurance company and find out if there are any discounts for healthy behavior, including weight, exercise, or not smoking. Do you think it is reasonable or ethical to charge higher health insurance premiums to people if they are rated as obese? Why or why not?

Using a sociological perspective also reveals the way disability is produced by institutional infrastructure, built environments, and the organized relationships of education, work, and family. For example, being in a wheelchair because your legs do not work like other people's legs can be defined as an impairment, but attending a school whose only means of upper-floor access are stairs is a crucial social framework that structures your experience of bodily difference. In this example, the design of the building is as important as the physical impairment in producing disability. A sociological model does not ignore physical difference, but "contends that societal, economic and environmental factors are at least as important in producing disability" (Scully 2004).

The experience of disability
The social model of disability emphasizes that disability is produced by the social conditions and policies that shape people's experiences of their bodily abilities.

Rather than physical or mental impairment of the body, then, a social model of disability emphasizes the experience of disability. This includes intersecting experiences of age, race, poverty, gender, and bodily differences that can all shape the lived reality of disability. In the United States, the civil rights of disabled people are recognized by the Americans with Disabilities Act of 1990 (ADA). In this legislation, Congress identified "a clear and comprehensive national mandate for the elimination of discrimination" and defined "clear, strong, consistent, enforceable standards addressing discrimination."

The ADA has resulted in sweeping improvements to building codes, educational policies, media formats, and workplace policies. Although discrimination against people with disabilities has not been eliminated, many social institutions have become more hospitable to disabled people since the pasage of the ADA. As the size of the disabled population continues to grow in the United States, with recent official estimates that 1 in 8 people are disabled (American Community Survey 2016), efforts to change institutional infrastructure and cultural understandings of disability are likely to expand too.

Medicalization A process where a social problem comes to be created or redefined as a medical issue.

MENTAL HEALTH. Definitions of mental health have also changed over time. The neurodiversity movement, for example, argues that a range of neurological conditions is a normal part of human variation (Jaarsma and Welin 2012). Neurodiversity activists resist the definition of their existence as pathological or medical, and they challenge social understandings of what is abnormal.

In fact, there has been a clear expansion of the number of mental health diagnoses for a range of conditions over the course of the 20th and 21st centuries. The American Psychiatric Association, which publishes the *Diagnostic and Statistical Manual of Mental Disorders*, began with a list 106 disorders in 1952 when the manual was first published. This rose to 297 in the fourth edition and now sits at 265 in the fifth edition (not counting modifiers to diagnoses).

The *DSM*
The *Diagnostic and Statistical Manual of Mental Disorders* defines and classifies mental disorders with the goal of improving diagnoses, treatment, and research. It is an authoritative handbook relied upon by medical practitioners, insurance companies, and government agencies.

Medicalization

Mental health is a central example of the process of **medicalization**, a process where a social problem comes to be created or redefined as a medical issue (Conrad and Schneider [1980] 1992). Peter Conrad's work on hyperkinesis, for example, describes how troublesome behavior, mostly among young boys, came to be diagnosed as the mental disorder of hyperactivity and later attention-deficit/hyperactivity disorder (Conrad 1975, 2006). Doctors were key to developing this diagnosis, as were companies offering newly available drugs for treatment, like Ritalin.

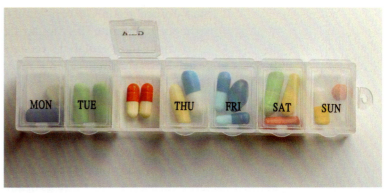

Medicalization

Medicalization is a process where a social problem comes to be created or redefined as a medical issue. In modern US culture, people increasingly interact with and rely on pharmaceuticals to shape and understand their experiences of social life, including their mood, gender, social behavior, and aging.

In more recent work, Conrad (2007) notes how big pharmaceutical companies, biotechnology industry research, insurance companies, and health maintenance organizations have extended medical solutions and medical markets into previously nonmedical areas of society. Wider ranges of disorders and bodily effects have become subject to pharmacological and/or surgical intervention over time. In his review, Schneider (2007) cites shyness, now defined as social anxiety disorder (Lane 2007); a wide range of cosmetic surgeries (Sullivan, 2001); and the pharmaceutical improvement of cognitive performance (Greely et al., 2008; Outram, 2010). Patients are increasingly consumers of drugs and other therapeutic interventions to enhance or improve their lives (Conrad 2007). Nikolas Rose describes this complicated process as one where people interact with pharmaceuticals in ways that entwine "products, expectations, ethics and forms of life" (2007b; Miller and Rose 1997).

The rise of medicalization and medical experts has had broad social implications, with doctors "involved in the mapping of disease in social space, collection of statistics on the illnesses of the population, design of sewers, town planning, regulation of foodstuffs and cemeteries and much more" (Rose 2007b: 701). At the same time, medical expertise is also increasingly state-mandated through education and licensure processes and institutionalized in facilities like clinics, asylums, and prisons.

MEDICAL PROFESSIONS AND MEDICAL AUTHORITY. The medical establishment has social power based on the authority to define what is healthy or pathological. Medical authority affects the education of health care professionals and the treatment of different populations, as we saw in the case of Lia Lee and her experience of epilepsy in the American medical system. The historical basis of medical authority in the United States is grounded in the professionalization of doctors. **Professionalization** is a process where a group of workers come to control a particular kind of work, defining training standards and credentials for entry into the occupation.

As Paul Starr documents in his landmark history, *The Transformation of American Medicine* ([1983] 2017), doctoring in the United States was not always a respected profession. Prior to the 20th century, most doctors made little money and were widely distrusted. Training was unstandardized and doctors competed with other practitioners, including midwives and herbalists. This changed in the early 20th century, as doctors began to organize

Professionalization A process where a group of workers come to control a particular space in the division of labor on the basis of their expertise.

as a unified group. Doctors formed relationships with hospitals and medical schools to promote the standardization of medical education, and began to participate in a regulated, credentialed profession. Organizations of doctors used the legal system to build an institutional monopoly to either drive out or control other practitioners. Working as a lobby group, the American Medical Association secured the passage of regulations that supported the autonomy and authority of medical doctors and prohibited noncertified practitioners from practicing medicine.

As the influence and authority of doctors grew over the 20th century, people's self-understanding of their own health also changed. Public trust in science increased, especially as deadly diseases such as tetanus and diphtheria were effectively controlled. At the same time, individuals came to understand that health and medicine were too complex for self-diagnoses and self-care. Doctors wielded greater influence in social institutions, as employees were frequently required to have a doctor sign off on their health before starting work, schools began to require medical records of checkups and immunization for students to enroll or participate on sports teams, and new immigrants became subject to more rigorous health screenings. By the middle of the 20th century, being a medical doctor had become one of the most prestigious and highly paid occupations in the United States.

By the end of the century, however, cultural and institutional changes had begun to undermine doctors' authority and autonomy, especially in the delivery of primary care (McKinlay and Marceau 2002, 2008; also see Timmermans 2008). As health care systems grew larger, the US government became less supportive of doctors in private practice. Their professional autonomy has also been threatened by rising numbers of medical school graduates and the "weakening of the physician's union (AMA)" (McKinlay and Marceau 2002). Importantly, social trust in doctors began to decline as more information became available about health care in an increasingly global context. More patients exercised autonomy over their own health by using the internet to become informed and by seeking out alternate health care providers such as pharmacists, nurse practitioners, counselors, massage therapists, and midwives. That said, doctors still remain an influential, well-educated, and highly paid group.

Medicine

Medicine The social response to illness that attempts to identify, prevent, and cure disease.

Medicine is the social response to illness that attempts to identify, prevent, and cure disease. It is the social organization of caring for sick people and ensuring the health of the wider population. This work can happen in many different ways.

Medical Institutions

Medical institutions Organizational arrangements in which medical therapies are developed and practiced.

Health care is delivered within **medical institutions** in which medical therapies are developed and practiced. These institutions include hospitals and other care facilities, the professional organization and education of medical practitioners, public health policy and the associated public institutions that implement it, and a wide range of medical business organizations, including the health insurance industry, and pharmaceutical and other corporate biomedical research organizations. Importantly, medical care is also practiced by lay people in the family and in community institutions.

HOSPITALS AND OTHER CARE FA-CILITIES. In the United States, medical care is increasingly delivered through large networks or **health care systems**, which are contractual connections between medical organizations. Most health care systems include doctors' offices and group practices with primary care and specialty services, hospitals, labs, clinics, and other services. The US Department of Health and Human Services reports nearly 45 percent of all physicians and nearly 70 percent of all hospitals are members of health care systems (Figure 12.3). Some of these networks are huge: the largest 5 percent have 18 or more hospitals (AHRQ 2016). There are many different kinds of care facilities too, not all of which are inside large systems. These include birth centers, blood banks, nursing homes, imaging and radiology centers, hospice homes for the dying, mental health and addiction treatment centers, and a range of emergency and urgent care organizations, among others.

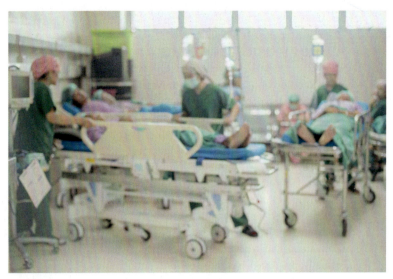

Hospitals

Hospitals are central medical institutions. They provide patient care and also serve as sites for medical education. They are connected to medical business organizations such as health insurance providers and pharmaceutical and other corporate biomedical research entities.

Health care systems Contractual connections between medical organizations.

Figure 12.3   Physicians and Hospitals in US Health Systems, 2016.
There are 626 health systems in the United States, according to AHRQ's Compendium of U.S. Health Systems, 2016. Nearly 45% of physicians and nearly 70% of hospitals are in those health systems.
Source: US Department of Health and Human Services. Agency for Health Research and Quality. 2018.

CAREERS

Sociology and Medicine

Medical education occurs in large health systems that include hospitals. Aspiring medical practitioners must first complete rigorous pre-medical training, which includes courses in advanced biology and chemistry. These classes prepare a student for the Medical College Admission Test (MCAT), the standardized exam required for medical school application. Undergraduates interested in a medical career are also advised to take classes in English, sociology, and psychology to prepare for the MCAT. Good communication skills and the ability to understand social context and group differences are crucial for medical practitioners.

Formally, the MCAT has four sections: Foundations of Living Systems, Foundations of Biological Systems, Foundations of Behavior, and Scientific Inquiry and Reasoning Skills/Critical Analysis and Reading Skills (CARS). The purpose of the CARS section is to measure how well students can apply what they know and integrate new information in complex environments, including biological, biochemical, and social information.

Many health-related occupations have been shaped by the idea that medical education should be science based, include a clinical component, and that it should develop a student's social capabilities and cultural awareness. These occupations include veterinary science, dentistry, public health, nursing, social work, community health education, pharmacy, nutrition, and many other associated roles. In each of these fields, awareness of social difference is a fundamental competence. For those interested in a career in a health field, exposure to key sociological concepts is an invaluable part of preparation.

Medical students
The medical education model in the United States is based on the idea that medicine should be science based, include a clinical component, and develop a student's social capabilities and cultural awareness. Sociology courses are good preparation for a medical career.

ACTIVE LEARNING

Find out: Pick two different health careers, such as surgical nurse, primary care doctor, midwife, social worker, or clinical psychologist. Visit your career center or go online to learn the requirements for training in each field. What kinds of training do these different fields have in common? What does this suggest about priorities in medical education?

Public Health

Illness is a personal, bodily experience, and it is also a social one. Our bodies are social objects because we live in groups and communities. If you have young children in school, you know kids often bring home colds and flu to the family. This is one reason schools have rules about illness, such as policies asking parents to keep children home if they have a fever so they will not spread infection.

Public health The health of the whole population.

At a wider social level, medical officials make policies to safeguard **public health**, understood as the health of the whole population. Many doctors and other medical practitioners work in government agencies concerned with public health. In the United States, the Centers for Disease Control and Prevention (CDC) focus on the immediate health and safety of the US population through monitoring and responding to national and international health threats. Another important government organization is the National Institutes of Health (NIH), which is the largest biomedical research agency in the world. The CDC and NIH both connect research to national public health.

Epidemiology The study of the social dimensions of disease patterns to discover the way diseases are spread and communicated.

An important kind of public health research is **epidemiology**, which investigates the social dimensions of disease patterns to discover the way diseases are communicated and spread. The goal of epidemiology is to develop

Solidarity and Conflict

Disruptive Behavior in Medical Settings

Doctors, nurses, and therapists must cooperate to deliver patient care, even though they come from different disciplines, have different kinds of training and education, earn different salaries, and work different schedules (Burdick et al. 2017; Gausvik et al. 2015; Epstein 2014). There is evidence that patients are harmed when health professionals do not communicate well (Weller, Boyd, and Cumin 2014). This makes disruptive behavior in medical settings a significant problem.

According to the Joint Commission, the oldest independent nonprofit accrediting body for medical standards in the United States, "intimidating and disruptive behavior" in health care organizations is defined as "overt actions such as verbal outbursts and physical threats, as well as passive activities such as refusing to perform assigned tasks or quietly exhibiting uncooperative attitudes during routine activities." Disruption, intimidation, and bullying in health care settings are a topic of increasingly urgent public concern. Recent online conversation threads include "5 steps nurses should take when dealing with difficult doctors," by Stephanie Stephens at Monster.com, a premier career website (2018); "How to Talk to Doctors" by Amy Keller on the *Daily Nurse* website (2016); or, "Don't tolerate disruptive physician behavior" by Stephen Lazoritz at *American Nurse Today* (2008). And it is not only nurses complaining about doctors. The Joint Commission's report emphasizes that there is a widespread culture of disruption and intimidation in health care. Nurses report disruption and disrespect from doctors (Klass 2017; Keller 2016; Ford 2009; Lazoritz 2008) as well as bullying and intimidation from other nurses (Robins 2015a, 2015b). Interns and medical students also report disruption, hazing, and disrespect from nurses and senior doctors (Slavin and Chibnall 2017; Dyrbye et al. 2014; Fried et al. 2012; Dyrbye, Thomas, and

Shanafelt 2005). There is also evidence that disruptive and intimidating behavior extends beyond nurses and doctors to pharmacists, therapists, support staff, and administrators (Joint Commission 2008; Wyatt 2013).

The consequences of disruption, intimidation, and bullying in health care are many. One concern is medical errors and adverse outcomes (Rosenstein and O'Daniel 2008). The Joint Commission (2008) also lists increased cost of care, staff turnover, and medical staff shortages (particularly of nurses) as key issues. These patterns of fractured solidarities in stressful workplaces with complicated hierarchies also seem especially problematic in the health care field, where the focus is on the care of others.

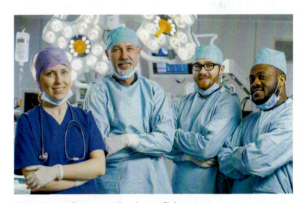

Diversity and cooperation in medicine
Doctors, nurses, and therapists must cooperate to deliver patient care, even though they come from different disciplines, have different kinds of training and education, earn different salaries, and work different schedules.

ACTIVE LEARNING

Find out: What are the pay differences between doctors and nurses? What accounts for them?

---

interventions to prevent or halt the worst health impacts of deadly diseases such as cholera, typhus, smallpox, yellow fever, measles, malaria, tuberculosis, influenza, HIV-AIDS, and Ebola. Some of these diseases have killed huge populations all around the world. Others have been brought under control by mass vaccination.

In our interconnected, globalized society, the spread of disease is of particular concern. This is why national public health organizations like the CDC and the international WHO pay close attention to the number of cases of infectious diseases that are reported around the world. This is what happened in 2009 when epidemiologists observed a much higher number of people with serious flu-like symptoms than expected, and eventually identified a previously

Epidemic A widespread or high incidence of an infectious disease.

Pandemic An epidemic that not only affects a large number of people but is also spread over a large geographical area of the world.

Public health education Educational efforts to prevent disease, promote healthy behaviors, and preempt risky ones.

undetected form of influenza. This was the H1N1 virus, later known as the swine flu. A vaccine was developed quickly to combat the **epidemic**. Swine flu was also classified as a **pandemic** since it not only affected a large number of people, but also spread over a large geographical area of the world. The WHO considers the likelihood of future epidemics and pandemics to be very high (Fan, Jamison, and Summers 2018), and advocates for investment in greater public health education, research, and preparedness to preempt mass deaths.

PUBLIC HEALTH EDUCATION. Complementing public health research are **public health education** efforts to prevent disease, promote healthy behaviors, and preempt risky ones. Public health education is delivered through government, medical, educational, and community institutions. These efforts might emphasize vaccination and sanitation while promoting health through educating people about nutrition, safety awareness, exercise, and support for smoking cessation or weight loss. Education efforts might occur at schools and workplaces or take the form of information provided to all patients during routine medical visits.

Mass media campaigns are an important part of public health education programs, and they have a long history. Some examples include early posters about handwashing and hygiene. These can be seen today in restaurant and supermarket bathrooms. More recently, advertisements and television appearances for First Lady Michelle Obama's "Let's Move" campaign targeted childhood obesity. Antismoking campaigns are among the most common public health campaigns, with some of them funded through taxes on tobacco products. Increasingly, public health advocates are turning to social media to spread health information.

The evidence for the positive impact of these kinds of campaigns is not straightforward. In a comprehensive meta-analysis of mass media campaigns, for example, interventions were found to be most effective when done on multiple fronts. For example, when antismoking ads were combined with making tobacco products more expensive via increased taxation, the campaign against smoking was more effective (Wakefield, Loken, and Hornick 2010). Mass media campaigns are also more effective when the targeted behavior is a single event (like getting a vaccine or a screening test) rather than an ongoing behavior (such as food choices or physical activity).

Public health media campaigns
Antismoking campaigns are among the most common public health campaigns, with some of them funded through taxes on tobacco products. Increasingly, public health advocates are turning to social media to spread health information.

Public health policy The norms, rules, and laws that attempt to shape public health behavior.

PUBLIC HEALTH POLICY. Public health policy consists of the norms, rules, and laws that attempt to shape public health behavior. Some public health policies, such as rules about sanitation and clean water, are widely accepted. In the case of acute disease outbreaks, most people follow quarantine restrictions at ports of entry like airports and docks. Most people understand that social cooperation is needed to respond to major health threats.

PAIRED CONCEPTS   Global and Local

Does Modern Society Make You Sick?

In *Love, Money, and HIV* (2014), Sanyu Mojola combines fieldwork and surveys in rural Kenya to analyze why young, educated African women are more susceptible to HIV-AIDS than less educated young women. This paradox is counterintuitive, since many policy-makers believe that education, and especially health education, can reduce the likelihood of contracting HIV-AIDS. In her award-winning study, Mojola shows that neither better information about HIV-AIDS nor the personal experience of attending funerals of AIDS victims affects the risky sexual behavior of these young educated women. Why not?

Mojola's explanation reveals that an unintended effect of education for girls in contemporary Kenya is that they develop a taste for cosmetics, smartphones, and the other high-status objects that circulate in the modern global marketplace. These are exciting symbols of elite and cosmopolitan identities. At the same time, the expansion of secondary education has led to credential inflation in Kenya, where there are not enough local jobs. High expectations around consumption, combined with weak income prospects, result in many young women choosing sexual relationships with men who can support their consumer aspirations and modern identities. This is problematic in the context of sex in contemporary Kenya, which is shaped by the history of the global HIV-AIDS epidemic.

Although it is well known that men traveling the main highways spread HIV-AIDS by having sex with multiple partners and being unwilling to use condoms, Mojola's interviews reveal that young, educated women in Kenya prefer these partners because they are older, wealthier, and more experienced. Such men provide gifts and support modern lifestyles. Similarly, although these young women attend funerals of women like themselves who have died from AIDS, this creates a context in which death is less remarkable (American Sociological Association 2016).

Does this mean that global modernity makes these young women sick? Mojola's analysis suggests that modern Kenya is a place where global forces of colonialism, capitalism, and consumption combine to produce increasing education and rising expectations in a local context marked by few job prospects and a mixture of traditional and modern ideas about sex and health. At this risky intersection of local and global forces, young educated women in contemporary Kenya have a higher risk of sickness and death than their less educated and less modern counterparts.

ACTIVE LEARNING

Reflect: Write a list of the places where you seek advice and/or information when you are sick. Do you consult different sources for different kinds of sickness? Who do you trust? Why? What is the difference between information learned in the family and information learned from a doctor, schoolteacher, or friend?

Other public health policies are resisted. For example, there are many institutional smoking bans in the United States, put in place by educational institutions, restaurants, and city and state governments. It is widely understood that tobacco products are unhealthy for individuals and communities, since it is harmful to inhale someone else's secondhand smoke. Despite growing public condemnation, the tobacco industry has long pursued multiple legal strategies to obstruct public health laws restricting tobacco use (Ibrahim and Glantz 2006; Brandt 2012). It is also the case that some individuals resist smoking bans and smoke in public and at home.

A different kind of example of resistance to public health policy is opposition to childhood vaccinations for preventable and highly contagious diseases such as measles and whooping cough. These diseases can be fatal, with babies and young children at higher risk than adults. Some parents believe that these vaccines are associated with autism and other negative outcomes in children. The great majority of public health experts disagree. They argue that not vaccinating children reduces protection against these diseases for everyone. Research from the Harvard School of Public Health shows that higher incidence of

National Infant Immunization Week poster, CDC
Vaccination to prevent deadly diseases like measles, mumps, and rubella is public health policy in the United States. In some countries it is illegal to resist vaccination, since lack of vaccination is understood to pose a public health risk to others. Do you think it is unreasonable to require parents to vaccinate children?

Curative medical care Care focused on curing disease or relieving pain to promote recovery.

Preventive medical care Care aimed at preventing disease before it occurs.

Palliative care Medical care offered to a person and that person's family when it is recognized that the illness is no longer curable.

Integrated medical care Systems of medical care that are coordinated to meet the multiple needs of clients.

Reproductive labor The work of producing and maintaining individuals for social participation in the economy and society.

Capitalist crisis of care The shortage of reproductive labor created by the capitalist organization of work.

diseases that vaccines prevent is concentrated in counties and schools with lower levels of vaccination (Aloe, Kulldorff, and Bloom 2017; Feldscher 2017). This finding is significant in the current US context where levels of whooping cough peaked in 2010 and 2012 (CDC 2019a), and where measles outbreaks are at their highest since 1992 "and since measles was declared eliminated in 2000" (CDC 2019b). Resisting vaccination recommendations is an example of how individual choices can affect the larger community by putting others at risk. It is also an example of how different groups of people disagree about the definitions of medical risk.

Social Responses to Sickness and Illness

In the United States and around the world, there are several different approaches to the organization of health care. **Curative medical care** is focused on curing disease or relieving pain to promote recovery (World Health Organization 2004: 20). A curative approach to care responds to crisis once a disease or injury has occurred. By contrast, **preventive medical care** aims to prevent disease before it occurs. Preventive (or "preventative") care might include exercising more, improving nutrition, or stopping smoking to prevent disease and improve quality of life. **Palliative care** provides pain relief for incurable illness and typically offers psychological and social support for the person who is suffering as well as their families. The World Health Organization (2004: 35) also recognizes **integrated medical care** as systems in which various kinds of care are coordinated by different care systems "to meet the multiple needs of clients." In practice, most health care systems contain elements of each kind of care.

CARE WORK. Much medical care occurs outside formal medical institutions in families and communities. The bulk of this is unpaid care in private households. Historically, this work has been done by women in their roles as wives and mothers. This is the **reproductive labor** of producing and maintaining individuals who participate in the economy and society. Even when reproductive work is paid, it tends to be dominated by women. Elementary and middle-school teachers, registered nurses, and psychiatric and home health aides are paid less, researchers argue, because these jobs are historically done by women (Carleton 2014).

Recent years have witnesses a widespread "crisis of care" in the United States and around the world, with fewer people available to care for children, elders, and the sick. The women who once did unpaid reproductive labor increasingly work in higher-paid employment—if they can get it. This has resulted in an unmet demand for care work.

Philosopher and social theorist Nancy Fraser describes this as a **capitalist crisis of care**, since capitalism has assumed but rarely paid for the value of socially reproductive care work. In early capitalism, care work was privatized in the family household. In the 20th century, care work was partly socialized

Structure and Contingency

Waiting for An Organ Transplant

There are about 80 organ transplants a day in the United States (Health Resources & Services Administration 2018). Kidneys are the most commonly transplanted organs, followed by the liver, heart, lungs, pancreas, and intestines. In addition to organs, human tissues can also be donated. Common donations include the cornea (the transparent covering over the eye), which can cure blindness. Other donations are skin for grafts, veins, and bones. For some transplants, donations are from deceased persons, while in other cases living donors give organs or tissues.

While rates of transplantation are high, demand for organs is much higher. Currently there are nearly 120,000 people on the transplant waiting lists in the United States. In this context, the question of who gets an organ for transplant is especially difficult for decision-makers.

Human organs can be purchased in some countries overseas, which raises hard choices as well as ethical and safety issues for people needing organs. In the United States, the sale of human organs is outlawed by the National Organ Transplant Act (1984). The law also contains provisions to establish the Organ Procurement and Transplantation Network (OPTN) and allows the establishment of nonprofit Organ Procurement Organizations. These laws and organizations define policies about who gets organs for transplant when they become available.

The process for selecting an organ recipient is highly rule governed (OPTN). In the first step, the OPTN screens out everyone on the list who is not a match for the organ because of blood type, height, weight, or other medical factors. The second step is geography; someone is more likely to receive an organ donation if they happen to be in the local donor service area when an organ becomes available. This is a highly contingent element in the transplant process. Some patients try to register in more than one service area to maximize their chances of donation, but the outcome still relies on the unpredictable unfolding of events that makes organs available. Even in the highly structured cooperative process of organ transplant, there are multiple contingencies that affect the decision of who will receive a donated organ. Stated another way, the policies and process of getting an organ for transplant are both highly structured and highly contingent.

Celebrating organ donors
In Louisville, Kentucky, on May 3, 2018, some participants in the annual Pegasus Parade wear shirts that say "Give the Gift of Life / Be an Organ Donor." The demand for organs is far higher than supply.

ACTIVE LEARNING

Discuss: Do you think it is ethical to register for the transplant list in more than one hospital donor zone to improve your odds for getting an organ donation? Why or why not?

---

in the form of state medical, disability, and family services. In the current era, where social welfare policies have been reduced or eliminated everywhere, Fraser observes that reproductive work is becoming commodified—that is, it has been transformed into something to be bought and sold on open markets (Fraser 2013).

Others have noted the globalization of care work. In the development of transnational markets in reproductive labor, many people have moved from the poorer countries of the Global South to the richer countries of the Global North to improve their economic well-being. Many of these migrants are women who find work in "in paid care, cleaning, or domestic service, looking after children, older people, and households in richer countries" (Williams 2018). Rather than being permanent settlers with citizenship rights, many of these workers have

Elder care
The global capitalist crisis of care contrasts young immigrant populations from poorer countries with aging citizen populations of wealthy countries. When these young Filipino nurses graduate, many will find work around the world. In fact, the Philippines exports so many nurses that there is a local crisis of nursing case in the Philippines.

Deinstitutionalization A historical process in the United States and other countries where populations once housed in long-term care facilities like psychiatric hospitals and centers for the developmentally disabled declined sharply over time.

the status of visitors or temporary workers. They leave their own families behind in their home countries, and support them by sending them their earnings. These are enormous global financial flows of labor and capital: for example, annual remittances from migrant Filipino workers to the Philippines were worth US $26.9 billion in 2016—or nearly half of the Philippines' national export economy (Rowley 2017). The Commission on Filipinos Overseas estimated that approximately 10.2 million people of Filipino descent lived or worked abroad, in over one hundred countries—about 10 percent of the national population.

Another factor affecting the US crisis in care work has been the **deinstitutionalization** of populations that were once housed in long-term care facilities, which included psychiatric hospitals and centers for the developmentally disabled. Where once these patients were incarcerated in institutions—sometimes against their will—the number of people in such long-term-care facilities has declined sharply (Prouty, Smith, and Lakin 2007; Eyal 2010, 2013). This was partly to do with moral critique of the conditions in these institutions, a resistance to the stigma and shame associated with mental illness and disability, and a move to community-based alternatives to care.

Greeted as a liberating and positive move by many, deinstitutionalization has had uneven consequences for some populations requiring care. Communities cannot always meet the needs created by deinstitutionalization, resulting in a lack of medical resources for people suffering from mental health crises and a disturbing rise in the criminalization of those same people. As the Treatment Advocacy Center reports, "nearly half of all individuals with schizophrenia or bipolar disorder will be jailed at some point in their lives. Individuals with serious mental illness also are significantly more likely to be injured or killed during an encounter with law enforcement" (TAC 2018).

Access to Health Care

The history of medical care and medical institutions is quite different across countries. For example, although the United States, Canada, and Australia share many standards for medical education and practice, Canada and Australia both have strong national health care systems, based on the idea that medical care is a right of citizenship. In the United States, by contrast, medical care is organized by the market. As the sociologist Paul Starr ([1983] 2017) notes in his definitive history of American medicine, this has the effect of associating the right to health care with hard work and employment rather than citizenship or human rights.

Health care systems are ranked by scholars and international agencies like the World Health Organization. They are evaluated along dimensions such as responsiveness, quality, and fairness. In 2018, Singapore, Luxembourg, Japan,

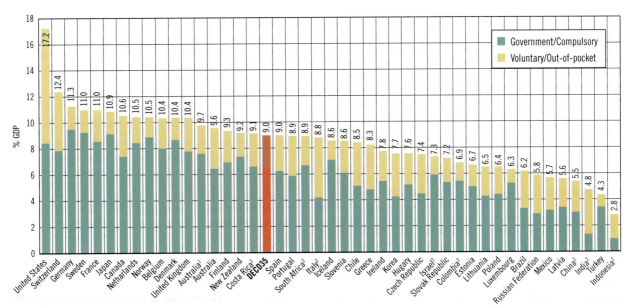

Note: Expenditure excludes investments, usless otherwise stated.
1. Australian expenditure estimates exclude all expenditure for residential aged care facilities in welfare (social) services.
2. Includes investments.

Figure 12.4   Health expenditure as a share of GDP, 2016 (or nearest year).
Source: OECD Health Statistics 2017, World Health Organization Global Health Expenditure Database.

Switzerland, and Qatar were the top five in health ranked by the Legatum Institute's annual report on global prosperity (Legatum 2018). These are all wealthy, capitalist, democratic countries, as are most countries with top health care systems. The United States is ranked 35th among the 149 countries studied. This is surprising because the United States spends far more per capita on health care than any other country in the world, with 17.2 percent of GDP spent on health care (Organization for Economic Cooperation and Development 2017, p. 132-134) (Figure 12.4).

In the United States, health care is a mix of private and public programs, with nearly 70 percent of people with health insurance paying for some form of private program. The basic idea in any **health insurance** scheme is that members pay a regular fee into a larger pool, to be drawn on if they need medical care. In this way, insurance programs enable participants to share risks and resources. There are many different ways of organizing and supporting insurance schemes for health care. In the United States in 2015, "employer-based insurance covered 55.7% of the population for some or all of the calendar year" (Barnett and Berchick 2017).

Historically, health insurance in the United States was organized by hospitals for a fixed fee to guarantee care in the case of unexpected hospitalization. A big improvement over out-of-pocket payment for medical services, such systems were developed by many countries prior to World War II. In an effort to control prices and inflation during the war, the US government offered tax incentives to employers for health benefits offered to employees. This was a large tax benefit to individuals, and it eventually resulted in the development of employer-based health insurance. While President Truman proposed a public health insurance program in 1945, and while it was popular with the US public, it was opposed by the US Chamber of Commerce, the American Hospital Association, and the American Medical Organization. These influential groups in

Health insurance A way to pay for health care where members pay a regular fee into a larger pool, to be drawn on when they need medical care.

the health care sector argued that such a proposal was socialist, and they feared that it would undermine the authority and autonomy of the medical profession (Corning 1969; Starr [1982] 2017). The resulting system was one where private health insurance coverage dominated, available to most people through their employer.

This arrangement left large populations without health coverage, importantly the aged, the poor, and certain disabled populations. It was not until 1965 that President Johnson signed into law the Medicaid and Medicare legislation that would cover these populations at a basic level. Some US states have additional programs to support the poor. In addition, military personnel and qualified veterans are covered through the military health system, and the government supports an Indian Health Service for eligible Native Americans.

Unlike most developed countries, however, the United States has no formal **national health care system** where all citizens are guaranteed access to basic medical services (Table 12.1). While the Affordable Care Act of 2010 was designed to extend health insurance to every citizen, the later Tax Cuts and Jobs Act of 2017 repealed key provisions, with analysts projecting a sharp increase in the rate of people without health insurance in the years to come (Jost 2017). As other countries such as India and Colombia weigh the pros and cons of developing national health care systems, the United States remains locked in struggle over the right way to organize and pay for health care.

National health care Government-based health care systems where all citizens are guaranteed access to a basic bundle of medical services.

Table 12.1: Countries with National Health Care Systems

	DATE FOUNDED
Norway	1912
Japan	1938
New Zealand	1938
Germany	1941*
Belgium	1945
United Kingdom	1948
Kuwait	1950
Sweden	1955
Bahrain	1957
Brunei	1958
Canada	1966
Netherlands	1966
Austria	1967
United Arab Emirates	1971
Finland	1972
Slovenia	1972
Denmark	1973
Luxembourg	1973
France	1974
Australia	1975
Ireland	1977
Italy	1978
Portugal	1979

	DATE FOUNDED
Cyprus	1980
Greece	1983
Spain	1986
South Korea	1988
Iceland	1990
Hong Kong	1993
Singapore	1993
Switzerland	1994
Israel	1995

Source: Ghanta 2013.

*Germany is sometimes identified with the oldest system of social insurance, beginning in 1883 (Bärnighausen and Sauerborn 2002; Carrin and James 2005). It was not until 1936 that health care was extended to dependents in Germany, and not until 1941 that the system was extended to pensioners (Busse and Riesberg 2004; Carrin and James 2005).

It is a paradox that the United States spends the most on health care in the world, but does not provide health care for its entire population and does not rank among the countries with the top health care systems in the world. Health care costs remain high and are rising, and insurance seems out of reach for many of the poor and members of other marginal populations. This makes it likely that health insurance will remain a potent political issue in the United States for years to come.

CASE STUDY

Genetic Testing

To explore the intersection between health, illness, and biomedical knowledge, the rise of commercial genetic testing, which uses laboratory methods to look at an individual's genes, provides a compelling case study. These tests rely on the *power* of biological and medical science to define human health and social welfare. While the National Institutes of Health emphasize the health benefits of genetic tests—such as diagnosing disease and identifying gene changes that can be passed on to children—they are also clear that genetic tests "cannot tell you everything about inherited diseases. For example, a positive result does not always mean you will develop a disease, and it is hard to predict how severe symptoms may be" (National Institutes for Health 2017).

Despite these attempts at caution by the NIH, popular and lay understandings link genetic risk to health, even though the *risk* of developing a disease is not the same as actually developing the disease. There are several forms of *resistance* to genetic diagnosis. One form of resistance is diet. Dr. Peter J. D'Adamo's book *The Geno-Type Diet* (2007) suggests that following genetically informed diet plans can help you "live the longest, fullest and healthiest life possible." There are also individuals sometimes referred to as "genetic superheroes" who resist "disease destiny" (Goldberg 2016).

DNA science for all
The saliva collection kit for ancestry testing by 23andMe.

Initially a limited medical practice, genetic testing is now widespread, with people using DNA testing kits at home. The Ancestry.com website, for example, offers "cutting edge DNA testing" along with "the world's largest online family history resource" to predict a person's genetic ethnicity. The website for 23andMe provides detailed "health reports" that offer "genetic health risk reports" for diseases including late-onset Alzheimer's, celiac, and Parkinson's, "carrier status reports" for over 40 hereditary conditions, including cystic fibrosis and sickle cell anemia, and "Wellness" and "Trait" reports

CASE STUDY CONTINUED

that provide information about freckles, male bald spot, and even unibrow.

Although it is offered as a medical service, 23andMe clearly advertises more when it says: "Find out where your DNA comes from and use it to take the trip of a lifetime." Clearly these new DNA tests go far beyond assessment of disease risks. Along with the rest of modern biomedicine, these DNA tests have immense authority to define the "normal" human body as well as its social characteristics. In this sense, genetic testing businesses like Ancestry and 23andMe share in the *power* of medical and biological science to define social understandings. They directly shape the social stories people tell about themselves, and the social actions they take as a result.

This is made clear in the account provided by Courtney, a client featured at Ancestry.com. She relates that her individual profile confirmed stories she had long told about her family, and especially about her mother and grandmother as strong women. The findings of her genetic test coupled with historical genealogical data allowed her to connect her self-understanding to traditions of African matrilineal authority. It allowed her to link her *local* biographical story to a larger *global* story and connect to a distant community on the Ivory Coast. This altered her identity in important ways. "It's fundamentally changed the way I think about myself," she says.

Similarly, Ancestry.com airs a television ad of a man dancing in traditional German lederhosen, joyfully expressing *solidarity* with his German ethnic community. After genetic testing, he discovers he has more Scottish and Irish ancestry than he thought. The advertisement closes with him in a kilt with bagpipes, suggesting that social practice should follow the revelation of ethnic heritage. It suggests there is a *conflict* between the celebration of German ethnicity when he is actually of Irish-Scottish ethnicity. These stories convey important lay understandings about race, ethnicity, and genetics. The social message in both cases seems to be that biological genetic information is what should define family narratives. In fact, the suggestion is that genetic information is more important than your prior understandings about where you are from. The scientific information is rooted in biological truth and is therefore "more real."

But does this make sense? Are race and ethnicity actually *structured* by genetics? Does your genetic information determine your ethnic and racial identity? There do seem to be group differences that are seen in aggregate genetic information. There are physical differences that appear to be related to risks of disease. It is also true that genetic information connects to stories of ethnic belonging for many people. Sociologists emphasize, however, that it is always important to see how these scientific facts are embedded in histories of racial difference. In the United States, as in other European settler societies, these are histories of colonization, slavery, and successive waves of immigration. This can also be seen in the collective genetic map of Americans.

Bryc et al. (2015) analyzed data from 145,000 cheek swabs collected by 23andMe and found that "a lot of Southern Whites are a little bit black" (Ingraham 2014). When compared to what people claim their racial and ethnic status to be, Bryc and her colleagues found that there is *contingency*, or a gray area in ethnic identification. As Ingraham (2014) reports, "People who are less than 15% African are highly unlikely to describe themselves as African-American. People who are 50% African or more are almost certain to describe themselves this way. In between, (grey shaded area), some uncertainty" (Figure 12.5).

This pattern of reporting is unsurprising considering the historical *privilege* associated with whiteness in the United States and the continuing pervasive *inequality* between black and white Americans. This preference for claiming a more privileged category also suggests pressing ethical questions in the wake of genetic technologies that allow scientists to engineer more desirable traits into human beings. Just because we can engineer humans genetically, should we? Are there limits on what we should do? Who decides?

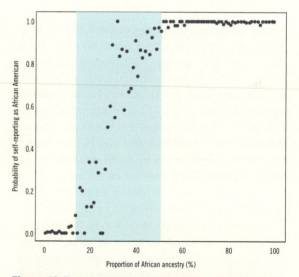

Figure 12.5   Proportion who claim African American identity compared to proportion of measured African ancestry.

Source: Bryc, Katarzyna, Eric Y. Durand, J. Michael Macpherson, David Reich, and Joanna L. Mountain. 2015. "The Genetic Ancestry of African Americans, Latinos, and European Americans across the United States." *The American Journal of Human Genetics* 96(1): 37–53 (additional tables: https://www.cell.com/cms/10.1016/j.ajhg.2014.11.010/attachment/cff15e7e-75da-48ac-ad13-2f6fe134fd48/mmc1.pdf).

LEARNING GOALS REVISITED

12.1 Know that health outcomes are stratified by race, class, gender, citizenship, education, geographical location, and income, as well as the interaction between these factors for any given individual.

- The sociology of health and illness studies the relationship between health and society. This includes health demography, which focuses on the prevalence, or the distribution, of disease and illness in a population.

- There are large differences in life expectancy between people who live in different parts of the world.

- Access to health care is a major determinant of health and life expectancy.

- The impact of environment on health outcomes can be understood through the concept of allostatic load, or the wear and tear on the body due to stress.

- Gender and race interact with other factors to shape life expectancy differently within and between nations.

- A wide range of environmental factors impact health outcomes.

- An intersectional health perspective emphasizes multiple systems of historical and current oppression that shape health outcomes, and draws attention to the epistemic privilege of Western, biomedical perspectives in health, illness, and medicine. Those using an intersectional perspective take a multilevel approach, and consider collective as well as individual health experiences.

12.2 Identify how health and illness are shaped by social factors such as cultural beliefs, historical experiences, social institutions, and the physical and social environment.

- While genetics are a major factor shaping health, they interact with social context to determine health outcomes. Medical researchers make this point by separating the study of genetics—the study of how genes function in the biological system—from the study of epigenetics—the study of how genes interact with wider natural and social environments.

- Different cultural understandings can have enormous effects on a patient's experience of health and illness.

- In the biomedical system of the United States, people are understood to occupy a sick role when they are sick. In the case of people suffering from chronic conditions, the expectation that they will always play the role of a patient is not always useful. Many patients reject the sick role and the model of medicine and health care it presumes.

- There is a difference between the physical fact of sickness and the social experience of illness that depends on social context and cultural understandings. The social *experience* of health, illness, disability, and medicine varies across social groups and environments.

12.3 Understand the way stigma, labeling, and medicalization affect the definition and experience of health.

- What counts as health, disease, or pathology varies over time.

- Being socially labeled as sick can carry social stigma, defined as a form of dishonor, discredit, or shame associated with illness. This is particularly problematic in the case of infectious diseases like HIV where failure to get treatment is a death sentence and can also lead to others becoming sick.

- Medicalization is the process where a social problem comes to be created, redefined, or labeled as a medical issue. The availability of pharmaceuticals and/or new surgical techniques can shape the definition of a physical condition as a medical condition requiring treatment.

- People who are disabled and some people with mental health diagnoses sometimes reject medicalization, medical labels, and the stigma that can attend them. Some groups argue that there is a wider range of human variation than most standard biomedical models define or accept.

12.4 Understand that the social responses to health, illness, and disability vary across time and place. There are different organizational and economic arrangements for health care, and these also change over time.

- Medicine is the social response to illness that attempts to identify, prevent, and cure disease. It is the social organization of caring for sick people and ensuring the health of the wider population.

- Curative approaches to medical care respond to acute events, while preventive care attempts to prevent disease before it occurs. Palliative care is care for people at the end of life. Integrative care combines many levels and systems of care to meet all care needs.

- Medical education occurs in large health systems that include hospitals.

- Medical professionalization in the United States is rooted in a science-based, highly credentialed form of medical education. Doctors have social authority beyond medicine in their roles as public health providers and guarantors of health in education and other institutions.

- Medical institutions are diverse. They include hospitals, medical schools and professions, public health agencies, governments, health insurance corporations, community groups, and nonprofit organizations. In the United States, much medical care is delivered in large health care systems.

- Alternative and complementary medical care is a growing part of the health care system.

- Much care work is provided in families and households, traditionally by women in their roles as wives and mothers. Some analysts argue there is a global capitalist crisis of care, with not enough care to meet demands for care work.

- Deinstitutionalization in the United States refers to the downsizing and closure of long-term care facilities for the mentally ill and developmentally disabled over the course of the 20th century.

- Medicine is organized differently among countries, with a different balance of care for acute and chronic conditions, and various economic models for funding heath care. National health care systems are arrangements where individuals are guaranteed basic medical services as a part of citizenship. Private insurance systems are arrangements where individuals and organizations fund health care through private insurance companies. The United States care system is a mix of private and public programs.

- By the end of the 20th century, cultural and institutional changes had begun to undermine doctors' authority and autonomy, especially in the delivery of primary care.

- Public health is the health of the entire population. Maintaining public health requires a high degree of cooperation.

- Public health research relies on epidemiology, which uses scientific research to investigate the social dimensions of disease patterns. Epidemiologists track epidemics—the high incidences of infectious diseases—so they do not become pandemic and spread across large parts of the world.

- Public health education efforts aim to prevent disease, promote healthy behaviors, and preempt risky ones.

- Public health policy refers to the norms, rules, and laws that shape public health behavior.

Key Terms

Review Questions

1. What is stigma? How is it related to labeling?

2. Give three reasons why the authority of medical doctors has declined in the 21st century.

3. What is epidemiology? What are some of the main medical institutions where epidemiologists work?

4. Describe the sick role.

5. What is the sociology of health and illness? What can it tell us about health disparities? Give an example.

6. Compare and contrast national health care systems and systems based on private insurance.

7. What is the difference between cultural competence and cultural humility? Why are they important?

8. Compare and contrast biomedical and intersectional approaches to health and illness.

9. Define medicalization and explain two examples.

10. What is public health? Name three ways public health is maintained.

11. In what ways is disability socially formed?

12. Describe the difference between disease and the illness experience.

Explore

RECOMMENDED READINGS

Conrad, Peter. 2007. *The Medicalization of Society: On the Transformation of Human Conditions into Treatable Disorders*. Baltimore: Johns Hopkins University Press.

Conrad, Peter, and Joseph W. Schneider. [1980] 1992. *Deviance and Medicalization: From Badness to Sickness*. Philadelphia: Temple University Press.

Foucault, Michel. 1965. *Madness and Civilization: A History of Insanity in the Age of Reason*. New York: Vintage Books.

Foucault, Michel. 1973 [1963]. *The Birth of the Clinic*. London: Tavistock.

Foucault, Michel. [1975] 1995. *Discipline & Punish: The Birth of the Prison*. New York: Vintage Books.

Fraser, Nancy. 2013. *Fortunes of Feminism: From State-Managed Capitalism to Neoliberal Crisis*. New York: Verso.

Fraser, Nancy, and Rahel Jaeggi. 2018. *Capitalism: A Conversation in Critical Theory*. New York: Polity.

Goffman, Erving. 1963. *Stigma: Notes on the Management of Spoiled Identity*. New York: Simon & Schuster.

Mojolo, Sanyu A. 2014. *Love, Money, and HIV: Becoming a Modern African Woman in the Age of AIDS*. Berkeley: University of California Press.

Saguy, Abigail C. 2014. *What's Wrong with Fat?* New York: Oxford University Press.

Starr, Paul. [1982] 2017. *The Social Transformation of American Medicine: The Rise of a Sovereign Profession and the Making of a Vast Industry*. New York: Basic Books.

ACTIVITIES

- *Use your sociological imagination*: Interview a family member about the medical services that are the most important to them: primary care, hospitalization for emergencies, pediatric care, dental, vision, public health care, someone to care for them at home when they are sick, etc.

- *Media+Data literacies*: Your medical data is legally private but also required for most individuals to participate in health care services in the United States. Can you identify the pros and cons of sharing your data as part of large medical data systems?

- *Discuss*: What is the difference in economic organization between health care systems based on private insurance and those based in government institutions? What are the pros and cons of each arrangement?

For additional resources, including Media+Data Literacy exercises, In the News exercises, and quizzes, please go to **oup.com/he/ jacobs-Townsley1e**

13

Politics, Media, and Social Movements

In June 2015, Donald Trump announced that he was running for the Republican Party's nomination for President. Trump had never held elected office, but this was not his first entry into a presidential race. In 1999 he announced his interest in running for the nomination of the much smaller Reform Party, but he withdrew from the race five months later. In the lead-up to the 2012 campaign he spoke at a number of conservative political events, but he did not enter the race that year. However, by 2015 he was ready to run.

Trump's campaign was controversial from the beginning. Adopting the slogan "Make America Great Again," he was strongly critical of immigrants and Islamic terrorism. He was against international trade agreements, China, and companies that sent jobs overseas. Trump was ridiculed by most policy experts, but he was an expert at getting media attention. He deliberately used inflammatory language and personal insults against his opponents, knowing that journalists would reward this behavior with abundant coverage. Les Moonves, the CEO of CBS Television, called Trump's campaign a "circus" that generated huge ratings and advertising revenue for the media. "It may not be good for America," Moonves said, "but it's damn good for CBS" (Bond 2016).

In a major surprise to pollsters and pundits, Donald Trump was elected President in November 2016. He had overcome significant opposition from leaders of his own political party, many of whom worked hard to try to prevent him from winning the nomination. He had overcome debate performances that were mocked by late-night television comedians and severely criticized by political experts. He had overcome allegations of sexual misconduct, including the release of a video in which he bragged about sexually assaulting women. He had overcome other scandals as well—charges that he had retweeted known white supremacists, that he had used anti-Semitic imagery, and that he had been publicly

US Presidential Inauguration, 2017
In 2017, Donald Trump was inaugurated as the 45th president of the United States. His election surprised pollsters and the media alike.

LEARNING GOALS

13.1 Understand the way sociologists define power.

13.2 Define the difference between coercive and persuasive power.

13.3 Understand how persuasive power is connected to the spread of democracy.

13.4 Understand how news media organizations influence politics and political debate.

13.5 Understand the different types of rights claims that social movements make against the powerful and how that helps create social solidarity.

endorsed by a number of openly racist and anti-Semitic groups. In the week after the election, and then again after his inauguration in January 2017, hundreds of thousands of people protested Trump's policies and his rhetoric. But Trump had prevailed. On January 20, 2017, he assumed the office of President of the United States. On that same day, he officially declared his candidacy for the 2020 election.

This chapter examines politics and the struggle for power. We begin by discussing different ways that individuals and groups exercise power. Next, we discuss the rise of democracy, and compare the different ways that democratic societies organize political power. In the second half of the chapter, we consider how media organizations shape the political process. We discuss why journalists cover political issues the way that they do, and we examine different sources of bias in that coverage. The chapter finishes with a discussion of political protest. We look at how social movements get created, what they do to attract and motivate members, and what kinds of strategies they use to increase their power and influence.

Politics as the Struggle for Influence

Power The ability of individuals or groups to get what they want, even against the resistance of others who are participating in the same action.

As we have emphasized throughout this book, one of the main ways of thinking sociologically is to consider the relationship between power and resistance. Writing at the end of the 19th century, Max Weber defined **power** as the ability of individuals or groups to get what they want, even against the resistance of others who are participating in the same action (Weber 1946). Weber's definition highlights the fact that people who have power would prefer not to face any resistance, but they have to be prepared for it.

State All of the institutions of government, which together rule over a clearly defined territory and have a monopoly on the legitimate use of force within the territory.

While power is an important aspect of almost all social settings, Weber argued that government or modern **state** power is distinctive in modern society. State power is unique in two respects. First, modern governments are responsible for establishing collective goals, and for creating public policies that will attempt to reach those goals (Parsons and Smelser 1956; Habermas 1975). Politicians compete with each other to define these collective goals, and propose different policies to respond to social problems. Using the media, they try to build public support for their different proposals. Interest groups, experts, and social movements try to catch the politicians' attention in order to influence their policy proposals. This struggle for influence defines **politics** in modern society.

Politics The struggle for influence and control over the state.

Second, the modern state is unique because it has exclusive control over the legitimate use of physical force within a given territory (Weber 1946). Because the state can use the police, the courts, and the military to enforce its decisions, it has the upper hand in most political conflicts. But state power, like any other exercise of power, works best when physical force is not used. In fact, if the state uses physical force too often, or in a way that is seen to be illegitimate, then political conflict and resistance can increase dramatically. This requires even more physical force by the state, leading to an escalating cycle of force and resistance. As sociologists have discovered, there is a delicate balance between the use of coercive power and persuasive power.

Coercive Power and Persuasive Power

The exercise of power almost always involves an asymmetrical relationship. In a political conflict, one side will generally have more resources at its disposal, and it will use those resources to try to exercise its will. There are two general types of resources that can be used to exercise power. **Coercive power** uses a system of punishments and rewards to try to force people to act in a particular way. **Persuasive power** is the attempt to convince other people that they actually want to act in a particular way, or at the least that it is the right thing for them to do. Each strategy has specific advantages and disadvantages.

In many ways, coercive power is easier to use than persuasive power. The threat that is built into coercive power is clear, and this is particularly true for the state. The US government, for example, can rely on the police, the courts, the Internal Revenue Service, and other state agencies to force compliance from its citizens.

Coercive power is often effective, but it comes with a cost. People resent being forced or threatened into action, and so the exercise of coercive power is often associated with resistance. This can create a spiral of escalating coercion and resistance. When this happens, coercive power becomes more expensive at the same time as it becomes less effective.

Given the risks associated with governments using coercive power, a more common strategy is persuasive power. Rather than trying to force or threaten people to do something, persuasive power has the goal of convincing them that a request for compliance is legitimate. They might argue that they are thinking about the common good rather than their own self-interest. They might appeal to shared values, or to the fact that they were elected by the people to their positions of power. In each of these instances, the exercise of power comes from influence rather than force.

Weber distinguished between three different types of persuasive power, which he referred to as legitimate authority (1946: 78–79). In premodern societies, the most common type of legitimate authority was **traditional authority**, where people follow a leader's orders because of the weight of tradition or custom. In modern societies, traditional authority has been mostly replaced by **rational-legal authority**, which is based on clearly defined and codified rules. With rational-legal authority, people believe in the authority of the rules or the laws. The third type that Weber identified is **charismatic authority**, which is based on the personal qualities that an individual leader possesses. Charisma can be particularly effective when combined with other types of power, because it creates a personal and emotional bond between leaders and their followers.

Persuasive power has different risks than coercive power. There is almost always an opposing side making an alternative argument. As a result, the use of persuasive power will often lead to a struggle for influence between competing groups. Despite these risks, however, most groups prefer persuasive power if they can use it successfully. The democratic revolution, which we discuss later in this chapter, led to forms of government that privilege noncoercive forms of power.

Coercive power The system of punishments and rewards that are used to try to force people to act in a particular way.

Persuasive power The ability to convince other people that a particular choice or action is the appropriate one.

Traditional authority A form of persuasive power in which people follow a leader's orders because of the weight of tradition or custom.

Rational-legal authority A form of persuasive power based on clearly defined rules that are written down.

Charismatic authority A form of persuasive power in which people follow a leader's orders because of the personal qualities that the leader possesses.

Power and Resistance

Public Protests in Tahrir Square

On January 25, 2011, tens of thousands of Egyptian citizens occupied Tahrir Square in Cairo to protest against President Hosni Mubarak's government. Similar protests erupted at the same time in other cities throughout Egypt. As the demonstrations spread, the police established a curfew, and the government shut down the internet to try to prevent protesters from spreading their message. Despite these efforts, the protests continued to grow. On February 4, hundreds of thousands of Egyptians protested in Cairo. By February 10, workers throughout Egypt went on strike in support of the growing movement.

The Egyptian government was ultimately unable to control the media or shut down the internet. International media organizations provided nearly 24-hour coverage of the scene at Tahrir Square, and Egyptian protesters used social media to report about their protests and to warn others about developing police activities. Ultimately frustrated in his attempts to stifle the protests, President Mubarak announced on February 11 that he would resign. The revolution had achieved success in only 18 days.

The revolution did not erupt spontaneously, however. Considerable planning and coordination took place well before 2011, as protests were organized against police abuse and coercion. The April 6 Youth Movement tried to organize a general strike in 2008, and within 10 days it had more than 70,000 members on its Facebook page. But the group was banned and its leaders arrested. In 2010, another Facebook page was created to protest the torture and killing of Khaled Said by Egyptian police. This Facebook page, "We Are All Khaled Said," had more than 400,000 members by January 2011, and was used to spread information about police abuse as well as to organize protests.

People who protest often know that they will be met with resistance. This picture was taken in Tahrir Square in 2011. Police are in riot gear, ready to use coercive force against the protesters. In fact, according to a news report in *The Guardian*, Egyptian police killed more than 800 protesters in 2011. Protesters did not only have to worry about the police in riot gear who confronted them directly, but also about police snipers stationed on rooftops throughout the city. But the threat of being hurt or killed did not deter the protesters. Instead, police violence reinforced the belief that protesting was the only way to rid Egypt of tyranny. Protesters knew that the images of police violence would be broadcast on televisions and computer screens throughout the world. Journalists, intellectuals, and government leaders worldwide condemned the actions of the police, lending international support to the protesters' goals and mobilizing thousands more to take to the streets.

Tahrir Square protests, 2011
The Egyptian government was unable to control the media coverage of the social protest at Tahrir square in 2011. Here, protesters watch TV during the protest. Within 18 days of the protest, Hosni Mubarak resigned as president.

ACTIVE LEARNING

Think about it: Try to imagine the things that protesters consider when they enter the scene of a public protest. What visual clues can they use to try to predict how dangerous the situation is going to be? Do you think their predictions about possible danger change how they act and how they participate in the protest? Are there things protesters can do to reduce their risk, or to make sure that any violent actions by the police will be reported by journalists? How can protesters use the danger of the situation to try to rally public support for their cause?

Hegemony, Critique, and Resistance

Because power involves an unequal relationship, dominant groups will always have resources and advantages over other groups. They may have more experts at their disposal, better access to the media, easier access to politicians, or more

Inequality and Privilege

Who Gets Elected to the US Senate?

The US Senate
Senators are predominantly old, male, white, educated, and wealthy. Of 100 senators in 2018, 77 are men, 79 have a higher degree, 89 are white, and their median net worth is $3 million.

The exercise of power is connected to the unequal distribution of resources. People who have more resources have an easier time gaining positions of political

leadership. This is a picture of the US Senate, taken in 2010. As of 2018, the average age for senators was 61.8 years. There are 77 men, and 23 women. Fifty-five of the senators have a law degree, 21 have a master's degree, and three have a medical degree. There are three African Americans, five Latinos, and three Asian Americans; the remaining 89 senators are white. The median net worth for this group of senators was more than $3 million. For comparison, the median net worth for American households in 2018 was only about $78,000 (Wolff 2012; see Manning 2019 for an update).

ACTIVE LEARNING

Discuss: Is it possible for these senators to represent all of their constituents when they come from a pretty narrow slice of the population? Are there any specific types of experiences that they might not have had, as compared to a lot of other Americans? Can you think of how these different experiences might influence the kinds of political projects that US senators think are important?

---

effective threats. Antonio Gramsci (1891–1937) described this relationship between dominant and nondominant groups in terms of hegemony (Gramsci 1971). **Hegemony** refers to the different strategies that dominant groups use to make their view of the world seem like "common sense" to the rest of the population. For example, if leaders of the automobile industry can get people to think about cars as an expression of individual freedom, it will be easier for them to shape a pro-automobile transportation policy. In this way, a hegemonic understanding that private cars are superior develops rather than widespread support for public transport infrastructure. It is much easier to exercise power if people cannot imagine an alternative to the current situation or perceive proposed alternatives as inferior to the status quo.

> **Hegemony** A form of power where dominant groups are able to make their worldview seem like "common sense" to the rest of the population.

The concept of hegemony emphasizes group struggle. In other words, while dominant groups try to convince the population that their vision of the world is the only one that makes sense, there are always other groups that propose a different way to look at an issue. This kind of critique is a central activity of social movements, which we discuss in greater detail at the end of the chapter.

Politics and Democracy

Persuasive power and the battle for hegemony became more important with the spread of democracy. Before the 16th century, political territories in Western Europe were poorly defined, and rulers delegated power to local elites and landowners. Most of the population had no political rights at all. With no connection to a central government and no chance to influence politics, people showed little interest in the monarchs who ruled over them (Anderson 1974). Political decisions usually involved a compromise between the monarch, the landowners, and church leaders, with little concern for the interests of "the people." Such societies were **absolute monarchies**, in which there were no laws restricting the power of the monarch over the people living in their territory.

The Democratic Revolution

By the end of the 18th century, democratic revolutions in France and the United States had changed the way people understood political power. During the English Civil War of the 1640s, a social movement known as the Levellers proposed that "all government is in the free consent of the people" (Hill 1984). The American Declaration of Independence expressed a similar idea in 1776, asserting that "governments are instituted among Men, deriving their just powers from the consent of the governed." The French Declaration of the Rights of Man and the Citizen asserted in 1789 that "no body nor individual may exercise any authority which does not proceed directly from the nation." All of these documents emphasized the idea of **popular sovereignty**, or the "rule of the people." Decisions are based on **deliberation** among citizens about matters of collective importance, so that after debating the merits of competing positions, people can reach a shared agreement about the best course of action.

The democratic revolutions that started in England, France, and the United States spread throughout the world, helped by advances in literacy and print technology. By the first decade of the 20th century 17 percent of the countries in the world were democracies; by the 1920s, 34 percent were democratic (Dahl 1989: 240). Today, more than 60 percent are democratic (Figure 13.1).

Comparing Systems of Representation

Today, not all countries have democratic forms of government. China, for example, holds indirect elections. Chinese citizens elect deputies to the National People's Congress, and those deputies elect the national officials. China is also a **single-party state**, which means that all candidates for national election come from the same political party. Because they do not have more than one political party, single-party states are generally not considered democracies, despite the fact that they hold elections.

Most democratic countries today are either **constitutional monarchies** or **democratic republics**. Constitutional monarchies still have a king or queen who acts as the ceremonial head of the nation, but their actual power is limited by law. Most of the power in a constitutional monarchy is held by elected officials. The first constitutional monarchy was established in England in 1688. Other examples of contemporary constitutional monarchies include Sweden, Belgium, and Japan. But most democratic countries today are democratic republics, in which there is no monarch and the

Absolute monarchy A form of government in which there are no laws restricting the power of the monarch over the people living in their territory.

Popular sovereignty The "rule of the people."

Deliberation The practice of discussing matters of collective importance, so that after debating the merits of competing positions, people can reach a shared agreement about the best course of action.

Single-party state A state in which all candidates in an election come from a single political party.

Constitutional monarchy A form of democratic government where power is held by elected officials and there is a king or queen who serves as the ceremonial head of the nation.

Democratic republic A form of democratic government where power is held by elected officials and there is no monarch.

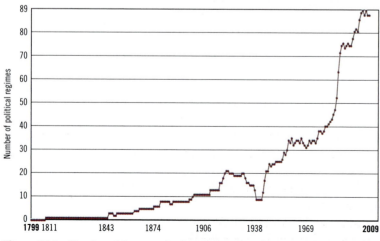

Figure 13.1   Number of democracies between 1800 and 2010.
Source: Max Roser. 2015. "Democratisation." Published online at OurWorldInData.org.

elected officials have all of the political power.

Another important difference is between **parliamentary** and **presidential** systems of democracy. In a parliamentary system the people vote for their elected officials in the legislature, but they do not vote for the head of government. Instead, the head of government is a member of the legislature. In most parliamentary systems, the person who becomes the head of government is the leader of the largest political party in the parliament. This is different from presidential systems, where there is a formal separation of powers between the head of government and the legislature. In such systems, the president is usually elected by a democratic vote of the people, and cannot be dismissed by the legislature except under unusual circumstances. Because they are elected by the people, presidents can claim to speak for the entire nation, and it is easier for them to develop a following that is separate from their political party (Lowi 1986). This is particularly true in today's media-saturated world, when presidents use social media to address the public directly and personalize their persuasive power (Eshbaugh-Soha and Peake 2011; Mast 2012).

Queen Elizabeth II
Queen Elizabeth II of Great Britain is a constitutional monarch, whose powers are limited by law.

On the other hand, it is usually much easier to pass legislation in a parliamentary system, and it is much easier to reach political compromises (Linz and Valenzuela 1994). In addition, because members of parliament can call an election at any time, some social scientists have argued that parliamentary systems are more sensitive to changes in public opinion (Linz 1990). There are stark exceptions to this, including the Australian constitutional crisis of 1974, where the Senate refused to fund the government, leading to a double dissolution of parliament; and the United Kingdom's 2019 parliamentary deadlock over Brexit, arising from disagreement about the process through which the UK will leave the European Union. Unlike in the presidential system of the United States, however, parliamentary deadlocks tend to trigger general elections so that a new government can be formed. Historically, there have been many more stable and successful parliamentary systems than presidential systems of democracy (Mainwaring and Shugart 1997).

Public Opinion and Popular Sovereignty

Because democratic societies place so much value on the "will of the people," those in power need a way to know what the people want. In the early years of democracy, there were no good ways to directly measure this **public opinion**. By the 19th century, politicians and journalists were using informal "straw polls" to try to predict the outcome of upcoming elections (Herbst 1995). As social scientists in the mid-20th century developed more sophisticated techniques of survey research, the modern opinion poll emerged.

Opinion polls made it possible to measure the attitudes and preferences of the population, and to communicate those preferences throughout society. Those in power came to rely on opinion polls to measure their public support,

Parliamentary system A form of democratic government where the head of government is chosen from the legislature, and is also usually the leader of the largest political party in parliament.

Presidential system A form of democratic government where there is a formal separation of powers between the head of government and the legislature, and the president is usually elected by a democratic vote of the people.

Public opinion The public expression of the different attitudes and beliefs that people have about a particular issue.

PAIRED CONCEPTS

Solidarity and Conflict

Push Polls and the Politics of Division

In 1946, Richard Nixon was running for the US House of Representatives, trying to unseat the incumbent Democratic congressman Jerry Voorhis. During the campaign, many Los Angeles residents received telephone calls from an anonymous person claiming to be a friend of theirs, who wanted to warn them that Voorhis was a communist (Sabato 1996). Even though the Nixon campaign was widely criticized for using such a dishonest campaign strategy, Nixon went on to win the election. From this experience, the "push poll" was born.

The American Association of Public Opinion Research (AAPOR 2015) defines a "push poll" as a type of negative campaigning that is designed as an opinion poll. Criticizing push polls as "unethical political telemarketing" more interested in influencing election outcomes than measuring opinions, professional pollsters complain that push polls take advantage of the trust people have in research organizations. The AAPOR has identified push polls as a violation of their professional code of ethics, and they have encouraged their members to help journalists and the public identify this form of fraudulent political telemarketing.

Push polls are designed to create conflict. Push pollsters do not identify the organization with which they are associated. They do not attempt to draw a representative sample, because they are not trying to discover any information. Instead, they will target specific groups of voters—for example, union workers, or suburban housewives. Rather than following the standard polling protocol of asking for basic demographic information from the person receiving the call, the push poller will instead ask the recipient for whom they intend to vote. If they are intending to vote for the candidate hired by the push poller, they will simply be encouraged to vote. However, should they express a preference for the "wrong" candidate, they will then be asked a series of leading questions trying to influence them not to vote for that candidate, or not to vote at all (Sabato 1996). Such questions are often hypothetical or blatantly false. An infamous example of this occurred in South Carolina during the 2000 US presidential campaign, when a push poll asked people, "Would you be more or less likely to vote for John McCain … if you knew he had fathered an illegitimate black child?" (Banks 2008).

Push polls create a number of social problems (Gerstmann and Streb 2004). First, they undermine public faith in legitimate polling, making people cynical about survey research in general. Second, they make people cynical about politics, encouraging them to believe that all politicians are untrustworthy. Finally, push polls are deliberately misleading, and often fraudulent in their intent. And all of these problems are compounded by the fact that political candidates routinely accuse their opponents of using push polls, while denying charges that they are using push polls themselves. These charges and counter-charges just increase the amount of confusion and cynicism among the electorate.

US Senator John McCain during the 2000 presidential campaign
McCain was the target of a series of push polls that hurt his candidacy.

ACTIVE LEARNING

Think about it: Several states have introduced legislation to ban or restrict push polls. But it is difficult to document how extensively push polls are being used, or to link push polls to the political candidates and their campaign organizations. Why do you think this is the case?

and to take action if they found their support declining. Declining poll numbers were an important factor in Lyndon B. Johnson's decision not to seek reelection as US president in 1968 (Dallek 1998; Bennett 2013). Public opinion had turned decidedly against the Vietnam War by 1968, with a Gallup poll reporting that 53 percent of Americans believed that it had been a mistake to send troops into Vietnam. Responding to these poll numbers, US presidential candidate Richard Nixon successfully campaigned with the argument that "new leadership will end the war and win the peace."

Representing the People

The power of public opinion operates most directly through voting, in which individuals express their preference for which political candidate they want to represent them or which policy proposal they support. Because voting is so important for the exercise of power, sociologists and other social scientists spend a lot of time studying social patterns and social consequences of voter behavior and public opinion (Brooks 2014).

VOTING. In the United States, every citizen who is at least 18 years old is eligible to vote. But democratic societies do not always extend voting rights to everyone. When the United States was first established as a democratic nation, most states restricted voting to white males who owned property. Many of these voting restrictions have been eliminated, usually as the result of political struggle by social movements. The Fifteenth Amendment to the US Constitution, which prohibited federal and state governments from denying the right to vote based on race, was ratified in 1870. In 1920, the Nineteenth Amendment gave women the right to vote. In 1964, the Twenty-fourth Amendment outlawed the "poll tax," which meant that the poor could no longer be excluded from voting. While most states continue to restrict voting privileges for convicted felons who are in prison (Uggen, Manza, and Thompson 2006), other restrictions have largely been eliminated.

While voting is one of the most important features of a democratic society, this does not mean that everyone who is eligible actually turns out to vote. As Figure 13.2 shows, the high point for voter turnout in the United States was between 1838 and 1898, when between 70 and 80 percent of eligible voters actually turned out to vote in presidential elections. Voter turnout has steadily declined since then. Fewer than 60 percent of eligible voters have turned out to vote for national elections since the 1960s. Voter turnout rates are even lower for state and local elections. Historically, voter turnout rates have been higher for whites, those with more education, and those who have more money. Older citizens are much more likely to vote than younger citizens. In some countries, such as Argentina, Australia, and Singapore, all eligible voters are required by law to vote.

Low voter turnout has a major impact on how political influence works. Politicians pay much more attention to the issues that concern actual voters, and they tend to ignore the issues that nonvoters care about.

INTEREST GROUPS. Interest groups also play an important role in the exercise of power. **Interest groups** bring people together on the basis of a common issue, and then try to influence political decision-makers on topics related to that issue. Some interest groups have millions of members, such as the National Rifle Association

Interest group An organization that brings people together on the basis of a common issue, and attempts to influence political decision-makers on topics related to that issue.

Figure 13.2   Voter turnout, 1789–2016.
Source: United States Election Project.

or the American Association of Retired Persons. Other interest groups represent a specific profession, such as the Association of Trial Lawyers of America or the American Medical Association. Interest groups have always been a distinctive feature of American politics; French observer Alexis de Tocqueville noted their importance when he visited the United States in the 1830s.

Interest groups exercise persuasive power through lobbying, research, and fundraising. Lobbyists meet with elected politicians and other important officials, and try to convince those officials to vote in a way that is consistent with the goals of the interest group. There are more than twelve thousand registered lobbyists in the United States, and they spend more than $3 billion each year trying to influence elected officials (Center for Responsive Politics 2019).

Interest group research is frequently conducted by "think tanks," which bring together social scientists, journalists, and public relations specialists to conduct policy-relevant research, which they share with journalists and elected officials (Medvetz 2012). One concern about interest-group research is that the agenda they pursue is different from the priorities of the larger public, and funding for such research may come from sources with very specific policy interests. Importantly, the size, number, and influence of think tanks are growing around the world (McGann 2019).

A third way that interest groups influence politics is through their fundraising activities. About a third of the money spent on congressional elections is raised by political action committees (PACs), which are created by interest groups to raise money for political candidates. A new type of interest group was established in 2010, the "super-PAC." Super-PACs are not allowed to give money directly to candidates, but they are allowed to run their own campaign ads designed to elect or defeat a specific candidate. The Center for Responsive Politics reports that super-PACs spent more than $600 million during the 2012 US presidential election and just over $1 billion in the 2016 election. In the 2018 midterm elections, interest groups spent $1.3 billion. All of these groups hope that their fundraising activities will increase the influence they have over elected officials.

The concern about interest groups is that they distort democracy. The most powerful interest groups are funded by trade and professional associations and by corporations, and their lobbying activities tend to focus on the narrow concerns of those groups rather than the general concerns of the public (Baumgartner et al. 2009). Another concern is that interest groups tend to support incumbents, which makes it harder for new candidates to win elections. In fact, in Congressional and Senate elections, incumbents are reelected more than 80 percent of the time. If incumbents pay most of their attention to interest groups, the result is that fewer people get to participate in policy debates about important public matters.

Mediated Politics

Public sphere The collection of places where private individuals and elected officials gather together to discuss matters of common concern.

In an ideal world, politics would take place in public rather than the hidden spaces populated by lobbyists and think tanks. The **public sphere** is a democratic idea that assumes that private citizens and elected officials should gather together to discuss matters of common concern (Jacobsen 2017; Habermas 1989). In principle, these discussions would include everyone who is affected by a particular issue and would be both open and transparent, so that people who do not wish to speak could still listen and form their own opinions.

Sociology and Politics

Because sociology helps us understand power and politics, sociology majors are well represented in political careers such as elected officials, political consultants and journalists, and social movement leaders. Fernando Cardoso was a sociology professor before he was elected president of Brazil in 1995, and Daniel Patrick Moynihan was a sociology professor at Harvard before he was elected to the US Senate in 1976. Former US president Ronald Reagan was a double major in sociology and economics as a student at Eureka College, and First Lady Michelle Obama was a sociology major at Princeton. E. J. Dionne, one of the most influential journalists and political commentators writing in the United States today, has a PhD in sociology from Oxford. Sociologists are particularly well represented in social movements. As we discussed in Chapter 1, many of the most important leaders of the Civil Rights Movement were sociology majors, including Jesse Jackson, Roy Wilkins, and Martin Luther King Jr.

Michelle Obama

ACTIVE LEARNING

Find out: Are there any current members of Congress who were sociology majors in college? What about contemporary journalists, editorial writers, or social movement leaders?

---

social consciousness and create social change within society itself (Bauman 2002). People who got involved in the new social movements often came to see themselves as "permanent activists," who affirmed their own identity through their protest activities (Polletta and Jasper 2001).

Since then, social movements have become more global. In the past, social movements made claims against specific governments. But today, there is a growing recognition that many of the most pressing social problems are beyond the control of a single country. Issues such as climate change, environmental sustainability, multinational corporate influence, global health crises, refugee populations, and the protection of human rights all require a coordinated global approach. Global social movements make demands on governments, but they also encourage journalists to expose wrongdoing, and organizers develop creative publicity stunts designed to influence global public opinion.

The environmental advocacy group Greenpeace is just one example of the global social movements that have become permanent fixtures in world politics. The most successful of them employ a large staff, have budgets in the millions of dollars, and operate in dozens of countries. But most social movements are quite small, and struggle to be noticed at all (Jacobs and Glass 2001; Sobieraj 2011). To succeed, social movements need material resources, as well as a strategy for capturing public attention.

Organizing for Change

Before the 1970s, most sociologists emphasized how social movements emerged from the grievances that people had in common. **Structural strain theory** sought to identify the things that helped turn grievances and structural inequalities into effective collective action (Smelser 1963). First, there would have

Structural strain theory
A theory about the connection between structural inequalities, grievances and collective action.

Global and Local

The Creation of Greenpeace

The environmental advocacy group Greenpeace was formed during the 1960s in Vancouver, Canada. Influenced by the emerging environmental movement (Chapter 16), its origins can be traced to the "Don't Make a Wave Committee," a movement protesting nuclear tests being conducted by the US military on Amchitka Island, in Alaska. Using the money raised from a benefit concert in Vancouver, they chartered a small fishing boat (which they renamed the *Greenpeace*) in 1971 to sail up to Alaska, bearing witness and protesting in the prohibited zone that the government had established. Their protests were successful, and the US military ceased nuclear testing in Amchitka.

Emboldened by their victory, the leaders of the group adopted the boat's name and vowed to expand their operations. They went to the South Pacific to protest French nuclear testing activities. They exposed the dumping of nuclear waste in the North Atlantic Ocean. They confronted Soviet, Norwegian, and Icelandic whaling ships, trying to get the International Whaling Commission to introduce a moratorium on whaling. They prevented the killing of seal pups in Newfoundland and Scotland. All of these protest activities were visually dramatic and broadcast by television journalists throughout the world, with Greenpeace's tiny boats confronting massive whaling and military ships.

Greenpeace's successes led to organizational growth, and Greenpeace International was formed in 1979 as an umbrella organization for the growing global movement. By the 1990s, Greenpeace had become a major force campaigning for international agreements to reduce greenhouse gas emissions. They brought attention to illegal logging in the Amazon forest. They convinced Ikea to use renewable timber in the construction of its furniture. They campaigned against genetically modified food. They supported and helped develop renewable and citizen-powered energy solutions. They established the Greenpeace Photo Award and the Greenpeace Design Awards to highlight photography, graphic design, and other visual arts that promote an environmentalist message.

Today, Greenpeace is the largest environmental movement in the world, with headquarters in the Netherlands and nearly three million members. They receive more than $30 million annually in contributions and grants, which they use to fund their movement activities and also to support a permanent staff of approximately 2,400 people. They also enjoy the support of more than 15,000 volunteers around the world. They still maintain an office in Vancouver—in fact, their Canadian offices are located only a few miles away from the original home of the Don't Make a Wave Committee.

International social movement organizations
Founded in 1971, the environmental activism organization Greenpeace reports operating 27 independent national/regional organizations in over 55 countries, with 250 staff in the head office in the Netherlands, and thousands more staff and volunteers worldwide. Greenpeace has revenue streams in the hundreds of millions of dollars.

ACTIVE LEARNING

Find Out: How important is Greenpeace in Vancouver's history? Is it a tourist destination? Are there museum exhibits about it? What can you find out?

to be social tension that made people more aware of their deprivation. Second, there would need to be a precipitating event that pushed some people into collective protest. If there was an excessively coercive response to the protest by those in power, then more people would be encouraged to protest together.

The 1965 Watts riots are an example of the kind of collective action that emerges from structural strain. In a context of extreme racial discrimination, segregation, and regular police violence against African Americans, a police arrest of a young black man from the Los Angeles neighborhood of Watts,

Marquette Frye, escalated quickly into a violent confrontation between police and residents. The confrontation turned into an urban uprising that lasted for several days and led to the destruction of more than two hundred buildings in Los Angeles. The Watts riots encouraged many local African Americans to join the Black Panther movement and the Nation of Islam; it also encouraged a "white backlash" that helped elect Ronald Reagan as governor of California in 1967 (Horne 1997).

MOBILIZING RESOURCES. Typically, social movements do not emerge spontaneously from collective grievances and precipitating events. They need leaders, and they need other people who have the time and the skills to manage the organization. All of this requires material resources. Social movements and political groups with these resources are more likely to

The Watts Rebellion, Los Angeles, 1965
In a context of extreme racial discrimination, segregation, and regular police violence against African Americans, the arrest of a young black man, Marquette Frye, escalated quickly into a violent confrontation between police and the residents of Watts, a neighborhood of Los Angeles. The resulting uprising lasted for several days and led to the deaths of 34 people and tens of millions of dollars in property damage.

achieve their goals. In the case of Watts, for example, the Black Panther Party already had a strong presence in Los Angeles, which allowed them to respond to the collective protests by recruiting new members.

Instead of focusing on the underlying inequalities that make people feel deprived or aggrieved, **resource mobilization theory** emphasizes the material and organizational resources that increase the chances that social movements will be able to achieve their goals (McCarthy and Zald 1977). There are four different types of resources that social movement organizations need if they want to increase their chances of success: money, legitimacy, facilities, and labor. Social movements can combine these resources in different ways. A social movement with a lot of money can hire professional staff to do the work needed to run the organization. Organizations with more legitimacy will have an easier time attracting money and labor, and will also have more success attracting media attention.

Resource mobilization theory suggests that groups that can capture the support of the wealthy will have an easier time achieving their objectives. It also suggests that wealthier societies will have more social movements, because they can rely on the extra discretionary time that their citizens enjoy (McCarthy and Zald 1977). This means that successful social movements are more likely to reflect the concerns of the wealthier classes. Environmental sustainability, Slow Food, bicycle advocacy, and lifestyle issues resonate more with the concerns of the privileged, and social movements based on these kinds of claims have a higher likelihood of success than other kinds of social movements. Because of their ability to attract resources, centrist and reformist movements are more likely to be successful than radical or revolutionary ones.

But material resources do not explain everything. If a social movement has committed and dedicated members, it can depend on them for volunteer labor, and it can succeed without having much money. If political opportunities allow them to attract the support of elected officials, they can get a lot of

Resource mobilization theory
A theory that links social movement success to resources of money, legitimacy, facilities, and labor.

public attention even if they lack good social connections. If they can create dramatic and visually compelling protest activities, they will be more likely to attract media attention. In an era of social media, community education and grassroots organizing can occur online. Movements such as Black Lives Matter and #MeToo have gained wide recognition using social media to communicate.

Some of the most important social movements have achieved success with very few material resources. These movements rely instead on the commitment of their members and the effectiveness of their protests. Piven and Cloward (1978) have argued, for example, that poor people's movements are the most successful when they rely on mass protests and disruptions. As soon as they develop into formal bureaucratic organizations, social movements become less concerned with the powerless, and they are more easily co-opted by the powerful (Piven and Cloward 1978).

GENERATING COMMITMENT. While the largest social movements can pay professional staff to do work for them, most rely primarily on volunteer labor. This creates a **free-rider problem**, where people who would benefit from a social movement's activities assume that others will do the work (Olson 1971). In order to overcome this problem, a social movement needs a critical mass of highly committed people who are willing to volunteer their time (Marwell and Oliver 1993).

Free-rider problem In social movement context, the situation where the people who benefit from a social movement's activities assume that others will do the work.

Many social movements use small groups and social networks to generate commitment. Because the free-rider problem becomes a bigger issue as group size increases, social movements try to create small-group situations where they can talk to people in a more intimate setting. The community organizer Fred Ross developed the house meeting technique during the 1940s and 1950s, as a way of generating commitment among a critical mass of supporters. Ross would hold a series of small meetings at people's homes, where he could describe the goals of the social movement, identify enthusiastic new recruits, and train them to become movement organizers. Cesar Chavez used the same approach when he organized the United Farm Workers movement during the 1960s and 1970s.

Social movements also encourage commitment by reinforcing emotional connections and collective identity. People are more likely to participate in a movement if doing so reinforces their sense of who they are (Polletta and Jasper 2001). The social movement ACT UP generated commitment among gays and lesbians by convincing them that protest around AIDS was an important way of expressing their gay identity (Polletta and Jasper 2001: 291). Protesters during the Egyptian revolution believed that they were saving the nation from decades of decline and humiliation, resurrecting Egypt's once-proud golden age (Alexander 2011: 31). The most effective kinds of movement identities clearly distinguish active members from bystanders. For example, students who participated in the 1960 lunch counter sit-ins emphasized the fact that they were actually *doing something* to protest racial oppression (Polletta 1998).

Getting Noticed

Social movements need to attract public attention if they want to achieve their goals. In general, there are two types of strategies for attracting attention. The first type is to pay close attention to the changing political context, and to frame the message in a way that connects to the larger public agenda. The second type is to stage visually compelling and dramatic cultural performances. The advent of online social networking has enhanced the ability of social movements to do both.

POLITICAL OPPORTUNITY STRUCTURE. Sociologists think about political context and social movements in terms of the **political opportunity structure**. Social movements have better opportunities in three types of situations: when there are changes in existing political alliances, when there are political conflicts among elites, and when there are clear alliances that can be made with specific political groups (Tarrow 1989). In these kinds of situations, elected officials and other groups with political power will be more willing to champion the cause of a social movement.

The American Civil Rights Movement offers a good case study of how the political opportunity structure can help a social movement. Leaders like Rosa Parks and Martin Luther King Jr. were very effective at creating dramatic protest events that attracted media attention. But they also benefited from a changing political context, as the sociologist Doug McAdam (1982) has shown. By the late 1940s, tensions between the United States and the Soviet Union had increased significantly, marking the start of the Cold War. President Truman and others in the US government were concerned that the Soviet Union would exploit American racism to discredit the government and weaken its international alliances. In this political context, Truman acted decisively to support a civil rights agenda. He created the Committee on Civil Rights in 1946, and he desegregated the military in 1948. Truman's actions divided the Democratic Party. In fact, southern Democrats ran their own candidate, Strom Thurmond, for president in 1948.

The changing political context of the late 1940s made it more likely that any civil rights protests in the South would be championed by the federal government and covered by national media. Leaders of the Civil Rights Movement recognized this opportunity, and they organized dramatic protest events in the 1950s and 1960s, culminating in the 1963 March on Washington.

CULTURAL PERFORMANCE. Social movements stage dramatic events of collective protest to attract public attention. We tend to see more collective protest during moments of political instability, and they are more likely to be effective during "unsettled times" (Swidler 1986; Habermas 1998). Still, for social movements to attract public attention, they need to produce compelling and meaningful events of collective protest.

Social movements carefully script their protests, in order to convey specific meanings to the larger public audience (Alexander 2011). They choose the site of their protest carefully. They try to plan how their protest activities will be choreographed together with police, bystanders, counterprotesters and others who are present on the scene. They work to convince journalists that their protests are legitimate and deserving of coverage (Sobieraj 2011). Sociologists think about this careful scripting of protest in terms of **symbolic politics**, in which the meanings associated with political actions are just as important as the policies or the social changes being proposed.

Good social movement leaders know how to create an effective cultural performance. When the American community organizer Saul Alinsky planned protest activities during the 1950s and 1960s, his goal was "to maneuver and bait the establishment so that it will publicly attack him as a 'dangerous enemy'" (Alinsky [1971] 2010). If he could manage to do this, he knew that he would get good media coverage, and he knew that most of the public would be outraged by the overreaction of the authorities. Similarly, Martin Luther King Jr. knew that every time his nonviolent protests met a violent reaction from Southern police, the images shown in newspapers and on television would anger Americans and increase public support for his movement. King also had a talent for creating visually compelling stages for his protests. The 1963 March on Washington is one of the most iconic

Political opportunity structure
The political opportunities available for successful social movement action that occurs when there are changes in political alliances, political conflicts among elites, or when there are clear alliances that can be made with specific political groups.

Symbolic politics A type of political activity in which the meanings associated with a political action are just as important as the policies or the social changes being proposed.

Getting noticed in a crowded attention space
Egyptian women (left) hold up a sign protesting the continued sexual harassment of women among protesters in the revolutionary actions in Tahrir Square in 2011, while Iranians living in Belgium hold up a placard in English reading "Where is My Vote?" during a 2009 protest against the Iranian election results (right). Using English on signs attracts English-language media coverage.

images in American history. Taking place 100 years after the Emancipation Proclamation, approximately 250,000 people marched from the Washington Monument to the Lincoln Memorial, where King gave his famous "I Have a Dream" speech as television stations broadcast the event live throughout the nation.

This remains true in the era of social media. The protestors in Egypt's Tahrir Square, for example, knew that their actions and the government response were being covered by social media and they scripted their protests accordingly. Indeed, it is not uncommon for protesters in non–English speaking countries to carry signs and placards written in English in the confident expectation that they will be read by a huge international media audience.

Other social movements use comedy and political satire in their cultural performances, using techniques such as "culture jamming" (Chapter 4). In a similar way, "Billionaires for Bush" was a regular presence during US Presidential campaigns in 2000 and 2004 (Chapter 2).

Movement Success

How do we know if a social movement is successful? All social movements attempt to change society, and all have specific goals they are trying to achieve. Sometimes it is easy to determine whether a movement met its goals. For example, the Human Rights Campaign fought for years against laws that prevented gay and lesbian couples from getting married. When individual states overturned these laws, and then when the Supreme Court ruled in 2013 that the Defense of Marriage Act was unconstitutional, and finally when the Supreme Court ruled in 2015 for freedom to marry nationwide, then the Human Rights Campaign could declare unambiguously that they had been successful in achieving their goals.

But it is not always easy to determine if a movement has met its goals. How would we know if the Slow Food movement has been successful? Would we need to see declining profits for McDonald's, or laws passed protecting regional cuisine? Would we need to see people spending more time eating dinner with family and friends, and less time eating alone in their cars? Would it be enough to see a growing awareness of sustainable agriculture and farm-to-table cooking? How would we measure this awareness?

For many movements, success in achieving their goals is often followed by a social backlash and higher levels of conflict. The feminist movement, which is widely regarded as one of the most successful social movements of the 20th century, faced a significant backlash during the 1980s (Faludi 2006). This backlash was part of a countermovement, which is often a consequence of social movement success. Many women today are reluctant to identify themselves as feminists, despite the fact that they believe in the idea of gender equality. The result is that feminists have to re-fight many of the battles they thought they had already won.

Many sociologists point to the fact that social movements do important things even when they fail to achieve their primary goals. When people participate in a social movement, they benefit from a sense of **social solidarity** that makes them feel more attached to society. People who participate in social movements learn important civic skills, and are more likely to join other voluntary associations and participate in politics (Minkoff 1997). All of this produces **social capital**, which refers to the relationships and experiences of social connection and cooperation that allow people to believe that they can work together to improve society. As Robert Putnam (2000) has argued, social capital is important for building and maintaining a democratic society.

White nationalists clash with counter-protesters in Charlottesville, Virginia, 2017
Backlash against social movements is one sign of movement success. Widespread social-movement conflict and violence suggest social and political instability.

Social solidarity A feeling of social connection and social belonging.

Social capital Relationships and experience of social connection and cooperation people have with each other that allow them to act together.

CASE STUDY

The Strange History of the US Electoral College

In the 2016 US election, Donald Trump was elected president despite the fact that he did not receive the most votes. His opponent, Hilary Clinton, received more than 2.8 million more votes than he did. This had happened before. In 1824, John Quincy Adams won the election despite receiving fewer votes than Andrew Jackson. In 1876, Rutherford B. Hayes was elected despite receiving fewer votes than Samuel Tilden. In 1888, Benjamin Harrison was elected despite receiving fewer votes than Grover Cleveland. And in 2000, George W. Bush became president despite receiving fewer votes than Al Gore. How could this happen in a democratic election? The answer has to do with the Electoral College.

The US Constitution states that the Electoral College is responsible for selecting the president and vice president of the United States. There are 538 electors, and an absolute majority of 270 electoral votes is needed to win the election. Each individual state decides how it will

select its electors. Each state gets one elector for each of its senators and representatives. The District of Columbia gets the number of electors that is proportional to its share of the national population, with its maximum number limited to that of the least populous state in the nation. In the original plan, each elector would cast two votes for president. The candidate who received the most votes would be elected president, and the candidate who received the second-highest number of votes would be elected vice president. This was changed in 1803, so that electors would cast one vote for president and one for vice president.

The creation of the Electoral College was a compromise. Many of the founders distrusted direct democracy, because they believed that ordinary people lacked sufficient knowledge to make good decisions and that they were easily swayed by emotional and misleading political arguments. But they were also concerned that

CASE STUDY CONTINUED

letting members of Congress make the decision would give them too much *power* over the President.

The decision to establish the Electoral College was also motivated by *inequality* and *privilege*, because it gave Congress a way of dealing with the fact that not everyone had the right to vote (Amar 2007). Because each state got a fixed number of electoral votes based on population (rather than the number of people eligible to vote, or the number of people who actually voted), there was no incentive to extend the vote to women. Similarly, there was no incentive to extend the vote to slaves, who were counted as three-fifths of a person for the purpose of determining the number of seats each state would have in the legislature. If the Constitution had required a direct election of the President by eligible voters, the slave states would have faced a choice; either extend the vote to slaves, or lose political power to the non-slave states.

There was *contingency* in the early Electoral College, as the states had not agreed about how to allocate their electoral votes. In most states, electors were chosen from congressional districts, and they would cast their vote for the candidate who won the election in their district. After Thomas Jefferson lost the 1796 election, however, the state of Virginia passed a "winner-take-all" law, in which all of the state's electoral votes would go to the candidate who won the state. With this change, Virginia gave all of its electoral votes to Jefferson in the 1800 election, and he became president. Other states quickly followed Virginia's lead. By 1836 all but one state had a winner-take-all system, and by 1880 all states were using this system. But this had a huge impact on the *structure* of presidential campaigns. Candidates now have little incentive to campaign in states where the outcome is obvious. Thirty-three states have voted for the same political party in the last five presidential elections, and 40 states have voted for the same party in every election since 2000. Candidates tend to ignore these states, instead focusing all their attention on those "battleground states" in which the election is closely contested.

Today, the Electoral College means that closely contested states get more attention and enjoy greater influence than other states, in a way that has led to some unusual political dynamics. Battleground states benefit significantly just because they are closely contested; they receive more federal grants, and they have more influence in general over federal policymaking (Hudak 2014). Voter turnout is higher in battleground states (Lipsitz 2009). They also tend to have more political division and higher levels of *conflict*. Political parties in these states work hard to encourage their members to vote,

Whose vote counts?
An Electoral College ballot from Illinois is seen during a joint session of Congress to count the votes in Washington, DC, in January 2017.

reinforcing the *solidarity* of their political party by demonizing the members of the other party. People who live in non-battleground states have become increasingly resentful of the Electoral College system (Alexander 2019).

While the US Electoral College was created as a response to *local* concerns by some of the Founders about direct democracy and other local concerns having to do with the political power of slaveholding states, it was not the first example of such a system to exist. Electoral colleges were used by elites throughout Europe to elect kings, princes, and high magistrates, going back as early as the 11th century (Colomer 2016). In the Catholic Church, the Pope is elected by a conclave of cardinals, which functions the same as the Electoral College. All of these systems provided a model that influenced the creation of the US Electoral College. And the US system, once established, created a *global* model for other national constitutions in the 19th century, including those of Argentina, Venezuela, Colombia, Mexico, Chile, and Peru (Colomer 2016). In each of these countries, though, there was a major political crisis in which a candidate won the Electoral College vote while losing the popular vote. They have all since replaced the old system with a direct presidential election, decided by the national popular vote.

There has been growing *resistance* to the US Electoral College system over the last 50 years, with several important social movements pushing to abolish the system in favor of a direct national vote. There have been more than seven hundred proposals to reform

CASE STUDY CONTINUED

or abolish the Electoral College through Constitutional amendment, but they have all failed to get the support they needed to be ratified (Alberta 2017). Today, there are several important movements continuing the effort. The National Popular Vote Interstate Compact is a movement to convince state legislatures to agree to give all of their electoral votes to the candidate who receives the most votes in the national election, regardless of the outcome in their state election. As of 2018, 12 states had signed the Compact, accounting for 172 of the 270 electoral college votes they need to control the election. The National Popular Vote plan has the support of dozens of advocacy groups, intellectuals, and major newspaper editorial staffs. Supporters of this movement have introduced legislation in favor of the Compact in all 50 states. But there has been consistent opposition by battleground states and small rural states, which have the most *power* in the current Electoral College system.

LEARNING GOALS REVISITED

13.1 Understand the way sociologists define power.

- Sociologists define power as the ability of individuals or groups to get what they want, even against the resistance of others who are participating in the same action.

- Sociologists emphasize that there are different types of power, but that every exercise of power encounters resistance.

- Sociologists emphasize that the exercise of power is shaped by the resources that the individuals or group has at its disposal. In other words, power is connected to the organization of inequality and privilege.

- In modern societies, state power organized by governments is centrally important in politics.

- Authority is the legitimate use of power that is based in the consent of the governed. Most commonly today, people respond to the authority of those who hold institutional positions anchored in law, such as elected officials or state representatives.

13.2 Define the difference between coercive and persuasive power.

- Coercive power involves the attempt to force people to do something by using the threat of punishment or violence, while persuasive power is the attempt to use influence to convince people to do what you want them to do.

- Coercive power and persuasive power have their own distinctive risks. Coercive power frequently results in an escalating spiral of violence and resistance. For persuasive power, the main risk is that the arguments of an opposing individual or group will be more convincing or more influential.

- Persuasive power is more effective than coercive power because people are more likely to resist coercive power. When this happens, coercive power becomes more expensive at the same time that it becomes less effective.

13.3 Understand how persuasive power is connected to the spread of democracy.

- The democratic revolutions in the 18th century in France and the United States made persuasive power more important because of the principle of popular sovereignty, which emphasized that power ultimately resided with the people.

- Candidates for elections today spend a lot of time and money trying to talk to ordinary people and civic groups as a way of learning what they want, so they can craft persuasive arguments in an attempt to win votes.

13.4 Understand how news media organizations influence politics and political debate.

- Media organizations influence politics by defining the agenda of issues that people will talk about. Elected officials influence the media agenda, but the media agenda is also influenced by economic considerations, by journalists' commitment to maintaining their professional autonomy, and by the actions of social movements.

- Hundreds of millions of dollars are spent on media campaigns by candidates for elected office in the United States. Incumbent presidents and other officials also rely on the media to speak to the large populations of contemporary societies.

- Social movements use a range of strategies to win attention in both the media and the wider political discussion.

- Media are important for maintaining hegemony, which is the vision of the world held by dominant groups.

13.5 Understand the different types of rights claims that social movements make against the powerful and how that helps create social solidarity.

- Social movements form when ordinary people act together to try to create social or political change. They are different from political parties or interest groups because they are led by people who are not professional politicians, and they try to achieve their goals outside of established institutions.

- Historically, excluded groups such as women and racial and ethnic minorities have formed social movements as the best way to advocate for change.

- Social movements are more likely to be successful if they have abundant resources, or if they connect to the concerns of wealthier groups.

- Some important social movements have achieved success with very few resources by generating commitment among their members, paying close attention to the changing political context, and creating dramatic cultural performances.

- Social movements express their political demands through identity claims that present the movement as a unified group with a unified interest, standing claims that assert that

a group must be more fully included in the society, and program claims of support for or opposition to specific laws or policy proposals.

- It is not always easy to determine whether a social movement is successful. Even the most successful social movements will often have to deal with political and cultural backlash. Despite these challenges, the people who participate in social movements develop a stronger sense of social solidarity, and they are more likely to participate in politics. In general, social movements encourage people to think about the ways that they might make their society a better place.

Key Terms

Absolute monarchy 380
Agenda-setting 386
Charismatic authority 377
Coercive power 377
Constitutional monarchy 380
Deliberation 380
Democratic republic 380
Free-rider problem 394
Hegemony 379
Interest group 383
Media concentration 388
Parliamentary system 381
Persuasive power 377
Political opportunity structure 395
Politics 376
Popular sovereignty 380
Power 376
Presidential system 381
Public opinion 381
Public sphere 384
Rational-legal authority 377
Resource mobilization theory 393
Single-party state 380
Social capital 397
Social movement 389
Social solidarity 397
State 376
Symbolic politics 395
Structural strain theory 391
Traditional authority 377

Review Questions

1. What is power? What is the difference between coercive and persuasive power? What are the advantages and disadvantages of each type?

2. How did the spread of democracy change the exercise of power?

3. While the United States has a presidential system of democracy, most successful democracies in the world today are parliamentary systems. What are the main differences between these two systems? What are the advantages and disadvantages of each system? Why do you think that parliamentary systems have tended to be more stable and more successful than presidential ones?

4. How do interest groups try to influence politics? How is this different from the model of politics expressed by the ideal of deliberation?

5. How do news organizations influence the political process?

6. What are some of the main limitations with mediated political discussions? What can ordinary people do to try to overcome these limitations and get their voices heard?

7. How does money influence the media agenda? How is this different for advertising-supported media organizations, as compared to government-funded media? What do professional journalists do to try to limit the influence of money?

8. What is a social movement? Why do people choose to organize social movements, rather than engage in a different kind of political action?

9. Describe the three different kinds of claims that social movements make against the powerful, according to Charles Tilly.

10. How have social movements changed since the 1960s?

11. What are the four different types of resources that social movement organizations need if they want to increase their chances of success?

12. What is the free-rider problem? What do social movements do to try to overcome the free-rider problem, and to make sure that people will participate in the movement?

13. What are some of the things that social movements can do if they want to increase their chances of getting noticed?

14. How do we know if a social movement is successful?

Explore

RECOMMENDED READINGS

Alexander, Jeffrey C. 2012. *The Performance of Power: Obama's Victory and the Democratic Struggle for Power.* New York: Oxford University Press.

Lukes, Steven. 2004. *Power: A Radical View*, 2nd ed. New York: Palgrave-Macmillan.

Schudson, Michael. 2003. *The Sociology of News.* New York: W. W. Norton.

Tilly, Charles, and Leslie Wood. 2012. *Social Movements, 1768–2012*, 3rd ed. New York: Paradigm Publishers

ACTIVITIES

- *Use your sociological imagination*: Select a social movement that interests you. What are the goals of this movement? How successful do you think the movement has been? Describe the resources the movement has, as well as the protest activities and the cultural performances that it uses to try to attract attention.

- *Data+Media Literacies*: Read the front section of the newspaper. Write down the stories that make the front page, and the different people who get quoted in the stories. What issues and voices are privileged?

- *Discuss*: Why do drivers slow down when they see a police car on the road? What does this say about power, the state, and the use of coercive and persuasive power?

For additional resources, including Media+Data Literacy exercises, In the News exercises, and quizzes, please go to **oup.com/he/ Jacobs-Townsley1e**

14

Economy, Education, Work, and Recreation

Before the 1980s, internships for college students were unusual. Plumbers, electricians, and others beginning a career in the skilled trades would often start out as apprentices, working with an experienced tradesperson until they had enough hands-on experience to be licensed. People who wanted to become doctors would complete a residency after completing medical school, where they worked under the supervision of an attending physician until they had enough experience to get an unrestricted license to practice medicine. But for nearly every other profession, the expectation was that if a new employee needed to learn additional skills, they would learn them on the job.

Internships emerged on a widespread basis in business schools in the 1980s. They were initially developed as a recruiting tool for students who intended to enter the finance, entertainment, and health care industries (Spradlin 2009). Internships helped students build relationships with potential employers and get work experience in their desired field. It was a good deal for both sides. Employers got free (or nearly-free) entry-level work from ambitious and motivated university students, and they also got a head start toward recruiting the most promising graduates. Students earned college credit toward their degree, while building networks and developing relationships with potential employers.

Internships proved to be very popular with students, and they spread quickly to other academic departments. By 2010, the general consensus among students and employers was that internships were one of the most important things a person could do to land a job in her chosen field. In England, a recent study found that about a third of all entry-level jobs were filled by college graduates who had already done internships with the organization that hired them (High Fliers 2016).

Hands-on learning
Direct experience is a useful form of learning. It is organized in paid apprenticeships, training academies, and internships.

LEARNING GOALS

14.1   Describe the different social purposes and social effects of education.

14.2   Describe the experience of going to school, and how it has changed over time.

14.3   Think about the kinds of characteristics that are associated with "good jobs," and describe how the distribution of good jobs is socially structured.

14.4   Describe the experience economy, and know where and how people are searching for satisfaction outside of work.

14.5   Describe how the economy has changed over time, and explain why economic insecurity is such a significant feature of modern social life.

Increasing numbers of employers were offering internships for first-year undergraduate students. Nearly half of all employers surveyed warned that college graduates with no work experience would have "little or no chance" of getting a job (High Fliers 2016: 26).

While internships are now considered a virtual requirement for getting a good job in most industries, they are not without controversy. Critics observe that too many internships are exploitative. While interns often work for little or no money in return for the promise of gaining direct work experience, they can also find themselves getting coffee, filing papers, and doing other menial tasks (Perlin 2012). Unpaid internships benefit wealthier students who do not need an income. Others complain that internships do not have a close enough connection to the larger educational mission of the university. Many colleges and universities are responding to these criticisms by establishing endowments to provide financial support for students in internships, and by creating courses that link the internship experience to the academic curriculum.

This chapter explores the relationship between education, work, and the economy. We begin by examining the different functions that education is supposed to perform. Next, we examine how schools are organized, and what the experience of going to school looks like. From there, we turn to the complementary worlds of work and recreation. The chapter ends with a discussion of the economy, paying particular attention to the forces that helped create the current global system.

What Is Education for?

In Germany, formal schooling begins at six years old. Between the ages of six and 10, most children attend a public elementary school in their neighborhood. At age 10, most German students and their parents choose between three different types of secondary schools: the *Gymnasium*, for students who plan to go to college; the *Realschule*, which ends in grade 10 and gives students the option to either go on to a *Gymnasium* (depending on exam results) or a vocational apprenticeship; or the *Hauptschule*, which also ends in grade nine or 10, and has a more vocational focus. All German schools require students to learn at least one foreign language.

Germany is unusual for how early it segregates students into university and vocational tracks, and it has been criticized for reproducing privilege and inequality by introducing these tracks so early in the students' lives. A 2000 study found that Germany had the worst inequality in its educational performance among all developed nations, although it has dramatically reduced educational inequality since then (Berwick 2015). But Germany has also received praise for its vocational training, which combines practical school training with apprenticeships in the private as well as the public sector. Culturally, German schools reinforce the respectability of the skilled trades and other manual labor. Germany has the lowest youth unemployment in the European Union. And for those students who are admitted to a public German university, there are no tuition fees.

Students at work in a vocational school in Ulm, Germany
Germany tracks students from age 10 into pathways to vocations in the trades or into university education.

Literacy, Socialization, Citizenship, and Job Training

As the discussion of Germany demonstrates, educational systems do many different things, and they pursue a variety of different goals. One goal for education is to promote **literacy**, which refers to the ability to read, write, and communicate well enough to participate fully in society. A second goal is to promote socialization (Chapter 5). A third goal is **citizenship education**, which involves learning about the history, laws, social institutions, and political organization of the nation. Finally, **job training**, in which schools teach students specific skills that will help them enter the workforce and earn a decent wage, is a goal of many educational systems.

MASS EDUCATION AND THE QUEST FOR LITERACY. Formal education used to be limited to children of the most privileged families. The first mass education systems developed in Western Europe and the United States during the 19th century (Soysal and Strang 1989), and soon emerged throughout the world as part of the larger spread of nation-states (Bendix 1964). Today, more than 90 percent of the children in the world go to school, and free elementary education is described as a basic human right by the United Nations (Meyer, Ramirez, and Soysal 1992).

According to the sociologists John Boli, Francisco Ramirez, and John Meyer, mass education has three basic features (Boli, Ramirez, and Meyer 1985). First, mass education is intended to be universal and standardized. This means that it should be available to everyone, and that students should be learning similar things and going to schools that are broadly similar. Second, mass education is strongly institutionalized, in the sense that schools around the world are organized in a strikingly similar and homogeneous way. And third, mass education is focused on the individual: each student is evaluated and expected to achieve a certain minimum level of proficiency in key literacy skills.

Literacy The ability to read, write, communicate, and use other skills that allow people to participate fully in their society.

Citizenship education Curriculum dealing with history, laws, main social institutions, and political organization of the nation in which students live.

Job training When schools teach students specific skills that will help them enter the workforce and earn a decent wage.

Children in a school classroom in Kenya
Mass literacy and education are policy goals in much of the world.

Despite its shortcomings, mass education has produced dramatic results. Only 12 percent of the world's population was literate in 1800, and only 21 percent was literate in 1900; by 2000, however, nearly 82 percent of the world's population had achieved literacy (Roser and Ortiz-Ospina 2018). There are still significant inequalities, which we discuss later in the chapter. But mass education has played a critical role in the socialization of children, helping them participate in their national societies as well as the larger global economy.

THE HIDDEN CURRICULUM. As we discussed in Chapter 5, schools are an important agent of socialization.

Moral education A form of education where students learn social skills, the values of self-determination and autonomy, and how to attach to social groups.

Émile Durkheim argued that one of the central functions of school was **moral education**. Durkheim emphasized three areas where schools prepared their students to be effective members of society: they encourage a spirit of discipline, they help create attachments to social groups, and they reinforce the values of self-determination and autonomy (Durkheim 1961). Talcott Parsons extended Durkheim's argument, writing that the school classroom is "an agency of socialization" (Parsons 1959: 297). According to Parsons, the classroom reinforces a commitment to a society's core values. It teaches students about citizenship, and what it means to be a good member of their society. It gets them to recognize that they are being evaluated in comparison to their classmates. And, on the basis of these evaluations, it encourages them to start thinking about the kinds of roles they will play in society when they are adults.

While Parsons and Durkheim emphasized the positive function of school socialization, others have emphasized how this socialization is connected to a "hidden curriculum" that reinforces power, privilege, and inequality. In his book *Life in Classrooms*, Philip W. Jackson (1968) argued that the classroom forces students to develop strategies for dealing with crowds and social distractions. It reminds them on a daily basis that there is an unequal power relationship between teachers and students, and it forces them to choose a side: Will they obey their teachers, or will they join other rebellious students to resist the power of school authorities? Rebellious students (who often come from more disadvantaged backgrounds) are often more popular and enjoy high status within the school, but bad grades and other negative evaluations limit their life chances as adults and reinforce their inequality (Willis 1977).

TEACHING PRACTICAL SKILLS FOR THE WORKFORCE. With the rise of mass education, schools took on a larger share of the responsibility for preparing people for the workforce. In *The Wealth of Nations* (1776), Adam Smith recognized the economic utility of the basic literacy taught in schools of the time, but today most jobs require more advanced literacy skills such as computer use, the ability to work collaboratively, and the ability to find and evaluate information.

Different kinds of schools teach students specific skills that are relevant to the workplace. The objective of vocational schools is to train students to enter the skilled trades. Vocational schools work closely with employers, establishing apprenticeship systems so that students can gain real-world experience and make connections with potential future employers. Graduate programs in professional fields such as law and medicine teach specific skills and knowledge, prepare students for their professional licensing exams, and facilitate connections with potential employers in hospitals and law firms. Last, the increasing expectations of many workplaces that college graduates will have completed at least one internship means that many contemporary students expect to learn practical work-related skills in their formal education.

There are disagreements about the importance of practical skills for education, as well as the preparation level of students when they enter the workforce. Employers believe that the most effective job candidates have a broad-based liberal arts education as well as a specific set of job-related skills, but they feel that colleges and universities need to place more emphasis on applied learning that takes place in real-world settings. Fewer than half of employers in a recent survey believed that college graduates were adequately prepared for the workforce, and fewer than one-quarter of employers believed that college graduates had developed the ability to use their knowledge and skills to solve real-world problems (Hart Research Associates 2015).

Many educators disagree with the argument that a school's most important mission is to help their students get a job. They argue instead that the mission of a school is "to encourage students to lead meaningful and thoughtful lives, to be informed and engaged citizens of the world, and to have a curiosity and a zest for learning that will help them to flourish throughout their lives" (Krislov 2013). They argue that the economy is moving so quickly that a narrow focus on a specific job skill is likely to produce workers whose skills are out of date almost as soon as they begin their jobs. The more effective approach, they argue, is to teach people how to become lifelong learners, who are flexible and creative in their orientation to the world.

University lecture hall
Employer surveys report that the most effective job candidates have a broad-based liberal arts education as well as a specific set of job-related skills, but they feel that colleges and universities need to put more emphasis on applied learning that takes place in real-world settings. What do you think?

CREDENTIALISM. Credentialism refers to a process in which formal educational qualifications are used to determine who is eligible to work in a given occupation. As Max Weber argued, credentialism is one of the most important social forces that shapes the modern stratification system. He further observed that college diplomas were being used as a credential to determine who was eligible for good management jobs in bureaucratic organizations. Credentialism is efficient for employers, because it reduces the number of applications they need to read carefully. But it also tends

Credentialism A process in which formal educational qualifications are used to determine who is eligible to work in a given occupation.

An unfair playing field?
Some wealthy parents go to extreme lengths to assure their children's education. This became clear in the 2019 college admissions scandal where actress Lori Loughlin (right) was revealed to have bribed college admissions officials at the University of Southern California to falsify her daughter's (left) application for admission.

Cultural capital Education, cultural knowledge, and cultural consumption that signals privilege to others; the knowledge and consumption of culturally valued things. Higher levels of cultural capital are associated with success in school.

to reinforce privilege and inequality, because people who come from a more privileged background are more likely to pursue advanced educational credentials.

Credentialism almost inevitably leads to credential inflation, in which there is a gradual and continual increase in the educational qualifications needed to get a specific job. As the sociologist Randall Collins has argued, credential inflation is a process that feeds on itself, almost guaranteeing that the educational requirements needed to get a job today will not be good enough to get the same job in the future (Collins 2011). While an undergraduate college degree was enough to get a management job in the 1940s and 1950s, today the same job usually requires a graduate degree. Collins further observes that "educational expansion and credential inflation could go on endlessly, until janitors need PhDs, and household workers and babysitters will be required to hold advanced degrees in household appliances and childcare" (2011: 235). The problem is that the costs for credential inflation are borne by students and their families, who have to spend more and more money on their education. They also have to delay their entry into the labor force, with each new educational qualification taking several years to complete. And while children from wealthy families often do not need to take out loans to cover tuition or living expenses, they may still feel intense social pressure to attend a prestigious college even if they are not interested in further education. Unfortunately, recent scandals have demonstrated the willingness of some wealthy parents to game the college-admissions system on behalf of their underqualified or uninterested children.

Social Sorting, Social Reproduction, and Social Mobility

The advantages of privilege assert themselves well before students get to college. Wealthy families can afford to send their children to schools that have more resources, more highly trained teachers, smaller classes, and better social networks that help their students get into better colleges and more prestigious (and higher-paying) jobs. They can afford to hire private tutors to make sure that their children don't fall behind. And they are quick to step in and intervene with teachers, in order to make sure that their children succeed (Chapter 5).

Schools also reinforce privilege and inequality by rewarding students who have the right kind of **cultural capital**. As we discussed in Chapter 4, cultural capital refers to the knowledge and consumption of culturally valued things. Being polite, knowing the right kinds of clothes to wear, or displaying an interest in and knowledge of art and high culture are all forms of cultural capital. Teachers tend to interpret these displays as evidence that a student is smart, curious, and precocious. They shower these students with attention, praise, and good grades. These students believe that their good grades were the result of their hard work and intellectual talents, but they fail to see how their academic success is also connected to their social and cultural privileges (Bourdieu and Passeron 1990).

There is strong evidence that education reinforces social privileges and inequalities. Children whose parents have more prestigious jobs, higher levels of education and income, and more wealth are significantly more likely to have higher levels of educational achievement (Conley 2001; Mare 1981). As inequality gets worse, so does the difference in educational achievement between high-income and low-income families (Mayer 2001). This is particularly true at the highest levels of education, where family resources are strongly associated with college enrollment (Morgan and Kim 2006). In fact, at the most prestigious universities in the United States, nearly three-quarters of the students come from families in the highest socioeconomic quartile (Haveman and Smeeding 2006).

The relationship between education and privilege is deeply concerning, because getting a college degree is the best route to achieving social mobility. A child born into a family in the lowest income quintile has about a 40 percent chance of staying at that income level as an adult; if she completes college, however, she has more than an 80 per-

The importance of college education
Children and teenagers at this college job fair in 2016 receive career counseling and information about what education is required for different careers.

cent chance of improving her socioeconomic standing, and nearly a 50 percent chance of entering the middle class (Reeves 2014). And these improvements are likely to last for generations, because children whose parents have a college degree are much more likely to complete college themselves. Improving access to college is a major public policy goal, as we discuss later in the chapter.

Childcare and Employment

Schools also serve purposes that may seem to have little to do with education. Social scientists have long argued that education helps keep the unemployment rate artificially low. When the job market is difficult, there is a higher likelihood that people will enroll in college or community college. This is the **warehousing theory** of education, which states that postsecondary education acts as a holding place that protects people from unstable labor market conditions (Bozick 2009).

> **Warehousing theory** A theory that focuses on the ways that postsecondary education acts as a holding place that protects people from unstable labor market conditions.

Schools are also a major source of employment. In the United States, there are more than five million full-time teachers working in elementary schools, high schools, colleges, and universities (NCES 2016). Schools employ just as many people in administration, clerical support, janitorial services, buildings and grounds maintenance, counseling and career services, and other non-teaching positions. In many communities, in fact, the schools are some of the biggest and most stable employers.

Finally, schools offer childcare for working parents, by giving their children a place to be during the workday.

Employment in education
Educational institutions, like this one, employ five million teachers in the United States. They also employ custodians, counselors, secretaries, and other support staff. In some communities schools are the largest employers.

Childcare is one of the most expensive household costs for working parents. On average, families with young children and working mothers spend more than 20 percent of the mother's income on childcare costs, and the proportion is even higher for low-income families (Glynn, Farrell, and Wu 2013). The cost for full-time infant daycare is often more expensive than a year of college tuition. Massive financial costs fall on young working parents, and it is a significant economic benefit for them when their children reach school age. Many schools also offer extended hours that more closely match parents' working schedules.

Going to School

Going to school is a common experience throughout the world. Still, even though more than 90 percent of the children in the world go to school, there are vast differences in what their schools look like. The school experience varies depending on the size of the school and how it is organized. Primary schools are different from secondary schools, which are different from colleges and universities. There are important differences in how schools teach, how they measure learning, and what kinds of technology they have at their disposal. There are differences in how well schools perform, what kinds of social relationships and networks they help create, and what kinds of social outcomes their graduates can expect.

Types of Schools

Private school A school that charges tuition for each student it educates.

Public school A school that is run by the state and receives all or most of its funding from the government.

One way to begin thinking about different types of schools is to investigate how they are funded and for whom they are designed. The historical trend is in favor of publicly funded schools, in which the cost of running the school is paid for by government rather than by the individuals attending the school. A second trend is toward a proliferation of different types of schools, which specialize in satisfying the needs of specific populations. Over time, this second trend has led to the general division into primary schools, secondary schools, and colleges and universities.

Public schools as an American institution
Founded in 1635, Boston Latin School is the oldest public school in the United States.

PRIVATE SCHOOLS AND PUBLIC SCHOOLS. Private schools charge tuition for each student they educate. Historically, private schools catered to the children of the elite, who could afford to pay for school and who did not need their children to be wage earners in the labor force. Private schools were the dominant form of education until the 18th century, when the state began to become more interested in encouraging mass literacy. Since then there has been a rapid growth of **public schools**, which are run by the state and which receive all or most of their funding from the government.

In the United States, more than 90 percent of students attend public schools today. The first public school in the United States was the Boston Latin

School, which was created in 1635. There are now about 100,000 public schools in the United States, which educate nearly 50 million students. The situation is similar in most of the world, where the public school has become by far the dominant type of educational institution.

Private schools continue to play a role in modern education. The majority of these are religious schools, which are supported through a combination of student tuition and church revenues. There are also elite private schools, which charge extremely high tuition and which historically have catered to the most privileged families in society.

Neither a public nor a private institution, **homeschooling** has gained in popularity since the 1970s. Homeschooling parents choose to educate their children at home instead of sending them to a traditional public or private school, although some homeschooling parents do coordinate certain kinds of activities or coursework with the local school system. Two types of families have been most attracted to homeschooling: fundamentalist Christians, and progressive families interested in exploring alternative approaches to teaching and learning (Stevens 2001). Mothers play a large role in the homeschooling movement, and they have established a national community for curriculum development while also maintaining a highly individualized approach to the education of their children.

Whether private or public, the kind of school that parents choose for their children is an emotional and moral matter, and school policy has frequently been the focus of public debate and controversy. For more than a century, there has been a strong desire to address the nation's social problems through educational reform, with a particular focus on the reform of public schools. In these debates, schools are seen as more than a place for learning skills and literacy; they are also a social space for promoting social inclusion and citizenship. Thus, in the landmark 1954 case of *Brown v. Board of Education*, the Supreme Court declared that segregated public schools were unconstitutional, and that in the field of public education, "separate but equal" had no place.

Homeschooling A type of schooling in which parents choose to educate their children at home instead of sending them to a traditional school.

PRIMARY SCHOOL AND SECONDARY SCHOOL. Beginning in the 1830s and 1840s, a growing movement in the United States called for increased government involvement in the organization of schools and the teaching of students. Studying the German educational system, Horace Mann and other leading educators laid the groundwork for the modern organization of schools. They created specialized schools to train teachers, and established a more standardized curriculum of instruction. They lobbied for funding to construct new schools that would be available to all children. And they created a system wherein each school was organized into single-age grades, with specific learning objectives for each grade and an overall plan for how learning was supposed to progress from one grade to the next.

The modern school system is organized into primary schools and secondary schools. **Primary school** is focused on the learning needs of children from the ages of five to 12, and places most of its emphasis on basic academic learning and socialization skills. Children between the ages of 12 and 17 attend **secondary school**, where they learn more specialized subject areas, and where they begin to develop the specific skills they will need to enter the workforce or to pursue more advanced studies in a college or university. The system of primary and secondary schools has been adopted by countries throughout the world.

Primary school The part of the education system that focuses on the learning needs of children from the ages of five to 12, with an emphasis on basic academic learning and socialization skills.

Secondary school The part of the education system in which students learn more specialized subject areas, and where they begin to develop the specific skills they will need to enter the workforce or university.

COLLEGES AND UNIVERSITIES. The modern organization of schools culminates with colleges and universities, in which experts in specialized fields teach students the most up-to-date knowledge in a specific area, and confer advanced degrees to students in those fields. As discussed, the undergraduate and graduate degrees that colleges award are some of the most valuable credentials in modern society. Colleges also aim to give their students the tools to think creatively, critically, and productively in order to prepare them for lifelong learning, which is an increasingly valuable skill in the economy.

The oldest university in the world is the University of Bologna (in Italy), which was established in 1088. The early universities focused on the study of law, medicine, philosophy, theology, mathematics, rhetoric, and astronomy. By the 19th century, with the growing influence of science (Chapter 11), the focus of most universities began to shift from religion to science. Intellectual freedom was emphasized, so that teachers and students could propose arguments without worrying about getting into trouble for the ideas they expressed. Most importantly, colleges and universities evolved from teaching already-established knowledge to prioritizing scientific discovery instead. This led to the creation of the modern research university.

Most of the world's top universities have adopted the model of the modern research university. Johns Hopkins University (established in 1876) was the first research university in the United States, but other colleges quickly reorganized themselves as research universities, and since the 1950s the research university has been the main organizational model for universities around the world (Schofer and Meyer 2005). But universities are not all the same. If we examine the entire field of colleges and universities, rather than just the most prestigious schools, we find that there is tremendous variation in the mission, clientele, prestige, size, and wealth of different institutions (Stevens, Armstrong, and Arum 2008: 128).

The most elite universities are characterized by extremely selective admissions policies and high levels of research activity by their faculty. Students who attend these universities spend most of their social energies on campus—not only attending classes, but also developing friendships, going to parties, looking for sexual and romantic partners, participating in sports and other clubs, and forging social bonds with other students on campus (Stevens, Armstrong, and Arum 2008: 132–33; Armstrong, and Hamilton 2013). Elite universities have a major impact on the social identities, social networks, and social opportunities of their students.

However, the biggest growth in the college and university sector is coming from colleges that do not have selective admissions policies, and that focus primarily on teaching students rather than producing research. In the United States today, there are more than 4,700 degree-granting colleges, which together enroll more than 20 million students. Approximately half of these students are enrolled in community

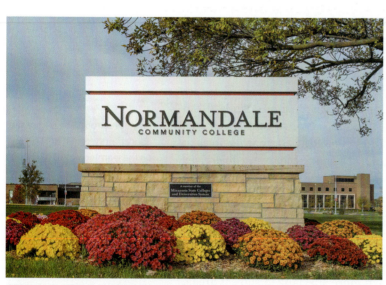

Community college as a gateway to success
Approximately half of all students in higher education in the United States are enrolled in community colleges, which have opened access to education for many people. Students who complete community college generally get better jobs than those who only complete high school, even though they do not tend to do as well in the labor market as those who complete a four-year degree.

colleges, which are characterized by open enrollment, lower tuition costs, more flexible attendance patterns, a nonresident student body, and a heavy focus on vocational training (Rosa 2008: 60). Community colleges expand access to college education, allowing people with less preparation and fewer resources to attend college. Students who complete community college generally get better jobs than those who only complete high school, even though they do not tend to do as well in the labor market as those who complete a four-year degree (Arum and Hout 1998). Further, there is not very good evidence to show that attending a community college significantly increases the likelihood that an individual will actually complete a four-year bachelor's degree (Rouse 1995).

SCHOOLS IN A DIGITAL AGE. One of the biggest recent changes to schools is the introduction of new digital technologies. In the United States, public schools now provide at least one computer for every five students, and they spend more than $3 billion per year on digital content (Herold 2016).

Digital technologies present promising opportunities for schools. They allow more personalization and flexibility in teaching and learning, because they enable students to move at their own pace and to follow their interests. They make it easier for students to store their work and share it with their teachers. They allow for a more active learning environment, and they free students from the physical confines of the classroom, allowing students and teachers to interact in online spaces and opening up learning environments to people who might not be able to attend traditional schools. Last, digital technologies teach students the media and computer skills they will need in the 21st-century economy.

Social scientists have identified concerns about digital learning. Digital technologies often reproduce inequality, because privileged students have better access to technology and receive more social support when they run into technical challenges (Robinson et al. 2015). Because schools have limited resources, an investment in learning technologies often forces them to reduce their investments in effective teacher training. In fact, schools from the elementary to the university level introduce digital technologies as a way to cut costs (Otterman 2011). And although some institutions of higher education have experimented with fully online programs, researchers have found that completion rates are substantially lower than for traditional courses (Parr 2013).

Teaching, Learning, and Assessment

Teachers and schools use different types of assessment in order to determine how much students are learning. Surprise quizzes, homework assignments, oral presentations, term papers, experiments, case studies, and examinations are all used regularly to measure how well students are mastering the course material. But tests and other forms of assessment are more than just a measure of learning. Most education scholars today, including sociologists, recognize that assessment can play an important role in the teaching and learning process (Sweet and Cardwell 2016; Chin, Senter, and Spalter-Roth 2011). Testing encourages students to study, aids in the retention of knowledge, encourages students to organize the course material more effectively, and improves the transfer of knowledge to new contexts (Clark and Filinson 2011; Roedifer et al. 2011).

STANDARDIZED TESTS AND THE DRIVE FOR ASSESSMENT. Students, their parents, and teachers are not the only people who are interested in measuring learning. Other interested stakeholders include school administrators, potential employers, admissions officers at selective colleges and universities,

Solidarity and Conflict

The Fight over Campus Speech Codes

Free speech rally, University of California, Berkeley, 2017
The fight over campus speech codes that intend to encourage tolerance and prohibit hate speech are contested by free speech advocates who argue they are a threat to freedom of thought and speech.

For many colleges and universities, 2017 was a challenging year, as they struggled to respond to conflicts erupting over who deserved to speak on campus, and how students should react to speakers with whom they disagreed. In Vermont, Middlebury College disciplined 67 of its students for repeatedly disrupting and shouting down a speaker, political scientist Charles Murray, who had been invited to the campus by a conservative student group. The University of California at Berkeley decided to cancel a speech by the right-wing provocateur Milo Yiannopoulos, when protests outside the venue became violent. By the end of the year, more than a dozen speakers had been disinvited by colleges and universities in the United States, in response to protests and complaints by student groups.

These conflicts over visiting speakers were connected to the larger issue of campus speech codes. Beginning in the 1980s, in an attempt to fight against discrimination and harassment and to build a more tolerant campus culture, many universities began to create speech codes to limit and punish speech that was deemed to be hateful and intolerant. By the end of the 1990s, nearly four hundred universities in the United States had established speech codes. A typical example was the speech code established in 1989 at the University of Michigan, which prohibited "any behavior, verbal or physical, that stigmatizes or victimizes an individual on the basis of race, ethnicity, religion, sex, sexual orientation, creed" or "creates an intimidating, hostile, or demeaning environment for educational pursuits, employment or participation in University[-]sponsored extra-curricular activities" (Hudson and Nott 2017).

The main advocates in favor of campus speech codes were antidiscrimination groups, which were offended by the continued use of racial stereotypes and racist language by others on campus. Buoyed by the successes of the Civil Rights Movement, these groups saw themselves as continuing the struggle to create more inclusion and a greater sense of social belonging on campus. But speech codes created conflicts with other groups. Libertarian groups criticized the speech codes as an infringement on free speech, which they argued needed to be protected regardless of how offensive the speech was. Conservative groups argued that speech codes were really a disguised attempt to silence conservative voices and to create campuses where only certain perspectives and opinions were allowed expression. Both groups filed lawsuits against universities and their speech code policies. And their lawsuits were almost always successful.

The spread of campus speech codes is surprising, given the historical commitment that universities have had to protecting open debate and the freedom of speech. The American Association of University Professors, in its 1915 Declaration of Principles, stated that the protection of academic freedom was absolutely essential to the fulfillment of the university's mission. The commitment to free speech on college campuses intensified during the 1960s, when students demanded that free speech and academic freedom needed to be extended to students as well as faculty. Facing repeated protests and sit-ins by hundreds of students, university administrators gave in to their demands. By the end of the 1960s, bans against political protest and political speech had been lifted on college campuses around the country.

From the beginning, though, movements to extend freedom of speech on college campuses have created conflicts with other groups. The professors who argued for the protection of academic freedom in the 1930s and the students who argued for free speech in the 1960s were opposed by conservative politicians, who viewed them as radicals threatening American values. The universities that were creating speech codes in the 1980s and 1990s were opposed by conservative activists and conservative media, who complained that the university

PAIRED CONCEPTS *continued*

was becoming a haven of "political correctness" that only tolerated certain types of beliefs and values. In all of these cases, the conflicts over campus speech have reinforced the boundaries between different social groups, as well as the solidarity and the commitment on each side to continue fighting.

ACTIVE LEARNING

Find out: Does your campus have a speech code? Can you find any examples where the speech codes on your campus have been used to block or limit speech? Can you find any examples where the speech codes on your campus have been criticized or have faced public protest?

and government officials. Because these groups need to compare large numbers of students from many different places (and even from different time periods), many of them have gravitated toward **standardized tests**, which are forms of assessment that are administered and scored under conditions that are the same for all students.

The use of standardized tests has a longer history than most people realize. In fact, standardized tests can be traced back to the 1840s, as a response to the rapid expansion of public schools. The initial goal of these tests was to sort students into classrooms of relatively equal ability, so that teaching and learning would be as efficient as possible. These tests were also designed to assess different types of schools—one-room schoolhouses in rural areas could be compared with large schools in urban areas, in order to see which types of schools were the most effective (US Congress, Office of Technology Assessment 1992: 108).

By the 1920s, standardized intelligence tests and achievement tests were being used in schools throughout the country. Multiple-choice questions had become the dominant format for standardized tests by the 1930s. Educational reformers used the results of these tests to push for changes in schools. Convinced that schools were doing a poor job of teaching students, they wanted to create a more uniform curriculum, reduce teachers' independence, and make schools accountable for their performance on the standardized tests (US Congress, Office of Technology Assessment 1992: 120–21). Standardized testing was also a large part of college admissions to assess candidates across the nation (Furuta 2017). By the late 20th century, the reliance on high-stakes standardized tests had become one of the defining features of education.

In a context of widespread institutional demands, sociologists have contributed to creating learning assessments, the educational assessment movement, and the wider scholarship of teaching and learning—albeit reluctantly at times (Crockett et al. 2018; Sweet, McElrath, and Kain 2014; Paino et al., 2012; Clark and Filinson 2011). Sociologists emphasize the difference between effective quality assessment and the political and institutional effects of the assessment projects of governments, educational administrators, and accreditors (Clark and Filinson 2011; Wilmoth 2004).

One catalyst for the spread of high-stakes standardized testing in recent decades was the 1983 release of *A Nation at Risk*, a report by Ronald Reagan's Department of Education that warned American schools were failing. In 2001, the US Congress passed the No Child Left Behind Act, which required all states to develop standardized tests, administered annually to all public school students, that could assess student knowledge of basic, grade-appropriate knowledge and skills. Schools were required to demonstrate annual improvement in their test scores, and those that consistently failed to do so faced increasingly harsh penalties, even closure.

Standardized tests Forms of assessment that are administered and scored under conditions that are the same for all students.

Education researchers, including those in sociology, criticized No Child Left Behind. In an article titled "No Child Left Behind? Sociology Ignored!" in the flagship journal *Sociology of Education*, David Karen argued that the politicians who claimed they were providing educational accountability to combat the "soft bigotry of low expectations" were instead reinforcing "the hard bigotries of inadequate funding, a poor understanding of the nature of educational and social inequality, and an even worse implementation plan" (2005: 165).

Other sociological researchers joined colleagues across the disciplines in identifying the way standardized tests encourage "teaching to the test," where the focus is on the narrow set of questions that students will see on the test rather than an attempt to develop a deeper knowledge of the topics being studied. This is especially true for low-performing schools where students are close to the boundary of proficiency standards (Jennings and Sohn 2014). Such tests also encourage schools to concentrate their resources only on subjects that are covered by the standardized tests, with the result that when schools face budget pressure, the first programs to be cut are art, music, languages, and other electives that are associated with a broad-based education (Hawkins 2012). And they do not effectively help reduce inequalities in student achievement, particularly those based on race, class, or disability (Au 2008).

NATIONAL AND INTERNATIONAL DIFFERENCES IN SCHOOL PERFORMANCE. Because a highly educated workforce is so important in today's global economy, there is a strong interest among politicians and policy-makers in comparing the educational performance of different countries. A test was developed to do this about 20 years ago, and was administered for the first time in 2000. Known as the Programme for International Student Assessment (PISA), the test is administered every three years to a representative sample of 15-year-old students in more than 70 different countries. It takes about two hours to complete, and assesses knowledge of mathematics, reading, and science. Countries that have scored the highest on the PISA test include Singapore, Hong Kong, Japan, Macau, and Estonia. In 2018, the United States scored 39th in mathematics, 24th in reading, and 25th in science.

What are the characteristics of the high-performing nations? They pay their teachers higher salaries, relative to the average national income. They tend to allocate resources more equitably, across socioeconomically advantaged and disadvantaged schools. They give their schools more autonomy in designing curricula and assessments, and they prioritize collaboration between teachers and school principals. There is less truancy and fewer disciplinary problems, even when controlling for socioeconomic background. They use more diverse instruments of assessment. And they tend to wait longer before they divide their students into different types of educational tracks (OECD 2013).

There are also important differences in school performance at the national level. For the United States, the PISA test separated out scores for North Carolina, Puerto Rico, and Massachusetts, and found that Massachusetts significantly outperformed the other two. In fact, Massachusetts scored about the same as Canada in reading and science, and about the same as Norway in mathematics. All three of its scores were significantly higher than the US average. North Carolina scored pretty close to the national average. Puerto Rico was significantly lower than the US average, with scores that were similar to Brazil, Indonesia, and other countries that are much poorer than the United States. In other comparisons of US states, the highest-performing schools tend to be

METHODS AND INTERPRETATION

Measuring Learning Outcomes and Teaching Effectiveness

Assessing learning
In standard classrooms, teachers lecture to students, but it is not always clear what or how much students actually learn. The development of learning assessments shifts the focus from individual grades to the effectiveness of teaching and learning. How much of student performance comes from teaching and how much from prior experience and family background?

Although schools and universities face increasing pressure to demonstrate student learning and teacher efficacy, there is widespread disagreement about how best to measure these things. For example, is it useful to give students the same test at the beginning and the end of the same year, to see what they have learned? Does it matter if students like their teachers, or if they develop a passion for the things they are learning? Should schools and teachers be rewarded for effective teaching, or be punished for ineffective teaching? And who should do the testing and evaluating?

The most common way of measuring teaching effectiveness is to use student ratings. Student ratings are used by virtually all colleges and universities, and they do a pretty good job of measuring whether students liked the teacher and whether they were engaged with the course material (Culver 2010). Still, there are many problems with student ratings. They display a significant gender and racial bias, with women and racial minorities receiving consistently lower student evaluations (Hamermesh and Parker 2005). They also display a bias in favor of smaller classes, despite the fact that teachers rarely have any control over class size. They are plagued by low response rates, particularly when they are conducted online (Ling, Phillips, and Wehrich 2012). There is no way to know whether different students mean the same thing when they evaluate a teacher as "satisfactory" or "poor." And there is no way to know whether students actually learned anything. The main advantage of student assessments is that they are easy and inexpensive to deploy. Other attempts to measure teaching effectiveness include peer ratings, self-evaluations, videos, alumni ratings, employer ratings, teaching awards, and teaching portfolios (Berk 2005). But these all have problems of their own, and still fail to measure whether students actually learned anything.

What about measuring learning outcomes? One approach is to look at performance on final exams. However, to make this approach effective, a school would have to either figure out how to compare different exams, or force all teachers of a particular course to give the same exam, which many teachers will resist. They can rely on standardized tests that are administered to all students at the end of the year, but if they do this they are only going to be measuring overall student performance. Standardized year-end exams make it nearly impossible to isolate the effectiveness of a specific teacher, unless that teacher has done all of the instruction for the student. An additional problem is that student performance is shaped by a variety of factors that are independent of teacher effectiveness, such as race, class, gender, school size, school resources, school culture, family background, and neighborhood characteristics (Schneider et al. 2011).

ACTIVE LEARNING

Think about it: If you were in charge of evaluating teaching effectiveness and learning outcomes at your school, which measures would you use? Why would you choose those measures instead of something else? What do you see as the main potential problems with those measurements?

located in wealthy suburbs surrounding Chicago, Boston, Philadelphia, New York City, and San Francisco. There are significant differences related to race and ethnicity, with African American and Hispanic students scoring lower than white and Asian American students. And there are significant class differences, with wealthier students performing better than poorer students.

The Spread of Singapore Math

Singapore has consistently scored at the top of international school exams, attracting considerable attention from education scholars. In the 2015 PISA exam, in addition to excelling in the science and mathematics section, Singapore's students scored higher on the reading and comprehension sections than students from other countries. In explaining Singapore's great success, experts point to educational policies that are meritocratic, offer good pay and high status to teachers, invest heavily in teachers as well as students, and provide strong remedial support as soon as a student begins to fall behind (Ng 2017).

As educators in other countries have sought to learn from Singapore's success, they have been particularly interested in the country's specific strategies for math instruction. Rather than the memorization and drilling that are emphasized heavily in more traditional arithmetic instruction for kindergarten and elementary school students, Singapore instead teaches students to master a limited number of concepts each school year before moving on to something new. The sequence of topics has been carefully planned, and is based on theories of child development. Teachers use a variety of strategies to help students solve increasingly difficult problems. Students draw pictures, diagram the elements of a problem, and use other aids such as blocks, cards, and bar charts (Hu 2010). By slowing down and making sure that students develop a deep understanding of each mathematic concept, students remember what they have learned and can build on their knowledge to tackle increasingly difficult skills. By the time they are in fourth or fifth grade, many Singaporean students are already performing one or two grade levels ahead of international standards.

Because of Singapore's success in international exams, programs in "Singapore math" have been successfully marketed to parents and schools around the world. Singapore Math Inc. was established in the United States in 1998, and now sells textbooks and other curricular materials to more than one thousand schools in the United States, Canada, Australia, and the Middle East.

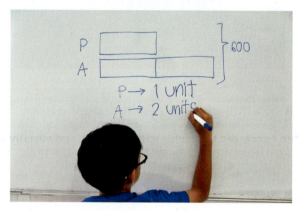

Singapore Math
In this pedagogical approach to math developed by educators in Singapore, the early curriculum moves slowly, and teachers use a variety of strategies to help students solve increasingly difficult problems. Advocates also point to educational policies in Singapore that are meritocratic, offer good pay and high status to teachers, invest heavily in teachers as well as students, and provide strong remedial support as soon as a student begins to fall behind.

ACTIVE LEARNING

Find out: Does your neighborhood school use Singapore math? Contact someone from your home school district (a teacher, principal, or assistant principal). Ask them about the math curriculum they use. Find out what they know about Singapore math, and what they think about it.

Making Friends and Building Networks

For most students, a key part of the school experience involves building friendships, social relationships, and social networks. As we discussed in Chapter 5, school is one of the most important agents of socialization. For many children, entering elementary school is the first time in their lives when they are spending long periods of time away from their homes, parents, and siblings. Primary schools, secondary schools, and colleges are places where students form peer groups and reference groups. As students move into adulthood, the relationships they develop in college become an important part of their social network, which they rely on to develop contacts and support resources throughout their working lives.

FRIENDS, CLIQUES, AND BULLIES. There are important social hierarchies in schools between different social groups, as well as hierarchies within each social group. These hierarchies are shaped by inequality and privilege, by solidarity and conflict, and by power and resistance. For most students, their school experience is impacted by their position in the overall pecking order of their school.

The importance that children place on being popular increases throughout elementary school, peaking during the early high school years (LaFontana and Cillessen 2010). In a classic study of clique dynamics, the sociologists Patricia Adler and Peter Adler found that the dominant and most popular groups in the school pecking order commanded the most interest, attention, and prestige from their classmates (Adler and Adler 1998). Individuals in the popular cliques carefully screen potential members, inviting them in for trial periods and ejecting them if they fail to win acceptance from the clique leaders. Hierarchies within the popular cliques are changing constantly, with less popular members trying to copy the fashion and behaviors of the group leaders. Practices of exclusion, rejection, humiliation, and physical intimidation are perpetrated, directed primarily at lower-status social groups but also at lower-status members of the popular groups. Regardless of where they are in the pecking order, students learn that school is a social minefield, in which popularity is often expressed through social exclusion and socially aggressive behavior, and where anyone can become a target.

The school pecking order reinforces privilege and inequality, because of the tendency for social groups to form on the basis of social similarities. Students who are wealthy and well dressed are more likely to be popular, as are students who conform to gender ideals (Adler, Kless, and Adler 1992). School cliques are highly segregated by race, to the general disadvantage of racial minorities. All of this means that the prestige hierarchy in most schools will reinforce other structures of privilege. But school popularity does not come without costs. Among teenagers, popular students are more likely to drink, use drugs, and engage in shoplifting, vandalism, and other forms of deviance (Allen and Allen 2009). These behaviors can have long-term costs, derailing students' successful transitions into college, the workplace, and adulthood.

For less popular students, the school pecking order presents different kinds of risks. Unpopular children are more likely to have academic troubles in school and to experience depression, anxiety, and isolation (Flook, Repetti, and Ullman 2005). They are also at greater risk of victimization, as the targets of aggressive behavior and bullying (Martin 2009). Bullying can include verbal insults, the spreading of rumors, and physical violence or intimidation. School bullying is shaped by homophobia, racism, sexism, and weight-based shaming, in a way that has the effect of stigmatizing marginalized populations and reinforcing structural inequalities (Pascoe 2011). In the United States, nearly one-third of students between the ages of 12 and 18 reported being

Bullying
Many students experience school as a social minefield, where they can be targeted at any time for social exclusion and bullying.

bullied at least once during the school year, with nearly 10 percent of them experiencing bullying almost daily (UNESCO 2017). Victims of bullying suffer well into adulthood; they have more health problems, higher levels of social isolation, and lower levels of educational attainment (Smith 2014).

NETWORKS AND NETWORKING. The social networks that students develop in school extend into their closest relationships, often becoming important primary groups in their adult lives. This is particularly true for students who attend college and university, because of where those schools are placed in the typical life cycle. In the United States, the average age of first marriage is 27 for women and 29 for men. Many of these couples cohabit before getting married (Chapter 10). In their early 20s, most students (and nearly all privileged students) are attending college and graduate school, which is why these schools are often seen as prime **marriage markets**. Indeed, sociological research shows that attending college increases the likelihood of marriage for men and women, and this effect is the highest for high-status students (Musick, Brand, and Davis 2012). More prestigious schools provide more valuable marriage markets.

At school, students develop useful social networks for their adult lives, particularly for those who attend elite private schools and prestigious universities. The students who go to such schools are surrounded by other students from elite families, and they are easily socialized into the hobbies and cultural tastes that are associated with that world. Prestigious schools also have powerful alumni networks, which provide new graduates with insider connections that can help them land high-paying and high-status jobs.

Marriage market Institutionalized spaces where individuals select potential sexual, romantic, and marriage partners.

Inequality and Privilege

How Elite Students Get Elite Jobs

Educational privilege
For the most prestigious and highest-paying jobs, the hiring process is designed to select candidates who come from the most privileged backgrounds and the highest-status universities.

In today's economy, some of the best-paying jobs are in the fields of investment banking, management consulting, and corporate law. This is particularly true for the top-tier firms in these fields, where starting salaries are close to $200,000 per year, and increase rapidly for people who continue employment with the top firms. Students know that these are the best-paying jobs, and there is intense competition to get them. But who gets these jobs? How do firms make their hiring decisions?

In *Pedigree: How Elite Students Get Elite Jobs*, the sociologist Lauren Rivera found that the hiring process at these top-tier firms is designed in a way that favors elite students from elite universities (Rivera 2015). This is due to the way that firms recruit for entry-level jobs, screen résumés to select applicants for interviews, and come to decisions about which interviewees will ultimately get a job offer.

The preference for elite students is built into the recruiting process, which is focused on campus recruitment events that are held at elite universities. The vast majority

PAIRED CONCEPTS *continued*

of people who are ultimately hired are identified through these events, where the firms come to campus and try to sell themselves to students. Only a small list of schools are included in these activities. Most top-tier firms identify about five "core schools" where they intend to invest most of their energy recruiting students. At these core schools, which are almost always Ivy League universities, firms will host information sessions, cocktail receptions, and dinners, where they interview dozens of potential candidates. Most firms also identify 10 or 15 "target schools," where they will interview candidates but will not invest as many resources. These schools are usually prestigious as well, but it is possible for a slightly less elite school to make it onto the list if one of the managing partners has a personal connection to the school. Students who do not graduate from a core or target school can still apply for positions in these firms, but their applications are kept in a separate stream and not considered very seriously; in many instances, they will be discarded without any review whatsoever (Rivera 2015: 35). Firms argue that pursuing this strategy makes it more likely that they will only hire the "best and the brightest," because of how difficult it is to get accepted into elite universities. But they also know that hiring employees from elite universities will make it easier for them to attract business, because their clients tend to come from those universities and to be invested in the social status that is associated with Ivy League degrees (Rivera 2015: 37).

Once the interviews begin, the preference continues for candidates who come from more elite backgrounds. After the screening preference for the highest-status universities has been accomplished, firms begin paying more attention to extracurricular activities and candidates' potential "fit" with the firm's culture and its employees.

Because these jobs require people to work very long hours, employers look to leisure activities and interests to gauge whether an applicant would be an interesting person to have on the team. High-status leisure pursuits that require significant investment of resources, such as tennis, squash, or crew, are weighted most heavily. People who lack extracurricular accomplishments are dismissed as "boring" people who would be "corporate drones"; as one recruiter commented, "I would trade an outgoing, friendly, confident person for a rocket scientist any day" (Rivera 2015: 94). These differences in cultural capital (Chapter 4) are closely related to social class background.

Ultimately, successful applicants are those deemed to have "polish," a fairly vague criterion of merit that tracks closely with the socioeconomic status of the candidates' parents (Rivera 2015: 250). There are exceptions to this, of course. Candidates who can tell a compelling story of overcoming major obstacles often fare well, and so do candidates from less elite places who had a personal connection to the firm, provided that they could display enough polish that one of the recruiters can make a strong case on their behalf. But on the whole, the hiring process is designed to select the most elite candidates, the ones from the most privileged backgrounds and the most high-status universities.

ACTIVE LEARNING

Find out: Do some research at your school's career services center. Does your school host on-campus recruiting events? What kinds of companies attend these events? What are they doing to sell themselves to potential employees? Are the companies coming to campus the top-tier firms in their industry? If not, try to find out where the top-tier firms are doing their on-campus recruiting.

Work and Recreation

Most students know that there is a relationship between education and work, and they are aware that the end of school marks the beginning of their careers. There is often overlap between these two parts of the life course. Many students work their way through school, and many others take on paid and unpaid internships with the hope of getting a better job when they graduate. Those who want to upgrade their skills and their credentials often return to school after a period of full-time work.

A widely shared goal in today's economy is to get a "good job," even though that can mean different things to different people. Some people place the most value on jobs that offer good pay and high status, while others emphasize satisfying working conditions and room for growth. Many workers also hope that their jobs will provide them enough time and resources to pursue hobbies, interests, and other forms of recreation that excite their passions or allow them to share fun experiences with friends and family.

Power, Privilege, and Inequality in the Workplace

For those who are fortunate to have a good job, the workplace can be a site of great passion and great reward. Such people tell you that they love their job. But this does not describe the working experience for most people. Work is also a place of domination, exploitation, and monotony.

As we discussed in earlier chapters, income inequality is shaped by race, class, and gender. Simply put, white men tend to have better jobs than other groups. They make more money for doing the same job, and they continue to be overrepresented in the best-paying and highest-status jobs. Among those who hold management jobs, white male overrepresentation is at virtually the same levels it was in the 1960s; while women and racial minorities hold more management positions than they used to, those positions are concentrated in the service sector, and in companies where they are mainly managing other women and other racial minorities (Stainback and Tomaskovic-Devey 2009).

In addition to the stratification of income and status, the workplace also reproduces massive inequalities in terms of how much control people have over their work and how much satisfaction they get out of their jobs. Most people have little control over their working conditions. Their work is closely monitored, and even if they do their job well they can be fired without any justification, due to the spread of "at-will" employment laws. For those who keep their jobs, their work is too often characterized by a soul-crushing monotony. This has been a consistent theme of social critics. In his 1854 novel *Hard Times,* the English writer Charles Dickens described the modern workplace as a prison in which workers were required to complete the same task every day, receiving starvation wages with little or no chance of improvement or advancement. More recently, in the 1999 film *Office Space,* writer and director Mike Judge depicts a world of office-park workers in cubicles, who hate their jobs and who are constantly harassed by their bosses.

In fact, exploitation and harassment are a regular feature of the work experience for many (if not most) workers. Bullying is a major problem in today's workforce, with most research reporting that between 10 and 20 percent of all workers are bullied annually (Einarson et al. 2003). Differences in power influence bullying in the workplace. Racial minorities and workers with high levels of job insecurity are more likely to be targets of workplace bullying (Hodson et al. 2006). More than 70 percent of the perpetrators of bullying are men, and more than 60 percent are bosses (Namie 2017). Sexual harassment is even more prevalent, with a recent study showing that three-quarters of all women in the United States have been sexually harassed at work (Johnson, Kirk, and Keplinger 2016). Victims of harassment rarely report their victimization, because of feared retaliation by bosses and ostracism by coworkers.

The Sociology of Job Satisfaction

What makes a job satisfying? And why will different workers derive different levels of satisfaction from the same job? These are important questions—not only because job satisfaction is associated with better health outcomes (Faragher, Cass, and Cooper et al. 2005), but also because it is connected to higher levels of worker productivity (Bockerman and Ilmakunnas 2012).

According to the sociologist Arne Kalleberg, the most important issue related to job satisfaction is whether the job's rewards match the worker's

Power and Resistance

The #MeToo Movement

Tarana Burke, founder of the #MeToo movement

In 2006, civil rights activist Tarana Burke created a non-profit organization to help support young women of color who had been victims of sexual abuse. The organization was called JustBeInc., and its motto was "me too."

In October 2017 the "me too" movement exploded into the public consciousness. Responding to multiple accusations of sexual harassment and assault made against the Hollywood movie producer Harvey Weinstein, the actress Alyssa Milano wrote the following on Twitter: "If you've been sexually harassed or assaulted write 'me too' as a reply to this tweet."

Within 24 hours, the hashtag #MeToo had been posted on Twitter nearly half a million times, and helped create a movement against sexual harassment and sexual assault in the workplace (Gilbert 2017). Harvey Weinstein was fired,

and later arrested on rape charges, as nearly a dozen women came forward with reports of sexual assault. #MeToo was used to publicize allegations of sexual harassment and assault against leading figures in the music industry, government, sports, finance, military, and other industries as well. Use of the hashtag spread to more than 80 countries. The European Union convened a session of parliament about how to combat sexual abuse, after the #MeToo movement publicized allegations of sexual harassment by EU workers (Schreuer 2017). In the US Congress, the ME TOO Congress Act was introduced in January 2018, in order to increase transparency surrounding how the US government responded to allegations of sexual harassment and assault.

Many people who have experience with previous women's movements fear that a backlash against #MeToo is inevitable. They point to complaints about how men are being fired before they have a chance to defend themselves, how the movement does not adequately distinguish between different types of sexual harassment, and how the movement might turn into a moral panic. But others reply that the potential of backlash is worth it, because the movement has shown powerful men that there are real risks to abusing the less powerful women who work for them. And because the movement has made retaliation by bosses much riskier, it encourages more women to report incidents of sexual abuse at work.

ACTIVE LEARNING

Think about it: Do you know anyone who tweeted or retweeted with the #MeToo hashtag? What has the response to the movement been among people you know?

---

expectations, interests, and values (Kalleberg 1977). Workers have different interests, and they expect different things from their jobs. Some workers want their job to be intrinsically interesting, while others are looking for good hours and pleasant physical surroundings. Some people want to be surrounded by friendly and interesting coworkers, while others place more importance on opportunities for career advancement. Some people want a big salary, while others are more interested in job security. Many workers are looking for a combination of these things. When the job meets their expectations and their values, then job satisfaction increases. Workers who have a wide variety of job opportunities have a higher likelihood of job satisfaction, because they have the luxury of choosing a job that matches their interests and values (Kalleberg 1977: 137).

Larger historical trends also shape the expectations and values that workers have about their jobs. Since the 1970s, there has been an increase in the value workers place on income and job security, as compared to other interests

Job satisfaction
Job satisfaction is more likely when the job's rewards match the worker's interests, expectations, and values.

and expectations (Kalleberg et al. 2006). Given the fact that job insecurity has increased significantly during this period and salaries have been stagnant for most workers (as we discuss later in the chapter), this has led to large increases in job dissatisfaction, with little expectation that it would return to levels seen during the 1970s or 1980s (McGregor 2017).

FINDING MEANING AND SATISFACTION OUTSIDE OF WORK. Economic success is not the only thing that matters for a happy and meaningful life. Jobs and money are important, to be sure, but they are not the most important factors contributing to overall happiness. Cross-national research finds that happiness levels are higher in societies with higher levels of economic development, higher levels of social tolerance, and more democracy (Inglehart et al. 2008). Other research has shown that, over the course of an individual's life, the most important thing is to have close relationships with family, friends, and people in the community. People who report that they have led meaningful lives tend to have strong social relationships; to do things that are challenging; and to participate in activities that allow them to connect their past, present, and future (Baumeister et al. 2013). Meaningful lives often include periods of stress and struggle, rather than periods of uninterrupted happiness.

Recognizing that people want more from life than a good job, a growing part of the economy is now focused on providing meaningful experiences that allow people to have authentic experiences, to express their true identities, and to reinforce their social connections with friends and family. The tourist and leisure industries have evolved in recent years to increasingly emphasize unique and memorable experiences that encourage self-discovery and growth (Morgan et al. 2009). Memorable experiences immerse people in a new cultural environment, allowing them to interact with locals, and to learn something new about the world and about themselves, in a way that helps them develop some aspect of their identity and to improve their self-confidence (Chandralal and Valenzuela 2013). These include things such as music festivals, food festivals and culinary tours, eco-tourism, spiritual tourism, and adventure travel.

These changes in the travel and leisure industry are part of a larger "experience economy," in which companies sell experiences and transformations rather than goods and services (Pine and Gillmore 1999). We can see this with the exploding popularity of marathons, obstacle races, Ironman triathlons, and other extreme challenges. The companies that sponsor these events are selling personal transformation and total immersion into a new lifestyle, and often into a social community of other enthusiasts. The race itself is the culmination of the experience, offering a festival-like event and a collective affirmation of the sacrifices that have been made and the new identity that has been embraced.

PAIRED CONCEPTS

Structure and Contingency

How Indoor Cycling Became a Multi-Billion-Dollar Industry

Soul Cycle class, Washington, DC

In the late 1980s, South African endurance cyclist Johnny Goldberg began to worry about all the time he was spending riding his bike. Living in Los Angeles, with a pregnant wife and a training schedule that often required riding at night, Goldberg built himself a stationary bike that would be able to accurately simulate what it was like to ride a road bike, and that would be strong enough to allow him to alternate between long periods of standing and sitting on the bike, which is necessary for endurance cyclists.

Goldberg, a successful fitness instructor with a large following in Los Angeles, began teaching small cycling classes with stationary bikes he built. The first classes were held in his garage, but they were so popular that he quickly created two "Spinning Centers" in Santa Monica and Hollywood. By 1994, he had contracted with the bicycle maker Schwinn to produce his Johnny G Spinner bikes, so that he could keep up with the demand for his classes. The program he developed included periods of high-intensity cycling combined with on-the-bike strength exercises, music, and motivational components. With a partner, he founded Madd Dogg Athletics to supervise the manufacturing of the Johnny G Spinner cycles as well as the training and licensing of official Johnny G spinning instructors.

In 1995 Goldberg presented his new spinning program to the annual meeting of the International Health, Racquet, and Sportsclub Association. There was an enthusiastic reception to the program, and spinning quickly became a global phenomenon. Today, Madd Dogg Athletics has more than 200,000 certified instructors and 35,000 licensed facilities; there are just as many unlicensed instructors and facilities, working at YMCAs as well as trendy new indoor cycling studios such as Soul Cycle and Flywheel. Indoor cycling is now one of the most profitable parts of the health club and fitness studio industry.

While Johnny Goldberg's distinctive biography was a big factor in spinning's development and success, the structural conditions were there for indoor cycling to take off. Group exercise classes exploded in popularity in the 1970s and 1980s, and health clubs had built or converted space to house the new aerobics studios that were in demand. But aerobics classes were much more popular among women, which meant that the studio spaces were only catering to some health club members and were left unused during long parts of the day. Health clubs saw spinning as a way to use those spaces for more of the day, and hopefully to cater to men just as much as women.

There are other structural reasons that explain the success of spinning and other indoor cycling studios. Most people already know how to ride a bike. Everybody was on their own bike, controlling their own resistance and intensity, which meant that the classes could include people of vastly different levels of fitness ability. The cycling studios became communities, where people could exercise together instead of spending their entire time at the gym by themselves. Relationships formed, and some people even met their future partners at spin class. Many of the more popular studios developed an almost cult-like following, with classes selling out instantly and with social status going to those who could score a space.

ACTIVE LEARNING

Think about it: One of the recent trends in indoor cycling is for the popular studios to be located in stand-alone studios rather than in larger, multipurpose health clubs. Using your sociological imagination, suggest a few explanations for why this is happening.

Historical Changes in the Economy

Economy All the activities and organizations that are involved in the production, distribution, and consumption of goods and services.

The **economy** refers to all the activities and organizations that are involved in the production, distribution, and consumption of goods and services. Like other institutions, the economy changes as society changes. In modern society, the biggest and most important change in the economy was the development of capitalism. Capitalism fundamentally changed the nature of work, and it continues to do so today.

According to the sociologist Immanuel Wallerstein, the modern economy emerged gradually in Europe between 1450 and 1640, as it changed from feudalism to capitalism (Wallerstein 1976). In **feudalism**, the main way that people created wealth was by owning land. A small number of people owned most of the land, and everyone else was completely dependent on the landowner. In exchange for using and living on part of the land, they were expected to provide services to the landowner. This included military service, agricultural work, maintaining roads and fences, and paying rent. Landowners also charged their dependents for other uses of the land, such as hunting, grazing livestock, or storing food. Dependents were generally not allowed to leave the area without the landowner's permission, and their children were often bound by the same relations of dependency.

Feudalism An economic system in which a small number of people owned most of the land, and everyone else was completely dependent on the landowner.

Feudalism lasted for hundreds of years, but it was not a very efficient system for producing goods and services. Small-scale and extremely local production was the norm, and virtually everything that was produced was consumed immediately. There was little incentive for landowners to invest in new productive technologies, or to engage in regional market transactions. Those who provided military services were relatively unskilled at fighting. Landowners had repeated conflicts with one another, and there was little incentive for them to cooperate. The dependent workers had no incentive to work hard, increase their skill, or develop new techniques of production. This left feudalism vulnerable to the more productive economic systems that developed with capitalism.

The Transition to Capitalism

Capitalism An economic system based on the private ownership of property, including the means of material life such as food, clothing, and shelter, and in which the production of goods and services is controlled by private individuals and companies, and prices are set by markets.

Capitalism is an economic system in which the production of goods and services is controlled by private individuals and companies; all economic activities are based on a calculation of potential profits; and the prices of all goods (including workers' wages) are determined by the marketplace (Chapter 2).

Capitalism began to develop during the 16th and 17th centuries, as an agricultural revolution swept across England that challenged the feudal system. New techniques of crop rotation as well as the shift toward higher-yield crops increased productivity beyond what was necessary for the immediate consumption of the feudal fiefdoms. New machinery made it easier to cut grain, which required fewer manual workers. All of this encouraged changes in how landowners related to the dependents living on their land. Rather than leaving their fields open for anyone to use, they enclosed the common lands so they could take advantage of the new farming techniques for their own benefit. Rather than relying on the rents and services of their dependent tenants for their wealth, they began to focus on selling their agricultural surplus in an ever-growing market. Farming became a business, motivated by the pursuit of profit (Overton 1996).

With fewer workers needed for farming, many of the peasants who had been living on the feudal fiefdoms were forced to move and to seek new types of work. Most of them ended up in towns and cities, where they were put to work producing goods and services. Merchants in these towns and cities expanded their businesses, selling their products to the new people living in the towns and also relying on the labor of those new arrivals to increase their production. Business owners, in pursuit of larger markets, encouraged governments to extend their reach by conquering overseas territories and by protecting the trading companies that were helping create a world market. Merchant banks developed to help finance this expansion of trade routes. Like the new farmers in the countryside, their motivation was the pursuit of profit.

The production of goods and the pursuit of profit accelerated rapidly during the Industrial Revolution. The development of new machines and new forms of energy to power those machines moved industrial production into urban factories. The factories did not need highly skilled workers; instead, they needed people to do highly repetitive tasks.

Mass production allowed factory owners to reduce the price of their goods, and new steamboats, canals, and railroads made it easier to get these products to distant markets. Small-scale producers could not compete; most of them were forced to move to cities and find jobs in factories. With more workers competing for fewer jobs, wages went down for most industrial workers. But for the owners of these factories and for the bankers who were financing their activities, profits soared.

The Industrial Revolution helped capitalism spread around the world, and changed the nature of work forever. Jobs became increasingly standardized, so that workers could be easily substituted for one another on assembly lines and other factory systems of mass production. As jobs became de-skilled, workers became easily replaceable, and business owners continually sought to reduce their wages. Many of them did this by increasing production for the same wage, often through the use of new technologies. Others reduced wages by moving factories to places where employees were willing to work for less. Still others used the threat of replacing their employees with cheaper workers in order to extract wage concessions.

Socialism A type of economy in which goods are produced according to social needs, and economic production is controlled and owned collectively by the workers themselves.

Soon, social movements against capitalism emerged throughout much of the capitalist world. Many of these movements were inspired by the critiques of Karl Marx, who argued that workers' lives would get worse unless they banded together, overthrew the capitalist system, and abolished private property. Once this happened, Marx believed, capitalism would be replaced by **socialism**, in which goods would be produced according to social needs, and economic production would be controlled and owned collectively by the workers themselves. Socialist movements spread throughout Europe during the second half of the 19th century and also in the United States, where the Socialist Labor Party was founded in 1877.

Industrial workers assemble radios at the Atwater Kent Factory in Philadelphia, 1925
Industrial jobs are standardized, so that workers can be easily substituted for one another on assembly lines and in other factory systems of mass production. Today, much industrial production has been moved to places where workers can be paid the lowest wages.

By the end of World War II in 1945, tensions between capitalism and socialism had developed into a Cold War between the United States and the Soviet Union. Each of the two world powers had its own sphere of alliances with countries whose political, military, and economic alliances were determined primarily by whether it had adopted a capitalist or a socialist economic system, or something in between. This lasted until 1991, with the disbanding of the Warsaw Pact alliance between the now-former Soviet Union and European state-socialist countries. By that point, organized resistance to capitalism had weakened considerably.

Post-Industrialism and the Changing Nature of the Economy

Post-industrialism An economy in which manufacturing becomes less important as a source of wealth, and where the production of information, knowledge, and services becomes more important.

Since the 20th century, the global economy has been changed by **post-industrialism**, which refers to an economy where manufacturing becomes less important as a source of wealth, and where the production of information, knowledge, and services becomes more important.

The rise and the social consequences of post-industrial society were described in books written by the sociologists Alain Touraine (1971) and Daniel Bell (1973). Beginning in the second half of the 20th century, Bell and Touraine argued, the advanced capitalist economies had experienced a shift away from manufacturing jobs and toward professional, technical, and service occupations. By 1970, half of all workers in the United States were employed in the service sector. Today, more than 80 percent of all American workers are employed in professional, technical, and service sector jobs. These jobs require access to information and information technology. They place a premium on knowledge, creativity, expertise, and communication skills, and require higher levels of education and more advanced credentials.

Post-industrialism has led to significant changes in the economy. Blue-collar jobs based on physical labor have declined in many countries, as they have been relocated to places that have less advanced economies and cheaper labor costs. The unions that protected blue-collar workers have lost political power, and the percentage of workers who belong to unions has also declined. Because of the emphasis on knowledge, creativity, and innovation, research universities have become major sources of economic growth (Berman 2012). Cities compete to attract the new tech companies that drive the information economy, and they try to make themselves attractive to the young college graduates who work for those companies (Castells 1999).

Economic Crisis and Insecurity in an Age of Globalization

Post-industrialism is good for the experts, the innovators, and the high-level professionals and managers who run the knowledge economy, but it is much worse for everyone else. As Kalleberg (2013) demonstrates in his book *Good Jobs, Bad Jobs*, there has

Protest against new Amazon headquarters, New York City, 2018
Community activists and union members protest the tax breaks and inducements offered to the commercial giant Amazon by the city and state of New York. Protesters successfully argued that the new opportunities Amazon would bring were unlikely to benefit local communities and workers and were instead likely to reinforce inequality in housing, jobs, and benefits.

been a dramatic rise in precarious employment since the 1970s. These jobs are defined by low wages, the elimination of benefits such as health insurance or retirement funds, and virtually no long-term security.

The trends in precarious work can be seen in the increasing use of temporary workers, involuntary part-time workers, independent contractors, and contingent or on-call workers. The jobs that have the most growth over the last 10 years are not the high-paying creative jobs celebrated by the knowledge economy. They are the precarious, low-paying service jobs that have high turnover and virtually no job security: home health care aides, retail salespeople, customer service representatives, and food preparation workers (Kalleberg 2013). These workers are more likely to experience periods of long-term unemployment (at least six months) and pay for more of their health insurance and retirement costs. Not surprisingly, workers' perception of job insecurity has increased dramatically since the 1970s.

Post-industrial work
Flexible workspaces like WeWork respond to shifting needs of the knowledge economy, where people may work from home and may need only a part-time office space that can be configured for meetings and working in teams.

These trends are magnified by globalization. As multinational corporations search the globe for cheap labor, workers lose bargaining power and governments lose control over economic policy. But for the innovators, knowledge workers, and professionals and managers who benefit the most from post-industrialism, globalization simply magnifies their sense of privilege and their isolation from the rest of society. According to the sociologist Zygmunt Bauman (2000), this new global elite is continually on the move, but they only experience an isolated and privileged version of the world. National boundaries are not very important for them, because their work as well as their recreation takes place all over the world. They have little understanding or empathy for the economic anxieties that are experienced by the less privileged.

CAREERS

The Uber-ization of the Economy

On a winter night in Paris in 2008, Travis Kalanick and Garrett Camp were frustrated with their inability to hail a cab. They wondered why cab hailing had not yet been integrated with smartphones to create a better user experience. Returning to San Francisco, they designed a smartphone app for cab hailing, and the result was a major innovation in global business. Today, Uber operates in 58 countries, (Hartmans and McAlone 2016), and

the company went public in 2019—albeit not at the price that was expected initially (Isaac, De La Merced, and Sorkin 2019).

Uber's success has as much to do with the way it relates to its employees as with its use of new technologies. From the beginning, Uber has treated the people who work for it as "independent contractors" rather than traditional employees. As such, Uber drivers have the

CAREERS CONTINUED

Uber driver, New York City
Uber's growth is part of a trend toward a "gig economy" where workers are independent contractors and frequently lack both health insurance and workers' compensation.

freedom to work when they want. Many of them drive for Uber as a second job, spending a few hours picking up passengers on nights, weekends, and other times they are free. Most of them like the flexibility of the arrangement. But this arrangement comes with costs. As independent contractors, they are not entitled to benefits that are legally owed to employees, such as a guaranteed minimum wage, workers' compensation, sick days, unemployment benefits, or reimbursed business expenses. State and local governments also lose in the arrangement, because Uber does not pay into state funds for workers' compensation and unemployment insurance. The federal government loses revenue too, because Uber does not pay Social Security taxes.

Uber's growth is part of a larger trend toward what is being called the "gig economy" or the "sharing economy," in which workers are expected to do their jobs as independent contractors. In addition to the taxi industry, where Uber and Lyft have become major players, these

kinds of arrangements are having a major impact in industries like construction and home repair services (TaskRabbit), home cleaning services (Homejoy), delivery services (Postmates, DoorDash), graphic design (Fiverr), and hotels and short-term rentals (Airbnb). Even the adult entertainment industry has started to get into the act; many strip clubs now treat their dancers as independent contractors. Recent surveys estimate that between 20 and 30 percent of working-age adults in the United States and Europe participate in the gig economy (Manyika et al. 2016).

For the vast majority of gig economy workers, wages are minimal. The median monthly income for Uber drivers is about $155; for TaskRabbit workers it is $110, and for Postmates couriers it is about $70 (Leasca 2017). Airbnb hosts make more money, with median monthly earnings of about $440.

In recent years, state labor commissions have gone to court to sue companies in the gig economy for misclassifying their workers as independent contractors instead of employees. These suits claim that such misclassification is costing hundreds of millions of dollars in lost tax revenue, and giving these companies an unfair advantage over law-abiding companies because of labor costs that can be as much as 40 percent lower (Wogan 2016). Workers have also filed lawsuits. In 2016, Uber settled a class-action lawsuit for $100 million. Once viewed as a place of innovation and freedom, many now see the gig economy as a place of exploitation.

ACTIVE LEARNING

Find out: Do you know anyone who does work in the gig economy? What do they see as the advantages and disadvantages of their jobs? Do they have another job where they are classified as an employee? If so, what are the differences in their two jobs?

CASE STUDY

What Kind of Education Do People Need in Today's Economy?

In 2011, Microsoft's cofounder Bill Gates declared in a speech to the National Governors Association that state universities should reduce support for the liberal arts and increase their investments in engineering, science, and other job-creating disciplines. Apple's cofounder Steve Jobs disagreed strongly. Jobs argued that Apple's success was the result of "technology married with liberal arts, married with the humanities," and that this

was truer than ever as their attention shifted to post-PC devices such as the iPhone and the iPad.

In some respects, it was strange for Gates and Jobs to be leading a public discussion about the future of higher education, given that neither of them had finished college—Gates left Harvard University after two years, and Jobs dropped out of Reed College after six months. But their disagreement provoked intense dispute about

CASE STUDY CONTINUED

the value of the liberal arts in the new tech economy. The argument in favor of a liberal arts education seems to have won the day, at least for the moment. In his 2018 book about the future of the tech economy, Microsoft president Brad Smith claimed that people with a liberal arts background would be absolutely crucial for realizing the full potential of artificial intelligence:

> . . . skilling-up for an AI-powered world involves more than science, technology, engineering, and math. As computers behave more like humans, the social sciences and humanities will become even more important. Languages, art, history, economics, ethics, philosophy, psychology and human development courses can teach critical, philosophical and ethics-based skills that will be instrumental in the development and management of AI solutions. (Smith and Shum 2018: 19)

Not everyone agrees with Jobs and Smith about the value of a liberal arts education. In a 2014 speech about job training and the manufacturing sector, President Barack Obama argued that "folks can make a lot more, potentially, with skilled manufacturing or the trades than they might with an art history degree." In 2011, Florida governor Rick Scott argued that his state did not need any more anthropologists, and that the state university should invest in degree programs that led to jobs. In 2016, Kentucky governor Matt Bevin suggested that the state's taxpayers should not be subsidizing the education of French literature majors.

The *conflict* between science and the humanities can be traced back to the earliest days of the modern research university. In his 1959 lecture "The Two Cultures," C. P. Snow argued that the conflict between scientists and humanists was a major obstacle preventing people from solving major social problems. Snow ([1959] 2001) argued that the *solidarity* of each group seemed to depend on criticizing the ignorance of the other. Humanists complained that scientists knew nothing about art, poetry, literature, or any of the other things that marked a refined or civilized person. Scientists, meanwhile, complained that humanists were scientific illiterates, that they knew little more about physics and other modern scientific disciplines than cavemen. The

identities of each group, it seemed, had been defined in opposition to the other, in a way that made cooperation difficult.

Throughout the history of the conflict between scientists and humanists, the *power* of the dominant group has allowed them to organize the university in a way that reinforced their own *privilege*. Today, professors in business and the sciences earn higher salaries, work in more modern buildings, have more research support, and tend to teach fewer courses than professors in the humanities. These professors may love their jobs, but institutional *inequality* means they are much more likely to be employed as contingent workers and less likely to have resources available for things like conference travel or even photocopying. Still, attempts by university administrators to close humanities departments altogether are met with *resistance*, as students and faculty protest the proposals, and as these protests get media coverage.

Today, the *structure* of the economy is one that largely favors scientific and technical education as the safest route to success. When Steve Jobs argued for the value of the liberal arts, he pointed to the *contingency* of his own biography as a major source of insight. Even though he had dropped out of Reed College, he continued to attend classes that interested him, including a course in calligraphy. Ten years later, when designing the Mac computer, his study of calligraphy inspired him to develop the Mac as the first computer with multiple typefaces and proportionally spaced fonts. This forever changed the interface of personal computers and other digital products.

In fact, in many parts of the world the focus on creativity is seen as the main advantage of the American education system and the main characteristic of American workers. In the United States, policy-makers and employers look at *global* comparisons that show American students lagging in science and math, and they urge the *local* schools to invest more heavily in those areas. In other parts of the world, and particularly in Asia, policy-makers look at a global economy in which innovation is heavily tilted toward the United States, and they encourage their local schools to try US-style creativity.

LEARNING GOALS REVISITED

14.1   Describe the different social purposes and social effects of education.

- Education is used to promote literacy, which refers to the ability to read, write, communicate, and use other skills that allow people to participate fully in their society. The promotion of mass literacy has been a major goal of schools since the 19th century, and today more than 82 percent of the world's population can read.

- Education promotes socialization, and for this reason it is often described as having a "hidden curriculum." In addition to teaching basic values, norms, and citizenship, schools also teach students how to deal with crowds and distractions; how to respond to the fact that they are being evaluated; and how to deal with power inequalities.

- Schools teach practical skills that students will need in the workforce, and they give out valuable credentials that are needed to gain entry into most of the high-paying and high-status professions. Schools sort students into different types of occupational futures, and they often do this in a way that reinforces privilege and inequality.

- Schools help the economy. They are a major source of employment, and they provide free childcare for working parents.

14.2   Describe the experience of going to school, and how it has changed over time.

- Most students today attend publicly funded schools. School systems around the world are organized into primary schools, secondary schools, and colleges and universities.

- Most private schools today are religious schools, which are supported through a combination of student tuition and church revenues. There are also elite private schools, which charge extremely high tuition and which historically have catered to the most privileged families in society. Since the 1970s the homeschooling movement has continued to grow.

- New digital technologies have become a significant presence in schools. These technologies offer the promise of a more flexible and personalized learning experience. They have also been used to cut costs, and there is evidence that they reinforce existing inequalities.

- High-stakes standardized tests have also become a major presence in many schools.

- For students, one of the most meaningful parts of going to school is the experience of building friendships and expanding social networks. The school experience is also shaped by a student's position in the overall "pecking order" of their school. This is particularly true during the early high school years, when the dynamics of social exclusion and bullying are a major issue.

14.3   Think about the kinds of characteristics that are associated with "good jobs," and describe how the distribution of good jobs is socially structured.

- Good jobs offer some combination of the following characteristics: good pay, high status, satisfying working conditions, room for growth, and enough free time and resources to pursue hobbies or other interests. People tend to be more satisfied when their job offers a good match with their expectations, interests, and values.

- Most people do not have good jobs, and they experience work as a place of domination, exploitation, and monotony. Good jobs are distributed unequally, in a manner that is shaped by race, class, and gender.

- Because of stagnating salaries and increasing job insecurity, there has been a general increase in job dissatisfaction since the 1970s.

14.4   Describe the experience economy, and know where and how people are searching for satisfaction outside of work.

- Happiness is not completely dependent on the job a person has. While economic security is associated with happiness, so are higher levels of social tolerance and democracy. Close relationships with family and friends are particularly important, and so is a life that allows people to do challenging things.

- The experience economy refers to the phenomenon in which companies sell experiences and transformations rather than goods and services. The experience economy has completely transformed the tourism, leisure, and recreation industries, and it is a growing part of the overall economy.

14.5 Describe how the economy has changed over time, and explain why economic insecurity is such a significant feature of modern social life.

- The most significant change in the modern economy was the transition from feudalism to capitalism. In capitalism, all economic activities are based on a calculation of potential profits, and the prices of all goods (including workers' wages) are determined by the marketplace.

- The Industrial Revolution helped capitalism spread around the world, and changed the nature of work forever. Jobs became increasingly standardized, so workers could be easily substituted for one another on assembly lines and in other factory systems of mass production. For many of them, this meant that their jobs became de-skilled, and they became more easily replaceable.

- The second half of the 20th century led to the development of post-industrial economies, in which manufacturing became less important as a source of wealth, and where the production of information, knowledge, and services became more important.

- Post-industrialism has been good for the experts, innovators, and high-level professionals who run the knowledge economy, but it has not been as good for everyone else. Most jobs have become much more precarious, with low wages, the elimination of benefits, and virtually no long-term security. The use of temporary workers, involuntary part-time workers, independent contractors, and contingent or on-call workers has increased dramatically.

The result has been an increase in economic inequality.

Key Terms

Capitalism 426
Citizenship education 405
Credentialism 407
Cultural capital 408
Economy 426
Feudalism 426
Homeschooling   411
Job training 405
Literacy 405
Marriage market 420
Moral education 406
Post-industrialism 428
Primary school   411
Private school 410
Public school 410
Socialism 427
Secondary school 411
Standardized tests 415
Warehousing theory 409

Review Questions

1. Describe the three main features of the mass literacy movements. What are the main achievements and shortcomings of the mass literacy movement?

2. Describe some of the ways that education reinforces social inequalities, and also some of the ways that it promotes social mobility.

3. Describe the main ways that education systems have changed over the last two hundred years.

4. What are standardized tests? Why were they developed, and how have they changed? What are some of their main advantages and disadvantages?

5. What are the characteristics of high-performing schools?

6. What are the characteristics of good jobs and bad jobs? What kinds of people are most likely to get these different types of jobs?

7. What is capitalism? How did capitalism change the nature of work and society? How has capitalism changed over the last hundred years?

Explore

RECOMMENDED READINGS

Adler, Patricia, and Peter Adler. 1998. *Peer Power: Preadolescent Culture and Identity*. New Brunswick, NJ: Rutgers University Press.

Bell, Daniel. 1973. *The Coming of Post-industrial Society. A Venture in Social Forecasting*. New York: Basic Books.

Boli, John, Francisco Ramirez, and John Meyer. 1985. "Explaining the Origins and Expansion of Mass Education." *Comparative Education Review* 29: 145–70.

Kalleberg, Arne. 2013. *Good Jobs, Bad Jobs*. New York: Russell Sage.

Rivera, Lauren. 2015. *Pedigree: How Elite Students Get Elite Jobs*. Princeton, NJ: Princeton University Press.

ACTIVITIES

- *Use your sociological imagination*: In October 2012 an article in the *Harvard Business Review* declared that data scientist was the "sexiest job of the 21st century." Read the article (https://hbr.org/2012/10/data-scientist-the-sexiest-job-of-the-21st-century), and do a sociological analysis of these jobs. Are they good jobs? What kinds of people are likely to get them? Are they more likely to reinforce social inequality or to promote social mobility? Are they likely to remain good jobs, or do you think they will eventually get influenced by the "Uber-ization of the economy" and the general tendency toward precarious work?

- *Media+Data Literacy*: Select a popular television show or movie set in a school, and another one set in a business environment. Describe the representations of teachers, students, bosses, and employees. What do you think these representations tell us about education and the economy?

- *Discuss*: Do you think your school sees itself as a research university, or as something else? Do you think your school's mission statement is an accurate description of what it is like to go to school there? Is there anything in the experience of going to your school that is not captured in the mission statement?

For additional resources, including Media+Data Literacy exercises, In the News exercises, and quizzes, please go to **oup.com/he/Jacobs-Townsley1e**

PART V CHANGE, ISSUES, AND THE FUTURE

15

Population, Immigration, and Urbanization

The town of Fossil, Oregon, has been slowly dying for decades. First established in 1876, the town has never had more than 700 residents. According to the 2010 US Census, there were only 473 people living in Fossil, with a median age of 56. There is only one restaurant, and the nearest hospital is more than an hour away. The town has virtually no racial or ethnic diversity, and no immigrant communities. The entire school district has only 60 students, and many of those students choose to participate in a distance learning program. There are very few jobs in the town, and average earnings per job in the county are the lowest in the state (Semuels 2016). Virtually all of the students who graduate from Fossil's lone high school leave the town.

The city of Houston could not be more different from Fossil. Established in 1836, the city now has more than two million residents, and it is one of the fastest-growing cities in the country. Houston has an extremely diverse economy, with major strengths in energy, health care, manufacturing, aerospace, education, and transportation. With affordable housing and a variety of good entry-level jobs, it is one of the best places in the United States for college graduates to begin a career. Houston is a global city, with extensive cultural attractions, an exciting restaurant scene, a large number of multinational corporate headquarters, a port for deep-sea ships, and a large international airport. It is also a major immigration destination; more than half a million immigrants live in Houston, and it has become the most racially and ethnically diverse major city in the country. With so much immigration and job growth, Houston is a young city, with a median age of 32.6.

Main street, Fossil, Oregon

LEARNING GOALS

15.1   Describe the basic trends in population growth, and understand how population changes influence society.

15.2   Think about the relationship between demography and social inequality.

15.3   Understand how urbanization has shaped social life, and describe how the organization of cities has changed over time.

15.4   Describe the basic historical trends in immigration.

15.5   Describe how immigrant communities are organized, and how they shape politics and the economy in both sending and receiving countries.

Demography The study of human populations.

Urbanization A social process in which the population shifts from the country into cities, and where most people start to live in urban rather than rural areas.

Immigration The movement of people from one nation to another.

This chapter explores how population, immigration, and urbanization shape social life. We begin by introducing some basic concepts in **demography**, which refers to the study of human populations. We consider historical trends in global population, discuss the kinds of social pressures that population growth and aging create, and explore how these population pressures are connected to social inequality. Next, we consider **urbanization**, which refers to the shift of populations into cities. We examine what it is like to live in cities, and we consider how the organization of cities has changed over time. Last, we examine historical trends in **immigration**, which refers to the movement of people between nations. We pay particular attention to how immigrant communities influence politics and the economy in the sending and receiving countries.

Population

Living in a town of five hundred people is much different than living in a city of several million. Living in a place where most of the people are old and retired is different than living in a city where most of the people are going to school or working. Living in a place where large numbers of people are continually arriving to establish new lives is different than living in a place where the same families have lived for generations. These basic features of a society's population have a massive impact on the nature of social life.

Demography and Population Growth

In the social sciences, the study of human populations is part of the subfield of demography. While theories about population dynamics can be traced back to ancient Rome and Greece, the field of demography did not really develop until the 19th century. Demography was initially a branch of statistics, and it still maintains a strongly quantitative orientation. By the 1920s it was becoming a distinct field of study. In the United States, demography has been a major influence in academic sociology since the 1930s (Hirschman and Tolnay 2005).

Census An official count of the population.

Demography is also a major research endeavor promoted by governments around the world. Nearly one hundred nations now carry out a **census**, which is an official count of the population. The United Nations has an official statistics division devoted to demography, which makes recommendations about best practices for conducting a national census and employs demographers to study global population trends. In fact, most wealthy countries employ demographers to measure population trends.

THE BASICS OF DEMOGRAPHY. Demography covers five basic research topics: the size of the population; its distribution across different geographic areas; its social composition, in terms of age, gender, race, ethnicity, and other relevant characteristics; historical changes in population; and the causes and consequences of population change (Baker et al. 2017). The kind of demographic research that most sociologists do is called **social demography**, which uses demographic data (such as censuses and population surveys) in order to study key social institutions and social processes (Hirschman and Tolnay 2005: 422). Social demographers study trends in marriage and divorce, population aging, immigration and social mobility, urbanization, and health disparities between different population groups.

Social demography Social research that uses demographic data in order to study key social institutions and social processes.

The key data sources that demographers use are the official censuses administered by national governments. The United Nations Statistics Division recommends that nations should undertake an official census once each decade. Conducting a census is one of the largest and most complicated peacetime activities that most nations will attempt. A census requires an accurate map of the country, as well as the recruitment and training of a large number of census counters. Census workers have to collect information from each individual household, compile all the information into a single data set, analyze the data, and disseminate the results to policy-makers as well as the public.

Demographers also rely on additional data sources. They examine official records of births, deaths, marriages, and migration. They rely on other population surveys sponsored by government and nongovernmental sources, such as the World Fertility Survey, the Current Population Survey, and the Demographic and Health Surveys. Last, based on a knowledge of how specific censuses undercount particular populations, they use modeling techniques to develop more accurate estimates of population trends.

Trends in Population Growth

The global population grew rapidly during the 20th century. World population did not top one billion until after 1800, and it did not exceed two billion until 1930. Global population reached four billion in 1975, and from that point it has increased by an additional billion people every 12 to 15 years. The global population reached seven billion in 2011, and it is projected to reach 9.8 billion by 2050 (UN 2017).

Demographic transition The historical decline in the birth rate and the death rate.

Rapid population growth was caused by the **demographic transition**, which refers to the historical decline in the birth rate and the death rate (or mortality rate). Before the 1800s, the birth rate and the death rate were both high. The infant mortality rate was particularly high, which resulted in a much slower rate of population growth. The average life expectancy was between 30 and 40 years, which was relatively unchanged from what it had been for

Population clock
The US Census Bureau website shows a live population clock for the United States and the 10 most populous countries in the world.

Careers in Gerontology

Gerontology is a field that studies the aging process and the social issues that are associated with an aging population. It is different from geriatrics, which is a medical specialty focusing on the care and treatment of the aged population. Gerontologists study the physical, mental, and social changes that happen to people when they get older. They examine the key issues and challenges that face a society with an aging population. And they try to develop policies that will improve quality of life—not only for older people, but also for the families and communities that care for them.

The aging population has increased the demand for health-related services, at the same time that it has reoriented those services toward the needs of the elderly. Hospitals, nursing and residential care facilities, and family services for the elderly have grown by nearly one-third over the last decade, and they are forecast to continue growing for the foreseeable future. People working in medical facilities, fitness centers, tourism, transportation, and many other industries will be able to perform their jobs more effectively if the study of gerontology is part of their formal schooling and continuing education.

Most universities offer options for people who want to study gerontology. People who are already working in nursing and home health care can earn a certificate in gerontology, which typically involves three or four sociology and psychology courses focused on the aging process. Many universities now offer a bachelor's degree in gerontology. These interdisciplinary programs combine coursework in sociology, psychology, and biology with community internships that connect students with hospitals, nursing homes, and assisted-living facilities. People who complete a master's degree in gerontology can find careers as administrators, directors, and

supervisors in these settings. Those with advanced degrees in gerontology are also working for banks, insurance companies, pharmaceutical companies, advocacy groups, and the government, helping these organizations serve the elderly population more effectively. They serve as consultants to architects and interior designers to come up with solutions that will help people modify their homes so they can "age in place." Increasingly, universities are making it possible for people to complete an online degree in gerontology, which allows them to upgrade their skills while remaining in their jobs.

Gerontology
Careers in gerontology respond to the social issues that are associated with an aging population.

ACTIVE LEARNING

Find out: What certificate and degree programs in gerontology does your university or college offer? Are these programs located in a separate department, or in a sociology or a psychology department?

---

significant health issues as they grow old. In fact, even for people who start out poor but experience positive social mobility during their adult lives, there is a tendency for their early disadvantage to reappear later in life, in the form of worse health outcomes (Nusslock and Miller 2016).

An aging population creates many social pressures for a society. One of these pressures is an increase in health costs. On average, medical expenses more than double between the ages of 70 and 90 (De Nardi et al. 2016). In wealthy countries such as Germany, Japan, and the United States, the elderly account for between one-quarter and one-third of all medical expenses (French and Kelly 2016). An aging population also creates pressures for family and friends, who are called upon to provide unpaid care for the elderly. Additional social pressures come from the effects that an aging population has on the workforce. People over the age of 65 are less likely to be in the labor force, particularly in wealthier nations. At the same time, most wealthy nations have a public pension system, in which workers are eligible to start receiving benefits sometime between the ages of 65 and 67. This means that an aging population faces a situation in which there is a smaller proportion of the population engaged in full-time work, and a larger proportion who are receiving public benefits. This creates a financial crisis for governments. With higher public pension expenses, there is less money available for other social programs.

While population aging is an issue that has confronted the wealthier countries first, it is increasingly becoming a global social issue. The world's older population is increasing faster than its younger population, a trend that is expected to continue. Total fertility rates have dropped to below replacement level on every continent except Africa, and they have been on the decline in Africa as well. Poorer countries are less prepared to face the health challenges associated with an aging population. They usually have a less-developed public pension system, which means that they have to confront higher levels of poverty among the elderly. And they often have to deal with an exodus of many of their younger workers, who are drawn away by the economic opportunities in wealthy countries.

Urbanization

The famous architect Frank Lloyd Wright (1867–1959) hated cities. He thought they were poorly designed, too crowded, too noisy, and too busy. In his 1932 book *The Disappearing City*, he wrote about his vision for the perfect community of the future, which he called Broadacre City. Because of new transportation and communication technologies, Wright argued, people no longer needed to live in crowded cities. They could live in new, modern homes filled with open space, glass, and natural light. Every family could live on a one-acre plot of land. Residential areas, commerce, industry, agriculture, and recreation could all be clearly separated, connected by spacious landscaped highways.

Jane Jacobs (1916–2006), a writer and a contemporary of Wright, had a different view of the city. In her 1961 book *The Death and Life of Great American Cities*, Jacobs argued that cities were exciting places to live precisely because they were crowded, disorganized, and full of strangers doing different things. Jacobs was an advocate of mixed-use development, and she thought that it was a mistake to separate various aspects of life into different parts of the city. Whether writing about sidewalks, neighborhoods, or

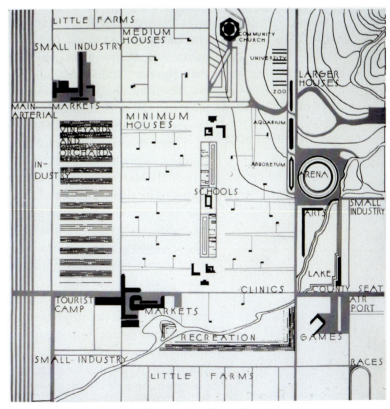

Frank Lloyd Wright's sketch of his futuristic Living City, Broadacre

parks, she emphasized that liveliness, density, and variety were the key elements to a successful city.

The contrasting visions of Jane Jacobs and Frank Lloyd Wright reflect the general ambivalence people feel about the role of cities in modern life. For some, the city is an exciting place, where the anonymity of the crowd gives them the freedom to be whoever they choose to be, where they have endless options for entertainment, where there are an endless variety of interesting people to meet, and where they can find the most economic opportunities. For others, the city is a concrete jungle of stress, congestion, pollution, and rudeness, where everybody is running some kind of scam, where rents are too high, and where all the ordinary tasks of the day are harder to complete than they need to be. But one thing is clear: urban life is a defining feature of the modern world.

Basic Concepts and Theories of Urbanization

The sociologist Louis Wirth (1857–1952) defined the city as "a relatively large, dense, and permanent settlement of heterogeneous individuals" (Wirth 1938: 1). Observing that the growth of great cities was one of the main features of modern civilization, Wirth argued that urbanization made social life more anonymous and impersonal, more superficial and impermanent, and more diverse and specialized. Wirth also argued that urban life increased social mobility, because the diversity and anonymity of the city tended to break down rigid social structures. The city was a place defined by opportunity as well as insecurity.

Other theories of urbanization have emphasized its connection to capitalism and to economic development in general. As we discussed in Chapter 14, changes in agricultural production during the 16th and 17th centuries forced people off farming lands and into cities in a search for work. The process accelerated rapidly during the Industrial Revolution of the 18th century, as more and more economic activity moved into urban factories. As the capitalist economy continued to expand, factory owners began to invest their profits into the urban built environment, which accelerated the growth of the city even further (Harvey 1985). Once this happened, the city became an economic "growth machine," with builders, bankers, real estate investors, business leaders, and politicians all working together to continue expanding the city and increasing property values (Logan and Molotch 1987).

Other theories have emphasized how urbanization encourages cultural changes. Georg Simmel (1858–1918) and Walter Benjamin (1892–1940) described the blasé detachment of city dwellers as they wandered the city streets, taking in its sights and sounds but not really engaging with any of it. Claude Fischer argued that the city's population density and heterogeneity made it an incubator of subcultures and social change (see Chapter 4). And Manuel Castells (1984) argued that the city has encouraged the growth of social movements and social change, with people joining together to demand the right to live in a more humane and tolerant city.

Interestingly, there is no standard definition of an urban area or an urban population. Each country has its own definition of who is an urban resident. But there are some common patterns and some central measurement concepts. The main concepts that demographers use to measure urbanization are population size and population density. For example, the Organisation for Economic Co-operation and Development (OECD) has established specific population thresholds (either 50,000 or 100,000 residents, depending on the country) and density thresholds (either 1,000 or 1,500 residents per square kilometer) to count as an urban area (OECD 2012). Other approaches factor in travel time and travel distance, recognizing that many people will choose to live just outside of a densely populated urban area and then travel into the city for work, shopping, and entertainment (Frey and Zimmer 1998). This helps account for suburban and exurban growth, which we discuss later in the chapter.

Historical Patterns and Current Trends in Urbanization

People have been living in cities for more than five thousand years. Between about 400 BCE and 100 CE, cities of more than 200,000 residents existed in Babylon, Patna (in India), and Rome (Frey and Zimmer 1998: 1). Evidence in-

Cities then and now
People have been living in cities for over five thousand years. Ancient Rome was home to more than 1 million people in the second century CE.

dicates that the city of Rome had more than one million residents during the second century CE These cities were important centers of trade, religious activity, and politics. For the most part, though, this was not a period of mass urbanization. Most people lived rural lives focused on agricultural production. Before 1850, the proportion of the world's population living in urban areas remained somewhere between 4 and 7 percent (Frey and Zimmer 1998).

As we discussed in Chapter 14, urbanization accelerated during the Industrial Revolution, when people moved from rural areas to work in large factories located in cities. The industrial city brought about a number of important social changes: a growing middle class, the spread of global trade and commerce, the development of modern banking systems, the shift to the nuclear family, and the growth of social reform movements.

By the time the cities of Beijing (in 1800) and London (in 1825) surpassed one million residents, urbanization had become a global phenomenon. There were more than 10 cities of one million residents in 1900; by 2016 there were more than 500 such cities, and today nearly one-quarter of the world's population lives in a city with more than one million inhabitants (United Nations, Department of Economic and Social Affairs, Population Division 2016a). UN demographers estimate that the urban population has quadrupled since 1960, and nearly 55 percent of the world's population now lives in a city.

Living in Cities

Living in a city is different than living in other kinds of places. The anonymity of city living means that people have more freedom to be who they want to be, but they also risk isolation and loneliness. The size and density of the city means that people have to deal with crowds, noise, and less living space. There are more things to do in the city, and there are more economic opportunities. And cities are constantly changing.

CITIES IN TRADITIONAL AND MODERN SOCIETIES. Pre-modern cities were much smaller, with lower levels of population density and less economic diversity. Most medieval cities had fewer than 10,000 inhabitants, and before the

Industrial Revolution it was rare for a city to have more than 50,000 people. These cities may have been smaller, but they were extremely crowded. They had narrow streets, and it was difficult for them to expand because they were often protected by stone perimeter walls. Air and water pollution presented a significant problem, and fires destroyed large numbers of buildings.

The pre-modern city may have been different than the city of today, but it was still a place of significant innovation and change. The city was the first type of society in which the residents lived primarily off trade and commerce rather than agriculture (Weber 1969). The city was a marketplace, where people specialized in the kinds of products they produced and then bought everything else they needed in the local market. The city was a place of consumption, where wealthy families and powerful government officials came to buy products that merchants had brought back from their distant travel and trading activity. Newspapers, banking and finance, democracy, and the idea of citizenship—all of these were created in the pre-modern city.

Modern cities have grown in population as well as geographical reach. Some urban areas have grown to be larger than 20 million people, spread over thousands of miles. Professional urban police departments began to form in the 19th century, in response to concerns about crime. Zoning laws and other forms of urban planning became increasingly important during the 20th century, as people grew concerned about social disorder and tried to manage the process of urban growth and suburban development.

Suburb A residential area located within commuting distance of a city.

SUBURBS AND EXURBS. A **suburb** is a residential area located within commuting distance of a city. Suburbs developed in the late 19th and early 20th centuries, first with improvements in railroad infrastructure and then with the spread of the automobile. Suburbs allowed middle-class families to escape the crowded, noisy, and dirty city and to purchase a newly built home surrounded by open spaces, parks, and new neighborhood schools. In addition to providing a lower-density space in which to live, these suburbs often had zoning laws that created separate and distinct spaces for residential and commercial activities. They also tended to have less socioeconomic, racial, and ethnic diversity among their residents.

One of the most influential suburban developments in the United States was Levittown, New York, a planned community on Long Island that was built between 1947 and 1951. Designing it as an affordable community within commuting distance of New York City, the owners of Levittown built detached homes, each with modern appliances, a lawn, and a white picket fence. Community swimming pools and other public amenities were part of the design. The houses could be purchased for less money than it would cost to live in a small urban apartment, particularly appealing for soldiers returning from World War II and their young families. The company that designed the community developed a 30-year mortgage with no down payment and monthly costs about the same as a rental property, and advertised Levittown as an opportunity to buy into the American Dream. Buying a house in Levittown was restricted to white applicants only, meaning that the suburb (like most that followed) would be racially segregated. Even today, more than 50 years after racial housing covenants were ruled to be illegal, Levittown remains nearly 80 percent white.

As more people moved to the suburbs, development pushed farther away from the central city. Older suburbs became more congested and less residential, as commercial builders constructed office parks near suburban freeway exits. In large metropolitan areas such as the New York Tri-State area, greater Boston,

Structure and Contingency

The Growth of Brambleton, Virginia

Brambleton, a planned community, was created in 2001 in Loudoun County, Virginia. It is located about 25 miles away from Washington, DC, near Dulles International Airport. It has a population of 17,000 people. Median household income is about $165,000, and the median property value for a home is about $550,000, making it one of the wealthiest communities in Virginia. Its residents are mostly white (52%), Asian (28%), and highly educated, with more than 30 percent of adults holding a graduate or professional degree.

There are good structural reasons for why Brambleton would be a good place to start a new wealthy community. Its location makes it part of the Washington, DC metropolitan area, which is one of the most important urban agglomerations in the country. It is conveniently located at the end of a new railway extension linking the area to Washington. Its proximity to Dulles International Airport makes it an attractive option to people whose jobs require travel. In addition, the "Dulles Corridor" has a booming economy of its own.

Like most of Loudoun County, Brambleton was a rural area for most of its history, but the decision to construct Dulles International Airport there in 1962 was a major contingency that changed Loudoun County's fortunes. The airport brought high-tech companies to the area, and developers built planned communities that catered to these new workers as well as to government workers who wanted to live in a suburban environment that retained a somewhat rural feel. By the 1990s the county was booming in population; nearly doubling in size each decade, there were more than 300,000 people living in Loudoun County in 2010, as compared to only 25,000 in 1960.

As a 21st-century planned community, Brambleton is wired for high-speed internet, television, and other digital entertainment services. There are neighborhood parks and pools, as well as 15 miles of paved trails that can be used for walking, running, or cycling. Houses, townhouses, and condominiums are all designed to emphasize open space, being close enough to the town's amenities that people can walk, ride their bikes, and interact with other town residents. Schools are located within the community.

Brambleton's town center has grocery stores, movie theaters, restaurants, banks, medical offices, salons, and fitness centers. There is a separate community of homes and condominiums for people aged 55 and older located within Brambleton, providing this aging population with their own lake, trails, swimming pools, and a clubhouse.

Brambleton's growth and success have created challenges and contingencies not imagined by its original architects. New schools were needed to prevent overcrowding. Pedestrian underpasses needed to be built to avoid roads that were becoming more crowded with cars. Plans for a golf course had to be abandoned, with the land repurposed for the construction of new homes. Like most of Loudoun County, Brambleton has been criticized for not having enough affordable housing for lower-income families. And while there are good mass transit options, the community's growth has contributed significantly to suburban sprawl and to traffic congestion that is among the worst in the nation.

The planned community of Brambleton, Virginia

ACTIVE LEARNING

Discuss: Brambleton is an example of a Master-Planned Community (MPC). While many wealthy people are attracted to MPCs, some find them to be too artificial, while others complain that they are just another example of rich people creating walled cities to exclude the less privileged. What do you think about MPCs?

and Washington-Baltimore, suburban development connected different cities together in a large, continuous space that geographers refer to as **conurbation**. Families in search of the original suburban experience—open space, more land, and less expensive housing costs—now find themselves moving to exurban communities, which are commuter towns on the outer fringes of an urban

Conurbation A process in which urban and suburban development reaches a point where different cities begin to be connected together in a large, continuous metropolitan space.

The emergence of the exurb
Exurbs are commuter towns on the outer fringes of an urban area, often more than 50 miles away from the central city. Some of these exurbs try to retain their rural character as they become connected to these ever-larger spaces of continuous urbanization and suburbanization.

Global city Cities that serve as the centers of global finance, international law, management consulting, and global marketing and communication.

area, often more than 50 miles away from the central city. Many of these exurban communities used to be rural areas, and they try to retain their rural character as they become connected to these ever-larger spaces of continuous urbanization and suburbanization.

GLOBAL CITIES. Urbanization and globalization have led to the creation of **global cities** such as London, Singapore, New York, and Tokyo. According to the sociologist Saskia Sassen, multinational corporations have become so complex that they need access to many different kinds of highly specialized professional service firms, in areas such as global finance, international law, management consulting, and global marketing and communication (Sassen 2001). These service firms locate themselves in a small number of global cities, where they have access to multinational corporate headquarters, other global service firms, and populations of highly educated young workers. Economically, these global cities have become disconnected from their surrounding region, because the work that the specialized global service firms are doing is not dependent on the fortunes of the regional or even the national economy. Socially and culturally, the people who work in these firms become part of a global elite. They travel between other global cities. They attain levels of wealth that are unimaginable to others living in the region, and they push up property values so high that the desirable neighborhoods are only attainable to other members of the global elite.

In its most recent ranking of global cities, the management consulting firm A. T. Kearney lists New York City as the most important global city, followed by London, Paris, Tokyo, and Hong Kong. These cities are all global centers of finance, with major stock exchanges and some of the largest international banking firms in the world. They have major international airports. Their universities attract students from around the world and train them in the kinds of specialized knowledge they will need to work for the global service firms. They are media and entertainment hubs, driving the global conversation about important social and political

Global cities
Global cities come to be disconnected from their surrounding region, because the work of the specialized global service firms that dominate them is not dependent on the fortunes of the regional or even the national economy. The global elite who live in these cities push up property values so that desirable neighborhoods are only attainable by other members of the global elite.

Inequality and Privilege

Why London Real Estate Is So Expensive

Housing markets in global cities seem almost immune to larger economic trends that influence other property markets. And while real estate is expensive in all global cities, London is in a class of its own. In the most desirable neighborhoods, potential buyers can expect to spend more than $5 million for a home, and potential renters can expect to pay about $8,000 per month for an apartment. Only about one-third of the buyers of properties in these neighborhoods are British; the rest come from the Middle East, Russia, Europe, India, Africa, and North America (Sullivan 2015).

According to the sociologist Roger Burrows, global financial institutions are encouraging their wealthiest clients to invest in London real estate, seeing it as a stable asset that has a very high rate of return (Burrows, Webber, and Atkinson 2017). More than $8 billion is invested in the London housing market from overseas each year. Some foreigners intend to use their London residence as a second home, while others use it as an investment property. They can get astronomically high short-term rents for their properties from members of the global business elite who need to be in London for short periods of time. Investors can usually expect an annual rate of return of more than 10 percent in the prime residential markets, based on the combination of rental income and resale profits.

As more of the world's super-rich have come to view the London real estate market as a valuable investment asset, the effects on construction patterns in the city have been significant. There is a strong incentive for builders and landowners to evict renters from older and more affordable housing properties, so they can demolish and then replace them with luxury buildings. Communities that were once affordable have gentrified rapidly, as the city becomes a destination that is only attainable for the super-rich. It is estimated that London now has half

a million residents with a net worth of over $1 million; the city is also home to approximately 80 people who are worth more than $1 billion (Burrows, Webber, and Atkinson 2017). Those who are not super-rich find themselves being pushed farther and farther outside of the city center, where they face longer commutes and where they unwittingly and unwillingly contribute to processes of suburbanization.

How the global elite live
London has one of the most desirable real estate markets in the world. The super-rich and corporate property investors have pushed up prices so far on properties like these townhouses in the central London neighborhood of Kensington that those who are not super-rich find themselves being pushed farther and farther outside of the city center.

ACTIVE LEARNING

Discuss: Do cities have a responsibility to build housing that is affordable and attainable to all of the people who work there?

issues. They are sources of cultural and scientific innovation. And they are extremely expensive places to live.

Global cities continue the processes of urbanization and conurbation, even though digital media make it possible to work anywhere in the world. As the sociologist Manuel Castells (2001) has shown, the rise of the internet has made cities more important. The young workers that tech companies are trying to hire want to live in cities. They are attracted to the economic opportunities, nightlife, cultural attractions, and diversity of the city. The same is true of the young lawyers, bankers, and consultants at the specialized global service firms

(Florida 2005). And this is particularly true for global cities like New York, San Francisco, London, and Tokyo.

Global cities also reinforce privilege and inequality. Housing in global cities has become a financial investment, which has led to rapidly accelerating housing prices (Florida 2017). Builders have focused on luxury apartments for the global elite, and they have reduced their investments in affordable housing. The result is that the poor, the working class, and even the middle class get pushed out of the city, or they are forced to accept substandard housing options. There is a very low likelihood that average people in these cities will be able to buy a house or even an apartment, meaning that they will be lifelong renters who are unable to accrue any wealth during their lives. Expensive housing also creates regional inequalities, as those who can afford to buy property in a global city—the same people who get the highest salaries—will see the value of their homes increase much faster than other homeowners. By concentrating wealth and power in a small number of massive urban regions, at the expense of the rest of the world, global cities reinforce global inequality (Sassen 2001).

URBANIZATION IN THE DEVELOPING WORLD. Urban growth in the developing world has occurred much faster than it did in the cities of Europe, North America, and Southeast Asia. Nations such as China, Nigeria, and Ecuador have rapidly transformed from rural to urban populations during the last 50 years, reaching levels of urbanization that took centuries to achieve in the developed nations of Europe and North America. Demographers estimate that most of the world's population increases are now occurring in cities in the developing world (Cohen 2006).

Rapid urbanization presents distinct challenges in poorer and developing countries. While wealthier and more developed countries typically have many different cities, which eventually connect through suburbanization and conurbation, developing countries typically have only one or two cities. This means that all of the rural migrants to the city are going to the same place, regardless of whether or not the city has the jobs or the resources to absorb them. Unable to find housing, they end up living in slums and shantytowns on the outskirts of the city, often without access to clean water, adequate public transportation, reliable power, or good schools. The cities lack the resources to deal with these challenges. They are unable to build adequate infrastructure, address poverty, deal with crime, or respond to the accelerating rates of pollution.

While urbanization has historically been associated with economic development and innovation, this has not been true to the same extent in the developing world. Urban residents in these countries are still better off than their rural counterparts in health outcomes, education, and employment, but the "urban bonus" is significantly smaller than it

Low-rise residential village contrasts with skyscrapers in Jakarta, Indonesia
Rapid urbanization presents distinct challenges in poor and developing countries. As cities struggle to build the infrastructure to support migrants from rural areas searching for economic opportunity, poorer residents live in older, deteriorating housing on the edges of the flourishing modern city.

Global and Local

How the H-1B Visa Program Transformed Tech and Education in the United States and India

The H-1B is a category of temporary visas that allows employers in the United States to hire highly educated foreign workers in specialized occupations, usually in the fields of science, technology, engineering, and mathematics. Created in 1990, the program grants visas to about 85,000 foreign workers each year. Employers petition for H-1B visas in order to fill specific job roles. They have to provide evidence that they will pay the H-1B visa at the same rate they would pay an American worker, and they have to demonstrate that their H-1B workers will not adversely impact the working conditions for their other employees.

The demand by employers for highly skilled foreign workers is much higher than the available supply of H-1B visas. If the number of applications exceeds the annual cap within the first five days of the application period (which has happened every year since 2014), the government conducts a lottery in order to select which applicants will receive the H-1B visa. The visa is good for a period of three years, and it can be extended for an additional three years.

Since 2001, more than half of all H-1B recipients have come from India (Ruiz 2017). The program has profoundly affected the economy as well as the education system in both nations. In India, the number of students studying computer science and engineering has increased significantly, with the hope of getting job offers from US companies through the H-1B visa program (Khanna 2017). These students have been a major resource for US tech companies, but they have also helped invigorate the tech sector in India. Not all of the Indian students can obtain the H-1B visa to work in the United States, and the ones who are unsuccessful have remained in India to help grow its own IT sector. In addition, many workers have returned to India after their visas expired, bringing their skills, networks, and resources to continue building this sector. The H-1B visa program has also contributed to the increase in graduate enrollments at US institutions by foreign students. In 1973, foreign students accounted for only about a quarter of PhD recipients in science and engineering fields in US universities; by 2003, they made up more than half (Bound et al. 2009). In fields like computer science and electrical engineering, international students earn more than three-quarters of all the graduate degrees in US universities (Redden 2017).

Some employers have abused the H-1B visa program, using it to outsource jobs and reduce labor costs in fields that are not very high tech. In 2014, 13 companies managed to obtain one-third of all H-1B visas (Park 2015). The largest of these companies, Tata Consultancy Services (TCS), received more H-1B visas than IBM, Google, Microsoft, Apple, Intel, and Amazon combined. TCS employs about 400,000 people, most of them based in India, where they provide human resources, finance, accounting, software tech support, and other business services to companies around the world. TCS uses its H-1B visas to send its Indian workers to US clients when they need someone on site, or when the TCS workers need a specific type of training that they cannot get in India. For the most part, companies like TCS are using the H-1B visa program to provide fairly routine services at a lower cost than the US companies could provide on their own. They end up eliminating jobs in America that could have been performed by American workers, at the same time that they reduce the number of H-1B visas that are available for innovative scientists and engineers (Torres 2017). The growing influence of business outsourcing firms such as TCS has made the H-1B via program much more controversial in the United States.

H-1B visa on an Indian passport
Created in 1990, the H-1B program grants US work visas to about 85,000 foreign workers each year.

ACTIVE LEARNING

Discuss: Supporters of the H-1B visa program argue that it makes the US economy stronger. They point to the fact that foreign scientists and engineers help create important new products and innovations. They also point to the fact that outsourcing companies make US businesses more competitive in the global economy, by reducing costs. Critics argue that the H-1B program hurts American workers by taking away jobs. What do you think?

is elsewhere in the world (Cohen 2006). These problems are made worse by the fact that most nongovernmental organizations continue to focus their development efforts on rural areas, based on an assumption that global poverty is primarily a rural phenomenon. There is also the issue of **brain drain**, in which the most highly educated people in poor countries move to places that have more economic opportunity. In fact, demographers estimate that about one-third of the scientists and engineers born in the developing world now live in global cities and other urban areas in the developed world (Lowell et al. 2004).

Brain drain When highly educated people in poor countries leave for places with more economic opportunity.

Immigration

The United States often describes itself as a nation of immigrants. About one-fifth of all international migrants currently live in the United States, and it has been the top immigrant destination in the world since at least 1960 (Zong et al. 2018).

The United States is not alone in its experiences with immigrants. Globally, there is more immigration than ever before. This has created significant consequences, both for communities receiving new immigrants and for the communities people leave behind. Immigration also has political consequences, in terms of citizenship policies, employment policies, and anti- and pro-immigrant and social movements.

Trends in Immigration

While human migration has been a feature of virtually all societies throughout recorded history, the pace of migration increased during the 18th century. Much of this increased movement was **internal migration**, which refers to the movement of people within the same country. Because of industrialization and urbanization, people were moving from rural areas into cities in search of better economic opportunities. International migration was also increasing during this time, mainly because of global trade, colonialism, and the forced migration associated with the international slave trade.

Internal migration The movement of people within the same country. Internal migration is different than international migration, which is what people usually refer to when they talk about immigration.

The pace of immigration accelerated during the 19th century, as capitalism spread from Europe to its colonies. Between 1864 and 1924, 48 million people (more than 10 percent of the population on the continent) left Europe (Massey 1999). More than half of these emigrants came to the United States, but large numbers also settled in Canada, Argentina, Australia, and New Zealand.

Immigration slowed considerably between 1920 and 1960. World War I encouraged anti-immigrant attitudes, which intensified even further with the global economic depression that began in 1929. In the United States, which had been the main immigrant destination, a series of new immigration laws banned entry from most Asian nations, established quotas for most European nations, and introduced a literacy test for potential new

The Statue of Liberty
The Statue of Liberty in New York Harbor has historically welcomed immigrants to the United States. As of 2018, immigrants and their US-born children numbered approximately 89.4 million people, or 28 percent of the US population.

METHODS AND INTERPRETATION

Measuring Immigration Flows

Getting good data on immigration is difficult. Countries all define and measure immigration differently. The strategies for measuring immigration often change over time, in response to changing immigration practices as well as better social-scientific knowledge about measurement errors.

The first step in getting good data about immigration is to have an accurate and consistent understanding of what is being measured. The United Nations defines an international migrant as a person who changes his or her usual place of residence. In addition, social scientists working at the United Nations have added several conceptual distinctions. They distinguish between long-term migrants (who stay for one year or more) and short-term migrants (who stay for between three and 12 months, for purposes other than recreation, business, or medical treatment). They distinguish between migrant flows (the number of people entering or leaving a country in a given year) and migrant stocks (the total number of international migrants present in a given country at a given point in time). And they have tried to identify special categories of migration, including temporary workers, highly skilled business migrants, undocumented migrants, forced migrants, family reunification migrants, and return migrants.

Social scientists and governments use a variety of data sources and collection strategies to measure immigration. Census data can be used to measure migration stocks and long-term immigration trends. But census data are only collected every 10 years in most countries, which makes it less useful for measuring migration flows. Furthermore, census data are not very good at measuring undocumented immigration. Since 2005, the United Nations Department of Economic and Social Affairs has collected annual data on migrant flows; their data currently include 45 countries. Just like the data used to measure migration stock, these data sets tend to undercount undocumented immigration. To complement these data sources, social scientists also use survey research to try to get a more accurate measure of the undocumented immigrant population, and to determine other possible sources of measurement error. Important examples of this kind of research include the Mexican Migration Project and the Latin American Migration Project, which are both directed by the Princeton University sociologist Douglas Massey in collaboration with colleagues from the University of Guadalajara in Mexico. With the knowledge they gain from this survey research, social scientists can get a more accurate picture of immigration flows by reweighting specific categories from the official population data.

ACTIVE LEARNING

Think about it: Politicians and journalists talk a lot about immigration, but do they ever discuss how complicated it is to provide an accurate measurement of immigration flows and immigration stocks?

immigrants. As a result of these new laws, immigration into the United States declined by more than 90 percent, as compared to prewar levels (Massey 1995). These restrictive laws remained in place throughout World War II. The only real increases in immigration levels came from the passage of laws in 1948 and 1953, which established special provisions for war refugees fleeing persecution.

Immigration increased again in the mid-1960s, when wealthy nations such as the United States began to increase their numerical quotas for the number of immigrants. The number of international migrants doubled between 1960 (71.8 million) and 1990 (152 million), and it has continued to increase since then, with a total of 222 million international migrants in 2010 (United Nations, Department of Economic and Social Affairs, Population Division 2016b). Immigration during this period became much more global, in terms of the places that immigrants were leaving as well as the places they were going. The new immigrants were much more likely to come from developing countries in Latin America, Africa, and Asia. The United States is still the largest immigrant destination, but there are also significant numbers of immigrants settling in Western Europe, Saudi Arabia, Japan, and South Korea (Massey 1999).

What Causes Immigration?

Immigration is shaped by "push factors" as well as "pull factors." Push factors include all those social forces that make people want to leave where they are living and find somewhere else to settle. With push factors, the desire to leave is the main cause of emigration. In this kind of situation, people will settle anywhere, as long as it is better than the place they are leaving. With pull factors, on the other hand, people are drawn to a specific place, usually in order to join family members who already live there, or to join an established community where they know they will be welcomed and supported.

The key push factors that are related to immigration are economic poverty, political instability, and violence. More than 80 percent of all immigrants end up settling in a country that is wealthier than the one they left (United Nations Development Programme 2009). Economic decision-making is a big part of the immigration decision, because moving to another country is expensive and risky. In fact, below a certain poverty threshold, the likelihood of immigration actually begins to decline, because people lack the financial resources to move. But for people living in poor countries who do have enough money to afford an international move, the promise of a better life is a significant motivation.

There are also strong motivations to immigrate from societies that are beset by political conflict and violence. When armed conflict between competing groups breaks out, there is often a surge in the refugee population, as residents of the war-torn region flee their homes in search of a safer place to live (Lischer 2014). In authoritarian countries, friends and family of opposition activists are often forced to flee their homes in order to avoid being jailed, tortured, or killed (Bank et al. 2016). Religious, ethnic, and racial minorities have frequently been forced to flee their homes and to become refugees in order to escape violence and persecution. Environmental changes in many parts of the world have led to widespread famine, forcing people to migrate to avoid starvation (Zetter and Morrissey 2014). These social forces have led to an explosion in the refugee population, with recent estimates suggesting that as many as 65 million people were forced to migrate in 2015 as a result of conflict and persecution (Edwards 2016).

The key pull factors that encourage immigration are family reunification, the desire to move to and join a well-known and established immigrant community, and recruitment into transnational work networks. Canada, Australia, and New Zealand have adopted a "points-based" immigration system that favors young workers who can fill jobs in high-demand occupations. America's H-1B visa system allows employers to bring in foreign workers in specialized and highly skilled occupations. In both of these types of arrangements, employers in high-tech and high-growth sectors of the economy have an incentive to create transnational recruiting networks that identify skilled foreign workers, help them move to the country to contribute to its economy, and provide resources that ease the transition to the new country. (We described an example of this type of immigration in Chapter 8, in a discussion of computer engineers recruited from Colombia to the United States.)

As with transnational work networks, there are immigration policies in place in many nations that encourage family reunification. In the United States, the 1965 Hart–Celler Act established preferences among those wishing to immigrate to the United States that favored relatives of US citizens as well as relatives of permanent residents. This quickly became the primary mechanism for immigration, and by 2000 about two-thirds of all permanent immigration to the United States came through the family reunification program (McKay 2003). Similarly, family reunification has become one of the main reasons for immigration into Europe, where the European Union established a directive in 2003 that encouraged the practice of reunification.

There are good reasons why family reunification would be a powerful draw for immigrants. The family is one of the most important sources of identity, solidarity, and social support (Chapter 10). Kinship networks provide financial and moral support, as well as useful local knowledge and connections that can help ease the transition for new immigrants. It is common for a new immigrant to stay with a family member when they first arrive, and to rely on their family's informal networks to help them find work and housing. These strategies work best when economic conditions are good, when the surrounding political environment is accepting of new immigrants, and when the place they arrive is connected to a vibrant and well-established immigrant community (Menjivar 1997).

Immigrant Communities

Immigrant communities in Miami have completely redefined the city (Portes and Stepick 1993). The transformation began in the 1950s with the arrival of Cuban immigrants fleeing a revolution in that country, who then settled in the area of the city that came to be known as Little Havana. It became a place where new arrivals could find a cheap place to live, continue to speak Spanish while learning more about US society, find a job (usually from a Cuban American business owner), and surround themselves with familiar elements of Cuban popular culture. Little Havana became known as a welcoming and attractive immigrant community throughout Latin America, and it was viewed as a desirable destination for others in the region trying to escape poverty and political instability. Nicaraguans began arriving in large numbers during the 1970s and 1980s, and they were followed shortly thereafter by immigrants from Guatemala, Haiti, and Honduras. Little Havana has become one of the most popular tourist destinations in Miami, and the Cuban "brand" is an important source of revenue for all business owners in the neighborhood, including many who are not Cuban American immigrants (Vasilogambros 2016). The city of Miami has become a multilingual and multicultural metropolis, the corporate gateway to Latin America.

IMMIGRANT ENCLAVES. Little Havana is an example of an **immigrant enclave**, where successful immigrant-owned businesses serve to anchor the community. Immigrant enclaves usually benefit from two phenomena: the arrival of immigrants who already have enough experience and financial resources to start their own businesses, and a large reserve of immigrant labor available for employment (Portes and Manning 1986). The relationship between employer and employee in an immigrant enclave is defined by solidarity and reciprocity. The employee works for a slightly lower salary, which allows the business to be effective in the market; the employer provides social and material support during emergencies, helps the workers develop the skills that enable them to advance in their jobs, and even provides aid when those workers are ready to start businesses of their own (Portes and Manning 1986: 62). In addition to Little Havana, other examples of successful immigrant enclaves include Korean communities in Los Angeles and New York City that developed

Immigrant enclave A community in which there are successful immigrant-owned businesses that serve to anchor the community.

historical example is the Jewish diaspora, which was the result of multiple incidents of exile over two thousand years. A large Chinese diaspora was caused by war and starvation during the late 19th century, and an Indian diaspora was initiated during the British colonization of India in the 18th and 19th centuries. The Irish diaspora began in the middle of the 19th century, as a result of widespread famine that forced more than half of the country's population to move to new communities in the United States, Canada, Australia, New Zealand, and Argentina. The African diaspora created by the transatlantic slave trade resulted in the forced resettlement of millions of West Africans in Europe, North America, and South America. The forced expulsion of populations continues today, leading to the formation of new diaspora communities. The Cuban immigrant community in Miami that we described earlier is a recent example; others include Iranians who were exiled after the 1979 Iranian Revolution, and Eritreans who fled after the government began arresting political opponents and critics in 2001.

Sociologist Rogers Brubaker identifies three key characteristics of diaspora populations that make it more likely they will be connected to transnational communities (Brubaker 2005). First, the population is dispersed across national borders, settling in different communities around the world. Second, there is a continued orientation to the homeland, as a source of identity, loyalty, and cultural heritage. The third characteristic is boundary maintenance, which means that the population maintains a distinctive identity that is different from the other people living in the society in which they settle. In other words, diaspora communities do not fully assimilate. It is common for them to have distinctive religious practices, to shop in different grocery stores, and to consume different news and entertainment media. They maintain a strong interest in the politics of their homeland, joining political organizations that might enable their eventual return.

Transnational communities are not all diasporas. In today's globalized world, the choice to immigrate to a new country is often a voluntary one. People immigrate because of opportunities in the global economy. When they decide to resettle in a new community, they know that computers, smartphones, and social media will make it easier to maintain social connections with the friends and family they leave behind. Improved transportation technologies mean that it will be easier to fly home to visit, at least for those who can afford it. They can choose to settle in an immigrant enclave, which means they will be surrounded by the sights, sounds, smells, and tastes associated with their cultural heritage. They can take advantage of changes in immigration policies, which allow them to hold dual citizenship and make travel visas easier to obtain. Those who are not fleeing persecution may even find themselves being actively encouraged to maintain social and emotional ties with their country of origin. In China, for example, the Overseas Chinese Affairs Office assists expatriates in doing business in China, and cultural exchange and language education programs targeted at overseas communities are designed to increase the attachment to Chinese culture (Liu 2016).

The Politics of Immigration

Immigration is a contentious issue. Countries have different laws about whom they will accept as immigrants, and different expectations about how much they expect immigrants to assimilate. Many countries have experienced anti-immigrant movements, which have been increasing in recent years. In countries that are experiencing population outflow, however, the political

Solidarity and Conflict

The Jewish American Diaspora and US Foreign Policy

American Jews are divided in support for the Zionist vision of a homeland for the Jewish people in the Middle East.

The 20th century witnessed a massive migration of Jews from brutal persecution in Europe, mostly to Israel and the United States. Europe had nearly nine million Jews in 1900, as compared to 1.5 million in the United States (the nation of Israel was established in 1948). By 2010 there were fewer than 1.5 million Jews living in Europe, as compared to more than five million in Israel as well as the United States. There are more Jews living in New York City today than there are in all of Europe.

The Jewish American diaspora has a number of distinctive characteristics. Jewish Americans are the most highly educated religious group in the United States, with heavy concentrations in professional occupations and large numbers living in the major urban and suburban areas of the country. More than two-thirds identify politically as moderate or liberal, and since the 1950s the Jewish American community has been a reliable supporter of the Democratic Party. More than half identify with either the Reform or Conservative denominations, neither of which is very popular in Israel. Nearly half of all married American Jews have a non-Jewish spouse, which has led to ongoing concerns about assimilation and Jewish American identity, concerns which are not present in Israel. At the same time, American Jews as a group have a very strong attachment to the nation of Israel, and they follow news about Israel and the Middle East closely.

Jewish Americans have had a strong interest in the future of Israel since before its establishment as a nation-state, and they have formed powerful political lobbying groups to try to influence United States foreign policy in the Middle East. Pro-Israel fundraising organizations were developed in the United States as early as 1939, with the goal of supporting Jewish refugees in the United States and the Middle East. A pro-Israel political lobby formed in the United States in 1953, after the escalation of military conflicts between Israelis and Palestinians led to a diplomatic crisis. With leaders of the United Nations criticizing the actions of the Israeli military, and with the United States announcing a temporary suspension of economic aid, the Jewish American lobby attempted to unite all Jewish Americans around the idea that the US government needed to support and protect Israel (Rossinow 2018).

Before the 1953 crisis there had been division among Jewish Americans. On one side were Zionists, who believed that all Jews had a duty to return to Israel. This group had already created a political lobbying group, called the American Zionist Council for Public Affairs (AZCPA). But not all Jewish Americans were Zionists. Many had reservations about the idea of Jewish nationalism, and wanted to build their lives in the United States. The conflict between the two groups made the AZCPA less effective. But the growing tension between the governments of Israel and the United States helped unite these two factions of the Jewish American population in support of the pro-Israel lobby, which was able to convince the US government to adopt a more strongly pro-Israel foreign policy. In 1959, the pro-Israel lobby changed its name to the American Israel Public Affairs Committee (AIPAC), in recognition that it represented the interests of Zionists as well as non-Zionists. Today, AIPAC continues to be the most influential pro-Israel lobby, and it is recognized as one of the most powerful political lobbying groups in Washington, DC.

ACTIVE LEARNING

Find out: AIPAC is not the only political lobby in the United States that is associated with a diaspora population. Choose another diaspora population (e.g., Irish Americans, Chinese Americans, Cuban Americans), and do some research on its lobbying presence in Washington, DC. How does this lobby group compare with AIPAC?

issues surrounding immigration are different. In such countries there is a concern about losing talented workers, as global immigration trends block national development and aggravate global inequality.

LAWS ABOUT CITIZENSHIP AND IMMIGRATION. In democratic societies, employers have been one of the most influential interest groups advocating for higher levels of immigration. Immigrants reduce labor costs in industries that depend on unskilled labor. Targeted policies aimed at high-skilled immigrants help companies that are working in technical and scientific fields. Real estate and construction companies benefit from the population growth that is associated with high levels of immigration. Civil and human rights groups have also been an important interest group, advocating for permissive immigration policies that are designed to help refugee populations. In settler societies such as Canada, Australia, New Zealand, and the United States, there are also powerful cultural influences that favor immigration, which rely on narratives about the country as a "nation of immigrants" and a "land of opportunity" (Freeman 1995: 887).

Citizenship The laws that define who is a legal member of a country.

Once immigrants settle in a new country, their experiences are shaped by the laws about **citizenship**, which define who is a legal member of a country. If they or their family can become citizens, it becomes easier for them to travel freely within the country, and they can leave the country with the full confidence that they will be allowed to return. In countries like France and the United States, anyone born in the country is automatically granted citizenship; in Germany, on the other hand, immigrants who are not ethnically German can live in the nation for generations without being granted citizenship (Brubaker 1992). The citizenship laws of Syria and Libya give preferences to people of Arab descent (Parolin 2009). Malta will give citizenship to anyone who is willing to live there for one year and to pay a fee of 1.15 million Euros. Some countries grant immediate citizenship to a person who marries a citizen of the nation, while others require a certain period of residence in the country before granting citizenship (Weil 2001). Many countries allow immigrants to hold dual citizenship, but others do not.

ANTI-IMMIGRANT MOVEMENTS. In some countries, increased immigration has ignited anti-immigrant movements. In the United States, anti-immigrant movements have occurred throughout the nation's history. Benjamin Franklin argued against German immigration in the 1770s, even before the founding of the nation. During the 1850s the American Party (commonly referred to as the "Know-Nothing Movement") campaigned against Irish and German Catholic immigrants. Anti-Chinese movements led to the passage of the Chinese Exclusion Act of 1882 (Chapter 8), which for more than 50 years barred the legal immigration of people from China. The early 20th century saw movements against Italian, Jewish, and Mexican immigrants.

With the global increase in immigration since the 1960s, and particularly since the 1990s, anti-immigrant

The oath of citizenship
Thousands of Latinos, including members of the armed forces, take the citizenship oath during a 2017 US naturalization ceremony in Los Angeles.

Calling for action on immigration
Protesters rally in downtown Los Angeles, February 17, 2017, in a show of support for immigration rights and against President Donald Trump's policies (left), while anti-immigration supporters wave signs and show their support for then-candidate Trump at a rally in Anaheim, California, on May 25, 2016.

political movements emerged throughout Europe and North America. Austria, Denmark, Italy, Poland, and Hungary have all formed coalition governments in which one of the parties was explicitly anti-immigrant. Anti-immigrant movements have also become much more influential in French, German, and British politics. In the United States, Donald Trump was elected president in 2016 after a campaign in which he described immigrants as murderers, rapists, and drug dealers. As president, Trump has moved to deport millions of undocumented immigrants, to refuse citizenship to the children of undocumented immigrants who were born in the United States, to sharply limit the admission of refugees and asylum seekers, and to reduce the overall levels of legal immigration, most infamously by attempting to build a wall across the entire US–Mexico border.

Sociologists have identified several social factors that increase the likelihood that an individual or group will support anti-immigrant movements. Racial and ethnic prejudice is a significant factor (Berg 2012). Differences in language, culture, and religion also increase the likelihood of anti-immigrant sentiment (Sackman et al. 2003), and so does the perception of economic threat (Quillian 1995). These different social factors combine into specific patterns and styles of anti-immigrant arguments (Bail 2008). In nations like Spain, Italy, and Hungary, where the number of immigrants is relatively small and where immigration is a more recent phenomenon, anti-immigration movements tend to focus on race and religion. In countries like France, Germany, the Netherlands, and the UK, which have a longer history with immigration, anti-immigrant movements focus more on language and culture.

The growing power of anti-immigrant movements has been met with resistance by immigrant-rights groups. In areas with large numbers of immigrants, churches, politicians, and business leaders have built successful coalitions that aim to recognize immigrants as valuable members of the community and to combat anti-immigrant political movements (Okamoto and Ebert 2016). In the United States these movements have been the most visible and successful in California, where immigrant and labor activist groups have worked together since the 1990s to campaign against anti-immigrant legislation in the state and to help elect progressive and pro-immigrant mayors in Los Angeles (Pastor 2015).

PAIRED CONCEPTS

Power and Resistance

A Day Without Immigrants

One significant immigrant rights movement in the United States is the Day Without Immigrants movement, which has organized national days of protest since 2006. The movement was formed by religious organizations, immigration advocacy organizations, and labor unions in Los Angeles who collaborated to protest against proposed legislation that would make it a felony to reside in the United States illegally. There had already been protests against the legislation elsewhere in the United States, and Congress had rejected the proposals. But the organizers of this movement, which they initially called the Great American Boycott, intended to show how important immigrants were to the economy and to the everyday lives of most Americans.

The organizers of the movement called for immigrants and those who supported immigrant rights to boycott US schools and businesses on May 1, 2006. Supporters of the movement were encouraged to stay home from work and school, to avoid buying anything for one day, and to join protests in cities around the country. It quickly became known as the Day Without Immigrants. It was a controversial movement, which was criticized by President George W. Bush as well as California governor Arnold Schwarzenegger. But it was very successful. More than a million people joined protests in Los Angeles, and there were also large protests in cities around the country. Businesses closed, and those that stayed open had to deal with high absentee rates. Goya Foods, which is one of the largest Hispanic-owned businesses in the United States, suspended deliveries in solidarity with the movement.

The immigrant rights movement continued to organize after the success of the 2006 protests. Many of the protesters joined United We Dream, a movement advocating for changes in immigration laws that would allow a pathway to citizenship for undocumented immigrants, and for general improvement in how schools, hospitals, and police interact with the community of undocumented immigrants. United We Dream was a major supporter and advocate for Deferred Action for Childhood Arrivals (DACA), a policy implemented by President Obama in 2012 that allowed some undocumented immigrants who had been brought to the United States as children to avoid deportation and to obtain a work permit in the United States. Donald Trump campaigned on a promise to end DACA on the first day of his presidency, and the Trump administration announced on September 5, 2017 that it was ending the DACA program.

President Trump's actions increased protest activity by immigrant rights movements, and led to the second Day Without Immigrants boycott and protest, which took place on February 16, 2017. A third Day Without Immigrants event was held on May 1, 2017, and since that time immigrant rights protests have been a regular occurrence in cities throughout the United States.

Day Without Immigrants
2017 saw the third national Day Without Immigrants, which called for immigrants and those who supported immigrant rights to boycott US schools and businesses.

ACTIVE LEARNING

Discuss: Do you think it is better for immigrant rights activists to work with politicians to change immigration policy, or to organize protests and other events that aim to change public opinion?

As immigrant rights movements achieve political successes and attract media attention, they influence public opinion about immigration. Public opinion research shows that attitudes toward immigrants have become much more supportive in California over the last 30 years (Skelton 2015), and there is some evidence that nationally organized immigrant-rights protests are beginning to have a similar effect (Voss and Bloemraad 2011).

Retirement Migration to Central America

For residents of the United States and Canada, two popular destinations for people who are looking to retire overseas are Panama and Ecuador. Both countries boast a warm climate, fresh fruits and vegetables, clean air and water, thriving metropolitan cities, beautiful mountain towns, and uncrowded beaches. They have excellent new medical facilities, modern digital technologies, and state-of-the-art airports that make them a short flight away from North America. Both have governments that are actively courting North American retirees, with tax incentives and other discounts. And they have a much lower cost of living. Most people who retire to these countries can live comfortably for less than two thousand dollars per month.

The idea of retirement migration to Central America first took root in Costa Rica more than 30 years ago. People were attracted by the idea of living at the beach, in a place that had great weather and incredible natural beauty. Costa Rica was already a stable democracy at that point, with an excellent health care system that expatriates could access for a monthly fee significantly lower than what they would pay in the United States. Costa Rica had a commitment to preserving its natural beauty, protecting more than one-quarter of the nation's land and investing heavily in renewable energy. And Costa Rica was the first country to actively court potential retirees with special incentives and tax breaks. Its pension program offered residency to anyone who

Retirement migration
Retirement migration is a globalized phenomenon where wealthy retirees from the United States and Canada retire to destinations of natural beauty, gentler climates, and lower cost of living, such as Costa Rica, Panama, and Ecuador. These countries offer retirees benefits such as tax incentives and pensions, as well as discounts on entertainment, hospital and energy bills, train fares, and airline tickets.

made a commitment to live in Costa Rica for at least four months each year, and who had a monthly income of at least $1,000 from a guaranteed government pension. Today, tens of thousands of North Americans live full time in Costa Rica.

While Costa Rica is still a popular destination for retirement migration, it now has competition from Ecuador and Panama. Costa Rica's popularity has made it more expensive than it used to be, and the large expatriate communities have made it seem less "exotic." Other Central American countries have begun to aggressively market themselves as retirement migration destinations. Panama and Ecuador both adopted their own version of the pension program, with additional perks to make themselves even more attractive to retirees. Panama offers retirees discounts on entertainment, hospital bills, energy bills, train fares, and airline tickets, and it guarantees that once they receive legal residency through the pension program they can never lose it. Ecuador allows people aged 65 years or older to skip to the front of the line in most establishments. And both countries are less expensive than Costa Rica.

Retirement migration is supported by a *global* network of magazines, websites, travel agencies, and internet forums. *International Living* magazine was established in 1979, promising "that an exotic life in a tropical paradise wasn't just for the rich and famous." Today, *International Living* (2019) has a website that attracts more than 500,000 readers a month as well as a monthly magazine with 100,000 print subscribers around the world. Ecuador, Panama, and Costa Rica ensure that retirees who move there can maintain their connections with the *local* community they are leaving behind, by providing high-speed internet, modern airports, and travel discounts that make it easy to visit friends and family in North America. There is also an important interaction of global and local in how retired migrants think about themselves. On the one hand, they imagine themselves as part of a global network of cosmopolitans, who are interested in experiencing different cultures (Hannerz 1990). On the other hand, they are looking to join specific local communities in Central America, and they work hard to be respectful guests of the new locations where they are moving—learning Spanish, interacting with "locals," and moving into neighborhoods that do not have too many expats living in them (Hayes and Carlson 2017).

CASE STUDY CONTINUED

While most people who choose retirement migration are looking for an improved quality of life, what this means depends on the *contingency* of an individual's biography and life circumstances. People who are still in good health seek to maintain an active lifestyle, while those who have had unsatisfying jobs are often looking for a community that places less value on work and money. Some people want to step outside of their comfort zones, while others are looking to spend lazy days at the beach. Some migrate together with friends and family, and others decide to move after major changes to family and life. Many decide to migrate after a sudden and surprising job loss, as evidenced by the surge in retirement migration after the global economic crisis of 2008. Regardless of the decisions shaping individuals' specific moves, however, there are clear *structural* patterns. There is a tendency for people to be attracted to places that were once colonial holdings of the countries in which they grew up; Americans going to Ecuador and Panama, people from the UK going to Malaysia, and people from France going to Morocco (Benson and O'Reilly 2009). Potential migrants often attach nostalgic meanings to the place they are moving, imagining it as a romanticized version of how the country they are leaving used to be; in fact, it is common for retirees living in Ecuador to describe their new home as being "like America in the 1950s" (Hayes 2018). And of course, people who choose retirement migration usually have a similar socioeconomic background.

There are strong elements of *privilege* and *inequality* at work in retirement migration too. The people who retire in Ecuador and Panama are neither poor nor rich. They are usually homeowners, and they tend to have a reliable pension, which gives them the resources they need to obtain residency and resettle in Central America. But they also find themselves in a position where they do not have the money to afford the kind of retirement they imagined for themselves if they stayed in the country where they grew up. They are privileged relative to the entire population in the United States, but they feel relative deprivation compared to other people they know and compared to the expectations they had from their earlier socialization. When they move to Central America, their privilege increases significantly. They can get more for their money, they are much higher up in the socioeconomic hierarchy, and they enjoy special incentives created by the government to encourage them to move.

The government incentives that are created to encourage people to retire to Ecuador and Panama bring social, political, and economic *power* to the new migrants. The new retirees quickly become employers, hiring native Central Americans as housecleaners, cooks, and home health care workers. Their presence has also led to a major restructuring of medicine and health care in Ecuador and Panama, with resources diverted toward the care of an aging immigrant population. There have been cases where indigenous communities are forcibly moved, to make way for new developments targeted at wealthier, newly retired immigrants. Not surprisingly, the direct and indirect power that the retirees possess has been met with *resistance*. People resent the gated communities that were built up to attract retirees; they resent the dramatic increase in land, housing, and food prices; and they resent the arrogance that often comes with the retirees' privileged position. This resentment displays itself in many forms of indirect resistance: pretending not to understand English, deliberately slowing down when working for or serving expats, complaining and gossiping about the new migrants, and charging an informal "gringo tax" for goods and services. There are also more direct forms of resistance, such as anti-American demonstrations, complaints made to politicians, burglaries, robberies, and thefts.

There are complicated *solidarities* and *conflicts* among retired migrants living in Central America. Many retirees know that a negative stereotype about loud, obnoxious, and culturally insensitive "ugly Americans" circulates in tourist places. Drawing on a distinction between "good guests" and "obnoxious gringos," they are drawn together in moral condemnation of bad behavior they see by some foreigners; by reinforcing their commitment to tolerance and cultural sensitivity, they hope to gain acceptance from their Ecuadorian and Panamanian neighbors (Hayes and Carlson 2017). There are also conflicted loyalties that are connected to national identity. Many of the American retirees in Ecuador maintain a strong identity as Americans, but they are deeply critical of US culture and foreign policy (Hayes 2018). This critical position can create tension and conflict when they return for visits to the United States, where family and friends see their criticisms of the United States as evidence of disloyalty.

LEARNING GOALS REVISITED

15.1 Describe the basic trends in population growth, and understand how population changes influence society.

- There has been rapid demographic change since the 20th century. World population did not top one billion until after 1800, and it did not exceed two billion until 1930. Global population reached four billion in 1975, and from that point it has increased by an additional billion people every 12 to 15 years. The global population reached seven billion in 2013, and it is projected to reach 9.8 billion by 2050.

- The birth rate and the death rate have both declined since the 19th century, but the death rate declined much faster than the birth rate.

- Population growth has created pressures on the food and water supply, and it has led to other environmental pressures as well.

- Population growth has been uneven, particularly since the 20th century, with poorer nations experiencing much faster rates of growth than wealthier nations.

15.2 Think about the relationship between demography and social inequality.

- Population growth increases social inequality because of the demographic divide, in which poor countries have higher birth rates and lower life expectancies, while wealthy countries have lower birth rates and higher life expectancies.

- In wealthier nations, one of the main social challenges is associated with a rapidly aging population, in which a larger proportion of people are retired. An aging population is associated with higher health care costs, higher public pension expenses, and fewer resources available for other social programs.

- People who live in poorer nations have a much lower life expectancy, a much higher infant mortality rate, and tend to have a less advanced economy with fewer opportunities for career advancement. As a result, there is a strong pressure for younger people living in these places to try to relocate to wealthier societies, where there will be more opportunities for themselves and their families.

15.3 Understand how urbanization has shaped social life, and describe how the organization of cities has changed over time.

- Urbanization has made social life more anonymous and impersonal, but it has also allowed people to pursue more diverse and specialized hobbies and occupations.

- Urbanization is associated with economic growth and the historical development of capitalism. It has also been associated with the growth of subcultures, social movements, and the increasing pace of social change.

- While people have been living in cities for more than five thousand years, the process of urbanization accelerated during the Industrial Revolution, and it has continued to accelerate ever since. The urban population has quadrupled since 1960, and nearly 55 percent of the world's population now lives in a city.

- Cities have expanded their geographical reach. Many people live in residential suburbs and exurbs, and commute into the city for work. In many metropolitan areas suburban development has expanded to the point that different cities are connected in a large, continuous space that geographers refer to as conurbation.

- Global cities like London, New York, and Tokyo have become more economically powerful, in a way that reinforces privilege and inequality. At the same time, there has been rapid urbanization in the developing world, which presents different kinds of opportunities and challenges.

15.4 Describe the basic historical trends in immigration.

- International immigration began to increase during the 19th century, as capitalism spread from Europe to its colonies in the New World. Immigration slowed considerably from 1920 to 1960, but then accelerated quickly after that.

The number of international migrants doubled between 1960 (71.8 million) and 1990 (152 million), and it has continued to increase since then, with a total of 222 million international migrants in 2010.

- Immigration has become much more global during the last 60 years, in terms of the places that immigrants were leaving as well as the places they were going. Immigrants during this period were much more likely to come from developing countries in Latin America, Africa, and Asia. The United States is still the largest immigrant destination, but there are also significant numbers of immigrants settling in Western Europe, Saudi Arabia, Japan, and South Korea

- People often choose to immigrate because of a desire to escape economic poverty, political instability, and violence. Other important factors that increase the likelihood of immigration are family reunification, the desire to move to and join a well-known and established immigrant community, and recruitment into transnational work networks.

15.5 Describe how immigrant communities are organized, and how they shape politics and the economy in both sending and receiving countries.

- Immigrants often settle in immigrant enclaves: areas in which there are successful immigrant-owned businesses that anchor the community. It is also common for them to face a segmented labor market, in which the jobs available to them are unskilled and poorly paid, with few opportunities for advancement.

- Remittances are a common practice within immigrant communities, which occur when immigrants send money back to family members living in their country of origin. In some countries remittances account for one-third of total GDP, and in most Latin American and Caribbean nations the value of remittances is greater than the value of foreign aid or government spending on social programs. In fact, many developing countries have policies that encourage immigration and the remittance economy associated with it; they permit dual citizenship, allow emigrants to vote while abroad, and sometimes even allow them to run for public office.

- Immigration is a contentious and political issue. Countries have different laws about who they will accept as immigrants, and what those immigrants have to do to become citizens of the nation. Many countries have experienced anti-immigrant movements at various points in their history, and these movements have been increasing in recent years.

- Immigration brings significant economic benefits to the nations that receive them. Immigrants reduce costs in industries that depend on unskilled labor. Targeted policies aimed at high-skilled immigrants help companies that are working in technical and scientific fields. Real estate and construction companies benefit from the population growth associated with high levels of immigration. Large immigrant enclaves have become popular tourist destinations, and an important part of the promotional branding of the cities that have them.

Key Terms

Brain drain 452
Census 438
Citizenship 460
Conurbation 447
Demographic divide 440
Demographic transition 439
Demography 438
Diaspora 457
Global city 448
Immigrant enclave 455
Immigration 438
Internal migration 452
Remittance 457
Social demography 439
Suburb 446
Transnational community 457
Urbanization 438

Review Questions

1. What do demographers study? What are the different data sources they use in their research?

2. What kinds of social pressures does population growth place on a society? What kinds of pressures are caused by an aging population? How are these pressures different for poor and wealthy societies?

3. Describe the main differences between pre-modern cities and the cities of today.

4. How are global cities different from other cities?

5. Describe some of the main ways that immigrant communities are different from nonimmigrant communities.

6. Does immigration contribute to global inequality? Be sure to address both sides of the question.

7. What are the social factors that increase the likelihood that an individual or group will take an anti-immigration position? What are the social factors that increase the likelihood of taking a pro-immigration position?

Explore

RECOMMENDED READINGS

Gans, Herbert. [1967] 2017. *The Levittowners: Ways of Life and Politics in a New Suburban Community.* New York: Columbia University Press.

Hayes, Matthew. 2018. *Gringolandia: Lifestyle Migration under Late Capitalism.* Minneapolis: University of Minnesota Press.

Magnus, George. 2008. *The Age of Aging: How Demographics Are Changing the Global Economy and Our World.* New York: Wiley.

Portes, Alejandro, and Alex Stepick. 1993. *City on the Edge: The Transformation of Miami.* Berkeley: University of California Press.

Sassen, Saskia. 2001. *The Global City: New York, London, Tokyo*, 2nd ed. Princeton, NJ: Princeton University Press.

ACTIVITIES

- *Use your sociological imagination*: With a metropolitan population of more than 30 million people, Jakarta (Indonesia) is one of the three largest cities in the world. Is it a global city? How is it similar to the most well-known global cities (London, Tokyo, New York)? How is it different?

- *Media+Data literacy*: With the aging population and the growth of the immigrant population, how are these trends represented on television? Take a look at the highest-rated television shows, and conduct a demographic profile of the characters portrayed in these shows. How do they compare to the demography of the real world?

- *Discuss*: With the value of remittances now exceeding $500 billion annually, some governments have proposed taxing them as a way of raising additional revenue. Do you think this is a good or a bad idea? Be sure to give specific reasons for your answer.

For additional resources, including Media+Data Literacy exercises, In the News exercises, and quizzes, please go to **oup.com/he/ Jacobs-Townsley1e**

16

Living on the Planet: Environment, Disaster, and Risk

In recent years, dramatic and dangerous natural disasters such as wildfires and hurricanes have been increasing in frequency and intensity. A 2018 wildfire in Northern California burned for more than a month, covering an area of nearly 500 square miles. The state of California now spends more than $500 million per year battling wildfires. And California is not alone. A 2014 fire in northwestern Canada covered 8 million acres; a 2003 fire in Siberia burned more than 47 million acres, which is nearly half the size of California.

The 2017 North Atlantic hurricane season was the most damaging and the most expensive in US history, with more than $200 billion of damage from 17 named storms (Drye 2017). Hurricane Harvey brought more than 27 trillion tons of rain to Texas, damaging or destroying more than 100,000 homes and leaving an even larger number of people without power for several weeks. Hurricane Irma was at one point the strongest hurricane the National Weather Service had ever recorded, with sustained winds of more than 157 miles per hour. Making landfall in the Caribbean and South Florida, this hurricane also destroyed nearly 100,000 homes. Hurricane Maria hit Puerto Rico with sustained winds of 155 miles per hour, leaving the entire island and its 3.4 million residents without power and damaging or destroying more than one-third of all the homes. Three months after Hurricane Maria had landed, half of the residents in Puerto Rico were still without power, and most of the schools were still closed. It will take years for the communities affected by these hurricanes to recover.

California burning, 2018
The 2018 wildfire season was the worst on record in California, with the highest number of fatalities and the largest amount of burned acreage (nearly 1.9 million acres) recorded in a single fire season.

LEARNING GOALS

16.1 Describe some of the key sociological theories that are useful for understanding environment and society.

16.2 Think about the relationship between culture, socialization, and environmental consciousness.

16.3 Describe how environmental risk is socially distributed, paying particular attention to the patterns of privilege and inequality.

16.4 Describe the political and economic forces that contribute to environmental crisis.

16.5 Know the history of environmentalist social movements, paying attention to their successes and failures.

Other environmental risks are also on the rise. There are more heat waves and weather extremes, with some areas experiencing extreme drought and others experiencing flooding due to heavy rainfall and overflowing rivers. Sea level has risen throughout the 20th century, and the rate of increase is projected to accelerate throughout the 21st century. Ocean acidification threatens coral reefs and the marine ecosystems that depend on them. Chemical spills, oil spills, and nuclear power accidents spread serious pollutants into the food and water supplies.

In this chapter, we use the environment and environmental crisis as a final case to demonstrate the value of thinking sociologically. We begin by discussing some sociological theories that are useful for understanding environment and society. Next, we consider the different ways that people learn about the environment, paying particular attention to culture, socialization, science, and religion. We also examine how environmental risk is distributed unequally, in a way that is connected to processes of privilege and inequality. We consider how the organization of politics and business shapes social practices that contribute to environmental protection or environmental destruction. Finally, we examine how social movements urge people to develop an environmental consciousness.

Living in Risk Society

The term "risk society" is the title of a 1992 book by sociologist Ulrich Beck. Society, Beck argued, has always had to deal with risks such as natural disasters, but for most of history these were believed to be produced by nonhuman forces. Today, however, people recognize that most of the significant risks we face are caused by modern society itself. Risks such as crime, industrial pollution, and the spread of new diseases are clearly caused by social activities. But natural risks such as floods, famines, hurricanes, and food contamination are also shaped by human activity, and their consequences are influenced by patterns of urban settlement and other forms of social organization. Dealing with risk is one of the main characteristics of living in the modern world.

Living in risk society means that people are always engaged in some form of risk management. Is the benefit of cheap energy worth the risk of pollution-related health crisis? Is the benefit of insecticide worth the risk of food contamination? And what if the proposed responses to risk are themselves risky? Beck argues that individuals and organizations lurch from one risk-produced crisis to the next, hoping to mitigate the damage while preparing themselves for the next disaster. The public gradually loses faith in the possibility that society can save them from these risks, leading to less trust in government, industry, and experts (Giddens 1990).

Living in risk society also means that people cannot protect themselves from risk-produced crisis. The consequences of ecological crisis are unevenly distributed, as we discuss later in this chapter. But pollution, food con-

Texas floods
Luxurious mansions prove vulnerable to climate-change-related flooding along the Colorado River after historic flooding near Austin, Texas.

tamination, and extreme weather affect everyone, regardless of their privilege. Pollution does not respect national borders, gated communities, or wealthy neighborhoods. Rising sea levels and increased hurricane activities threaten luxury beachfront developments. The world's wealthiest cities, such as London, Tokyo, and New York, face the same significant environmental challenges as impoverished megacities around the world.

Influenced by Beck's theory of risk society, environmental sociologists developed a theory of **ecological modernization** in order to highlight the ways that economic and political policies might change to create a more sustainable future (Mol and Spaargaren 2000). With growing expert knowledge about and public awareness of environmental risks, economic markets could begin promoting "green" products. National and international policy-makers could coordinate their efforts to create globally effective ecological strategies. The global social movement of environmentalism continues to encourage people to think critically about their everyday interactions with the natural world. But the ability to solve any of these issues once and for all is limited, because each new development in politics, in the market, and in public life results in the creation of new risks and new threats.

Ecological modernization A sociological theory focused on the expectation that growing expert knowledge and public awareness of environmental risks will lead to the development of more sustainable policies and practices.

Learning about the Environment: Culture and Socialization, Science and Religion

Although environmental issues and crises feature more prominently than ever before in public and policy debates, they are still frequently displaced by other issues. "For most people," argues the sociologist Anthony Giddens, "there is a gulf between the familiar preoccupations of everyday life and an abstract, even apocalyptic, future of climate chaos" (Giddens 2009: 1). Most people are not doing very much to change their everyday habits in their interactions with the environment. These habits are much more likely to change if people learn about the environment in a way that is connected to their socialization and their other cultural experiences.

As we discussed in Chapters 4 and 5, our understandings about the world develop through cultural meanings and socialization. These meanings are organized into relationships of similarity and difference, which are always changing. Some meanings exist in language and other types of ideal culture, while others can be found in the objects we use and display to others. Shared meanings bring people together, and they are an important part of our socialization. But cultural conflicts are also a common occurrence, and these conflicts are shaped by power, privilege, and inequality.

Thinking about culture and socialization helps us think about the kinds of environmental understandings that are likely to resonate with people in their social lives. In his book *The Politics of Climate Change*, Giddens talks about this in terms of the "Giddens Paradox." This paradox states that, "since the dangers posed by global warming aren't tangible, immediate, or visible in the course of day-to-day life, however awesome they appear, many will sit on their hands and do nothing of a concrete nature about them" (Giddens 2009: 2). Neither utopian dreams about technology coming to the rescue nor dystopian dreams about a planet already beyond saving will get people to change their everyday behaviors or their lifestyles. To change everyday behaviors, people need to believe that those everyday behaviors matter. Working through all the agents of socialization—the family, peer group, schools, media, the workplace, and beyond—people have to be resocialized to think about how their ordinary behaviors are connected to environmental risk.

The importance of culture can be seen in the phenomenal success of the 2006 documentary film *An Inconvenient Truth*, which chronicled the attempts by former vice president Al Gore to get people to take environmental crisis more seriously (Smith and Howe 2015). In many ways, the film was an unlikely candidate to be a runaway success, given that more than half of it consisted of Gore lecturing with PowerPoint slides. But the film took in more than $50 million at the box office, received an Academy Award for best documentary film, and led to a Nobel Peace Prize for Gore. In their book on culture and the climate change debate, sociologists Philip Smith and Nicholas Howe give four reasons why the film was able to convey its environmental message so powerfully (Smith and Howe 2015). First, Gore was a compelling character; having just lost the Presidential election, environmentalism became the source for his private and public redemption. Second, because he was a non-expert, Gore was able to tell a story about his own environmental consciousness that resonated with most viewers. Third, in addition to offering scientific evidence in support of his case, Gore relied on powerful historical analogies of moments when people failed to act in spite of mounting evidence; specifically, he mentioned the ignored warnings about Hitler and the health risks associated with tobacco. Last, he offered the audience a positive collective purpose,

Al Gore and *An Inconvenient Truth*

reinforced with examples of previous times when society came together to respond to great challenges.

Public debates about environmental risk are also shaped by the ongoing cultural tension between science and religion. As we discussed in Chapter 11, religious and scientific cosmologies have been the two dominant providers of meaning and order to the world in which people live. There is an inherent tension between these two systems of meaning, in the sense that religion emphasizes faith and science emphasizes skepticism. There is also a historical tension between the two, because many scientists were publicly critical of religious belief and argued that the world would be a better place if science simply replaced religion. More recently, scientists and religious leaders have begun to think about how they might more effectively coexist. In fact, the attempt to communicate better about the dangers confronted by environmental risk has been a major focus of this effort to create a post-secular approach to social problems. But these efforts are in their early stages, and they face significant resistance from both religious and scientific institutions.

Last, debates about environmental risk are shaped by the culture of journalism. As sociologists and media scholars have pointed out, journalists tend to show that they are not biased by making sure they present two opposing positions on most issues (Tuchman 1978). In the debate about environmental risks, this has meant that climate change skeptics continue to get a lot of media coverage (Giddens 2009). Among the skeptics are some scientists who argue that the threat of environmental risk has been overstated, that climate change is a constant feature of world history, and that there is not yet definitive scientific proof that human activity is the primary cause of environmental risk. While 97 percent of published scientific articles agree that climate change is real, and is caused by human activity (Cook et al. 2016), the culture of journalism means that news reports will generally emphasize "both sides" of the story.

The Unequal Distribution of Environmental Risk

As we have seen, there are clear patterns to the organization of privilege and inequality. Race, gender, and class are important dimensions of stratification (Chapter 7), which tends to privilege men, racially dominant groups, wealthier families, and the more educated. There is also a global dimension to stratification, with the most privileged people clustered in North America and Western Europe, and with global poverty concentrated in sub-Saharan Africa and Latin America. Rural areas tend to be poorer than urban areas. Inequality and poverty have significant social consequences, resulting in worse health outcomes, higher death rates, and higher levels of incarceration. And while the consequences of environmental risk are felt by everyone on the planet, they are felt more strongly by people who are lower in the stratification system.

Social science research has consistently found that ecological crises have a more severe impact on poor and vulnerable populations. Drawing on their research about lead exposure, sociologists developed a model of **concentrated disadvantage**, in which the poorest and most racially segregated communities suffer the most from environmental risk (Muller, Sampson, and Winter 2018). Even after controlling for education, household income, and other individual characteristics, sociologists have found that African American and Latino families move into more environmentally hazardous neighborhoods than white

Concentrated disadvantage A structural outcome in which the poorest and most racially segregated communities suffer the most from environmental risk.

Environmental risk
Exposure to environmental hazards and potential harm is stratified. These children play near a Houston oil refinery. Sulfur dioxide is a common byproduct of oil refineries that can damage the health of young children and unborn babies.

families (Crowder and Downey 2010). It is not only that poor families of color are most likely to live in neighborhoods where dangerous toxins and pollutants are present. It is also the fact that the neighborhoods where they live lack powerful community organizations that can demand change. Property values in their communities are so low that developers have no incentive to improve housing stock, and residents lack the material resources to move to a safer community.

Exposure to environmental hazards is also stratified globally, with poor nations suffering more than wealthy ones. Whether measuring changes in crop yields, loss of land due to rising sea levels, economic damage from floods and hurricanes, or changes in health care expenditures, the worst impacts will be felt in Africa, Latin America, and South Asia (World Economic Forum 2018). Poor countries respond much more slowly to environmental risk. They have fewer material resources to deal with infrastructure challenges, and they often lack the expertise to develop green technologies that will be competitive in the global marketplace (Bell and Russell 2002). In fact, many poor countries complain that global environmental policies are just a way for wealthy countries to force them to import expensive green technologies, in a way that increases their economic dependence and inequality (Bapna and Talberth 2011).

While environmental risk increases inequality, it is also the case that inequality increases environmental risk (Laurent 2015). Inequality forces poorer countries to focus on fast-paced economic growth, which in the developing world has always been associated with higher levels of carbon dioxide emissions and higher rates of natural resource consumption. Inequality also encourages large corporations to shift the pollution-intensive parts of their operations into poorer countries, where they will face less opposition and the compensation costs for polluting will be much lower. And, despite the prevalence of hybrid cars and bans on plastic bags that we see in wealthy countries, it remains the case that the higher levels of consumption in those societies are associated with significantly higher levels of per-capita waste (Hoornweg and Bhada-Tata 2012).

The Politics and Business of Environmental Destruction and Conservation

There are many reasons why corporations and other business organizations contribute to environmental degradation. In *The Environment: From Surplus to Scarcity* (1980), sociologist Allan Schnaiberg developed a theory about the **treadmill of production**, which explains why business and economic activity increases environmental risk. Schnaiberg argues that the continuous quest for economic growth encourages businesses to pursue strategies that cause environmental damage. Corporations are the main forces powering the treadmill. They produce more products than people need, which increases waste and energy consumption. They rely on the cheapest forms of energy, which increases pollution. But consumers also help power the treadmill, by buying more things

Treadmill of production A social process in which the continuous quest for economic growth encourages businesses to pursue strategies that cause large and unsustainable environmental damage.

than they really need and by basing their purchasing decisions on the lowest price, without regard for the environmental consequences of their consumption decisions.

Political forces also contribute to environmental risk. As we discussed in Chapter 14, the growing power of multinational corporations means that governments have less power to regulate businesses, because of the fear that companies will move their operations to a more business-friendly place. This has led to a general loss of confidence in government's ability to solve complicated social problems. There is also a short-term bias in political decision-making, which privileges issues that are of immediate concern to voters (the price of gasoline and food, the availability of good jobs, etc.). Politicians easily lose focus on long-term issues such as environmental policy, which require extensive planning and political cooperation (Giddens 2009). And when they do focus on environmental policy, they are easily influenced by political lobbying. In the United States, more than $3 billion was spent from 2009 to 2014 on lobbying related to environmental issues (Delmas 2016; Delmas, Lim, and Nairn-Birch 2015).

The politics of environmentalism have begun to change in recent years, creating new openings for clean energy and conservation policies. While environmental lobbying used to focus on anti-regulation efforts, there has been a significant increase in lobbying expenditures by clean energy firms that favor pro-environment policies (Hulac 2016). Natural gas producers have begun to form alliances with these clean energy firms, based on an assessment that clean energy policies will benefit them at the expense of coal producers (Kim, Urpelainen, and Yang 2016).

The rapid growth in renewable energy technologies, including solar, wind, geothermal, and hydroelectric power, may account for this increase in pro-environment political lobbying. Solar power capacity increased by 50 percent globally in 2017, and it is now the fastest-growing energy source (IEA 2017). Prices have come down dramatically, and scientists now estimate that renewable energy will be less expensive than fossil fuels sometime around 2020 (Leary 2018). The leading manufacturers of solar panels and related equipment have become multinational corporations, with annual revenues in the billions of dollars. Many countries with the worst environmental problems have embraced renewable energy, giving them economic reasons to pursue and support pro-environment policies. For example, China, which has had the highest level of greenhouse gas emissions globally since 2006, has become the undisputed global leader in renewable energy production and manufacturing (IEA 2017).

Making Wastefulness Deviant: Movements of Environmental Consciousness

Environmentalist social movements have become a powerful cultural and social force. While conservation movements can be traced back to the late 19th century, and are responsible for the creation of national park systems, the modern environmental movement emerged in the 1950s and 1960s. The movement was initially concerned with the dangers of nuclear weapons and nuclear power, but soon embraced the need to protect the environment, conserve natural resources, and reduce waste.

Earth Day march, New York City, 1970

Environmental movements work to change public opinion and get people to think differently about their everyday activities. A key initiative is Earth Day, April 22, first celebrated in 1970. Now observed by nearly 200 nations, Earth Day has become one of the largest secular holidays in the world, with more than one billion participants each year. Organized as an environmental teach-in, Earth Day has become a hub for grassroots activism. Thousands of environmental groups use the occasion for outreach and education. Environmental organizations also organize protests to raise public awareness and influence policy after major pollution catastrophes, such as the 1989 *Exxon Valdez* oil spill in Alaska, the 2010 BP *Deepwater Horizon* oil spill in the Gulf of Mexico, and the 2011 nuclear accident in Fukushima, Japan. They also coordinate acts of civil disobedience to protest corporations that are major polluters, such as the 2016 Break Free campaign against coal mines and coal power plants on six continents.

Many of the activities of social movements are designed to change people's everyday consciousness about nature and the environment. Global organizations such as Greenpeace and the World Wildlife Fund produce public service advertisements designed to get people thinking about conservation and wildlife protection, as well as the dangers of polluting industries. Over the last 20 years, social movements focused on **corporate social responsibility** have targeted business leaders, trying to convince them to adopt more sustainable and environmentally responsible business practices (Bendell 2009). Such practices include socially responsible investment strategies, the reduction of waste, the adoption of more environmentally sound production strategies, and the promotion of brand loyalty through strategies that appeal to environmentally conscious consumers (such as fair-trade production practices, charitable contributions to environmental organizations, etc.) (Porter and Kramer 2006).

Environmentalists have also formed political parties, in order to elect candidates who will advocate for pro-environment government policies. Developing out of the student and antinuclear movements of the 1960s, the Green Party emerged in Europe, Australia, and New Zealand during the

Corporate social responsibility
A social movement to convince business leaders to adopt sustainable and environmentally responsible practices.

Climate change march to support the Paris Agreement, May 8, 2016
Hundreds of climate protestors marched in London on May 8, 2016, against apparent backtracking on the 2015 Paris agreement (Paris COP 21). That agreement called for signatories to reduce their greenhouse gas emissions as well as provide financial support to emerging countries to help them address the impact of climate change.

1970s. By the 1980s, Green Party candidates had won elections throughout Europe, North America, and Australasia. By the end of the 20th century the Green Party had become a global political force, campaigning for clean energy, environmental conservation, and a greater environmental consciousness in everyday life. The electoral and legislative successes of Green Party candidates have helped increase global support for the environment (Dunlap and York 2008). Furthermore, where the Green Party has had national success, it has been very effective at linking local environmental campaigns to national environmental organizations (Rootes 1999).

Sociological Realism: Limits on Environmental Progress

While environmental movements have had important successes, these victories have been uneven, and they often (if inadvertently) reinforce privilege and inequality. With the exception of the corporate social responsibility movement, whose influence is relatively recent, most successful environmental campaigns have tended to focus on individual habits instead of structural changes. While campaigns aimed at the actions of ordinary people are certainly important, they can also take the burden of responsibility off the companies that are actually producing waste. In fact, some of the earliest antilittering campaigns were actually created by corporations, with this very purpose in mind. One of the most famous of these is the "Keep America Beautiful" campaign (which began in the 1950s, and still exists today), which was funded by some of the biggest companies in the packaging industry. By focusing on the littering consumer, these companies diverted attention from their production of single-use bottles and packages instead of the more expensive (but less wasteful) multi-use and refillable ones (Plumer 2006).

Another challenge is the tendency for successful movements to be followed by a social backlash, which polarizes public attitudes and leads to the formation of countermovements (Chapter 13). Countermovements criticize both the original movement's diagnosis of a specific social problem as well as the movement's policy goals. Often, the countermovement receives support from established political and economic elites, who stand to benefit from a reversal of the movement's successes. Ironically, the successes of the environmental movement have helped create an anti-environmentalist countermovement, which has aligned itself with conservative political parties as well as corporate lobbying groups that have an economic interest in rolling back environmental regulations. In the United States, Donald Trump campaigned for president in 2016 on a policy of protecting the coal industry and reversing environmental protections. Similar backlash movements have won the support of conservative political parties in Europe, Canada, and Australia (Lockwood 2018; Dunlap and McCright 2015).

The structure of global privilege and inequality also limits the effectiveness of environmental movements. Environmental movements have been most successful in the affluent nations of Western Europe, North America, and Asia, where global privilege makes a post-materialist politics possible (Rootes 1999). In other words, when people have a reliable food supply, a safe social infrastructure, and the individual rights that come with democracy, they can afford to start thinking about reducing their personal carbon footprint and buying products from companies that are committed to sustainable production practices. In other parts of the world, where basic political freedoms and economic needs have yet to be fully satisfied, people often have other priorities. Complicating things further, in countries that have been the victims of colonialism, people are often suspicious of Western-based social movement organizations that convince (or force) them to change the way they live their lives (Doherty and Doyle 2006). In general, the communication strategies of environmental movements are less successful when they come from outsiders who are not part of the community (Brulle 2010). People are more open to changing their opinions and behaviors when they are treated as partners in a mutual dialogue.

Free-rider problem A collective action problem, in which people in large groups will not act in a way that helps the common good unless it benefits their own personal interests.

The last major obstacle to reducing environmental risk is the **free-rider problem**. The free-rider problem is common to all large-scale collective action problems (Rolfe 2017). Put simply, the free-rider problem states that people in large groups will not act in a way that helps the common good unless it benefits their own personal interests. If people are in a small group, they are more likely to act in an environmentally responsible way, out of fear they will be criticized for creating unnecessary waste. If they are part of the environmental movement and have taken on an identity as environmentalists, they also will be more likely to act in an environmentally responsible way. But the problem of reducing environmental risk requires good behavior on the part of everyone. If it is hard to be more environmentally responsible (e.g., separating recyclables into glass, paper, and plastic), people are less likely to participate. If it is more expensive to buy a sustainable product, people will choose the less expensive one that creates more environmental risk. They may tell a survey researcher that they share the values of environmentalism, but their behaviors tell a different story.

The free-rider problem helps explain why pollution, waste, and greenhouse gas emissions continue to increase. The United Nations Framework Convention on Climate Change (UNFCCC) was first established in 1992, as an agreement among nations to set guidelines for stabilizing and eventually reducing greenhouse gas emissions. While there were no enforcement mechanisms, individual guidelines were established for each nation that wanted to participate. This was replaced by the 1997 Kyoto Protocol, which created legally binding emissions targets for the 37 industrialized nations that signed the agreement, as well as commitments by these nations to supply technology and funding for climate-related projects in less-developed nations. Despite these agreements, global greenhouse gas emissions from human activities increased by 35 percent between 1990 and 2009 (EPA 2016). Developing nations, which did not have any binding targets, increased their emissions significantly. The United States refused to sign on to the agreement, and also saw its emissions increase. Russia, Japan, and Canada announced in 2011 that they would not continue the agreement unless it included China and the United States, which were the two largest polluters in the world. A new agreement was reached in Paris in 2015, which included 194 nations including China and India. But the Paris Agreement allowed each nation to establish its own targets, and it took away all binding enforcement mechanisms. Even this watered-down agreement proved to be too much for the US government, and in 2017 President Trump announced his intention to withdraw from the agreement. Not surprisingly, most nations have failed even to meet the targets they set for themselves, causing the UN Secretary General to warn that the world's nations had arrived at a "dangerous tipping point" on climate change (Sengupta 2018).

While the obstacles for environmental change remain significant, individuals and groups continue to organize to push for more ecologically sensitive policies and practices. In the United States, the governors of California, New York, Washington, and 20 other states announced that they would continue to follow the Paris Agreement despite the fact that the federal government had withdrawn. One hundred and seventy communities in the United States have successfully campaigned to ban gas-powered leaf blowers, which are a significant source of noise pollution and greenhouse emissions. The city of Barcelona has banned cars that are more than 20 years old. In the city of Copenhagen, more than half of the people bike to work, and there is a mandatory green roof policy for all new buildings. Cities all over the world are banning plastic bags. There is a growing competition among many cities and countries to create innovative new policies of ecological sustainability, and to provide incentives for businesses and other organizations to make environmental protection a central element of new projects. Environmental scientists at Yale University have created the Environmental Performance Index, which ranks the environmental health and ecosystem vitality of 180 nations, publishing its results every two years (Switzerland is the global leader, with the United States ranked 27th). In short, there are many efforts to improve the environmental health of societies at local, regional, and global levels. Like most social things, they involve the actions of individuals, families, communities, and larger organizations, including government and business organizations. Together, these efforts are slowly shifting the culture around environmental responsibility.

LEARNING GOALS REVISITED

16.1 Describe some of the key sociological theories that are useful for understanding environment and society.

- The theory of risk society is based on the realization that most of the significant risks that people face are caused by modern society itself. Living in risk society means that people are always engaged in some form of risk management. Regardless of how much wealth and privilege people have, they cannot protect themselves from risk-produced crisis, nor can they solve these risks once and for all.

- The theory of ecological modernization points to the ways that growing expert knowledge and public awareness of environmental risks are leading to the development of more sustainable policies and practices.

- The theory of the Giddens Paradox describes why the individual and collective responses to environmental crisis are so much less dramatic than the reality of the threat being posed. Because the dangers of climate change are not typically concrete realities facing people in their everyday lives, people tend to spend most of their energy dealing with their problems and concerns of the moment.

16.2 Think about the relationship between culture, socialization, and environmental consciousness.

- The development of environmental consciousness depends on all the agents of socialization—the family, peer group, schools, media, the workplace, and beyond—and the way those agents of socialization encourage people to think about how their ordinary behaviors are connected to environmental risk.

- Culturally, environmental messages will tend to be more persuasive and effective if they have compelling characters; if they include nonexperts; if they include scientific evidence as well as nonscientific analogies; and if they offer the audience a positive collective purpose.

- Public debates about environmental risk are shaped by the ongoing cultural tension between science and religion.

- Debates about environmental risk are also shaped by the culture of journalism, which tends to emphasize two sides to every issue in a way that has increased the likelihood that climate science skeptics will more easily get media coverage.

16.3   Describe how environmental risk is socially distributed, paying particular attention to the patterns of privilege and inequality.

- While the consequences of environmental risk are felt by everyone on the planet, they are felt more strongly by people who are lower in the stratification system.

- Poor families are more likely to move into neighborhoods where toxins and pollutants are present. They are less likely to be able to move to safer neighborhoods, and they are less likely to have access to community organizations that can effectively advocate for better environmental safety.

- Even after controlling for education, household income, and other individual characteristics, racial minorities are more likely to move into environmentally hazardous neighborhoods.

- Exposure to environmental hazards is also stratified globally, with poor nations suffering more than wealthy ones.

- Global inequality increases global environmental risk.

16.4   Describe the political and economic forces that contribute to environmental crisis.

- A focus on economic growth increases environmental risk, because it leads to the production of more goods as well as an emphasis on cheap energy. This increases the creation of waste as well as the production of higher levels of greenhouse gases.

- The power of multinational corporations increases environmental risk, because it weakens the ability of government to create and enforce regulations on business.

- Politicians have a difficult time doing the kind of long-term planning that is associated with environmental policy. When they do focus on the environment, they are often influenced by the large amount of lobbying money spent by business interests opposed to regulation.

- Climate change skepticism has become an important part of conservative politics.

16.5   Know the history of environmentalist social movements, paying attention to their successes and failures.

- The modern environmental movement began in the 1950s and 1960s. It was initially focused on the dangers of nuclear weapons and nuclear power, but movement leaders quickly developed a more general focus on protecting the environment, conserving natural resources, and reducing waste.

- Social movements have organized major global events such as Earth Day, which is designed to help people develop a more environmental consciousness. They have also organized protest events targeted at large polluting corporations. And they have produced thousands of public service advertisements designed to get people thinking about conservation and wildlife protection.

- Environmentalists have also organized themselves into political parties, in order to elect candidates who will advocate for pro-environment government policies. By the end of the 20th century the Green Party had become a global political force, campaigning for clean energy, environmental conservation, and a greater environmental consciousness in everyday life.

- Environmental movements have been more successful at changing individual habits than business practices, and they have been more successful in wealthier nations. The successes of environmental movements have also been challenged by backlash from countermovements.

Key Terms

Concentrated disadvantage 473
Corporate social responsibility 476
Ecological modernization 471
Free-rider problem 478
Treadmill of production 474

Review Questions

1. In what ways do the environmental crises of today threaten the social lives of the privileged? How do these differ from the threats facing the less privileged?

2. What is the Giddens Paradox, and how does it complicate the attempt to respond effectively to environmental risk?

3. Describe one case in which culture has helped promote environmental consciousness, and one case in which it has hindered environmental consciousness from forming.

4. Describe the main ways that inequality makes it more difficult to deal effectively with environmental risk.

5. Describe two reasons why we should be optimistic about the social responses to global environmental risk. Describe two reasons why we should not be optimistic.

Explore

RECOMMENDED READINGS

Dunlap, Riley, and Robert Brulle. 2015. *Climate Change and Society: Sociological Perspectives*. New York: Oxford University Press.

Giddens, Anthony. 2009. *The Politics of Climate Change*. Malden, MA: Polity Press.

Schnaiberg, Allan. 1980. *The Environment: From Surplus to Scarcity*. New York: Oxford University Press.

ACTIVITIES

- *Use your sociological imagination*: Hurricane Harvey, which landed in Texas in 2017, did much more damage than people thought it would. Do some research about the hurricane, and discuss the sociological factors that helped make it such a major catastrophe for the city of Houston.

- *Media+Data Literacy*: Watch the documentary film *An Inconvenient Truth*. Do you agree with Smith and Howe's analysis of why it was successful?

- *Discuss*: If technological developments made renewable energy the same price as fossil fuels, how do you think this would change the social responses to environmental risks? What major challenges do you think would still exist?

For additional resources, including Media+Data Literacy exercises, In the News exercises, and quizzes, please go to **oup.com/he/Jacobs-Townsley1e**

Glossary

Absolute mobility Change in social position, regardless of what is happening with other people.

Absolute monarchy A form of government in which there are no laws restricting the power of the monarch over the people living in their territory.

Achieved status A status that can be earned through action.

Active audiences The idea that people are active, skillful interpreters of the world who have the ability to recognize and resist cultural power.

Acute disease A single or repeated episode of relatively rapid onset and short duration from which the patient usually returns to his/her normal or previous state or level of activity.

Agenda-setting The idea that news media set the public agenda. They do not shape *what people think*, but they do have great influence on *what people think about*.

Agents of socialization The people, groups, and organizations that most powerfully affect human socialization. The five primary agents of socialization are family, school, peer groups, media, and the workplace.

Alienation A condition where humans have no meaningful connection to their work, or to each other

Allostatic load The wear and tear on the body due to stress.

Anomie The condition of feeling isolated and disconnected in the absence of rich social connection.

Applied research Research with the goal of solving practical problems in society.

Ascribed status A status assigned to people by society, which is not chosen and which cannot be changed easily.

Ascriptiveness The degree to which characteristics at birth like race, gender, ethnicity, parents' background, or nationality determine life outcomes in a stratification system.

Assimilation When minority groups fully embrace the culture of the dominant group and lose their distinctive racial and/or ethnic characteristics.

Basic research Research with the goal of advancing our fundamental knowledge and understanding of the world.

Beliefs All the things we think are true, even in the absence of evidence or proof; ideas about the world that come through divine revelation or received tradition.

Big data Refers to the large amount of data produced by our technological ability to capture the behavior of humans (and machines and others) over huge populations and time spans.

Blended family A household that includes a step-parent, step-sibling, or half-sibling.

Blockbusting A practice where real estate agents would go to a neighborhood where racial minorities were beginning to move in, convince the white residents there that their property values were going to decrease, and encourage them to sell their houses below market value.

Boomerang kids Young adults who move back home to live with their parents after a period of independence

Brain drain When highly educated people in poor countries leave for places with more economic opportunity.

Broken windows theory A theory of policing stating that ignoring small crimes and minor violations creates a spiral of increasing deviance and more serious criminality.

Bureaucracy An organizational form with a clearly defined hierarchy where roles are based on rational, predictable, written rules and procedures to govern every aspect of the organization and produce standardized, systematic, and efficient outcomes.

Canon The set of thinkers and ideas that serve as a standard point of reference for a scholarly or artistic tradition.

Capitalism An economic system based on the private ownership of property, including the means of material life such as food, clothing, and shelter, and in which the production of goods and services is controlled by private individuals and companies, and prices are set by markets.

Capitalist crisis of care The shortage of reproductive labor created by the capitalist organization of work.

Case study research Research that relies on a small number of cases that offer special insight into a particular social process and are studied in depth, typically using comparative methods.

Caste systems An extremely unequal stratification system in which people are born into a particular social group and have virtually no opportunity to change their social position.

Categorical inequality The inequality between social categories or social groups.

Categorical or nominal variable A variable that measures phenomena that are not inherently numerical, such as gender, race, or ethnicity. In this case the numerical code assigned to a quality is more a name than a number.

Causation Causation occurs when two variables share a pattern because one variable produces the pattern in the other.

Cause Something that produces an outcome. Technically, a cause is where a first event is understood to produce a material effect on a second event.

Census An official count of the population.

Charismatic authority A form of persuasive power in which people follow a leader's orders because of the personal qualities that the leader possesses.

Chronic disease A permanent, nonreversible condition that might leave residual disability, and that may require long-term treatment and care

Citizenship The laws that define who is a legal member of a country.

Citizenship education Curriculum dealing with history, laws, main social institutions, and political organization of the nation in which students live.

Civil law Law that deals with disputes between individuals and organizations. Most legal cases are civil cases.

Classification systems Elaborate and nuanced identifications of similarity and difference based on cultural patterns that develop over time when people place beliefs, practices, and cultural objects into groups of similar things and groups of different things.

Code-switching Adapting behavior to meet different role expectations across interactional contexts.

Coercive power The system of punishments and rewards that are used to try to force people to act in a particular way.

Cohabitation An arrangement in which romantic couples choose to live together instead of getting married.

Collective representations Pictures, images, or narratives that describe the social group and are held in common.

Colonialism A global stratification system in which powerful nations used their military strength to take political control over other territories and exploit them economically.

Colorblind racism A form of racism based on the refusal to discuss or notice race.

Commercial culture Cultural commodities that exist to be bought and sold.

Commodity An object that is bought and sold in a market. Commodity production is a system of producing goods and services to be bought and sold on markets.

Comparative-historical methods A set of research methods that uses comparison of events and processes in the past to understand the development and operation of social things.

Complicit masculinity A form of masculinity where an individual may not meet all the requirements of hegemonic masculinity but still benefits from the gender order in which they are viewed as masculine.

Compulsory heterosexuality A social order in which sexual desire between males and females is understood to be the only normal form of sexuality, and is enforced through medical, legal, religious and other social institutions.

Concentrated disadvantage A structural outcome in which the poorest and most racially segregated communities suffer the most from environmental risk.

Confirmation bias The tendency to look for information that reinforces prior beliefs; when research is biased to confirm the researcher's preexisting beliefs or hypotheses.

Conflict Disagreement, opposition, and separation between individuals or groups.

Conflict theory Conflict theorists argue that social structures and social systems emerge out of the conflicts between different groups.

Consensus theory Consensus theorists focus on social equilibrium, which is the way that different parts of society work together to produce social cohesion.

Conspicuous consumption A way to display privilege, wealth, and social status to others.

Constitutional monarchy A form of democratic government where power is held by elected officials and there is a king or queen who serves as the ceremonial head of the nation.

Consumerism A widespread ideology grounded in conspicuous consumption that encourages buying and consuming goods, including buying more than an individual needs.

Content analysis A sociological method to systematically evaluate and code text documents in which word frequencies or other textual features can be turned into quantitative variables.

Contentious politics The use of social conflict and other disruptive techniques to make a political point in an effort to change government policy.

Contingency Openness in social life produced by human choices and actions.

Continuous or linear variable A measure of inherently numerical phenomena that can be counted, divided and multiplied, such as money or time.

Controlled experiment Scientific method that systematically controls the factors that affect some outcome of interest and studies it systematically to isolate the causal logic that produces the observed effects.

Conurbation A process in which urban and suburban development reaches a point where different cities begin to be connected together in a large, continuous metropolitan space.

Convenience sample A sample collected from a research population on the basis of convenience, or easy access.

Corporate social responsibility A social movement to convince business leaders to adopt sustainable and environmentally responsible practices.

Correlation A correlation is an observed statistical dependence between two variables, but it does not mean the variables are *causally* related.

Cosmology The system of knowledge and beliefs that a society uses to understand how the world works and how it is organized.

Counterfactual reasoning An analytical strategy for investigating the causal logic of research that asks what factors might have led to a different social outcome.

Credentialism A process in which formal educational qualifications are used to determine who is eligible to work in a given occupation.

Crime Deviant behavior that is defined and regulated by law.

Crime rate Calculated in the United States as the number of criminal offenses committed per 100,000 people in the population.

Criminal justice system All the government agencies that are charged with finding and punishing people who break the law.

Criminal recidivism The likelihood that a person will engage in future criminal behavior.

Critical race theory A theory that first developed in critical legal studies to show the ways that the law reinforced racial injustice and domination.

Crystallization The degree to which one dimension of inequality in a stratification system is connected to other dimensions of inequality.

Cultural capital Education, cultural knowledge, and cultural consumption that signals privilege to others; the knowledge and consumption of culturally valued things.

Cultural competence The ability to perceive and engage other cultural ideas. In medical settings cultural competence means the ability to meet the cultural, social, and linguistic needs of patients.

Cultural gatekeepers Decision-makers who control access to or influence what kind of culture is available to an audience.

Cultural hierarchies Socially organized inequality based on ideas about what counts as "good" or worthwhile culture.

Cultural humility An approach to health care where medical professionals develop a stance that is open to the patient and that seeks to learn from them how they perceive the situation on an ongoing basis.

Cultural imperialism When a small number of countries dominate the market for culture and destroy smaller, local cultures.

Cultural pluralism An alternative to the idea of assimilation that imagines a society where people maintain their unique cultural identities while also accepting the core values of the larger society.

Cultural relativism The idea that all meaning is relative to time and place.

Cultural turn An interdisciplinary movement in sociology and other disciplines that emphasizes the collective cultural dimension of social life.

Culture The entire set of beliefs, knowledge, practices, and material objects that are meaningful to a group of people and shared from generation to generation.

Culture war A profound, society-threatening conflict over values.

Curative medical care Care focused on curing disease or relieving pain to promote recovery.

Cybercrime Crime conducted using computer networks.

Davis–Moore theory of inequality The theory that some level of inequality is necessary to motivate people to do the most difficult and important jobs in a society.

Decoding The process in which cultural messages are interpreted by specific people.

Degree of inequality The level of concentration of a specific asset within the larger population.

Deinstitutionalization A historical process in the United States and other countries where populations once housed in long-term care facilities like psychiatric hospitals and facilities for the developmentally disabled declined sharply over time.

Deliberation The practice of discussing matters of collective importance, so that after debating the merits of competing positions, people can reach a shared agreement about the best course of action.

Democratic republic A form of democratic government where power is held by elected officials and there is no monarch.

Demographic divide A general pattern of global population growth, in which poor countries have higher birth rates and lower life expectancies, while wealthy countries have lower birth rates and higher life expectancies. The demographic divide is a significant cause of global inequality and global immigration patterns.

Demographic transition The historical decline in the birth rate and the death rate. The demographic transition began during the 19th century, and accelerated throughout the 20th century.

Demography The study of human populations.

Denomination A religious sect that has begun to develop a more established bureaucracy and a common set of ritual practices.

Dependent variable The outcome to be explained in a research study; the researcher wants to identify what produces the effects on the dependent variable.

Deviance Any behavior that is outside social boundaries for what counts as normal and acceptable.

Deviant subculture A group of people who set themselves apart as being different from the larger mainstream culture of the society.

Diaspora A type of transnational community that develops when specific populations are forced to leave their homeland and to scatter across different communities around the globe.

Discourses Organized systems of knowledge and power that define what meanings we count as normal, and what kinds of meanings we attach to people who are "not normal."

Discrimination Negative and unequal treatment directed at a particular group.

Disease A disorder in the structure or function of the human organism.

Disenchantment The condition of rationalized bureaucratic societies characterized by the growing importance of skepticism and the decline of belief as a source of social action.

Division of labor A central principle for organizing the productive work in society that sorts different people into different work roles to ensure the production and reproduction of human life. This includes the separation of work and life into different, more specialized parts.

Dominant culture The ideas, values, beliefs, norms, and material culture of society's most powerful groups.

Dramaturgical theory A theory of society developed by Erving Goffman that refers to social life as a series of theatrical performances.

Dyad A group of two people with one relationship.

Ecological modernization A sociological theory focused on the expectation that growing expert knowledge and public awareness of environmental risks will lead to the development of more sustainable policies and practices.

Economy All the activities and organizations that are involved in the production, distribution, and consumption of goods and services.

Ego The part of the mind that balances the demands of the id and the superego to determine the most practical course of action for an individual in any given situation.

Elites An elite is formed through high-status behavior and the formation of institutions to create a community of privilege and control.

Emphasized femininity A counterpart to the idea of hegemonic masculinity, where women perform in stereotypically feminine ways that conform to a patriarchal gender order.

Empirical evidence Fact-based information about the social or natural world.

Encoding The process through which people with power try to create forms of material and ideal culture that encourage cultural consumers to adopt specific shared meanings.

Epidemic A widespread or high incidence of an infectious disease.

Epidemiology The study of the social dimensions of disease patterns to discover the way diseases are spread and communicated.

Epigenetics The study of how genes interact with wider natural and social environments.

Epistemic privilege The privilege that attaches to the knowledge of powerful people.

Epistemology A branch of philosophy that explores how we know whether a statement or a fact is actually true.

Ethics Critical reasoning about moral questions. Ethical research weighs the benefits of research against possible harm to human subjects of research.

Ethnic cleansing The forcible removal of an entire group of people from a society because of their race, ethnicity, or religion.

Ethnic enclaves Geographical areas defined by high levels of ethnic concentration and cultural activities and ethnically identified economic activities.

Ethnicity A system for classifying people into groups on the basis of shared cultural heritage and a common identity.

Ethnocentrism When people assume that their society is superior to others and when they use their own cultural standards to judge outsiders.

Ethnography A sociological research method based on participant-observation in the field where researchers try to capture social life in all of its detail and complexity.

Experiments A sociological research method that controls the conditions of observation with the goal of isolating the effects of different factors on some outcome of interest.

Extended family A type of family in which the household includes parents, children, grandparents, aunts, uncles, and other relatives.

Falsifiability The idea that scientific statements define what condition or evidence would prove them wrong.

Family A group of related people, who are connected together by biological, emotional, or legal bonds.

Feminine The set of personal, social, and cultural qualities associated with females and women.

Feminism A theoretical critique and historical series of social movements that proposed women as equal to men and argued that women should be treated as equals in major social institutions.

Feudalism An economic system in which a small number of people owned most of the land, and everyone else was completely dependent on the landowner.

Field experiments Research using experimental methods in natural settings outside of the laboratory.

Focus groups A sociological research method that gathers groups of people together for discussion of a common question or a particular social issue to collect data.

Folkways Common sense and fairly unserious norms.

Free-rider problem A collective action problem, in which people in large groups will not act in a way that helps the common good unless it benefits their own personal interests. In social movement contexts, the situation where the people who benefit from a social movement's activities assume that others will do the work.

Game stage A stage of social development when children are around seven years old and begin to make friends, learn to pick games that other people want to play, and learn how to avoid or to quickly resolve arguments that arise when a game is being played.

Gender The socially constructed roles for women and men that define expected behaviors for individuals of each sex.

Gender cue Part of a social script that tells other people what gendered behavior to expect in the future and how to orient their own behavior in the present.

Gender dysphoria A diagnosis in the fifth edition of the *Diagnostic and Statistical Manual of Mental Disorders* to describe when people experience "intense, persistent gender incongruence."

Gender order A characterization of society as fully organized by gender.

Gender performance Actions and behaviors that conform to widespread gendered understandings of social roles and social identities.

Gender script A set of social norms that direct people to act in accordance with widely understood gender expectations.

Gender socialization The social interactions and experiences through which individuals learn how to occupy the gender roles considered appropriate to their sex status.

Gender stereotypes Widespread cultural understandings about the different and contrasting qualities associated with women and men.

Genealogy The study of family history in order to document how family members are related to each other.

Generalize To make the argument that the finding from a particular sample of people or a single research study applies to a wider research population.

Generalized other The rules of society that the child internalizes through the process of socialization.

Generation A group of individuals who are of a similar age and are marked by the same historical events that take place during their youth.

Genetics The study of how genes function in the biological system.

Genocide The systematic killing of people on the basis of their race, ethnicity, or religion.

Global/globalization The interconnection of social life on the planet.

Global city Cities that serve as the centers of global finance, international law, management consulting, and global marketing and communication. Examples include London, New York, and Tokyo.

Global culture Beliefs, knowledge, practices, and material objects that are shared all around the world.

Globalization A concept that refers to the growing social, economic, cultural, and political interdependence of the world's people; the process of international integration in many domains affecting cultural, economic, and political relationships and made possible by changes in transportation, telecommunications, media, and information technology.

Hate crime Acts of violence and intimidation against people because of their race, ethnicity, national origin, religion, gender identity, sexual orientation, gender or disability.

Health care systems Contractual connections between medical organizations.

Health demography The study of the prevalence, or the distribution, of disease and illness in a population.

Health insurance A way to pay for health care where members pay a regular fee into a larger pool, to be drawn on when they need medical care.

Hegemonic masculinity A form of power that enshrines an ideal standard of masculinity and justifies all the ways our society is organized to reinforce the leading role of men.

Hegemony A form of power where dominant groups are able to make their worldview seem like "common sense" to the rest of the population.

Heteronormative A social order that assumes compulsory heterosexuality and links it to binary sex categories, to gender roles at work, in the family, and in the nation, and also to heterosexual sex roles.

Heterosexuality Sexual desire and sexual relations between males and females.

Hidden curriculum The rules of behavior students need to learn to function effectively in the school and the larger society.

Hierarchy of masculinities A social order where some masculinities are seen as superior to others, and all are superior to femininity.

High culture All the cultural products that are held in the highest esteem by a society's intellectuals and elites.

Homeschooling A type of schooling in which parents choose to educate their children at home instead of sending them to a traditional school.

Horizontal mobility Social movement in people's life that occurs without changing their overall position in the socioeconomic stratification system.

Horizontal occupational segregation A pervasive pattern of gender segregation where women are concentrated into female-typed, lower-earning jobs.

Hypothesis A specific statement about the causal relationship between variables that is falsifiable, which means it is a statement that can be proved wrong on the basis of empirical evidence.

Id The unconscious part of the mind, which seeks immediate pleasure and gratification.

Ideal culture All the social meanings that exist in nonmaterial form, such as beliefs, values, expectations, and language.

Identity theft When criminals use stolen personal and financial information to assume a person's identity in order to obtain credit and other financial advantages in that person's name.

Ideology A system of shared meaning that is used to justify existing relationships of power and privilege.

Illness experience The way in which illness is understood and managed by patients and their carers.

Immigrant enclave A community in which there are successful immigrant-owned businesses that serve to anchor the community. Immigrant enclaves are highly desirable destinations for new immigrants.

Immigration The movement of people from one nation to another.

Incarceration A form of punishment in which the offender is confined in prison.

Income The flow of earnings over a delimited time period including rents, salaries, and income transfers like pensions or dividends.

Independent variable The factor that produces a change in the dependent variable.

In-depth interviews A sociological research method that uses extended, open-ended questions to collect data.

Inequality The unequal distribution of social goods such as money, power, status, and social resources.

Informed consent The idea that people must consent to being studied and that researchers must give their subjects enough information about the study so that they can make a truly voluntary decision about whether or not to participate.

In-group A reference group that a person is connected to in a positive way and feels bonded to, whether or not they know people in the group personally.

Institution An established system of rules and strategies that defines how people are related to each other and how they should act in a given social situation.

Institutional level of analysis The intermediate level of analysis, between microsociology and macrosociology, of specific institutions and social relationships.

Institutional reflexivity The phenomenon where people change their behavior in response to social research.

Institutional Review Board (IRB) A governing group that evaluates proposed research with the goal of protecting human subjects from physical or psychological harm.

Integrated medical care Systems of medical care that are coordinated to meet the multiple needs of clients.

Interest group An organization that brings people together on the basis of a common issue, and attempts to influence political decision-makers on topics related to that issue.

Intergenerational mobility The change in social status between different generations in the same family, or the change in the position of children relative to their parents.

Internal migration The movement of people within the same country. Internal migration is different than international migration, which is what people usually refer to when they talk about immigration.

Intersectional health perspective A multilevel approach to health care and medicine that emphasizes the multiple systems of oppression that shape health outcomes and how they interact.

Intersectionality A perspective that identifies the multiple, intersecting, and situational nature of the categories that shape people's identities.

Intersex The medical term for people born with primary sex characteristics that are not easily classified into the dichotomous male/female categories. More recently the term "disorders of sex development" (DSD) has been recommended by persons with intersex conditions.

Job training When schools teach students specific skills that will help them enter the workforce and earn a decent wage.

Kinship system The set of rules that define who counts as a member of the family, the names that are given to different types of family members, and the expectations about how different family members will relate to one another.

Labeling theory A theory that people become deviant when they are labeled as deviant people.

Laws Attempts by governments to establish formal systems of rules about how people are allowed to behave, as well as a system of punishments for when they break those rules.

Level of analysis The size or scale of the objects sociologists study.

Life expectancy The amount of time an individual can expect to live.

Literacy The ability to read, write, communicate, and use other skills that allow people to participate fully in their society.

Local The specific particular settings of everyday life, including face-to-face relationships.

Logic Valid reasoning.

Looking-glass self A concept that describes how we develop a social self based on how we think other people perceive us.

Lower-middle class A social class group below the middle class composed of families with a household income of between $15,000 and $60,000 per year.

Macrosociology The analysis of large-scale structural patterns and historical trends, including the workings of the economic, political, and cultural systems.

Male breadwinner A social role for adult men based on the expectation that men should earn enough in wages to support a dependent wife and family.

Marginal productivity theory The theory that inequality is a way of rewarding people who make a greater contribution to society, by encouraging them to work hard and use their talents.

Marriage market Institutionalized spaces where individuals select potential sexual, romantic, and marriage partners.

Masculine The set of personal, social, and cultural qualities associated with males and men.

Master status A single status that becomes so important that it is the only one that matters in social interactions.

Material culture All the cultural objects that are produced by a social group or a society.

Matthew Effect A tendency in science in which the most eminent scientists get most of the recognition and rewards for scientific research.

Means of symbolic production The organized social resources for creating, producing, and distributing communications.

Mechanical solidarity A system of social ties that produces social cohesion on the basis of similar work and life in less complex divisions of labor.

Media concentration A situation when a few large companies control the majority of commercial culture.

Medical institutions Organizational arrangements in which medical therapies are developed and practiced.

Medical risk Any condition or factor that increases the likelihood of disease or injury.

Medicalization A process where a social problem comes to be created or redefined as a medical issue.

Medicine The social response to illness that attempts to identify, prevent, and cure disease.

Meritocracy Stratification systems where high position is held by those who perform the best on examinations and other formal tests of ability.

Microsociology The analysis of individuals and small-group interaction.

Middle class A social class group below the upper-middle class composed of families with an annual income of between $60,000 and $90,000.

Modern era/modernity The period of history in which the combined effects of industrialization, colonization, and the democratic revolutions created massive social change.

Modern world system A term coined by Immanuel Wallerstein to describe the economic integration that occurred with the massive expansion of global trade in modernity.

Monotheism A religious cosmology in which there is only one deity.

Moral education A form of education where students learn social skills, the values of self-determination and autonomy, and how to attach to social groups.

Moral indifference When we distance ourselves from the consequences of our actions for others.

Moral order A social arrangement that is organized around widely understood and institutionally enforced ideas of right and wrong; the gender order is a moral order since it defines what is right and wrong for women and men.

Moral panic When an event, situation, individual or group comes to be defined as a threat to social values.

Mores Norms that define serious expectations about behavior that invoke central values.

Multicultural marketing Advertising that tailors specific messages to target minority groups.

Multiculturalism A culturally pluralist society that officially recognizes the existence of different cultural groups and identities, and that develops policies promoting cultural diversity.

Multilevel approach to health and illness A part of an intersectional health perspective that emphasizes the systemic sources of health and illness as well as individual characteristics.

Multilineal A kinship system that traces both the maternal and the paternal lines of descent, giving equal significance to each.

National health care Government-based health care systems where all citizens are guaranteed access to a basic bundle of medical services.

Net worth Wealth and income minus any debt owed.

Network centrality A network position with many individual direct ties with many people in the network, or someone who is highly influential in a network.

Normalization The process through which social standards of normal behavior are used to judge people and to reform those who are determined not to be normal

Norms Shared expectations, specific to time and place, about how people should act in any particular situation.

Nuclear family A traditional image of the family, which consists of a heterosexual couple living together with their children.

Operationalization The process of defining measures for a sociological study.

Opinions Ideas about the world that stem from common values or experience.

Ordinal variable A measure of categorical order, such as more and less, where the distances between categories are not numerically precise.

Organic solidarity A system of social ties that produces social cohesion based on differences in a complex division of labor.

Organizational culture The distinctive beliefs and patterns of behavior that develop within an organization.

Out-group A reference group toward which a person has a negative connection.

Palliative care Medical care offered to a person and that person's family when it is recognized that the illness is no longer curable.

Pandemic An epidemic that not only affects a large number of people but is also spread over a large geographical area of the world.

Parliamentary system A form of democratic government where the head of government is chosen from the legislature, and is also usually the leader of the largest political party in parliament.

Parole A process through which prisoners who appear to have reformed themselves can earn an early release from their prison sentence.

Participant-observation A research method of observing people in social settings by participating in those social settings with them.

Party system A stratification system where power and privilege come from the effective leadership of important organizations.

Patriarchy A social system rooted in male power, where men and qualities associated with men are considered to be superior to women and to qualities associated with women.

Patrilineal A kinship system that privileges the male line of descent.

Peer groups Groups of people of similar age who share the same kinds of interests.

Peer pressure Peer groups encourage adolescents and teens to engage in behaviors that they would not perform if their parents were watching.

Peer review The process of review of proposed research or publication by the community of scientific experts in a profession or scientific field.

Persuasive power The ability to convince other people that a particular choice or action is the appropriate one.

Pink-collar jobs A term coined to describe the kinds of jobs done by women entering the labor force in the 1970s and 1980s.

Play stage A stage of social development when children around three years old begin to engage in role-playing games.

Plea bargaining A process in which a defendant pleads guilty to a lesser charge that has been negotiated by the prosecuting and defense attorneys.

Police A group of people authorized to enforce the law, prevent crime, pursue and bring to justice people who break the law, and maintain social order.

Political opportunity structure The political opportunities available for successful social movement action that occur when there are changes in political alliances, political conflicts among elites, or when there are clear alliances that can be made with specific political groups.

Politics The struggle for influence and control over the state.

Polytheism A religious cosmology in which there is a group of deities

Popular culture Objects of material culture industrially produced and distributed for the masses.

Popular sovereignty The "rule of the people."

Post-colonial theory A critical perspective that argues that the ways we see globalization, power, and economic systems in the modern world are all shaped by the conquest and subordination of the world's peoples by Western European powers dating from the 15th and 16th centuries.

Post-industrialism An economy in which manufacturing becomes less important as a source of wealth, and where the production of information, knowledge, and services becomes more important.

Post-secular society A society in which religion and science coexist harmoniously, and where there is an attempt to create mutual learning and respect between religious ideas and scientific ideas.

Power A social relationship in which one individual or group is able to influence the conduct of other individuals or groups either directly through force or indirectly through authority, persuasion, or cultural expectation; the ability of individuals or groups to get what they want, even against the resistance of others who are participating in the same action.

Presidential system A form of democratic government where there is a formal separation of powers between the head of government and the legislature, and the president is usually elected by a democratic vote of the people.

Preventive medical care Care aimed at preventing disease before it occurs.

Primary deviance A deviant act or behavior that does not result in the person adopting an identity as a deviant person.

Primary groups Small groups typically based in face-to-face interaction that foster strong feelings of belonging.

Primary school The part of the educationsystem that focuses on the learning needs of children from the ages of five to 12, with an emphasis on basic academic learning and socialization skills.

Primary sexual characteristics The organs required for physical reproduction.

Primogeniture A system in which the first-born child (or, more commonly, the first-born son) inherits the entire family estate.

Prison-industrial complex A profit-making system that uses prison labor and prisons to support a wide array of economic activities.

Private school A school that charges tuition for each student it educates.

Privilege The greater resources possessed by some individuals and groups compared to others.

Professionalization A process where a group of workers come to control a particular space in the division of labor on the basis of their expertise.

Property crime Defined by the Uniform Crime Reporting Program as burglary (entering a home or business to commit theft) motor vehicle theft, larceny (other forms of theft), and arson.

Proselytizing The attempt by an individual or an organization to convert other people to their own religious beliefs.

Public health The health of the whole population.

Public health education Educational efforts to prevent disease, promote healthy behaviors, and preempt risky ones.

Public health policy The norms, rules, and laws that attempt to shape public health behavior.

Public opinion The public expression of the different attitudes and beliefs that people have about a particular issue.

Public religion A situation in which individuals and organizations make faith-based moral arguments about the public good.

Public school A school that is run by the state and receives all or most of its funding from the government.

Public sociology A commitment to bringing sociological knowledge to a general public audience, and participating in wider public conversations and struggles for social justice.

Public sphere The collection of places where private individuals and elected officials gather together to discuss matters of common concern.

Punishment A social response to deviance that controls both deviant behavior and the offender, and that aims to protect the social group and its social standards.

Qualitative methods Sociological research methods that collect nonnumerical information, such as interview transcripts or images.

Quantitative methods Sociological research methods that collect numerical data that can be analyzed using statistical techniques.

Queer Any idea or practice that actively disturbs the binaries describing a neat concurrence of sex, gender, and desire in society.

Queer theory A critical perspective that identifies the logic of homophobia and heterosexism in social practice and social institutions, and how that logic works to maintain social order.

Race A system for classifying people into groups on the basis of shared physical traits, which people in society treat as socially important and understand to be biologically transmitted.

Racial determinism A dominant social theory in the 19th century that argued that the world was divided into biologically distinct races, and that there were fundamental differences in ability between the different racial groups.

Racial formation theory A critique that analyzes modern Western society and particularly US society as structured by a historically developed "racial common sense." Racial stereotypes and institutionalized patterns of inequality are embedded in the fundamental fabric of modern social life at both the individual and the institutional levels.

Racial profiling The police practice of targeting an individual because of their race or ethnicity.

Racial steering A practice in which realtors would encourage people to look for homes in specific neighborhoods depending on their race, as a way to ensure the "desirable" neighborhoods were reserved for whites.

Random sample A selection from a research population based on a random mechanism, such as a dice roll, a flipped coin, or a random number generator.

Rationalization A major dynamic of modernity in which social relationships become more predictable, standardized, systematic, and efficient.

Rational-legal authority A form of persuasive power based on clearly defined rules that are written down.

Reactivity When the researcher has an effect on the behavior and the responses of the interview subject.

Redlining A practice where banks would not give mortgages to people who lived in minority-dominated neighborhoods.

Reference group A group that people use to help define how they fit in society by providing standards to measure themselves.

Reflexivity The imaginative ability to move outside of yourself in order to understand yourself as part of a wider social scene.

Rehabilitation An approach to punishment that seeks to improve offenders and restore them to society.

Relationality The idea that social things take on meaning only in relationship to social other things.

Relative deprivation A form of inequality between groups where people believe that they are being treated unequally in comparison to another group they view as similar to themselves.

Relative mobility The understanding of change in social position compared to other groups.

Relativism The idea that truth depends on the group, the community, the society, and the culture to which a person belongs.

Reliability The consistent measurement of the object over units in a population or over repeated samples.

Religion A unified system of beliefs and practices related to sacred things, which unite all of its adherents into a single moral community.

Remittance A practice in which immigrants send money back to family members living in their country of origin.

Representative sample A selection from a research population that contains all the features of the wider population from which it is drawn.

Reproductive labor The work of producing and maintaining individuals for social participation in the economy and society

Research methods Strategies to collect accurate and useful information about the world.

Research population The entire universe of individuals or objects in a study.

Residential segregation A social practice in which neighborhoods are separated on the basis of group differences.

Resistance Opposition to the exercise of power.

Resocialization The process through which we adjust our lives, attitudes, and behaviors in response to new circumstances.

Resource mobilization theory A theory that links social movement success to resources of money, legitimacy, facilities, and labor.

Rigidity The degree to which movement is possible in a stratification system.

Ritual An event where people come together to reaffirm the meaning of the sacred, to acknowledge its special qualities and its separateness from ordinary (profane) life.

Role The set of expected behaviors associated with a particular status.

Role conflict When there are competing expectations coming from different statuses and role expectations clash, individuals become conflicted.

Role strain When the different expected behaviors associated with a status are in tension with one another, individuals experience strain trying to meet expectations.

Sample A selection from a research population for the purposes of research.

Sanctions Actions that punish people when they do not act in a way that accords with norms.

Sandwich parents The generational position where people are raising their children at the same time as their own parents are becoming elderly and need care.

Second shift The unpaid housework and childcare women perform after returning home from their paid job.

Second-wave feminism. The movements and activism around women's rights in the 1960s and 1970s, with a focus on reproductive rights, work, family, and equal pay.

Secondary deviance A deviant act or behavior that occurs when a person has taken on the role of the deviant person.

Secondary groups Large, impersonal groups usually organized around a specific activity or interest.

Secondary school The part of the education system in which students learn more specialized subject areas, and where they begin to develop the specific skills they will need to enter the workforce or university.

Secondary sex characteristics Physical features that emerge at puberty like body hair and breasts.

Sects A smaller and more loosely organized group of religious believers who disagree with the established church and try to create their own authentic expression of religious faith.

Secularization thesis The argument that religion will become less important in modern society.

Secular-rational values Widely held social beliefs that emphasize the importance of individualism, science, and critique.

Segregation A social practice in which neighborhoods, schools, and other social organizations are separated by race and ethnicity.

Selection effect The bias produced in data by the way the data are chosen, or selected.

Self A sociological term used in the symbolic interactionist tradition to describe the individual person and their social being. The self is produced and only takes on meaning in interaction and relationships with others.

Self-expression values Widely held social beliefs that emphasize the importance of tolerance, political participation, personal happiness, and environmental protection.

Separate spheres The idea that there are and should be separate social domains for women and men.

Sex The status of male or female, which is assigned at birth and is associated with physical attributes such as chromosomes and anatomical differences.

Sick role An idea developed by Talcott Parsons to describe social expectations for the behavior of sick people.

Single-party state A state in which all candidates in an election come from a single political party.

Snowball sample A selection from a research population taken by asking the first few research subjects to identify and recommend others for study.

Social capital Group ties and network attachments people have and the sense of trust and security that they get from their group memberships and network attachments; the relationships and experience of social connection and cooperation people have with each other that allow them to act together.

Social control theory A theory that people who have strong social bonds and attachments in their community are less likely to engage in deviant behavior.

Social demography Social research that uses demographic data in order to study key social institutions and social processes. Social demographers study trends in marriage and divorce, population aging, immigration and social mobility, urbanization, and health disparities between different population groups.

Social facts Facts about the collective nature of social life that have their own patterns and dynamics beyond the individual level.

Social group A set of people that are connected in some way.

Social mobility A change in a person's social status or a movement to a different place in the stratification system.

Social movement A group of people acting together to try to create social or political change, usually outside the channels of institutionalized politics.

Social network A group organized through social ties between individuals that works through the connections that link individuals to one another.

Social research The systematic investigation of some aspect of the social world, which aims to contribute to our general understanding of society.

Social sciences The disciplines that use systematic scientific and cultural methods to study the social world, as distinct from the natural and physical worlds.

Social stratification A central sociological idea that describes structured patterns of inequality between different groups of people.

Socialism A type of economy in which goods are produced according to social needs, and economic production is controlled and owned collectively by the workers themselves.

Socialization All of the different ways that we learn about our society's beliefs, values, and expected behaviors; the ongoing process of learning the social meanings of a culture.

Socioeconomic status A general term referring to sociological measures of social position that include income, educational attainment, and occupational prestige.

Sociological imagination The ability to see the connections between individual lives, wider social structures, and the way they affect each other.

Sociological research methods All the different strategies sociologists use to collect, measure, and analyze data.

Sociology of health and illness A field of sociology that studies the relationship between health and society.

Solidarity The sense of belonging and the connection that we have to a particular group.

Standardized tests Forms of assessment that are administered and scored under conditions that are the same for all students.

State All of the institutions of government, which together rule over a clearly defined territory and have a monopoly on the legitimate use of physical force within the territory.

Status A specific social position that an individual occupies in the social structure.

Status group A group held together by a common lifestyle and shared characteristics of social honor.

Stereotypes A form of ideology that encourages people to believe in the natural superiority or inferiority of different groups of people.

Stigma A form of dishonor, discredit, or shame associated with illness; a spoiled identity.

Stratification A central sociological idea that describes structured patterns of inequality between different groups of people.

Structural mobility Changes in social position in the stratification system that occur because of structural changes in the economy and wider society.

Structural strain theory A theory about the connection between structural inequalities, grievances, and collective action.

Structure The seen and unseen regular, organized patterns of social life.

Subcultures The ideas, values, beliefs, norms, and material culture of all the nondominant groups in the society.

Suburb A residential area located within commuting distance of a city. Suburbs began to spread out from cities in the late-19th and early-20th centuries, first with improvements in railroad infrastructure and then with the spread of the automobile.

Superego The moral part of the mind, which acts as the conscience.

Surveillance Monitoring other people's activites, often by using video and other media technologies.

Surveys A sociological research method that asks a series of defined questions to collect data from a large sample of the research population.

Survival values Widely held social beliefs that emphasize the importance of economic and physical security.

Symbolic ethnicity The way dominant groups feel an attachment to specific ethnic traditions without being active members of the ethnic group.

Symbolic interactionism A perspective associated with the Chicago school of sociology that argues that people develop a social self through interaction with others.

Symbolic meaning The broader cultural content of a cultural object, idea, or event which is based on the other images, emotions, meanings, and associations that come from the larger culture.

Symbolic politics A type of political activity in which the meanings associated with a political action are just as important as the policies or the social changes being proposed.

Theodicy The attempt to explain why suffering and injustice exist in the world.

Theoretical sample A selection from a research population that focuses a sample as research progresses and where the sampling strategy changes after the initial data have been collected, based on what is theoretically important.

Theories of the middle range Theories that focus on particular institutions and practices rather than an overarching theory of society

Thomas theorem The proposition that the way people interpret a situation has real consequences for how they act.

Total institutions Institutions like prisons, nursing homes, or the military that control every aspect of their members' lives.

Traditional authority A form of persuasive power in which people follow a leader's orders because of the weight of tradition or custom.

Traditional values Widely held social beliefs that emphasize the importance of traditional religion, family, national pride, and obedience to authority.

Transgender people People whose gender identity does not correlate with the sex status they were assigned at birth.

Transnational community A community that reaches beyond national boundaries.

Transnational family A household that is maintaining strong family bonds and simultaneous connections to multiple countries.

Treadmill of production A social process in which the continuous quest for economic growth encourages businesses to pursue strategies that cause large and unsustainable environmental damage.

Triad A group of three people with three relationships.

Underclass A social group described by William Julius Wilson that experiences long-term unemployment and social isolation, and often lives in impoverished urban neighborhoods.

Upper-middle class A social class group at the top of the middle-class system with good job security and high-paying salaries of over $100,000 per year.

Urbanization A social process in which the population shifts from the country into cities, and where most people start to live in urban rather than rural areas.

Utopia An image of an imaginary, perfect world in which there is no conflict, hunger, or unhappiness.

Validity When data accurately measure the phenomenon under study.

Values General social ideas about what is right and wrong, good and bad, desirable and undesirable, important or unimportant.

Variable A quantity that changes, or varies, in a research population.

Vertical occupational segregation A pattern in occupations where men tend to hold higher, better-paid positions within the same occupation as women.

Vertical social mobility Social mobility up or down in the socioeconomic stratification system.

Violent crime Defined by the Uniform Crime Reporting Program as homicide, aggravated assault, rape, and robbery.

Warehousing theory A theory that focuses on the ways that postsecondary education acts as a holding place that protects people from unstable labor market conditions.

Wealth The stock of valuable assets including physical and intellectual property, art, jewelry, and other valuable goods.

White-collar crime Financially motivated nonviolent crime, usually committed by business professionals in the course of doing their jobs.

Working poor People and families in poverty despite having at least one person who works for a wage.

Workplace sexual harassment Unwelcome and offensive conduct that is based on gender that has become a condition of employment, or conduct that creates an intimidating, hostile, or abusive work environment.

World society The view that there is a common global culture consisting of shared norms about progress, science, democracy, human rights, and environmental protection.

World systems theory A way to think about global stratification that emphasizes the relative positions of countries in the world economy as crucial determinants of inequality.

Xenophobia Fear and hatred of strangers who have a different cultural background.

Zone of permitted variation A social space around a boundary where rules can be contested.

References

Abbasi, Daniel. 2006. *Americans and Climate Change: Closing the Gap between Science and Action*. New Haven, CT: Yale School of Forestry and Environmental Studies. https://climatecommunication.yale.edu/publications/americans-and-climate-change/.

Abbott, Andrew. 1988. *The System of Professions: An Essay on the Division of Expert Labor*. Chicago: University of Chicago Press.

Abbott, Andrew. 2001. *Chaos of the Disciplines*. Chicago: University of Chicago Press.

Abelman, Nancy, and Jiyeon Kang. 2014. "Memoir/Manuals of South Korean Pre-College Study Abroad: Defending Mothers and Humanizing Children." *Global Networks* 14: 1–22.

Acker, J. (1973). "Women and Social Stratification: A Case of Intellectual Sexism." *American Journal of Sociology* 78(4): 936–45.

Adler, N. E., and D. H. Rehkopf. 2008. "US Disparities in Health: Descriptions, Causes, and Mechanisms." *Annual Review of Public Health* 29: 235–53.

Adler, Patricia, and Peter Adler. 1998. *Peer Power: Preadolescent Culture and Identity*. New Brunswick, NJ: Rutgers University Press.

Adler, Patricia, Steven Kless, and Peter Adler. 1992. "Socialization to Gender Roles: Popularity among Elementary School Boys and Girls." *Sociology of Education* 65: 169–87.

Adorno, Theodor W., Else Frenkel-Brunswik, Daniel J. Levinson, and R. Nevitt Sanford. 1950. *The Authoritarian Personality*. New York: Harper & Brothers.

Alarcón, R. 1999. "Recruitment Processes Among Foreign-Born Engineers and Scientists in Silicon Valley." *American Behavioral Scientist* 42(9): 1381–97.

Alba, Richard D. 1976. "Social Assimilation Among American Catholic National-Origin Groups." *American Sociological Review* 41(6): 1030–1046.

Alba, Richard D. 1990. *Ethnic Identity: The Transformation of White America*. New Haven, CT: Yale University Press.

Alba, Richard, and Victor Nee. 2003. *Remaking the American Mainstream: Assimilation and Contemporary Immigration*. Cambridge, MA: Harvard University Press.

Alberta, Tim. 2017, September/October. "Is The Electoral College Doomed?" *Politico*. https://www.politico.com/magazine/story/2017/09/05/electoral-college-national-popular-vote-compact-215541.

Alexander, Jeffrey C. 1987. *Twenty Lectures: Sociological Theory since World War II*. New York: Columbia University Press.

Alexander, Jeffrey C. 1990. "Beyond the Epistemological Dilemma: General Theory in a Postpositivist Mode." *Sociological Forum* 5: 531–44.

Alexander, Jeffrey C. 2003. *The Meanings of Social Life: A Cultural Sociology*. New York: Oxford University Press.

Alexander, Jeffrey C. 2006. *The Civil Sphere*. New York: Oxford University Press.

Alexander, Jeffrey C. 2011. *Performative Revolution in Egypt: An Essay in Cultural Power*. London: Bloomsbury Academic.

Alexander, Robert, 2019. *Representation and the Electoral College*. New York: Oxford University Press.

Alex-Assensoh, Yvette, and Lawrence Hanks, eds. 2000. *Black and Multiracial Politics in America*. New York: NYU Press.

Alinsky, Saul. [1971] 2010. *Rules for Radicals*. New York: Random House.

Allen, Joseph, and Claudia Allen. 2009. *Escaping the Endless Adolescence*. New York: Ballantine Books.

Almond, Gabriel, R. Scott Appleby, and Emmanual Sivan. 2003. *Strong Religion: The Rise of Fundamentalisms around the World*. Chicago: University of Chicago Press.

Aloe, Carli, Martin Kulldorff, and Barry R. Bloom. 2017. "Geospatial Analysis of Nonmedical Vaccine Exemptions and Pertussis Outbreaks in the United States." *Proceedings of the National Academy of Sciences of the United States of America* 114(27): 7101–5.

Alschuler, Albert. 1968. "The Prosecutor's Role in Plea Bargaining." *The University of Chicago Law Review* 36(1): 50–112. doi:10.2307/1598832.

Alschuler, A. 1975. The Defense Attorney's Role in Plea Bargaining. *The Yale Law Journal* 84(6): 1179–1314. doi:10.2307/795498.

Amaldoss, Wilfred, and Sanjay Jain. 2008. "Trading Up: A Strategic Analysis of Reference Group Effects." *Marketing Science* 54: 932–42.

Amar, Akhil Reed. 2007. "Some Thoughts on the Electoral College: Past, Present, and Future." Faculty Scholarship Series. Paper 790. http://digitalcommons.law.yale.edu/fss_papers/790.

Amato, Paul R. 2010. "Research on Divorce: Continuing Trends and New Developments." *Journal of Marriage and Family* 72: 650–666. https://doi.org/10.1111/j.1741-3737.2010.00723.x.

Amato, Paul, Laura Loomis, and Alan Booth. 1995. "Parental Divorce, Marital Conflict, and Offspring Well-Being During Early Adulthood." *Social Forces* 73: 895–15.

American Association of Public Opinion Researchers. 2015. "AAPOR Statement on 'Push Polls.'" https://www.aapor.org/Standards-Ethics/Resources/AAPOR-Statements-on-Push-Polls.aspx.

American Association of University Women. 2016. "The Simple Truth about the Gender Pay Gap." http://www.aauw.org/research/the-simple-truth-about-the-gender-pay-gap/.

American Psychological Association. 2017a. "Answers to Your Questions about Individuals with Intersex Conditions." http://www.apa.org/topics/lgbt/intersex.aspx.

American Psychological Association. 2017b. "Transgender People, Gender Identity and Gender Expression." http://www.apa.org/topics/lgbt/transgender.aspx.

American Sociological Association, Research and Development Department, 2006. *What Can I Do with a Bachelor's Degree in Sociology?* A National Survey of Seniors Majoring in Sociology: First Glances: What Do They Know and Where Are They Going? Washington, DC: American Sociological Association. http://www.asanet.org/galleries/default-file/B&B_first_report_final.pdf.

Americans with Disabilities Act of 1990, as amended. https://www.ada.gov/pubs/adastatute08.htm#12101.

Anderson, Benedict. 2006. *Imagined Communities: Reflections on the Origin and Spread of Nationalism.* New York: Verso.

Anderson, C. A., and Bushman, B. J. 2018. "Media Violence and the General Aggression Model." *Journal of Social Issues* 74: 386–13. doi:10.1111/josi.12275.

Anderson, Elijah. 1999. *The Code of the Street: Decency, Violence and the Moral Life of the Inner City.* New York: W.W. Norton and Company.

Anderson, James. 2007. *Daily Life during the French Revolution.* Westport, CT: Greenwood Press.

Anderson, James, 2015. *Criminological Theories.* Burlington, MA: Jones and Bartlett.

Anderson, Monica. 2015, April 9. "A Rising Share of the US Black Population Is Foreign Born." Pew Research Center Social and Demographic Trends. http://www.pewsocialtrends.org/2015/04/09/a-rising-share-of-the-u-s-black-population-is-foreign-born/.

Anderson, Perry. 1974. *Lineages of the Absolutist State.* London: Verso.

Anderson, Tom. 2015, March 12. "'Boomerang Kids' Are Ruining Their Parents Retirement." *CNBC.* http://www.cnbc.com/2015/03/12/saving-for-retirement-boomerang-kids-are-ruining-their-parents-retirement.html.

Appadurai, Arjun. 1996. *Modernity at Large: Cultural Dimensions of Globalization.* Minneapolis: University of Minnesota Press.

Appiah, Kwame Anthony, and Amy Gutmann. 1998. *Color Conscious: The Political Morality of Race.* Princeton, NJ: Princeton University Press.

Apted, Michael. 2009. "Interview with Michael Apted." *Ethnography* 10: 321–25.

Arum, Richard, and Michael Hout. 1998. "The Early Returns: The Transition from School to Work in the United States." In *From School to Work: A Comparative Study of Educational Qualifications and Occupational Destination,* ed. Yossi Shavit and Walter Muller (pp 471–510). Oxford, England: Clarendon Press.

Ariens, Chris. 2014, October 30. "Weather Channel Distances Itself from Founder's Climate Change Comments," *Adweek.* http://www.adweek.com/tvnewser/weather-channel-distances-itself-from-founders-climate-change-comments/245200.

Armstrong, Elizabeth, and Laura Hamilton. 2013. *Paying for the Party: How College Maintains Inequality.* Cambridge, MA: Harvard University Press.

Arsenault, Mark. 2012, May 11. "Beverly Mother Gets Jail for Permitting Teenage Drinking" *Boston Globe.* http://www.bostonglobe.com/metro/2012/05/11/salem-woman-gets-six-months-jail-six-months-house-arrest-for-providing-alcohol-daughter-party/2InVsVtiBXkHVK0dd4zKVM/story.html.

Artiga, Samantha, Julia Foutz, Elizabeth Cornachione, and Rachel Garfield. 2016. *Key Facts on Health and Health Care by Race and Ethnicity.* Kaiser

Foundation. https://www.kff.org/report-section/key-facts-on-health-and-health-care-by-race-and-ethnicity-section-4-health-coverage/.

Asante-Muhammad, Dedrick, and Natalie Gerber. 2018, January 8. "African Immigrants: Immigrating into a Racial Wealth Divide." *Huffington Post*. https://www.huffpost.com/entry/african-immigrants-immigrating-into-a-racial-wealth_b_5a539aa9e4b0cd114bdb353c.

Aspers, Patrik. 2010. *Orderly Fashion: A Sociology of Markets*. Princeton, NJ: Princeton University Press.

Aspers, Patrik, and Frédéric Godart. 2013. "Sociology of Fashion: Order and Change." *Annual Review of Sociology* 39: 171–92.

Assari, Shervi. 2017, March 8. "Why Do Women Live Longer Than Men?" *The Conversation*. https://theconversation.com/if-men-are-favored-in-our-society-why-do-they-die-younger-than-women-71527.

Associated Press. 2003, October 23. "Buick's Name Means 'Masturbate' in Quebec Slang." https://www.sfgate.com/news/article/Buick-s-name-means-masturbate-in-Quebec-slang-2581410.php.

Associated Press. "Louisiana: Chinese Drywall Maker Settles Claims." *New York Times*, December 15, 2011. https://www.nytimes.com/2011/12/16/us/louisiana-chinese-drywall-maker-settles-claims.html.

Au, Wayne. 2008. "Devising Inequality: A Bernsteinian Analysis of High-Stakes Testing and Social Reproduction in Education." *British Journal of Sociology of Education* 29(6): 639–51.

Austin, Joe. 2001. *Taking the Train: How Graffiti Art Became an Urban Crisis in New York City*. New York: Columbia University Press.

AVERT. "Hiv Stigma And Discrimination." Information on HIV. https://www.avert.org/professionals/hiv-social-issues/stigma-discrimination#footnote8_yr7pkpo.

Ayres, Ian, and Peter Siegelman. 1995. "Race and Gender Discrimination in Bargaining for a New Car." *American Economic Review* 85: 304–21.

Ayres-Brown, A. 2014, April 21. "McDonald's Gave Me the 'Girl's Toy' with My Happy Meal. So I Went to the CEO." *Slate*. https://slate.com/human-interest/2014/04/mcdonald-s-and-me-my-fight-to-end-gendered-happy-meal-toys.html.

Back, Les, Andy Bennett, Laura Desfor Edles, Margaret Gibson, David Inglis, Ronald Jacobs, and Ian Woodward. 2012. *Cultural Sociology: An Introduction*. Hoboken, NJ: Wiley-Blackwell.

Bagdikian, Ben. 2004. *The New Media Monopoly*, 20th ed. New York: Beacon Press.

Baierl, Edgar. 2004. "Why is life expectancy longer for women than it is for men?" *Scientific American* 291(6): 120.

Bail, Christopher. 2008. "The Configuration of Symbolic Boundaries against Immigrants in Europe." *American Sociological Review* 73: 37–59.

Bail, Christopher A. 2014. "The Cultural Environment: Measuring Culture with Big Data." *Theory and Society* 43: 465–82.

Baiocchi, Gianpaolo. 2012. "The Power of Ambiguity: How Participatory Budgeting Travels 8, 2: 1–12. 8: Article 8.

Baker, C. Edwin. 2006. *Media Concentration and Democracy: Why Ownership Matters*. Cambridge: Cambridge University Press.

Baker D. P., and G. K. LeTendre. 2005. *National Differences, Global Similarities: World Culture and the Future of Schooling*. Stanford, CA: Stanford University Press.

Baker, Jack, David A. Swanson, Jeff Tayman, and Lucky M. Tedrow. 2017. *Cohort Change Ratios and Their Applications*. New York: Springer.

Baker Jr., Houston. 1987. *Modernism and the Harlem Renaissance*. Chicago: University of Chicago Press.

Baldassarri, Delia. 2017. "Collective Action." In *The Oxford Handbook of Analytical Sociology*, eds. P. Bearman and P. Hedstrom (web). New York, NY: Oxford University Press. doi:10.1093/oxfordhb/9780199215362.013.17.

Baltzell, Digby E. 1958. *The Philadelphia Gentleman. The Making of a National Upper Class*. New York: Free Press.

Bandarage, Asoka. 2015, March 3. "Proselytism or a Global Ethic?" *Huffington Post*. https://www.huffingtonpost.com/asoka-bandarage/proselytism-or-a-global-e_b_6779640.html.

Bank, Andre, Christiane Froehlich, and Andrea Schneiker. 2016. "The Political Dynamics of Human Mobility: Migration out of, as and into Violence" *Global Policy* 8. https://onlinelibrary.wiley.com/doi/full/10.1111/1758-5899.12384.

Banks, Ann. 2008, January 14. "Dirty Tricks, South Carolina, and John McCain." *The Nation*. https://www.thenation.com/article/dirty-tricks-south-carolina-and-john-mccain/.

Banerjee, A., Duflo, E., Ghatak, M., and Lafortune, J. (2013). Marry for What? Caste and Mate Selection in Modern India. *American Economic Journal: Microeconomics* 5(2), 33–72.

Bapna, Manish, and John Talbert. 2011, April 5. "What Is a Green Economy?" World Resources Institute. https://www.wri.org/blog/2011/04/qa-what-green-economy-0.

Barker, Martin, and Julian Petley, eds. 2001. *Ill Effects: The Media/Violence Debates,* 2nd ed. New York: Routledge.

Barlett, C. P., D. A. Kowalewski, S. S. Kramer, and K. M. Helmstetter. 2018. "Testing the Relationship between Media Violence Exposure and Cyberbullying Perpetration." *Psychology of Popular Media Culture* 8(3), 280-286. http://dx.doi.org/10.1037/ppm0000179.

Barnett, Jessica C., and Edward R. Berchick. 2017, September 12. *Health Insurance Coverage in the United States: 2016* (Report No. P60-260). US Census. https://www.census.gov/library/publications/2017/demo/p60-260.html.

Bärnighausen, Till, and Rainer Sauerborn. 2002. "One Hundred and Eighteen Years of the German Health Insurance System: Are There Any Lessons for Middle- and Low Income Countries?" *Social Science & Medicine* 54 (10): 1559–1587.

Barrett, Frank. 1996. "The Organizational Construction of Hegemonic Masculinity: The Case of the U.S. Navy." *Gender, Work, and Organization* 3: 129–42.

Barro, Robert, and Rachel McCleary. 2004. "Which Countries Have State Religions?," NBER Working Paper 10438. http://www.nber.org/papers/w10438.

Bauman, Zygmunt. 2000. *Liquid Modernity*. Malden, MA: Polity Press.

Bauman, Zygmunt. 2002. *Society Under Siege*. Cambridge: Polity Press.

Bauman, Zygmunt. 2003. *Wasted Lives: Modernity and Its Outcasts*. Malden, MA: Polity Press.

Bauman, Zygmunt. 2004. *Wasted Lives: Modernity and Its Outcasts*. Indianapolis, IN: Wiley.

Baumeister, Roy, Katherine Vohs, Jennifer Aaker, and Emily Garbinsky. 2013. "Some Key Differences between a Happy Life and a Meaningful Life." *The Journal of Positive Psychology* 8: 505–16.

Baumgartner, Frank R., Jeffrey M. Berry, Marie Hojnacki, Beth L. Leech, and David C. Kimball. 2009. *Lobbying and Policy Change: Who Wins, Who Loses, and Why*. Chicago: University of Chicago Press.

Beal, Becky. 1995. "Disqualifying the Official: An Exploration of Social Resistance through the Subculture of Skateboarding." *Sociology of Sport Journal* 12: 252–67.

Bearman, Peter. 2005. *Doormen*. Chicago: University of Chicago Press.

Beck, Ulrich, 1992. *Risk Society*. Thousand Oaks, CA: SAGE.

Beck, Ulrich. 2005. *Power in the Global Age: A New Global Political Economy*. Indianapolis, IN: Wiley.

Beck, Ulrich. 2006. *Cosmopolitan Vision*. Malden, MA: Polity.

Becker Howard, S. 1963. *Outsiders. Studies in the Sociology of Deviance*. New York: Free Press.

Beckhusen, Julia, and Rochelle Cooper. (2018). *Full-Time, Year-Round Workers by Education, Sex, and Detailed Occupation: ACS 2016*. US Census. https://www.census.gov/data/tables/2016/demo/industry-occupation/acs-2016.html.

Beisel, Nicola. 1998. *Imperiled Innocents: Anthony Comstock and Family Reproduction in Victorian America*. Princeton, NJ: Princeton University Press.

Bekhuis, Hidde, Marcel Lubbers, and Ultee Wout. 2014. "A Macro-sociological Study into the Changes in the Popularity of Domestic, European, and American Pop Music in Western Countries." *European Sociological Review* 30(2): 80–193.

Bell, Daniel A. 2015. *The China Model: Political Meritocracy and the Limits of Democracy*. Princeton, NJ: Princeton University Press.

Bell, Daniel. 1973. *The Coming of Post-industrial Society. A Venture in Social Forecasting*. New York: Basic Books.

Bell, Ruth, and Clifford Russell., 2002. "Environmental Policy for Developing Countries," *Issues in Science and Technology* 18. http://issues.org/18-3/greenspan/.

Belyea, Ashley. 2011. "Thinking Outside the Blog: Women's Voices and a New Generation of Communications Technology." *Yale Journal of International Affairs* 6: 53–63.

Bem, S. L. 1974. "The Measurement of Psychological Androgyny." *Journal of Consulting and Clinical Psychology* 42: 155–62.

Bem, S. L. 1993. *The Lenses of Gender: Transforming the Debate on Sexual Inequality*. New Haven, CT: Yale University Press.

Benavot, Aaron, Yun-Kyun Cha, David Kamens, John W. Meyer, and Suk-Ying Wong. 1991. "Knowledge for the Masses: World Models and National Curricula: 1920–1987." *American Sociological Review* 56: 85–100.

Bendell, Jem, ed. 2009. *The Corporate Responsibility Movement*. Greenleaf Publishing, Sheffield.

Bendix, Reinhard. 1964. *Nation-Building and Citizenship: Studies of Our Changing Social Order*. New York: Wiley.

Bennett, Anthony J. 2013. *The Race for the White House from Reagan to Clinton: Reforming Old Systems, Building New Coalitions*. New York: Palgrave Macmillan.

Bennett, Tony, Mike Savage, Elizabeth Bortolaia Silva, Alan Warde, Modesto Gayo-Cal, and David Wright. 2009. *Culture, Class, Distinction*. New York: Routledge.

Bennett, W. Lance, Regina G. Lawrence, and Steven Livingston. 2008. *When the Press Fails: Political Power and the News Media from Iraq to Katrina*. Chicago: University of Chicago Press.

Bennett, W. Lance and Robert M. Entman. 2001. *Mediated Politics: Communication in the Future of Democracy*. Cambridge: Cambridge University Press.

Benson, Etienne. 2013. "The Urbanization of the Eastern Gray Squirrel in the United States." *The Journal of American History* 100(3): 691–710.

Benson, Michaela, and O'Reilly, Karen. 2009. "Migration and the Search for a Better Way of Life: A Critical Exploration of Lifestyle Migration." *The Sociological Review* 57(4): 608–25.

Benson, Rodney. 2009. "What Makes News More Multiperspectival? A Field Analysis." *Poetics* 37 (5–6): 402–18.

Benson, Rodney. 2010. "Futures of the News." In *New Media, Old News: Journalism and Democracy in the Digital Age*, ed. N. Fenton. Thousand Oaks, CA: SAGE Publications.

Benson, Rodney, and Daniel C. Hallin. 2007. "How States, Markets and Globalization Shape the News: The French and US National Press, 1965–97." *European Journal of Communication* 22(1): 27–48. http://ejc.sagepub.com/content/22/1/27.

Berg, Justin. 2012. "Opposition to Pro-immigrant Public Policy: Symbolic Racism and Group Threat." *Sociological Inquiry* 83: 1–31.

Berger, Peter. 1967. *The Sacred Canopy: Elements of a Sociological Theory of Religion*. New York: Penguin.

Berger, Peter, ed. 1999. *The Desecularization of the World*. Washington, DC: Eerdmans.

Berk, Ronald. 2005. "Survey of 12 Strategies to Measure Teaching Effectiveness," *International Journal of Teaching and Learning in Higher Education* 17: 48–62.

Berk, Sarah Fenstermaker. 1985. *The Gender Factory: The Apportionment of Work in American Households*. New York: Plenum.

Berman, Eli. 2009. *Radical, Religious, and Violent: The New Economics of Terrorism*. Cambridge, MA: MIT Press.

Berman, Elizabeth. 2012. *Creating the Market University: How Academic Science Became an Economic Engine*. Princeton, NJ: Princeton University Press.

Bertrand, Natasha. 2015. "'Fifty Shades of Grey' Started Out as 'Twilight' Fan Fiction before Becoming an International Phenomenon." *Business Insider*. http://www.businessinsider.com/fifty-shades-of-grey-started-out-as-twilight-fan-fiction-2015-2.

Berwick, Carly. 2015, November 3. "The Great German School Turnaround." *The Atlantic*. https://www.theatlantic.com/education/archive/2015/11/great-german-scool-turnaround/413806/.

Bhambra, Gurminder K. 2009. "Postcolonial Europe : Or, Understanding Europe in Times of the Post-Colonial." In *The SAGE Handbook of European Studies*, ed. C. Rumford (pp. 69–86). Los Angeles: SAGE.

Bianchi, Suzanne M., Liana C. Sayer, Melissa A. Milkie, and John P. Robinson. 2012. "Housework: Who Did, Does or Will Do It, and How Much Does It Matter?, *Social Forces* 91(1): 55–63.

Bianchi, S., L. Subaiya, and J. Kahn. 1999. "The Gender Gap in the Economic Well-Being of Nonresident Fathers and Custodial Mothers." *Demography* 36: 195–203.

Bibbins-Domingo, K., and A. Fernandez. 2007. "BiDil for Heart Failure in Black Patients: Implications of the U.S. Food and Drug Administration Approval." *Annals of Internal Medicine* 146(1): 52–56.

Biblarz, Timothy J., and Evren Savci. 2010. "Lesbian, Gay, Bisexual, and Transgender Families." *Journal of Marriage and Family* 72(3): 480–97. http://www.jstor.org/stable/40732492.

Bidwell, Allie. 2014, February 5. "STEM Job Market Much Larger Than Previously Reported." *U.S. News & World Report*. https://www.usnews.com/news/stem-solutions/articles/2014/02/05/report-stem-job-market-much-larger-than-previously-reported.

Bittman, M., P. England, L. Sayer, N. Folbre, and G. Matheson. 2003. "When Does Gender Trump Money? Bargaining and Time in Household Work." *American Journal of Sociology* 109: 186–214.

Black, Sandra E., and Paul J. Devereux. 2011. "Recent Developments in Intergenerational Mobility." In *Handbook of Labor Economics, Vol. 4B*, eds. Orley

Ashenfelter and David Card (pp. 1487–1541). Amsterdam: North Holland.

Black, Sandra, Paul Devereux, and Kjell Salvanes. 2005. "The More the Merrier? The Effects of Family Size and Birth Order on Children's Education." *The Quarterly Journal of Economics* 120(2): 669–700.

Blair-Loy, Mary, and Stacey J. Williams. 2013. "Male Model of Career." In *Sociology of Work: An Encyclopedia,* ed. Vicki Smith (pp. 550–53). Thousand Oaks, CA: SAGE.

Blau, Francine D., and Lawrence M. Kahn. 2017. "The Gender Wage Gap: Extent, Trends, and Explanations." *Journal of Economic Literature* 55(3), 789–865.

Blau, Peter, and Otis Dudley Duncan 1967. *The American Occupational Structure.* New York: Wiley.

Blossfeld, Hans-Peter. 1986. "Career Opportunities in the Federal Republic of Germany: A Dynamic Approach to the Study of Life Course, Cohort, and Period Effects." *European Sociological Review* 2: 208–25.

Blum, Ben. 2018. "The Lifespan of a Lie." *Medium.* https://medium.com/s/trustissues/the-lifespan-of-a-lie-d869212b1f62.

Blumberg, Rae, ed. 1991. *Gender, Family, and Economy: The Triple Overlap.* Newbury Park, CA: SAGE.

Blumer, Herbert. 1968. *Symbolic Interactionism: Perspective and Method.* Berkeley, CA: University of California Press.

Bobo, Lawrence, and Camille L. Zubrinsky. 1996. "Attitudes on Residential Integration: Perceived Status Differences, Mere In-Group Preference, or Racial Prejudice?" *Social Forces* 74(3): 883–909. doi:10.2307/2580385.

Bockerman, Petri, and Pekka Ilmakunnas. 2012. "The Job Satisfaction–Productivity Nexus: A Study Using Matched Survey and Register Data." *Industrial & Labor Relations Review* 65: 244–62.

Boczkowski, Pablo. 2010. *News at Work: Imitation in an Age of Information Abundance.* Chicago: University of Chicago Press.

Boli, John, Francisco Ramirez, and John Meyer. 1985. "Explaining the Origins and Expansion of Mass Education." *Comparative Education Review* 29: 145–70.

Bond, Paul. 2016, February 29. "Leslie Moonves on Donald Trump: 'It May Not Be Good for America, but It's Damn Good for CBS.'" *Hollywood Reporter.*

Bonilla-Silva, Eduardo [2003] 2018. *Racism without Racists: Color-Blind Racism and the Persistence of Inequality in America.* Lanham, MD: Rowman and Littlefield.

Boorstin, Daniel J. 1961. *The Image: A Guide to Pseudo-events in America.* New York: Vintage.

Borkum, Jared. 2016, June 9. "Local Content Quotas on TV Are Global—They Just Don't Work Everywhere." *The Conversation.* https://theconversation.com/local-content-quotas-on-tv-are-global-they-just-dont-work-everywhere-60656.

Bound, John, Sarah Turner, and Patrick Walsh, 2009. "Internationalization of US Doctorate Education." NBER Working Paper No. 14792. https://www.nber.org/papers/w14792.

Bourdieu, Pierre. 1984. *Distinction: A Social Critique of the Judgement of Taste.* Cambridge, MA: Harvard University Press.

Bourdieu, Pierre. 1986. "The forms of capital." Pp. 241-258 in Richardson, J., *Handbook of Theory and Research for the Sociology of Education.* Westport, CT: Greenwood.

Bourdieu, Pierre. 1998. *The State Nobility: Elite Schools in the Field of Power.* Stanford, CA: Stanford University Press.

Bourdieu, Pierre. 2000. *The Weight of the World. Social Suffering in Contemporary Society.* Stanford, CA: Stanford University Press.

Bourdieu, Pierre. 2010. *Sociology Is a Martial Art: Political Writings by Pierre Bourdieu.* New York: New Press.

Bourdieu, Pierre, and Jean Claude Passeron. 1979. *The Inheritors: French Students and Their Relation to Culture.* Chicago: University of Chicago Press.

Bourdieu, Pierre, and Jean Claude Passeron. 1990. *Reproduction in Education, Society and Culture.* Newbury Park, CA: SAGE.

Bowles, Samuel, Herbert Gintis, and Melissa Groves, eds. 2008. *Unequal Chances: Family Background and Economic Success.* Princeton, NJ: Princeton University Press.

Bowman, Karlyn. 2017, January 13. "Interracial Marriage: Changing Laws, Minds, and Hearts," *Forbes.* https://www.forbes.com/sites/bowmanmarsico/2017/01/13/interracial-marriage-changing-laws-minds-and-hearts/#ecd5ee67c597.

boyd, dana. 2018. "Media Manipulation, Strategic Amplification, and Responsible Journalism." Presentation at the Online News Association conference, Austin, Texas.

Bozick, Robert. 2009. "Job Opportunities, Economic Resources, and the Postsecondary Destinations of American Youth." *Demography* 46: 493–512.

Brake, Mike. 2013. *The Sociology of Youth Culture and Youth Subcultures: Sex and Drugs and Rock 'n' Roll.* New York: Routledge.

Brandt, Allan M. 2012. "Inventing Conflicts of Interest: A History of Tobacco Industry Tactics." *American Journal of Public Health* 102(1): 63–71.

Brenner, Philip. 2016. "Cross-National Trends in Religious Service Attendance," *Public Opinion Quarterly* 80: 563–83.

Broadhurst, Roderic, Peter Grabosky, Mamoun Alazab, and Steve Chon. 2014. "Organizations and Cyber crime: An Analysis of the Nature of Groups Engaged in Cyber Crime." *International Journal of Cyber Criminology* 8 (1): 1–20.

Brooks, Arthur. 2003. "Religious Faith and Charitable Giving." *Policy Review* 121: 39–48.

Brooks, Clem. 2014. "Introduction: Voting Behavior and Elections in Context." *The Sociological Quarterly* 55: 587–95.

Brooks, Roy L. 1994. "Critical Race Theory: A Proposed Structure and Application to Federal Pleading." *Harvard BlackLetter Law Journal* 11: 85–113.

Brown, Simon. 2015. "Crowdsourcing Social Research." Technology Research Stream. Social Science Matrix. University of California, Berkeley. http://matrix.berkeley.edu/research/crowdsourcing-social-research.

Brubaker, Rogers. 1992. *Citizenship and Nationhood in France and Germany.* Cambridge, MA: Harvard University Press.

Brubaker, Rogers. 2005. "The 'Diaspora' Diaspora." *Ethnic and Racial Studies* 28: 1–19.

Brulle, Robert. 2010. "From Environmental Campaigns to Advancing the Public Dialog: Environmental Communication for Civic Engagement." *Environmental Communication* 4: 82–98.

Bryc, Katarzyna, Eric Y. Durand, J. Michael Macpherson, David Reich, and Joanna L. Mountain. 2015. "The Genetic Ancestry of African Americans, Latinos, and European Americans across the United States." *The American Journal of Human Genetics* 96(1): 37–53.

Buckles, Kasey, and Elizabeth Munnich. 2012, Summer. "Birth Spacing and Sibling Outcomes." *Journal of Human Resources* 47(3): 613–642.

Budig, Michelle, and Paula England. 2001. "The Wage Penalty for Motherhood," *American Sociological Review* 66: 204–25.

Burawoy, Michael. 1998. "The Extended Case Method." *Sociological Theory* 16: 4–33.

Burawoy, Michael. 2005. "2004 American Sociological Association Presidential Address: For Public Sociology." *British Journal of Sociology* 56: 259–94.

Burdick, Kailee, Areeba Kara, Patricia Ebright, and Julie Meek. 2017. "Bedside Interprofessional Rounding. The View from the Patient's Side of the Bed." *Journal of Patient Experience* 4(1): 22–27.

Bureau of Justice Statistics. 2019. "Victims of Identity Theft, 2016." https://www.bjs.gov/index.cfm?ty=pbdetail&iid=6467.

Burning Glass. 2014, February. "Real-Time Insight into the Market for Entry-Level STEM Jobs." http://burning-glass.com/wp-content/uploads/Real-Time-Insight-Into-The-Market-For-Entry-Level-STEM-Jobs.pdf.

Burrows, R., Webber, R., and Atkinson, R. 2017. Welcome to 'Pikettyville'? Mapping London's alpha territories. *The Sociological Review*, 65(2):184–201.

Burt, Martha, Laudan Aron, Edgar Lee, and Jesse Valente. 2001. *Helping America's Homeless: Emergency Shelter or Affordable Housing?* Washington, DC: Urban Institute Press.

Burt, Ronald. 1995. *Structural Holes: The Social Structure of Competition.* Cambridge, MA: Harvard University Press.

Busse, Reinhard and Annette Riesberg. 2004. *A Health care systems in transition: Germany.* Copenhagen, WHO Regional Office for Europe on behalf of the European Observatory on Health Systems and Policies.

Butler, J. (2006). *Gender Trouble: Feminism and the Subversion of Identity.* New York: Routledge.

Caiola, C., S. Docherty, M. Relf, and J. Barroso. 2014. "Using an Intersectional Approach To Study the Impact of Social Determinants of Health for African-American Mothers Living with HIV." *Advances in Nursing Science* 37(4): 287–98.

Camacho, Keith L. 2016. "Filipinos, Pacific Islanders, and the American Empire." In *The Oxford Handbook of Asian American History*, eds. David K. Yoo and Eiichiro Azuma. New York: Oxford University Press. http://www.oxfordhandbooks.com/view/10.1093/oxfordhb/9780199860463.001.0001/oxfordhb-9780199860463-e-8.

Campbell, Don. 1997. *The Mozart Effect: Tapping the Power of Music to Heal the Body, Strengthen the Mind, and Unlock the Creative Spirit.* New York: Avon Books.

Campbell, Don. 2000. *Mozart Effect for Children: Awakening Your Child's Mind, Health & Creativity with Music*. New York: William Morrow.

Carleton, Cheryl. 2014, February 13. "Why We Pay Teachers, Secretaries, and Home Health Aides So Little." *Business Insider*. https://www.businessinsider.com/low-pay-caring-industry-2014-2.

Carney, Stephen, Jeremy Rappleye, and Iveta Silova. 2012. "Between Faith and Science: World Culture Theory and Comparative Education." *Comparative Education Review* 56: 336–93.

Carrin, Guy, and Chris James. 2005. "Social Health Insurance: Key Factors Affecting the Transition Towards Universal Coverage." *International Social Security Review* 58 (1): 45–64.

Carrington, Daisy. 2013, June 3. "Iran Tightens Grip on Cyberspace with 'Halal Internet.'" CNN. http://www.cnn.com/2013/06/03/world/meast/iran-internet-restrictions-halal-internet/index.html.

Carson, E. Ann, and Daniela Golinelli. 2013, December. "Prisoners in 2012," Bureau of Justice Statistics. http://www.bjs.gov/content/pub/pdf/p12tar9112.pdf.

Carver, Lisa F., Afshin Vafaei, Ricardo Guerra, Aline Freire, and Susan P. Phillips. 2013. "Gender Differences: Examination of the 12-item Bem Sex Role Inventory (BSRI-12) in an Older Brazilian Population." *Plos ONE* 8: e76356. https://journals.plos.org/plosone/article?id=10.1371/journal.pone.0076356.

Casanova, Jose, 1994. *Public Religions in the Modern World*. Chicago: University of Chicago Press.

Cashin, S. 2005. *The Failures of Integration: How Race and Class Are Undermining the American Dream*. New York: Public Affairs.

Castells, Manuel. 1984. *The City and the Grassroots*. Berkeley, CA: University of California Press.

Castells, Manuel. 1999. *The Information Age*. New York: Blackwell Press.

Castells, Manuel. 2001. *The Internet Galaxy*. New York: Oxford University Press.

Center for Constitutional Rights. 2009. "Racial Disparity in NYPD Stops-and-Frisks: The Center for Constitutional Rights Preliminary Report on UF-250 Data from 2005 through June 2008." https://ccrjustice.org/sites/default/files/assets/Report-CCR-NYPD-Stop-and-Frisk_3.pdf.

Center for Responsive Politics. n.d. "Lobbying Database." https://www.opensecrets.org/lobby.

Centers for Disease Control. 2019a. Measles (Rubeoloa). Cases and Outbreaks. https://www.cdc.gov/measles/cases-outbreaks.html.

Centers for Disease Control. 2019b. Pertussis (Whooping Cough). Surveillance and Reporting. Trends. https://www.cdc.gov/pertussis/surv-reporting.html#trends.

Centers for Disease Control and Prevention. 2013, December. "U.S. Public Study Health Service Syphilis Study at Tuskegee." http://www.cdc.gov/tuskegee/index.html.

Champagne, Duane. 2008. "From First Nations to Self-Government: A Political Legacy of Indigenous Nations in the United States." Special Issue on Indigenous Peoples: Struggles Against Globalization and Domination, eds. James V. Fenelon and Salvador J. Murguia. *American Behavioral Scientist* 51(13): 1672–93.

Chandralal, Lalith, and Fredy-Roberto Valenzuela, 2013. "Exploring Memorable Tourism Experiences: Antecedents and Behavioral Outcomes." *Journal of Economics, Business and Management* 1: 177–81.

Chase-Dunn, Christopher, Yukio Kawano, and Benjamin Brewer. 2000. "Trade Globalization since 1795: Waves of Integration in the World-System." *American Sociological Review* 65: 77–95.

Chaves, Mark. 1994. "Secularization as Declining Religious Authority." *Social Forces* 72(3): 749–74. doi:10.2307/2579779.

Chaves, Mark. 2017. *American Religion: Contemporary Trends*. Princeton, NJ: Princeton University Press.

Chaves, Mark, and Alison J. Eagle. 2016. "Congregations and Social Services: An Update from the Third Wave of the National Congregations Study." *Religions* 7: 55.

Chawla, Sandeep, Anja Korenblik, Suzanne Kunnen, Thibault Le Pichon, Aruna Nathwani, Thomas Pietschmann, Wolfgang Rhomberg, Ali Saadeddin, Johny Thomas, and Melissa Tullis. 2005. *World Drug Report 2005: Volume 1: Analysis(Report)*. United Nations Office on Drugs and Crime.

Chawla, Sandeep, Justice Tettey, Beate Hammond, Matthew Nice, Barbara Remberg, Angela Me, Coen Bussink, Phil Davis, Kamran Niaz, Preethi Perera, Catherine Pysden, Martin Raithelhuber, Anousha Renner, Ali Saadeddin, Antoine Vella, Thibault le Pichon, Hakan Demirbüken, Raggie Johansen, Anja Korenblik, Suzanne Kunnen, Kristina Kuttnig, Ted Leggett, Hayder Mili, and Thomas Pietschmann. 2010. *World Drug Report 2010*. United Nations Office on Drugs and Crime.

Chen, Feinian. 2009. "Family Division in China's Transitional Economy." *Population Studies* 63: 53–69.

Chen, Stephanie. 2011, January 3. "Hitting Up the Family Bank." *CNN*. http://www.cnn.com/2011/LIVING/01/03/borrow.money.family.bank/.

Chen, Te-Ping, and Miriam Jordan. 2016, May 1. "Why So Many Chinese Students Come to the US." *Wall Street Journal*. http://www.wsj.com/articles/why-so-many-chinese-students-come-to-the-u-s-1462123552.

Cheng, Simon, and Brian Powell. 2015. "Measurement, Methods, and Divergent Patterns: Reassessing the Effects of Same-Sex Parents." *Social Science Research* 52: 615–26.

Cherlin, Andrew, and Frank F. Furstenberg, Jr. 1988. "The Changing European Family: Lessons for the American Reader." *Journal of Family Issues* 9(3):291–97. doi:10.1177/019251388009003001.

Chetty, Raj, Nathaniel Hendren, Patrick Cline, and Emmanuel Saez. 2014. "Where Is the Land of Opportunity? The Geography of Intergenerational Mobility in the United States." *The Quarterly Journal of Economics* 129: 1553–1623.

Childs, Dennis. 2015. *Slaves of the State: Black Incarceration from the Chain Gang to the Penitentiary.* Minneapolis: University of Minnesota Press.

Childs, Erica. 2005. *Navigating Interracial Borders: Black-White Couples and their Social Worlds.* New Brunswick, NJ: Rutgers University Press.

Chin, Christine B. N. 2013. *Cosmopolitan Sex Workers: Women and Migration in a Global City.* New York: Oxford University Press.

Chin, J., Senter, M. S., and Spalter-Roth, R. 2011. "Love to Teach, but Hate Assessment?" *Teaching Sociology* 39(2): 120–26. https://doi.org/10.1177/0092055X11401562.

Chomsky, Noam. 2006. *Language and Mind.* New York: Cambridge University Press.

Choo, Hae Yeon, and Myra Marx Ferree. 2010. "Practicing Intersectionality in Sociological Research: A Critical Analysis of Inclusions, Interactions, and Institutions in the Study of Inequalities." *Sociological Theory* 28(3): 129–49.

Chou, Rosalind S., and Joe R. Feagin. 2008. *Myth of the Model Minority: Asian Americans Facing Racism,* 2nd ed. Boulder, CO: Paradigm Publishers.

Christakis, Nicholas, and James Fowler. 2009. *Connected.* New York: Little, Brown.

Chung, Angie. 2007. *Legacies of Struggle: Conflict and Cooperation in Korean-American Politics.* Stanford, CA: Stanford University Press.

Clark, Jenna L., Sara B. Algoe, and Melanie C. Green. 2017. "Social Network Sites and Well-Being: The Role of Social Connection." *Current Directions in Psychological Science* 27(1): 32–37.

Clark, R., and Filinson, R. (2011). "Kicking and Screaming: How One Truculent Sociology Department Made Peace with Mandatory Assessment." *Teaching Sociology* 39(2): 127–37. https://doi.org/10.1177/0092055X11400439.

Clarke, Matt. 2013, January. "Dramatic Increase in Percentage of Criminal Cases Being Plea Bargained." *Prison News*, p. 20. https://www.prisonlegalnews.org/news/2013/jan/15/dramatic-increase-in-percentage-of-criminal-cases-being-plea-bargained.

Clarke, Tainya C., Lindsey I. Black, Barbara J. Stussman, Patricia M. Barnes, and Richard L. Nahin. 2015, February 9. "Trends in the Use of Complementary Health Approaches among Adults: United States." *National Center for Health Statistics Reports* 95.

Clear, Todd. 1994. *Harm in American Penology: Offenders, Victims, and Their Communities.* Albany, NY: State University of New York Press.

Cohen, Barney. 2006. "Urbanization in Developing Countries: Current Trends, Future Projections, and Key Challenges for Sustainability." *Technology in Society* 28: 63–80.

Cohen, Philip. 2014. *The Family: Diversity, Inequality, and Social Change.* New York: W. W. Norton.

Cohen, Stanley. 2002. *Folk Devils and Moral Panics: The Creation of the Mods and Rockers.* New York: Routledge.

Cohn, Carol. 1987. "Within and Without: Women, Gender, and Theory." *Signs* 12: 687–718.

Cohn, D'Vera. 2015, June 18. "Census Considers New Approach to Asking About Race—By Not Using the Term at All." Pew Research Center. http://www.pewresearch.org/fact-tank/2015/06/18/census-considers-new-approach-to-asking-about-race-by-not-using-the-term-at-all/.

Cohn, D'Vera, Jeffrey Passel, Wendy Wang, and Gretchen Livingston. 2011, December 14. "Barely Half of US Adults Are Married—A Record Low." Pew Research Center Social and Demographic Trends. http://www.pewsocialtrends.org/2011/12/14/barely-half-of-u-s-adults-are-married-a-record-low/.

Coleman, James Samuel. 1996. *Equality of Educational Opportunity.* Washington, DC: US Department of Health, Education, and Welfare, Office of Education.

Coleman, M., M. A. Fine, L. H. Ganong, K. J. M. Downs, and N. Pauk. 2001. "When You're Not the Brady Bunch: Identifying Perceived Conflicts and

Resolution Strategies in Stepfamilies." *Personal Relationships* 8: 55–73.

Colley, A., G. Mulhern, J. Maltby, and A. M. Wood. 2009. "The Short Form BSRI: Instrumentality, Expressiveness and Gender Associations among a United Kingdom Sample." *Personality and Individual Differences* 46: 384–87.

Collins, Randall. 2011. "Credential Inflation and the Future of Universities." *Italian Journal of Sociology of Education* 2: 228–51.

Colomer, Josep. 2016, December 11. "The Electoral College Is a Medieval Relic. Only the US Still Has One." *Washington Post.* https://www.washingtonpost.com/news/monkey-cage/wp/2016/12/11/the-electoral-college-is-a-medieval-relic-only-the-u-s-still-has-one/?noredirect=on&utm_term=.14d6f2affdb5.

Common Sense Media. 2016a. "Media Use by Tweens and Teens." San Francisco, CA: Common Sense Media Inc. https://www.commonsensemedia.org/research/the-common-sense-census-media-use-by-tweens-and-teens.

Common Sense Media. 2016b. "Plugged-in Parents of Tweens and Teens." San Francisco, CA: Common Sense Media Inc. https://www.commonsensemedia.org/research/the-common-sense-census-plugged-in-parents-of-tweens-and-teens-2016.

Community Speedwatch. n.d. https://www.communityspeedwatch.org/FRONT-Main.php?m=0.

Comte, Auguste, Harriet Martineau, and Frederic Harrison. 1896. *The Positive Philosophy of Auguste Comte.* London: G. Bell & Sons.

Conk, M. A. 1978. "Occupational Classification in the United States Census: 1870–1940." *The Journal of Interdisciplinary History* 9(1): 111–30.

Conk, M. A. 1989. "Accuracy and Efficiency and Bias: The Interpretation of Women's Work in the U.S. Census of Occupations, 1890–1940." *Historical Methods* 14(2), 65–72.

Conley, Dalton. 2001. "Capital for College: Parental Assets and Postsecondary Schooling." *Sociology of Education* 74: 59–72.

Conley, Dalton, 2005. *The Pecking Order: Which Siblings Succeed and Why.* New York: Pantheon Books.

Connell, R. W. 1987. *Gender and Power: Society, the Person and Sexual Politics.* Stanford, CA: Stanford University Press.

Connell, Raewyn. 1995. *Masculinities.* Berkeley: University of California Press.

Conrad, Peter. 1975. "The Discovery of Hyperkinesis: Notes on the Medicalization of Deviant Behavior." *Social Problems* 23(1): 12–21.

Conrad, Peter. 2006. "Introduction to Expanded Edition." *Identifying Hyperactive Children: The Medicalization of Deviant Behavior*, Expanded ed. Aldershot, UK: Ashgate.

Conrad, Peter. 2007. *The Medicalization of Society: On the Transformation of Human Conditions into Treatable Disorders.* Baltimore: Johns Hopkins University Press.

Conrad, Peter, Joseph W. Schneider, and Joseph R. Gusfield. 1992. *Deviance and Medicalization: From Badness to Sickness.* Philadelphia: Temple University Press.

Contreras, Randol. 2012. *The Stickup Kids: Race, Drugs, Violence, and the American Dream.* Berkeley: University of California Press.

Cook, John, Naomi Oreskes, Peter T. Doran, William R. L. Anderegg, Bart Verheggen, Ed W. Maibach, J. Stuart Carlton, Stephan Lewandowsky, Andrew G. Skuce, Sarah A Green, Dana Nuccitelli, Peter Jacobs, Mark Richardson, Bärbel Winkler, Rob Painting, and Ken Rice. 2016, April 13. "Consensus on Consensus: A Synthesis of Consensus Estimates on Human-Caused Global Warming." *Environmental Research Letters* 11(4): 1–7. doi:10.1088/1748–9326/11/4/048002.

Cook, Karen S., Toshio Yamagishi, Coye Cheshire, Robin Cooper, Masafumi Matsuda, and Rie Mashima. 2005. "Trust Building via Risk Taking: A Cross-Societal Experiment." *Social Psychology Quarterly* 68: 121–42.

Cooley, Charles Horton. [1922] 2012. *Human Nature and the Social Order.* Lenox, MA: HardPress Publishing.

Copen, C. E., K. Daniels, and W. D. Mosher. 2013. "First Premarital Cohabitation in the United States: 2006–2010 National Survey of Family Growth (National Health Statistics Reports, No. 64)." Hyattsville, MD: National Center for Health Statistics.

Corning, Peter A. 1969. "Chapter 2: The Second Round—1927–1940." In *The Evolution of Medicare: From Idea to Law.* Washington, DC: Office of Research and Statistics, Social Security Administration. OCLC 25869. https://www.ssa.gov/history/corningchap2.html.

Cornwell, Erin, and Linda Waite. 2009. "Social Disconnectedness, Perceived Isolation, and Health among Adults." *Journal of Health and Social Behavior* 50: 31–48.

Corsaro, William. 2005. *The Sociology of Childhood*, 2nd ed. Newbury Park, CA: Pine Forge Press.

Corse, Sarah M. 1997. *Nationalism and Literature: The Politics of Culture in Canada and the United States.* Cambridge, UK: Cambridge University Press.

Coser, Lewis A. 1977. *Masters of Sociological Thought: Ideas in Historical and Social Context.* New York: Harcourt Brace Jovanovich.

Crank, John. 2004. *Understanding Police Culture*, 2nd ed. New York: Routledge.

Crenshaw, Kimberlé. 2016. "The Urgency of Inter-sectionality." TEDWomen 2016. https://www.ted.com/talks/kimberle_crenshaw_the_urgency_of_intersectionality.

Crenshaw, Kimberlé, Neil Gotanda, Garry Peller, and Kendall Thomas. 1996. *Critical Race Theory: The Key Writings That Formed the Movement.* New York: New Press.

Crimmins, Eileen M., Mark D. Hayward, and Teresa E. Seeman. 2004. "Race/Ethnicity, Socioeconomic Status, and Health in Critical Perspectives on Racial and Ethnic Differences in Health in Late Life." In *Panel on Race, Ethnicity, and Health in Later Life*, ed. N. B. Anderson, R. A. Bulatao, and B. Cohen (pp. 310-352). Washington, DC: National Academies Press.

Crockett, Jason L., Albert S. Fu, Joleen L. Green-wood, and Mauricia A. John. 2018. "Integrated Sociology Program Assessment: Inclusion of a Senior Portfolio Graduation Requirement." *Teaching Sociology* 46(1): 34–43. https://doi.org/10.1177/0092055X17726833.

Crowder, Kyle, and Liam Downey. 2010. "Inter-Neighborhood Migration, Race, and Environmental Hazards: Modeling Micro-Level Processes of Environmental Inequality." *American Journal of Sociology* 115: 1110–1149.

Culver, Stephen. 2010. "Course Grades, Quality of Student Engagement, and Students' Evaluation of Instructor." *International Journal of Teaching and Learning in Higher Education* 22: 331–36.

Curry, Jennifer, Christopher Belser, and Ian Binns. 2013. "Integrating Postsecondary College and Career Options in the Middle Level Curriculum," *Middle School Journal* 44: 26–32.

Cyphers, Luke, and Ethan Trex. 2011, September 19. "The History of the National Anthem in Sports." *ESPN The Magazine.* http://espn.go.com/espn/story/_/id/6957582.

D'Addario, Daniel. 2014, March 4. "'The Bachelor' Host on Why There'll Never Be a Gay Bachelor: 'Is It a Good Business Decision?'" *Salon.* https://www.salon.com/2014/03/04/the_bachelor_host_on_why_therell_never_be_a_gay_bachelor_is_it_a_good_business_decision/.

Dahl, Robert Alan. 1989. *Democracy and Its Critics.* New Haven, CT: Yale University Press.

Dallek, Robert. 1998. *Flawed Giant: Lyndon Johnson and His Times, 1961–1973.* Oxford, UK: Oxford University Press.

Damian, Rodica, and Brent Roberts. 2015. "Settling the Debate on Birth Order and Personality," *PNAS* 112(46): 14119–20.

Danielian, Lucig, and Stephen Reese. 1989. "A Closer Look at Intermedia Influences On Agenda Setting: The Cocaine Issue of 1986." In *Communication Campaigns about Drugs: Government, Media, and the Public* (pp. 47–66). Hillsdale, NJ: Erlbaum.

Davidson, Adam. 2014, June 20. "It's Official: The Boomerang Kids Won't Leave." *New York Times.* https://www.nytimes.com/2014/06/22/magazine/its-official-the-boomerang-kids-wont-leave.html?_r=1.

Davis, Angela. 2001. *The Prison Industrial Complex* (audio CD). Chico, CA: AK Press.

Davis, Kingsley, and Wilbur E. Moore. 1945. "Some Principles of Stratification." *American Sociological Review* 10: 242–49.

Dayan, Daniel, and Elihu Katz. 1992. *Media Events: The Live Broadcasting of History.* Cambridge, MA: Harvard University Press.

De Graaf, N. D., P. De Graaf, and G. Kraaykamp. 2000. "Parental Cultural Capital and Educational Attainment in the Netherlands: A Refinement of the Cultural Capital Perspective." *Sociology of Education* 73: 92–111.

De La Rey, C. 2005. "Gender, Women and Leadership." *Agenda: Empowering Women for Gender Equity* 65: 4–11. http://www.jstor.org/stable/4066646.

De Nardi, M., E. French, J. Jones, and J. McCauley. 2016. "Medical Spending of the US Elderly." *Fiscal Studies* 37: 717–47.

Deegan, Mary Jo. 1990. "Review of *The Chicago School: A Liberal Critique of Capitalism*; Myths of the Chicago School of Sociology." *British Journal of Sociology* 41: 587–90.

Deegan, Mary Jo. 1991. *Women in Sociology: A Bio-Bibliographical Sourcebook.* New York: Greenwood.

Deegan, Mary Jo. 2002. *Race, Hull-House, and the University of Chicago: A New Conscience against Ancient Evils.* Westport, CT: Praeger.

Deegan, Mary Jo. 2007. "The Chicago School of Ethnography." In *Handbook of Ethnography* (pp. 11–25). Thousand Oaks, CA: SAGE.

Deegan, Mary Jo. 2014. *Annie Marion MacLean and the Chicago Schools of Sociology, 1894–1934.* New Brunswick, NJ: Transaction Publishers.

Delmas, Magali. 2016. "Research: Who's Lobbying Congress on Climate Change." *Harvard Business Review*. https://hbr.org/2016/10/research-whos-lobbying-congress-on-climate-change.

Delmas, Magali, Jinghui Lim, and Nicholas Nairn-Birch. 2015. "Corporate Environmental Performance and Lobbying." *Academy of Management Discoveries* 2: 175–97.

Demby, Gene. 2016, March 2. "Combing through 41 Million Tweets to Show How #BlackLivesMatter Exploded." *NPR Code Switch*. http://www.npr.org/sections/codeswitch/2016/03/02/468704888/combing-through-41-million-tweets-to-show-how-blacklivesmatter-explode.

Demerath, N. Jay III, and Yonghe Yang. 1997. "What American Culture War? A View from the Trenches as Opposed to the Command Posts and the Press Corps." In *Cultural Wars in American Politics* (pp. 17–38). Hawthorne, NY: Aldine de Gruyter.

Devers, Lindsay. 2011. "Plea and Charge Bargaining. Research Summary." Bureau of Justice Assistance, US Department of Justice. https://www.bja.gov/Publications/PleaBargainingResearchSummary.pdf.

Dewan, Shaila, and Robert Gebeloff. 2012, May 21. "More Men Enter Fields Dominated by Women." *New York Times*. https://www.nytimes.com/2012/05/21/business/increasingly-men-seek-success-in-jobs-dominated-by-women.html.

Dhaouadi, Mahmoud. 1990. "Ibn Khaldun: The Founding Father of Eastern Sociology." *International Sociology* 5: 319–35.

Diamond, Anna. 2016, November 17. "South Korea's Testing Fixation," *The Atlantic*. https://www.theatlantic.com/education/archive/2016/11/south-korean-seniors-have-been-preparing-for-today-since-kindergarten/508031/.

DiMaggio, Paul. 1982. "Cultural Capital and School Success: The Impact of Status Culture Participation on the Grades of US High School Students." *American Sociological Review* 47: 189–201.

DiMaggio, Paul, Manish Nag, and David Blei. 2013. "Exploiting Affinities between Topic Modeling and the Sociological Perspective on Culture: Application to Newspaper Coverage of U.S. Government Arts Funding." *Poetics* 41: 570–606.

Doherty, Brian, and Timothy Doyle. 2006. "Beyond Borders: Transnational Politics, Social Movements, and Modern Environmentalisms." *Environmental Politics* 15: 697–12.

Domhoff, G. William. 2013. *Who Rules America? The Triumph of the Corporate Rich*, 7th ed. New York: McGraw-Hill.

Donaldson, M. 1993. "What Is Hegemonic Masculinity?" *Theory & Society, 22*(5), 643–57.

Doniger, Wendy. 2013. *On Hinduism*. New Dehli: Aleph Book Company.

Dordick, Gwendolyn. 1997. *Something Left To Lose: Personal Relations and Survival among New York's Homeless*. Philadelphia: Temple University Press.

Doyle, Aaron, Randy Lippert, and David Lyon. 2012. *Eyes Everywhere: The Global Growth of Camera Surveillance*. New York: Routledge.

Drake, St. Clair, and Horace R. Cayton. [1945] 1993. *Black Metropolis: A Study of Negro Life in a Northern City*. Chicago: University of Chicago Press.

Drescher, J. 2015. "Out of DSM: Depathologizing Homosexuality." *Behavioral Sciences* 5(4), 565–75. http://doi.org/10.3390/bs5040565.

Drori, G. S., J. W. Meyer, F. O. Ramirez, and E. Schofer. 2003. *Science in the Modern World Polity*. Stanford, CA: Stanford University Press.

Drye, Willie. 2017, November 30. "2017 Hurricane Season Was the Most Expensive in US History." *National Geographic*. https://news.nationalgeographic.com/2017/11/2017-hurricane-season-most-expensive-us-history-spd/.

Du Bois, W. E. B. 1903. "The Talented Tenth." In *The Negro Problem: A Series of Articles by Representative American Negroes of To-Day*, ed. Booker T. Washington (pp. 31–75). New York: James Pott & Co.

Du Bois, W. E. B. 1935. *Black Reconstruction in America 1860–1880*. New York: Simon & Schuster.

Du Bois, W. E. B. 1947. *The World and Africa: An Inquiry into the Part Which Africa Has Played in World History*. New York: Viking.

Du Bois, W. E. B. [1899] 1967 *The Philadelphia Negro: A Social Study*. New York: Schocken Books.

Du Bois, W. E. B. [1903] 1994. *The Souls of Black Folk*. New York: Dover Publications.

Duneier, Mitchell. 1992. *Slim's Table: Race, Respectability, and Masculinity*. Chicago: University of Chicago Press.

Duneier, Mitchell. 2000. *Sidewalk*. New York: Farrar, Straus and Giroux.

Dunlap, Riley E., and Aaron M. McCright. 2015. "Challenging Climate Change: The Denial Countermovement." In *Climate Change and Society: Sociological Perspectives (Report of the ASA Task Force on Sociology and Global Climate Change)*, eds. R. E. Dunlap and R. J. Brulle (pp. 300–32). New York: Oxford University Press.

Dunlap, Riley E., and Richard York. 2008. "The Globalization of Environmental Concern and the

Limits of the PostMaterialist Explanation: Evidence from Four Cross-National Surveys." *Sociological Quarterly* 49: 529–63.

Durkheim, Émile. 1961. *Moral Education*. New York: Free Press.

Durkheim, Émile. 1997. *Suicide: A Study in Sociology*. New York: Free Press.

Durkheim, Émile. 2008. *The Elementary Forms of Religious Life*. Oxford, UK: Oxford University Press.

Durkheim, Émile. [1893] 2014. *The Division of Labour in Society*. New York: Free Press.

Durkheim, Émile. [1895] 2014. *The Rules of Sociological Method*. New York: Free Press.

Durose, Matthew R., Smith, Erica L., and Patrick A. Langan. 2005. "Contacts between Police and the Public, 2005." U.S. Department of Justice, Office of Justice Programs, Bureau of Justice Statistics Special Report. http://www.bjs.gov/content/pub/pdf/cpp05.pdf.

Duru, O. K., N. T. Harawa, D. Kermah, and K. C. Norris. 2012. "Allostatic Load Burden and Racial Disparities in Mortality." *Journal of the National Medical Association* 104(1–2): 89–95.

Duster, Troy. 2016. "Review." In *Decoding Racial Ideology in Genomics: Why We Pretend Race Exists in America* by Johnny E. Williams. Cover. Lanham, MD: Lexington Books.

Dyrbye, L. N., West, C. P., Satele, D., Boone, S., Tan, L., Sloan, J., and Shanafelt, T. D. 2014. "Burnout Among U.S. Medical Students, Residents, and Early Career Physicians Relative to the General U.S. Population." *Academic Medicine* 89(3):443–51. doi: 10.1097/ACM.0000000000000134.

Dyrbye L. N., M. R. Thomas, and T. D. Shanafelt. 2005. "Medical Student Distress: Causes, Consequences, and Proposed Solutions." *Mayo Clinical Proceedings* 80: 1613–22.

Eagly, A. H., and B. T. Johnson. 1990. "Gender and Leadership Style: A Meta-analysis." *Psychological Bulletin* 108(2), 233–56. http://dx.doi.org/10.1037/0033–2909.108.2.233.

Ebadi A, and A. Schiffauerova. 2015. "How to Receive More Funding for Your Research? Get Connected to the Right People!" PLoS ONE 10(7): e0133061. https://doi.org/10.1371/journal.pone.0133061.

Ecklund, Elaine, David Johnson, Christopher Scheitle, Kirstin Matthews, and Steven Lewis. 2016. "Religion among Scientists in Comparative Context: A New Study of Scientists in Eight Regions." *Socius* 2: 1–9. doi:10.1177/2378023116664353.

Edin, Kathryn, and Maria Kefalas. 2005. *Promises I Can Keep: Why Poor Women Put Motherhood before Marriage*. Berkeley: University of California Press. DOI: 10.1080/10911350802427480.

Edin, Kathryn, Laura Lein, and Christopher Jencks. 1997. *Making Ends Meet: How Single Mothers Survive Welfare and Low-Wage Work*. New York: Russell Sage Foundation.

Edmonds-Poli, Emily, and David Shirk. 2012. *Contemporary Mexican Politics*. Lanham, MD: Rowman and Littlefield.

Edwards, Adrian. 2016, June 30. "Global Forced Displacement Hits Record High." United Nations High Commissioner for Refugees. http://www.unhcr.org/en-us/news/latest/2016/6/5763b65a4/global-forced-displacement-hits-record-high.html.

Einarsen, Stale, Helge Hoel, Dieter Zapf, and Cary Cooper, eds. 2003. *Bullying and Emotional Abuse in the Workplace: International Perspectives in Research and Practice*. New York: Taylor and Francis.

Eliasoph, Nina and Jade Lo. 2012. "Broadening Cultural Sociology's Scope: Meaning-making in Mundane Organizational Life." In *The Oxford Handbook of Cultural Sociology*, eds. Jeffrey Alexander, Philip Smith, and Ronald Jacobs (pp. 763–787). New York: Oxford University Press.

Elder, Glenn. 1998. *Children of the Great Depression*. Boulder, CO: Westview Press.

Elliott, Annabel Fenwick. 2014, July 8. "'Do You Wanna Be White?' Korean Skincare Brand Sparks Backlash by Posing Controversial Question on a Billboard in New York." *Daily Mail*. https://www.dailymail.co.uk/femail/article-2684956/Do-wanna-white-Korean-skincare-brand-sparks-backlash-posing-controversial-question-billboard-New-York.html.

Ellison, Christopher G., and Marc A. Musick. 1993. "Southern Intolerance: A Fundamentalist Effect?" *Social Forces* 72: 379–398.

Emerson, Michael, and David Hartman. 2006. "The Rise of Religious Fundamentalism," *Annual Review of Sociology* 32: 127–44.

Emery, Robert. 2009, March 18. "Joint Physical Custody." *Psychology Today*. https://www.psychologytoday.com/blog/divorced-children/200905/joint-physical-custody.

England, P. 2010. "The Gender Revolution: Uneven and Stalled." *Gender & Society* 24(2), 149–166.

Enss, C. (2005). *Hearts West: True Stories of Mail-Order Brides on the Frontier*, 1st ed. Guilford, CT: TwoDot Globe Pequot Press.

Enten, Harry J. 2013, 25 September. "The Public Policy Polling Controversy." *The Guardian*. http://www.theguardian.com/commentisfree/2013/sep/25/public-policy-polling-controversy.

Environmental Protection Agency. 2016. "Climate Change Indicators: Global Greenhouse Gas Emissions." https://www.epa.gov/climate-indicators/climate-change-indicators-global-greenhouse-gas-emissions.

Epstein, Cynthia Fuchs, and William Josiah Goode. 1971. *The Other Half: Roads to Women's Equality*. Upper Saddle River, NJ: Prentice-Hall.

Epstein, Nancy E. 2014. "Multidisciplinary In-Hospital Teams Improve Patient Outcomes: A Review." *Surgical Neurology International* 5(Suppl 7): S295–S303.

Equal Employment Opportunity Commission. 2017. "Harassment." https://www.eeoc.gov/laws/types/harassment.cfm.

Equality Now. 2017. "Sex Trafficking Fact Sheet." http://www.equalitynow.org/traffickingFAQ.

Ericson, Richard V., and Kevin D. Haggerty. 2006. *The New Politics of Surveillance and Visibility*. Toronto: University of Toronto Press.

Eshbaugh-Soha, Matthew, and Jeffrey S. Peake. 2011. *Breaking through the Noise: Presidential Leadership, Public Opinion, and the News Media*. Stanford, CA: Stanford University Press.

Espiritu, Yen Le. 2003. *Home Bound: Filipino American Lives Across Cultures, Communities and Countries*. Berkeley, CA: University of California Press.

ESPN. 2015, July 16. "Caitlyn Jenner Vows to 'Reshape the Landscape' in ESPYS speech." ESPN.com. http://www.espn.com/espys/2015/story/_/id/13264599/caitlyn-jenner-accepts-arthur-ashe-courage-award-espys-ashe2015.

Esposito, John, Darrell Fasching, and Todd Lewis. 2014. *World Religions Today*, 5th ed. New York: Oxford University Press.

Essig, Laurie. 2011, June 24. "Divorce Makes You a Bad person...Again." *Psychology Today* https://www.psychologytoday.com/us/blog/love-inc/201106/divorce-makes-you-bad-person-again.

Etzioni, Amitai. 2007. "Citizen Tests: A Comparative, Communitarian Perspective." *The Political Quarterly* 78: 353–64.

Evans, John, 2011. "Epistemological and Moral Conflict between Religion and Science." *Journal for the Scientific Study of Religion* 50: 707–27. doi:10.1111/j.1468–5906.2011.01603.x.

Eyal, Gil. 2010 *The Autism Matrix*. Cambridge, MA: Polity.

Eyal, Gil. 2013. "For a Sociology of Expertise: The Social Origins of the Autism Epidemic." *American Journal of Sociology* 118(4): 863–907. doi:10.1086/668448.

Eyerman, Ron, and Andrew Jamison. 1998. *Music and Social Movements: Mobilizing Traditions in the Twentieth Century*. Cambridge, UK: Cambridge University Press.

Fahmy, Dalia. 2018, April 25. "Key Findings about Americans' Belief in God." Pew Research Center. Fact Tank. https://www.pewresearch.org/fact-tank/2018/04/25/key-findings-about-americans-belief-in-god/.

Faist, Thomas. 2000. "Transnationalization in International Migration: Implications for the Study of Citizenship and Culture." *Ethnic and Racial Studies* 23: 189–222.

Faist, Thomas, and Eyüp Özveren. 2004. *Transnational Social Spaces: Agents, Networks, and Institutions*. Burlington, VT: Ashgate.

Faludi, Susan. 2006. *Backlash: The Undeclared War against American Women*. New York: Three Rivers Press.

Fan, Victoria Y., Dean T Jamison, and Lawrence H Summers. 2018. "Pandemic Risk: How Large Are the Expected Losses?" *Bulletin of the World Health Organization* 96: 129–34.

Fang, Marina. 2013, August 5. "Public Schools Slash Arts Education and Turn to Private Funding." https://thinkprogress.org/public-schools-slash-arts-education-and-turn-to-private-funding-f16ff3b0bda5/#.6avz40f22.

Faragher, E. B., M. Cass, and C. L. Cooper. 2005. "The Relationship between Job Satisfaction and Health: A Meta-analysis." *Occupational and Environmental Medicine* 62: 105112.

Fawaz, Leila. 2014. *A Land of Aching Hearts: The Middle East in the Great War*. Cambridge, MA: Harvard University Press.

Feagin J. R., and M. P. Sikes. 1994. *Living with Racism: The Black Middle-Class Experience*. Boston: Beacon.

Federal Bureau of Investigation. 2017. *Crime in the United States*. https://ucr.fbi.gov/crime-in-the-u.s/2017/crime-in-the-u.s.-2017/topic-pages/tables/table-43.

Feldscher, Karen. 2017, July 11. "Increase in Pertussis Outbreaks Linked with Vaccine Exemptions, Waning Immunity." Harvard T. H Chan School of Public Health News. https://www.hsph.harvard.edu/news/features/

increase-in-pertussis-outbreaks-linked-with-vaccine-exemptions-waning-immunity/.

Ferguson, Priscilla Parkhurst. 2014. *Word of Mouth: What We Talk about When We Talk about Food.* Berkeley, CA: University of California Press.

Fingerhut, Hannah. 2016, May 12. "Support Steady for Same-Sex Marriage and Acceptance of Homosexuality." Pew Research Center Fact Tank. http://www.pewresearch.org/fact-tank/2016/05/12/support-steady-for-same-sex-marriage-and-acceptance-of-homosexuality/.

Finke, Roger, and Rodney Stark. 1988. "Religious Economies and Sacred Canopies: Religious Mobilization in American Cities, 1906." *American Sociological Review* 53(1): 41–49. http://www.jstor.org/stable/2095731.

Finke, Roger, and Rodney Stark. 1998 "Religious Choice and Competition." *American Sociological Review* 63(5): 761–66. http://www.jstor.org/stable/2657339.

Firebaugh, Glenn, and Laura Tach. 2012. "Income, Age, and Happiness in America." In *Trends in the United States, 1972–2006: Evidence from the General Social Survey*, ed. P. Marsden (pp. 267–87). Princeton, NJ: Princeton University Press.

Fischer, Claude S. 1975. "Toward a Subcultural Theory of Urbanism." *American Journal of Sociology* 80(6): 1319–41.

Fisher, George. 2003. *Plea Bargaining's Triumph: A History of Plea Bargaining in America.* Stanford, CA: Stanford University Press.

Fletcher, P. 2016, November 30. "Native Advertising Will Provide a Quarter of News Media Revenue by 2018." *Forbes.* https://www.forbes.com/sites/paulfletcher/2016/11/30/native-advertising-will-provide-a-quarter-of-news-media-revenue-by-2018/#75950afa2d0c.

Flook, Lisa, Rena Repetti, and Jodie Ullman. 2005. "Classroom Social Experiences and Predictors of Academic Performance." *Developmental Psychology* 41: 319327.

Florida, Richard. 2005. *Cities and the Creative Class.* New York: Routledge.

Florida, Richard. 2017. *The New Urban Crisis: How Our Cities Are Increasing Inequality, Deepening Segregation, and Failing the Middle Class—And What We Can Do about It.* New York: Basic Books.

Foley, Kristie, David Altman, Robert Durant, and Mark Wolfson. 2004. "Adults Approval and Adolescent Alcohol Use." *Journal of Adolescent Health* 35: 17–26.

Foner, Nancy, and Joanna Dreby. 2011. "Relations between the Generations in Immigrant Families." *Annual Review of Sociology* 37: 545–64.

Fontenot, Kayla, Jessica Semega, and Melissa Kollar. 2018, September. "Income and Poverty in the United States: 2017." Current Population Reports. https://www.census.gov/content/dam/Census/library/publications/2018/.../p60-263.pdf.

Food and Drug Administration. 2016, October 26. *Collection of Race and Ethnicity Data in Clinical Trials Guidance for Industry and Food and Drug Administration Staff.* https://www.fda.gov/regulatory-information/search-fda-guidance-documents/collection-race-and-ethnicity-data-clinical-trials.

Forbes. 2019. Largest Public Companies, 2019 rankings. *Forbes.* https://www.forbes.com/global2000/list/#header:revenue_sortreverse:true_industry:Broadcasting%20%26%20Cable_country:United%20States.

Ford, Steve. 2009, November 10. "US Nurses and Doctors at Loggerheads." https://www.nursingtimes.net/news/hospital/us-nurses-and-doctors-at-loggerheads/5008121.article.

Forret, Monica L., and Thomas W. Dougherty. 2004. "Networking Behaviors and Career Outcomes: Differences for Men and Women." *Journal of Organizational Behavior* 25(3): 419–37.

Foucault, Michel. 1965. *Madness and Civilization.* New York: Bantam Books.

Foucault, Michel. [1963] 1973. *The Birth of the Clinic.* London: Tavistock.

Foucault, Michel. 1988. *Madness and Civilization: A History of Insanity in the Age of Reason.* New York: Knopf Doubleday.

Foucault, Michel. [1977] 1995. *Discipline and Punish: The Birth of the Prison.* New York: Vintage Books.

Frank, D. J., and J. W. Meyer. 2007. "University Expansion and the Knowledge Society." *Theory & Society* 36: 287–311.

Frank, Thomas. 2004. *What's the Matter with Kansas? How Conservatives Won the Heart of America.* New York: Metropolitan Books.

Frankel, Fred. 1996. *Good Friends Are Hard to Find.* New York: Perspective Publishing.

Frankfurt, Harry. 1987. "Equality as a Moral Ideal." *Ethics* 98: 21–43.

Fraser, Nancy. 2013. *Fortunes of Feminism: From State-Managed Capitalism to Neoliberal Crisis.* New York: Verso.

Fraser, Nancy, and Rahael Jaeggi. 2018. *Capitalism: A Conversation in Critical Theory*. New York, Cambridge, MA: Polity.

Freeman, Gary P. 1995. "Modes of Immigration Politics in Liberal Democratic States." *The International Migration Review* 29(4): 881–902.

Freeman, Jo. 1974. "Political Organization in the Feminist Movement." *Acta Sociologica* 18: 222–24.

Freidson, Eliot. [1970] 1988. *Profession of Medicine: A Study of the Sociology of Applied Knowledge*. Chicago: University of Chicago Press.

French, Eric, and Elaine Kelly. 2016. "Medical Spending around the Developed World." *Fiscal Studies* 37: 327–44.

Frey, William H. 2018, December 17. "Black-white segregation edges downward since 2000, census shows." https://www.brookings.edu/blog/the-avenue/2018/12/17/black-white-segregation-edges-downward-since-2000-census-shows/.

Frey, William H., and Zachary Zimmer. 1998, September. "Defining the City and Levels of Urbanization." PSC Research Report No. 98-423.

Fried, J. M., M. Vermillion, N. H. Parker, and S. Uijtdehaage. 2012. "Eradicating Medical Student Mistreatment: A Longitudinal Study of One Institution's Efforts." *Academic Medicine: Journal of the Association of American Medical Colleges* 87: 1191–98.

Fried, SueEllen. 1998. *Bullies and Victims: Helping Your Children through the Schoolyard Battlefield*. Lanham, MD: M. Evans and Company.

Friedan, Betty. [1963] 2001. *The Feminine Mystique*. New York: W.W. Norton.

Friedland, Roger. 2001. "Religious Nationalism and the Problem of Collective Representation." *Annual Review of Sociology* 27: 125–52. http://www.jstor.org/stable/2678617.

Friedmann, Alex. 2012, January. "The Societal Impact of the Prison Industrial Complex, or Incarceration for Fun and Profit—Mostly Profit." *Prison Legal News* 23(1): 20–23.

Fulcher, Megan, Erin L. Sutfin and Charlotte J. Patterson. 2008. "Individual Differences in Gender Development: Associations with Parental Sexual Orientation, Attitudes, and Division of Labor." *Sex Roles* 58(5–6): 330–341.

Fullerton, Howard, N., Jr. 1999. "Labor Force Participation: 75 Years of Change, 1950–98 and 1998–2025." *Monthly Labor Review* 122(12): 3–12.

Furuta, J. 2017. "Rationalization and Student/School Personhood in U.S. College Admissions: The Rise of Test-Optional Policies, 1987 to 2015." *Sociology of Education* 90(3): 236–54. https://doi.org/10.1177/0038040717713583.

Gabler, Neil. 2016, May. "The Secret Shame of Middle-Class Americans." *The Atlantic*. http://www.theatlantic.com/magazine/archive/2016/05/my-secret-shame/476415/.

Gabriel, R. 2016. "A Middle Ground? Residential Mobility and Attainment of Mixed-Race Couples" *Demography* 53: 165188.

Gac, Scott. 2007. *Singing for Freedom: The Hutchinson Family Singers and the Nineteenth-Century Culture of Reform*. New Haven, CT: Yale University Press.

Gajanan, M. 2017. "Read What the Head of the U.S. Marines Said to Female Marines after the Naked Photo Scandal." http://time.com/4701509/robert-neller-marine-nude-photo/.

Ganong, Lawrence H., and Marilyn Coleman. 1997. "How Society Views Stepfamilies." *Marriage & Family Review* 26(1–2): 85–106.

Gans, Herbert J. 1979. *Deciding What's News: A Study of CBS Evening News, NBC Nightly News, Newsweek, and Time*. Evanston, IL: Northwestern University Press.

Ganzeboom, Harry, Donald Treiman, and Wout Ultee. 1991. "Comparative Intergenerational Stratification Research: Three Generations and Beyond." *Annual Review of Sociology* 17: 277–302.

Gao, Helen. 2012, March 28. "How China's New Love Affair with US Private Schools Is Changing Them Both." *The Atlantic*. http://www.theatlantic.com/international/archive/2012/03/how-chinas-new-love-affair-with-us-private-schools-is-changing-them-both/255154/.

Garfinkel, Harold. 1967. *Studies in Ethnomethodology*. Englewood Cliffs, NJ: Prentice-Hall.

Gates, Warren E. 1967. "The Spread of Ibn Khaldûn's Ideas on Climate and Culture." *Journal of the History of Ideas* 28: 415–22.

Gatta, Mary L., and Patricia A. Roos. 2005. "Rethinking Occupational Integration." *Sociological Forum* 20(3): 369–402. http://www.jstor.org/stable/4540905.

Gausvik C., A. Lautar, L. Miller, H. Pallerla, and J. Schlaudecker. 2015. "Structured Nursing Communication on Interdisciplinary Acute Care Teams Improves Perceptions of Safety, Efficiency, Understanding of Care Plan and Teamwork As Well

As Job Satisfaction." *Journal of Multidisciplinary Healthcare* 14(8): 33–37.

Gelfand, M. J., J. L. Raver, L. H. Nishii, L. M. Leslie, J. Lun, B. C. Lim, L. Duan, A. Almali-ach, S. Ang, J. Arnadottir, Z. Aycan, K. Boehnke, P. Boski, R. Cabecinhas, D. Chan, J. Chhokar, A. D'Amato, M. Ferrer, I.C. Fischlmayr, R. Fischer, M. Fülöp, J. Georgas, E.S. Kashima, Y. Kashima, K. Kim, A. Lempereur, P. Marquez, R. Othman, B. Overlaet, P. Panagiotopoulou, K. Peltzer, L.R. Perez-Florizno, L. Ponomarenko, A. Realo, V. Schei, M. Schmitt, P. B. Smith, N. Soomro, E. Szabo, N. Taveesin, M. Toyama, E. Van de Vliert, N. Vohra, C. Ward, and S. Yama-guchi. 2011. "Differences between tight and loose cultures: A 33-nation study." *Science* 332(6033): 1100–1104. doi: 10.1126/science.1197754.

Geronimus A. T., M. Hicken, D. Keene, and J. Bound. 2006. "'Weathering' and Age Patterns of Allostatic Load Scores among Blacks and Whites in the United States." *American Journal of Public Health* 96(5): 826–33.

Gerstel, Naomi. 1987. "Divorce and Stigma." *Social Problems* 34: 172–86.

Gerstmann, Evan, and Matthew Streb. 2004. "Putting an End to Push Polling: Why It Should Be Banned and Why the First Amendment Lets Congress Ban It." *Election Law Journal* 3: 37–46.

Ghanta, Praveen. 2013. "List of Countries with Universal Healthcare." True Cost Blog. https://truecostblog.com/2009/08/09/countries-with-universal-healthcare-by-date/.

Ghilarducci, Teresa. 2008. *When I'm Sixty-Four: The Plot against Pensions and the Plan to Save Them.* Princeton, NJ: Princeton University Press.

Gibson-Davis, C. M., K. Edin, and S. McLanahan. 2005. "High Hopes but Even Higher Expectations: The Retreat from Marriage among Low-Income Couples." *Journal of Marriage and Family* 67: 1301–12.

Giddens, A. 1992. *The Transformation of Intimacy: Sexuality, Love and Eroticism in Modern Society.* Cambridge, MA: Polity.

Giddens, Anthony. 1990. *Consequences of Modernity.* Stanford, CA: Stanford University Press.

Giddens, Anthony. 1991. *Modernity and Self-Identity: Self and Society in the Late Modern Age.* Stanford, CA: Stanford University Press.

Giddens, Anthony. 2009. *The Politics of Climate Change.* Cambridge, MA: Polity.

Giddens, Anthony, and Simon Griffiths. 2006. *Sociology.* New York: Polity.

Gieryn, Thomas. 1999. *Cultural Boundaries of Science.* Chicago: University of Chicago Press.

Gilbert, Sophie. 2017, October 16. "The Movement of #MeToo." *The Atlantic.* https://www.theatlantic.com/entertainment/archive/2017/10/the-movement-of-metoo/542979/.

Gilliam, F. D., and S. Iyengar. (2000) "Prime Suspects: The Influence of Local Television News on the Viewing Public." *American Journal of Political Science* 44: 560–573.

Giroux, Henry, and David Purpel, eds. 1983. *The Hidden Curriculum and Moral Education: Deception or Discovery.* San Pablo, CA: McCutchan Publishers.

Gitlin, Todd. 1995. *The Twilight of Common Dreams: Why America Is Wracked by Culture Wars.* New York: Henry Holt & Co.

Gitlin, Todd. 2001. *Media, Unlimited. How The Torrent of Images and Sounds Overwhelms Our Lives.* New York: Metropolitan Books.

Glaser, Barney G. 1978. *Theoretical Sensitivity: Advances in the Methodology of Grounded Theory.* Mill Valley, CA: The Sociology Press.

Glazer, N. 1993. "Is Assimilation Dead?" *The Annals of the American Academy of Political and Social Science, 530,* 122–136.

Glick, Jennifer. 2010. "Connecting Complex Processes: A Decade of Research on Immigrant Families." *Journal of Marriage and Family* 72: 498–515.

Global Industry Analysts Inc. 2015. "The Global Skin Lighteners Market: Trends, Drivers and Projections." http://www.strategyr.com/Market-Research/Skin_Lighteners_Market_Trends.asp.

Glynn, Sarah, Jane Farrell, and Nancy Wu. 2013, May 7. "The Importance of Preschool and Childcare for Working Mothers." Report. *Center for American Progress.* https://www.americanprogress.org/issues/education-k-12/reports/2013/05/08/62519/the-importance-of-preschool-and-child-care-for-working-mothers/.

Goel, Vindu. 2014, June 29. "Facebook Tinkers With Users' Emotions in News Feed Experiment, Stirring Outcry." *New York Times.* https://www.nytimes.com/2014/06/30/technology/facebook-tinkers-with-users-emotions-in-news-feed-experiment-stirring-outcry.html.

Goffman, Erving. 1959. *The Presentation of Self in Everyday Life.* New York: Anchor.

Goffman, Erving. 1963. *Stigma: Notes on the Management of Spoiled Identity*. Englewood Cliffs, NJ: Prentice-Hall.

Goldberg, Carey. 2016, April 11. "'Genetic Superheroes': Rare Exceptions Resist Mutations Thought to Be Disease Destiny." *WBUR Radio Boston*. http://www.wbur.org/commonhealth/2016/04/11/genetic-superheroes.

Goldin, Claudia, and Maria Shim. 2004. "Making a Name: Women's Surnames at Marriage and Beyond." *Journal of Economic Perspectives* 18: 143–160.

Goldthorpe, John, and Clive Payne. 1986. "Trends in Intergenerational Class Mobility in England and Wales, 1972–1983." *Sociology* 20: 1–24.

Goodenough, Ward. 1970. *Description and Comparison in Cultural Anthropology*. Chicago: Aldine.

Gordon, Raymond G., ed. 2005. *Ethnologue: Languages of the World*, 15th ed. Dallas: SIL International.

Gorski, Philip. 2004. "The Poverty of Deductivism: A Constructive Realist Model of Sociological Explanation." *Sociological Methodology* 34: 1–33.

Gottshalk, Marie, 2007. "Dollars, Sense, and Penal Reform: Social Movements and the Future of the Carceral State," *Social Research* 74(2): 669–694.

Gouldner, Alvin Ward. 1979. *The Future of Intellectuals and the Rise of the New Class*. London: Palgrave.

Gowan, Teresa. 2010. *Hobos, Hustlers, and Backsliders: Homeless in San Francisco*. Minneapolis: University of Minnesota Press.

Graber, Doris. 1980. *Crime News and the Public*. New York: Praeger.

Graf, Nikki, Anna Brown, and Eileen Patten. 2019, March 22. "The Narrowing, but Persistent, Gender Gap in Pay." Pew Research Center. Fact Tank. https://www.pewresearch.org/fact-tank/2019/03/22/gender-pay-gap-facts/.

Gramlich, John. 2017, March 1. "Most Violent and Property Crimes in the U.S. Go Unsolved." Pew Research Center. Fact Tank. http://pewrsr.ch/2mKD7R8.

Gramsci, Antonio. 1971. *Prison Notebooks*. New York: International Publishers.

Granovetter, Mark S. 1973. "The Strength of Weak Ties." *American Journal of Sociology* 78(6): 1360380. http://www.jstor.org/stable/2776392.

Granovetter, Mark S. 1995. *Getting a Job: A Study of Contacts and Careers*. Chicago: University of Chicago Press.

Grant, Adam. 2014. *Give and Take: Why Helping Others Drives Our Success*. New York: Penguin.

Grasgruber, P., J. Cacek, T. Kalina, and M. Sebera. 2014. "The Role of Nutrition and Genetics as Key Determinants of the Positive Height Trend." *Economics and Human Biology* 15: 81–100.

Grattet, Ryken, and Valerie Jenness. 2001. "Examining the Boundaries of Hate Crime Law: Disabilities and the Dilemma of Difference." *Criminology* 91: 653–698.

Greely, Henry T., Barbara Sahakian, John Harris, Ronald C. Kessler, Michael S. Gazzaniga, Phillip Campbell, and Martha J. Farah. 2008, December 11. "Toward Responsible Use of Cognitive Enhancing Drugs by the Healthy." *Nature* 456 (7223): 702–5.

Greenwood, Jeremy, Nezih Guner, Georgi Kocharkov, and Cezar Santos. 2014, May, revised. "Marry Your Like: Assortative Mating and Income Inequality." *American Economic Review (Papers and Proceedings)* 104(5): 348–53.

Gregoire, Carolyn. 2015, May 15. "How Being an Oldest, Middle, or Youngest Child Shapes Your Personality." *Huffington Post*. http://www.huffingtonpost.com/2015/05/13/birth-order-personality_n_7206252.html.

Grinburg, Emanuella. 2015, July 15. "Why Caitlyn Jenner's Transgender Experience Is Far from the Norm." *CNN*. http://www.cnn.com/2015/06/03/living/caitlyn-jenner-transgender-reaction-feat/.

Groves, Robert. Women at Work. Census blog. Friday August 12, 2011. https://www.census.gov/newsroom/blogs/director/2011/08/women-at-work.html.

Grunebaum, H. (2007). "Thinking about Romantic/Erotic Love." *Journal of Marital and Family Therapy* 23(3): 295–307.

Grusky, David. 1994. "The Contours of Social Stratification." In *Social Stratification: Class, Race, and Gender in Sociological Perspective*, ed. D. Grusky (pp. 3–35). Boulder, CO: Westview Press.

Grusky, David, and Tamar Kricheli-Katz, eds. 2012. *The New Gilded Age*. Stanford, CA: Stanford University Press.

Gudykunst, William B. 2004. *Bridging Differences: Effective Intergroup Communication*, 4th ed. Newbury Park, CA: SAGE.

Gusfield, Joseph. 1963. *Symbolic Crusade: Status Politics and the American Temperance Movement*. Urbana: University of Illinois Press.

Habermas, Jürgen. 1975. *Legitimation Crisis*. Boston: Beacon Press.

Habermas, Jürgen. 1989. *The Structural Transformation of the Public Sphere: An Inquiry into a Category of Bourgeois Society.* Cambridge: Polity Press.

Habermas, Jürgen. 1996. *Between Facts and Norms: Contributions to a Discourse Theory of Law and Democracy.* Boston: Polity Press.

Habermas, Jürgen. 2008. "Notes on Post-secular Society." *New Perspectives Quarterly* 25(4): 17–29.

Habermas, Jürgen. 2014. *Religion and Rationality: Essays on Reason, God and Modernity.* Malden, MA: Wiley.

Haddad, L. 1977. "A Fourteenth-Century Theory of Economic Growth and Development." *Kyklos* 30: 195–213.

Hagan, John, and R. Dinovitzer. 1999. "Collateral Consequences of Imprisonment for Children, Communities and Prisoners." In *Crime and Justice: Prisons, Vol. 26*, ed. M. Tonry and J. Petersilia (pp. 121–62). Chicago: University of Chicago Press.

Hale, Jo Mhairi. 2017. "Cognitive Disparities: The Impact of the Great Depression and Cumulative Inequality on Later-Life Cognitive Function." *Demography* 54: 2125–58.

Hall, John R., Laura Grindstaff, and Ming-cheng Miriam Lo. 2010. *Handbook of Cultural Sociology.* New York: Routledge.

Hall, Stuart. 1973. *Encoding and Decoding in the Television Discourse.* Birmingham, UK: University of Birmingham.

Hall, Stuart, Chas Critcher, Tony Jefferson, John Clarke, and Brian Roberts. 1978. *Policing the Crisis: 'Mugging', the State and Law and Order.* London: Macmillan.

Hallin, Daniel C., and Paolo Mancini. 2004. *Comparing Media Systems: Three Models of Media and Politics.* Cambridge, MA: Cambridge University Press.

Halperin, David M. 1997. *Saint Foucault: Towards a Gay Hagiography.* Oxford, UK: Oxford University Press.

Hamermesh, D. S., and A. Parker. 2005. "Beauty in the Classroom: Instructors' Pulchritude and Putative Pedagogical Productivity." *Economics of Education Review* 24(4), 369–76.

Hamilton, J. T. 2004. *All the News That's Fit to Sell: How the Market Transforms Information into News.* Princeton, NJ: Princeton University Press.

Hamilton, Vivian. 2006. *Principles of U.S. Family Law,* 75 Fordham Law Review 31(1): 31-73. https://ir.lawnet.fordham.edu/flr/vol75/iss1/2.

Hampton, Keith, Inyoung Shin, and Weixu Lu, 2017. "Social Media and Political Discussion: When Online Presence Silences Offline Conversation." *Information, Communication and Society* 20: 1090–1107.

Hannerz, Ulf. 1990. "Cosmopolitans and Locals in World Culture." *Theory, Culture & Society* 7(2): 237–251.

Harcourt, Bernard E. 2012. *The Illusion of Free Markets: Punishment and the Myth of Natural Order.* Cambridge, MA: Havard University Press.

Hargittai, Eszter, and Gina Walejko. 2008. "The Participation Divide: Content Creation and Sharing in the Digital Age." *Information, Communication & Society* 11: 239–56.

Harper, Christopher, and T. Alan Lacey, 2016, July 28. "Get at STEM Job with Less Than a Four-Year Degree." US Department of Labor Blog. https://blog.dol.gov/2016/07/28/get-a-stem-job-with-less-than-a-4-year-degree/.

Harris, Cheryl I. 1993. "Whiteness as Property." *Harvard Law Review* 106: 1707.

Harris, David. 1999. "The Stories, the Statistics, and the Law: Why 'Drivin While Black' Matters," *Minnesota Law Review* 84: 265–326.

Harrison, R. J. 2002. "Inadequacies of Multiple-Response Race Data in the Federal Statistical System." In *The New Race Question: How the Census Counts Multiracial Individuals*, eds. J. Perlmann and M.C. Waters (pp. 137–60). New York: Russell Sage Foundation.

Hart Research Associates. 2015. Falling Short? College Learning and Career Success Selected Findings from Online Surveys of Employers and College Students Conducted on Behalf of the Association of American Colleges & Universities. https://www.aacu.org/leap/public-opinion-research/2015-survey-falling-short.

Hartley, John. 1999. *Uses of Television.* London, UK: Routledge.

Hartmans, Avery, and Nathan McAlone, 2016, August 1. "The Story of How Travis Kalanick Built Uber into the Most Feared and Valuable Startup in the World," *Business Insider.* http://www.businessinsider.com/ubers-history.

Harvey, David. 1985. *The Urbanization of Capital: Studies in the History and Theory of Capitalist Urbanization.* Baltimore: Johns Hopkins University Press.

Haskins, Ron. 2008. "Education and Economic Mobility." Economic Mobility Project, Pew Charitable Trusts. https://www.brookings.edu/wp-content/uploads/2016/07/02_economic_mobility_sawhill_ch8.pdf.

Hausladen, Gary J. 2000. "The Evolution of the Place-Based Police Procedural." In *Places for Dead Bodies* (pp. 11–32). Austin: University of Texas Press. http://www.jstor.org/stable/10.7560/731271.6.

Haveman, Robert, and Timothy Smeeding. 2006. "The Role of Higher Education in Social Mobility." *The Future of Children* 16: 125–50.

Havocscope. (2015). *Global Black Market Information. Prostitution: Price and Statistics of the Global Sex Trade.* https://www.amazon.com/Prostitution-Prices-Statistics-Global-Trade-ebook/dp/B00ZZBFXO2.

Hawkins, Tyleah. 2002, December 28. "Will Less Art and Music in the Classroom Really Help Students Soar Academically?" *Washington Post.* https://www.washingtonpost.com/blogs/therootdc/post/will-less-art-and-music-in-the-classroom-really-help-students-soar-academically/2012/12/28/e18a2da0-4e02-11e2-839d-d54cc6e49b63_blog.html?utm_term=.d08ea6922669.

Hayes, Matthew. 2018. *Gringolandia: Lifestyle Migration under Late Capitalism.* Minneapolis: University of Minnesota Press.

Hayes, Matthew, and Jesse Carlson. 2017. "Good Guests and Obnoxious Gringos: Cosmopolitan Ideals among North American Migrants to Cuenca, Ecuador." *American Journal of Cultural Sociology* 6: 189–211.

Hays, Sharon. 1998. *The Cultural Contradictions of Motherhood.* New Haven, CT: Yale University Press.

Hazir, Irmak Karademir. 2018. "Cultural Omnivorousness." Oxford Bibliographies. http://www.oxfordbibliographies.com/view/document/obo-9780199756384/obo-97801997563840134.xml.

He, Wan, Daniel Goodkind, and Paul Kowal. 2016. *U.S. Census Bureau, International Population Reports, P95/16-1, An Aging World: 2015.* Washington, DC: US Government Publishing Office. https://www.census.gov/content/dam/Census/library/publications/2016/demo/p95-16-1.pdf.

Health Resources and Services Administration. 2018. "Organ Donation Statistics" U.S. Government Information on Organ Donation and Transplantation. Department of Health and Human Services. Web. https://www.organdonor.gov/statistics-stories/statistics.html.

Heath, L., and K. Gilbert. 1996. "Mass Media and the Fear of Crime." *American Behavioral Scientist* 39(4): 379–86.

Hebdige, Dick. 1979. *Subculture: The Meaning of Style.* New York: Routledge.

Hegewisch, Ariane, and Asha DuMonthier. 2015. "The Gender Wage Gap by Occupation 2015 and by Race and Ethnicity." Institute for Women's Policy Research. http://www.iwpr.org/publications/pubs/the-gender-wage-gap-by-occupation-2015-and-by-race-and-ethnicity/.

Held, David. 1999. *Global Transformations: Politics, Economics and Culture.* Stanford, CA: Stanford University Press.

Helland, M. S., T. von Soest, K. Gustavson, E. Røysamb, and K. S. Mathiesen. 2014. "Long Shadows: A Prospective Study of Predictors of Relationship Dissolution over 17 Child-Rearing Years." *BMC Psychology* 2: 40.

Herbst, Susan. 1995. *Numbered Voices: How Opinion Polling Has Shaped American Politics.* Chicago: University of Chicago Press.

Herold, Benjamin. 2016, February 5. "Technology in Education: An Overview," *Education Week.* https://www.edweek.org/ew/issues/technology-in-education/.

Hesmondhalgh, Davis. 2019. The Cultural Industries, 4th ed. London: Sage.

Hickel, Jason. 2016, April 8. "Global Inequality May Be Much Worse Than We Think." *The Guardian.* https://www.theguardian.com/global-development-professionals-network/2016/apr/08/global-inequality-may-be-much-worse-than-we-think.

High Fliers Research Limited. 2016. *The Graduate Market in 2016.* London: High Fliers Research Limited. https://www.highfliers.co.uk/download/2016/graduate_market/GMReport16.pdf.

Hill, Catherine, Christianne Corbett, and Andresse St. Rose, 2010. *Why So Few? Women in Science, Technology, Engineering, and Mathematics.* Washington, DC: American Association of University Women.

Hill, Christopher. [1972] 1984. *The World Turned Upside Down: Radical Ideas During the English Revolution.* London: Penguin.

Hill, Michael R. 2002. *Harriet Martineau: Theoretical and Methodological Perspectives.* New York: Routledge.

Hirsch, A. R. 1983. *Making the Second Ghetto: Race and Housing in Chicago, 1940–1960.* Cambridge, UK: Cambridge University Press.

Hirschi, Travis. 1969. *Causes of Delinquency.* Los Angeles, CA: University of California Press.

Hirschman, Charles, and Stewart Tolnay. 2005. "Social Demography." In *Handbook of Population,* ed. D. Poston and M. Micklin (pp. 419–49). New York: Springer.

Historic England. 2019. "A History of Disability: From 1050 to the Present Day." https://historicengland.org.uk/research/inclusive-heritage/disability-history/.

Ho, Karen. 2009. *Liquidated: An Ethnography of Wall Street*. Durham, NC: Duke University Press.

Hoang, Kimberly Kay. 2015. *Dealing in Desire: Asian Ascendancy, Western Decline, and the Hidden Currencies of Global Sex Work*. Oakland: University of California Press.

Hobsbawm, E. J. 1996. *The Age of Revolution 1789–1848*. New York: Vintage.

Hochschild, Arlie. 2012. *The Second Shift*. NY: Penguin.

Hochschild, Arlie. 2018. *Strangers in Their Own Land. Anger and Mourning on the American Right*. New York: New Press.

Hochschild, J., and V. Weaver. 2010. "There's No One as Irish as Barack O'Bama: The Politics and Policy of Multiracialism in the United States." *Perspectives on Politics* 8: 737–60.

Hodson, Randy, Vincent Rosigno, and Steven Lopez. 2006. "Chaos and the Abuse of Power: Workplace Bullying in Organizational and Interactional Context." *Work and Occupations* 33: 382–416.

Holzer, Harry. 1996. *What Employers Want: Job Prospects for Less-Educated Workers*. New York: Russell Sage Foundation.

Homans, Charles. 2010, January/February. "Hot Air: Why Don't TV Weathermen Believe in Climate Change?" *Columbia Journalism Review*. http://archives.cjr.org/cover_story/hot_air.php.

hooks, bell. 2000. *Feminist Theory: From Margin to Center*. Boston: South End Press.

Hoornweg, Daniel, and Perinaz Bhada-Tata. 2012. "What a Waste: A Global Review of Solid Waste Management." *Urban Development Series; Knowledge Papers No. 15*. Washington, DC: World Bank. https://openknowledge.worldbank.org/handle/10986/17388.

Horne, Gerald. 1997. *Fire This Time: The Watts Uprising and the 1960s*. New York: Da Capo Press.

Hout, Michael, and Claude S. Fischer. 2002. "Why More Americans Have No Religious Preference: Politics and Generations." *American Sociological Review* 67(2):165–90.

Hout, M., and Greeley, A. M. 1998. "What Church Officials' Reports Don't Show: Another Look at Church Attendance Data." *American Sociological Review* 63(1): 113–19.

Hsu, Francis. 1981. *Americans and Chinese: Passages to Differences*. Honolulu: University of Hawaii Press.

Hu, Winnie. 2010, September 30. "Making Math as Easy as 1, Pause, 2, Pause...". *New York Times* https://www.nytimes.com/2010/10/01/education/01math.html.

Hudson, David, and Lata Nott. 2017, March. "Hate Speech and Campus Speech Codes." *Newseum Institute*. http://www.newseuminstitute.org/first-amendment-center/topics/freedom-of-speech-2/free-speech-on-public-college-campuses-overview/hate-speech-campus-speech-codes/.

Huffington Post. 2012, March 19. "Sofia Vergara: Is She Taking The Latino Stereotype Too Far?" https://www.huffpost.com/entry/sofia-vergara-is-she-taking-the-latino-stereotype-too-far_n_1363193.

Hulac, Benjamin. 2016, September 9. "Clean Energy Firms Lobby Congress as Much as Dirty Firms Do." *Scientific American*. https://www.scientificamerican.com/article/clean-energy-firms-lobby-congess-as-much-as-dirty-firms-do/.

Hunter, James Davison. 1991. *Culture Wars: The Struggle to Define America*. New York: Basic Books.

Hunter, James Davison, and Alan Wolfe. 2006. *Is There a Culture War?: A Dialogue on Values and American Public Life*. Washington, DC: Brookings Institution Press.

Iannaccone, Laurence. 1997. "Toward an Economic Theory of 'Fundamentalism.'" *Journal of Institutional and Theoretical Economics* 153: 100–16.

Ibarra, H. 1993. "Personal Networks of Women and Minorities in Management: A Conceptual Framework." *The Academy of Management Review* 18(1), 56–87. http://www.jstor.org/stable/258823.

Ibrahim, J. K., and Stanton A. Glantz. 2006. "Tobacco Industry Litigation Strategies to Oppose Tobacco Control Media Campaigns." *Tobacco Control* 15(1): 50–58.

Ignatiev, Noel. 2008. *How the Irish Became White*. New York: Routledge.

Inglehart, Ronald, and Christian Welzel. 2005. *Modernization, Cultural Change, and Democracy: The Human Development Sequence*. Cambridge, UK: Cambridge University Press.

Inglehart, Ronald, Roberto Foa, Christopher Peterson, and Christian Welzel. 2008. "Development,

Freedom, and Rising Happiness: A Global Perspective (1981–2007)." *Perspectives on Psychological Science* 3: 264–85.

Ingraham, Christopher. 2014, December 22. "A lot of southern whites are a little bit black." *Washington Post*. https://www.washingtonpost.com/.../a-lot-of-southern-whites-are-a-little-bit-black/.

Internal Revenue Service. 2019. *IRS Provides Tax Inflation Adjustments for Tax Year 2019* https://www.irs.gov/newsroom/irs-provides-tax-inflation-adjustments-for-tax-year-2019.

International Labour Organization. 2017. *Labour Force Participation Rate—ILO Modelled Estimates, July 2018*. http://www.ilo.org/ilostat/faces/oracle/webcenter/portalapp/pagehierarchy/Page3.jspx?MBI_ID=15&_afrLoop=1079054415126282&_afrWindowMode=0&_afrWindowId=npx41s27r_1#!%40%40%3F_afrWindowId%3Dnpx41s27r_1%26_afrLoop%3D107905441 5126282%26MBI_ID%3D15%26_afrWindowMode%3D0%26_adf.ctrl-state%3Dnpx 41s27r_33.

International Living. 2019. "Advertize With Us." https://internationalliving.com/about-il/advertise-with-us/.

Isaac, Mike, Michael J. De La Merced and Andrew Ross Sorkin. 2019, May 17. "How Enthusiasm for Uber Evaporated Before I.P.O." *New York Times*. https://www.nytimes.com/2019/05/15/technology/uber-ipo-price.html.

Ishizuka P. 2018. "The Economic Foundations of Cohabiting Couples' Union Transitions." *Demography* 55(2): 535–57.

Ising, M., and F. Holsboer. 2006. "Genetics of Stress Response and Stress-Related Disorders." *Dialogues in Clinical Neuroscience* 8: 433–44.

Jaarsma, Pier, and Stellan Welin. 2012. "Autism as a Natural Human Variation: Reflections on the Claims of the Neurodiversity Movement." *Health Care Analysis* 20(1): 20–30.

Jackson, K. T. 1985. *Crabgrass Frontier: The Suburbanization of the United States*. New York: Oxford University Press.

Jackson, Philip W. 1968. *Life in Classrooms*. New York: Holt, Rinehart and Winston.

Jacobi, Carina, Wouter van Atteveldt, and Kasper Welbers. 2015. "Quantitative Analysis of Large Amounts of Journalistic Texts Using Topic Modelling." *Digital Journalism* 4(1): 89–106. https://doi.org/10.1080/21670811.2015.1093271.

Jacobs, Ronald, 2000. *Race Media and the Crisis of Civil Society: From Watts to Rodney King*. Cambridge University Press.

Jacobs, Ronald N., and Daniel J. Glass. 2001. "Media Publicity and the Voluntary Sector: The Case of Nonprofit Organizations in New York City." *Voluntas: International Journal of Voluntary and Nonprofit Organizations* 13(3): 235–52.

Jacobs, Ronald N., and Eleanor Townsley. 2011. *The Space of Opinion: Intellectuals, Media and the Public Sphere*. New York: Oxford University Press.

Jacobs, Ronald N., and Eleanor Townsley. 2014. "The Hermeneutics of Hannity: Format Innovation in the Space of Opinion after September 11." *Cultural Sociology* 8(3):1–18.

Jacobsen, Linda, Mark Mather, and Genevieve Depuis. 2012. "Household Change in the United States." *Population Reference Bureau* 67(1): 1–13.

Jacobson, Thomas. 2017. "Trending Theory of the Public Sphere." *Annals of the International Communication Association* 41(1): 70–82. doi:10.1080/23808985.2017.1288070.

Jæger, Mads Meier. 2010. "Does Cultural Capital Really Affect Academic Achievement?" Aarhus, Denmark: Centre for Strategic Research in Education DPU, Aarhus University.

James, Paul. 1996. *Nation Formation: Towards a Theory of Abstract Community*. Thousand Oaks, CA: SAGE.

Jamison, Anne. 2013. *Fic: Why Fanfiction Is Taking over the World*. Dallas, TX: SmartPop.

Jencks, Christopher. 1995. *The Homeless*. Cambridge, MA: Harvard University Press.

Jennings, Jennifer, and Heeju Sohn. 2014. "Measure for Measure: How Proficiency-Based Accountability Systems Affect Inequality in Academic Achievement." *Sociology of Education* 87(2): 125–41.

Jerolmack, Colin, and Shamus Khan. 2014. "Talk Is Cheap: Ethnography and the Attitudinal Fallacy." *Sociological Methods & Research* 43: 178–209.

Johnson, Stephanie, Jessica Kirk, and Ksenia Keplinger, 2016, October 4. "Why We Fail to Report Sexual Harassment," *Harvard Business Review*. https://hbr.org/2016/10/why-we-fail-to-report-sexual-harassment.

Johnson, Suzanne, and Elizabeth O'Connor. 2002. *The Gay Baby Boom: The Psychology of Gay Parenthood*. New York: NYU Press.

Joint Commission. 2008, July 9. *Behaviors that undermine a culture of safety. Sentinel Event Alert.*

http://www.jointcommission.org/sentinel_event_alert_issue_40_behaviors_that_undermine_a_culture_of_safety/.

Jones, Megan A. 2002. "Deafness as Culture: A Psychosocial Perspective." *Disability Studies Quarterly* 22(2): 51–60.

Jones, Robert Alun. 1986. *Émile Durkheim: An Introduction to Four Major Works*. Thousand Oaks, CA: SAGE.

Joppke, Christian. 2004. "The Retreat of Multiculturalism in the Liberal State: Theory and Policy." *British Journal of Sociology* 55: 237–57.

Joppke. Christian. 2015. *The Secular State Under Siege: Religion and Politics in Europe and America*. Cambridge: Polity.

Jordan, Lucy, and Elspeth Graham. 2015. "Early Childhood Socialization and Wellbeing." In *Routledge Handbook of Families in Asia*, ed. S. Quah (pp. 175–90). New York: Routledge.

Jost, Timothy. 2017, December 20. "The Tax Bill and The Individual Mandate: What Happened, and What Does It Mean?" *Health Affairs Blog*. https://www.healthaffairs.org/do/10.1377/hauthor20091027.990764/full/.

Juergensmeyer, Mark. 2003. *Terror in the Mind of God: The Global Rise of Religious Violence*. Berkeley: University of California Press.

Julian, Tiffany, and Robert Kominski. 2011. *Education and Synthetic Work-Life Earnings Estimates*. Washington, DC: US Department of Commerce, Economics and Statistics Administration, Census Bureau.

Juster R. P., B. S. McEwen, and S. J. Lupien. 2010. "Allostatic Load Biomarkers of Chronic Stress and Impact on Health and Cognition." *Neuroscience and Biobehavioral Reviews* 35(1): 2–16. doi:10.1016/j.neubiorev.2009.10.002.

Kahn, Johnathan. 2007. "Race in a Bottle." *Scientific American* 297(2): 40–45.

Kahn, Jonathan. 2013. *Race in a Bottle: The Story of BiDil and Racialized Medicine in a Post-Genomic Age*. New York: Columbia University Press.

Kahneman, Daniel, Paul Slovic, and Amos Tversky, eds. 1982. *Judgment under Uncertainty: Heuristics and Biases*. Cambridge, UK: Cambridge University Press.

Kalleberg, Arne. 1977. "Work Values and Job Rewards: A Theory of Job Satisfaction." *American Sociological Review* 42: 124–43.

Kalleberg, Arne 2013. *Good Jobs, Bad Jobs*. NY: Russell Sage Foundation.

Kalleberg, Arne L. 2011. *Good Jobs, Bad Jobs: The Rise of Polarized and Precarious Employment Systems in the United States, 1970s–2000s*. New York: Russell Sage Foundation.

Kalleberg, A. L., Marsden, P. V., Reynolds, J., and Knoke, D. 2006. "Beyond Profit? Sectoral Differences in High-Performance Work Practices." *Work and Occupations* 33(3): 271–302.

Kane, J., and A. D. Wall. 2005. *National Public Survey on White-Collar Crime*. Fairmont, VA: National White-Collar Crime Center.

Kanter, R. M. 1977. *Men and Women of the Corporation*. New York: Basic Books.

Kaplan, Dana, 2003. *American Reform Judaism: An Introduction*. New Brunswick, NJ: Rutgers University Press.

Karabel, Jerome. 2005. *The Chosen: The Hidden History of Admission and Exclusion at Harvard, Yale, and Princeton*. New York: Houghton Mifflin.

Karen, David. 2005. "No Child Left Behind? Sociology Ignored!" *Sociology of Education* 78(2): 165–69.

Katz, Elihu, and Paul Lazarsfeld. 1955. *Personal Influence*. Chicago: Transaction Publishers.

Kearney, Melissa, and Benjamin Harris. 2013. "A Dozen Facts about America's Struggling Lower-Middle Class." Hamilton Project Policy Paper, Brookings Institution. https://www.brookings.edu/research/a-dozen-facts-about-americas-struggling-lower-middle-class/.

Keller, Amy. 2016, April 26. "How to Talk to Doctors." *Daily Nurse*. https://dailynurse.com/how-to-talk-to-doctors/.

Kempner, Joanna. 2008. "The Chilling Effect: How Do Researchers React to Controversy?" *PLoS Medicine* 5(11). http://www.ncbi.nlm.nih.gov/pmc/articles/PMC2586361/.

Kempner, Joanna, Jon F. Merz, and Charles L. Bosk. 2011. "Forbidden Knowledge: Public Controversy and the Production of Nonknowledge." *Sociological Forum* 26: 475–500.

Kennedy, Randall. 1997. *Race, Crime and the Law*. New York: Pantheon Books, Random House.

Khaldûn, Ibn. 2004. *The Muqaddimah: An Introduction to History*. Princeton, NJ: Princeton University Press.

Khan, Shamus. 2012. *Privilege: The Making of an Adolescent Elite at St. Paul's School*. Princeton, NJ: Princeton University Press.

Khanna, Gaurav. 2017, August 8. "Technology, Innovation, and the American Dream: New Study Finds H-1B Visas Benefit US and Indian Workforce."

Center for Global Development. https://www .cgdev.org/blog/technology-innovation-and-american-dream-new-study-finds-h-1b-visas-benefit-us-and-indian.

Khazan, Olga. 2015. "The Bro Whisperer. Michael Kimmel's Quest to Turn College Boys into Gentlemen—and Improve Sex on Campus." *The Atlantic* 315(1): 20–21.

Khosrokhavar, Farhad. 2008. *Inside Jihadism*. New York: Routledge.

Kidd, Dustin. 2010. *Legislating Creativity: The Intersections of Art and Politics*. New York: Routledge.

Kim, Eun Kyung. 2018, December 11. "TIME's 2018 Person of the Year: 'The Guardians and the War on Truth.'" *Today* 2018. December 11, 2018. https://www.today.com/news/time-person-year-2018-guardians-war-truth-t144911.

Kim, Kyounghee. 2009. "Change and Challenge of Korean Family in the Era of Globalization: Centering Transnational Families." *Journal of Ritsumeikan Social Sciences and Humanities* 1: 167–81.

Kim, S., J. Urpelainen, and J. Yang. 2016. "Electric Utilities and American Climate Policy: Lobbying by Expected Winners and Losers." *Journal of Public Policy* 36(2): 251–75.

Kimmel, Michael. 2010. *Misframing Men: Essays on the Politics of Contemporary Masculinities*. New Brunswick, NJ: Rutgers University Press.

King, Gary. 2011. "Ensuring the Data Rich Future of the Social Sciences." *Science* 331: 719–21.

King, Mary C. 1992. "The Evolution of Occupational Segregation by Race and Gender, 1940–1988." *Monthly Labor Review* 115(4): 30–36.

King, Ryan S., and Marc Mauer. 2002, February. *State Sentencing and Corrections Policy in an Era of Fiscal Restraint*. Washington, DC: The Sentencing Project.

Klass, Perri. 2017, April 10. "Rude Doctors, Rude Nurses, Rude Patients." *New York Times*. https://www.nytimes.com/2017/04/10/well/family/rude-doctors-rude-nurses-rude-patients.html.

Klinenberg, Eric. 2012. *Going Solo: The Extraordinary Rise and Surprising Appeal of Living Alone*. NY: Penguin.

Koffler, Jacobs. 2015, June 29. "Here Are Places Women Can't Take Their Husband's Name When They Get Married." *Time*. http://time.com/3940094/maiden-married-names-countries/.

Kopelman, Richard, Rita Fossen, Eletherios Paraskevas, Leanna Lawter, and David Prottas.

2009. "The Bride Is Keeping Her Name: A 35-Year Retrospective Analysis of Trends and Correlates." *Social Behavior and Personality* 37(5): 687–700.

Korteweg, Anna, and Gökçe Yurdakul. 2014. *The Headscarf Debates: Conflicts of National Belonging*. Stanford, CA: Stanford University Press.

Krauss, Lawrence. 2010, August 1. "Faith and Foolishness: When Religious Beliefs Become Dangerous." *Scientific American*. https://www.scientificamerican.com/article/faith-and-foolishness/.

Krislov, Marvin. 2013, December 5. "The Enduring Relevance of a Liberal Arts Education." *The Hechinger Report*. http://hechingerreport.org/the-enduring-relevance-of-a-liberal-arts-education/.

Kuhn, Thomas S. 1979. "Metaphor and Science." In *Metaphor and Thought* (pp. 409–19). Cambridge, UK: Cambridge University Press.

Kuisel, Richard. 1996. *Seducing the French: The Dilemma of Americanization*. Berkeley: University of California Press.

Kuo, Hsiang-Hui Daphne, Hyunjoon Park, Taissa S. Hauser, Robert M. Hauser, and Nadine F. Marks. 2019. "Surveys of the Life Course and Aging: Some Comparisons." Working Paper No. 2001-06. Center for Demography and Ecology, University of Wisconsin, Madison. https://cde.wisc.edu/wp-2001-06/.

Kutateladze, Besiki, Whitney Tymas, and Mary Crowley. 2014. "Race and Prosecution in Manhattan." Research Summary. Vera Institute of Justice. Prosecution and Racial Justice Program. https://www.vera.org/publications/race-and-prosecution-in-manhattan.

Kwiatkowski, Elizabeth. 2016, August 5. "Jubilee Sharpe—9 Things to Know about the 'Bachelor in Paradise' Bachelorette." *Reality TV World*.

Lachmann, Richard. 2000. *Capitalists in Spite of Themselves: Elite Conflict and European Transitions in Early Modern Europe*. New York: Oxford University Press.

Lachmann, Richard. 2003. "Elite Self-Interest and Economic Decline in Early Modern Europe." *American Sociological Review* 68: 346–72.

LaFontana, Kathryn, and Antonius Cillessen. 2010. "Developmental Changes in the Priority of Perceived Status in Childhood and Adolescence." *Social Development* 19(1): 130–47.

Lakatos, Imre. 1978. *The Methodology of Scientific Research Programmes: Philosophical Papers*. Cambridge, UK: Cambridge University Press.

Lamont, Michèle. 2002. *The Dignity of Working Men: Morality and the Boundaries of Race, Class, and Immigration*. Cambridge, MA: Harvard University Press.

Lamont, Michèle, Graziella Moraes Silva, Jessica Welburn, Joshua Guetzkow, Nissim Mizrachi, Hanna Herzog, and Elisa Reis. 2016. *Getting Respect: Responding to Stigma and Discrimination in the United States, Brazil, and Israel*. Princeton, NJ: Princeton University Press.

Lamothe, D. 2014, October 31. "The U.S. Military's Long, Uncomfortable History with Prostitution Gets New Attention." *Washington Post*. https://www.washingtonpost.com/news/checkpoint/wp/2014/10/31/the-u-s-militarys-long-uncomfortable-history-with-prostitution-gets-new-attention/?utm_term=.bd5ce7cb39df.

Landivar, Liana. 2013. "Disparities in STEM Employment by Sex, Race, and Hispanic Origin." American Community Survey Reports, September 2013. Washington, DC: US Census Bureau.

Lane, Christopher. 2007. *Shyness: How Normal Behavior Became a Sickness*. Princeton, NJ: Princeton University Press.

Lareau, Annette. 2003. *Unequal Childhoods: Class, Race, and Family Life*. Berkeley, CA: University of California Press.

Lareau, Annette, and Kimberly A. Goyette. 2014. *Choosing Homes, Choosing Schools*. New York: Russell Sage Foundation.

Larson, Reed, and Maryse Richards. 1991. "Daily Companionship in Late Childhood and Early Adolescence: Changing Developmental Contexts." *Child Development* 62: 284–300.

Laurent, Eloi. 2015, March. "Social Ecology: Exploring the Missing Link in Sustainable Development." Working Paper, OFCE-Sciences-Po, Stanford University. https://www.ofce.sciences-po.fr/pdf/dtravail/WP2015-07.pdf.

Lauzen, M., ed. 2015. *It's a Man's (Celluloid) World*. Report of the Center for the Study of Women in Television and Film, San Diego University. http://womenintvfilm.sdsu.edu/files/2014_Its_a_Mans_World_Report.pdf.

Lazoritz, Stephen. 2008. "Don't Tolerate Disruptive Physician Behavior." *American Nurse Today* 3(3). https://www.americannursetoday.com/dont-tolerate-disruptive-physician-behavior/.

Lea, John, and Jock Young. 1984. *What Is to Be Done about Law and Order?* New York: Penguin.

Leary, Kyrie. 2018, January 17. "Renewable Energy Will Be Cheaper Than Fossil Fuels by 2020, According to a New Report." *Business Insider*. https://www.businessinsider.com/renewable-energy-will-be-cheaper-than-fossil-fuels-by-2020-2018-1.

Leasca, Stacey. 2017, July 17. "These Are the Highest Paying Jobs in the Gig Economy." *Forbes*. https://www.forbes.com/sites/sleasca/2017/07/17/highest-paying-jobs-gig-economy-lyft-taskrabbit-airbnb/#6abf5d127b64.

Lee, D., and S. McLanahan. 2015. "Family Structure Transitions and Child Development: Instability, Selection, and Population Heterogeneity." *American Sociological Review* 80: 738–63.

Legatum. 2018. Prosperity Index. London: The Legatum Institute Foundation. https://www.prosperity.com/rankings.

Lele, Uma, and Steven W. Stone. 1989. *Population Pressure, the Environment and Agricultural Intensification: Variations on the Boserup Hypothesis*. Managing Agricultural Development in Africa (MADIA) discussion paper no. 4. Washington, DC: The World Bank. http://documents.worldbank.org/curated/en/809971468739234405/Population-pressure-the-environment-and-agricultural-intensification-variations-on-the-Boserup-hypothesis.

Lemert, Edwin. 1967. *Human Deviance, Social Problems and Social Control*. Englewood Cliffs, NJ: Prentice-Hall.

Lemert, Charles C. 2008. *Social Things: An Introduction to the Sociological Life*. Lanham, MD: Rowman & Littlefield.

Lengermann, Patricia M., and Jill Niebrugge-Brantley. 1998. *The Women Founders: Sociology and Social Theory, 1830–1930: A Text/Reader*. Boston: McGraw-Hill.

Lenhart, Amanda. 2015, April 9. "Teens Social Media and Technology Overview 2015," Pew Research Center. http://www.pewinternet.org/2015/04/09/teens-social-media-technology-2015/.

Levanon, Asaf, Paula England, and Paul Allison. 2009. "Occupational Feminization and Pay: Assessing Causal Dynamics Using 1950–2000 US Census Data." *Social Forces* 88(2): 865–91.

Levitt, Peggy. 2001. *The Transnational Villagers*. Stanford: University of California Press.

Levitt, Peggy, and Deepak Lamba-Nieves. 2011. "Social Remittances Revisited." *Journal of Ethnic and Migration Studies* 37(1): 1–22.

Levitt, Peggy, and Nina Glick Schiller. 2004. "Conceptualizing Simultaneity: A Trans-national Social

Field Perspective on Society." *International Migration Review* 38 (3): 1002–1039.

Levitt, Steven. 2004. "Understanding Why Crime Fell in the 1990s: Four Factors That Explain the Decline and Six That Do Not." *Journal of Economic Perspectives* 18: 163–90.

Lewis, C. E., and M. A. Lewis. 1984. "Peer Pressure and Risk-Taking Behaviors in Children." *American Journal of Public Health* 74: 580–94.

Lieberson, Stanley. 1980. *A Piece of the Pie: Blacks and White Immigrants Since 1880*. Berkeley: University of California Press.

Liebman, Charles S. 1973. *The Ambivalent American Jew*. Philadelphia: Jewish Publication Society.

Lienesch, Michael. 1993. *Redeeming America: Piety and Politics in the New Christian Right*. Chapel Hill: University of North Carolina Press.

Lindner, Andrew M., Melissa Lindquist, and Julie Arnold. 2015. "Million Dollar Maybe? The Effect of Female Presence in Movies on Box Office Returns." *Sociological Inquiry* 85(3): 407–428.

Ling, T., J. Phillips, and S. Weihrich. 2012. "Online Evaluations vs In-Class Paper Teaching Evaluations: A Paired Comparison." *Journal of the Academy of Business Education* 12: 150–61.

Link, Bruce, Jo Phelan, Ann Stueve, Robert Moore, and Ezra Susser. 1995. "Lifetime and Five-Year Prevalence of Homelessness in the United States: New Evidence on an Old Debate." *American Journal of Orthopsychiatry* 65: 347–54.

Linz, J. J. 1990. "Presidents vs. Parliaments: The Virtues of Parliamentarism." *Journal of Democracy* 1(4): 84–91.

Linz, Juan J., and Arturo Valenzuela, eds. 1994. *The Failure of Presidential Democracy: Comparative Perspectives*. Baltimore, MD: The Johns Hopkins University Press.

Lipka, Michael, and Conrad Hackett. 2017, April 6. "Why Muslims Are the World's Fastest-Growing Religious Group." Pew Research Center. http://www.pewresearch.org/fact-tank/2017/04/06/why-muslims-are-the-worlds-fastest-growing-religious-group/.

Lipset, Seymour Martin. 1960. *Political Man: The Social Bases of Politics*. Garden City, NY: Anchor Books.

Lipsitz, Keena. 2009. "The Consequences of Battleground and 'Spectator' State Residency for Political Participation." *Political Behavior* 31: 187–209.

Liu, Leah. 2016, July 27. "China Has Its Own Birthright Tour." *Foreign Policy*. https://foreignpolicy.com/2016/07/27/china-has-its-own-birthright-tour-overseas-chinese-diaspora-soft-power/.

Livingston, Gretchen. 2018, April 8. "About One-Third of U.S. Children Are Living with an Unmarried Parent." Pew Research Center Fact Tank. https://www.pewresearch.org/fact-tank/2018/04/27/about-one-third-of-u-s-children-are-living-with-an-unmarried-parent/.

Lochner, Lance. 2011. "Nonproduction Benefits of Education: Crime, Health, and Good Citizenship." In *Handbook of the Economics of Education, Vol. 4*, eds. Eric A. Hanushek, Stephen Machin, and Ludger Woessmann (pp. 183–282). Amsterdam: North Holland.

Lockwood, Matthew. 2018. "Right-Wing Populism and the Climate Change Agenda: Exploring the Linkages." *Environmental Politics* 4: 712–32.

Logan J. G., and D. J Barksdale. 2008. "Allostasis and Allostatic Load: Expanding the Discourse on Stress and Cardiovascular Disease." *Journal of Clinical Nursing*. 17(7B): 2018.

Logan, John, and Harvey Molotch. 1987. *Urban Fortunes: The Political Economy of Place*. Berkeley: University of California Press.

Lopes, Paul. 2009. *Demanding Respect: The Evolution of the American Comic Book*. Philadelphia: Temple University Press.

Lyonette, Clare, and Rosemary Crompton. 2015. "Sharing the Load? Partners' Relative Earnings and the Division of Domestic Labour." *Work, Employment and Society* 29: 23–40.

Madden, Mary, Amanda Lenhart, Sandra Cortesi, Urs Gasser, Maeve Duggan, Aaron Smith, and Meredith Beaton. 2013, May 21. "Teens, Social Media, and Privacy." Pew Research Center, Internet Science And Tech. http://www.pewinternet.org/2013/05/21/teens-social-media-and-privacy/.

Mahnken, Kevin. 2017, January 29. "An Arts Education Crisis? How Potential Federal Cuts Could Decimate School Arts Programs." *The 74*. https://www.the74million.org/article/potential-federal-cuts-may-decimate-school-arts-programs/.

Mainwaring, Scott, and Matthew S. Shugart. 1997. "Juan Linz, Presidentialism, and Democracy: A Critical Appraisal." *Comparative Politics* 29(4): 449–71.

Mann, Michael. 1993. *The Sources of Social Power: The Rise of Classes and Nation-States, 1760–1914*. Cambridge, UK: Cambridge University Press.

Mannheim, Karl. 1952. "The Problem of Generations." In *Essays on the Sociology of Knowledge: Collected Works, Volume 5*, ed. Paul Kecskemeti (pp. 276–322). New York: Routledge.

Manning, Jennifer E. 2019, June 7. "Membership of the 116th Congress: A Profile." *Congressional Research Service*. https://crsreports.congress.gov R45583.

Manyika, James, Susan Lund, Jacques Bughin, Kelsey Robinson, Jan Mischke, and Deepa Mahajan. 2016, October. "Independent Work: Choice, Necessity, and the Gig Economy." *McKinsey Global Institute*. https://www.mckinsey.com/global-themes/employment-and-growth/Independent-work-Choice-necessity-and-the-gig-economy.

Mare, Robert D. 1981. "Change and Stability in Educational Stratification." *American Sociological Review* 46(1): 72–87.

Margalit, Avishai. 1996. *The Decent Society*. Cambridge, MA: Havard University Press.

Martin, E. 1990. "Science and Women's Bodies." In *Body/Politics: Women and the Discourses of Science*, eds. Mary Jacobus, Evelyn Fox Keller, and Sally Shuttleworth, eds. (pp. 69–82). New York and London: Routledge.

Martin, Steven P. 2006. "Trends in Marital Dissolution by Women's Education in the United States." *Demographic Research* 15: 537–60.

Martin, Wednesday. 2013, January 23. "Banning the 'Blended' Family: Why Step-families Will Never Be the Same as First Families." *Telegraph*. http://www.telegraph.co.uk/women/mother-tongue/9820359/Banning-the-blended-family-why-step-families-will-never-be-the-same-as-first-families.html.

Martineau, Harriet. 1837. *Society in America*. London: Saunders and Otley.

Martineau, Harriet. 1838. *How to Observe: Morals and Manners*. Whitefish, MT: Kessinger Publishing.

Marwell, Gerald, and Pamela Oliver. 1993. *The Critical Mass in Collective Action. A Micro-Social Theory*. Cambridge: Cambridge University Press.

Marx, Karl, and Friedrich Engels. 1848. *The Communist Manifesto*. New York: Penguin.

Mason, Mary Ann, Sydney Harrison-Jay, Gloria Messick Svare, and Nicholas H. Wolfinger. 2002. "Stepparents: De Facto Parents or Legal Strangers?" *Journal of Family Issues* 23(4): 507–22. doi: 10.1177/0192513X02023004003.

Massey, Douglas. 1995. "The New Immigration and Ethnicity in the United States." *Population and Development Review* 21: 631–52.

Massey, Douglas S. 1999. "International Migration at the Dawn of the Twenty-First Century: The Role of the State."*Population and Development Review* 25(2): 303–322.

Massey, Douglas S., and Nancy A. Denton. 1993. *American Apartheid: Segregation and the Making of the Underclass*. Cambridge, MA: Harvard University Press.

Mast, Jason L. 2012. *The Performative Presidency. Crisis and Resurrection During the Clinton Years*. Cambridge: Cambridge University Press.

Matthews, Jennifer. 2009. *Chicle: The Chewing Gum of the Americas, From the Ancient Maya to William Wrigley*. Tuscon, Arizona: University of Arizona Press.

Mayer, Susan E. 2001. "How Did the Increase in Economic Inequality between 1970 and 1990 Affect Children's Educational Attainment?" *American Journal of Sociology* 107:1–32.

McAdam, Doug. 1982. *Political Process and the Development of Black Insurgency, 1930-1970*. Chicago: University of Chicago Press.

McCarthy, John D., and Mayer N. Zald. 1977. "Resource Mobilization and Social Movements: A Partial Theory." *American Journal of Sociology* 82(6): 1212–241.

McGann, James G. 2019. "2018 Global Go To Think Tank Index Report." Think Tanks and Civil Societies Program, University of Pennsylvania. https://repository.upenn.edu/think_tanks/16.

McGregor, Jena, 2017, September 1. "Job Satisfaction Is Up, but Well Below All-Time Highs," Washington: *Washington Post*. Web. https://www.washingtonpost.com/news/on-leadership/wp/2017/09/01/job-satisfaction-is-up-but-still-well-below-one-time-highs/?utm_term=.eb466e925414.

McKay, Ramah. 2003, May 1. "Family Reunification." Migration Policy Institute. https://www.migrationpolicy.org/article/family-reunification.

McKernan, Brian. 2013. "The Morality of Play: Video Game Coverage in the *New York Times* from 1980 to 2010." *Games and Culture* 8: 307–29.

McKinlay, J. B. and L. D. Marceau. 2002. "The End of the Golden Age of Doctoring." *International Journal of Health Services* 32(2): 379–416.

McKinlay, J. B., and L. D. Marceau. 2008. "When There Is No Doctor: Reasons for the Disappearance of Primary Care Physicians in the US during the Early 21st Century." *Social Science & Medicine* 67(10): 1481–91.

McLanahan, S., L. Tach, and D. Schneider. 2013. "The Causal Effects of Father Absence." *Annual Review of Sociology* 39: 399–427.

McMillen, Matt. 2011, February 1. "Complementary and Alternative Medicine on the Rise." *WebMD*

Archives. https://www.webmd.com/a-to-z-guides/news/20110201/complementary-and-alternative-medicine-on-the-rise.

Mead, George Herbert. 1967. *Mind, Self, and Society from the Standpoint of a Social Behaviorist*. Chicago: University of Chicago Press.

Mead, M. (1928). *Coming of Age in Samoa*. New York: William Morrow.

Medhora, S. 2015, January 8. "ACT Moves to Expunge Historic Convictions of Homosexuality." *The Guardian*. https://www.theguardian.com/world/2015/jan/09/act-moves-expunge-historic-convictions-homosexuality.

Medvetz, Thomas. 2012. *Think Tanks in America*. Chicago: University of Chicago Press.

Melucci, Alberto, John Keane, and Paul Mier. 1989. *Nomads of the Present: Social Movements and Individual Needs in Contemporary Society*. Philadelphia: Temple University Press.

Menjivar, C. 2000. *Fragmented Ties: Salvadoran Immigrant Networks in America*. Berkeley: University of California Press.

Menjivar, Cecilia. 1997. "Immigrant Kinship Networks and the Impact of the Receiving Context: Salvadorans in San Francisco in the Early 1990s." *Social Problems* 44: 104–23.

Merton, Robert. 1968. "The Matthew Effect in Science." *Science* 159: 56–63.

Merton, Robert. 1968. *Social Theory and Social Structure*. New York: Free Press.

Merton, Robert. [1942] 1973. *The Sociology of Science: Theoretical and Empirical Investigations*. Chicago: University of Chicago Press.

Merton, Robert K. 1988. "The Matthew Effect in Science, II: Cumulative Advantage and the Symbolism of Intellectual Property." *Isis* 79(4): 606–23. http://www.jstor.org/stable/234750.

Messner, Steven F., Sandro Galea, Kenneth J. Tardiff, Melissa Tracy, Angela Bucciarelli, Tinka Markham Piper, Victoria Frye, and David Vlahov. 2007. "Policing, Drugs, and the Homicide Decline in New York City in the 1990s." *Criminology* 45(2): 385–413.

Messner, Steven F., and Richard Rosenfeld. 2007. *Crime and the American Dream*. Belmont, CA: Wadsworth.

Meyer, John W. 2010. "World Society, Institutional Theories, and the Actor." *Annual Review of Sociology* 36: 1–20.

Meyer, John W., John Boli, George M. Thomas, and Francisco O. Ramirez. 1997. "World Society and the Nation-State." *American Journal of Sociology* 103(1): 144–81.

Meyer, John W., Francisco O. Ramirez, and Yasemin N. Soysal. 1992. "World Expansion of Mass Education, 1870–1970." *Sociology of Education* 65(2): 128–49.

Milanovic, Branco. 2010. *The Haves and the Have-Nots: A Brief and Idiosyncratic History of Global Inequality*. New York: Basic Books.

Milanovic, Branco. 2016. *Global Inequality: A New Approach for the Age of Globalization*. Cambridge, MA: Harvard University Press.

Miller, Claire Cain. 2016, March 18. "As Women Take Over a Male-Dominated Field, the Pay Drops." *New York Times*. Web. https://www.nytimes.com/2016/03/20/upshot/as-women-take-over-a-male-dominated-field-the-pay-drops.html.

Miller, Marc. 2016, August 17. "To Get A Job, Use Your Weak Ties." *Forbes*. https://www.forbes.com/sites/nextavenue/2016/08/17/to-get-a-job-use-your-weak-ties/#2ea3dd846b87.

Miller, Peter, and Nikolas Rose. 1997. "Mobilising the Consumer: Assembling the Subject of Consumption." *Theory, Culture & Society* 14(1): 1–36.

Mills, C. Wright. 2000. *The Sociological Imagination*. New York: Oxford University Press.

Minkoff, Debra C. 1997. "Producing Social Capital: National Social Movements and Civil Society." *American Behavioral Scientist*, 40(5): 606–619.

Misner, Ivan, Hazel M. Walker, and Frank J. De Raffelle Jr. 2012. *Business Networking and Sex: Not What You Think*. Irvine, CA: Entrepreneur Press.

Moffitt, T. E. 2005. "The New Look of Behavioral Genetics in Developmental Psychopathology: Gene–Environment Interplay in Antisocial Behavior." *Psychological Bulletin* 131: 533–54.

Mohanty, C. T. 1984. "Under Western Eyes: Feminist Scholarship and Colonial Discourses." *boundary 2*, 12(3): 333–58.

Mohr, John W., Robin Wagner-Pacifici, Ronald L. Breiger, and Petko Bogdanov. 2013. "Graphing the Grammar of Motives in U.S. National Security Strategies: Cultural Interpretation. Automated Text Analysis and the Drama of Global Politics." *Poetics* 14: 670–700.

Mojola, Sanyu A. 2014. *Love, Money and HIV: Becoming a Modern African Woman in the Age of AIDS*. Berkeley: University of California Press.

Mok, Diana, Barry Wellman, and Juan Carrasco. 2010 "Does Distance Matter in the Age of the Internet?" *Urban Studies* 47(13): 2747–783. http://www.jstor.org/stable/43079957.

Mol, Arthur, and Gert Spaargaren. 2000. "Ecological Modernisation Theory in Debate: A Review." In *Ecological Modernisation around the World*, eds. A.

Mol and D. Sonnenfeld (pp. 17–49). London: Frank Cass Publishers.

Molina-Guzmán, Isabel. 2010. *Dangerous Curves: Latina Bodies in the Media*. New York: New York University Press.

Molla, Rani, and Peter Kafka. 2019, April 3. "Here's Who Owns Everything in Big Media Today. It Probably Won't Look Like This for Long." *Recode*. https://www.recode.net/2018/1/23/16905844/media-landscape-verizon-amazon-comcast-disney-fox-relationships-chart.

Molotch, Harvey. 2005. *Where Stuff Comes From: How Toasters, Toilets, Cars, Computers and Many Other Things Come to Be As They Are*. New York: Routledge.

Moore, L., and Diez-Roux, A. 2006. "Associations of Neighborhood Characteristics with the Location and Type of Food Stores." *American Journal of Public Health* 96: 325–31.

Moore, Randy, and William McComas, 2016. The Scopes Monkey Trial. Charleston, SC: Arcadia Publishing.

Mora, G. Christina. 2015. *Making Hispanics: How Activists, Bureaucrats, and Media Constructed a New American*. Chicago: University of Chicago Press.

Morales, Manolo. Out Magazine. 2016, May 31. "After many complaints, MultiChoice bans Caitlyn Jenner's show across Africa." *Out* https://www.out.com/popnography/2016/5/31/i-am-cait-banned-africa.

Morgan, Michael, Jorgen Elbe, and Javier Curiel. 2009. "Has the Experience Economy Arrived? The Views of Destination Managers in Three Visitor Dependent Areas." *International Journal of Tourism Research* 11: 201–16.

Morgan, Stephen, and Youn-Mi Kim. 2006. "Inequality of Conditions and Intergenerational Mobility: Changing Patterns of Educational Attainment in the United States." In *Mobility and Inequality: Frontiers of Research From Sociology and Economics*, eds. S. Morgan, D. Grusky, and G. Fields (pp. 165–94). Stanford, CA: Stanford University Press.

Morran, C. 2014, April 21. "McDonald's Trying to Stop Differentiating between 'Girls' and 'Boys' Toys in Happy Meals." *The Consumerist* (archives). Yonkers, NY: Consumer Reportshttps://consumerist.com/2014/04/21/mcdonalds-trying-to-stop-differentiating-between-girls-and-boys-toys-in-happy-meals/.

Morrione, Thomas J. 1988. "Herbert G. Blumer (1900–1987): "A Legacy of Concepts, Criticisms, and Contributions." *Symbolic Interaction* 11: 1–12.

Morris, Aldon. 2015. *The Scholar Denied: W. E. B. Du Bois and the Birth of Modern Sociology*. Los Angeles: University of California Press.

Motion Picture Association of America. 2018. *Theme Report. A comprehensive analysis and survey of the theatrical and home entertainment market environment (THEME) for 2018*. https://www.mpaa.org/wp-content/uploads/2019/03/MPAA-THEME-Report-2018.pdf.

Moynihan, Ray. 2003. "The Making of a Disease: Female Sexual Dysfunction." *British Medical Journal* 326(45). https://www.bmj.com/content/326/7379/45?ijkey=1100a4d8cd38ed-943debc246da5f84e93b5c71b2&keytype2=tf_ipsecsha.

Mukerji, Chandra, and Michael Schudson, eds. 1991. *Rethinking Popular Culture: Contempory Perspectives in Cultural Studies*. Berkeley, CA: University of California Press.

Muller, Christopher, Robert Sampson, and Alix Winter. 2018. "Environmental Inequality: The Social Causes and Consequences of Lead Exposure." *Annual Review of Sociology* 44: 263–82.

Mullings, L., and A. J. Schulz. 2006. "Intersectionality and Health: An Introduction." In *Gender, Race, Class & Health: Intersectional Approaches*, eds. A. J. Schulz and L. Mullings (pp. 3–17). San Francisco: Jossey-Bass.

Munnell, Alicia. 2015, March. "The Average Age of Retirement—An Update." *Center for Retirement Research at Boston College Brief* 15(4): 1–5.

Murdock, George. 1949. *Social Structure*. New York: Free Press.

Murrell, Nathaniel Samuel. 1998. *Chanting Down Babylon: The Rastafari Reader*. Philadelphia: Temple University Press.

Musick, Kelly, Jennie E. Brand, and Dwight Davis. 2012. "Variation in the Relationship Between Education and Marriage: Marriage Market Mismatch?" *Journal of Marriage and Family* 74(1): 53–69.

Musick, K., and A. Meier. 2010. "Are Both Parents Always Better Than One? Parental Conflict and Young Adult Well-Being." Los Angeles: California Center for Population Research. http://papers.ccpr.ucla.edu/papers/PWP-CCPR-2008-022/PWP-CCPR-2008-022.pdf.

Nahin, Richard L., Patricia M. Barnes, and Barbara J. Stussman. 2016. "Expenditures on Complementary Health Approaches: United States, 2012." *National Health Statistics Reports* 95. Hyattsville, MD: National Center for Health Statistics.

Namie, Gary. 2017. "2017 WBI US Workplace Bullying Survey." http://www.workplacebullying.org/wbiresearch/wbi-2017-survey/.

Nanos, Janelle. 2016, June 22. "Millennials' Strange Love Affair with Greeting Cards." *Boston Globe*. 2016. https://www.bostonglobe.com/business/2016/06/21/stationery/cB8ULjVpWBDiJfrlJGpzxH/story.html.

Nash, Gary B. 2014. *Red, White and Black: The Peoples of Early America*, 7th ed. London: Pearson.

National Center for Children in Poverty. 2019. "Measuring Poverty." http://www.nccp.org/topics/measuringpoverty.html.

National Center for Health Workforce Analysis. 2017, July 21. *Supply and Demand Projections of the Nursing Workforce: 2014–2030*. Rockville MD: US Department of Health and Human Services, Health Resources and Services Administration, Bureau of Health Workforce, National Center for Health Workforce Analysis.

National Endowment for the Arts. 2012. "How the United States Funds the Arts, 3rd edition." NEA Office of research and Analysis. https://www.arts.gov/publications/how-united-states-funds-arts.

National Endowment for the Arts. 2015. "A Decade of Arts Engagement: Findings from the Survey of Public Participation in the Arts, 2002–2012." *NEA Research Report* #58. Office of Research and Analysis. https://www.arts.gov/sites/default/files/2012-sppa-feb2015.pdf.

National Institute of Environmental Health Sciences. 2019. "Health and Education. Women's Health." https://www.niehs.nih.gov/health/topics/population/whealth/index.cfm.

National Institutes of Health. 2017. "Genomic Medicine for Patients and the Public. Frequently Asked Questions about Genetic Testing." https://www.genome.gov/19516567/faq-about-genetic-testing/

National Science Board. 2018. *Science and Engineering Indicators 2018*. NSB-2018-1. Alexandria, VA: National Science Foundation. Available at https://www.nsf.gov/statistics/indicators/.

Neckerman, Kathryn, and Florencia Torche. 2007. "Inequality: Causes and Consequences," *Annual Review of Sociology* 33: 335–57.

Newport, Frank. 2013, July 25. "In US, 87% Approve of Black-White Marriage, vs. 4% in 1958." http://www.gallup.com/poll/163697/approve-marriage-blacks-whites.aspx.

Ng, Pak Tee. 2017, September 20. "The Education Paradoxes of Singapore." *International Herald News*. Web. https://internationalednews.com/2017/09/20/the-education-paradoxes-of-singapore/.

Nielsen. 2016, April 26. "Nearly 75% Of Global Consumers List Brand Origin As Key Purchase Driver." https://www.nielsen.com/us/en/press-room/2016/nielsen-75-percent-of-global-consumers-list-brand-origin-as-key-purchase-driver.html.

Noam, Eli M. 2016. *Who Owns the World's Media? Media Concentration and Ownership around the World*. Oxford, UK: Oxford University Press.

Nock S. L. 1995. "A Comparison of Marriages and Cohabiting Relationships." *Journal of Family Issues* 16: 53–76.

North, Douglass C. 1961. *The Economic Growth of the United States, 1790–1860*. Englewood Cliffs: Prentice-Hall.

Nusslock, R., and G. Miller. 2016. "Early-Life Adversity and Physical and Emotional Health across the Lifespan: A Neuroimmune Network Hypothesis." *Biological Psychology* 80: 23–32.

O'Barr, W. M. (2012). "Sexuality, Race, and Ethnicity in Advertising." *Advertising & Society Review* 13(3). muse.jhu.edu/article/491084.

Office for Human Research Protections. United States. 1978. *The Belmont report: ethical principles and guidelines for the protection of human subjects of research*. [Bethesda, Md.]: The Commission. https://www.hhs.gov/ohrp/regulations-and-policy/belmont-report/read-the-belmont-report/index.html.

Office of the United States Trade Representative. 2017. *2017 National Trade Estimate Report on Foreign Trade Barriers*. https://ustr.gov/sites/default/files/files/reports/2017/NTE/2017%20NTE.pdf.

Okamoto, Dina, and Kim Ebert. 2016. "Group Boundaries, Immigrant Inclusion, and the Politics of Immigrant-Native Relations." *American Behavioral Scientist* 60: 224–50.

Oliver, Melvin L., and Thomas M. Shapiro. 2006. *Black Wealth/White Wealth. A New Perspective on Racial Inequality*. New York: Routledge.

Olson, Mancur. 1971. *The Logic of Collective Action: Public Goods and the Theory of Groups*. Cambridge MA: Harvard University Press.

Olzak, Susan. 1994. *The Dynamics of Ethnic Competition and Conflict*. Stanford, CA: Stanford University Press.

Omi, Michael, and Howard Winant. 1994. *Racial Formation in the United States: From the 1960s to the 1990s*. New York: Routledge.

Onwuachi-Willig, Angela, and Jacob Willig-Onwuachi. 2009. "A House Divided: The Invisibility of the Multiracial Family." *Harvard Civil Rights–Civil Liberties Law Review* 44: 231–53.

Organ Procurement and Transplantation Network. n.d. "How Organ Allocation Works." Washington, DC: US Department of Health and Human Services. https://optn.transplant.hrsa.gov/learn/about-transplantation/how-organ-allocation-works/.

Organization for Economic Cooperation and Development. 2012. Redefining "Urban": A New Way to Measure Metropolitan Areas. Paris: OECD Publishing. https://doi.org/10.1787/9789264174108-en.

Organization for Economic Cooperation and Development. 2013. PISA 2012 Results: What Makes Schools Successful (Volume IV): Resources, Policies and Practices. Paris: OECD Publishing. https://doi.org/10.1787/9789264201156-en.

Organization for Economic Cooperation and Development. 2017. Health at a Glance 2017: OECD Indicators. Paris: OECD Publishing. https: //doi.org/10.1787/health_glance-2017-en.

Organization for Economic Cooperation and Development. 2018. "Marriage and Divorce Rates." Family Database. OECD, Social Policy Division, Directorate of Employment, Labour and Social Affairs. Web. http://www.oecd.org/els/family/database.htm.

Ostrower, Francie. 2004. *Partnerships between Large and Small Cultural Organizations: A Strategy for Building Arts Participation*. Washington, DC: Urban Institute.

Otterman, Sharon, 2011. "In City Schools, Tech Spending to Rise Despite Cuts", *New York Times*, March 29, 2011. https://www.nytimes.com/2011/03/30/nyregion/30schools.html.

Otto, Amy. 2014, April 23. "Feminists Fighting McDonald's Are Learning the Wrong Lessons." *The Federalist*. FDRLST Media. Web. https://thefederalist.com/2014/04/23/feminists-fighting-mcdonalds-are-learning-the-wrong-lessons/.

Outram, Simon. 2010. "The Use of Methylphenidate among Students: The Future of Enhancement?" *Journal of Medical Ethics* 36(4): 198–202.

Overton, Mark. 1996. *Agricultural Revolution in England: The Transformation of the Agrarian Economy 1500–1850*. Cambridge: Cambridge University Press.

Pager D. 2007a. "The Use of Field Experiments for Studies of Employment Discrimination: Contributions, Critiques, and Directions for the Future." *Annual American Academy of Political and Social Sciences* 609: 104–33.

Pager, Devah. 2007b. *Marked: Race, Crime, and Finding Work in an Era of Mass Incarceration*. Chicago: University of Chicago Press.

Pager, Devah. 2003. "The Mark of a Criminal Record." *American Journal of Sociology* 108: 937–75.

Pager, D., and Shepherd, H. 2008. "The Sociology of Discrimination: Racial Discrimination in Employment, Housing, Credit, and Consumer Markets." *Annual Review of Sociology* 34: 181–209.

Pager, Devah, Bruce Western, and Bart Bonikowski. 2009. "Discrimination in a Low-Wage Labor Market: A Field Experiment." *American Sociological Review* 74: 777–99.

Paino, M., C. Blankenship, L. Grauerholz, and J. Chin. 2012. "The Scholarship of Teaching and Learning in Teaching Sociology: 1973–2009." *Teaching Sociology* 40(2): 93–106. https://doi.org/10.1177/0092055X12437971.

Parente, V., L. Hale, and T. Palermo. 2013. "Association between Breast Cancer and Allostatic Load by Race: National Health and Nutrition Examination Survey 1999–2008." *Psychooncology* 22(3): 621–28. doi:10.1002/pon.3044.

Park, Haeyoun. 2015, November 10. "How Outsourcing Companies Are Gaming the Visa System." *New York Times*. https://www.nytimes.com/interactive/2015/11/06/us/outsourcing-companies-dominate-h1b-visas.html.

Park, Robert Ezra. 1922. *The Immigrant Press and Its Control*. New York: Harper & Brothers.

Parker, Kim. 2012, March 15. "Who Are the Boomerang Kids?" Pew Research Center Social and Demographic Trends. http://www.pewsocialtrends.org/2012/03/15/who-are-the-boomerang-kids/.

Parker, Kim, Nikki Graf, and Ruth Igielnik. January 17, 2019. Generation Z Looks A Lot Like Millennials On Key Social And Political Issues. Pew Research Center. Fact Tank. https://www.pewsocialtrends.org/2019/01/17/generation-z-looks-a-lot-like-millennials-on-key-social-and-political-issues/.

Parolin, Gianluca, 2009. *Citizenship in the Arab World*. Amsterdam: Amsterdam University Press.

Parr, Chris, 2013. "Not Staying the Course," *Inside Higher Ed*, May 10, 2013. http://www.insidehighered.com/news/2013/05/10/new-study-low-mooc-completion-rates.

Parsons, Talcott, 1943. "The Kinship System of the Contemporary United States," *American Anthropologist* 45: 22–38.

Parsons, Talcott, 1959. "The School Classroom as a Social System: Some of Its Functions in American Society." *Harvard Educational Review* 29(4): 297–318.

Parsons, Talcott, and Robert Bales. 1955. *Family, Socialization and Interaction Process*. Glencoe, IL: Free Press.

Parsons, Talcott, and Neil Joseph Smelser. 1956. *Economy and Society: A Study in the Integration of Economic and Social Theory*. New York: Free Press.

Pascoe, C. J. 2011. *Dude, You're a Fag: Masculinity and Sexuality in High School*. Berkeley: University of California Press.

Pastor, Manuel. 2015, Winter. "How Immigrant Activists Changed LA." *Dissent*. https://www.dissentmagazine.org/article/how-immigrant-activists-changed-los-angeles.

Pasura, Dominic, 2016. "Transnational Religious Practices and Negotiation of Difference among Zimbabwean Catholics." In *Migration, Transnationalism, and Catholicism: Global Perspectives*, ed. D. Pasura and M. Erdai (pp. 121–144). London: Palgrave Macmillan.

Patten, Eileen. 2013, August 28. "The Black-White and Urban-Rural Divides in Perceptions of Racial Fairness." *Pew Research Center Fact Tank*. https://www.pewresearch.org/fact-tank/2013/08/28/the-black-white-and-urban-rural-divides-in-perceptions-of-racial-fairness/.

Patterson, Orlando. 1982. *Slavery and Social Death*. Cambridge, MA: Harvard University Press.

Pattison, Mark, 2015. "Africa's Catholic Population Has Grown by 238 Percent Since 1980." *Catholic Herald*, June 3, 2015. http://www.catholicherald.co.uk/news/2015/06/03/africas-catholic-population-has-grown-by-238-per-cent-since-1980/.

Payne, Brian, 2011. *White Collar Crime*. New York: Sage Publications.

Pedulla, David S., and Sarah Thébaud. 2015. "Can We Finish the Revolution? Gender, Work-Family Ideals, and Institutional Constraint." *American Sociological Review* 80(1): 116–39.

Pelaez, Vicky. 2008, March 10. "The Prison Industry in the United States: Big Business or a New Form of Slavery?" *El Diaro-La Prensa, New York and Global Research*. https://www.globalresearch.ca/the-prison-industry-in-the-united-states-big-business-or-a-new-form-of-slavery/8289.

Perlin, Ross, 2012. *Intern Nation: How to Earn Nothing and Learn Little in the Brave New Economy*. New York: Penguin.

Perlmann, Joel, and Mary C. Waters, eds. 2002. *The New Race Question: How the Census Counts Multiracial Individuals*. New York: Russell Sage Foundation.

Peterson, Richard A. 1992. "Understanding Audience Segmentation: From Elite and Mass to Omnivore and Univore." *Poetics* 21: 243–58.

Peterson, Richard. 1996. "A Re-evaluation of the Economic Consequences of Divorce." *American Sociological Review* 61: 528–36.

Pew Research Center. 2007. "World Publics Welcome Global Trade—but Not Immigration." https://www.pewglobal.org/2007/10/04/world-publics-welcome-global-trade-but-not-immigration/.

Pew Research Center. 2010a. "A Balance Sheet at 30 Months: How the Great Recession Has Changed Life in America." Pew Research Center's Social and Demographic Trends Project. http://www.pewsocialtrends.org/files/2010/11/759-recession.pdf.

Pew Research Center. 2010b. "The Decline of Marriage and Rise of New Families." Social and Demographic Trends. https://www.pewsocialtrends.org/2010/11/18/the-decline-of-marriage-and-rise-of-new-families/.

Pew Research Center. 2011, January 13. "A Portrait of Stepfamilies." Social and Demographic Trends. https://www.pewsocialtrends.org/2011/01/13/a-portrait-of-stepfamilies/.

Pew Research Center. 2012a. "Overview of Same-Sex Marriage in the United States." http://www.pewforum.org/2012/12/07/overview-of-same-sex-marriage-in-the-united-states/.

Pew Research Center, 2012b, December 18. "The Global Religious Landscape", Pew Research Center Religion and Public Life. http://www.pewforum.org/2012/12/18/global-religious-landscape-exec/.

Pew Research Center. 2013, March 20. "Growing Support for Gay Marriage: Changed Minds and Changing Demographics." US Politics and Policy. http://www.people-press.org/2013/03/20/growing-support-for-gay-marriage-changed-minds-and-changing-demographics/.

Pew Research Center. 2014, March 7. "Millennials in Adulthood: Detached from Institutions, Networked with Friends." Social and Demographic Trends. https://www.pewsocialtrends.org/2014/03/07/millennials-in-adulthood/.

Pew Research Center. 2015a, June 10. "What Census Calls Us: A Historical Timeline." Social and Demographic Trends. https://www.pewsocialtrends.org/interactives/multiracial-timeline/.

Pew Research Center. 2015b, June 11. "Multiracial in America: Proud, Diverse, and Growing in Numbers." Social and Demographic Trends. http://www.pewsocialtrends.org/2015/06/11/multiracial-in-america/#fnref-20523-7.

Pew Research Center. 2017, September 8. "Indians in the U.S. Fact Sheet." Social and Demographic Trends. https://www.pewsocialtrends.org/fact-sheet/asian-americans-indians-in-the-u-s/.

Pew Research Center. 2018, May 31. "Media Use among US Teens." From "Teens, Social Media and Technology 2018." Internet and Technology. http://www.pewinternet.org/2018/05/31/teens-social-media-technology-2018/.

Phelan, Jo, Bruce Link, Robert Moore, and Anne Stueve. 1997. "The Stigma of Homelessness: The Impact of the Label 'Homeless' on Attitudes about the Poor." *Social Psychology Quarterly* 60: 323–37.

Pierret, Janine. 2003. "The Illness Experience: State of Knowledge and Perspectives for Research." *Sociology of Health and Illness* 25(3): 4–22.

Piketty, Thomas. 2014. *Capital in the Twenty First Century*. New York: Belknap.

Pine, B. Joseph II, and James H. Gillmore. 1999. *Experience Economy*. Cambridge, MA: Harvard Business School Press.

Pinsker, Joe. 2015, February 26. "White Privilege, Quantified." *The Atlantic*. http://www.theatlantic.com/business/archive/2015/02/white-privilege-quantified/386102/.

Piore, Michael J. 1979. *Birds of Passage: Migrant Labor and Industrial Societies*. New York: Cambridge University Press.

Piven, Frances Fox, and Richard Cloward. 1978. *Poor People's Movements: Why They Succeed, How They Fail*. New York: Vintage Books.

Plumer, Bradford. 2006, May 22. "The Origins of Anti-Litter Campaigns." *Mother Jones*. https://www.motherjones.com/politics/2006/05/origins-anti-litter-campaigns/.

Pollack, Craig Evan, Catherine Cubbin, Ayesha Sania, Mark Hayward, Donna Vallone, Brian Flaherty, and Paula A. Braveman. 2013. "Do Wealth Disparities Contribute to Health Disparities within Racial/ethnic Groups?" *Journal of Epidemiology and Community Health (1979–)* 67(5): 439–45. http://www.jstor.org/stable/43281547.

Polletta, Francesca. 1998. "'It Was Like a Fever . . .' Narrative and Identity in Social Protest." *Social Problems* 45(2): 137–59.

Polletta, Francesca, and James M. Jasper. 2001. "Collective Identity and Social Movements." *Annual Review of Sociology* 27: 283–305. http://www.scribd.com/doc/33978101/Collective-Identity-and-Social-Movements.

Popper, Karl. 2005. *The Logic of Scientific Discovery*. New York: Routledge.

Population Reference Bureau. 2015, December 1. "The Demographic Divide: What It Is and Why It Matters." https://www.prb.org/thedemographicdividewhatitisandwhyitmatters/.

Porter, M. E., and Kramer, M. R. 2006. "Strategy & Society: The Link between Competitive Advantage and Corporate Social Responsibility." *Harvard Business Review* 84: 78–92.

Portes, Alejandro. 1995. "Children of Immigrants: Segmented Assimilation and its Determinants." In *The Economic Sociology of Immigration*, ed. A. Portes (pp. 248–80). New York: Russell Sage Foundation.

Portes, Alejandro, and Robert D. Manning. 1986. "The Immigrant Enclave: Theory and Empirical Examples." In *Competitive Ethnic Relations*, eds. J. Nagel and S. Olzak (pp. 47–64). Orlando, FL: Academic Press.

Portes, Alejandro, and Alex Stepick. 1993. *City on the Edge: The Transformation of Miami*. Berkeley: University of California Press.

Powers, William. 2016, February 23. "Who's Influencing Election 2016?" Lab for Social Machines. MIT. https://medium.com/@socialmachines/who-s-influencing-election-2016-8bed68ddecc3.

Prasad, Sunila J., Pooja Nair, Karishma Gadhvi, Ishani Barai, Hiba Saleem Danish, and Aaron B. Philip. 2016, February 3. "Cultural Humility: Treating the Patient, Not the Illness." *Medical Education Online* 21, 30908. doi:10.3402/meo.v21.30908.

Prince, Martin J., Fan Wu, Yanfei Guo, Luis M. Gutierrez Robledo, Martin O'Donnell, Richard Sullivan, and Salim Yusuf. 2014. "The Burden of Disease in Older People and Implications for Health Policy and Practice." *Lancet* 385(9967): 549–62.

Prouty, Robert W., Gary Smith, and K. Charlie Lakin. 2007. *Residential Services for Persons with Developmental Disabilities: Status and Trends through 2006*. Minneapolis: University of Minnesota, Research and Training Center on Community Living.

Pugh, Allison. 2009. *Longing and Belonging*. Oakland: University of California Press.

Putnam, Robert. 2000. *Bowling Alone*. New York: Simon & Schuster.

Quah, John. 2010. *Public Administration, Singapore Style*. Bingley, West Yorkshire, England: Emerald Group Publishing.

Quillian, Lincoln. 1995. "Prejudice as a Response to Perceived Group Threat: Population Composition and Anti-immigrant and Racial Prejudice in Europe." *American Sociological Review* 60: 586–611.

Raley, R. Kelly, Megan Sweeney, and Danielle Wondra. 2015. "The Growing Racial and Ethnic Divide in US Marriage Patterns." *Future Child* 25: 89–109.

Rapaport, Abby. 2013, March 22. "Take That, Political Science!" *The American Prospect*. Web. https://prospect.org/article/take-political-science.

Rauscher, Frances H., Gordon L. Shaw, and Catherine N. Ky. 1993. "Music and Spatial Task Performance." *Nature* 365: 611.

Rauscher, Frances H., Gordon L. Shaw, Linda J. Levine, Catherine N. Ky, and Eric L. Wright. 1994. "Music and Spatial Task Performance: A Causal Relationship." Paper presented at the 102nd Annual Convention of the American Psychological Association, Los Angeles.

Redden, Elizabeth. 2017, October 11. "Foreign Students and Graduate STEM Enrollment." *Inside Higher Ed*. https://www.insidehighered.com/quicktakes/2017/10/11/foreign-students-and-graduate-stem-enrollment.

Reed, Bronwen, 2015, June 16. "'Wild Geese Families': Stress, Loneliness, for South Korean Families Heading Overseas to Gain Edge in 'Brutal' Education System." *ABC News*. http://www.abc.net.au/news/2015-06-16/thousands-of-south-korea-families-apart-for-australian-education/6547604.

Reed, Isaac Ariail. 2011. *Interpretation and Social Knowledge: On the Use of Theory in the Human Sciences*. Chicago: University of Chicago Press.

Reeves, Richard. 2014, August 20. "Saving Horatio Alger: Equality, Opportunity, and the American Dream." Washington DC: Brookings Institution Press. http://csweb.brookings.edu/content/research/essays/2014/saving-horatio-alger.html#.

Reiner, R., S. Livingstone, and J. Allen. 2003. "From Law and Order to Lynch Mobs: Crime News Since the Second World War." In *Criminal Visions: Media Representations of Crime and Justice*, ed. P. Mason (pp. 13–32). Devon, UK: Willan Publishing.

Reuter, Peter H. 2009. *Assessing the Operation of the Global Drug Market. Report 1*. RAND Corporation. https://www.rand.org/pubs/technical_reports/TR705.html.

Revers, Matthias. 2014. "Journalistic Professionalism as Performance and Boundary Work: Source Relations at the State House." *Journalism* 15(1): 37–52.

Ridgeway, Cecilia L., Kristen Backor, Yan E. Li, Justine E. Tinkler, and Kristan G. Erickson. 2009. "How Easily Does a Social Difference Become a Status Distinction? Gender Matters." *American Sociological Review* 74: 44–62.

Rincón, Lina. 2015. "Between Nations and the World: Negotiating Legal and Social Citizenship in the Migration Process." Unpublished PhD dissertation, State University of New York at Albany.

Riordan, Bruce. 2018, September 26. "The Evolution of the Police Procedural. 50 Years and 2 Golden Ages of Cops on Screen. *CrimeReads*. https://crimereads.com/the-evolution-of-the-police-procedural/.

Ritzer, George. 2013. *The McDonaldization of Society* 7. Thousand Oaks, CA: SAGE.

Rivera, Lauren, 2015. *Pedigree: How Elite Students Get Elite Jobs*. Princeton, NJ: Princeton University Press.

Roberts, Donald, and Ulla Foehr. 2004. *Kids and Media in America*. Cambridge, UK: Cambridge University Press.

Roberts, Donald, and Ulla Foehr. 2008, Spring. "Trends in Media Use." *Future Child*. 18(1): 11–37.

Roberts, Dorothy. 2012. *Fatal Invention: How Science, Politics, and Big Business Re-create Race in the Twenty-first Century*. New York: New Press.

Robins, Alexandra. 2015a. *The Nurses: A Year of Secrets, Drama, and Miracles with the Heroes of the Hospital*. New York: Workman.

Robins, Alexandra. 2015b, April 27. "Mean Girls of the ER: The Alarming Nurse Culture of Bullying and Hazing." *Marie Claire*. May 2015. https://www.marieclaire.com/culture/news/a14211/mean-girls-of-the-er/.

Robinson, Laura, Sheila Cotten, Hiroshi Ono, Anabel Quaan-Haase, Gustavo Mesch, Wenhong Chen, Jeremy Schulz, Timothy Hale, and Michael Stern, 2015. "Digital Inequalities and Why They Matter," *Information, Communication and Society* 5: 569–82.

Roby, Pamela A. 1992. "Women and the ASA: Degendering Organizations Structures and Processes, 1964–1974." *The American Sociologist* 23(1): 18–48.

Rodriguez, Clara E. 2004. *Heroes, Lovers, and Others: The Story of Latinos in Hollywood*. Washington, DC: Smithsonian Books.

Roedifer, Henry, Adam Putnam, and Megan Smith. 2011. "The Benefits of Testing and Their Applications to Educational Practice." *Psychology of Learning and Motivation* 55: 1–36.

Rogers, Everett. 1962. *Diffusion of Innovation*. New York: Free Press.

Rogers, Everett M., and James W. Dearing. 2012. "Agenda-Setting Research: Where Has It Been, Where Is It Going?" *Communication Yearbook 11* (pp. 555–94). New York: Routledge.

Romalino, Carly. 2014, December 16. "Millennials Embrace Sending Christmas Cards." *South Jersey Courier-Post.* http://www.courierpostonline.com/story/news/local/south-jersey/2014/12/16/millennials-embrace-sending-christmas-cards/20517669/.

Rootes, Christopher. 1999. "Environmental Movements: From the Local to the Global," *Environmental Politics* 8: 1–12.

Roscigno, Vincent, Sherry Mong, Reginald Byron, and Griff Tester. 2007. "Age Discrimination, Social Closure, and Employment." *Social Forces* 83: 313–44.

Rose, Nikolas. 2007a. *The Politics of Life Itself: Biomedicine, Power, and Subjectivity in the Twenty-First Century*. Princeton, NJ: Princeton University Press.

Rose, Nikolas. 2007b. "Beyond Medicalisation." *Lancet*, 369 (February 24): 700–702.

Rose, Peter, 1993. " 'Of Every Hue and Caste': Race, Immigration, and Perceptions of Pluralism." *The Annals of the American Academy of Political and Social Science* 530, 1: 187–202.

Rosenfeld, Richard. 2002. "Crime Decline in Context." *Contexts* 1(1): 25–34.

Rosenstein, A. H., and M. O'Daniel. 2008. "A Survey of the Impact of Disruptive Behavior and Communication Defects on Patient Safety." *The Joint Commission Journal on Quality and Patient Safety* 34(8): 464–71.

Roser, Max. 2015, December 4. "Democratisation." OurWorldInData.org. https://ourworldindata.org/democracy.

Roser, Max, and Esteban Ortiz-Ospina. 2018. "Literacy." OurWorldInData.org. https://ourworldindata.org/literacy.

Rossi, Alberto G., David Blake, Allan Timmermann, Ian Tonksk, and Russ Wermers. 2016. "Network Centrality and Delegated Investment Performance." *Journal of Financial Economics* 128(1): 183–206.

Rossi, Alice S. 1970. "Status of Women in Graduate Departments of Sociology, 1968–1969." *The American Sociologist* 5(1): 1–12.

Rossi, Alice S. 1985. *Gender and the Life Course*. New York: Aldine.

Rossi, Peter H. 1989a. *Down and Out in America: The Origins of Homelessness*. Chicago: University of Chicago Press.

Rossi, Peter H. 1989b. *Homelessness in America: Selected Topics*. Amherst, MA: Social and Demographic Research Institute.

Rossiter, Margaret, 1993. "The Matthew Matilda Effect in Science." *Social Studies of Science* 23(2): 325-341. doi:10.1177/030631293023002004, ISSN 0306-3127.

Rothwell, Jonathan. 2014, September 30. "How the War on Drugs Damages Black Social Mobility." Brookings Institution. http://www.brookings.edu/blogs/social-mobility-memos/posts/2014/09/30-war-on-drugs-black-social-mobility-rothwell.

Rouse, Cecilia. 1995. "Democratization or Diversion? The Effect of Community Colleges on Educational Attainment." *Journal of Business and Economic Statistics* 13: 217–24.

Rowley, Anthony. 2017, October 11. "Remittances Remain Crucial to Philippines Economy. Cash Sent Home from All over the World Was Worth US$26.9 Billion in 2016." *The National.* https://www.thenational.ae/business/remittances-remain-crucial-to-philippines-economy-1.666517.

Rubin, Kenneth, and Hildy Ross, eds. 1982. *Peer Relationships and Social Skills in Childhood*. New York: Springer.

Rucke, Katie. 2013, September 10. "P&G Pledges to Remove Controversial Chemicals from Its Products." *Mint Press News.*

Ruggles, Steven. 2012. "The Future of Historical Family Demography." *Annual Review of Sociology* 38: 423–41.

Ruiz, Neil. 2017, April 27. "Key Facts about the US H1-B Visa Program," Pew Research Center Factank. http://www.pewresearch.org/fact-tank/2017/04/27/key-facts-about-the-u-s-h-1b-visa-program/.

Rumbaut, Rubén G., and Egon Bittner. 1979. "Changing Conceptions of the Police Role: A Sociological Review." *Crime and Justice* 1: 239–288.

Sabato, Larry. 1996. "When Push Comes to Poll." *Washington Monthly* 28(6): 26–31.

Sackmann, Rosemarie, Bernhard Peters, and Thomas Faist. 2003. *Identity and Integration: Migrants in Western Europe*. Aldershot, UK: Ashgate.

Sadker, Myra, and David Sadker. 1995. *Failing at Fairness: How America's Schools Cheat Girls*. New York: Scribner.

Saenz, Rogelio. 2005, August. "The Changing Demographics of Roman Catholics." *Population Reference Bureau*. http://www.prb.org/Publicationsof/Articles/2005/TheChangingDemographicsof RomanCatholics.aspx.

Saez, Emmanuel. 2019. "Striking It Richer: The Evolution of Top Incomes in the United States (Updated with 2017 final estimates)." https://eml.berkeley.edu/~saez/saez-UStopincomes-2017.pdf.

Saguy, Abigail C. 2014. *What's Wrong with Fat?* New York: Oxford University Press.

Said, Edward W. 1994. *Culture and Imperialism*. New York: Vintage.

Sampson, R. J., S. W. Raudenbush, and F. Earls. 1997. "Neighborhoods and Violent Crime: A Multilevel Study of Collective Efficacy." *Science* 277: 918–24.

Sampson, Robert J., and John H. Laub. 1995. *Crime in the Making: Pathways and Turning Points through Life*. Cambridge, MA: Harvard University Press.

Samuel, Lawrence. 2012. *The American Dream: A Cultural History*. Syracuse, NY: Syracuse University Press.

Sanders, Bernie. 2016. "Issues. Income and Wealth Inequality" (Campaign website). https://berniesanders.com/issues/income-and-wealth-inequality/.

Sarche, Michelle, and Paul Spicer. 2008. "Poverty and Health Disparities for American Indian and Alaska Native Children: Current Knowledge and Future Prospects." *Annals of the New York Academy of Sciences* 1136: 126–36.

Sassen, Saskia. 2001. *The Global City*. Princeton, NJ: Princeton University Press.

Satran, Joe. 2013, December 14. "The Secret History of the War on Public Drinking." *Huffington Post*. http://www.huffingtonpost.com/2013/12/14/public-drinking-laws_n_4312523.html.

Saussure, Ferdinand. 1998. *Course in General Linguistics*. London: Open Court Classics.

Savage, Mike. 2015. *Social Class in the 21st Century*. New York: Penguin.

Savitsky, D. 2012. "Is Plea Bargaining a Rational Choice? Plea Bargaining as an Engine of Racial Stratification and Overcrowding in the United States Prison System." *Rationality and Society* 24(2): 131–167. https://doi.org/10.1177/1043463112441351.

Schiller, Herbert. 1991. *Culture, Inc: The Corporate Takeover of Public Expression*. New York: Oxford University Press.

Schlossberg, Nancy. 2009. *Revitalizing Retirement: Reshaping Your Identity, Relationships, and Purpose*. Washington, DC: American Psychological Association.

Schmidt, Samantha. 2017, May 26. "Breaking Down Trump's 'Shove.'" *Washington Post*.

Schmitt, Christopher. 1991, December 8. "Plea Bargaining Favors Whites, as Blacks, Hispanics Pay Price," *San Jose Mercury News*, p. 1A.

Schnaiberg, Allan. 1980. *The Environment: From Surplus to Scarcity*. New York: Oxford University Press.

Schneider, Barbara, Erin Grogan, and Adam Meier, 2011. "Improving Teacher Quality: A Sociological Presage." In *Frontiers in Sociology of Education*, ed. M. Hallinan (pp. 163–80). London: Springer.

Schneider, Joseph. 2015. "The Medicalization of Deviance: From Badness to Sickness." In *The Handbook of Deviance,* ed. Erich Goode (pp. 137–53). New York: Wiley-Blackwell.

Schofer, Evan, and John W. Meyer. 2005. "The Worldwide Expansion of Higher Education in the Twentieth Century." *American Sociological Review* 70(6): 898–920.

Schor, Juliet B. 2004. *Born to Buy: The Commercialized Child and the New Consumer Culture*. New York: Scribner.

Schreuer, Milan. 2017, October 25. "A #MeToo Moment for the European Parliament." *New York Times*. https://www.nytimes.com/2017/10/25/world/europe/european-parliament-weinstein-harassment.html.

Schudson, Michael. 1978. *Discovering the News: A Social History of American Newspapers*. New York: Basic Books.

Schudson, Michael. 2011. *The Sociology of News*, 2nd ed. New York: W. W. Norton.

Schuster, J. Mark Davidson. 1991. *The Audience for American Art Museums. Research Division Report #23*. Washington, DC: National Endowment for the Arts. http://eric.ed.gov/?id=ED351242.

Schwarz, H. 2015, April 28. "There Are 390,000 Gay Marriages in the U.S. The Supreme Court Could Quickly Make It Half a Million." *Washington Post*. https://www.washingtonpost.com/news/the-fix/wp/2015/04/28/heres-how-many-gay-marriages-the-supreme-court-could-make-way-for/?utm_term=.1c6c3dd8e67d.

Scientific American. 2007. "The Association of Black Cardiologists Responds to 'Race In A Bottle.'" July

30, 2007. https://www.scientificamerican.com/article/the-association-of-black-cardiologists-responds-to-article/.

Scientific American. 2007. "BiDil Maker NitroMed Responds to 'Race In A Bottle.'" July 30, 2007. https://www.scientificamerican.com/article/bidil-maker-nitromed-responds-to-race-in-a-bottle/.

Scientific American. "Race-Based Medicine: A Recipe for Controversy." https://www.scientificamerican.com/article/race-based-medicine-a-recipe-for-controversy/.

Sclafane, Susanne. 2010, May 23. "Chinese Drywall Maker Settles Lawsuit; Terms Undisclosed, but Agreement Sets Stage for More Moves with Homebuilders." *Property and Casualty.* https://www.propertycasualty360.com/2010/05/23/chinese-drywall-maker-settles-lawsuit/?slreturn=20190622170220.

Scott, James. 1985. *Weapons of the Weak: Everyday Forms of Peasant Resistance.* New Haven, CT: Yale University Press.

Scott, John. 2006. *Social Theory: Central Issues in Sociology.* Thousand Oaks, CA: SAGE.

Scully, Jackie Leach. 2004. "What Is a Disease?" *EMBO Reports* 5(7): 650–53. http://doi.org/10.1038/sj.embor.7400195.

Sedgewick, E. K. (2008). *Epistemology of the Closet* (updated with a new preface). Los Angeles: University of California Press.

Seeman, T. E., E. Crimmins, M. H. Huang, B. Singer, A. Bucur, T. Gruenewald, L. F. Berkman, and D. B. Reuben. 2004. "Cumulative Biological Risk and Socio-economic Differences in Mortality: MacArthur Studies of Successful Aging." *Social Science and Medicine* 58(10): 1985–97.

Seidman, Steven. 1985. *Contested Knowledge: Social Theory in the Postmodern Era.* Malden, MA: Blackwell.

Seidman, Steven. 2002. *Beyond the Closet: The Transformation of Gay and Lesbian Life.* New York: Routledge.

Seidman, Steven. 2013. *Contested Knowledge: Social Theory Today,* 5th ed. Hoboken, NJ: Wiley.

Seidman, Steven, and Jeffrey C. Alexander. 2001. *The New Social Theory Reader.* New York: Routledge.

Semotiuk, Andy J. 2019, January 2. "Recent Changes to the H1B Visa Program and What Is Coming in 2019." *Forbes* https://www.forbes.com/sites/andyjsemotiuk/2019/01/02/recent-changes-to-the-h1b-visa-program-and-what-is-coming-in-2019/#161cd0af4a81.

Semuels, Alana. 2016, June 2. "The Graying of Rural America." *The Atlantic.* https://www.theatlantic.com/business/archive/2016/06/the-graying-of-rural-america/485159/.

Sengupta, Somini. 2018, September 10. "U.N. Chief Warns of a Dangerous Tipping Point on Climate Change." *New York Times.* https://www.nytimes.com/2018/09/10/climate/united-nations-climate-change.html.

Sennet, Richard. 1972. *The Hidden Injuries of Class.* New York: Knopf.

Sennet, Richard. 2005, September 13. *The Culture of the New Capitalism.* New Haven, CT: Yale University Press.

Shafer, Emily. 2006. "Are Men or Women More Reluctant to Marry in Couples Sharing a Non-Marital Birth?" *Gender Issues* 23(2): 20–43.

Shakespeare, Tom, and Nicholas Watson. 2001. "The Social Model of Disability: An Outdated Ideology?" In *Research in Social Science and Disability,* Vol 2, eds. Sharon N. Barnartt and Barbara Altman eds. (pp. 9–28). Amsterdam and New York: JAI.

Shanahan, James, and Michael Morgan. 1999. *Television and Its Viewers.* Cambridge, UK: Cambridge University Press.

Shapin, Steven, 1995. "Here and Everywhere: Sociology of Scientific Knowledge." *Annual Review of Sociology* 21: 289–321.

Shapiro, Ariel. 2019, May 15. "World's Biggest Media Companies." Forbes Global 2000. *Forbes.* https://www.forbes.com/sites/arielshapiro/2019/05/15/worlds-largest-media-companies-2019/#7a0ee5a754bb.

Shapiro, Thomas. 2005. *The Hidden Costs of Being African-American: How Wealth Perpetuates Inequality.* New York: Oxford University Press.

Shin, Laura. 2015, March 26. "The Racial Wealth Gap: Why a Typical White Household Has 16 Times the Wealth of a Black One." *Forbes.* http://www.forbes.com/sites/laurashin/2015/03/26/the-racial-wealth-gap-why-a-typical-white-household-has-16-times-the-wealth-of-a-black-one/#36a044b66c5b.

Shlay, Anne B., and Peter H. Rossi. 1992. "Social Science Research and Contemporary Studies of Homelessness." *Annual Review of Sociology* 18: 129–60.

Short, Kevin. 2014, October 21. "Next Time Someone Says 'White Privilege Isn't Real,' Show Them This." *Huffington Post.* http://www.huffingtonpost.com/

2014/10/21/upward-mobility-race_n_6016154. html.

Shrader, Brad, Jeffrey Kaufmann, and Sue Pickard Ravenscroft. 2006, June 15. "Why Do Some Students Cheat? They Rationalize It, ISU Research Finds." (press release). https://www.news.iastate. edu/news/2006/jun/rationalizing.shtml.

Shrum, Wesley. 1996. *Fringe and Fortune: The Role of Critics in High and Popular Art.* Princeton, NJ: Princeton University Press.

Shrum, Wesley, Meil Creek, and Suadra Hunter, 1988. "Friendship in School: Gender and Racial Homophily." *Sociology of Education* 61: 227–39.

Shuey, K. M., and Willson, A. E. (2008). "Cumulative Disadvantage and Black-White Disparities in Life-Course Health Trajectories." *Research on Aging* 30(2): 200–25.

Shumow, Lee B., and Jennifer A. Schmidt. 2013. *Enhancing Adolescents' Motivation for Science: Research-Based Strategies for Teaching Male and Female Students.* Thousand Oaks, CA: Corwin.

Shumway, D. (2003). *Modern Love. Romance, Intimacy, and the Marriage Crisis.* New York: NYU Press.

Sidibé, Michel. 2012, July 5. "Giving Power to Couples to End the AIDS Epidemic." *Huffington Post.* https://www.huffpost.com/entry/hiv-aids _b_1477206.

Siegel, Robert, and Michele Norris. 2007, June 11. "*Loving* Decision: 40 Years of Legal Interracial Unions," *NPR.* http://www.npr.org/templates/ transcript/transcript.php?storyId=10889047.

Sikora, A. G., and Mulvihill, M. (2002). "Trends in Mortality Due to Legal Intervention in the United States, 1979 through 1997." *American Journal of Public Health* 92(5): 841–43.

Silverman, Rachel Emma, and Michelle Higgins. 2003, September 17. "When the Kids Get the House in a Divorce." *Wall Street Journal.* https:// www.wsj.com/articles/SB106374829921566600.

Simonson, Peter. 2005. "The Serendipity of Merton's Communications Research." *International Journal of Public Opinion Research* 17: 277–97.

Simpson, Brent, Ashley Harrell, and Robb Willer. 2013. "Hidden Paths from Morality to Social Order: Moral Judgments Promote Prosocial Behavior." *Social Forces* 91: 1529–48.

Skelton, George. 2015, March 26. "Attitudes Shift on Illegal Immigration, but Unity Eludes Other Issues." *Los Angeles Times.* http://www.latimes. com/local/politics/la-me-cap-california-poll-20150326-column.html.

Skocpol, Theda. 1995. *Social Policy in the United States: Future Possibilities in Historical Perspective.* Princeton, NJ: Princeton University Press.

Skocpol, Theda, 1996. "The Politics of American Social Policy, Past and Future," in Individual and Social Responsibility: Child Care, Education, Medical Care, and Long-Term Care in America, ed. V. Fuchs. University of Chicago Press, pp. 309–34.

Slavin, Stuart J., and John T. Chibnall. 2017. "Mistreatment of Medical Students in the Third Year May Not Be the Problem." *Medical Teacher* 39(8): 891–93.

Smedley, Audrey. 1993. *Race in North America: Origin and Evolution of a Worldview.* Boulder, CO: Westview Press.

Smelser, Neil J. 1963. *The Sociology of Economic Life.* Englewood Cliffs, NJ: Prentice-Hall.

Smith, Aaron, and Monica Anderson. 2018, March 1. "Social Media Use in 2018." Pew Research Center. http://www.pewinternet.org/2018/03/01/ social-media-use-in-2018/.

Smith, Anthony D. 2004. *Chosen Peoples: Sacred Sources of National Identity.* New York: Oxford University Press.

Smith, Brad, and Harry Shum, 2018. *The Future Computed: Artificial Intelligence and the Future of Society.* Microsoft. https://blogs.microsoft .com/wp-content/uploads/2018/02/The-Future-Computed_2.8.18.pdf.

Smith, Christian, ed., 1996. *Disruptive Religion: The Force of Faith in Social Movement Activism.* New York: Routledge.

Smith, Lawrence, Lisa Best, D. Alan Stubbs, John Johnston, and Andrea Archibald, 2000. "Scientific Graphs and the Hierarchy of the Sciences." *Social Studies of Science* 30: 73–94.

Smith, Philip. 2008. *Punishment and Culture.* Chicago: University of Chicago Press.

Smith, Philip, and Nicolas Howe. 2015. *Climate Change as Social Drama: Global Warming in the Public Sphere.* Cambridge University Press.

Smith, Philip, Timothy L. Phillips, and Ryan D. King. 2010. *Incivility: The Rude Stranger in Everyday Life.* New York: Cambridge University Press.

Smith, Philip, and Alexander Riley. 2008. *Cultural Theory: An Introduction.* Malden, MA: Wiley-Blackwell.

Smith, Rebecca. 2014, April 18. "Bullying at School Affects Health 40 Years Later." *The Guardian.* https://www.telegraph.co.uk/news/health/children/10772302/Bullying-at-school-affects-health-40-years-later.html.

Smock, Pamela. 2000. "Cohabitation in the United States: An Appraisal of Research Themes, Findings, and Implications." *Annual Review of Sociology* 26: 1–20.

Smock, Pamela J., and Fiona Rose Greenland. 2010. "Diversity in Pathways to Parenthood: Patterns, Implications, and Emerging Research Directions." *Journal of Marriage and Family* 72(3): 576–93. http://www.jstor.org/stable/40732497.

Snow, Charles Percy. [1959] 2001. *The Two Cultures.* London: Cambridge University Press.

Snow, David A., and Leon Anderson. 1993. *Down on Their Luck: A Study of Homeless Street People.* Oakland: University of California Press.

Snyder, Gregory. 2009. *Graffiti Lives: Beyond the Tag in New York's Urban Underground.* New York: NYU Press.

Sobieraj, Sarah. 2011. *Soundbitten: The Perils of Media-Centered Political Activism.* New York: NYU Press.

Soper, Taylor. 2013, May 22. "Report: Teens Leave Facebook for Twitter, Because They Want Less Drama." *Geekwire.* http://www.geekwire.com/2013/pew-report-teens-facebook-twitter-instagram/.

Sorensen, Aage, and Arne Kalleberg. 1981. "An Outline of a Theory of the Matching of Persons to Jobs." In *Sociological Perspectives on Labor Markets,* ed. I. Berg (pp. 49–74). New York: Academic Press.

Southern Poverty Law Center. 2004, December 21. "Wal-Mart Drops Protocols, but Controversy Lives On." *Intelligence Report.* https://www.splcenter.org/fighting-hate/intelligence-report/2004/wal-mart-drops-protocols-controversy-lives.

Soysal, Yasemin, and David Strang, 1989. "Construction of the First Mass Education Systems in Nineteenth-Century Europe." *Sociology of Education* 62: 277–88.

Spierenberg, Pieter, 1984. *The Spectacle of Suffering.* New York: Cambridge University Press.

Spradlin, J. Isaac. 2009, April 27. "The Evolution of Interns." *Forbes.* https://www.forbes.com/2009/04/27/intern-history-apprenticeship-leadership-careers-jobs.html#32c6b3a746b7.

Stacey, Judith, and Barrie Thorne. 1985. "The Missing Feminist Revolution in Sociology." *Social Problems* 32: 301–16.

Staggenborg, Suzanne. 2010. *Social Movements.* New York: Oxford University Press.

Stainback, Kevin, and Donald Tomaskovic-Devey. 2009. "Intersections of Power and Privilege: Long-Term Trends in Managerial Representation." *American Sociological Review* 74: 800–20.

Stampler, Laura. 2011, April 20 "SlutWalks Sweep The Nation". *Huffington Post.* https://www.huffpost.com/entry/slutwalk-united-states-city_n_851725?guccounter=1.

Starr, Paul. [1982] 2017. *The Social Transformation of American Medicine: The Rise of a Sovereign Profession and the Making of a Vast Industry.* New York: Basic Books.

Stenmark, Mikael, 2014. "Relativism: A Pervasive Feature of the Contemporary Western World?" *Social Epistemology* 29: 31–43.

Stepler, Renee, and Anna Brown. 2016, April 19. "Statistical Portrait of Hispanics in the United States." Pew Research Center Hispanic Trends. http://www.pewhispanic.org/2016/04/19/statistical-portrait-of-hispanics-in-the-united-states/.

Stevens, Mitchell. 2001. *Kingdom of Children: Culture and Controversy in the Homeschooling Movement.* Princeton, NJ: Princeton University Press.

Stevens, Mitchell L., Elizabeth A. Armstrong, and Richard Arum. 2008. "Sieve, Incubator, Temple, Hub: Empirical and Theoretical Advances in the Sociology of Higher Education." *Annual Review of Sociology* 34: 127–51.

Stevenson, Betsy, and Justin Wolfers. 2007. "Marriage and Divorce: Changes and Their Driving Factors." NBER Working Paper 12944. http://www.nber.org/papers/w12944.pdf.

Strauss, A., and Glaser, B., eds. 1975. *Chronic Illness and the Quality of Life.* St. Louis: Mosby.

Strauss, William, and Neil Howe, 2000. *Millennials Rising: The Next Great Generation.* New York: Vintage.

Streib, Jessi. 2017. "The Unbalanced Theoretical Toolkit: Problems and Partial Solutions to Studying Culture and Reproduction but Not Culture and Mobility." *American Journal of Cultural Sociology,* 5(1–2): 127–153. https://doi.org/10.1057/s41290-016-0015-5.

Student Doctor Network. 2016, May 3. "The MCAT: A History and Current Overview" https://www.studentdoctor.net/2016/05/03/the-new-mcat/.

Su, Dejun, and Lifeng Li. 2011. "Trends in the Use of Complementary and Alternative Medicine in the United States: 2002–2007." *Journal of Health Care for the Poor and Underserved* 22(1): 296–310.

Suarez-Orozco, C., and Suarez-Orozco, M. 2001. *Children of Immigration.* Cambridge, MA: Harvard University Press.

Sullivan, Andrew. 2004. *Same-Sex Marriage: Pro and Con*. New York: Vintage.

Sullivan, Deborah A. 2001. *Cosmetic Surgery: The Cutting Edge of Medicine in America*. New Brunswick, NJ: Rutgers University Press.

Sullivan, Laura, Tatjana Meschede, Lars Dietrich, and Thomas Shapiro. 2015. "The Racial Wealth Gap: Why Policy Matters." *Demos*. http://www.demos.org/sites/default/files/publications/RacialWealthGap_1.pdf.

Sullivan, Ruth. 2015, September 18. "Is London's Knightsbridge Still a Golden Postcode for Homebuyers?" *Financial Times*. https://www.ft.com/content/e71a4138-587c-11e5-9846-de406ccb37f2.

Sundt, J. (2002). "Rehabilitation Model." In *Encyclopedia of Crime and Punishment*, ed. D. Levinson (pp. 1361–67). Thousand Oaks, CA: SAGE.

Sutherland, Anna. 2014. "The Rise of Cohabitation." *Institute for Family Studies* (blog). https://ifstudies.org/blog/the-rise-of-cohabitation/.

Sweeney, Megan M. 2010. "Remarriage and Stepfamilies: Strategic Sites for Family Scholarship in the 21st Century." *Journal of Marriage and Family* 72(3): 667–84. http://www.jstor.org/stable/40732502.

Sweet, S., and Cardwell, M. 2016. "Editor's Comment: Considering Assessment." *Teaching Sociology*, 44(3): 149–50. https://doi.org/10.1177/0092055X16650659.

Sweet, S., McElrath, K., and Kain, E. L. 2014. "The Coordinated Curriculum: How Institutional Theory Can Be Used to Catalyze Revision of the Sociology Major." *Teaching Sociology* 42(4): 287–97. https://doi.org/10.1177/0092055X14541551.

Swidler, Ann. 1986. "Culture in Action: Symbols and Strategies." *American Sociological Review* 51(2): 273–86.

Swire, Peter. 2015. "The USA FREEDOM Act, the President's Review Group and the Biggest Intelligence Reform in 40 Years." Privacy Perspectives. https://iapp.org/news/a/the-usa-freedom-act-the-presidents-review-group-and-the-biggest-intelligence-reform-in-40-years.

Tach, L. M., and Eads, A. 2015. "Trends in the Economic Consequences of Marital and Cohabitation Dissolution in the United States. *Demography* 52: 401–32.

Tarrow, Sidney G. 1989. *Democracy and Disorder: Protest and Politics in Italy, 1965–1975*. Oxford, UK: Oxford University Press.

Tatum, Beverly. 1997. *"Why Are All the Black Kids Sitting Together in the Cafeteria?" and Other Conversations about Race*. New York: Basic Books.

Taylor, Charles. 1994. *Multiculturalism: Examining the Politics of Recognition*. Princeton, NJ: Princeton University Press.

Taylor, Charles. 2007. *A Secular Age*. Cambridge, MA: Harvard University Press.

Telep, Cody, and David Weisburd, 2012. "What Is Known about the Effectiveness of Police Practices in Reducing Crime and Disorder?" *Police Quarterly* 20: 1–27.

Telles, Edward E. 2002. "Racial Ambiguity among the Brazilian Population." *Ethnic and Racial Studies* 25(3):415–441.

Tepper, Steven J. 2011. *Not Here, Not Now, Not That!* Chicago: University of Chicago Press.

Terpstra, Jan. 2011. "Two Theories on the Police—The Relevance of Max Weber and Emile Durkheim to the study of the police." *International Journal of Law Crime and Justice* 39(1): 1–11. 10.1016/j.ijlcj.2011.01.009.

Tervalon, M., and J. Murray-Garcia. 1998. "Cultural Humility versus Cultural Competence: A Critical Distinction in Defining Physician Training Outcomes in Multicultural Education." *Journal of Health Care for the Poor and Underserved* 9(2): 117–125.

Thoits, Peggy. 2010. "Stress and Health: Major Findings and Policy Implications." *Journal of Health and Social Behavior* 51: S41–S53.

Thomas, Kevin J. A. 2012. "Demographic Profile of Black Caribbean Immigrants in the United States." Washington DC: Migration Policy Institute.

Thompson, Caroline. 2017, May 4. "Fat-Positive Activists Explain What It's Really Like to Be Fat." *Vice*. https://www.vice.com/en_us/article/gvzx94/fat-positive-activists-explain-what-its-really-like-to-be-fat.

Thompson, John. 1991. *Ideology and Modern Culture: Critical Social Theory in the Era of Mass Communication*. Stanford, CA: Stanford University Press.

Thompson, Kenneth, 2012. "Globalization and Religion." In *The Oxford Handbook of Cultural Sociology*, eds. Jeffrey Alexander, Philip Smith, and Ronald Jacobs (pp. 471–486). New York: Oxford University Press.

Thornton, Arland. 1989. "Changing Attitudes toward Family Issues in the United States." *Journal of Marriage and Family* 51(4): 873-93. doi:10.2307/353202.

Tilly, Charles. 1999. *Durable Inequality*. Berkeley: University of California Press.

Tilly, Charles. 2004. *Social Movements, 1768-2004*. Boulder, CO: Paradigm.

Tilly, Charles, and Lesley J. Wood. 2012. *Social Movements 1768–2012*. New York: Routledge.

Timmermans, Stefan. 2008. "Oh Look, There Is a Doctor after All: About the Resilience of Professional Medicine: A Commentary on McKinlay and Marceau's 'When There Is No Doctor.'" *Social Science & Medicine* 67(10): 1492–96.

Tocqueville, Alexis de. [1835, 1840] 2003. *Democracy in America*, ed. L. Kramnick. London: Penguin Classics.

Tolnay, Stewart. 2003. "The African-American 'Great Migration' and Beyond." *Annual Review of Sociology* 29: 209–32.

Tomaskovic-Devey D., M. Thomas, and K. Johnson. 2005. "Race and the Accumulation of Human Capital across the Career: A Theoretical Model and Fixed-Effects Application." *American Journal of Sociology* 111: 58–89.

Tomaskovic-Devey, Donald, and Patricia Warren. 2009. "Explaining and Eliminating Racial Profiling." *Contexts* 8: 34–39.

Tong, Elisa K., and Stanton A. Glantz. 2007. "Tobacco Industry Efforts Undermining Evidence Linking Secondhand Smoke with Cardiovascular Disease." *Circulation* 116(16): 1845–54.

Tonry, Michael. 1995. *Malign Neglect*. New York: Oxford University Press.

Tonry, M. 2007. "Looking Back to See the Future of Punishment in America." *Social Research* 74(2): 353–378.

Tonry, Michael. 2014. "Remodeling American Sentencing: A Ten-Step Blueprint for Moving Past Mass Incarceration." *Criminology and Public Policy* 13: 503–33.

Touraine, Alain. 1971. *The Post-industrial Society: Tomorrow's Social History: Classes, Conflicts and Culture in the Programmed Society*. New York: Random House.

Touraine, Alain, 1981. *The Voice and the Eye*. Cambridge: Cambridge University Press.

Tresch, A. 2009. "Politicians in the Media: Determinants of Legislators' Presence and Prominence in Swiss Newspapers." *The International Journal of Press/Politics*. 14(1): 67–90.

Tuchman, Gaye. 1978. *Making News: A Study in the Construction of Reality*. New York: Free Press.

Tunstall, Jeremy. 2007. *The Media Were American: U.S. Mass Media in Decline*. New York: Oxford University Press.

Turnbull, Sue. 2014. "The Roots of Crime." In *The TV Crime Drama* (pp. 20–43). Edinburgh: Edinburgh University Press. http://www.jstor.org/stable/10.3366/j.ctt1g0b60z.6.

Turner, William B. 2000. *A Genealogy of Queer Theory*. Philadelphia: Temple University Press.

Turow, Joseph. 1998. *Breaking Up America: Advertising and the New Media World*. Chicago: University of Chicago Press.

Twenge, J. M. 1997. "Changes in Masculine and Feminine Traits over Time: A Meta-analysis." *Sex Roles* 36(5): 305–25.

Uggen, Christopher, Jeff Manza, and Melissa Thompson. 2006. "Citizenship, Democracy, and the Civic Reintegration of Criminal Offenders." *The Annals of the American Academy of Political and Social Science* 605: 281–310.

UNAIDS. 2017. "Make Some Noise for Zero Discrimination on 1 March 2017." http://www.unaids.org/sites/default/files/media_asset/2017-zero-discrimination-day_en.pdf.

UNESCO. 2017. *School Violence and Bullying: Global Status Report*. http://unesdoc.unesco.org/images/0024/002469/246970e.pdf.

Unger, Roberto, 1976. *Law in Modern Society*. New York: Free Press.

United Nations, Department of Economic and Social Affairs, Population Division. 2016a. *The World's Cities in 2016—Data Booklet (ST/ESA/SER.A/392)*. New York, NY: United Nations. https://www.un.org/en/development/desa/population/publications/databooklet/index.asp.

United Nations, Department of Economic and Social Affairs, Population Division. 2016b. *International Migration Report 2015: Highlights (ST/ESA/SER.A/375)*.

United Nations Development Programme, 2009. *Human Development Report 2009*. "Overcoming Barriers: Human mobility and development." New York: Palgrave Macmillan. http://hdr.undp.org/sites/default/files/reports/269/hdr_2009_en_complete.pdf.

Upchurch D. M., B. W. Rainisch, and L. Chyu. 2015. "Greater Leisure Time Physical Activity Is Associated with Lower Allostatic Load in White, Black, and Mexican American Midlife Women: Findings from the National Health and Nutrition Examination Survey, 1999 through 2004." *Women's Health Issues*. 25(6): 680–87. doi:10.1016/j.whi.2015.07.002.

US Census. 2018. "Estimated Median Age at First Marriage: 1890 to present. Current Population survey. Table MS-2." https://www.census.gov/

data/tables/time-series/demo/families/marital.html.

US Census. 2018. Current Population Survey, 1968 to 2018. Annual Social and Economic Supplements. https://www.census.gov/content/dam/Census/library/visualizations/2018/demo/p60-263/figure1.pdf.

US Centers for Disease Control and Prevention, US Health Disparities & Inequalities Report 2011. https://www.cdc.gov/mmwr/pdf/other/su6001.pdf.

US Centers for Disease Control and Prevention and National Cancer Institute. 2019. "Cancer Statistics Data Visualizations Tool, based on November 2018 submission data (1999-2016)." U.S. Cancer Statistics Working Group. U.S. Department of Health and Human Services. www.cdc.gov/cancer/dataviz.

US Congress, Office of Technology Assessment. 1992, February. "Testing in American Schools: Asking the Right Questions, OTA-SET-519." Washington, DC: US Government Printing Office.

US Department of Heath and Human Services. 2017. "Defining Health Systems." Agency for Healthcare Research and Quality. https://www.ahrq.gov/chsp/chsp-reports/resources-for-understanding-health-systems/defining-health-systems.html.

US Department of Health and Human Services. 2016. "Physicians and Hospitals in U.S. Health Systems, 2016." Data Infographics. Agency for Health Research and Quality. https://www.ahrq.gov/sites/default/files/wysiwyg/data/infographics/physicians-hospitals.pdf.

US Food and Drug Administration. 2005. *Collection of Race and Ethnicity Data in Clinical Trials*. Silver Spring, MD: US Department of Health and Human Services, US Food and Drug Administration.

Vagianos, A. 2015, February 19. "1 in 3 Women Has Been Sexually Harassed at Work, According to Survey." *Huffington Post*. http://www.huffingtonpost.com/2015/02/19/1-in-3-women-sexually-harassed-work-cosmopolitan_n_6713814.html.

Vaillant, George. 2012. *Triumphs of Experience: The Men of the Harvard Grant Study*. Cambridge, MA: Belknap Press.

Valdivia, Angharad N. 2010. *Latina/os and the Media*. Cambridge, UK: Polity.

Valenzuela, Angela. 1999. *Subtractive Schooling: U.S.-Mexican Youth and the Politics of Caring*. Albany: SUNY Press.

Van Atteveldt, Wouter, Nel Ruigrok, Kasper Welbers, and Carina Jacobi. 2018. "News Waves in a Changing Media Landscape 1950–2014." *From Media Hype to Twitter Storm: News Explosions and Their Impact on Issues, Crises, and Public Opinion*, ed. Peter Vasterman (pp. 61–82). Amsterdam: Amsterdam University Press. http://www.jstor.org/stable/j.ctt21215m0.7.

van Emmerik, Hetty I., M. C. Euwema, M. Geschiere, and M. F. A. G. Schouten. 2006. "Networking Your Way through the Organization." *Women in Management Review* 21(1): 54–66.

Van Zuylen-Wood. 2013, 12 December. "Philly was the First City in America to have Squirrels." *Philadelphia*. https://www.phillymag.com/news/2013/12/12/philly-first-city-america-squirrels/.

Vasilogambros, Matt. 2016, April 7. "Cuba, The Brand." *The Atlantic*. https://www.theatlantic.com/business/archive/2016/04/little-havana-miami/477204/.

Vaughan, Diane. 1990. *Uncoupling: Turning Points in Intimate Relationships*. New York: Vintage.

Veblen, Thorstein. 1899. *The Theory of the Leisure Class*. New York: Macmillan.

Vercayie, Diemer, and Marc Herremans. 2015. "Citizen Science and Smartphones Take Roadkill Monitoring to the Next Level." *Nature Conservation* 11: 29–40. doi:10.3897/natureconservation.11.4439.

Verhoeven, Beatrice, and Rasha Ali. 2016, June 7. "'The Bachelorette' So White: Inside the Show's Diversity Deficit. ABC's 'The Bachelorettte' and 'Bachelor' Always Have the Same Relationship Status with Race: It's Complicated." *The Wrap*.

Vogt, Evon, 1969. *Zincantan: A Maya Community in the Highlands of Chiapas*. Cambridge, MA: Harvard University Press.

Voss, Kim, and Irene Bloemraad, eds. 2011. *Rallying for Immigrant Rights: The Fight for Inclusion in 21st Century America*. Berkeley: University of California Press.

Wacquant, Loïc. 2006. *Body & Soul: Notebooks of an Apprentice Boxer*. New York: Oxford University Press.

Waddington, P.A.J., 2002. *Policing Citizens: Police, Power, and the State*. New York: Routledge.

Wakefield, Melanie A., Barbara Loken, and Robert C. Hornik. 2010. "Use of Mass Media Campaigns to Change Health Behaviour." *Lancet* 376(9748): 1261–71.

Wallerstein, Immanuel. 1976. "From Feudalism to Capitalism: Transition or Transitions?" *Social Forces* 55: 273–83.

Wallerstein, Immanuel Maurice. 2004. *World-Systems Analysis: An Introduction*. Durham, NC: Duke University Press.

Wallerstein, Judith. 1991. "The Long-Term Effects of Divorce on Children: A Review." *Journal of the American Academy of Child and Adolescent Psychiatry* 30: 349–60.

Wallsten, Kevin. 2015. "Non-Elite Twitter Sources Rarely Cited in Coverage." *Newspaper Research Journal* 36 (1): 24–41. doi:10.1177/0739532915580311.

Wang, Wendy. 2012, February 16. "The Rise of Intermarriage." Pew Research Social and Demographic Trends. http://www.pewsocialtrends.org/2012/02/16/the-rise-of-intermarriage/.

Ware, Bronnie. 2011. *The Top Five Regrets of the Dying*. London: Hay House.

Warner, Michael. 1993. *Fear of a Queer Planet: Queer Politics and Social Theory*. Minneapolis: University of Minnesota Press.

Waters, Mary. 1990. *Ethnic Options: Choosing Identities in America*. Berkeley: University of California Press.

Waters, Mary. 2001. *Black Identities: West Indian Immigrant Dreams and American Realities*. Cambridge, MA: Harvard University Press.

Weber, Max. 1946. *From Max Weber: Essays in Sociology*. New York: Oxford University Press.

Weber, Max, 1969. *The City*. New York: Free Press.

Weber, Max. [1905] 2011. *The Protestant Ethic and the Spirit of Capitalism*. New York: Oxford University Press.

Webley, K. 2010, April 30. "A Brief History of the Happy Meal." *Time*. http://content.time.com/time/nation/article/0,8599,1986073,00.html.

Weil, Patrick. 2001. "Access to citizenship: A comparison of twenty five nationality laws." In *Citizenship Today: Global Perspectives and Practices*, eds. T. Alexander Aleinikoff and Douglas Klusmeyer (pp 17–35). Carnegie Endowment for International Peace, Washington DC.

Weiss, A., and S. M. Chermak. 1998. "The News Value of African American Victims: An Examination of the Media's Presentation of Homicide." *Journal of Crime and Justice* 21: 71–88.

Weiss, Rick, and Justin Gillis. 2000, June 27. "Teams Finish Mapping Human DNA." *Washington Post*. https://www.washingtonpost.com/archive/politics/2000/06/27/teams-finish-mapping-human-dna/3af9bfcf-e7b6-4ac1-bcdb-f4fc117c19bd/?utm_term=.b3e595005bb8.

Weller, Jennifer, Matt Boyd, and David Cumin. 2014. "Teams, Tribes and Patient Safety: Overcoming Barriers to Effective Teamwork in Healthcare." *Postgraduate Medical Journal* 90(1061): 149–54.

Welsh, Brandon C., and David P. Farrington. 2009, October. "Public Area CCTV and Crime Prevention: An Updated Systematic Review and Meta-Analysis." *Justice Quarterly* 26(4): 716–45.

Welzel, Christian, and Ronald Inglehart. 2009. "Political Culture, Mass Beliefs and Value Change." In *Democratization* (pp. 126–44). Oxford, UK: Oxford University Press.

Western, Bruce. 2006. *Punishment and Inequality in America*. New York: Russell Sage Foundation.

Western, Bruce, and Sara McLanahan. 2000. "Fathers behind Bars: The Impact of Incarceration on Family Research." *Contemporary Perspectives in Family Research* 2: 309–24.

Western, Bruce, and Becky Petit. 2005. "Black-White Earnings Inequality, Employment Rates, and Incarceration." *American Journal of Sociology* 111: 553–78.

Wilkinson, Richard, and Kate Pickett. 2009. *The Spirit Level: Why Greater Equality Makes Societies Stronger*. London: Bloomsbury Press.

Williams, C. L. 1992. "The Glass Escalator: Hidden Advantages for Men in the "Female" Professions." *Social Problems* 39(3): 253–67.

Williams, C. L. (2013). "The Glass Escalator, Revisited. Gender Inequality in Neoliberal Times." *Gender & Society, 27*(5): 609–29.

Williams, Fiona. 2018. "A Global Crisis in Care?" *Global Dialogue* 8(2). http://globaldialogue.isa-sociology.org/a-global-crisis-in-care/.

Williams, Johnny E. 2016. *Decoding Racial Ideology in Genomics: Why We Pretend Race Exists in America*. Lanham, MD: Lexington Books.

Williams, Raymond. 1983. *Culture and Society: 1780–1950*. New York: Columbia University Press.

Willis, Paul. 1977. *Learning to Labor*. New York: Columbia University Press.

Wilmoth, Janet. 2004. "Questions and Comments about National, Externally Graded Assessment Exams: A Response to Wagenaar." *Teaching Sociology* 32(2): 241–43.

Wilson, James Q. 1968. *Varieties of Police Behavior*. Cambridge, MA: Harvard University Press.

Wilson, James Q., and Georle L. Kelling. 1982. "Broken Windows: The police and neighborhood safety." *The Atlantic*. 248(March). https://www.theatlantic.com/magazine/archive/1982/03/broken-windows/304465/.

Wilson, William J. 1987. *The Truly Disadvantaged: The Inner City, the Underclass, and Public Policy*. Chicago: University of Chicago Press.

Wingfield, Adia Harvey. 2009. "Racializing the Glass Escalator: Reconsidering Men's Experiences with Women's Work." *Gender and Society*, 23(1): 5–26.

Wirth, Louis. 1938. "Urbanism as a Way of Life." *American Journal of Sociology* 44(1): 1–24.

Wogan, J. B. 2016, June. "Who's an Employee? The Uber-Important Question of Today's Economy." Management and Labor. *Governing. The States and Localities*. Web. http://www.governing.com/topics/mgmt/gov-uber-employee-lawsuits-sharing-economy.html.

Wolf, Michael, Bruce Friedman and Daniel Sutherland, 1998. *Religion in the Workplace*. Chicago, IL: American Bar Association.

Wolfe, Michelle, Bryan D. Jones, and Frank R. Baumgartner. 2013. "A Failure to Communicate: Agenda Setting in Media and Policy Studies." *Political Communication* 30(2): 175–92. doi:10.1080/10584609.2012.737419.

Wolff, Edward. 2012. "The Asset Price Meltdown and the Wealth of the Middle Class." NBER Working Paper Number 18559. https://www.nber.org/papers/w18559.

Wolfson, Evan. 2004. *Why Marriage Matters: America, Equality, and Gay People's Right to Marry*. New York: Simon & Schuster.

Wood, Molly. 2014, July 28. "OKCupid Plays with Love in User Experiments." *New York Times*. https://www.nytimes.com/2014/07/29/technology/okcupid-publishes-findings-of-user-experiments.html.

Woodhouse, Kellie, 2015, May 22. "Doing Their Fair Share," *Slate*. http://www.slate.com/articles/life/inside_higher_ed/2015/05/wealthy_universities_like_harvard_leave_low_income_students_behind_despite.html.

Woodward, Ian. 2012. "Consumption as Cultural Interpretation: Taste, Performativity and Navigating The Forest Of Objects." In *The Oxford Handbook of Cultural Sociology*, eds. Jeffrey Alexander, Philip Smith, and Ronald Jacobs (pp. 671-97). New York: Oxford University Press.

World Atlas. n.d. "The Nations of Europe by the Average Age At First Marriage." https://www.worldatlas.com/articles/the-nations-of-europe-by-the-average-age-at-first-marriage.html.

World Bank. 2018. *Piecing Together the Poverty Puzzle. Poverty and Shared Prosperity*. Washington, DC: The World Bank.

World Economic Forum. 2018. "Global Risks Report 2018," 13th ed. http://reports.weforum.org/global-risks-2018/.

World Health Organization. 1946. "Constitution of the World Health Organization as adopted by the International Health Conference, New York, 19–22 June 1946." Quoted in Grad, Frank P. 2002. "The Preamble of the Constitution of the World Health Organization." Bulletin of the World Health Organization. 80(12): 982.

World Health Organization. 2004. *A Glossary of Terms for Community Health Care and Services for Older Persons* (WHO Centre for Health Development Ageing and Health Technical Report Vol. 5). http://www.who.int/kobe_centre/ageing/ahp_vol5_glossary.pdf.

World Health Organization. 2016. "World Health Statistics 2016: Monitoring Health for the SDGs Annex B: Tables of Health Statistics by Country, WHO Region and Globally." http://www.who.int/gho/publications/world_health_statistics/2016/en/ 2018).

Wu, Xiaoxu, Yongmei Lu, Sen Zhou, Lifan Chen, and Bing Xu. 2016. "Impact of Climate Change on Human Infectious Diseases: Empirical Evidence and Human Adaptation." *Environment International* 86:14–23.

Wuthnow, Robert. 1989. *The Struggle for America's Soul: Evangelicals, Liberals, and Secularism*. Grand Rapids, MI: Wm. B. Eerdmans Publishing Co.

Wuthnow, Robert. 1997. *The Crisis in the Churches: Spiritual Malaise, Fiscal Woe*. New York: Oxford University Press.

Wyatt, Ian, and Daniel Hecker. 2006. "Occupational Changes during the Twentieth Century." *Monthly Labor Review* 129(3): 35–57.

Wyatt, Ronald M. 2013, October 2. "Revisiting Disruptive and Inappropriate Behavior: Five Years after Standards Introduced." Center for Transforming Healthcare Leaders. https://www.jointcommission.org/jc_physician_blog/revisiting_disruptive_and_inappropriate_behavior/.

Yancy, Clyde W. 2007, July 30. "The Association of Black Cardiologists Responds to "Race in a Bottle. A Misguided Passion." *Scientific American*. https://www.scientificamerican.com/article/the-association-of-black-cardiologists-responds-to-article/.

Yang, Guobin. 2011. *The Power of the Internet in China: Citizen Activism Online*. New York: Columbia University Press.

Yousafzai, Malala. 2013. *I Am Malala: The Girl Who Stood Up for Education and Was Shot by the Taliban*. London: Weidenfeld and Nicolson.

Young, Jacob T. N., and Frank M. Weerman. 2013. "Delinquency as a Consequence of Misperception:

Overestimation of Friends' Delinquent Behavior and Mechanisms of Social Influence." *Social Problems* 60(3): 334–56. doi:10.1525/sp.2013.60.3.334.

Young, Robert J. C., and Homi Bhabha. 2004. *White Mythologies*. New York: Routledge.

Zarulli, Virginia, Julia A. Barthold Jones, Anna Oksuzyan, Rune Lindahl-Jacobsen, Kaare Christensen, and James W. Vaupel. 2018. "Women Live Longer Than Men Even During Severe Famines and Epidemics." *Proceedings of the National Academy of Sciences of the United States of America*. 115(4): 832–40.

Zhou, M. 1998. "'Parachute Kids' in Southern California: The Educational Experience of Chinese Children in Transnational Families." *Education Policy* 12: 682–702.

Zhou, M., and C. Bankston. 1998. *Growing Up American: How Vietnamese Children Adapt to Life in the United States*. New York: Russell Sage Foundation.

Zhou, Min, 1997. "Segmented Assimilation: Issues, Controversies, and Recent Research on the New Second Generation." *International Migration Review* 31(4): 825–58.

Zimmerman, Frederick J., Dimitri A. Christakis, and Andrew N. Meltzoff. 2007. "Associations between Media Viewing and Language Development in Children under Age 2 Years." *Journal of Pediatrics* 151: 364–68.

Zong, Jie, Jeanne Batalova, and Jeffrey Hallock. 2018, February 8. "Frequently Requested Statistics on Immigrants and Immigration in the United States." Migration Policy Institute. https://www.migrationpolicy.org/article/frequently-requested-statistics-immigrants-and-immigration-united-states.

Zuckerman, Harriet. 1977. *Scientific Elite: Nobel Laureates in the United States*. New York: Free Press.

Zweigenhaft, Richard, and G. William Domhoff. 2006. *Diversity in the Power Elite*. Lanham, MA: Rowman and Littlefield.

Credits

Index

Page numbers in bold indicate figures or tables.